Professions in Ethical Focus
An Anthology

EDITED BY

Fritz Allhoff and Anand J. Vaidya

broadview press

Library and Archives Canada Cataloguing in Publication

Professions in ethical focus : an anthology / edited by Fritz Allhoff and Anand J. Vaidya.

Includes bibliographical references.
ISBN 978-1-55111-699-0

1. Professional ethics. I. Allhoff, Fritz II. Vaidya, Anand
BJ1725.P764 2008   174   C2008-904103-8

Broadview Press is an independent, international publishing house, incorporated in 1985. Broadview believes in shared ownership, both with its employees and with the general public; since the year 2000 Broadview shares have traded publicly on the Toronto Venture Exchange under the symbol BDP.

We welcome comments and suggestions regarding any aspect of our publications—please feel free to contact us at the addresses below or at broadview@broadviewpress.com.

North America   PO Box 1243, Peterborough, Ontario, Canada K9J 7H5
2215 Kenmore Ave., Buffalo, New York, USA 14207
Tel: (705) 743-8990; Fax: (705) 743-8353
email: customerservice@broadviewpress.com

UK, Ireland, and continental Europe   NBN International, Estover Road, Plymouth, UK PL6 7PY
Tel: 44 (0) 1752 202300; Fax: 44 (0) 1752 202330
email: enquiries@nbninternational.com

Australia and New Zealand   UNIREPS, University of New South Wales
Sydney, NSW, Australia 2052
Tel: 61 2 9664 0999; Fax: 61 2 9664 5420
email: info.press@unsw.edu.au

www.broadviewpress.com

Copy-edited by John Burbidge

PRINTED IN CANADA

The interior of this book is printed on 100% recycled paper.

CONTENTS

Why Study Professional Ethics?

FRITZ ALLHOFF and ANAND VAIDYA

Volume Introduction

In this volume, we will offer various readings on professional ethics: professional ethics is a branch of applied ethics which, in turn, is part of philosophical ethics (and, thereafter, philosophy) more generally. We have chosen the five professions that receive the most discussion in professional ethics: accounting and finance; engineering; journalism; law; and medicine (we will treat these alphabetically as there seems no motivated conceptual priority of one over another). One unit is dedicated to each of these professions, and the most prevalent ethical questions within each are raised. A prior set of questions regards the nature of professions in the first place: what is a profession? What makes one field professional in ways that another is not? And why have professional *ethics* at all; is it necessary or superfluous? In this introduction, we will briefly consider some of these questions.

So, first, what is a profession? If we think about some of the enterprises enumerated above, something seems to set them apart from other things that people might do for a living. Take gardening, for example, and compare it with law. In some important sense, law differs from gardening insofar as the former seems more rigorously codified by responsibility, ethical obligation, significant outcomes, accredited and lengthy professional training, and so on. While that might seem intuitively compelling—and some people, surely, do not share all of those intuitions—it is a little more challenging to systematize the differences between professions and non-professions. Ernest Greenwood, in his classic article "Attributes of a Profession" (reprinted in this volume) identifies the following elements of a profession: a systematic body of knowledge; professional authority and credibility; regulation and control of mem-

bers; a professional code of ethics; and a culture of values, norms, and symbols. Law, for example, has all five of these things, whereas gardening lacks at least the last three.

As mentioned above, we have chosen five professions to highlight in this volume because these are the ones that are most frequently discussed in ethical contexts. And, of course, part of this has to do with their public nature. Accounting and finance and journalism have each suffered various scandals in recent years; the former because of corporate improprieties and the latter because of high-profile cases involving plagiarism and source confidentiality. There have also been some notable cases in recent years (e.g., product recalls) that have increased the attention paid to engineering ethics, particularly with regard to issues that affect public safety. Medicine and law have long traditions of ethical self-regulation by member-based organizations (the American Medical Association and the American Bar Association, respectively). Furthermore, a lot of the ethical issues in these professions are highlighted on extremely popular television shows; much of this exposure—albeit fictitious, unlike the cases in accounting and finance and journalism—also draws attention to and interest in medical and legal ethics.

Thus far, we have identified several professions in which ethical inquiry might be appropriate. But we could still ask what sorts of questions would be fruitful here and, in particular, whether we expect to derive professional ethics from these investigations. What is professional ethics? Most fundamentally, such a concept would espouse a sort of role-differentiated morality, which is to say that various individuals would have various obligations because of the *role* that they play (e.g., accountant, engineer, journalist, lawyer, or physician). Lawyers, for example, are employed to represent certain clients because of their greater knowledge of the intricacies of the legal system. This role places on them specific obligations both to the client and to the system of law and the courts, which would not apply to a non-lawyer. Similar stories could be told for other cases and for other professions.

But this raises an interesting question, which is whether professional ethics are really necessary at all. For we already have general moral theory; for example, utilitarianism, which says that the right actions are the ones that maximize total aggregate happiness. If utilitarianism is correct, then a professional ethic would seem irrelevant or superfluous because we already have the tools to obligate the professional in this moral framework without invoking any further professional ethic. Perhaps, then, the lawyer should represent the needy client because so-doing would maximize happiness (let us assume that an exoneration would, in fact, do this). Similarly, the non-lawyer need not represent the client because such representation would not likely be successful and therefore not maximize happiness. In other words, we get the same results (*viz.*, obligation for the lawyer and no obligation for the non-lawyer) through our espousal of a general moral theory as we would have gotten with a role-differentiated morality: does this render the latter irrelevant or superfluous?

Some people certainly think so, and this skepticism will be apparent through some of the readings in this volume. Alternatively, some people think not, and that line of argumentation will also present itself. Or indeed we might take some intermediate stance wherein *even if* the professional ethic can be subsumed under general moral philosophy, there is still something to be gained by tending to the issues that present themselves within professional contexts; this might not give us a metaphysically independent professional ethic but nevertheless license our forthcoming investigations.

A final element to keep in mind throughout the volume has to do with professional codes of ethics. Within some professions, let us assume that we have identified some salient ethical feature, and furthermore assume that it is clear to us what the appropriate response should be toward that feature. For example, consider medicine and the question of whether we should protect patient confidences. In this case, we might think that there are both deontic (e.g., respect for persons) and consequentialist (e.g., confidences engender better care since patients will be more likely to disclose, and therefore receive better care) moral reasons to endorse confidentiality. As a philosophical investigation, this might be the end of the line, but, practically and publicly, there may still be work to do. In particular, those moral obligations could be codified into some code of ethics, and promulgated to the constituents of the profession.

Thus, some professions chose to codify various ethical tenets, which serve the professional practice. The American Medical Association, for example, publishes its *Code of Medical Ethics*. Once such a code exists, its status can be of various sorts, ranging from advisory to regulatory. Once we decide to codify professional ethics, then there is a further question about *who* should effect such codification. Again, consider the AMA, which has a Council of Ethical and Judicial Affairs to develop the *Code*. Other professions, however, might not have a similar body, and then we might wonder how such a codification is even possible.

Finally, *enjoy* this book, and enjoy studying ethics. As you progress through the volume, think about what should be *done* with some of the ethical conclusions that you reach; they are not only of academic interest, but also have social implications. A lot of the topics raised in this book are extremely important and enjoy tremendous public attention. Applied ethics is one of the few branches of philosophy that enjoys that sort of status, which makes it a very compelling enterprise.

ERNEST GREENWOOD

Attributes of a Profession

The professions occupy a position of great importance on the American scene.[1] In a society such as ours, characterized by minute division of labor based upon technical specializations, many important features of social organization are dependent upon professional functions. Professional activity is coming to play a predominant role in the life patterns of increasing numbers of individuals of both sexes, occupying much of their waking moments, providing life goals, determining behavior, and shaping personality. It is no wonder, therefore, that the phenomenon of professionalism has become an object of observation by sociologists.[2] The sociological approach to professionalism is one that views a profession as an organized group which is constantly interacting with the society that forms its matrix, which performs its social functions through a network of formal and informal relationships, and which creates its own subculture requiring adjustments to it as a prerequisite for career success.[3]

Within the professional category of its occupational classification the United States Census Bureau includes, among others, the following: accountant, architect, artist, attorney, clergyman, college professor, dentist, engineer, journalist, judge, librarian, natural scientist, optometrist, pharmacist, physician, social scientist, social worker, surgeon, and teacher.[4] What common attributes do these professional occupations possess which distinguish them from the nonprofessional ones? After a careful canvass of the sociological literature on occupations, this writer has been able to distill five elements, upon which there appears to be consensus among the students of the subject, as constituting the distinguishing attributes of a profession.[5] Succinctly put, all professions seem to possess: (1) systematic theory, (2) authority, (3) community sanction, (4) ethical codes, and (5)

a culture. The purpose of this article is to describe fully these attributes.

Before launching into our description, a preliminary word of caution is due. With respect to each of the above attributes, the true difference between a professional and a nonprofessional occupation is not a qualitative but a quantitative one. Strictly speaking, these attributes are not the exclusive monopoly of the professions; nonprofessional occupations also possess them, but to a lesser degree. As is true of most social phenomena, the phenomenon of professionalism cannot be structured in terms of clear-cut classes. Rather, we must think of the occupations in a society as distributing themselves along a continuum.[6] At one end of this continuum are bunched the well-recognized and undisputed professions (e.g., physician, attorney, professor, scientist); at the opposite end are bunched the least skilled and least attractive occupations (e.g., watchman, truckloader, farm laborer, scrubwoman, bus boy). The remaining occupations, less skilled and less prestigeful than the former, but more so than the latter, are distributed between these two poles. The occupations bunched at the professional pole of the continuum possess to a maximum degree the attributes about to be described. As we move away from this pole, the occupations possess these attributes to a decreasing degree. Thus, in the less developed professions, social work among them, these attributes appear in moderate degree. When we reach the mid-region of the continuum, among the clerical, sales, and crafts occupations, they occur in still lesser degree; while at the unskilled end of the continuum the occupations possess these attributes so minimally that they are virtually nonexistent. If the reader keeps this concept of the continuum in mind, the presentation will less likely appear as a distortion of reality.

Systematic Body of Theory[7]

It is often contended that the chief difference between a professional and a nonprofessional occupation lies in the element of superior skill. The performance of a professional service presumably involves a series of unusually complicated operations, mastery of which requires lengthy training. The models referred to in this connection are the performances of a surgeon, a concert pianist, or a research physicist. However, some nonprofessional occupations actually involve a higher order of skill than many professional ones. For example, tool-and-die making, diamond-cutting, monument-engraving, or cabinet-making involve more intricate operations than schoolteaching, nursing, or social work. Therefore, to focus on the element of skill per se in describing the professions is to miss the kernel of their uniqueness.

The crucial distinction is this: the skills that characterize a profession flow from and are supported by a fund of knowledge that has been organized into an internally consistent system, called a *body of theory*. A profession's underlying body of theory is a system of abstract propositions that describe in general terms the classes of phenomena comprising the profession's focus of interest. Theory serves as a base in terms of which the professional rationalizes his operations in concrete situations. Acquisition of the professional skill requires a prior or simultaneous mastery of the theory underlying that skill. Preparation for a profession, therefore, involves considerable preoccupation with systematic theory, a feature virtually absent in the training of the nonprofessional. And so treatises are written on legal theory, musical theory, social work theory, the theory of the drama, and so on, but no books appear on the theory of punch-pressing or pipe-fitting or bricklaying.

Because understanding of theory is so important to professional skill, preparation for a profession must be an intellectual as well as a practical experience. On-the-job training through apprenticeship, which suffices for a nonprofessional occupation, becomes inadequate for a profession. Orientation in theory can be achieved best through formal education in an academic setting. Hence the appearance of the professional school, more often than not university affiliated, wherein the milieu is a contrast to that of the trade school. Theoretical knowledge is more difficult to master than operational procedures; it is easier to learn to repair an automobile than to learn the principles of the internal combustion engine. There are, of course, a number of free-lance professional pursuits (*e.g.*, acting, painting, writing, composing, and the like) wherein academic preparation is not mandatory. Nevertheless, even in these fields various "schools" and "institutes" are appearing, although they may not be run along traditional academic lines. We can generalize that as an occupation moves toward professional status, apprenticeship training yields to formalized education, because the function of theory as a groundwork for practice acquires increasing importance.

The importance of theory precipitates a form of activity normally not encountered in a nonprofessional occupation, *viz.*, theory construction via systematic research. To generate valid theory that will provide a solid base for professional techniques requires the application of the scientific method to the service-related problems of the profession. Continued employment of the scientific method is nurtured by and in turn reinforces the element of *rationality*.[8] As an orientation, rationality is the antithesis of traditionalism. The spirit of rationality in a profession encourages a critical, as opposed to a reverential, attitude toward the theoretical system. It implies a perpetual readiness to discard any portion of that system, no matter how time honored it may be, with a formulation demonstrated to be more valid. The spirit of rationality generates group self-criticism and theoretical controversy. Professional members convene regularly in their associations to learn and to evaluate innovations in theory. This produces an intellectually stimulating milieu that is in marked contrast to the milieu of a nonprofessional occupation.

In the evolution of every profession there emerges the researcher-theoretician whose role is that of scientific investigation and theoretical systematization. In technological professions[9] a division of labor thereby evolves, that between the theory-oriented and the practice-oriented person. Witness the physician who prefers to attach himself to a medical research center rather than to enter private practice. This division may also yield to cleavages with repercussions upon intraprofessional relationships. However, if properly integrated, the division of labor produces an accelerated expansion of the body of theory and a sprouting of theoretical branches around which specialties nucleate. The net effect of such developments is to lengthen the preparation deemed desirable for entry into the profession. This accounts for the rise of graduate professional training on top of a basic college education.

Professional Authority

Extensive education in the systematic theory of his discipline imparts to the professional a type of knowledge that highlights the layman's comparative ignorance. This fact is the basis for the professional's authority, which has some interesting features.

A nonprofessional occupation has customers; a professional occupation has clients. What is the difference? A customer determines what services and/or commodities he wants, and he shops around until he finds them. His freedom of decision rests upon the premise that he has the capacity to appraise his own needs and to judge the potential of the service or of the commodity to satisfy them. The infallibility of his decisions is epitomized in the slogan: "The customer is always right!" In a professional relationship, however, the professional dictates what is good or evil for the client, who has no choice but to accede to professional judgment. Here the premise is that, because he lacks the requisite theoretical background, the client cannot diagnose his own needs or discriminate among the range of possibilities for meeting them. Nor is the client considered able to evaluate the caliber of the professional service he receives. In a nonprofessional occupation the custom-

er can criticize the quality of the commodity he has purchased, and even demand a refund. The client lacks this same prerogative, having surrendered it to professional authority. This element of authority is one, although not the sole, reason why a profession frowns on advertising. If a profession were to advertise, it would, in effect, impute to the potential client the discriminating capacity to select from competing forms of service. The client's subordination to professional authority invests the professional with a monopoly of judgment. When an occupation strives toward professionalization, one of its aspirations is to acquire this monopoly.

The client derives a sense of security from the professional's assumption of authority. The authoritative air of the professional is a principal source of the client's faith that the relationship he is about to enter contains the potentials for meeting his needs. The professional's authority, however, is not limitless; its function is confined to those specific spheres within which the professional has been educated. This quality in professional authority Parsons calls *functional specificity*.[10] Functional specificity carries the following implications for the client-professional relationship.

The professional cannot prescribe guides for facets of the client's life where his theoretical competence does not apply. To venture such prescriptions is to invade a province wherein he himself is a layman, and, hence, to violate the authority of another professional group. The professional must not use his position of authority to exploit the client for purposes of personal gratification. In any association of superordination-subordination, of which the professional-client relationship is a perfect specimen, the subordinate member—here, the client—can be maneuvered into a dependent role. The psychological advantage which thereby accrues to the professional could constitute a temptation for him. The professional must inhibit his impulses to use the professional relationship for the satisfaction of sexual need, the need to manipulate others, or the need to live vicariously. In the case of the therapeutic professions it is ideally preferred that client-professional intercourse not overflow the professional setting. Extraprofessional intercourse could be used by both client and professional in a manner such as to impair professional authority, with a consequent diminution of the professional's effectiveness.

Thus far we have discussed that phase of professional authority which expresses itself in the client-professional relationship. Professional authority, however, has professional-community ramifications. To these we now turn.

Sanction of the Community

Every profession strives to persuade the community to sanction its authority within certain spheres by conferring upon the profession a series of powers and privileges. Community approval of these powers and privileges may be either informal or formal; formal approval is that reinforced by the community's police power.

Among its powers is the profession's control over its training centers. This is achieved through an accrediting process exercised by one of the associations within the profession. By granting or withholding accreditation, a profession can, ideally, regulate its schools as to their number, location, curriculum content, and caliber of instruction. Comparable control is not to be found in a nonprofessional occupation.[11] The profession also acquires control over admission into the profession. This is achieved via two routes. First, the profession convinces the community that no one should be allowed to wear a professional title who has not been conferred it by an accredited professional school. Anyone can call himself a carpenter, locksmith, or metal-plater if he feels so qualified. But a person who assumes the title of physician or attorney without having earned it conventionally becomes an impostor. Secondly, the profession persuades the community to institute in its behalf a licensing system for screening those

qualified to practice the professional skill. A *sine qua non* for the receipt of the license is, of course, a duly granted professional title. Another prerequisite may be an examination before a board of inquiry whose personnel have been drawn from the ranks of the profession. Police power enforces the licensing system; persons practicing the professional skill without a license are liable to punishment by public authority.[12]

Among the professional privileges, one of the most important is that of confidentiality. To facilitate efficient performance, the professional encourages the client to volunteer information he otherwise would not divulge. The community regards this as privileged communication, shared solely between client and professional, and protects the latter legally from encroachments upon such confidentiality. To be sure, only a select few of the professions, notably medicine and law, enjoy this immunity. Its very rarity makes it the ultimate in professionalization. Another one of the professional privileges is a relative immunity from community judgment on technical matters. Standards for professional performance are reached by consensus within the profession and are based on the existing body of theory. The lay community is presumed incapable of comprehending these standards and, hence, of using them to identify malpractice. It is generally conceded that a professional's performance can be evaluated only by his peers.

The powers and privileges described above constitute a monopoly granted by the community to the professional group. Therefore, when an occupation strives toward professional status, one of its prime objectives is to acquire this monopoly. But this is difficult to achieve, because counter forces within the community resist strongly the profession's claims to authority. Through its associations the profession wages an organized campaign to persuade the community that it will benefit greatly by granting the monopoly. Specifically the profession seeks to prove: that the performance of the occupational skill requires specialized education; that those who possess this education, in contrast to those who do not, deliver a superior service; and that the human need being served is of sufficient social importance to justify the superior performance.

Regulative Code of Ethics

The monopoly enjoyed by a profession vis-à-vis clients and community is fraught with hazards. A monopoly can be abused; powers and privileges can be used to protect vested interests against the public weal.[13] The professional group could peg the price of its services at an unreasonably high level; it could restrict the numbers entering the occupation to create a scarcity of personnel; it could dilute the caliber of its performance without community awareness; and it could frustrate forces within the occupation pushing for socially beneficial changes in practices.[14] Were such abuses to become conspicuous, widespread, and permanent, the community would, of course, revoke the profession's monopoly. This extreme measure is normally unnecessary, because every profession has a built-in regulative code which compels ethical behavior on the part of its members.

The profession's ethical code is part formal and part informal. The formal is the written code to which the professional usually swears upon being admitted to practice; this is best exemplified by the Hippocratic Oath of the medical profession. The informal is the unwritten code, which nonetheless carries the weight of formal prescriptions. Through its ethical code the profession's commitment to the social welfare becomes a matter of public record, thereby insuring for itself the continued confidence of the community. Without such confidence the profession could not retain its monopoly. To be sure, self-regulative codes are characteristic of all occupations, nonprofessional as well as professional. However, a professional code is perhaps more explicit, systematic, and binding; it certainly possesses more altruistic overtones and is more public service-oriented.[15]

These account for the frequent synonymous use of the terms "professional" and "ethical" when applied to occupational behavior.

While the specifics of their ethical codes vary among the professions, the essentials are uniform. These may be described in terms of client-professional and colleague-colleague relations.

Toward the client the professional must assume an emotional neutrality. He must provide service to whoever requests it, irrespective of the requesting client's age, income, kinship, politics, race, religion, sex, and social status. A nonprofessional may withhold his services on such grounds without, or with minor, censure; a professional cannot. Parsons calls this element in professional conduct *universalism*. In other words, only in his extraoccupational contacts can the professional relate to others on particularistic terms, *i.e.*, as particular individuals with concrete personalities attractive or unattractive to him. In his client contacts particularistic considerations are out of place. Parsons also calls attention to the element of *disinterestedness* in the professional-client relationship.[16] In contrast to the nonprofessional, the professional is motivated less by self-interest and more by the impulse to perform maximally. The behavior corollaries of this service orientation are many. For one, the professional must, under all circumstances, give maximum caliber service. The nonprofessional can dilute the quality of his commodity or service to fit the size of the client's fee; not so the professional. Again, the professional must be prepared to render his services upon request, even at the sacrifice of personal convenience.

The ethics governing colleague relationships demand behavior that is co-operative, equalitarian, and supportive. Members of a profession share technical knowledge with each other. Any advance in theory and practice made by one professional is quickly disseminated to colleagues through the professional associations.[17] The proprietary and quasi-secretive attitudes toward discovery and invention prevalent in the industrial and commercial world are out of place in the professional. Also out of place is the blatant competition for clients which is the norm in so many nonprofessional pursuits. This is not to gainsay the existence of intraprofessional competition; but it is a highly regulated competition, diluted with co-operative ingredients which impart to it its characteristically restrained quality. Colleague relations must be equalitarian; intraprofessional recognition should ideally be based solely upon performance in practice and/or contribution to theory.[18] Here, too, particularistic considerations must not be allowed to operate. Finally, professional colleagues must support each other vis-à-vis clientele and community. The professional must refrain from acts which jeopardize the authority of colleagues, and must sustain those whose authority is threatened.[19]

The ways and means whereby a profession enforces the observance of its ethical code constitute a case study in social control. Self-discipline is achieved informally and formally.

Informal discipline consists of the subtle and the not-so-subtle pressures that colleagues exert upon one another. An example in this connection is the phenomenon of consultation and referral.[20] Consultation is the practice of inviting a colleague to participate in the appraisal of the client's need and/or in the planning of the service to be rendered. Referral is the practice of affording colleagues access to a client or an appointment. Thus, one colleague may refer his client to another, because lack of time or skill prevents his rendering the needed service; or he may recommend another for appointment by a prospective employer. Since professional ethics precludes aggressive competition and advertising, consultation and referral constitute the principal source of work to a professional. The consultation-referral custom involves professional colleagues in a system of reciprocity which fosters mutual interdependence. Interdependence facilitates social control; chronic violation of professional etiquette arouses colleague resentment, resulting in the cessation of consultation requests and referrals.

A more formal discipline is exercised by the professional associations, which possess the power to criticize or to censure, and in extreme cases to bar recalcitrants. Since membership in good standing in the professional associations is a *sine qua non* of professional success, the prospect of formal disciplinary action operates as a potent force toward conformity.

The Professional Culture

Every profession operates through a network of formal and informal groups. Among the formal groups, first there are the organizations through which the profession performs its services; these provide the institutionalized setting where professional and client meet. Examples of such organizations are hospital, clinic, university, law office, engineering firm, or social agency. Secondly, there are the organizations whose functions are to replenish the profession's supply of talent and to expand its fund of knowledge. These include the educational and the research centers. Third among the formal groups are the organizations which emerge as an expression of the growing consciousness-of-kind on the part of the profession's members, and which promote so-called group interests and aims. These are the professional associations. Within and around these formal organizations extends a filigree of informal groupings: the multitude of small, closely knit clusters of colleagues. Membership in these cliques is based on a variety of affinities: specialties within the profession; affiliations with select professional societies; residential and work propinquity; family, religious, or ethnic background; and personality attractions.

The interactions of social roles required by these formal and informal groups generate a social configuration unique to the profession, *viz.*, a professional culture. All occupations are characterized by formal and informal groupings; in this respect the professions are not unique. What is unique is the culture thus begotten. If one were to single out the attribute that most effectively differentiates the professions from other occupations, this is it. Thus we can talk of a professional culture as distinct from a nonprofessional culture. Within the professions as a logical class each profession develops its own subculture, a variant of the professional culture; the engineering subculture, for example, differs from the subcultures of medicine and social work. In the subsequent discussion, however, we will treat the culture of the professions as a generic phenomenon. The culture of a profession consists of its *values*, *norms*, and *symbols*.

The social values of a professional group are its basic and fundamental beliefs, the unquestioned premises upon which its very existence rests. Foremost among these values is the essential worth of the service which the professional group extends to the community. The profession considers that the service is a social good and that community welfare would be immeasurably impaired by its absence. The twin concepts of professional authority and monopoly also possess the force of a group value. Thus, the proposition that in all service-related matters the professional group is infinitely wiser than the laity is regarded as beyond argument. Likewise nonarguable is the proposition that acquisition by the professional group of a service monopoly would inevitably produce social progress. And then there is the value of rationality; that is, the commitment to objectivity in the realm of theory and technique. By virtue of this orientation, nothing of a theoretical or technical nature is regarded as sacred and unchallengeable simply because it has a history of acceptance and use.

The norms of a professional group are the guides to behavior in social situations. Every profession develops an elaborate system of these role definitions. There is a range of appropriate behaviors for seeking admittance into the profession, for gaining entry into its formal and informal groups, and for progressing within the occupation's hierarchy. There are appropriate modes of securing appointments, of conducting referrals, and of handling consultation.

There are proper ways of acquiring clients, of receiving and dismissing them, of questioning and treating them, of accepting and rejecting them. There are correct ways of grooming a protégé, of recompensing a sponsor, and of relating to peers, superiors, or subordinates. There are even group-approved ways of challenging an outmoded theory, of introducing a new technique, and of conducting an intraprofessional controversy. In short, there is a behavior norm covering every standard interpersonal situation likely to recur in professional life.

The symbols of a profession are its meaning-laden items. These may include such things as: its insignias, emblems, and distinctive dress; its history, folklore, and argot; its heroes and its villains; and its stereotypes of the professional, the client, and the layman.

Comparatively clear and controlling group values, behavior norms, and symbols, which characterize the professions, are not to be encountered in nonprofessional occupations.

Our discussion of the professional culture would be incomplete without brief mention of one of its central concepts, the *career* concept. The term career is, as a rule, employed only in reference to a professional occupation. Thus, we do not talk about the career of a bricklayer or of a mechanic; but we do talk about the career of an architect or of a clergyman. At the heart of the career concept is a certain attitude toward work which is peculiarly professional. A career is essentially a *calling*, a life devoted to "good works."[21] Professional work is never viewed solely as a means to an end; it is the end itself. Curing the ill, educating the young, advancing science are values in themselves. The professional performs his services primarily for the psychic satisfactions and secondarily for the monetary compensations.[22] Self-seeking motives feature minimally in the choice of a profession; of maximal importance is affinity for the work. It is this devotion to the work itself which imparts to professional activity the service orientation and the element of disinterestedness. Furthermore, the absorption in the work is not partial, but complete; it results in a total personal involvement. The work life invades the after-work life, and the sharp demarcation between the work hours and the leisure hours disappears. To the professional person his work becomes his life.[23] Hence the act of embarking upon a professional career is similar in some respects to entering a religious order. The same cannot be said of a nonprofessional occupation.

To succeed in his chosen profession, the neophyte must make an effective adjustment to the professional culture.[24] Mastery of the underlying body of theory and acquisition of the technical skills are in themselves insufficient guarantees of professional success. The recruit must also become familiar with and learn to weave his way through the labyrinth of the professional culture. Therefore, the transformation of a neophyte into a professional is essentially an acculturation process wherein he internalizes the social values, the behavior norms, and the symbols of the occupational group.[25] In its frustrations and rewards it is fundamentally no different from the acculturation of an immigrant to a relatively strange culture. Every profession entertains a stereotype of the ideal colleague; and, of course, it is always one who is thoroughly adjusted to the professional culture.[26] The poorly acculturated colleague is a deviant; he is regarded as "peculiar," "unorthodox," "annoying," and in extreme cases a "troublemaker." Whereas the professional group encourages innovation in theory and technique, it tends to discourage deviation from its social values and norms. In this internal contradiction, however, the professional culture is no different from the larger culture of society.

One of the principal functions of the professional schools is to identify and screen individuals who are prospective deviants from the professional culture. That is why the admission of candidates to professional education must be judged on grounds in addition to and other than their academic qualifications.[27] Psychic factors presaging favorable adjustment to the professional culture are granted an importance equivalent to mental abilities. The professional school provides test situations through initial and graduated exposures of the novice to the professional culture. By his behavior in these social situations involving colleagues, clients, and community, the potential deviant soon reveals himself and is immediately weeded out. Comparable preoccupation with the psychic prerequisites of occupational adjustment is not characteristic of nonprofessional occupations.

Implications for Social Work

The picture of the professions just unveiled is an ideal type. In the construction of an ideal type some exaggeration of reality is unavoidable, since the intent is to achieve an internally coherent picture. One function of the ideal type is to structure reality in such manner that discrete, disparate, and dissimilar phenomena become organized, thereby bringing order out of apparent disorder. We now possess a model of a profession that is much sharper and clearer than the actuality that confronts us when we observe the occupational scene. What is the utility of this model for social work?

The preoccupation of social workers with professionalization has been a characteristic feature of the social work scene for years. Flexner,[28] Johnson,[29] Hollis and Taylor,[30] and others have written on the subject, proposing criteria which must be met if social work is to acquire professional status. Whenever social workers convene there is the constant reaffirmation of the urgency to achieve the recognition from the community befitting a profession. The union of the seven separate organizations into the National Association of Social Workers is generally regarded as an important milestone in social work history, precisely because of its potential stimulus toward professionalization.

In view of all this, it is proper for social workers to possess clear conceptions of that which they so fervently seek. The model of the professions portrayed above should contribute to such clarification;

it should illuminate the goal for which social workers are striving. It is often contended that social work is still far from having attained professional status.[31] But this is a misconception. When we hold up social work against the model of the professions presented above, it does not take long to decide whether to classify it within the professional or the nonprofessional occupations. Social work is already a profession; it has too many points of congruence with the model to be classifiable otherwise. Social work is, however, seeking to rise within the professional hierarchy, so that it, too, might enjoy maximum prestige, authority, and monopoly which presently belong to a few top professions.

The model presented above should also serve to sensitize social workers to anticipate some of the problems that continued professionalization must inevitably precipitate. The model indicates that progressive professionalization will involve social workers in novel relationships with clients, colleagues, agency, community, and other professions. In concluding this paper we refer briefly to one such problem. It is no secret that social workers are not all uniformly enthusiastic about the professionalization of social work. Bisno[32] has given verbalization to a prevailing apprehension that social workers might have to scuttle their social-action heritage as a price of achieving the public acceptance accorded a profession. Extrapolation from the sociologists' model of the professions suggests a reality basis for these fears. It suggests that the attainment of professional prestige, authority, and monopoly by social workers will undoubtedly carry disturbing implications for the social action and social reform components of social work philosophy. The anticipated developments will compel social workers to rethink and redefine the societal role of their profession.

These and other dilemmas flowing from professionalization are bound to tax the best minds among social workers for their resolution. In this connection a proper understanding of the attributes of a profession would seem to be indispensable.

NOTES

1 Talcott Parsons, "The Professions and Social Structure," *Social Forces*, Vol. 17 (May 1939), 457-67.

2 Theodore Caplow, *The Sociology of Work* (Minneapolis: University of Minnesota Press, 1954).

3 Oswald Hall. "The Stages of a Medical Career," *American Journal of Sociology*, Vol. 51 (March 1948), 327-36; "Types of Medical Careers," *American Journal of Sociology*, Vol. 55 (November 1949), 243-53; "Sociological Research in the Field of Medicine: Progress and Prospects," *American Sociological Review*, Vol. 16 (October 1951), 639-44.

4 US Bureau of the Census, *1950 Census of Population: Classified Index of Occupations and Industries* (Washington, DC: Government Printing Office, 1950).

5 The writer acknowledges his debt to his former students at the School of Social Welfare, University of California, Berkeley, who, as members of his research seminars, assisted him in identifying and abstracting the sociological literature on occupations. Their conscientious assistance made possible the formulation presented in this paper.

6 The occupational classification employed by the US Census Bureau is precisely such a continuum. The categories of this classification are: (a) professionals and semiprofessional technical workers; (b) proprietors and managers, both farm and non-farm, and officials; (c) clerical, sales, and kindred workers: (d) craftsmen, skilled workers, and foremen; (e) operatives and semiskilled workers; and (e) laborers, unskilled, service, and domestic workers (US Bureau of the Census, *op. cit.*).

7 The sequence in which the five attributes are discussed in this paper does not reflect upon their relative importance. The order selected has been dictated by logical considerations.

8   Parsons, *op. cit.*

9   A technology is a profession whose aim is to achieve controlled changes in natural relationships. Convention makes a distinction between technologists who shape nonhuman materials and those who deal with human beings. The former are called engineers; the latter practitioners.

10 Parsons, *op. cit.*

11 To set up and run a school for floral decorating requires no approval from the national florists' association, but no school of social work could operate long without approval of the Council on Social Work Education.

12 Many nonprofessional occupations have also succeeded in obtaining licensing legislation in their behalf. Witness the plumbers, radio operators, and barbers, to mention a few. However, the sanctions applied against a person practicing a nonprofessional occupation are much less severe than is the case when a professional occupation is similarly involved.

13 Abraham Flexner, "Is Social Work a Profession?" in *Proceedings of the National Conference of Charities and Corrections* (Chicago: 1915), 576-90. Robert K. Merton, "Bureaucratic Structure and Personality," in Alvin Gouldner, ed., *Studies in Leadership* (New York: Harper & Brothers, 1950), 67-79.

14 Merton, *op. cit.*

15 Flexner, *op. cit.* Parsons, *op. cit.*

16 Parsons, *op. cit.*

17 Arlien Johnson, "Professional Standards and How They Are Attained," *Journal of American Dental Association*, Vol. 31 (September 1944), 1181-89.

18 Flexner, *op. cit.*

19 This partly explains why physicians do not testify against each other in malpractice suits.

20 Hall, *op. cit.*

21 The term *calling* literally means a divine summons to undertake a course of action. Original-ly, it was employed to refer to religious activity. The Protestant Reformation widened its meaning to include economic activity as well. Henceforth divinely inspired "good works" were to be both secular and sacred in nature. Presumably, then, any occupational choice may be a response to divine summons. In this connection, it is interesting to note that the German word for vocation is *Beruf,* a noun derived from the verb *berufen,* to call.

22 Johnson, *op. cit.*

23 The all-pervading influence of work upon the lives of professionals results in interesting by-products. The members of a profession tend to associate with one another outside the work setting (Oswald Hall, "The Stages of a Medical Career," *op. cit.*). Their families mingle socially; leisure time is spent together; "shop talk" permeates social discourse; and a consensus develops. The profession thus becomes a whole social environment, nurturing characteristic social and political attitudes, patterns of consumption and recreation, and decorum and *Weltanschauung* (Caplow, *op. cit.*; and William H. Form. "Toward an Occupational Social Psychology," *Journal of Social Psychology*, Vol. 24, February 1946, 85-99).

24 Oswald Hall, "The Stages of a Medical Career" and "Types of Medical Careers," *op. cit.*

25 R. Clyde White, "'Social Workers in Society': Some Further Evidence," *Social Work Journal*, Vol. 54 (October 1955), 161-64.

26 The laity also entertain a stereotypic image of the professional group. Needless to say, the layman's conception and the professional's self-conception diverge widely, because they are fabricated out of very different experiences. The layman's stereotype is frequently a distortion of reality, being either an idealization or a caricature of the professional type.

27 Oswald Hall, "Sociological Research in the Field of Medicine: Progress and Prospects," *op. cit.*

28 Flexner, *op. cit.*

29 Johnson, *op. cit.*

30 Ernest V. Hollis and Alice L. Taylor, *Social Work Education in the United States* (New York: Columbia University Press, 1951).

31 Flexner considered that the social work of his day was not a profession. Hollis and Taylor regard present-day social work as still in its early adolescence.

32 Herbert Bisno, "How Social Will Social Work Be?" *Social Work*, Vol. 1, No. 2 (April 1956), 12-18.

◆ ◆ ◆ ◆ ◆

DON WELCH

Just Another Day at the Office: The Ordinariness of Professional Ethics

Much of the work in professional ethics in recent years has focused on the distinctiveness of the ethics of the professions. Alan Goldman has described the view that professional duties must override what would otherwise be moral obligations because special norms and principles should guide a professional's conduct.[1] We've been told that professionalism embodies a standard of good conduct that is not the same as the norms of morality that ordinarily govern relations among persons.[2] Often the claim is not that professionals must meet the same moral standards as the rest of us and then go beyond those, but that their distinctive moral standards may conflict with the requirements of "ordinary morality."[3]

A prevailing assumption among many professionals is that they are called on to conform to ethical standards that are "higher" than those that apply to ordinary people.[4] Professional morality places its values "at a higher position in the ethical hierarchy. It gives them greater ethical importance than does ordinary morality."[5] On reflection, however, it is not at all clear what "higher" means. Consider one statement of the ethical meaning of professionalism:

> In ethical terms, to be a professional is to be dedicated to a distinctive set of ideals and standards of conduct. It is to lead a certain kind of life defined by special virtues and norms of character. And it is to enter into a subcommunity with a characteristic moral ethos and outlook.[6]

Because of these presumably distinctive ideals and standards, it is argued, professional ethics may sometimes justify, even require, a practitioner to do something different than what would otherwise be morally obligatory. This is an approach that "implies that the rules which decide what is ethical for ordinary people do not apply equally, if at all, to those with social responsibility."[7] These standards clearly establish a certain immunity for professionals from the moral requirements placed on "laypeople"; we shall return to the question of whether they are "higher."

The standards that are to govern the work of professionals are often written into canons or codes of professional ethics, which Michael Davis describes as conventions among professionals that are produced when an occupation becomes a profession. "What conscience would tell us to do *absent* a certain convention is not necessarily what conscience would tell us to do *given* that convention."[8] The existence of such professional codes, as well as conventions that tale other forms, means that professionals are not permitted to engage in the weighing of the kinds of interests and factors that is allowed by ordinary morality.[9] Therefore, they are, to an extent, exempt from judgment based on moral standards outside the particular subcommunity that has its own distinctive moral ethos.

Given this heightened status that is accorded to professional ethics, it is understandable that entry into the club of professionalism is quite desirable. To the long-accepted entries of such occupations as law and medicine have been added such areas as engineering, accounting, nursing, social work, journalism, management, education, policy analysis and scientific research. The insistence of many occupational groups that they too be recognized as "professionals" has led one commentator to fear that the label "professional" is being threatened with evacuation of part of its meaning.[10]

Those who have been writing about the unique qualities and characteristics of professional ethics are themselves professionals. It is not surprising that, writing from their particular standpoints, they view their own moral dilemmas to be more noteworthy and different in kind from those faced by the masses. The sense one gets from reading much of the professional ethics literature is that, compared to the world of ordinary ethics, the demands placed on professionals are more compelling, the reasoning required of them is more sophisticated, and the compromises they make are morally superior. I am convinced, for the reasons stated below, that the distinctions are overdrawn.

Stephen F. Barker has attempted to establish the distinctiveness of professional ethics while avoiding the idea that professional obligations are more demanding and harder to comply with than those of nonprofessional occupations.[11] He identifies three features that distinguish the ethical ideology of a profession from nonprofessional ideology: (1) the ethical ideology of a profession does not stem merely from a business contract between employer and employee; (2) this professional ethical ideology involves requirements that those in the occupation have largely agreed to impose on themselves; and (3) this ideology includes an ethical ideal of service to society.[12]

A focus on the employer-employee contract, however, narrows the inquiry much too quickly. Certainly not all self-employed people are inherently more professional than all salaried people. It is true that professional obligations do not stem "merely" from an employer-employee business contract. But, as Barker recognizes, many professionals are employees and so some of their obligations *do* stem from such contracts. Further, it is also the case that all of the obligations of nonprofessionals cannot be traced to such an employer-employee contract.

Barker gives the following example, in his comparison of nonprofessional firefighters and professional physicians, to illustrate the distinctiveness of the non-contractual professional obligation: "[I]t will be unethical for the physician publicly to endorse medicines or treatments which have no proven medical value, though nonphysicians may do this blamelessly."[13] If one agrees with this conclusion, it is only because of the distinctive content of the practice of medicine, not because of some generalized sense of the distinctive nature of professional obligation. I would argue that a parallel obligation does apply to the firefighter: that it would be unethical for a firefighter who is making a presentation in an elementary school classroom during fire prevention week to endorse fire safety practices that are not safe.

We need to avoid taking the position that professionals impose upon themselves obligations to serve society in ways that nonprofessionals do not because the only ethical obligations nonprofessionals have is to adhere to the employee contract. Confining the moral obligations of non-professionals to those embodied in such a contract is overly restrictive. Certainly there are firefighters, cafeteria workers, construction workers, secretaries, and a host of other nonprofessionals who, as members of those groups, have felt that they should respond to moral expectations that were not a part of a business contract.

Professionals do not have a monopoly on responding to the ideal of service to society. As Barker points out, many nonprofessionals are indeed called into service to society. Nor are professionals immune from employment arrangements that override a duty they have to service a larger community good. For example, physicians reject "bedside rationing" of scarce services for the good of society because of their obligation to the single patient before them; attorneys reject being drawn into seeking justice for the good of society because of their obligation to the single client before them. Of course service to an individual is one way in which a professional can be of service to society. But the same is true for nonprofessionals. One could reply that sometimes nonprofessionals act professionally and sometimes professionals act in a nonprofessional manner. The question still remains whether it is appropriate to maintain such a generalized ideal of professionalism that calls for a different form of ethical analysis.

My point is that any claim for a stronger ethical content and a substantially different ethical structure for professional ethics is dubious. All of us, professionals and nonprofessionals, experience and respond to ethical problems in fundamentally the same way. The efforts to identify special concepts of morality for professionals create distracting distinctions that separate out pieces of the moral life that can be better understood as integral parts of a whole. I am not arguing that professionals do not have to respond to particular expectations that make a difference in the moral choices they make. Particular contexts do require particular kinds of ethical attention. My argument, rather, is that everyone is continuously engaged in exactly the same kind of process of moral deliberation....

... Most lists of features of the professions include something like the criteria mentioned earlier. One such feature is providing services that are important to society. In recent years we have seen many examples in other countries of people starving to death because of a lack of a food distribution system. Truck drivers provide this important service to society. Airplane mechanics, firefighters and farmers, to mention only a few others, also feel that they provide important services but find themselves on few lists of professionals. Even if service to society does provide a basis for separating the professions from other occupational pursuits, it seems that that feature would argue for less moral insularity, not more. The more crucial a service is to a community, the greater the community's stake is in seeing that the service is rendered in ways that are morally appropriate in light of prevailing societal standards.

Not unrelated to this first feature of the professions is a second characteristic: professionals are committed to some good larger than their own self-interest, e.g., the welfare of society. Accordingly, we expect morally superior behavior from those engaged in a profession. But it may well be that this self-proclaimed adoption of a higher calling was rooted in economic self-interest and a desire for social status, and a gap often exists between this vision and actual professional practice. Indeed, the adoption of some ethical codes can be seen as ways of protecting professionals' self-interests by exempting them from the moral claims placed on the rest of us, rather than obligating them to higher moral aspirations in the service of the common good. And, since we're seeking distinctive features of the professions, it should be noted that we expect many others to be committed to some good larger than their own self-interest: mothers and fathers, United Way volunteers, scout masters and lay religious leaders, to name a few.

A third kind of feature often associated with the professions is the fact that they are often granted a degree of autonomy by society, sometimes including a societally granted monopoly for the services they render. This autonomy usually entails a judgment by peers, a certain insulation from lay judgment and control. Rather than providing grounds for the claimed moral distinctiveness, this feature seems to be a result of having found such distinctiveness. A measure of autonomy is granted because of a recognition that there is something distinctive about a profession that warrants this special treatment. The issue in this inquiry is not whether this degree of moral autonomy and insulation exists, nor whether additional responsibilities are generated by such a grant of autonomy; rather, the issue is why it is appropriate to separate out certain professions in this way.

A fourth feature of the professions also gives a basis for arguing for this autonomy and thus for moral distinctiveness: the nature of professional services requires skills and knowledge not possessed by the population at large. Professions entail extensive training with a significant intellectual component. The problems and moral dilemmas encountered by professionals simply cannot be accurately assessed by laypeople.

While this fourth feature seems on point, it is important that we not claim too much for it. This characteristic of professions may say much about who engages in moral assessments of professional behavior; it may say very little about how those people should make such assessments. Esoteric knowledge and specialized training may limit the number of people who can ably analyze a professional problem. These features, however, do not require that those able people analyze that problem using ethical modes of reasoning that are different from those of "ordinary morality."

If I want to emphasize the continuities rather than the discontinuities, it is obviously important to identify what the truck driver has in common with the doctors and lawyers. In fact, at this point, I want to enlarge the conversation to address the continuities between the ethics of the professionals and those of every other person who plays a distinctive role in our community—which is all of us. So the discussion includes not only those driving trucks and engaged in other occupations, but also mothers and fathers, participants in political parties and neighborhood organizations, citizens, members of churches and synagogues. Davis is right that the conventions that exist among us affect our moral choices. We face such conventions, however, in every role we play.

In this regard, we should look at one other feature that is sometimes mentioned as being characteristic of the professions. Individuals incur certain obligations as they enter into a profession. They pledge to abide by a code of ethics, their covenant with others to uphold the standards of that profession, they agree to act in accordance with professional expectations. This kind of contracting among members of a profession creates limits on the extent to which one can act as an individual agent. Of course, our truck driver may have certain kinds of contractual obligations—to a company from which she leases the trailer or the bank that holds a note on the cab or the shipper who relies on a delivery. But it is important to look beyond these kinds of obligations that flow from normal arrangements. Agreements like bank loans and official codes of ethics are not the only sources for moral decision-making. Many of the professional conventions are matters of less formal expectations than those codified in rules and officially adopted standards. We are also subject to the conventions and expectations of family, friends and members of nonvocational groups, i.e., the expectations of ordinary morality.

The common thread, the source of the "ordinariness of professional ethics," is that all of us, in all aspects of our lives, are subject to moral claims inherent in the roles we play. The term "positional obligation" refers to the concept that holding a particular position or filling a particular role carries with it obligations that that person would not otherwise have. This feature of role morality is not, of course, a new thought. But the well-established insights of role morality render unremarkable the weaker claims of professional ethics—that professional roles entail obligations. Further, the insights of role morality cast doubt upon the stronger claims—that professional ethics require resort to moral norms and forms of moral reasoning that are different from that required by "ordinary" roles. Professional ethics conventions—in codes and in other forms—do create prima facie duties. We can only think about the ethical issues a professional confronts in the context of the conventions of that particular profession. But this insight applies to the conventions associated with all aspects of our lives.

All of the other relationships that we establish create prima facie duties as well. The difficult questions arise when we find ourselves subject to contradictory prima facie duties.

The inevitability of facing contradictory prima facie duties lies in the reality that each of us embraces multiple roles. We may be truck drivers or physicians. But at the same time we may also be mothers, citizens, church members and neighbors—to name only a few possibilities. Our continuing task is to respond to a variety of role expectations which inevitably conflict with one another from time to time. Insofar as professional obligations impose only prima facie duties and our response to these should be similar in character to our response to other prima facie duties, then we can avoid the danger Steven Salbu has identified as lurking in professional ethical standards: "A prefabricated, externally imposed code of ethics, taken literally to be what it pretends to be, suggests that the ethical issues have been addressed by the experts. The person who accepts the code at face value replaces the honest and difficult confrontation of ethical questions with a mindless conformity to the rules"[14] ...

... The moral dilemmas faced by professionals are fundamentally the same as those we face in all arenas of life. The challenge raised by conflicting expectations in the professions is similar to the challenge raised in everyday life. How do we balance incompatible demands? How do we weigh competing priorities? How do we determine the appropriate answer to the question, "What ought I to do?" I do not believe that the external demands of "ordinary morality" are always of secondary importance to the expectations that are generated by professional conventions. I cannot accept a moral system that asserts that professional duty always overrides other duties such as the obligations accompanying one's role as a father or as a citizen. Unless one is willing to make such a claim of unqualified preeminence for professional obligations, those obligations are recognized to be one set of

moral expectations alongside others, to be responded to in the same way that we respond to ordinary moral expectations.

It does not follow that there is no such thing as professional ethics. We can recognize a particular ethic to be professional because it is marked by the realities of the relationships that exist in what we consider to be a professional setting—not by some distinctive structures for ethical reasoning. There is such a thing as professional ethics. There are also such things as parental ethics, political ethics, business ethics and religious ethics. In each case the distinctive character of the enterprise derives from the particular relationships and the content associated with particular contexts. These kinds of ethics do not call for different kinds of ethical reasoning than that called for by ordinary ethics. Rather, it is in ordinary ethics that we find the understandings of moral obligation that are common to all of these more particularized forms of ethics.

NOTES

1 Alan Goldman, *The Moral Foundations of Professional Ethics* (Totowa, NJ: Rowman and Littlefield, 1980). Goldman himself finds these assertions unconvincing in most cases.

2 Albert Flores, *Professional Ideals* (Belmont, CA: Wadsworth, 1988), 1.

3 Rob Atkinson has described the distinction, "firmly ensconced in the literature," between legal professional morality and ordinary morality in "Beyond the New Role Morality for Lawyers," *Maryland Law Review* 51 (1992): 855-60.

4 Gerald J. Postema, "Moral Responsibility in Professional Ethics," *New York University Law Review* 55 (1980): 63.

5 Benjamin Freedman, "A Meta-Ethics for Professional Morality," *Ethics* 89 (1978): 10.

6 Bruce Jennings, Callahan and Wolf, "The Professions: Public Interest and Common Good," in "The Public Duties of the Professions," Spe-

cial Supp, *Hastings Center Report* 17, No. 1 (1987): 5.

7 Peter F. Drucker, "What Is 'Business Ethics'?" *The Public Interest* No. 63 (Spring 1981): 24.

8 Michael Davis, "Thinking Like an Engineer: The Place of a Code of Ethics in the Practice of a Profession," *Philosophy and Public Affairs* 20, No. 2 (1991): 154-55.

9 Ibid., 162.

10 Paul F. Camenisch, *Grounding Professional Ethics in a Pluralistic Society* (New York: Haven Publications, 1983), 4.

11 Barker, "What Is a Profession?" *Professional Ethics* 1 (Spring/Summer 1992): 73-99.

12 Ibid., 88-89.

13 Ibid., 89.

14 Steven R. Salbu, "Law and Conformity, Ethics and Conflict," *Indiana Law Journal* 68 (1992): 106.

◆ ◆ ◆ ◆ ◆

JOHN T. SANDERS

Honor Among Thieves: Some Reflections on Professional Codes of Ethics[1]

As complicated an affair as it may be to give a fully acceptable general characterization of professional codes of ethics that will capture every nuance, one theme that has attracted widespread attention portrays them as contrivances whose primary function is to secure certain obligations of professionals to clients, or to the external community.[2] In contrast to such an "externalist" characterization of professional codes, it has occasionally been contended that, first and foremost, they should be understood as *internal conventions*, adopted among professionals as a de-vice for securing the "interests" of the professionals themselves.[3]

In what follows, I will argue that both of these lines are incomplete. As important as service to the community and the interests of professionals may be in the full understanding of the multiple role that "codes of ethics" play in many professions, it is equally important to see them as expressive of the romance of a profession. Professional codes should be understood not only in terms of their utility to the community, or in terms of their utility to practitioners, but as expressions of callings. Analyses of professional codes of ethics that do not take into consideration their role in evoking the romance of a professional calling are thus not entirely adequate.

Professional standards and codes can be fully understood only if one appreciates that they are designed to contribute to and evoke feelings of dignity, self-worth—and, for better or for worse, even the superiority—of the professionals themselves; the code may seem to *them* to express essential features of what the profession really is.[4]

To understand the importance of this issue, it is useful first to address briefly a variety of issues that are best described as conceptual or linguistic. When this ground has been lightly covered, the way will have been prepared for more substantive matters.

1. "Professional" and Its Cognates

In addressing these issues, it is important to acknowledge the squishiness of the conceptual terrain. When we speak of "professionals," we may mean to indicate different, even conflicting things in different contexts. In calling a person a "professional," for example, we may mean to indicate no more than that the person has a certain competence in a certain demanding task, or we may mean no more than that the person has completed a certain course of training, or has a certain occupation (whether or not any particular competence is possessed). We may mean something praiseworthy, or something condemnatory, depending upon context. Our standards for tightness in the definition of the term will similarly vary with context.

Deploying the term in some ways makes it conceptually impossible for a person to be a professional without ever having received monetary compensation for working in the field in question. If I have been working as a waiter for the last twenty years, and have never found a position as an attorney, it might seem disingenuous for me to tell people that I am a professional lawyer, even though I might have all the certification of competence I need to prove it. Yet it would not be at all out of order for a legal periodical to note the fact that, perhaps due to hard economic times, many professionals have not been able to find work in the field.

Sometimes the difference between professional and amateur practitioners seems to betoken different competencies, sometimes nothing more than a difference between getting paid for what is done as opposed to doing it for free. Everything hangs on context.

Things get even more complicated when one begins to sort through the jungle of nuance surrounding various commonalities and differences in the meanings of cognate terms. The adjectival use of the term "professional" does not always work precisely in the way that the substantive usage does. And similar subtle differences are to be found in the various usages of terms like "profession" and "professionalism," and in the relations between these several cognates.

Many efforts have been made to bring order to this potentially confusing area of discourse,[5] and I suspect that all who have involved themselves in such efforts would concede that considerable ambiguity must always remain, given the general imprecision of natural language.

Nevertheless, it seems to me that some success can be gleaned if one steps back to a suitable level of generality. It appears that a common thread that runs through nearly all deployments of the cognates of the term "professional" is the idea of *competence* at a relatively *difficult* task. Where sometimes it seems that competence is *not* involved—for example, where we may wish to say that some members of the medical profession are not competent at all—it is often because of an intervening social/linguistic factor that somehow itself involves issues of competence. In the example of "incompetent doctors," we are talking about people who have successfully met what are deemed to be the standards of competence set for physicians (that's what allows us to identify them as doctors), but who aren't really competent after all.[6]

Similarly, where we are inclined to make a distinction between professionals and amateurs based on receiving pay for the work, this is often because of a widespread background belief that those who don't get money for what they do must not really be very good at it (unless such unremunerated work is done for reasons of charity—in which case it might actually be an *indicator* of true professionalism, at least from some perspectives).

There are bound to be counterexamples to the claim that competence at some difficult task is central to understanding these several concepts; natural language flourishes and grows just because of such fuzziness at the edges. But the first substantive claim of this paper may be formulated in the following rather conservative fashion: competence at some difficult task is more central to the notion of a profession, a professional, or professionalism, than are either service or the interests of the professionals. While *any* of these ideas may be superficially absent in some uses of these terms, competence at some difficult task is more central, and more universal, than any of the other ideas often mentioned as possible necessary conditions. Such competence, I claim, is involved either explicitly or implicitly as a necessary (if not sufficient) condition for the legitimate application of any of these related terms. A "professional" is one who is competent at some difficult task; the term "profession" describes either the pursuit of the work in question, or the (perhaps institutionalized) aggregate of persons doing that work; "professionalism" and other cognates must similarly involve reference to this central idea.7

II. "Platonic" versus "Social" Standards of Competency

Interesting complications—ones that serve to explain many conflicting judgments about the nature of professional *codes* of ethics—arise when one focuses attention on the fact that the notion of "competence at a difficult task" involves two evaluational terms whose satisfaction criteria are controversial. Which tasks are difficult? What are the standards of competence that are to be applied? Differences about these matters will yield differences in judgments about the propriety of describing particular kinds of activity as "professions" and particular individuals as "professionals."

An especially important area of controversy, at least for the purposes of the present paper, involves perspectival factors that come into play in deciding that a particular activity is performed "competently." One interesting way of distinguishing among evaluational perspectives involves the difference between standards that are *internal* to the task, on the one hand, and standards that are *external*, on the other. A professional athlete, for example, might become completely caught up in details of her sport that completely ignore whatever values *the fan* may wish to apply. Nevertheless, such an athlete may very well be among those most appreciated by fans. The question arises: how much should the *fans* (or any other non-professional's) criteria of "competence" affect the standards of professionalism used by the athlete? To what extent is *professionalism proper* (as opposed to social value) a function of contributions made to those *outside* the profession?

A philosopher may have no interest in attempting to make contributions to humanity (or in other philosophers who make such contributions their ex-

plicit goal), but may focus all of his attention on trying to get the argument straight. A physicist might have no concern about technological applications, and may feel that too much concern of this kind is antithetical to the pursuit of pure science. Whether such attitudes among professionals are good or bad for society at large is debatable. But this question seems to be quite independent of the question concerning professionalism proper. If the very idea of professionalism or of the professional were held to include provisions about service to the community or service to professionals themselves, then it should be paradoxical to speak of true professionals who care for neither of these things, but who only care about the quality of the job they did. Not only does this not seem paradoxical, it seems quite easy to imagine.

Because the terms "internal" and "external" are used elsewhere in this paper to indicate differences between how things look from perspectives within and outside of particular professional groups, and because this is not *precisely* what I am getting at in this section, it will be desirable to find better terms. What I wish to highlight is the difference between what I call "Platonic" standards of competence and what may be called "social" standards.

In the first book of Plato's *Republic*, there is a discussion about the nature of various professions, which arises in the course of Socrates' attempt to refute the contention of Thrasymachus that "justice is the interest of the stronger."8 There, the general contention of Socrates is that the nature of any profession—and the nature of proper professional behavior—may largely be determined through an analysis of the particular activity engaged in by the professional in question. Thus a doctor's interest is in health, a ship's captain's proper interest is in getting the ship safely from one place to another, and the ruler's interest is in running the city-state well.

Complications arise, though, depending upon how one describes a person's profession. While a doctor's job may be to heal patients, a heart specialist's job may be to fix hearts. Some things that are necessarily a part of the business of doing everything possible to fix a heart might imperil other aspects of a patient's health. So what determines one's professional responsibility? While this particular potential conflict may seem relatively easy to resolve, others won't be. Much depends on how one sees the profession. Once a particular profession has been described in terms of a particular sort of task, however, the *Platonic* criteria of competency will arise, more or less as a matter of *logic*, from the nature of the task itself.

Social criteria of competency are not the same. One might become as competent as you please at some odd task or another, and this task might be very difficult, involving skills of a high order and, even, considerable training; one will not thereby have established any *social* value. And where people other than the professional have any interest at all in what that professional does, there arises at least the possibility of conflict over criteria of competency in that profession. For any activity at all, whether legitimately to be described as a "profession" or not, the same distinction can be made: Platonic criteria of competency measure how well the activity is performed, given the internal logic of that activity; social criteria of competency measure how well the activity is performed, given various external goals and values.

Finally, the issue comes to a head when conflict arises, as it often does, over how the Platonic and social criteria of competency may best be measured against one another. Especially interesting, in this regard, are the contentions of some professionals that the best way to serve general *social* goals may be to ignore them, in the short term, and to favor, instead, Platonic goals.

Thus doctors may argue, rightly or wrongly, that the best overall care for the patient may come from specialists who concentrate on their special domains of expertise, rather than on anything so ambiguous as general well-being. Or physicists may argue that

less ultimate social good will come from scientists who worry too much about social good itself than from scientists who stick to pure research. Or teachers may contend that too much attention to styles of classroom presentation distract attention from substance, which is most important to students in the long run.

The Platonic and social criteria of professional competence are often hard to distinguish, since there can be no doubt that many professions have service (for example) as part of their internal value system. Even in such professions, it is possible to distinguish between different emphases among practitioners upon relatively Platonic and relatively social criteria, and debates about the relative importance of each are widespread in virtually all professions.

Since such debates often come to a head in discussions surrounding the design and development of professional codes of ethics, it is important to attempt to shed as much light as possible on the way professions look from the inside. And in order to expose the particular features of professions that seem to me to be most central to professionalism taken generally, it is helpful to focus attention on professions other than the commonly chosen examples like law, medicine, or engineering. Indeed, it is useful to get as far away as possible from all professions whose contributions are deemed fundamental to social well-being.

As I hope to show, the perceived importance of these professions in social life has led to a persistent failure to see the most fundamental features of what the professions mean to the professionals themselves, and to an attempted co-optation of the writing of professional codes by people outside the profession (or by people whose goals are to increase the level of appreciation for the profession by outsiders). Such externally oriented motivations are not unreasonable, nor is it likely, in realistic terms, that they can be altogether ignored in the construction and development of professional codes. But even an attempt to get a clearer understanding of *their* role in the construction of professional codes of ethics is best served if we put them, for the moment, aside.

III. Solidarity among Professionals

So far I have briefly sketched some reasons for doubting that the idea of external service must be involved in the definition of "profession" or any of its cognates. A bit more tentatively, I have suggested that whether such considerations are central to the nature of professional codes of ethics is debatable. By way of moving toward consideration of some nonstandard professions, and thereby to a consideration of a central element within professional codes of ethics that is too frequently missed or underestimated, it is useful to say a word or two about the thesis that the idea of *solidarity among professionals* is somehow central to the very concept of a profession, and plays a necessary role in the design of professional codes of ethics.

Some of the problems that I will address are identified in a valuable recent article by Michael Davis, where he writes:

> ... a code of ethics is primarily a *convention between professionals*. According to this explanation, a profession is a group of persons who want to cooperate in serving the same ideal better than they could if they did not cooperate. Engineers, for example, might be thought to serve the ideal of efficient design, construction, and maintenance of safe and useful objects. A code of ethics would then prescribe how professionals are to pursue their common ideal so that each may do the best she can at minimal cost to herself and those she cares about (including the public, if looking after the public is part of what she cares about). The code is to protect each professional from certain pressures (for example, the pressure to cut corners to save money) by making

it reasonably likely (and more likely than otherwise) that most other members of the profession will *not* take advantage of her good conduct. A code protects members of a profession from certain consequences of competition. A code is a solution to a co-ordination problem.[9]

Davis clearly describes a code of ethics as being fundamentally conventional. Such a reading is bound to meet with resistance among professionals who think of their codes as getting at something objective about the profession, or who aspire to capturing the real character of their profession in their code.[10] One might expect to find arguments that run as broad and as deep in this area as the ones about "natural law" in ethics proper, and the arguments deployed on both sides are likely to have implications that run deep into standard considerations of ethical theory.

Davis goes on to suggest that a profession is a group of persons who want to cooperate in serving common ideals. This is not obvious. Why should professions be defined in terms of a desire for cooperation? No doubt professionals often do hope to gain support from colleagues in pursuit of a common cause, but this is hardly necessary. And differences in the degree to which cooperation is called for—or even possible—depend in large measure upon the differing characteristics of the various professions.

It is not altogether impossible to imagine, for example, professionals who take it as a fundamental part of their profession that they do what they do alone, without the support of anyone. For such a profession, one might also imagine a code of ethics that found expression for this ideal. Being an individualist is not itself a profession, but is it not conceptually possible to imagine a genuine profession which involved solitary activity in a fundamental way? And is it not also possible that such professionals would recognize and admire one another, and that they might further adhere to some—at least tacit—code of professional ethics, which might explicitly call for individuality and non-cooperation? If these are conceptually possible, then we should at least be cautious in defining the term "profession" in such a way as to exclude them.

Finally, Davis describes the task of a code of professional ethics as prescribing "how professionals are to pursue their common ideal so that each may do the best she can at minimal cost to herself and those she cares about (including the public, if looking after the public is part of what she cares about)." Why should there be any assumption at all about whether professional codes of ethics will or will not include provisions about common pursuits, individual interests of professionals, or concern for outsiders? Davis's formulation, quite clearly contrary to the views of those who take service to be *central* to the very idea of the "professional," seems to presume that "looking after the public" will *not* be among the ideals of the profession, the pursuit of which the code aims at clarifying. Instead, he includes them among things that the professional herself might (or might not) "care about."

What warrants this presumption? One might actually expect (as some of the authors mentioned earlier clearly do) that such an ideal is quite central to many professions, and that codes of ethics in those professions would attempt to give expression to this ideal. It is hard to avoid the conclusion that *this* difference among the "internalists" and "externalists" about the nature of professions and the nature of professional codes stems, in large part, from concentration on different professions, or at least on different *models* of professional life. If this is true, then what is revealed is an insufficiently general notion of professions and professional codes. What should be sought is an analysis that is general enough as to underwrite the debates about substantive detail that professionals (and outsiders) may argue about.

A further consideration illuminates even more the concerns I have with an understanding of professional codes of ethics like that expressed by Davis.

If the interests of professionals were central to their codes of ethics, and if concern for outsiders were only peripheral and contingent upon the interests of the professionals, why would honesty or fair dealing to outsiders play such a fundamental role in many of them?[11] I certainly admit that honesty and fair dealing can be defended on grounds of self-interest—this is the claim, anyway, of ethical eudaemonists and egoists from Plato to Rand—but is that why they appear in professional codes? Or is this phenomenon better understood as more directly founded on considerations of professional pride and personal self-respect, whether these latter are themselves to be defended egoistically or not? Is it solely because professional groups hope to gain respectability in the broader community that it promotes such values? Is this just public relations?

Where does any sense of duty or obligation enter into Davis's analysis of professional codes of ethics? And wherever such consideration does enter the analysis—if at all—to whom or what are the several obligations owed? Must the obligations all be directed toward the community? Or toward other professionals? How about toward certain standards that themselves appear to professionals to be intrinsic to the very idea of their particular professions? Like accuracy in the case of accountants? Or like healing in the case of physicians? Surely it is reasonable to expect that professional codes of ethics will contain explicit or implicit references not only to rights and interests, but to obligations of these and other kinds, not all directed to one overarching behavioral or moral end, but directed in every which way. Indeed, it seems likely that codes of ethics are deemed valuable—or even necessary, sometimes—because of a need to establish some balance among rights, interests and obligations that point in several different directions at once.[12]

Imagine a code of professional ethics that asserts an (at least *prima facie*) obligation to obey one's employer, regardless of consequences to the public (perhaps on the ground of discretion, comparable to the similar rule applicable to one or another extent to ministers, lawyers, doctors, and accountants). Imagine professionals who might involve themselves in such a profession.

It is possible that G. Gordon Liddy once thought of himself as just this kind of professional.[13] We on the outside might dislike—might even be horrified—by Liddy's profession. But it is not at all difficult to imagine that a group of such professionals might have an explicit or implicit code of ethics.

IV. Honor among Thieves— Romancing the Code

What are the initial internal motivators that lead professionals to establish codes of ethics, independently of outside pressure? They need not have anything to do with obligations to the public. They need not have to do with interests of professionals as normally construed. They might have a lot to do with certain more or less romantic pictures not only of a line of work, but of a way of life.

Professionals, both traditionally and in modern life, frequently identify themselves in a certain way with certain of their activities. Professional codes of ethics often strive to capture the essence of the character and style that animates the self-image common among practitioners.[14] Professions, and their codes, mean something to practitioners that is not shared with outsiders.

With this general theme in mind, I offer as an exemplar not engineering and not medicine—professions whose importance to the public makes it hard to see them purely as professions, rather than as service organizations—but professional crime.[15]

If the mark of a professional is competency at some difficult task, then not any or every criminal (i.e., breaker of the law) could be understood as a professional. But there is no reason to suppose that undesirable or illegal activity is in any way *excluded* from the domain of professionalism. Indeed, there is a considerable body of romantic fiction that focuses

on criminals who are really quite good at accomplishing the most remarkable criminal feats. Our attitude toward them is characteristically torn: we are (for the most part) critical of their dirty deeds, but we admire their skill and, perhaps, their panache. It is not at all hard to understand the claim that they are real professionals, even though we are not pleased with their activities and even though they may be acting quite alone. It is not at all unheard of that such professionals can band together, and even establish codes of ethics. For the most vivid example of such a phenomenon, one need only turn to what is widely known as the realm of "organized crime."

Modern criminal brotherhoods—like the Mafia, the Cosa Nostra, or the Unione Corse—all seem to have descended from the Garduna of fifteenth-century Spain. The descent is in almost every case quite straightforward: a cadre sent out by a parent organization into new territory collaborates with native criminals to form a new society, organized along structural lines set out by the old one.[16] The parallel with political colonization is quite interesting, especially in the subsequent development of the new societies: sometimes the new organizations remain loyal to the parent, sometimes they rebel.

The Spanish Garduna appears to have been organized in about 1417. It was thus already a venerable institution by 1598, when Luis Zapata described it:

> In Seville there is said to be a brotherhood of thieves with a chief magistrate and captains who sell services; it has a depository for stolen goods and a chest with three keys in which the loot is kept; from this chest they take what they need to defray expenses and to bribe those who are in a position to help them when they are in trouble. They are very careful to accept only men who are strong and active and old Christians, their membership being limited to the servants of powerful and high-placed individuals

such as agents of the law; and the first oath to which they swear is that, even though they may be drawn and quartered, they will endure it and will not inform on their companions.[17]

Now, there is certainly no concern for the public reflected in this oath, but it is equally plain that other members of the group stand to benefit from each member's abiding by it. The question is: what motivates any member, when under such duress, to even *think* of abiding by it? We are talking about being drawn and quartered, after all. But the success of the criminal brotherhood over the centuries is to a great extent attributable to the fact that members were indeed inclined to abide by their oaths. What accounts for this fact?

In order to further clarify the nature of the professional society we are talking about, it is important to realize that these were not political or religious organizations that had turned to crime to support other, more commonly accepted undertakings. As David Chandler has explained, the character of the Garduna was historically unique:

> Nothing like the brotherhood existed prior to the fifteenth century. There had been earlier "criminal societies," most notably the Assassins of eleventh-century Persia; the Thugs, founded in thirteenth-century India; and the Chauffeurs, founded in thirteenth-century France. But each of those claimed non-criminal motives to justify their existence. The Assassins were political terrorists. The Thugs and Chauffeurs were religious cults.
>
> The men of the Spanish brotherhood did not lean on such rationales. Their conceptual innovation was to provide their services for church, state, criminals, or virtually any client with the required fee. They conducted themselves as a business, investing some of their revenues in police and political protection, setting some aside for pensions, and sharing the rest as profit. A rigorous code of conduct was imposed and secrecy and discipline were strict.
>
> Their most inflexible law was the application of the death penalty for those who violated either secrecy or discipline. The brotherhood's adherence to that law has subsequently caused a relative absence of historical treatment.[18]

It seems obvious that the motivation to maintain silence in the face of dire threats is mixed. The threat of death to those who squeal, imposed by the brotherhood itself, is not to be ignored. Under all but the most life-threatening of situations, one can easily imagine that the force behind the society's rigorous code was the threat of punishment.

But it is just as easy to imagine that members of the society were frequently enough placed in just the kind of life-threatening situations that make it difficult to see why they would have remained silent. Is it really in one's interest to avoid death at the hands of the brotherhood by allowing oneself to be drawn and quartered?

While it is possible to imagine that the vows of secrecy and the like that were part of the Garduna code were further enforced by threats to family and loved ones, surely one ingredient is missing from this picture: honor and self-respect. For whatever reason, members of Garduna were encouraged to think of themselves as part of a special society, with special requirements. Those who violated the code were dishonored, were outcasts.

This theme is to be found, of course, in professional societies, guilds, and leagues throughout the Middle Ages. Professional groups like these represent genuine micro-societies which, by virtue of the fact that they are to some extent voluntarily chosen by individual professionals—or at least aspired to—can expect members to have personal, internal motivation to abide by the rules. Since this is the case, professional codes have the potential of being significantly more compelling than general social mores, even more compelling than the law. For they speak to people with the voice of what they aspire to—they speak to their self-image. And they speak from a platform that may be expected to command the respect of the professional more than would someone who did not share a healthy part of that professional's self-image.

V. Conclusion—Romancing the Professions

Among the consequences of this understanding of professional codes of ethics are these: where they are not simply imposed from the outside that is, where they grow from internal need within the profession—they may be expected to have considerable force. While part of this force involves threats made against non-compliance, a large part may be expected to be the result of the identification of the professional with her colleagues. Thus they may serve as ideals, evocations of the romance of the profession, and as expressions of certain general characteristics and modes of behavior deemed within the profession to be the mark of the professional.

Where they are well crafted, they have the support of the individuals who think of themselves as professionals within that field. They will not be seen as burdens, but as badges or banners. They are not rules that must slavishly be followed on threat of disbarment or other similar penalty, but proclamations of the line drawn between professionals and non-professionals, between us and them.

Thus, where they are well crafted, professional codes of ethics have great personal force in the lives of professionals. If this comes as a surprise, it is probably because contemporary examples of codes of ethics are frequently not well crafted. They do not manage to evoke the self-images of the professions. They seem to speak to the professions from outside, offering threats and compulsion rather than ideals

and solidarity. Thus they do not have the force that they might have.[19] That force is reserved for the not-so-public shared commitment to ideals that are part of the "common law" among engineers, doctors, lawyers, or whomever. And where some small part of that common law actually does survive in contemporary professional codes of ethics, so does that force.

The struggle over professional codes of ethics is a classical political one. Precisely because a professional code can speak with a powerful and compelling voice to professionals within a particular area, it is in the interest of those who depend on those professionals to capture the code, so to speak. Those of us who aren't engineers but who depend on engineers want them to do this, to never do that, and always to think of us in whatever they do. We want them to ostracize anyone who doesn't make us and our welfare the first priority. And we want the professional code to speak to this, because it is so compelling a force in the lives of professionals. But, of course, to the extent that those outside the profession actually do manage to capture the code, it thereby loses the desired force among professionals. The code comes to be perceived by them as something external.

The worst part of all of this is that, in the case of most professional codes, a dedication to honest service probably would have been central even without external prompting: most people do not aspire to membership in the Unione Corse. And, in most cases, such a dedication would have had all the force that internally-generated codes always have—it would have spoken to the very self-images of those who aspire to cast their lives in the mold of the profession in question. But, as part of an externally motivated code, dedication to honest service and the like may become discredited, looking for all the world like selfish demands directed by society at professionals: "Think of us!" "Think of us!" If goals like honest service have come to seem like burdensome obligations, rather than matters of honor, it may be in large part because we have not left our professionals alone.

Should professionals, then, be left to their own devices? Should we let them do anything they want? Certainly not. We must, for example, protect ourselves from those who would collude to violate our rights. But it is the job of the law to do this, however law may be institutionalized.[20]

The upshot of the suggestions offered in this paper may be that, in the end, keeping professionals honest and otherwise righteous in their dealings with outsiders is not as fundamental a part of the role of professional codes of ethics as might be thought. It is, however, a mistake to understand professional codes as nothing more than conventions established by professionals for the pursuit of their individual or common interests.

Instead, such codes should be seen as having as their most fundamental job the expression of whatever common ideals, images, or goals there may be among professionals. As such they have considerable power, and may be expected to include, at least as a general rule, some provisions concerning fair dealing with outsiders.[21]

If we as outsiders try to capture these codes for our own purposes, we will inevitably rob them of their power. If we try to slide our interests into such codes of ethics surreptitiously—without explicitly trying to capture them—then we may have some success. But the codes will have been corrupted, from the point of view of the professionals, and will accordingly lose some of their power. And we risk alienating professionals from ideals and goals that they might have chosen for themselves, if left alone.

It might be best simply to leave the professional codes entirely to the professionals. Where some profession's code bothers us, let us take this up in the appropriate public forum, and let us make illegal what we cannot allow. But let *us* do that. Let us not expect professional codes of ethics to do the work of law. And let us be more tolerant and respectful of the human needs and aspirations that lead to professionalism in the first place. We stand to gain a great deal if we can do *anything* that encourages people to

bring ethical standards back in out of the cold, to a position closer to the heart.

NOTES

1   This paper was read and discussed at the 138th Semiannual Meeting of the Creighton Club (The New York State Philosophical Association), held at Hobart and William Smith Colleges in Geneva, New York, in April of 1993. I am grateful to Steven Lee, Scott Brophy, and the participants in the discussion for their stimulating commentary. I must also thank Wade Robison and Victoria Varga, along with the editor and referees of *Professional Ethics*, for various helpful suggestions and references.

2   See, for example, Karen Lebacqz, *Professional Ethics* (Nashville: Abingdon Press, 1985), as well as sources she refers to, especially A.M. Carr-Saunders and P.A. Wilson, *The Professions* (Oxford: Clarendon Press, 1933) and Carnegie Samuel Calian, *Today's Pastor in Tomorrow's World* (New York: Hawthorne Books, 1977). While Lebacqz orients her careful discussion of professional ethics to issues that especially confront the ministry, the impact of her argument about professional ethics is in no way restricted to that profession alone. Nevertheless, this focus does tend to highlight features of professionalism that, while shared by a number of professions, are not fully universal. Lebacqz ultimately argues for an understanding of professional ethics which emphasizes injunctions about character, rather than about action, and the emphasis is on *other-regarding* character traits. For a more explicitly general attempt to link other-regarding injunctions with the very idea of a profession, see Stephen F. Barker, "What is a Profession?" *Professional Ethics*, vol. I (1 & 2): 73-99.

3   June Goodfield, for example, warns that professional codes of ethics may be misnamed, since they so frequently emphasize issues that

are better understood as matters of etiquette among professionals, "Reflections on the Hippocratic Oaths," *The Hastings Center Studies*, 1(2): 90. Similarly, Lisa Newton has contended that a professional code can become no more than "a code of Professional Manners oriented toward a Professional Image for the protection of Professional Compensation." See Newton, "A Professional Ethic: A Proposal in Context," John E. Thomas (ed.), *Matters of Life and Death* (Toronto: Samuel Stevens, 1978, 264). Just as is true of the more "externalist" characterization of professional codes, this "internalist" picture can be supported with empirical evidence taken from actual codes representing a wide variety of disciplines. But, as will be contended in what follows, to adopt either of these views of codes involves the underemphasis of crucial features of professional codes of ethics that have nothing at all to do with *anyone's* "interests," whether professional, client, or third party.

4 An important similar argument is offered by Bill Puka in his "Commentary" on Heinz C. Luegenbiehl's "Codes of Ethics and the Moral Education of Engineers." Both papers may be found in the *Business and Professional Ethics Journal*, 2(4): 41-66. It must also be noted that it is not unusual to find reference to the importance of "calling" in *many* accounts of professional codes of ethics. This is especially true in discussions of the ministry, where the idea of being "called" to the profession has a literal intent. The argument of this paper is not that the involvement of this factor in professional codes of ethics has never before been noticed; rather, the point is that its importance and centrality in a *general* understanding of professions, professionalism—and, especially, professional codes—has been underestimated. See Mark S. Frankel, "Professional Codes: Why, How, and with What Impact?" *Journal of Business Ethics*, 8(2 & 3): 109-15, for an account which at-

tempts to balance several frequently conflicting factors that contribute to the development of professional codes of ethics. While Frankel acknowledges "aspirational" factors, he does not do full justice to the importance and the romance of "calling" as it plays a role in the perception professionals have of their codes.

5 Some of these papers are collected in an outstanding anthology, edited by Albert Flores, *Professional Ideals* (Belmont, California: Wadsworth, 1988). See especially the articles collected in Section I.

6 It is quite common for terms to shift meaning in this way over time as they become institutionally co-opted. For a thorough discussion of another example of this phenomenon, see John T. Sanders, "Political Authority," *The Monist*, 66(4): 545-56.

7 I do not at all wish to deny that there may be other—even many other—necessary conditions. I argue here only for the centrality and special importance of the one I call attention to. As will become apparent in what follows, for example, I am especially interested in calling attention to the importance, especially in attempting to understand professional *codes* of ethics, of a sense of *commitment* to the "difficult task" in question. Sometimes this sense of commitment will be referred to in what follows as a "calling," and sometimes it will be discussed in terms of the "romance" of a profession. I have resisted, however, the strong temptation to identify this commitment factor as central to the definition of "professional" and its cognates. This is because of the unfortunately widespread phenomenon of people who are plainly (and legitimately) to be referred to as professionals, but who just as plainly despise their work. As hard as it is for me to understand personally, I even know *philosophers* like this. They are not at all committed to their profession, nor do they find it at all romantic. They believe themselves

to be stuck, usually by virtue of their age and of what they perceive to be the difficulty of seeking an alternative profession, in a line of work which they no longer have much interest in. I am afraid that this is not at all anomalous, and have therefore come to the conclusion that the idea of commitment, calling, and the "romance" of a profession, while fundamentally a part of a genuine understanding of professional codes, is not at all central to the more general concept of "professional" and its cognates.

8   I am indebted to Steven Lee for reminding me of the relevance of this passage to my argument.

9   Michael Davis, "Thinking Like an Engineer: The Place of a Code of Ethics in the Practice of a Profession," *Philosophy and Public Affairs*, 20(2): 150-67.

10   Davis acknowledges that thinking of professional codes as "conventions between professionals" has the potential of being misleading. He tries to avoid the problems he sees by urging that the conventions he has in mind are not *contracts*. Instead, they are more like "quasi-contracts" (Davis, *op. cit.*, 156). This move, however, does not succeed in allaying the concerns that I am outlining here.

11   I hope it is clear, by now, that I am objecting as much to the universal *omission* of provisions about service to the community as to the universal *inclusion* of such provisions. An adequate understanding of professionalism, taken generally, ought to accommodate the fact that the inclusion of such provisions will vary from profession to profession, not as a function of professional convention, but as a function of the internal logic of what the various professionals *do*. I will thus be arguing, in what follows, for the primacy of Platonic criteria of competency over social criteria in the analysis of professional codes of ethics.

12   There are individual self-interests, obligations to other professionals and *their* interests, obli-

gations to clients and to the community at large, and obligations that may best be understood as being owed to the very idea of the profession. *All* of these—and many more—may come to play roles in the construction of professional codes of ethics, and all may tug in different directions. The play among the different interests, rights, and obligations may pull the code in different directions at different times during its development. And, of course, different professions will accommodate themselves differently to the sundry demands placed upon them. But as professional codes get pulled away from expression of fundamental ideals and virtues respected by the professionals themselves, they will necessarily play an increasingly less important role in their actual lives and work. Such an eventuality is in *no one's* interest.

13   Acknowledgment of the possibility that people like this may very well be acting "professionally," or even that such professions may exist, is not equivalent to approving or admiring either the professionals themselves or their work. I am contending that the key to whether such activities are reasonably to be labeled "professions" is not whether they make contributions to social life that we approve of, nor is it whether they involve collaboration among professionals for their mutual benefit, I hope it is plain that I also reject the view that merely *declaring* oneself a professional (and one's occupation a profession) is sufficient to make it so. Instead, the mark of a professional is competency at a difficult task. Arguments against calling a particular field a "profession" are thus on the mark where they challenge the difficulty of the work, and arguments against honoring a person as a "professional" are appropriate where they challenge competency *or* difficulty. They are, in my view, *off* the mark if they merely call attention to unsavory features of what is done, or to the lack of suitable organizations and common

motivations among professionals. These latter arguments serve only to support the perfectly reasonable claims that there are some professions that are bad for society and that some professions are unorganized. It is worth noting that, if public service and some mode of organization were part of the very *definition* of "profession," we would be unable to make these latter claims, on logical grounds. It is largely because of the unacceptability of this consequence that I urge the analysis present in the text.

14   For a thorough discussion of such factors, see Lebacqz, *op. cit.*

15   One subgroup among professional criminals is, of course, frequently referred to as "the oldest profession." That modern prostitutes continue to have a professional self-image of themselves is indicated clearly in a 1992 *New York Times* article, in which it was reported that prostitution in the New York City area had begun to move across the river to New Jersey because of a crack epidemic in the city. As one prostitute who made the move explained, "You could say the crack addicts ruined everything ... Here it's more professional" (quoted in Evelyn Nieves, "For Better Business, Prostitutes Leave Manhattan for Jersey City," *New York Times*, 22 September 1992, sections B1 and B6). Outsiders may not take such self-perceptions seriously, but insiders certainly do.

16   For an extraordinarily compelling history of the criminal societies, see David Leon Chandler, *Brothers in Blood: The Rise of the Criminal Brotherhoods* (New York: E.P. Dutton, 1975).

17   Quoted in Chandler, *op. cit.*, 5.

18   Chandler, 2.

19   The journal *Chemical Engineering*, for example, after conducting a survey concerning what engineers would do in a collection of hypothetical "ethical" cases, found that "Although the American Institute of Chemical Engineers, the professional society of many of our US read-

ers, has a code of ethics, this was almost universally ignored in determining the solutions to our survey problems. Fewer than a half-dozen [out of 4318] respondents even mentioned a code of ethics at all." See Roy V. Hughson and Philip M. Kohn, "Ethics," *Chemical Engineering*, 87(19): 132.

20   It is crucial that all who depend upon the work of professionals recognize that *no* perspective on the permissability of behavior that affects others is privileged. Just because respected professionals and their societies insist that certain behaviors ought to be permitted by the wider community (perhaps because these behaviors are alleged to be necessary to the continuing effectiveness of the profession in question), this is by no means a sufficient ground for community approval. Judgments made by professionals, like all judgments, are influenced by a wide variety of factors, some of them relatively Platonic, some of them (both for better and for worse) social. For discussion of some of the effects of this fact on decisions made within and about academic science, see John T. Sanders and Wade L. Robison, "Research Funding and the Value-Dependence of Science," *Business and Professional Ethics Journal*, 11(1): 33-50. For an even darker picture of the consequences of putting too much faith in scientific professionals, see William Broad and Nicholas Wade, *Betrayers of the Truth* (New York: Simon and Schuster, 1982).

21   It is interesting to note that even the code of the Garduna had provisions mandating discretion and quality service to clients.

◆ ◆ ◆ ◆ ◆

MICHAEL DAVIS

Professional Responsibility: Just Following the Rules?

My subject is a criticism of conduct something like this: "That's not acting responsibly, that's just following the rules." The criticism appears as an attack on "legalism" in both business and professional ethics. While my focus here will be on professional ethics, everything I say should, with minor changes, apply equally well to following corporate or other business codes of ethics.

Legalism (it is said) reduces professional responsibility to doing as the profession's code of ethics requires; professional responsibility, like moral responsibility generally, is more open-ended, including (among other things) certain virtues. My subject thus overlaps the larger debate in moral theory between "principle ethics" and "virtue ethics." I shall draw some conclusions relevant to that debate.

My thesis is that following "the rules," while not all there is to professional ethics, is generally enough for responsible conduct (or, at least, is so when the profession's code of ethics is reasonably well written, as most are). Rules set the standard of professional conduct; just following those rules, in a relatively robust but not unusual sense of "following those rules," is acting as a responsible professional.

I. Some Preliminaries

The attack on legalism need not be put in terms of rules. One can make it in terms of "just satisfying one's obligations [or duties]" or "just respecting others' rights." Indeed, Caroline Whitbeck recently combined all three versions in one omnibus attack on legalism: "If rights and obligations or rules about what acts to perform or refrain from performing

were all there were to professional ethics, it would be a simple matter and hardly worthy of attention in a college course."[1]

I shall, however, have little more to say about obligations or rights here for two reasons. First, obligations and rights can be, and often are, stated as rules. Hence, any discussion of rules implicitly includes obligations and rights (more or less). Second, any separate discussion of obligations or rights would complicate my defense of legalism a good deal without adding much of substance. So, I shall concentrate on rules.

When mere rule following is contrasted with acting responsibly, there is always something that mere rule following is supposed to leave out (hence the "mere"). Whitbeck, for example, explains why professional ethics deserve attention in a college course in this way: "The exercise of responsibility typically requires the exercise of discretion and consideration of many technical matters and matters of value."[2] For her, what mere rule following must leave out is, it seems, all exercise of discretion, technical knowledge, and consideration of value. She does not explain why mere rule following might leave all this out. The explanation is not obvious—as I shall now show.

Consider this brief rule of engineering ethics having its counterpart in the code of ethics of most professions: "Engineers shall perform services only in areas of their competence."[3] Sometimes engineers do not need discretion or even much technical knowledge to know that the service in question is beyond their competence. (Think of an engineer asked to do brain surgery because she has a doctorate—in engineering.) Often, however, engineers do need discretion, technical knowledge, and an understanding of the values inherent in engineering's conception of competence to decide whether a certain service is within their competence. For example, whether writing a certain computer program is within the competence of an engineer may depend in part on whether the errors she is likely to commit given her skill would create substantial risks for users or third parties. Deciding whether a risk is substantial combines technical judgments (such-and-such errors are likely) with judgments of value (the risks are, or are not, substantial).

We must, I think, assume that Whitbeck knows this. So, her criticism of rules must make a different point—one her words leave us to guess. We are, then, in no position to decide whether her criticism of rules—or the similar criticism of others—is justified until we understand what "just following the rules" leaves out. And we are not likely to understand that until we understand what just following the rules might be. For that reason, I devote the body of this paper to considering seven different interpretations of "just following the rules," all that I have found in the literature, noticed in conversation, or made up on my own: blind obedience, strict obedience, malicious obedience, negligent obedience, accidental obedience, stupid obedience, and interpretative obedience. Having examined these seven, I conclude that, for professional ethics at least, the criticism of just following the rules is unjustified. Under but one interpretation of just following the rules, the rules are not in fact being followed. Under that one (the interpretative), there is nothing obviously wrong with just following the rules.

II. Following Rules Blindly or Strictly

Mere rule following is doing what the rule says without concern for context or consequence, a "mechanical" or "blind" obedience. Finding a clear example of such obedience is hard. Here is the best I have (blind obedience, though not exactly to a rule): One day, at age two, my son was having trouble opening a cabinet door because of a safety latch. Instead of opening the door for him, I advised him to "use his head." He immediately obeyed, giving the door a hard rap with his forehead, apparently without thought to any alternative interpretation of my ad-

vice or even to past experience of banging his head against a hard surface. He has not given me such blind obedience since.

Though rational in some contexts, strict obedience does not seem rational as a general way to practice a profession. Strict obedience makes sense where judgment is justifiably separated from performance (for example, where some "higher" authority is in the best position to "reason why" and others, subordinates, to "do or die"). The general name for the separation of judgment from performance is "hierarchy." Since hierarchy tends to ignore what subordinates think, however well-informed and judicious the subordinates may be, any justification of strict obedience must identify a compensating advantage. On the battlefield, the compensating advantage is pretty clear. The coordination of large masses in movement is difficult under the best of conditions. In battle, with the noise and confusion, there is little opportunity for joint deliberation even in a unit as small as a platoon or squad. The alternative to obeying the order of a superior is disorder or delay, potentially disastrous when coordination and speed matter.

Few, if any, professions demand strict obedience to an ethical authority. But even if they all did, the result would not be relevant to our subject. Where one has rendered strict obedience to an ethical authority, the proper description is "I was just obeying orders" or "I was just following controlling precedent" rather than "I was just following the rules."

III. Malicious Obedience

Sometimes the description, "I was just following the rules," occurs in defense of conduct. To have acted according to the rules, however bad the outcome and however foolish the rules, is to have acted in a way insulating one from (full) responsibility. The most common use of "just following rules" in this sense, or at least the most visible, is when employees "strike" their employer by "working to rule" or "going by the book." This form of strike is particularly satisfying to employees and maddening for the employer. The employees continue to be paid, though they are costing their employer money, time, and grief. The employer cannot complain without admitting that "the book" is wrong. For many employers, the point of having "the book" is to have a basis for disciplining employees when they fail to do as they should. So, working to rule catches the employer in his own trap. One way or another, the employer must "eat his words." Think, for example, how the police can bring traffic to a halt on a busy highway simply by ticketing every traffic violation they observe—as many police manuals require.

What does working to rule leave out? Another name for working to rule, "malicious obedience," suggests an answer. What working to rule leaves out is the good will employees otherwise give their employer. Ordinarily, employees interpret the rules to take into account the inability of general language to anticipate special cases; they try to understand what the employer is trying to achieve by laying down such rules; they use "common sense."

Working to rule resembles strict obedience. In both, there is an obvious disconnection between what a reasonable person would think should be done, all else equal, and what the person in question is doing. In both too, there is a reason, though not the same reason, for the disconnection. The difference between strict obedience and working to rule is that, in strict obedience, the reason for the disconnection is the overall good of the enterprise; in working to rule, the reason is the exact opposite. The employee takes into account what would be good for the employer only in order to choose an interpretative strategy to defeat it.

We may distinguish a weak sense and a strong sense of malicious obedience. In the weak sense, malicious obedience is the malicious adoption of an interpretative strategy that is not itself malicious. For example, the principle "Be literal" might be adopted for reasons other than malice. But, in working to rule, it is adopted maliciously, that is, with the in-

tent, expectation or hope that literalness will make trouble for the employer. Malicious obedience in the strong sense carries malice one step further. Not only is the interpretative strategy adopted maliciously but what is adopted also has malice built into it, for example, "Choose the most damaging interpretation the language allows."

What do these two forms of working to rule have to do with just following a code of professional ethics? For most of these codes, the answer must be: little. The codes themselves contain rules of interpretation. Often gathered at the front under the heading "preamble," "principles," or "canons" to distinguish them from less general directives, these rules of interpretation effectively rule out malicious obedience. For example, the NSPE's "Code of Ethics for Engineers" includes at least two "Fundamental Canons" that seem to rule out malice:

> Engineers, in the fulfilment of their professional duties, shall:
> 1. Hold paramount the safety, health, and welfare of the public in the performance of their professional duties, [and]
> 4. Act in professional matters for each employer or client as faithful agents or trustees. Specific rules of practice must then be read to protect the public welfare and to serve the employer as a faithful agent or trustee. An engineer cannot simply work to rule.

I do not claim that such general principles of interpretation make following the rules easy. On the contrary, I admit they make following the rules hard. My point is that, as they do that, they also rule out most, perhaps all, the malicious interpretations of rules necessary for malicious obedience.

Or, rather, that is one of my points. Malicious obedience requires a conscious misunderstanding of the rules; there can also be unconscious misunderstanding. For example, engineers have been known to argue that the rule requiring them to serve each client or employer as a faithful agent or trustee imposes a professional obligation to cut costs even when doing so endangers the public. These engineers neither reject the obligation to the public welfare nor misinterpret it. They just do not think of it as they try to do what they should. They fail to exercise reasonable care in interpreting their professional code. If malicious obedience is a conscious failure to exercise reasonable care in interpreting the rules, then what we are now contemplating is an unconscious failure. We must now consider three forms of unconscious failure to just follow the rules.

IV: Negligent and Accidental Obedience

Some writers have recently taken to contrasting the law's "malpractice" or "negligence" standard of tort liability with the "due care" (or "reasonable care") standard of true professionalism. Until I read these writers, I had supposed that negligence was a relatively clear concept. I now see that it is not. So, to avoid misunderstanding, let me explain what I once supposed obvious.

In the common law, both American and English, negligence is, almost by definition, a failure to exercise due care in our relations with others. In negligence law, the interesting question is not whether anyone, especially a professional, should be held to the due-care standard. Due care is the minimum standard even for a child or a madman. The interesting question is what due care requires. For example, Prosser, the leading authority on torts, understands a failure of due care as "[conduct] which should be recognized as involving unreasonable danger to others."[4]

Any distinction between what one's profession requires and what is merely legally required cannot be made in terms of "due care"—or, at least, cannot be so made without inviting confusion. A profession does not need a code of ethics to be held to the standard of due care. The law already does that; the

any malpractice suit (for negligence) will allege a failure of due care. What a code of professional ethics does, if it does anything beyond restating existing legal obligations is to set a new standard of care, one higher than existed before. That new standard can, in virtue of the code, become what may reasonably be expected of members of the profession; it is reasonable to expect members of a profession to do what they commit themselves to doing. Some dangers that had been reasonable before would then become unreasonable, raising the legal minimum for members of the profession and thereby turning into malpractice conduct previously allowed to the profession (and still allowed to others). A profession's code of ethics helps define what care is due from members of that profession and, in doing that, to set the standard of malpractice for them. But, whatever the standard, anything less than good practice is malpractice.[5]

Negligent obedience is, then, a failure to exercise due care in following the relevant rules, whether the failure unreasonably risks harm to others or is in some other way faulty. Negligent obedience differs from (what we shall call) stupid obedience in that the failure need not arise from an inability to act as one should. Stupid obedience is a matter of competence; negligent obedience is not (or, at least, need not be).

The term "negligent obedience" may seem paradoxical. Insofar as the obedience in question is negligent, how can it be obedience? Is it not literally failure to obey? But, insofar as the obedience in question is literally obedience, how can it be negligent? The paradox is resolved by distinguishing the subjective side of obedience from the objective. Subjectively that is, from the point of view of the agent, negligent obedience is obedience. The agent must believe that she is acting as she should or her disobedience would be malicious, not negligent. She must, in other words, mean well even as she in fact fails to do what meaning well would ordinarily lead her, or at least someone of ordinary prudence, to do.

What she does fails to be obedience only objectively, that is, from the point of view of people of ordinary prudence not directly involved.

What if, from the point of view of ordinary prudence, she seemed to follow the rule, but did so without knowing or intending it? Her act would correspond to what the rule required, but only by accident.[6] This is an exotic form of acting according to the rule rather than following it. Though she might (truthfully and effectively) defend her conduct by saying, "I followed the rule," she could not defend it by saying, "I was just following the rule." "I followed the rule" means I did nothing contrary to the rule. "I was just following the rule" may, or may not, mean that, but it always means that one satisfied the subjective condition that is, that one at least tried to determine what the rule requires.

What if she did try to follow the rule, though in a way we would regard as clearly negligent had she not in fact acted in accordance with the rule? We would be inclined to say (something like): "Well, all's well that ends well, but you really should learn how to interpret the rule." We would not, in other words, regard her as someone who was just following the rules (in a sense requiring no apology). Trying to follow the rule is not all there is to the subjective side; the trying must meet a certain standard of care. The trying must be of a sort likely to result in following the rule.

Negligent obedience is always a failure to follow the rule; accidental obedience, while not a failure to follow the rule, is at least a failure to follow the rule for the right reason, that is, because one has understood it properly. Negligent failure to understand the rule properly may arise from lack of the appropriate virtue (such as carefulness). But it need not. Lack of virtue is neither necessary nor sufficient for negligent obedience.

Some negligent obedience may arise even where everyone is as virtuous as humanly possible. The prudent person (a human being), acting as judge, may see error the prudent person as agent (also a human being) might overlook (even though she should not). Lack of virtue is not a necessary condition for negligent obedience.

Lack of virtue is also not a sufficient condition for negligent obedience. Even a relatively careless person can (sometimes) exercise due care—though she may have to try hard to do it. Her trying hard enough may, as a matter of fact, arise (in part) from other virtues, such as practical wisdom or concern for others; but it might also arise from less noble grounds, such as greed or fear of punishment. Whatever the ground, if she tries hard, she may be able to do as the rule requires; and doing that, she does not act negligently, however lacking in the virtue of care she may be. Nor is her obedience merely accidental; it is the ordinary consequence of her deliberate effort.

Since lack of virtue is neither necessary nor sufficient for negligent obedience, negligent obedience cannot be understood as a failure of virtue (a failure to have, or to act from, the virtue of due care). Negligent obedience must, instead, be understood as a failure to follow certain rules (for example, "Avoid unreasonable risk to others").

In saying this, I am not denying that acting well is easier if one is virtuous than if one is not. I agree that, for example, a competent engineer is more likely to exercise due care in his professional work if he is meticulous, alert, thoughtful, and serious than if he is not. All I am denying is that the link between good conduct and any particular virtue (or virtue in general) is close enough that, even under the best of conditions actually possible, the one can guarantee the other: acting from virtue is no substitute for just following the rules.

V. Stupid Obedience

Those who obey stupidly resemble the negligent in unconsciously failing to exercise due care in interpreting the relevant rules. They differ from the negligent only in the cause of failure. Unlike the negligent, the stupid fail because they do not know better. The cause of not knowing better may be original, that is, a lack of native wit, or educational, for example, never having been taught how to interpret the rule in question. In law, the most common form of stupid obedience is the layman's trying to follow a statute without considering how case law may have made the statute's simple language treacherous. In professional ethics, the most common form of stupid obedience is, I think, reading a code of ethics as if each rule were independent of the others.

The stupid have an excuse the negligent do not. They are not free of blame. One can blame another for an act or for its consequences. To blame someone for an act is to declare the act bad and his; to blame him for some state of affairs is to declare the state of affairs bad and some act or omission of his the cause. To excuse someone's failure to follow a rule by saying, "He doesn't know better," does not save him from blame; it only changes the terms.

Whether the change of terms even amounts to a reduction in blame is a matter of opinion: many of us might prefer to be thought malicious or negligent rather than stupid. In any case, for a professional, stupidity is as objectionable as malice.

Perhaps many of those professionals who seek to excuse themselves for misconduct with the answer, "I was just following the rules," are pleading stupidity. It is therefore worth pointing out that whenever this plea is necessary, the professional in question was not in fact following the rules (even if she was doing her best to follow them). In this respect, stupid obedience resembles the other forms of "just following the rules" discussed so far. It is a failure to follow the rules.

VI. Interpretative Obedience

Except for blind obedience, all the forms of rule following discussed so far acknowledged, however implicitly, that rules must be interpreted. In strict obedience, the interpretation is largely left to others

("higher authority"). In malicious obedience, interpretation is deliberately abused; in negligent or accidental obedience, interpretation is not given the attention it deserves; and in stupid obedience, interpretation is not done skillfully enough, whether from lack of wit or learning. This list of ways in which one can fail to follow the rules suggests that just following the rules is not simple. We must now consider just how complicated it can be.

In law, there are many methods of interpreting a rule. They are not exclusive, though some are likely to be more important in one area of the law and others in another. When interpreting a particular rule, one important question is always how that rule fits with the others in the particular document in which it appears. All else equal, a particular will, contract, statute, or other document should, if possible, be interpreted so that each term keeps the same meaning throughout, none of its rules is inconsistent with any other, and all serve the document's avowed purpose (or at least that none works against it). This "internalist" approach may yield one defensible interpretation but more often yields several. Where there are several internally defensible interpretations, there may be no way to choose except to go outside the document.

There may, in any case, be other reasons to go outside the document. For example, the internalist interpretation may have yielded an immoral or irrational result, or violated the intentions of those who composed the document (intentions indicated by evidence outside the document itself).

Lawyers often describe an interpretation of a rule as a "construction." The description is hardly metaphorical. Interpreting a rule is as much construction as discovery. There are, therefore, differences in style that, though well within the bounds of competence, may lead well-meaning lawyers to quite different results. Some lawyers may, all else equal, think going back to the intentions of the actual authors the best guide to what a rule means; others, that the best guide is what decent, well-informed, and rational authors would have meant when the document was drafted or would mean today; others may think the best guide is what the "plain man" would suppose such words to mean; and others how a particular interpretation fits with the way the law is developing. Some may think that a particular method of interpretation pre-empts the rest. Others may think that each method is relevant, carrying a certain weight, the overall construal being determined by some combination of methods. And so on. When a lawyer speaks of "just following the rule," she is likely to mean "just following the interpretation of the rule I find obvious using the method of interpretation I take for granted."[7]

We have a profession, lawyers, who make their living in part by offering possible interpretations of rules, and another, judges, who make theirs in part by deciding between lawyers' interpretations. This at least suggests that following some rules, the rules of a legal system, can be quite complicated. While there is no profession in which the rules of professional ethics reach the complexity of even a relatively simple legal system, we need not be surprised that learning how to follow a code of professional ethics should require college course work. After all, lawyers need three years of law school to learn how to interpret the law.

What must we teach students in order to teach them how to follow the code of ethics of their hoped-for profession? We must, of course, teach them the context in which the code is to be applied, that is, something of the history of the profession, of the organizations in which members of the profession work, of the expectations other members of the profession will have of their colleagues, and of what members do (and the effect what they do can have on others). We must also teach something about the purpose of the rules, the structure of the code (the relation of one rule to another), the interpretative strategies considered appropriate, and the consequences of certain mistakes in interpretation. We should help students to see their profession's code

of ethics as the work of human beings much like themselves, human beings who have specific purposes in developing such rules and should therefore be open to revising them, or standing interpretations of them, as new information comes in. Last, and perhaps most important, we should give practice in following the rules, that is, in analyzing specific "fact situations," applying the rules to those facts, reaching conclusions about what is required, allowed, or forbidden, making arguments in defense of the conclusions, and inventing ways to do as the rules so interpreted say. One does not know how to follow a rule unless one knows how to develop, state, defend, and carry out workable courses of action in accord with the rule in contexts in which the rule ordinarily applies.

VII. What Is Left Out?

This (interpretative) way of understanding "just following the rules" leaves us with the question with which we began: what does just following the rules leave out? What I have argued so far is that the rules of professional ethics themselves exclude certain forms of "just following the rules" (malicious, negligent, accidental, and stupid obedience); other forms (blind and strict obedience) are not following the rules at all. Only one interpretation of just following the rules of professional ethics, the interpretative, seems robust enough to count as just following the rules (without some apologetic qualification). That interpretation seems to leave nothing important out.

My argument, even admitting its soundness, may seem to miss what underlay the objection to "*just* following the rules" with which we began, the idea (introduced by "just") of trying to get by with the minimum, a failure to make room for the "spirit" of the rules as well as the "letter." To this fundamental objection, I have two replies, one general and one particular. The general reply is that "the spirit of the rule" is a metaphor. By itself, it tells us little. My own view is that the appropriate interpretative strategy is the rule's spirit. It is what gives life to the otherwise dead letters of a rule. Those who try to follow a rule without the appropriate interpretative strategy may think of themselves as "just following the rule" but they are likely to fail to follow it. That is the lesson of negligent and stupid obedience. Those who have criticized "just following the rules" seem not to have realized how much goes into following a rule. That is not to say that virtue is not relevant to following the rules. It is, instead, to point to a particular rarely-mentioned virtue, the disposition to interpret rules correctly, as crucial to responsible professional conduct (though not defining of it), to come a long way down from the airy world in which rules are hardly worth mention to one in which teaching the rules is central to developing the crucial virtue.

That is my general reply. My particular reply is a challenge to individual critics: show me a clear case of professional responsibility that is not just following the profession's code of ethics. By "clear case" I mean one that most members of the profession would agree is uncontroversial.

I feel safe making this challenge because I think the critics of legalism badly underestimate what rules can do. Rules can set high standards; set positive standards as well as negative; and provide guidance on when to make exceptions to otherwise binding rules. Rules can also require virtues such as competence and caring.[8] There is no reason, except oversight, why a profession's code should leave out anything most members of the profession consider important.

But, surely (it may be asked), is there not something wrong with a professional trying to get by with the minimum required? This question may be understood as raising one of two objections. If we emphasize "trying" (an attitude), we get an objection to a certain interpretative strategy one to which few, if any, professional codes allow. Consider again the preamble of the NSPE code. Does it not point the faithful interpreter toward "the highest principles"

rather than "the minimum"? How can an engineer follow that code and try to do the minimum?

If, instead of emphasizing the trying, we emphasize the outcome ("the minimum required"), we get an objection to doing only what the code in fact requires. The point of the objection so interpreted escapes me. Why would a professional not be acting responsibly if she did only what her profession code of ethics required? The attack on legalism (the call to "go beyond" the rules) may be a confused way of proposing reforms—in the rules themselves or in their interpretation. If so, the professional responsibilities put forward are beyond the rules— the rules as written if not the rules as they could be written—will, upon examination, turn out to be controversial.[9]

NOTES

1 Caroline Whitbeck, *Ethics in Engineering Practice and Research* (Cambridge, UK: Cambridge University Press, 1998), 83.

2 Whitbeck, 83.

3 National Society of Professional Engineers, *Code of Professional Ethics* (1997), II.2.

4 "The almost universal use of the phrase 'due care' to describe conduct that is not negligent, should not be permitted to obscure the fact that the real basis of negligence is ... behavior which should be recognized as involving an unreasonable danger to others." William L. Prosser, *Law of Torts, 4th Ed.* (St. Paul, MN: West Publishing, 1971), 145.

5 Or, to be more exact, it is malpractice if the other conditions of negligence are also present (an unreasonable risk to others, a resulting harm, measurable loss, and so on).

6 I owe the identification of accidental obedience to Robert McCutcheon, Davis and Elkins College.

7 For some idea of how complicated interpretation of rules can be, see Ronald Dworkin, *Laws Empire* (Cambridge, MA: Harvard

University Press, 1986)—or any good text in jurisprudence.

8 For example, engineering could have some such rule as this: "Engineers shall be competent" or "Engineers shall care deeply about the environment." But how (it might be asked) can a rule require one to have a virtue? Mustn't rules—as guides to conduct—require conduct? Well, no—and yes. Rules need not explicitly require conduct. They can simply set qualifications (as our two examples do). Since those who cannot meet the qualifications cannot be as the rule requires, they can only follow the rule by avoiding coming under it, that is, by staying out of the profession in question or, having got in before the lack of virtue was discovered, by leaving. Rules explicitly requiring virtue implicitly require conduct (that is, the not-getting-into-situations-where-one-cannot-be-as-required).

9 Lest my own words in *Thinking Like an Engineer* (New York: Oxford University Press, 1998), 59, be quoted against me, I should point out that I am not here speaking (as I was there) of tasks professionals have "good reason" to take on or assign, but of tasks they have taken on already in virtue of membership in a profession having a certain code of ethics and are therefore required of them.

UNIT 1

Ethics in Accounting and Finance

ANAND VAIDYA

Ethics in Accounting and Finance

Unlike issues in legal and medical ethics that are highly visible because of their constant presence in our lives, the news media, and through television programs that dramatize them, ethical issues pertaining to accounting and finance are, by comparison, far less known to the general public. It is safe to say that until recently the general public's perception of accounting and finance was one on which both were thought of as containing relatively few ethical issues of importance. However, this point of view is due more to a lack of awareness of the ethical issues than to any other factor concerning the importance of the issues.

In the case of finance, one issue, that of insider trading, has been around at least since the middle of the twentieth century. It is a highly complex issue involving both cultural and economic factors. Some of the ethical issues surrounding insider trading were brought to the public's attention by the classic American movie *Wall Street*. However, it was not until the late 1990s when a slew of corporate scandals involving principal accounting firms, such as Arthur Andersen, and huge corporations, such as Enron, that the general public became aware that both accounting and finance were areas ripe with ethical issues of a great consequence.

One central issue in accounting ethics involves the identification and navigation of conflicts of interest, an issue that is also at play in legal and medical ethics. Conflicts of interest often arise for accountants out of the fact that they have an obligation to the public to accurately and to the best of their judgment audit the financial statements of a corporation when hired to do so. However, as a member of an independent corporation, such as an accounting firm, they have a fiduciary responsibility to their employer to attract and to maintain clients through providing accounting services. Although these roles need not conflict, they may come into conflict through internal corporate pressure.

The conflicting responsibilities that an accountant may face are further exacerbated by the fact that, although there are rules governing the reporting of financial statements, these rules are open to reasonable disagreement and allow for a plurality of reporting strategies. This plurality of reporting strategies places an accountant in a situation where they could report financial statements one way to the public, and another way to the board of the corporation or to the SEC. The possibility of reporting things two different ways brings forth the issue of whether both parties have a moral right to the same information. If both parties have a right to the same information, then an accountant must choose from amongst the methodologies available a best method.

The possibility of reporting financial statements in different ways arises from The Generally Accepted Accounting Principles (GAAP), which is, in part, a guide to the reporting of financial statements. GAAP has gaps, which allow for a plurality of reporting methodologies. For example, an accountant could restructure the financial holdings of a corporation so as to reduce tax liability, or to represent an increase in profit. Given the plurality of reporting methodologies in GAAP, an accountant faced with the responsibility to maintain a client for a firm, could choose to exploit one methodology in order to retain a client at the cost of the accuracy or validity of the reporting for the purposes of the public's interest. In addition, the different reporting methodologies consistent with GAAP may fall into "best practice" for reporting x, or "inappropriate" for reporting x. Though there are agreed upon best practices for reporting in many cases, it is fundamentally the possibility of interpretation and reasonable disagreement amongst working accountants that allows for the reporting holdings in different ways.

One issue that arises here is over whether accountants have an *additional* responsibility to the public over and above consistency with GAAP. If GAAP is understood in part as a document that regulates the duties of an accountant, one may argue that exploiting gaps and methodologies allowable by GAAP is simply an ethical form of creative accounting. Unethical creative accounting would be outright violating a principle (explicit or reasonably implied) of GAAP, some agreed "best practice" for reporting, or one of the official ethics codes for accountants.

Another important ethical issue that accountants face derives from the role they play in middle-management. One responsibility they take on in this area is controlling, requesting, and reporting on performance targets. In regard to performance targets, certain ethical questions can arise. Performance targets, such as project budgets, are often negotiated between middle- and upper-management. Upper-management wants to distribute the minimum amount of funds required to get a project done. Middle-management, on the other hand, wants to achieve the performance target, such as bringing the project in on or under budget, because they often lead to rewards, such as promotion or bonuses. So, employees have an incentive to negotiate for more than what they actually need in order to protect against unforeseen contingencies that would lead to the project coming in over budget. If the employers had perfect information they would not give employees extra funds because they want to distribute the minimum required to get the project done. As a consequence of information asymmetry, slack can be introduced. Accountants play a crucial role insofar as they are the conduit through which negotiations are made.[1]

There are general ethical questions about the introduction of slack. When is the introduction of slack, if ever, morally permissible? And if so, how much? Does slack lead to complacency and an overall decline in work productivity? What are the positive outcomes of the introduction of slack?

Although insider trading is legally impermissible, there is still a further question about what the moral grounding, if any, is for the ethical impermissibility of insider trading. Insider trading simply understood is the practice of buying or selling a security while in possession of, or on the basis of, information that

is not publicly known. Insider trading occurs when one trades on information that is confidential or acquired in a way that is in violation of SEC regulations. The basic moral question concerning insider trading is the following: in virtue of what is it morally impermissible, if at all, to buy and sell securities on the basis of non-public information?

One important issue at the center of the debate is whether the moral permissibility of insider trading rests on the claim that all interested parties have a right to relevant information. If all interested parties have a moral right to all relevant information, then trading on the basis of information that is not open to the public would violate this right. Of course the claim that all parties interested in acquiring some security have a right to all relevant information about it can be challenged. So, the question becomes what, if anything, is special about trading in virtue of which all traders have a right to all relevant information.

Another issue at the center of the debate concerns whether or not insider trading is actually better for the market because when there is insider trading stock prices accurately reflect true value. When there is no insider trading, supposedly, more speculation occurs, the greater the speculation, the less accurate the price. However, even if this economic result were true, additional claims, such as that a trading system in which prices are more accurate is morally better than one that is not, would have to be added to get to the conclusion that insider trading is morally permissible.

The articles in this unit reveal the growth of interest in ethical issues in accounting and finance. The editors include them in this volume with the hope that more attention will be given to these important areas of professional ethics.

NOTE

1   For further discussion of "slack," see Mary Beth Armstrong, "Ethical Issues in Accounting" in Norman E. Bowie (ed.), *The Blackwell Guide to Business Ethics*, (Oxford: Blackwell Publishing, 2002).

ACCOUNTANTS' OBLIGATIONS AND VIRTUES

MOHAMMAD J. ABDOLMOHAMMADI and MARK R. NIXON

Ethics in the Public Accounting Profession

I know only that what is moral is what you feel good after and what is immoral is what you feel bad after.

—Ernest Hemingway

Introduction

The American Heritage Dictionary defines profession as "the body of qualified persons in an occupation or field." A major characteristic of a "qualified person" is the specialized knowledge of the profession: medical knowledge for medical doctors, accounting knowledge for certified public accountants (CPAs). Professionals have an ethical responsibility to have acquired the specialized knowledge before offering their professional services. Professionals are also expected to keep abreast of the knowledge enhancements through continuing professional education. Another characteristic of professionals is that they possess the mental attitude of serving the public with the best of their ability so as to earn the public trust. How does a profession enforce these ethical responsibilities? By self-monitoring, supported by a viable code of conduct. In fact, the existence of a code of professional conduct is considered a hallmark of any profession.

The Code of Professional Conduct of the American Institute of Certified Public Accountants (AICPA) is the primary source of guidance for accountants in public practice. Similar codes, issued by the Institute of Management Accountants (IMA) and the Institute of Internal Auditors (IIA), govern accountants and auditors in private practice. In recent times, the accounting profession has developed several recognized subspecialties, such as Certified Personal Financial Planner, or Certified Fraud Examiner. Each of the subspecialties have also adopted professional codes of conduct that are consistent with AICPA's Code of Professional Conduct. The focus of this chapter is on professional accountants in public practice. Consequently, we limit our discussion to the CPAs who are obliged to adhere to the Code of Professional Conduct of the AICPA. The AICPA Code (hereafter, the Code) is designed to serve a multitude of purposes:

- A message that the professional CPA has a duty to serve the public (Collins and Schulz, 1995, 32)
- A means of conferring legitimacy upon the professional body, i.e., the AICPA (Preston et al., 1995, 509)
- Protecting public interest or a client where the professional delivers a specialized service which cannot be easily measured or judged as to its quality (Preston et al., 1995, 508; Neale, 1996, 223)
- Providing a filtering mechanism to limit the number of professionals to those who are willing and capable of adhering to the Code and unattractive to those who do not abide by it (Neale, 1996, 223).

In the remainder of this chapter, first, we briefly discuss the types of services that are provided by CPAs.

Of particular importance to the discussion of ethics is ethics audit services as an emerging area of assurance services that major public accounting firms have begun to offer in recent years. Second, we provide a brief discussion of the AICPA's Code of Professional Conduct with a focus on its principles, but also examples of its rules. Third, the elaborate professional ethics enforcement program is discussed, where illustrative cases and descriptive statistics about the AICPA's disciplinary actions over a 20-year period are provided. The chapter ends with a concluding section where some observations about controversial ethical issues facing the profession are discussed.

Public Accounting Services

The AICPA has approximately 350,000 members, all of whom are CPAs. To be a CPA, most states require that an individual have had some experience in public accounting. The most distinguishing characteristic of a public accounting practice is to provide audit services for financial statements of various businesses. These financial statements are normally used by the CPA's clients to provide information to stockholders, potential investors, creditors and regulatory agencies. However, not all CPAs remain in public practice. A large number of members of the AICPA are in industry, such as those working in accounting departments of private or public companies. Others are in private practice (provide clients with unaudited financial statements, tax and business consulting), government or education. While there are some minor differences in the ways in which these members keep their AICPA membership in "good standing," they all are required to adhere to the provisions of the Code. (For example, members in public practice are generally subject to more stringent continuing professional education requirements than those in industry or education.) However, due to the importance of the public trust to the profession, those in public practice are scru-

tinized more closely than others. For this reason, it is important to identify various areas of services provided by the CPAs in public practice with some emphasis on those in ethics audit services.

CPAs in public practice provide these services:

- Audit services
- Compilation and review services
- Attestation services
- Management advisory services, including internal audit services
- Tax services
- Assurance services, including ethics audit services.

The purpose of an *audit service* is to add credibility to financial statements of clients by issuing a report on the fair presentation of the financial statements taken as a whole. A vast majority of clients receive a standard three paragraph audit opinion (called an "unqualified" opinion) which is essentially a bill of health. Variations of this opinion indicate that the auditor is either taking some exceptions (called "modified wording" or a "qualified opinion" depending on the extent of the exception), or states that the financial statements are not presented fairly (called an "adverse opinion"). If the auditor finds that he/she is not independent of the client, then a "disclaimer of opinion" is issued. The Auditing Standards Board of the AICPA is responsible for developing the *Statements of Auditing Standards* that must be followed by auditors in the conduct of their audits. It is important to note that the issuance of an independent audit opinion can *only* be made by a CPA. The other services listed below can be provided by individuals that are not CPAs.

A *compilation* is the presentation of financial information, in the form of financial statements, without the CPA expressing any opinion on them. A review is where a CPA has conducted only limited procedures and can give only limited assurance that the financial statements require no material modification. Compilation and review services are normally for non-public companies that may not require full audited statements, but do want some limited assurance about the reliability of their financial statements.

The Statement of Standards for Attestation Engagements, *Attestation Standards* (AT Section 100) defines an attest engagement as "one in which a practitioner is engaged to issue or does issue a written communication that expresses a conclusion about the reliability of a written assertion that is the responsibility of another party." If the written communication is about historical financial statements, then the attestation is the same as an audit. However, a client may want an opinion on its representations related to its own internal controls, or investment performance history, or remaining reserves in an oil field. In these types of engagements, the CPA will still be held to the same level of professional standards as if they were auditing financial statements.

Management advisory services, including internal audit services, are often referred to as *consulting services*. Most of the consulting is related to the internal operations or planning for a client. A practitioner has developed an expertise in a client's affairs and is probably also an expert in the client's industry. This background makes the practitioner a logical choice to consult on matters related to accounting information systems (including hardware and software choices), inventory planning and flows, executive compensation arrangements, or designing pension and profit-sharing plans.

Tax services relate to corporations, other businesses, and individuals. The services can be limited to only the preparation of federal, state, and local tax returns, but frequently include advice on merger and acquisition, tax planning for current tax minimization or estate planning, and representation in tax audits from the Internal Revenue Service. The tax services area is an example where a practitioner is not required to be strictly independent from the client. The practitioner is expected to be an advocate for the client and to minimize the client's total tax liability.

Assurance services, including ethics audit services are defined by an AICPA special committee as "independent professional services that improve the quality of information, or its context, for decision makers" (Pallais, 1996, 16). Assurance services can include audit and attestation, but also include other non-traditional services. Assurance services are centered on improving the quality of information, and frequently involve situations when one party wants to monitor another, even when both parties work for the same company (Pallais, 1996). Ethics audit services would be an example of the latter service and will be discussed further in a later section.

A recent meeting of the National Association of State Boards of Accountancy concluded that regardless of the type of service provided, CPAs are required to have seven "competencies" (Haberman, 1998, 17): four of these competencies are technical in nature (e.g., the ability to assess the achievement of an entity's objectives); one relates to decision making, problem solving, and critical thinking; and another one concerns the ability to communicate the scope of work, findings and conclusions; but the one that is most relevant to ethics is "an understanding of the Code of Professional Conduct." Also, in a National Future Forum held in January 1998, five core values were identified for CPAs: continuing education and life-long learning, competence, integrity, attunement with broad business issues, and objectivity (CPA Vision Project, 1998). Of particular importance to this chapter are integrity and objectivity that are part of the Code as well. This Code is discussed in the next section.

Among the services identified above, assurance services have gained much attention in recent years as an area of significant growth for the accounting profession. These services are provided to improve the quality of information or its context, for decision makers. An example of these assurance services is the CPA *WebTrust*sm service by which CPAs assess the reliability of information in company web sites, and if the information is found to be reliable, the *Web-Trust*sm seal is stamped on the client's web site.

The AICPA's Special Committee on Assurance Services (also known as the Elliott Committee after its chairman, Robert Elliott) has proposed many areas of assurance services. Of special interest to ethicists is "assessment of ethics-related risk and vulnerabilities" (Elliott and Pallais, 1997, 63). Some accounting firms (e.g., Arthur Andersen, KPMG Peat Marwick) have already begun offering ethics audit services, According to KPMG Peat Marwick, the ethics audit has four components (KPMG, 1997):

- An assessment of the ethical climate of the client encompassing culture, environment, motives, and pressures
- An assessment of performance incentives—the issue is whether the performance incentives provide a motivation to behave outside the moral norm
- The communication of the message about what is acceptable or unacceptable ethical behavior—this communication covers issues of ethical policies, procedures, and training downstream from management to employees; it also covers the nature of upstream communication from employees to management
- Compliance where the policies, procedures, and offices involved in the enforcement of the client's ethics program are assessed.

Although an ethics audit is designed for a company's internal purposes, it is clear that there could be external ramifications. The fact that a company has conducted an ethics audit may have positive implications with outside regulatory agencies, suppliers, customers or prospective employees.

Ethics audit services are partly governed by *Statements on Auditing Standards* promulgated by the Auditing Standards Board (1997). However, there are significant differences between ethics audits and financial audits. For example, an ethics audit is used

to identify a client's areas of vulnerability in comparison with its industry benchmarks. This is different from comparison of a company's ethical performance with absolute ethical philosophies. It is also different from a financial audit where the fairness of financial statements is assessed against generally accepted accounting principles. KPMG Peat Marwick LLP states that an ethics audit is a "positive confirmation of the existence and effective implementation of best ethical practices" (KPMG, 1996).

A concern about the multitude of services provided by CPAs is that conflict of interest may arise from an auditor performing the financial audit as well as other services. This is said to threaten auditor independence. As discussed in the next section, independence is one of the major rules in the Code. In the past, it was not uncommon for auditors to decline engagements or not provide additional services if there was any threat, real or perceived, to their independence. We will return to a discussion of the magnitude of this issue in the final section. Suffice it to say here that, today, it is common for CPAs to avoid this problem by offering various services from separate divisions of the audit firm so as to minimize issues of conflict of interest. In one case, the accounting firm split into two separate entities: Andersen World-wide split into Arthur Andersen to provide audit and tax services and Andersen Consulting to provide management advisory services. Recently, however, Andersen Consulting has alleged that Arthur Andersen is also providing management advisory services to its big clients against the contract that resulted in the split of Andersen in the first place.

AICPA's Code of Professional Conduct

The AICPA's mission statement charges its CPA members with the responsibility to "serve the public interest in performing the highest quality of professional services" (AICPA, 1988, vii). The Code calls for honorable behavior, even at the sacrifice of personal interest. Various steps are necessary to prepare the CPA for these services. These steps include education, certification, licensing, and practice, but also a mental ability and commitment to discharging one's responsibility with care and diligence. (Note that all states require that CPAs in public practice be licensed. A CPA may choose not to be a member of the AICPA, and thus not subject to the AICPA Code. However, most state licensing authorities have adopted the AICPA Code as their ethical and professional standards.)

The AICPA's Code of Professional Conduct states, in its preamble, that being a member is voluntary, but by accepting membership one assumes an obligation to the public, clients, and colleagues. To guide behavior, the AICPA has instituted a Code that has four components:

- Principles of professional conduct
- Rules of conduct
- Interpretations of rules of conduct
- Rulings by the Professional Ethics Division of the AICPA and its Trial Board.

There are six principles in the Code. These principles and the AICPA directives related to them are listed in Table 1. They provide the basic

Table 1: AICPA's Principles of Professional Conduct

Principle	AICPA Directive
1. Responsibilities	In carrying out their responsibilities as professionals, members should exercise sensitive professional and moral judgments in all their activities.
2. The Public Interest	Members should accept the obligation to act in a way that will serve the public interest, honor the public trust and demonstrate commitment to professionalism.
3. Integrity	To maintain and broaden public confidence, members should perform all professional responsibilities with the highest sense of integrity.
4. Objectivity and Independence	A member should maintain objectivity and be free of conflicts of interest in discharging professional responsibilities. A member in public practice should be independent in fact and appearance when providing auditing and other attestation services.
5. Due Care	A member should observe the profession's technical and ethical standards, strive continually to improve competence and the quality of services, and discharge professional responsibility to the best of the member's ability.
6. Scope and Nature of Services	A member in public should observe the Principles of the Code of Professional Conduct in determining the scope and nature of services to be provided.

Source: AICPA (1988).

foundation of ethical and professional conduct that is expected of the CPA. However, due to their conceptual nature, these principles are not enforceable. Nevertheless, they point to the importance of public interest (Principles 1 and 2) and the requisite moral characteristics of CPAs in public practice (Principles 3-6).

The Rules of Conduct and the Interpretations of the Rules of Conduct are more specific in nature than the Principles, and as such, they are enforceable. A detailed discussion of these rules and their interpretation is beyond the scope of this chapter but may be found in the AICPA publications and standard auditing texts. To show the general tenet of the rules, we provide a summary here:

- Section 100: Independence, Integrity, and Objectivity (e.g., Rule 102-2 prohibiting conflict of interest)
- Section 200: General Standards and Accounting Principles (e.g., Rule 201-1 requiring competence)
- Section 300: Responsibilities to Clients (e.g., Rule 301-1 prohibition of dissemination of any confidential client information obtained during the course of an audit)
- Section 500: Other Responsibilities and Practices (e.g., Rule 501-1 forbidding retention of client records).

Section 400 that related to responsibilities to colleagues no longer has any rules at this time. However, concurrent with the issuance of the new Code in 1988, the AICPA also approved a mandatory quality peer review program where CPA firms provide reviews of the quality of practice in other CPA firms and present recommendations for improvement. The AICPA also established a number of practice-monitoring committees to facilitate these peer reviews for CPA firms.

The final component of the Code, Rulings by the Professional Ethics Division and the Trial Board of the AICPA, relates to the AICPA's activities to en-force the rules and their interpretations. These issues are discussed in the next section.

Enforcement of the Code of Conduct

Violations of the Code can be diverse and numerous. A detailed listing and discussion of these violations is beyond the scope of this chapter. Here are several examples:

- A CPA was engaged to prepare the financial statements of a company and then audited those same financial statements—a violation of the rule of independence.
- A practitioner prepared a fraudulent tax return on a client's behalf.
- A practitioner did not have the necessary technical skills to perform required work for an engagement—a violation of competence.
- A CPA did not release documents to a client—a violation of Rule 501-1 requirements.

These violations result in disciplinary actions by the AICPA such as admonishment, termination or suspension of membership in the Institute. Since 1975, the Joint Trial Board of the AICPA has been the source of disciplinary action with the participation of some state societies. This cooperation has recently been expanded to include virtually all 50 states and has resulted in the establishment of the Joint Ethics Enforcement Program (JEEP) since 1995. JEEP maximizes the resources for investigation and eliminates duplication (News Report, 1995).

Penalties for violation of the Code range from a recommendation that a member take remedial or corrective action, to a permanent expulsion from the AICPA. For example, a member who has violated the Code may be recommended by the Professional Ethics Division to take a continuing professional education course. If the member does not comply with the recommendation, the Ethics Division may refer him/her to the Trial Board for a hearing. The Trial Board may suspend a member for up to two years or expel him or her for violating the Code. In cases where a crime punishable by imprisonment for more than one year has occurred the member is automatically suspended or terminated from AICPA membership. A similar penalty can be imposed for filing a false income tax return on a client's behalf.

The disciplinary actions of the Joint Trial Board are publicized in the AICPA's newsletter, *The CPA Letter*. Generally, this means that a similar action has been taken by the professional state society of CPAs in the state where the violator has membership. (Note that a CPA can have membership in more than one state society. Furthermore, a CPA can get licensing from various state boards of CPA for practice in multiple states.) These state societies have codes of professional conduct for their membership that are identical with, or similar to, the AICPA Code (AICPA, 1997, 6).

On the surface, the actions taken by the AICPA and/or state societies of CPAs may appear to be insignificant in nature since membership in these associations is voluntary and one can resign at any time. In reality, an action such as termination of membership, may indeed tarnish one's reputation as a CPA to the extent that one would voluntarily leave the profession altogether. Also, consider the fact that the practice of public accounting requires licensing by governmental regulatory agencies such as state boards of public accountancy. The AICPA and/or state society actions to terminate or suspend membership may precede or succeed revocation or suspension of practice licenses by state boards of accountancy. Thus, the CPA may be barred from practice, involuntarily, for a period of time or forever, depending on the nature of the violation.

State boards of public accountancy have been set up to enforce state accounting laws. These boards are generally charged with the responsibility of overseeing the accounting profession in their states. Consequently, they have mechanisms by which complaints against CPAs are documented, investigated, and adjudicated. These complaints "can come from a variety of sources, including clients, third parties such as federal, state and local governments; and other CPAs, especially successor accountants and auditors. The state board must investigate each complaint to assess its merit and, if necessary, determine the appropriate corrective action" (Ruble, 1997).

The disciplinary actions taken by state boards of accountancy and state societies of CPAs may also be the result of court action against a member. For example, a criminal conviction in a court of law may automatically result in suspension or termination of membership in state societies and the AICPS, as well as loss of practice license by the state board of public accountancy.

As stated earlier, violations of the AICPA Code may require a hearing by the Ethics Division of the AICPA or its Trial Board. State societies of CPAs have similar mechanisms, and they cooperate closely with the AICPA. Virtually all state boards have joined with the AICPA to create the Joint Ethics Enforcement Program (JEEP). This program has developed a detailed manual for effective and efficient treatment of code violations. According to the AICPA professional standards and the provisions of the JEEP manual (AICPA, 1997), there are two distinct methods of dealing with member violations. The first is suspension or termination of membership without a hearing, i.e., automatic disciplinary actions. The second is the AICPS disciplinary action process where provisions are made for a hearing.

The automatic sanctions are generally the result of court actions or other governmental (e.g., Securities and Exchange Commission) actions against CPAs. As soon as notification is received by the secretary of the AICPA, a suspension or termination notice is automatically mailed to the member via registered or certified mail. If the member does not appeal, then the action is viewed as final and publicized in *The CPA Letter*. However, if the member appeals in writing, then the Trial Board forwards the appeal to an *ad hoc* committee for a decision. If the appeal is granted. then the case is forwarded to the Ethics Division for appropriate action. Otherwise, the automatic decision is affirmed and publicized in *The CPA Letter*. The disciplinary action is termination in cases of:

- crime punishable by imprisonment for more than a year;
- willful failure to file an income tax return when required by law;
- filing false or fraudulent income tax return on own or client behalf; and
- willful aid in preparation and presentation of a false and fraudulent income tax return of a client.

Membership will be revoked or suspended without a hearing if the member's practice license is suspended or revoked as a disciplinary action by a governmental agency.

The cases that do not result in automatic suspension or termination of membership are Code violations that have been brought to the attention of state societies or the AICPA through complaints made by individuals, clients, or other CPAs. JEEP processes these cases. The member can plead guilty and/or resign from the AICPA and state society membership. In this case, the Trial Board may recommend acceptance of the member's resignation, but require that the member appear for a hearing by the Trial Board at a later date. If the member does not plead guilty or the Trial Board does not accept the member's resignation a panel is set up by the Trial Board for investigation of the case. The Trial Board may choose not to accept a member's resignation due to the seriousness of a violation. They may feel that, to serve the public interest, the member needs to be publicly expelled. The panel may decide that no action is necessary or may schedule a hearing. The result of the hearing may be that no action is necessary or that the member must be admonished, suspended, terminated, or must perform some activity such as taking x hours of continuing

professional education. The member can appeal this decision within thirty days, and if granted, the Trial Board will review the decision and will uphold it, change it, or find the member innocent and inform the member of its decision. If the decision is that a violation had occurred for which disciplinary action is taken, then the decision is publicized in *The CPA Letter*.

Illustrative Disciplinary Actions

To illustrate the disciplinary actions against CPAs, we first present the facts about an individual who was found to have violated the AICPA Code. We will then present descriptive data to show the extent of the disciplinary actions taken over a 20-year period. This information is extracted from a disciplinary action database we have compiled from an examination of *The CPA Letter* published from 1977 till 1996.

Case 353 occurred in 1990. The individual was found to have violated the AICPA Code by having assisted in the preparation of a false tax return and having obstructed justice by lying about it (i.e., perjury). The information came from conviction in the court of law and automatically resulted in termination of AICPA membership.

A summary of the 20-year data is presented in Table 2. The data are classified by the type of disciplinary action (termination, suspension, and other) and by the source of action (automatic or hearing). Also provided are the averages per year. These averages are calculated by dividing the raw numbers by 20 years (1977-96). Finally, we have divided the average yearly disciplinary actions by the average number of members in the AICPA over the 20-year period to find the average number of disciplinary actions per 10,000 AICPA members.

Several observations from Table 2 are interesting to note. First, a majority of cases were automatic disciplinary actions. Of the 488 terminations, 330 were automatic as compared with 158 that resulted from the Joint Trial Board hearings. Similarly, of the 250 cases of suspension, 138 were automatic as compared with 112 that resulted from hearings. The exception was "other" cases that resulted in admonishment, censure or other types of disciplinary actions. None of these cases was the result of an automatic disciplinary action. Thus, overall, of the 803 cases, 468 were subjects of automatic action as compared with 335 hearings by the Joint Trial Board.

Second, a related observation is that a majority of the cases, automatic or hearing, resulted in the termination of the violator from the AICPA membership. Of the 468 automatic cases, 330 resulted in termination of membership. Similarly, 158 of the 330 hearing cases resulted in termination of the violator. Suspension was next followed by "other" disciplinary actions.

Third, the average per 10,000 membership indicates that overall, only 1.7 persons (1 automatic and 0.7 from hearing) were disciplined per year. Of these 1.1 were terminated, 0.5 were suspended, and 0.15 were subjected to other disciplinary actions.

A conclusion from this data is that violations of the Code by the AICPA members are rare. The assumption is that all major cases are detected and adjudicated by the AICPA, state boards of accountancy, and state societies of CPAs. There are, of course, unreported or undetected violations of the Code as well. Thus, the true level of ethical behavior is not possible to observe. However, it is in the best interest of a self-regulating profession to expose unethical behavior. With this in mind, there are several significant overall ethical controversies facing the profession and these are discussed in the next section.

Table 2: AICPA's Disciplinary Action Statistics 1977-96

Disciplinary action	Source			Average per 10,000
	Automatic	Hearing	Trial	
Termination	330 (16.5/year)	158 (7.9/year)	488 (24.4/year)	1.1
Suspension	138 (6.9/year)	112 (5.6/year)	250 (12.5/year)	0.5
Other (e.g., admonish or censure)	0 (0/year)	65 (3.25/year)	65 (3.25/year)	0.15
Total	468 (23.4/year)	335 (16.75/year)	803 (40.15/year)	1.7
Average per 10,000	1.0	0.7	1.7	

	Membership size:	1977	130,331
		1996	394,938
	Average		227,634

Source: Disciplinary Action Database compiled by the authors from *The CPA Letter*.

Controversial Ethical Issues in the Accounting Profession

As discussed in the previous sections, the accounting profession has developed a code of conduct and has an elaborate disciplinary program in place to enforce the Code. Surveys of CPAs (e.g., Cohen and Pant, 1991) indicate that the Code and its enforcement are viewed as effective for the professional body. This does not, however, mean that the profession has been free from criticism. While CPAs, in general, do not believe that unethical behavior leads to success, they do perceive that opportunities exist in the accounting profession to engage in unethical behavior. This is because surveys of CPAs indicate that some clients request fraudulent alteration of tax returns or financial statements (Finn et al., 1988).

Critics allege that these client pressures, causing ethical problems for the profession, are partly due to the professionals having abandoned the legitimacy of ethical character that was the norm in the early 1900s. Critics support this allegation by noting that, in the early 1900s, there were virtually no general auditing or accounting standards, while today there is a large complicated set of standards and rules. Critics claim that today's CPAs rely on "following the rules" rather than focusing on what is the best, fairest, or clearest presentation of accounting information. As technical expertise has become the cornerstone of the CPA practice, the legitimacy of technique has replaced the legitimacy of character (Abbott, 1988, 190). Even within this technical expertise, critics argue that some CPAs have ignored their clients' creative accounting in which earnings have been manipulated in some cases. For example, Lomas Financial Corporation has filed a $300 million lawsuit against its auditors, alleging that two audit partners collaborated with the management of Lomas Financial Corporation to conceal risky financial practices that contributed to the company's failure (MacDonald, 1997).

Similarly, a large potential area of concern for CPA firms is the exposure to lawsuits from consulting engagements. The largest lawsuit yet filed against a CPA firm ($4 billion) was related to a consulting engagement by an accounting firm to develop and implement a "turnaround plan" for Merry-Go Round Enterprises (MacDonald, 1997). The suit alleges fraud, fraudulent concealment, negligence, and lack of independence. These are issues that are normally raised in an audit engagement lawsuit. William Brewer, an attorney, states "It's an unusual suit. Big Six accounting firms have generally not been sued for their consulting work. However, it's a sign of the times. You'll see many more of these cases in the future as accountants hold themselves out as business consultants" (MacDonald, 1997, 312).

In other cases, rapid changes in the information technology have brought the CPA's knowledge under question. The new information technology has also changed the public need for CPA services. For example, whereas traditional audited financial statements were issued three or four months after the closing of the client's fiscal year, the new technology has made it possible to provide the information on line and in real time. As mentioned earlier, the profession has responded by developing the *WebTrust*sm service to respond to this need.

Perhaps the most significant ethical challenge to the profession is the question of independence. It has been alleged that auditors systematically violate the Code's independence rule. The Code is clear in its direction of the need for independence, not only in fact which is unobservable, but also in appearance which can be observed by third parties. The auditor may, in fact, exercise independence from the client even if he or she has financial interest in the company. However, to assure independence in appearance, the auditor is prohibited from having any direct interest such as stock ownership in the client, or significant indirect interest such as ownership of stocks in the client by the CPA's close relatives.

Critics argue that independence rules must also be addressed in cases of providing conflicting services to the client. For example, how can an auditor be independent of his or her client in conducting a financial audit if the auditor is also the one who had provided advice in the development or purchase of the client's accounting system. Similarly, the profession has been criticized for taking inadequate responsibility for detecting fraudulent financial reporting by clients in situations where auditor's self-interest has been on the line. These allegations have resulted in Congressional investigations of the profession. For example, Senator Metcalf investigated the profession in 1976 (US Senate, 1976) while Senator Moss did the same in 1978 (US Senate, 1978). (A detailed discussion of these investigations and the profession's response to them is beyond the scope of this chapter; they are stated here to show the significance of the issues.)

The profession's response has been to set up commissions to investigate these issues, and to provide recommendations, based on which new pronouncements could be issued. For example, in response to Senators Metcalf and Moss investigations, the AICPS established The Commission on Auditors' Responsibilities in the mid-1970s (The Cohen Commission, 1978). The recommendations from this commission led to the establishment of another commission later to investigate fraudulent financial reporting (The Treadway Commission, 1987) and later to yet another commission (COSO, 1992) that made a long list of recommendations. As a result of the recommendations of these commissions, the profession has taken significant steps to enhance its guidance for practitioners by issuing new pronouncements. The revised Code of Conduct issued in 1988 (AICPA, 1988) tightened the Code requirements by eliminating some ambiguous and controversial sections. Specifically, the new Code allows for advertising by CPAs that was prohibited by the earlier code. In the same year, the Auditing Standards Board issued a package of nine new *Statements on*

Auditing Standards (dubbed expectation gap standards) to provide better guidance to the auditors in their conduct of the financial audit. More recently, the Auditing Standards Board responded to the Treadway Commission (1987) and COSO (1992) reports by issuing a new *Statement on Auditing Standards No. 82* that requires auditors to plan the audit so that if fraud exists, it can be detected (Auditing Standards Board, 1997). In the past, the profession steadfastly denied responsibility to plan the audit for the purpose of detecting fraud although it maintained that if fraud was indicated in the course of the normal audit, it would be investigated.

Other contemporary ethical issues confronting the profession include confidentiality, public confidence, and serving the public interest.

Confidentiality

The CPA is entrusted with a large amount of information from the client. The auditor is prohibited to share this information with others, except in response to court order and other exceptional situations. For example, the auditor can provide financial ratios to industry trade groups so long as specific client information is not revealed. However, the auditor cannot use confidential information for self or other financial interests such as trading stocks based on the insider information gathered in the course of the audit.

Public Confidence

The profession allows CPAs to advertise, but through its ethics rulings limits the type of advertising to those that enhance public confidence. For example, contingent fees and commissions are not allowed for referral of attest function services (i.e., audits, compilation and reviews), but allowed for management advisory services. Contingent fees and referral commissions were prohibited altogether until 1988 when under pressure from the Federal Trade Commission, the AICPA council voted to change the rule (Mintz,

1990, 3). Nevertheless, critics argue that advertising has helped change public accounting from a profession to a business (Mason, 1994).

Serving the Public Interest

As stated earlier, the profession only recently has begun to accept responsibility for planning the audit for detection of fraud and other illegal acts (Auditing Standards Board, 1997). More needs to be done to clarify the CPA's responsibility to the public. For example, should the CPA engage in whistle-blowing when an illegal act or fraud is detected to have been committed by a client? As critics argue, at the present time, "the resolution of conflicts between an accountant's client, on the one hand, and the general public, on the other, is usually balanced in favor of the client. The legal system supports this outcome, at least for the time being" (Epstein and Spalding, 1993, 271). Others argue that the source of this problem is the weight that is placed on confidentiality at the expense of public interest (Collins and Schulz, 1995).

Conclusion

The accounting profession has developed an elaborate Code of Conduct complete with a continuing education and an effective enforcement program. However, more needs to be done to make accountants more responsive to public expectations to enhance public trust. While the profession has been forthcoming in its responses to Congressional hearings and private commission recommendations in the past two decades more is needed to continue building a more trustworthy profession. This is especially urgent in light of the speedy change that is fostered by the age of information technology.

REFERENCES

Abbott, A. 1988: *The System of Professions: An Essay on the Division of Expert Labor*. Chicago, IL: University of Chicago Press.

AICPA 1988: *Code of Professional Conduct*. New York: AICPA.

AICPA 1997: *Joint Ethics Enforcement Program (JEEP): Manual of Procedures*. New York: AICPA.

Auditing Standards Board 1997: *Statement on Auditing Standards No. 82: Consideration of Fraud in a Financial Statement Audit*. New York: AICPA.

Cohen, J.R. and Pant, L.W. 1991: "Beyond Bean Counting: Establishing High Ethical Standards in the Public Accounting Profession." *Journal of Business Ethics* Vol. 10, 45-56.

Collins, A. and Schulz, N. 1995: "A Critical Examination of the AICPA Code of Professional Conduct." *Journal of Business Ethics* Vol. 14, 31-41.

COSO (Committee of Sponsoring Organizations of the Treadway Commission) 1992: *Internal Control: Integrated Framework*. Harborside, NJ: AICPA.

CPA Vision Project 1998: "CPA Vision Project Identifies Top Five Core Values." *The CPA Letter*. Vol. 1 (June), 9.

Elliott, R.K. and Pallais, D.M. 1997: "First: Know Your Market." *Journal of Accountancy*, (July), 56-63.

Epstein, M.J. and Spalding, A.D. 1993: *The Accountant's Guide to Legal Liability and Ethics*. Boston, MA: Irwin.

Finn, D.W., Chenko, L.B., and Hunt, S.D. 1988: "Ethical Problems in Public Accounting: The View from the Top." *Journal of Business Ethics* Vol. 7, 605-15.

Haberman, L.D. 1998: "Regulatory Reform at NASBA." *Journal of Accountancy* (February), 16-17.

KPMG 1996: *Innovating Best Ethical Practices*. Montvalle. NJ: KPMG Peat Marwick, LLP.

KPMG 1997: "Creating the Moral Organization." *KPMG Internet Web Site*. Montvalle, NJ: KPMG Peat Marwick, LLP.

MacDonald, E. 1997: "Trustee Files $4 Billion Lawsuit against Ernst & Young." *The Wall Street Journal*, December 2, Vol. 240, B12.

Mason, E. 1994: "Public Accounting: No Longer a Profession?" *The CPA Journal* Vol. 64(6) July, 34-37.

Mintz, S. 1990: *Cases in Accounting Ethics and Professionalism*. New York: McGraw-Hill.

Neale, A. 1996: "Conduct, Misconduct and Accounting." *Journal of Business Ethics* Vol. 15, 219-96.

News Report 1995: "New Era in Ethics Enforcement." *Journal of Accountancy* Vol. 13, August.

Pallais, D. 1996: "Assurance Services: Where We Are: Where We're Going." *Journal of Accountancy* Vol. 182(3) September, 16-17.

Preston, A.M., Cooper, D.J., and Scarbrough, D.P. 1995: "Changes in the Code of Ethics of the US Accounting Profession. 1917 and 1988: The Continual Quest for Legitimization." *Accounting. Organizations and Society*. August, 507-46.

Ruble, M.R. 1997: "Letter from the State Board: What Should You Do Next?" *Journal of Accountancy* Vol. 183(5) May, 75.

The Cohen Commission 1978: *Report, Conclusions, and Recommendations*. New York: AICPA.

The New York Times December 27, 1997 Vol. 147, B147.

The Treadway Commission 1987: *Report of the National Commission on Fraudulent Financial Reporting*. New York: AICPA.

US Senate Subcommittee on Reports, "Accounting and Management of the Committee on Governmental Affairs; the Metcalf Committee 1976: *The Accounting Establishment*." Washington, DC: US Government Printing Office.

US Senate; the Moss Committee 1978: *Report of the Committee on Auditors' Responsibilities*. Washington, DC: US Government Printing Office.

♦ ♦ ♦ ♦ ♦

DOMÈNEC MELÉ
Ethical Education in Accounting: Integrating Rules, Values, and Virtues

Introduction

Ethics in accounting has seen an increased interest in the last decade, although it is not by any means a new subject. In the USA, public accounting has had some form of ethical standards since at least the beginning of the twentieth century (Casler, 1964, mentioned by Loeb, 1988). Issues regarding ethics in accounting are briefly touched on in some early European textbooks on business ethics (e.g., Azpiazu, 1964; Baudhuin, 1954). However, specific training on accounting ethics for accounting students or a systematic presentation of this matter had rarely been undertaken until the 1970s (Loeb and Bedingfield, 1972). In 1978, Loeb edited *Ethics in the Accounting Profession*, a pioneering monograph on this topic.

Since the mid-1980s several institutions related with accounting associations have encouraged ethical education in accounting, starting in 1986 with the report of the American Accounting Association Committee on the "Future Structure, Content, and Scope of Accounting Education" and continuing, in 1987, with the National Commission on Fraudulent Financial Reporting (Treadway Commission). Since then many other institutions have adopted a similar focus (Armstrong et al., 2003, note 1).

Nowadays, accounting ethics is part of the curriculum in several colleges and business schools, and a number of scholars have written textbooks and casebooks on accounting ethics (Armstrong, 1993; Cottell and Perlin, 1990; Duska and Duska, 2003; Gowthorpe and Blake, 1998; Maurice, 1996; Mintz, 1997; among others). Thus, considerable steps have been made in ethical accounting education, but, after the well-known recent accounting scandals, it seems absolutely essential to pay increasing attention to ethics in accounting and to improve ethical education for accountants. In line with this, this paper aims to contribute to a better understanding of accounting ethics and to provide some insights on ethical education in accounting.

First, this article examines some relevant current approaches in accounting ethics and ethical education in accounting and the corresponding role given to rules and principles, ethical theories, values, and virtues. Second, it presents an approach in which rules, values and virtues are presented in an interrelated consistent manner. Finally, some implications of this approach for ethical education in accounting are discussed.

Ethics for Professional Accountants: Only a Set of Standards for Moral Behavior?

Accountants can perform their work in many different areas, including auditing, managerial accounting, tax accounting, financial planning, consulting and, of course, simply preparing accounts. In each of these spheres, ethical issues appear (Armstrong, 2002), and accountants perceive that opportunities exist in their work to engage in unethical behavior.[1]

Codes of conduct for accountants give guidelines for proper behavior in the profession. For accountants, as in any other profession, codes are the most concrete cultural form in which professions acknowledge their societal obligations (Abbott, 1983). Codes, and possibly some procedures for reinforcing them, are a public commitment of the profession and a basic element in achieving social recognition of, and public trust in the profession.

Codes of conduct contain a set of principles and rules, which specify what society expects to be considered in decision making. According to Bowie and Duska (1985), from a practical perspective, codes of conduct are useful in several ways: (1) motivat-

ing through the use of peer pressure; (2) providing a stable and permanent guide to right or wrong rather than leaving the question to continual ad hoc decisions; (3) giving guidance, especially in ambiguous situations, guiding the behavior of the employees and controlling the autocratic power of employers over employees; (4) helping to specify the social responsibility of business itself; (5) contributing to the interest of business itself, for if businesses do not police themselves ethically, others will do it for them.

Although some ethical standards with sound foundations could easily be recognized in most codes of conduct for accountants, in practice, the rules are often applied in a mechanical way. There also exists the risk that people might confuse ethics in accounting with a set of rules, legal standards or other regulations. Adams et al. (1995) believe that, in today's legalistic society, the question of "what is the right thing to do?" is often confused with "what is legal?" While they refer to accountants in the USA this statement could readily be extended to many other countries.

Velayutham (2003) points out that the focus of codes of ethics has been to progressively replace the "true and fair view" requirement by "compliance with accounting standards." Thus, codes have moved from focusing on moral responsibility to a public good to that of a technical specification for a product or service. In this way, technique has supplanted character. Velayutham adds that the term "code of ethics" is now misleading, and it would be more appropriate to talk about "code of quality Assurance."

On the other hand, Lere (2003), an Accounting Professor, suggests that it is often rare to have a situation where codes of ethics impact on decision making. While enforcement provisions can increase the likelihood that an individual will select (forego) the action that a code of ethics indicates to be ethical (unethical), there are limits as to how effective enforcement provisions can be.

Another fault of codes and rules appears when questioning whether the best ethical behavior is always to follow the established rules. Adams et al. (1995) have studied several cases regarding auditing client confidentiality in which disclosure could be the best ethical behavior, in spite of the applicable rules, which state that a Certified Public Accountant (CPA) member acting in public practice shall not disclose any confidential information without the specific consent of the client. A survey among CPAs showed that a substantial percentage (between 30% and 47%) thought that the best ethical behavior would be not following the rules of the code for these specific cases.[2]

The range and limitations of these codes could be understood from what Louis Vlasco affirmed in 1983, as chairman of the National Association of Accountants (NAA) of the USA, when he presented the association's code of conduct:[3]

> "I make no claim that the NAA standards, in and of themselves, are the ultimate solution to all ethical dilemmas that management accountants may face. In the future, however, if a management accountant is asked, for example, to recalculate certain figures to make his or her division appear to be more profitable than is warranted, that accountant has somewhere to turn for guidance. He or she will be able to point to the standard that explicitly states that management accountants have a responsibility to communicate information fairly and objectively."[4]

Summarizing, codes of conduct have a role to play, although ethics in accounting cannot be reduced to simply what codes of conduct state. In fact, textbooks in accounting ethics usually include some relevant codes of conduct, or significant excerpts, with the corresponding rules and principles, but generally they agree that ethical education in accounting should be more than just knowing and applying rules. As, Loeb and Rockness, two experts in ethical education in accounting, recognized: "our (the auth-ors) collective experience indicates that both college students and practicing accounting professionals are interested in accounting ethics education that moves beyond the rules of a code of ethics and the code's corresponding official interpretation" (Loeb and Rockness, 1992, 488).

Principles and Moral Reasoning

In some fields of professional activity there is a tendency to emphasize basic principles from which particulars norms derive. Thus, in 1957, the American Medical Association replaced its Code of Ethics, which stated the duties that American physicians owed to their patients, their society, and to one another, with a statement of moral principles, supplemented by opinions and commentaries on specific cases and questions (Roth, 1994, 695). This tendency is also perceived in accounting ethics, although in a much less extended fashion.

Numerous accounting codes of conduct, especially those in the USA, emphasize specific standards rather than generic principles. Thus, the Code of Professional Conduct of the American Institute of Certified Public Accountants (AICPA), revised significantly in 1988,[5] specifies that independence requires fulfilling the standards promulgated by bodies designated by the Council (Rule 101); objectivity and integrity involve being free of conflict of interests, and not knowingly misrepresenting facts and not subordinating one's judgments to others (Rule 102). This also occurs with compliance in the general standards and accounting principles (section 200); responsibility to clients, including issues related with confidential client information and contingency fees (section 300); responsibility to colleagues (section 400) and other responsibilities and practices (section 500). The Code of the Institute of Management Accountants, much more succinct than the AICPA's code, presents generic principles as well as a heading grouping the rules.

In contrast, other codes, generally with a more international approach, stress general principles as a foundation for accounting ethics, without omitting, of course, specific standards of behavior. This is the case of the *Code of Ethics for Professional Accountants* of the International Federation of Accountants (IFAC) which highlights a crucial principle as the main reference for the whole code: the public interest. In the Introduction to this code it states:

> "The IFAC Board and the IFAC Ethics Committee believes that the establishment of a conceptual framework that requires professional accountants to identify, evaluate and address threats to compliance with the fundamental principles, rather than merely comply with a set of specific rules which may be arbitrary, is in the public interest."[6]

This code also includes a set of principles and values (technical and moral), with a brief explanation of each: integrity, objectivity, professional competence and due care, confidentiality, professional behavior and technical standards.[7] This emphasis on values and principles is made even sharper by an explicit recognition of the superiority of principles over the rules. The latter, according to this code, "may be arbitrary."

Considering the general principles that serve as a rule's basis provides a broader perspective for ethical behavior in accounting. With this approach, it may well be easier to avoid a legalistic vision of ethics in accounting or a mechanistic application of rules in decision making.

Frequently principles adopted come from rationalistic theories which propose diverse methods of moral reasoning to apply properly these principles for solving dilemmas or to justify certain actions. For this purpose, ethical education in accounting usually includes teaching several normative theories, such as Kantianism, Utilitarianism and other rationalistic ethical theories. These theories help to iden-

tify moral dilemmas and to provide a pathway for moral reasoning.

These approaches reflect on the idea, implicitly or explicitly, that ethics in accounting, as in other matters, is an "application of ethics or morality ... to practical issues" (Cottell and Perlin, 1990, x). Here, by ethics or morality it is understood that ethical systems or ethical theories, such as those above, are rooted in the philosophy of modernity and oriented to solve ethical dilemmas.

Certainly, "identifying moral conflicts, thinking them through, discussing them with colleagues and others, and utilizing the tools of ethical analysis are useful, in fact, indispensable activities" (Cottell and Perlin, 1990, ix-x). No doubt exists that encouraging professionals or students to use ethical reasoning is valuable. But presenting Kantian theory, with its categorical imperatives or the Utilitarian principle of "the greatest happiness for the greatest number" or any other ethical theory based on aprioristic principles of morality has some shortcomings.

First, depending on the aprioristic principle accepted, the action can be seen only as a set of duties (Kantian and Neo-Kantian theories) or only as the set of consequences (Utilitarianism, if they are evaluated in terms of satisfaction or consequentialism, if they are evaluated in terms of other chosen values). Authors in favor of understanding ethics only as duties criticize others that think only consequences are relevant. Contrasted with these approaches, many people consider relevant both the action itself and also the action's foreseeable and avoidable consequences.

Second, well-known post-modern philosophers, such as Derrida, Foucault, Lyotard, Wittgenstein, Rorty and others, repudiate all these aprioristic theories, because they believe that modern philosophy, including Kantianism and Utilitarianism, err by accepting the unshakable foundation of knowledge. From a different perspective, an Aristotelian critique can also be made against the foundations of modern moral theories (Duska, 1993).

Third, even though teaching these theories develops students' skills in solving ethical dilemmas, applying theories and determining what is right according to a set of duties or systematically analyzing the consequences, this does not motivate students to act well. Ethics cannot become so mechanical as merely applying a rule, a "technology" for solving moral dilemmas. In teaching business ethics, Cooley (2004) has observed that students memorize enough of the moral theories to pass their tests, but never understand the motivating spirit underlying the theories. He concludes that students know how to apply the moral principles to various situations, but produce the wrong results due to their illicit biases and rationalizations. Fulfilling your (self-evident) duties (Kantianism) or calculating the consequences in terms of satisfaction (Utilitarianism) does not seem enough for ethical behavior, because human behavior is far more complex than accepting aprioristic principles and knowing how to apply them. As will be discussed afterwards, motivation and habits are also very important for correct behavior.

The fourth shortcoming has to do with the lack of consideration of the decision maker's character in moral reasoning (Anscombe, 1958; MacIntyre, 1984; Veatch, 1968; among others). Since the enlightenment, modern moral philosophy has emphasized duties and norms without examining the personal disposition of the person making the moral judgment in a concrete situation and without considering the habits acquired by deciding and acting in a certain way. In contrast to modern moral philosophy, the Aristotelian view argues that moral judgment "is not merely an intellectual exercise of subsuming a particular under rules or hyper-norms. Judgment is an activity of perceiving while simultaneously perfecting the capacity to judge actions and choices and to perceive being" (Koehn, 2000, 17). This vision contrasts with Kantian theory and Utilitarianism, which, as has been pointed out, take for granted this capacity and consider it irrelevant in making moral judgments.

Values and Virtues

Teaching values could also counter a concept of ethical training reduced to a mere application of rules or the shortcoming of the rationalistic theories mentioned before. Values can also go as far as providing a motivation to act well.

"Value in general may best be glossed as that which is worth having, getting, or doing ... Value, thus understood, is essentially relational, i.e., it is value for some person(s) or living being(s)" (Bond, 2001, 1745). Values, in the context of business, belong to whatever is necessary, or makes a positive contribution, for maintaining and improving business, as human activity. These include moral values, which express what is worth for a human activity.

Many codes present the grounding values. Thus, the AICPA Code includes the following values: service to others or public interest, competency, integrity, objectivity, independence, professionalism, including continuing education, and accountability to the profession, which are similar to considerations that appear in most professional codes (Duska and Duska, 2003, 77). For its part, the Standards of Ethical Conduct for Management Accountants of the NAA of the USA defined the ethical responsibilities of managers through four values: competence, confidentiality, integrity and objectivity. Afterwards, this code was the basis for the current Standards of Ethical Behavior for Practitioners of Management Accounting and Financial Management adopted in 1997 by the Institute of Management Accountants (the former National Association of Accountants),[8] which also presents these values, although they add a fifth section devoted to resolving ethical conflicts.

But values are not enough. Accountants, as with every professional, have to make practical judgments about concrete situations and, above all, have to behave correctly. Both conditions require not only bearing values in mind but having good character, as we will try to explain later.

Pioneers in ethical education in accounting, in spite of their praiseworthy task, focused on dilemmas and ethical theories rather than on the role of virtues. This is the case of Loeb (1988), Langenderfer and Rockness (1989), and others at the end of the 1980s.[9] Although Loeb (1988, 322) included "setting the stage for" a change in ethical behavior, "he does not go so far as to imply accounting educators have the power to bring about good or bad behavior on the part of students" (Armstrong et al., 2003, 10).

Similarly, from a practitioner perspective, up until recently, perhaps the only virtue, at least implicitly stressed, is the disposition to fulfill the obligations prescribed by code or by normative ethical theories. Thus, the *Standards* of the Institute of Management Accountants states: "Practitioners of management accounting and financial management have an obligation to the public, their profession, the organization they serve, and themselves to maintain the highest standards of ethical conduct."

Several scholars have strongly criticized those approaches which reduce ethical education to presenting ethical theories to solve ethical dilemmas without considering personal virtues and behavior. Pincoffs (1986, 4-6) pointed out the problems with theories used to solve ethical dilemmas. He stated deontological or utilitarian ethical theories are reductive, since they eliminate what is morally relevant (character) and they legislate the form of moral reflection (duties and consequences). In similar terms, Shaub (1994) focused on several potential weaknesses in implementing accounting ethics education in the classroom and criticized the current overreliance on ethical dilemmas.

As an alternative to teaching ethical theories, Pincoffs (1986, 150) presented the primary objective of moral education as encouraging the development of the person. This means encouraging the development of virtues, that is to say, permanent dispositions that favor ethical behavior.

Subsequently, other scholars have presented significant insights into the role of virtue in accounting, both in practice and education. Francis (1990) emphasized the role of the agent beyond rules and the capacity of accounting to be a virtuous practice. Mintz (1995, 1996), following Pincoffs (1986) and McIntyre (1984), presented significant pedagogical insights in the teaching of virtue to accounting students and mentioned several virtues which enable accountants to withstand environment pressures and to act in accordance with the moral point of view: (1) benevolence and altruism; (2) honesty and integrity; (3) impartiality and open-mindedness; (4) reliability and dependability; (5) faithfulness and trustworthiness.

The Crucial Importance of the Agent's Character

Regarding practical judgments, Armstrong (2002, 145) affirms that "accounting is an art, not a science. It requires significant judgments and assumptions and 10 accountants, given complex circumstances, will probably arrive at several different net income or taxable income figures." Accountants must determine the significance of each situation while acting with objectivity, independence, professional competence, due care, professional behavior, confidentiality, integrity, and so on. Rules cannot determine what to do in every situation. Universal principles can give guidelines, but each situation is unique. Accountants have to judge each situation and judge what objectivity, integrity, etc. mean in a given situation; and then act according to this judgment.

It has been rightly said that a "practical judgment is, at the very least, crucially dependent upon perception" (Koehn, 2000, 4). The ethical perception depends on certain human capacities, related with character, which is different from others, such as logic or aesthetics. This capacity to perceive the ethical dimension of the reality is no more than practical wisdom or prudence (in the moral sense), an intellectual virtue, called "phronesis" by Aristotle

(*Nichomachean Ethics*, bk 5, chap. 7). Practical wisdom may be expressed, for instance, in being sincerely objective, truly unbiased and independent, and in following the "spirit of the law" rather than the letter of the law.

Character of a person, in which practical wisdom forms an important part, is made up of habits (good habits, or virtues, or bad habits, or vices). Habits shape personal character, which combines with personality (understanding by personality mainly the innate features and non-moral qualities). Aristotle described personality as the following:

> "virtues we get by first exercising them, as also happens in the case of the arts as well. For the things we have to learn before we can do them, we learn by doing them, e.g., men become builders by building and lyre-players by playing the lyre; so too we become just by doing just acts, temperate by doing temperate acts, brave by doing brave acts ...; by doing the acts that we do in our transaction with other men we become just or unjust, and by doing the acts that we do in the presence of danger, and being habituated to feel fear or confident, we become brave or cowardly." (*Nichomachean Ethics*, bk 2, chap. 1; 1103a31 and 1103b15)

The virtue of man is "the state of character which makes a man good and which makes him do his own work well" (*Nichomachean Ethics*, bk 2, chap. 6; 1106a22). In other words, virtuous individuals habitually perform moral actions. Thus, courage drives us to do what is good and justice to give to each what is his or hers by right.

To sum up, virtues should be introduced in ethical education as a crucial element to overcome the limitations previously discussed. However, a new problem arises: how to harmonize virtues with rules and values. Some versions of "virtues" only judge as virtues those which foster outcomes: industriousness for a productive life: justice for achieving good rela-

tions: loyalty to maintain a sound adhesion: truthfulness to garner more the reputation of being a reliable person. Similarly, for some authors virtues are virtues only if they are accepted in a particular context. Thus, Solomon, defines virtue as "a pervasive trail of character that allows one to 'fit into' a particular society and excel in it" (1992, 107). In spite of Solomon's valuable contribution in introducing virtues in business ethics, and his general directive that all the virtues of everyday life apply to business, the definition he gives can be criticized (Ewin, 1995) because some "virtues" which are accepted as such in a particular society, would be dubious examples of human excellence in another.[10]

Another problem is found in certain approaches in which virtues are proposed without any reference to norms or principles, which according to some authors is a failure to supply the means to resolve moral dilemmas (Messerly, 1994, 109; among others).

Both problems arise from considering virtues apart from rules and values or principles instead of simultaneously considering rules, values and virtues.[11] But, are rules, values and virtues really interrelated?

Understanding the Interrelation between Rules, Values and Virtues

Rules, values and virtues are indeed interrelated if one accepts the basic anthropological and ethical concepts presented by Aristotle and his main commentator, Thomas Aquinas (MacIntyre, 1993). A crucial point in this approach is that values have to be considered as "intrinsic moral values," or "moral goods" rooted in human nature.

This makes sense, since values, although frequently considered either as subjective or as social agreements, can also be understood objectively. Some scholars have even distinguished values, in general, from "moral or ethical values." The latter are defined as those which, when one lives in accordance with them, contribute to "the good of the person," that is to say, to the perfection or flourishing of individuals as human beings. In this sense, Guardini (1999, 30-31) wrote that the good (of the person) "is different from any other values." These other values "drive our behavior here and now, depending on the situation, while the good compels us always ..." In other words, the requirements of values are always specific; the requirements of good are universal. The former is presented to men and women in certain circumstances ..., while the requirement of good drives men and women for the simple fact of being human. If moral values, relate to "the good of the person," they can be distinguished from other values (technical, economics, aesthetics, etc.).

Following Aquinas (*Summa Theologica*, I-II, q. 94, a. 2), moral goods can be known by human reason from the spontaneous inclinations of human nature, such as the good of life from the inclination to conserve life, the good of true knowledge from the inclination to know, and the good of a harmonic and peaceful social life, from the inclination to live in society.[12] Truthfulness, justice and loyalty, which are crucial values in accounting, are ethical values tied to the goods of true knowledge and sound social life. Without these values social life deteriorates and trust—a cement of social life—is destroyed.

Humans are responsible for their own acts and, therefore, for their human development, which at the same time produces a good society. It requires the following of rules associated with moral goods. Some rules need extensive study due to complicated issues in each profession or environment. But there are some elemental moral rules relatively easy to learn. Thus, practically everyone can discover the "golden rule" (treat others in the same way you would like to be treated), the rule of respecting human dignity, "giving people their rights," honoring promises and fulfilling contracts, and some others. Likewise, abusing power by exploiting human need, manipulating people and considering persons as mere instruments

for the sake of one's own interests, are ethical rules regarding what must be avoided.[13]

By acting in accordance with these rules and consequently in accordance with moral goods, the individual acquires virtues. These virtues acquired by acting according to moral goods and the corresponding rules can be called "human virtues." Understanding rules, goods (values), and virtues in this way is, by definition, interrelated.

Because human virtues are habits, they provide promptness or readiness to do good, ease or facility in performing a good action and joy or satisfaction while doing it. Human virtues, or virtues proper to human beings as such, are traditionally grouped in four major categories called "cardinal virtues": practical wisdom (or prudence); justice, which includes all "transitive virtues" or virtues related with dealing with others; and two self-master virtues: fortitude (sometimes known as courage) and temperance (or moderation) (Houser, 2004; Pieper, 1965), which many consider genuine human virtues (Geach, 1977).

Moral values (goods) entail rules and acting in accordance with these rules develops human virtues, and these virtues make it easier to grasp moral values (see Figure 1). In grasping moral values, practical wisdom has a crucial role, since this virtue provides the capacity for perceiving human good in every action[14] and to determine what is the content of each

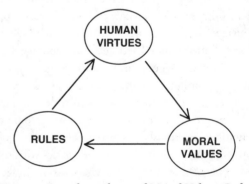

Figure 1. Interdependence of Moral Values, Rules, and Human Virtues

virtue (e.g., pointing out what does it mean to be courageous in a particular situation). Other human virtues are united among them, and practical wisdom requires the existence of the other virtues. For Aristotle, "it is not possible to be good in the strict sense without practical wisdom, or practically wise without moral virtues" (*Nichomachean Ethics*, bk VI, chap. 13; 1144b31).[15]

In other words (see Figure 2), practical wisdom points out what is the right means in each situation regarding transitive and self-mastering virtues. Practicing these latter virtues develops practical wisdom as a necessary condition. Finally, transitive and self-mastering virtues have reciprocal influences (e.g., fairness requires courage, and being fair is fostered by the development of courage needed to act fairly).[16] Rules, goods and virtues, understood in this way, are indeed interconnected. Furthermore, "virtues, rules and goods ... have to be understood in their relationship or not at all"; and "rules, conceived apart from virtues and goods, are not the same as rules conceived in dependence upon virtues and goods; and so it is also with virtues apart from rules and good and good apart from rules and virtues" (MacIntyre, 1993, 144).

Ethical Education for Good Behavior

In line with the Aristotelian tradition, I suggest ethical behavior of a person in accounting, as in any other human activity, depends on (see Figure 3)

- *Moral sensitivity*, which could be described as how the subject comprehends the ethical dimension of a situation. Human beings have a certain capacity to feel other people's needs. In the face of certain situations we experience feelings of compassion, solidarity, sympathy for a noble cause, and other moral sentiments. In accounting, one can feel that a practice can adversely or favorably affect some people. But there are also sentiments of greed, self-sufficiency or even

Figure 2. Practical Wisdom as a Driver of Moral Virtues

fear which can be stronger than those related to good behavior. Sentiments can also lead to attitudes of sentimentalism, the morality of which could be questioned. Therefore, moral sentiments seem not sufficient for an authentic moral sensibility; they need practical wisdom to bring about moral sensibility. Practical wisdom helps one to grasp the moral good in each particular action. External influences, including the perceptions of peers, education, and ethical knowledge can cultivate (or discourage) moral sentiments.

- *Moral judgment*, or capacity to judge which alternatives are ethically acceptable and which are not and to determine the uprightness of the intention. Good behavior requires deliberation

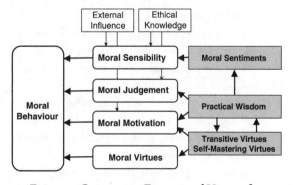

Figure 3. Constituent Factors and Virtues for a Moral Behaviour

and deciding to carry out an action. Making sound moral judgments is previous to making a good decision. In this deliberation, practical wisdom plays a crucial role. It fosters upright moral reasoning by taking into account universal principles and the pertinent circumstances of each situation. Furthermore, some other relevant virtues in accounting, such as objectivity, open-mindedness, insight and perspicacity can be considered as integrated within practical wisdom.

Ethical knowledge, including a right understanding of rules, principles and values, which could be seen as accumulation of wisdom throughout time, can also help one to make sound ethical judgments. This latter is especially valuable for those without experience and with low practical wisdom. However, rules, principles and values have to be considered only as an aid and not as a substitute for practical wisdom.

- *Moral motivation*, understood as willingness to take the moral course of action, placing moral values (human goods) above other values, and taking personal responsibility for moral outcomes. Frequently, moral motivation is the driving force for making good moral judgments but it plays a crucial role in selecting the right action and in executing it. Practical wisdom and transitive moral virtues (indirectly also self-mastering virtues) foster moral motivation, since they give a permanent motivation for acting well. External motivation, such as moral role modeling, ethical leadership, culture, education, etc., can also play a significant role in motivating people towards moral behavior.

- *Moral virtues* or permanent attitudes and interior strength for moral behavior. Among these virtues, those which have special relevance to accounting are fairness, integrity, truthfulness, honesty, loyalty, faithfulness, trustworthiness, service to the common good, gratitude and benevolence ("transitive virtues" or justice in

a broad sense). Courage, perseverance, competence, diligence, professional will, humility, and other self-mastering virtues help to defeat inner resistance to act as one should. Practical wisdom, as has been said, provides capacity to perceive the right means for each virtue.

If this sketch is correct, character, shaped by the virtues of the subject, is crucial for moral behavior.

Rules, Values (Goods) and Virtues in Ethical Education in Accounting

If the goal of ethical education is achieving good behaviors, it should insist on awaking moral sensibility, help make sound moral judgments, induce moral motivation and encourage moral virtues. Possibly some people would argue that ethical education is only about developing moral reasoning in students. I side with those that think that this is not enough. What does it matter if students know how to reason well in ethics if they are not motivated to act ethically? Thus, in my view, ethical education requires not only the development of intellectual skills but also the development of attitudes for good behavior.

Another problem, as we have seen, is that generally, rules, principles, values and virtues in current ethical education are presented in a fragmented fashion in accounting. But, if moral values, rules and virtues are so closely intertwined, ethical education ought to present all of these elements in their interrelation, although the main orientation should be toward virtues (character) since virtues are critical for moral behavior, as explained in the preceding section.

Teaching rules, starting with prohibitive rules, makes sense and should be promoted. The order of learning is "that we first have to learn in certain initial situations what is always enjoined or always prohibited, in order that we may become able to extrapolate in a non-rule-governed way to other types of situations in which what courage or justice or truthfulness, together with prudence, demands is more than conformity to the universal rule" (MacIntyre, 1993, 143). Thus, the knowledge of rules contained in codes of conduct is still necessary but they have to be critically examined and understood in their relation with human values.

Thus, human values and general principles related to them should occupy a central role in ethical education as well. Rather than presenting enlightened ethical theories to students I would suggest challenging them to reflect on what is really good. This question is not so common since many view the answer to it as a mere personal choice. Certainly, each person has to discover what is good for him or her. But such a choice entails great responsibility.

According to MacIntyre (1993), the starting point of moral reasoning for ordinary and plain people—by which I mean those who have not received any philosophical influence—is the question "What is my good?" When an ordinary person asks "what is my good?" he or she is asking about what he or she values, but he or she could be wrong and might rethink the real value for him or her. This leads to the further, already philosophical question: "What in general is the good, for my kind of history in this kind of situation?" And that in turn will lead to a fundamental philosophical question "What is the good as such for human beings as such?" (MacIntyre, 1993, 136-37).

An accountant is involved in a professional practice which demands good reputation and a contribution to the public interest or the common good, but he or she is, above all, a person who asks him or herself, "what is my good here and now?" From a relatively early age we follow rules given by parents, teachers, clergy or other people who elicit our confidence. Afterwards, we may have realized that some of these were social conventions, or organizational rules and came from reasons of efficacy or utility, but others we discover to have a moral sense (fairness, truthfulness, loyalty, ...). Through this process of trial and error, one discovers moral values and the difference between them and their opposites.

Wisdom accumulated over centuries recognizes some ethical values rooted in human nature, which ordinary persons have a certain capacity to take hold of, for instance, the value of human life, contributing to the well being of others or living together in a peaceful and amiable way. This latter includes a set of moral values that most people can understand as such. Ethical education should be aware of this and present questions and comments regarding human values and how rules correspond to them.

Regarding virtues, ethical education is different from rules and values since the acquisition of virtues is not a question of knowledge, but a result of personally deliberated and free actions. As Aristotle realized, it takes place by repetition of good actions. Here arises the age old question, coming from Socrates and Plato's time about whether virtues can be taught. If virtues are acquired through deliberate and free actions, it is clear that ethical education cannot produce virtues by itself, but virtues can be shown. Furthermore, the importance of virtues can be emphasized to motivate students toward moral behavior, which generates virtues. Several authors have given suggestions in this respect. For Mintz (1995) educators should inform students about the importance of virtues and facilitate the learning of virtue through case analysis, cooperative and collaborative learning techniques and role-playing. Dobson and Armstrong (1995) stressed the essential role played by moral exemplars or role models, or "white-hat" accountants. Stewart (1997) urges the use of narrative to enhance moral motivation. At the same time, he points out how the accounting faculty must be role-models to students in their professional responsibilities. All these proposals can contribute to fostering ethical behavior, if it is taught together with rules and human good in an integrated manner.

Conclusion

This paper has attempted to present some shortcomings to approaches of ethical education in accounting that separately consider rules and principles, values and virtues in a fragmentary manner. I have considered that values are "intrinsic moral values" or "moral goods" rooted in human nature and virtues are human virtues, that is to say, virtues of the person as such. Values (in the intellect) have a correspondence with virtues (in character). It has been argued that rules, values and virtues are interrelated and form a unity. This should lead us to re-think ethics in accounting by considering simultaneously rules, values and virtues and their interrelation.

This paper also holds that the main goal for ethical education in accounting—and of course, in any other professional field—should be to impact on the ethical behavior of those receiving this education and not only to provide a set of theories tools to solve ethical dilemmas. Ethical behavior primarily has to do with character, although ethical knowledge and external motivation must also be an influence. Consequently, ethical education has to be oriented toward motivating moral behavior and acquiring virtues, as some scholars have pointed out in recent years.[17] However, virtues are not a matter of knowledge but personal moral development. What ethical education can do is to show virtues, exhort and motivate the student to acquire them and explain how to do so. This includes the presentation and discussion of rules, generally from codes, principles and values which are necessary for acquiring virtues.

From a practical perspective, this proposal requires, first of all, changing the status quo of teaching which exclusively presents rules and enlightened ethical theories. Teaching material should also seek a different focus than what is common in many places, which is presenting dilemmas based on cases and providing little or no information about the people involved. What I have proposed is a comprehensive ethical approach interrelating rules, values and virtues. Case studies should include not only dilemmas but also descriptions of specific people involved in a particular situation, significant facts of their life, traits of their character, as well as other relevant information about factors with an influence on moral behavior, such as how people are motivated by their organization (incentives, moral role modeling, leadership, organizational culture and so on) and by the socio-cultural environment.

Acknowledgements

I am grateful to Ronald Duska, Mary B. Armstrong and Josep M. Rosanas for their thoughtful comments on an early draft of this paper.

NOTES
1 Finn et al. (1988) surveying the responses of 332 members of the AICPA found that the most frequent ethical issues in the accounting profession (CPAs) were: client proposals of tax alteration and tax fraud (47%), conflict of interest and independence (16%), client proposal of alteration of financial statements (10%) and other issues (15%).
2 The authors of this study interpret this percentage for different moral development among respondeees, many would not surpass level 4 of Kohlberg (1976) for whom the right thing is respecting authority and preserving the rules of society, while others will be at level 5, related to individual rights or level 6, which employs universal moral and ethical principles.
3 It was the *Standards of Ethical Conduct for Management Accountants* of the NAA, which afterwards become the current *Ethical Behavior for Practitioners of Management Accounting and Financial Management*.
4 Published in *Management Accounting*, September 1983, 68.
5 <http://www.aicpa.org/about/code/index.htm> (April 16, 2004).
6 <http://www.ifac.org/Guidance/EXD-Download.php?EDFID=00058> (April 16, 2004).
7 <http://www.ifac.org/Guidance/EXD-Download.php?EDFID=00058> (April 16, 2004).

8   <http://www.imapdx.org/ethics.htm>   (April 16, 2004).

9   Loeb proposed the following goals for ethics education in accounting, taken from Callahan (1980), who wrote about goals in the teaching of ethics: (1) relating accounting education to moral issues; (2) recognizing issues in accounting that have ethical implications; (3) developing a "sense of moral obligation" or responsibility; (4) developing the abilities needed to deal with ethical conflicts or dilemmas; (5) learning to deal with the uncertainties of the accounting profession; (6) "setting the stage for" a change in ethical behaviour; (7) appreciating and understanding the history and composition of all aspects of accounting ethics and their relationship to the general field of ethics (1988, 322).

10 "Given Solomon's account of what virtues are, the obvious virtues in business might well seem to be those traits that make somebody, for example, a good salesperson—traits which include excellence in persuading people to accept falsehood as much as honesty" (Ewin, 1995, 823).

11 Mintz (1995, 1996), who has emphasized the role of virtues in accounting education, as has been said, seems to have been aware of the necessity to integrate virtues with rules (standards), duties and values. He states: "Ethics refers to standards of conduct that indicate how one ought to behave based on values and moral duties and virtues arising from principles about right and wrong" (1995, 251). However, he did not go further by integrating these three elements. In fact, it would be very difficult to do so, since he considers universalistic perspectives ("principles about right and wrong") and subjective perception of values: ("values are basic and fundamental beliefs that guide or motivate attitudes or actions": 251) which are one of the sources for standards of conduct (standards of conduct ... based on values and moral duties).

12 The idea develops an original approach of Thomas Aquinas (*Summa Theologica*, I-II, q. 94, a. 2).

13 According to Thomas Aquinas (*Summa Theologica*, I-II, q.100, a.1), the Ten Commandments, apart from being a set of fundamental moral rules both for Jews and Christians, contain the whole of natural law. These rules contribute to the good of the person who fulfills them and one can easily realize that the Commandments are indispensable rules of all social life.

14 It is "right reason about things to be done," says Thomas Aquinas (*Summa Theologica*, I-II, q. 65, a. 1).

15 Aquinas insists on the same point: "no moral virtue can be without prudence; since it is proper to moral virtue to make a right choice, for it is an elective habit. Now right choice requires not only the inclination to a due end, the inclination to which is the direct outcome of moral virtue, but also the correct choice of things conducive to the end, which choice is made by prudence, that counsels, judges, and commands in those things that are directed to the end" (*Summa Theologica*, I-II, q. 65, a. 1). Elsewhere, he adds: "... discretion belongs to prudence, rectitude to justice, moderation to temperance, and strength of mind to fortitude, in whatever matter we consider these properties to be. In this way the reason for the connection is evident: for strength of mind is not commended as virtuous, if it be without moderation or rectitude or discretion: and so forth" (*Summa Theologica*, I-II, q. 58, a. 4).

16 On the interdependence of virtues, see, e.g., Simon (1986, chap. 6).

17 See a similar goal for ethical education, although from a different perspective in Armstrong et al. (2003).

REFERENCES

Abbott, A.: 1983, "Professional Ethics," *American Journal of Sociology* 88, 856-85.

Adams, B.L., F.L. Malone and W. James: 1995, "Confidentiality Decisions: The Reasoning Process of CPAs in Resolving Ethical Dilemmas," *Journal of Business Ethics* 14(12), 1015-20.

American Accounting Association Committee on the Future Structure, Content and Scope of Accounting Education: 1986, "Future Accounting Education: Preparing for the Expanding Profession," *Issues in Accounting Education*, Spring, 168-95.

Anscombe, E.: 1958, "Modern Moral Philosophy," *Philosophy* 33, 1-19. Reproduced in R. Crisp and M. Slote (eds.), 1997, *Virtue Ethics* (Oxford: Oxford University Press).

Aquinas, T.: (1273/1947). *Summa Theologica*, translation: Fathers of the English Dominican Province (New York: Benziger Brothers).

Aristotle, *Nichomachean Ethics* in R. McKeon (ed.), 1941, *The Basic Works of Aristotle* (New York: Random House).

Armstrong, M.B.: 1993, *Ethics and Professionalism for CPAs* (Cincinnati: South-Western).

Armstrong, M.B.: 2002, "Ethics Issues in Accounting," in N.E. Bowie (ed.), *The Blackwell Guide to Business Ethics* (Oxford: Blackwell).

Armstrong, M.B., J.E. Ketz and D. Owsen: 2003, "Ethics Education in Accounting: Moving Toward Ethical Motivation and Ethical Behavior," *Journal of Accounting Education* 21(1), 1-16.

Azpiazu, J.: 1964, *La moral del hombre de negocios* (Zaragoza: Fax).

Baudhuin, F.: 1954, *D'ontologie des affaires*, 4th edition (Bruxelles: Universelle).

Bond, E.J.: 2001. "The Concept of Value," in L.C. Becker and C.B. Becker (eds.), *Encyclopedia of Ethics* (New York, London: Routledge), 1745-50.

Bowie, N. and R. Duska: 1985, *Business Ethics* (New Jersey: Prentice-Hall).

Callahan, D.: 1980, "Goals in the Teaching of Ethics," in D. Callahan and S. Bok (eds.), *Ethics Teaching in Higher Education* (New York: Plenum Press).

Cooley, D.R.: 2004, "The Moral Paradigm Test," *Journal of Business Ethics* 50(3), 289-94.

Cottell Jr., P.G. and T.M. Perlin: 1990, *Accounting Ethics: A Practical Guide for Professionals* (New York: Quorum Books).

Dobson, J. and M.B. Armstrong: 1995, "Application of Virtue Ethics Theory: A Lesson from Architecture," *Research in Accounting Ethics* 1, 315-30.

Duska, R.F.: 1993, "Aristotle: A Pre-modern Post-Modern? Implications for Business Ethics," *Business Ethics Quarterly* 3(3), 227-49.

Duska, R.F. and B.S. Duska: 2003, *Accounting Ethics* (Oxford: Blackwell).

Ewin, R.E.: 1995, "The Virtues Appropriate to Business," *Business Ethics Quarterly* 5(4), 823-32.

Finn, D.W., L.B. Chonko and S.D. Hunt: 1988, "Ethical Problems in Public Accounting: The View from the Top," *Journal of Business Ethics* 7(8), 605-15.

Francis, J.R.: 1990, "After Virtue? Accounting as a Moral and Discursive Practice," *Accounting, Auditing and Accountability Journal* 3(3), 5-17.

Geach, P.T.: 1977, *The Virtues* (Cambridge: Cambridge University Press).

Gowthorpe, C. and J. Blake, (eds.), 1998, *Ethical Issues in Accounting* (New York, London: Routledge).

Guardini, R.: 1999, *Ética. Lecciones en la Universidad de Munich* (BAC, Madrid). Original: 1993, *Ethik. Vorlesungen an der Universitat München* (Mainz: Matthias-Grünerwald- Verlag).

Houser, R.E. (ed.): 2004, *The Cardinal Virtues. Aquinas, Albert and Philip the Chancelor* (Toronto: Pontifical Institute of Mediaeval Studies).

Koehn, D.: 2000, "What is Practical Judgment?" *Professional Ethics Journal* 8(3/4), 3-18.

Langenderfer, H.Q. and J.W. Rockness: 1989, "Ethics into Accounting Curriculum: Issues, Problems and Solutions," *Issues in Accounting Education* 4, 58-69.

Lere, J.C.: 2003, "The Impact of Codes of Ethics on Decision Making: Some Insights from Information Economics," *Journal of Business Ethics* 48(4), 365-79.

Loeb, S.E. and J.P. Bedingfield: 1972, "Teaching Accounting Ethics," *The Accounting Review*, October, 811-13.

Loeb, S.E. (ed.): 1978, *Ethics in the Accounting Profession* (New York: Wiley).

Loeb, S.E.: 1988, "Teaching Students Accounting Ethics: Some Crucial Issues," *Issues in Accounting Education* 3(2), 316-29.

Loeb, S.E. and J. Rockness: 1992, "Accounting Ethics and Education: A Response," *Journal of Business Ethics* 11(7), 485-90.

MacIntyre, A.: 1984, *After Virtue. A Study in Moral Theory*, 2nd edition (Notre Dame, IN: Notre Dame University Press).

MacIntyre, A.: 1993, "Plain Persons and Moral Philosophy: Rules, Virtues and Goods," *Convivium* (2nd series) 5, 63-80.

Maurice, J.: 1996, *Accounting Ethics* (London: Pitman).

Messerly, J.G.: 1994, *An Introduction to Ethical Theories* (Lanham, New York, London: University Press of America).

Mintz, S.M.: 1995, "Virtue Ethics and Accounting Education," *Issues in Accounting Education* 10(2), 247-67.

Mintz, S.M.: 1996, "The Role of Virtue in Accounting Education," *Accounting Education: A Journal of Theory, Practice and Research* 1, 67-91.

Mintz, S.M.: 1997, *Cases on Accounting Ethics and Professionalism*, 3rd edition (New York: McGraw-Hill).

National Commission on Fraudulent Financial Reporting (Treadway Commission): 1987, "Report of the National Commission on Fraudulent Financial Reporting," <http://www.coso.org/NCFFR.pdf> (accessed on July 13, 2004).

Pieper, J.: 1965, *Four Cardinal Virtues* (Notre Dame, IN: Notre Dame University Press).

Pincoffs, E.L.: 1986, *Quandries and Virtues* (Lawrence: University Press of Kansas).

Roth, J.K. (consulting editor): 1994, *Ethics* (Pasadena, CA: Salem Press).

Shaub, M.K.: 1994, "Limits to the Effectiveness of Accounting Ethics Education," *Business & Professional Ethics Journal* 13(1/2), 129-45.

Simon, Y.: 1986, in V. Kuic (ed.) *The Definition of Moral Virtue* (New York: Fordham University Press).

Solomon, C.R.: 1992, *Ethics and Excellence: Cooperation and Integrity in Business* (New York: Oxford University Press).

Stewart, I.: 1997, "Teaching Accounting Ethics: The Power of Narrative," *Accounting Education: A Journal of Theory, Practice and Research* 2, 173-84.

Veatch, H.: 1968, *For an Ontology of Morals* (Evaston, IL: Northwestern University Press).

Velayutham, S.: 2003, "The Accounting Professions' Code of Ethics: Is It a Code of Ethics or a Code of Quality Assurance?" *Critical Perspectives on Accounting* 14(4), 483-503.

LEARNING FROM CORPORATE SCANDALS

The Lessons from Enron

After the Energy Firm's Collapse, the Entire Auditing Regime Needs Radical Change

The mess just keeps spreading. Two months after Enron filed for Chapter 11, the reverberations from the Texas-based energy-trading firm's bankruptcy might have been expected to fade; instead, they are growing. On Capitol Hill, politicians are engaged in an investigative orgy not seen since Whitewater, with the blame pinned variously on the company's managers, its directors, its auditors and its bankers, as well as on the Bush administration; indeed on anybody except the hundreds of congressmen who queued up to take campaign cash from Enron. The only missing ingredient in the scandal—so far—is sex.

The effects are also touching Wall Street. In the past few weeks, investors have shifted their attention to other companies, making a frenzied search for any dodgy accounting that might reveal the next Enron. Canny traders have found a lucrative new strategy: sell a firm's stock short and then spread rumours about its accounts. Such companies as Tyco, PNC Financial Services, Invensys and even the biggest of the lot, General Electric, have all suffered. Last week Global Crossing, a telecoms firm, went bust amid claims of dubious accounts. This week shares in Elan, an Irish-based drug maker, were pummelled by worries over its accounting policies.

All this might create the impression that corporate financial reports, the quality of company profits and the standard of auditing in America have suddenly and simultaneously deteriorated. Yet that would be wide of the mark: the deterioration has actually been apparent for many years. A growing body of evidence does indeed suggest that Enron was a peculiarly egregious case of bad management, misleading accounts, shoddy auditing and, quite probably, outright fraud. But the bigger lessons that Enron offers for accounting and corporate governance have long been familiar from previous scandals, in America and elsewhere. That makes it all the more urgent to respond now with the right reforms.

Uncooking the Books

The place to start is auditing. Accurate company accounts are a keystone for any proper capital market, not least America's. Andersen, the firm that audited Enron's books from its inception in 1985 (it was also Global Crossing's auditor), has been suggesting that its failings are representative of the whole profession's. In fact, Andersen seems to have been unusually culpable over Enron: shredding of incriminating documents just ahead of the investigators is not yet a widespread habit. But it is also true that this is only the latest of a string of corporate scandals involving appalling audit failures, from Maxwell and Polly Peck in Britain, through Metallgesellschaft in Germany, to Cendant, Sunbeam and Waste Management in America. In the past four years alone, over 700 American companies have been forced to restate their accounts.

At the heart of these audit failures lies a set of business relationships that are bedevilled by perverse incentives and conflicts of interest. In theory, a company's auditors are appointed independently by its shareholders, to whom they report. In practice, they are chosen by the company's bosses, to whom they all too often become beholden. Accounting firms frequently sell consulting services to their audit clients; external auditors may be hired to senior management positions or as internal auditors; it is far too easy to play on an individual audit partner's fear of losing a lucrative audit assignment. Against such a background, it is little wonder that the quality of the audit often suffers.

What should be done? The most radical change would be to take responsibility for audits away from private accounting firms altogether and give it, lock, stock and barrel, to the government. Perhaps such a change may yet become necessary. But it would run risks in terms of the quality of auditors; and it is not always so obvious that a government agency would manage to escape the conflicts and mistakes to which private firms have so often fallen prey. As an intermediate step, however, a simpler suggestion is to take the job of choosing the auditors away from a company's bosses. Instead, a government agency—meaning, in America, the Securities and Exchange Commission (SEC)—would appoint the auditors, even if on the basis of a list recommended by the company, which would continue to pay the audit fee.

Harvey Pitt, the new chairman of the Securities and Exchange Commission, is not yet willing to be anything like so radical. He has been widely attacked because, when he acted in the past as a lawyer for a number of accounting firms, he helped to fend off several reforms. Yet he now seems ready to make at least some of the other changes that the Enron scandal has shown to be necessary.

Among these are much fiercer statutory regulation of the auditing profession, including disciplinary powers with real bite. Hitherto, auditors have managed to get away with the fiction of self-regulation, both through peer review and by toothless professional and oversight bodies that they themselves have dominated. There should also be a ban on accounting firms offering (often more profitable) consulting and other services to their audit clients. Another good idea is mandatory rotation, every four years or so, both of audit partners—so that individuals do not become too committed to their clients—and of audit firms. The most effective peer review happens when one firm comes in to look at

a predecessor's books. The SEC should also ban the practice of companies' hiring managers and internal auditors from their external audit firms.

In Search of Better Standards

Then there is the issue of accounting standards themselves. Enron's behaviour has confirmed that in some areas, notably the treatment of off-balance-sheet dodges, American accounting standards are too lax; while in others they are so prescriptive that they have lost sight of broader principles. Past attempts by the Financial Accounting Standards Board to improve standards have often been stymied by vociferous lobbying. It is time for the SEC itself to impose more rigorous standards, although that should often be through sound principles (including paying less attention to single numbers for earnings) rather than overly detailed rules. It would also be good to come up with internationally agreed standards.

Although audit is the most pressing area for change, it is not the only one. The Enron fiasco has shown that all is not well with the governance of many big American companies. Over the years all sorts of checks and balances have been created to ensure that company bosses, who supposedly act as agents for shareholders, their principals, actually do so. Yet the cult of the all-powerful chief executive, armed with sackfuls of stock options, has too often pushed such checks aside.

It is time for another effort to realign the system to function more in shareholders' interests. Companies need stronger non-executive directors, paid enough to devote proper attention to the job; genuinely independent audit and remuneration committees; more powerful internal auditors; and a separation of the jobs of chairman and chief executive. If corporate America cannot deliver better governance, as well as better audit, it will have only itself to blame when the public backlash proves both fierce and unpleasant.

◆ ◆ ◆ ◆ ◆

HOWARD ROCKNESS and
JOANNE ROCKNESS

Legislated Ethics: From Enron to Sarbanes-Oxley, the Impact on Corporate America

Enron, WorldCom, HealthSouth, Adelphia, Parmalat, Elan, Andersen ... the list goes on and on. In the past three years the world economic system has witnessed in monetary terms the largest dollar level of fraud, accounting manipulations and unethical behavior in corporate history and certainly the most economic scandals and failures since the 1920s. Unlike the Savings and Loan failures of the 1980s, the current ethical crisis is broadly based and spreads across industries and countries. In July, 2002 the US Congress responded with the Sarbanes-Oxley Act which legislates ethical behavior for both publicly traded companies and their auditor firms. Can a government legislate ethical behavior or does the corporate or firm culture determine individual and group actions? This paper explores that question through review of the recent corporate scandals along with the requirements of the Sarbanes-Oxley legislation.

"Historical Perspective" Section presents a historical perspective on previous attempts to legislate corporate ethical behavior followed by discussion of some of the largest recent corporate financial reporting scandals and the underlying unethical and fraudulent actions in "Recent Corporate Frauds" Section. "Sarbanes-Oxley Act of 2002" section outlines specific provisions of the Sarbanes-Oxley Act as the most recent attempt to legislate ethical behavior followed by discussion of the potential outcomes. "Basic Premises for Ethical Financial Reporting" Section of the paper develops a framework positing four premises of corporate management's behavior

followed by conclusions on the likely impact of the current attempts to legislate ethical behavior.

Historical Perspective

The historical perspective illustrates that the frauds and failures of recent years are not a new phenomena.

The twentieth century witnessed the growth of enormous international corporations and very large international Certified Public Accounting (CPA) firms. This growth has not been without struggle, controversy and regulation. Corporate fraud, unethical management behavior, and questionable financial reporting have surfaced repeatedly throughout the century with resulting regulation and studies calling for ethical behavior. Table I presents a summary of key regulatory acts of the century that attempted to impose ethical conduct on the US securities markets, corporate America and the CPA profession. The early legislation was aimed at financial institutions and the security of the monetary system. However, the most sweeping legislation followed the excesses of the 1920s.

The 1920s were a period of industrial growth with a corresponding surge in stock prices. A new economy of automobiles, oil, steel, radio communications and expensive real estate drove market prices to unprecedented levels (Pearlstein, 2002). Accounting standards were developed privately, often poorly defined and unregulated. As a result, they were subject to manipulation with accurate financial reporting easily compromised to drive stock prices, meet loan covenants or attract new investors. The unregulated securities markets were characterized by short sales, fraudulent trading practices and margin purchases that pushed investors and management to attempt to drive prices in search of even higher returns. The incentives for management to engage in unethical practices were driven by personal gain, ego and greed illustrated by opportunistic and exploitative executive behavior to achieve personal objectives. The results were famous frauds such as the Ponzi scheme, fraudulent financial reporting, unsubstantiated market values and the crash of 1929.

The Securities Acts of 1933 and 1934 were the US Congress' response to the 1920s and the first broadly based attempt to elicit ethical behavior by corporations, the securities markets and the accounting profession through legislation. The Acts established the US Securities and Exchange Commission (SEC), regulated securities trading, mandated common accounting standards and required CPA firm audits of publicly traded companies. These Acts signified a landmark change in corporate accountability and provided the foundation for growth of the CPA profession as external auditors. Prior to the Sarbanes-Oxley Act of 2002, the SEC Acts were considered the most significant pieces of legislation in the history of both the CPA profession and US corporate financial reporting.

The 1933 and 1934 SEC Acts did not solve the systemic problems. Between 1934 and 2002, there were many instances of ethical transgressions in US corporate financial reporting. The 1960s were marked by real estate scandals filled with creative accounting and the 1970s saw international frauds and bribery resulting from numerous unethical behaviors. This time the regulatory response was the 1977 Foreign Corrupt Practices Act. The Act imposed new ethical standards on corporations dealing in foreign countries, attempted to curtail bribery and illegal payments and precipitated increased audit procedures (Shearman and Sterling, 2001). The SEC proposed management attestation of internal control systems following the Foreign Corrupt Practices Act, but under pressure from corporate America the requirement was dropped.

The 1980s experienced the failure of real estate driven savings and loans as well as widespread Wall Street corruption, fraudulent reporting, insider trading and junk-bond schemes (Vickers and France, 2002). By 1991, the FBI had budgeted more than $125 million to pursue cases of financial fraud in the

S&L industry (US Congress: Senate, 1992) and the Big Six CPA firms paid $1.6 billion to settle fraudulent reporting charges levied against them by the federal government (Arthur Andersen et al., 1992). Zimring and Hawkins (1993) argued that deregulation of banking with relaxation of regulations created conditions that made regular fraudulent practices the norm. The Federal Deposit Insurance Corporation Improvement Act in 1991 (US Congress, 1991) dealt directly with the fraud in savings and loans and required attestation of internal control in financial institutions. Litigation resulting from the savings and loan failures precipitated the Private Securities Litigation Reform Act of 1995 (US Congress, 1995) that attempted to limit CPA firm liability and was the first requirement for auditors to report fraud externally to the SEC.

In addition to legislation, unethical actions of the 1970s and 1980s precipitated the National Commission on Fraudulent Financial Reporting (Treadway Commission, 1987) report calling for ethical behavior by corporations. The report made numerous recommendations to prevent fraudulent financial reporting including strong recommendations for internal control systems. Emphasis was placed on the tone at the top, ethics education and codes of conduct. However, the Treadway Commission focused more on employee fraud, not management fraud, and centered on detection, not prevention, providing no clear effective strategy for preventing management fraud (Tipgos, 2002). Following the Treadway Report, the SEC once again proposed management attestation of internal control systems as well as disclosure of responses to auditor recommendations, but they backed down under pressure from corporate America. In 1992, the Committee of Sponsoring Organizations of the Treadway Commissions (COSO, 1992) again responded to the ethical problems of the 1980s with their framework for internal control framework guidance.

The 1990s brought an unprecedented era of fraudulent reporting and unethical corporate man-

Table I. U.S. Legislation Attempting to Prevent Behaviors Viewed as Unethical

Legislation	Timing	Ethical focus	Requirement	Result
Owens-Glass (Federal Reserve) Act of 1913	1913	Banking failures due to inadequate or fraudulent reserves	Rules for operations of banks including maintenance of reserves, financial reporting requirements	Creation of Federal Reserve System, in part, for more effective supervision of banking activities. Required annual independent audits of Federal Reserve Banks and Board
Glass-Stegall Act of 1933	1933	Conflict of interest and fraud by banks	Prohibited commercial banks from engaging in investment banking. Similarly, prohibited investment banks from engaging in commercial banking directly or through employees, officers, or directors	Intended to keep banks from selling securities to pay off loans made by the bank to failing company or country
US Securities and Exchange Act of 1933	1933	Prohibited deceit, misrepresentations, and other fraud in sale of securities	Required disclosure of relevant information through registration of securities	Made commitment of fraud in conjunction with sale of securities (registered or unregistered) illegal
US Securities and Exchange Act of 1934	1934	Insider stock trading, manipulation of financial markets, fraudulent financial reporting	Self-policing by stock exchanges and National Association of Security Dealers, filing of quarterly and audited annual reports by registered companies	Established CPA as the independent outside auditor of published financial statements. Provided for civil actions by the SEC and private investors for fraud, insider trading, and market manipulation
Investment Company Act of 1940	1940	Abuses in investment companies (principally mutual funds investing in stocks of other companies) including conflicts of interest	Periodic disclosure of structure, operations, financial condition, and investment policies. Established fiduciary responsibilities of investment company's directors and trustees	Registration of mutual fund management companies and disclosure of transaction between the management company and affiliates
Foreign Corrupt Practices Act	1977	Bribery of foreign government and business officials. US political campaign contributions by US corporations.	Required companies to design and maintain internal control systems and detailed records which accurately and fairly reflect financial activities	Made payments to officials of foreign government, companies, or their agents in order to obtain business illegal. Established direct link between internal audit function and board of directors
FIDCA improvement act	1991	Fraud and conflict of interest on the part of officers and directors of failed savings and loan institutions	Required report by officers on internal control over financial reporting and compliance with federal law. Required independent auditor attestation on management reports on internal control and compliance	First instance of separate management assertion with respect to internal control and auditor attestation of management's assertion
Private Securities Litigation Reform Act	1995	Frivolous litigation against SEC companies for alleged wrong-doing	Required lawyer to make specific allegations of wrongdoing but also required outside auditor to notify SEC of serious financial wrongdoing	Outside auditor must report evidence of serious financial wrongdoing to board of directors and then to SEC if board does not take appropriate action
Sarbanes-Oxley Act (See Table IV for detailed analysis of content)	2002	Fraudulent financial reporting	Regulates CPA profession and service provided to external public company audit clients, and legislates control requirements, corporate management certifications, audit committees responsibilities, and corporate culture changes	Significant civil and criminal penalties for certification by management of inaccurate financial statements or inoperative internal controls. Established increased oversight responsibilities for audit committees of board of directors. Requires external auditor certification of internal controls

agement behavior. The dot.com phenomena, a new economy of technology, communications, day-trading, a roaring bull market, and a surge of initial public offerings often creating instant wealth made this period unlike any time in history. The use of incentive-based compensation schemes provided the incentives, and continued development of computer technology and the transfer of records from paper to machine paved the way to countless opportunities for fraudulent financial reporting.

A new round of corporate failures began in the late 1990s and early 2000s. The unethical actions of corporate leaders led to bankruptcies and restatements of a magnitude unimagined in prior decades. Since 1997, more than 10% of US public companies have restated their reports resulting in market capitalization losses in excess of $100 billion (GAO, 2002). In the twelve-month period ending June 30, 2003 alone, 354 companies restated earnings (Huron Consulting Group, 2003). The sheer size of the failures dwarfed previous scandals. "It is not that our leaders are worse than ever, it's just that the bad ones can do more damage than ever before, and on a spectacular scale" (Morris, 2002).

The response this time was the Sarbanes-Oxley legislation (Sarbanes) of 2002, which is the focus of this paper and is discussed in detail in "Conclusion" Section. Will Sarbanes be different or will unethical and fraudulent management behavior continue resulting in more corporate failures? The parallels of the 1920s, the 1980s and the past decade are strong and raise serious doubts as to whether ethical behavior can be legislated. "Recent Corporate Frauds" Section discusses some of the most glaring illustrations of ethical misconduct and fraud in corporate America to set the stage for US legislature's perceived need to respond with the Sarbanes-Oxley Act in 2002.

Recent Corporate Frauds

"Losses from financial frauds total approximately $200 billion dollars. On Enron alone those losses are more than two times the aggregate losses suffered when the stock market crashed in 1929." (Turner, 2002)

Enron

Enron's failure will most likely go down in history as not only one of the most spectacular financial failures, but also as a turning point in professional accounting regulation and corporate financial reporting. It was the driving force behind the Sarbanes-Oxley legislation. However, it was only one of many corporate failures resulting from unethical and fraudulent behavior that led to landmark legislation.

Table II presents a summary of significant recent corporate and accounting frauds. The unethical behaviors represented in Table II include fraudulent financial reporting (most common), obstruction of justice, theft of assets, unauthorized loans to senior management, bribery, manipulation of markets, perjury, and insider trading. The types of fraud were pervasive, extended over years rather than single episodes, and involved very large sums of money. The most consistent common element across all these firms is the involvement of senior management in the frauds including members of the Board of Directors, the CEO, the CFO, and other key executives.

The tone at the top has been cited as the primary driver of corporate ethical conduct by many professional sources (e.g., AICPA, 2002; COSO, 1992; Treadway Commission, 1987). Ethicists have long argued that tone drives the corporate culture (Buchholz and Rosenthal, 1998, 177). Sweeney (2003) argued that the tone at the top sets the corporate culture and in many cases was a root cause of the unethical conduct and fraudulent activities. He cites two common characteristics: overly aggressive financial performance targets and a can-do culture that did not tolerate failure (Sweeney, 2003).

In this culture, what often began as questionable accounting adjustments grew into massive fraud in an attempt to fix each quarter's numbers to close the

Table II. Example Companies Charged with Financial Irregularities

Company	Industry	Fraud	Activity	Participants	Outcome
Sunbeam: 1996–1997 ($60 million)	Consumer durables	Fraudulent financial reporting	Understating inventory value, underreporting cost of goods sold, recognizing revenue from undelivered goods, bill and hold sale, channel stuffing, and establishing false reserves in 1996 to improve 1997 income	Senior management including CEO	CEO and CFO settled SEC civil charges, termination of senior management, barred from serving in senior positions in public companies
Waste Management (1997) ($1.7 billion)	Trash collection and disposal	Fraudulent financial reporting	Misrepresentation of asset lives and salvage values, overvaluation of landfill site assets, excess reserves, and reporting expenses as assets	Senior management	Senior management sued for fraud, settled insider trading charge. Company settled civil litigation for $457 million.
Global Crossing (2002)	Telecommunications	Fraudulent financial reporting	Overstatement of revenue from barter transactions	Senior management	Chapter 11 bankruptcy, congressional investigation, SEC charged senior management with fraud
Xerox (1997–2000) ($1.5 billion)	Office equipment	Fraudulent financial reporting	Booking revenue from foreign subsidiaries before earned and failure to appropriately classify lease assets	Senior management for South America	$10 million fine
WorldCom/MCI (2002) ($3.8 billion income and $400 million in loans, alleged $11 billion in revenue)	Telecommunications	Fraudulent financial reporting	Reporting of line rental expense as capital lease asset, underreporting of line rental expenses, and off-books loans to CEO	Senior management	CEO charged with fraud, CFO and other financial executives plead guilty to criminal fraud, active jail sentences
Andersen (2002)		Obstruction of justice	Destruction of documentary evidence after SEC launch of Enron investigation	Andersen legal department and professional staff	Convicted of obstruction of justice. Firm dissolved
HealthSouth (2003) ($4.2 billion overstatement of income)	Healthcare delivery	Fraudulent financial reporting	Reporting non-existent assets and underreporting revenues	Senior management	Guilty pleas by over 25 of senior financial managers, CEO charged with civil and 85 counts of criminal fraud
Tyco (2002) ($600 million)	Diversified manufacturer	Theft of assets, unauthorized loans to senior management, and fraudulent financial reporting	Unauthorized loans and payments to senior executives	Senior management including CEO, CFO, and chief legal officer	Senior management indicted for corruption, conspiracy, grand larceny and falsifying records. CEO and CFO pleaded innocent. Six-month trial ended with hung jury
Adelphia Communications (2001) ($3.1 billion including $300 million in unauthorized cash withdrawals and loans by founding family/senior management)	Cable television	Theft of assets and fraudulent financial reporting	Unauthorized payments and loans to principal owners, inflated capital expenditures, hidden debt	Founding family/senior management	SEC/Department of Justice indictment

Company	Industry	Fraud	Activity	Participants	Outcome
Parmalat (2003) (estimated 8.0 billion euros overstatement of assets and 500 million euros diverted to family accounts)	Dairy products	Fraudulent financial reporting, looting of company	Reporting non-existent assets (Cash)	Founder/family/senior management	
Ahold NV (2003) (overstatement of income by at least 900 million euros)	Groceries and food distribution	Management fraud in US and European subsidiaries	Overstating income in subsidiaries in part by recognizing manufacturer rebates and special discounts prior to sale of goods	Subsidiary management	CEO and CFO of company resign
Cendant	Diversified services				
Enron (over $1 billion)	Energy	Fraudulent financial reporting, bribery of foreign government officials, manipulation of energy markets	Overstating income by hiding losses, and understatement of liabilities by transferring debt to related companies	Senior management	Guilty pleas by senior financial management, indictment of CEO
Imclone Systems Inc. (2002)	Biotechnology/Pharmaceuticals	Insider trading, perjury, and obstruction of justice	Sale of owned shares by senior management ahead of announcement of bad news	Senior management, family, and friends	CEO pleaded guilty, friend convicted

variance between income targets and actual results. The classic slippery slope of unethical behavior prevailed as otherwise honest people came to believe they were acting in the best interest of the company and consented to participating in unethical and fraudulent behavior. Personal gain, ego and survival were perhaps all motivating factors for the individuals involved. The impact of senior management on the corporate culture and resulting frauds are illustrated by taking a closer look at three of the biggest scandals: Enron, WorldCom, and HealthSouth.

Sims and Brinkmann (2003) provide an in-depth analysis of the culture at Enron. They describe how Jeffrey Skilling, former CEO, set the tone at the top by creating a culture that would push limits and where employees were expected to perform to a continually increasing standard. Bartlett and Glinska (2001) quoted employees stating "… it was all about

an atmosphere of deliberately breaking the rules …" Complex accounting strategies and manipulations were utilized to meet ever-higher expectations.

The Enron issues were relatively sophisticated requiring knowledge of difficult accounting regulations and an understanding of ways to manipulate the rules. Approximately 3000 non-consolidated special purpose entities were created to move debt off the balance sheet, complicated hedge and derivative transactions were improperly accounted for, related party transactions were improperly disclosed (or not disclosed at all), and the accounting for the sale of Enron's stock in exchange for notes receivable was questionable.

Enron's slippery slope got steeper. It started as utilization of accounting rules to the company's advantage. It then progressed to fraudulent reporting and, finally, to destruction of documents. Numerous people were involved with many having full knowledge of the fraudulent accounting. One mid-level executive, Sherron Watkins, tried to blow the whistle but was ignored (Morse and Bower, 2002). Control systems failures were evident in both the corporation and in their external audit firm, Andersen, as the warnings of Sherron Watkins and others within Andersen went unheeded. The result was the then largest corporate bankruptcy of the century and the resulting demise of Andersen.

Unprecedented levels of Enron related litigation are underway including lawsuits brought by investors, the SEC, the US Justice Department, pension plans, and employees (SEC, 2004a). Major investment firms including Citibank and J.P. Morgan already have paid $135 million and $120 million, respectively, to settle SEC charges that they aided Enron in the fraud (Forbes, 2003). Fifteen former executives were criminally indicted and seven have pleaded guilty. Andrew Fastow, the former CFO, pleaded guilty to fraud in January 2004 and negotiated a ten-year prison sentence (CNN Money, 2004). He will be a major witness against the former CEO Jeffrey Skilling. On February 19, 2004, the US Justice Department charged Skilling with 42 counts conspiracy, fraud, and other security laws violations (Flood, 2004).

WorldCom

At WorldCom, CEO and founder, Bernie Ebbers, set the tone at the top. Richard Breeden, former chairman of the SEC, says Ebbers "scoffed at ethics and controls ... real men only worry about revenue growth" (Sweeney, 2003). In the WorldCom culture, promotions were given to those who claimed credit for things they did not do, were willing to twist reality, and promised what they could not deliver. Trouble began at WorldCom when they failed to meet the revenue expectations communicated earlier to the investment community. In 2004, the CFO pleaded guilty stating that he and the CEO met con-

cerning the problem. The CEO refused to meet with the investment community to announce the shortfall. Rather, the CFO said he was instructed by the CEO to fix the problem. Allegations are that the CEO was keenly aware of the likely impact on share price and was more concerned about $400 million he had personally borrowed from WorldCom secured by WorldCom stock (Padgett, 2002).

The WorldCom unethical and fraudulent accounting practices resulted in a $9 billion dollar restatement ... the largest in US history. Recent evidence now places the total fraudulent reporting at $11 billion (Perrotta, 2004). Over a five-year period, accountants at WorldCom systematically altered records, often after the books were closed, to meet analyst's expectations. According to the WorldCom indictment, CEO Ebbers, CFO Sullivan and others created a process called "close the gap" which identified improper accounting adjustments and then instructed staff to carry out the manipulations. Initially reserves were used to absorb expenses. When the reserves ran out a variety of accounting frauds were used to enhance revenues and decrease expenses. For example, costs for annual operating leases for lines were capitalized as assets to reduce expenses (SEC, 2004b). Unlike Enron, this did not involve manipulation of complex accounting rules, but rather a straight-forward capitalization of expenses.

Members of the financial staff including the CFO, the controller and head of general accounting have pleaded guilty to fraud and the CEO has been charged with securities fraud (Washington Post, 2004). David Myers the former controller told a US district judge that he was "instructed on a quarterly basis by senior management to ensure that entries were made to falsify WorldCom's reported actual costs and therefore increase WorldCom's reported earnings. I knew there was no justification or documentation" (Taub, 2002). Accounting managers were given promotions, raises, and made to feel responsible for the likely collapse of the stock price if they did not manipulate the books (Pulliam, 2003).

The WorldCom corporate culture encouraged unethical behavior both by appealing to individuals' sense of promoting the greatest common good for the workers, shareholders, and community and by raising fears of losing their jobs if they did not comply with requests to falsify records. Arguably, many of the financial staff at Enron may not have had the knowledge to recognize the sophisticated transactions as fraudulent. However, WorldCom staff knew it was wrong and went along with the schemes anyway (Pulliam, 2003). Again, an individual, Cynthia Cooper, blew the whistle to the audit committee and started the resulting disclosure of the fraudulent financial practices (Ripley, 2002).

HealthSouth

HealthSouth is perhaps the most egregious illustration of unethical and fraudulent behavior. Recent estimates indicate the accounting fraud may have manufactured $4 billion of false earnings (MSNBC, 2004). Once again, the tone at the top led to a slippery slope of unethical actions. According to the SEC indictment, senior officers would present actual results to the CEO each quarter and, if they were short of expectations, he would tell them to fix it. The accounting personnel then convened in "family meetings" and discussed what false accounting entries to make to inflate earnings. The focus was on altering the contractual adjustments account (common in health care to recognize differences between gross billings and what health care providers will pay) to increase net revenue. The adjustment was balanced by falsifying fixed assets accounts. To further the fraud, many of HealthSouth's accounting personnel were prior employees of the auditor, Ernst and Young, and knew adjustments they could make that would not be detected in audit procedures. If the auditors did question an entry, the HealthSouth accountants created false documents to support it (SEC, 2003c). The CEO Scrushy personally profited selling 7.7 million shares of stock when the price was

artificially inflated by accounting numbers as well as bonus payments and salary payments.

HealthSouth's ethical problems also existed at the Board level. Three directors had significant ties to the company: one earned $250,000 in consulting fees, one owned expensive resort property with the CEO, and one had a $5.6 million contract to install glass at a HealthSouth hospital. The same three served on the combined audit and compensation committee (Lublin and Carms, 2003).

The SEC accused former HealthSouth management of fabricating $2.74 billion in earnings and charged them with fraud, reporting violations, and internal controls violations. Fifteen financial employees have pleaded guilty. Scrushy has been indicted on 85 counts and he has pleaded not guilty (Bassing, 2003). Scrushy was the first CEO to be charged under the Sarbanes-Oxley Act for signing a false certification of financial statements. Scrushy's attorneys have fought the charge with a rebuttal that Sarbanes is unconstitutional and should be repealed (National Accounting News, 2003). Meanwhile, Scrushy has become a religious talk show host (CBSNEWS, 2004).

All three of these cases illustrate a corrupt tone at the top that emphasized making the numbers at the expense of doing the right thing. Collusion, top management pressure on employees to act unethically, personal greed and gain, audit failures, and a corrupt corporate culture were common across these corporations. Similar patterns can be seen in the other companies listed in Table II. Is it possible for legislation to prevent further unethical and fraudulent behavior in corporations like we have witnessed in these cases? The US Congress has attempted to do so with the Sarbanes-Oxley legislation of 2002. However, the regulations are aimed not only at corporate America but also at the CPA firms who perform their audits. The major international CPA firms have demonstrated similar ethical problems. Before we discuss the specific provisions of the Sarbanes Act, we present a brief review of the most notable recent ethical issues raised by actions of CPA firms.

The Big Five ... No, the Final Four: Ethical Failure in CPA Firms

> "Too many CFO's are being judged today not by how effectively they manage operations, but by how they manage the street. And, too many auditors are being judged not just by how well they manage an audit, but by how well they cross-market their firm's non-audit services." (Levitt, 2000)

The corporate ethical failures of the past decade have taken their toll on the US public accounting profession. Table III links a number of the major financial reporting scandals to their respective external auditors along with the related litigation against the CPA firms. One conclusion that may be drawn from Table III is that none of the firms have been immune from scandal and all have been subject to litigation.

All of the Big Five were subject to criticism in the 1990s for inadequate audit procedures, a strong focus on increasing the breadth and volume of consulting services, providing internal audit services to external audit clients, and utilizing the accounting rules to the advantage of audit clients rather than focusing on underlying economic substance. Articles in the business press such as "Accounting Wars" (Business Week, 2000), "Lies, Damned Lies, and Managed Earnings" (Fortune, 1999) became widespread. Arthur Levitt, then chairman of the SEC, reprimanded the CPA profession for flaws in revenue recognition practices, utilization of "cookie-jar" reserves, and capitalization of in-process R&D. He also expressed strong concerns about a perceived lack of independence (Levitt, 1998). Based on his concerns, Levitt predicted an Enron, just not specifically by name (Business Week, 2000). Arthur Wyatt, a former FASB member, argued that greed became a driving force within the accounting firms just as it did within many corporations. He further argued,

"the cultures of the firms—changed from a central emphasis on delivering professional services in a professional manner to an emphasis on growing revenues and profits" (Wyatt 2004, 49).

In June of 2000, the SEC believed that the potential for ethical failures was sufficient to justify proposing new regulations on auditor independence to impose limits on services to audit clients to avoid conflicts of interest. The proposal would have banned external auditors from providing the same non-audit services to audit clients that Sarbanes banned two years later (Business Week, 2000). The proposal met with strong opposition from the Big Five, the American Institute of Certified Public Accountants (AICPA), and corporate America and resulted in a compromise regulation in November, 2000 which permitted information systems design and implementation consulting as well as limited internal audit outsourcing to continue as long as fees were disclosed. The Sarbanes-Oxley Act of 2002 subsequently has prohibited these services.

Under the 2000 SEC regulations, Andersen continued providing significant consulting services to Enron in addition to external audit services. Total Enron-based revenue was $55 million in 2000 with $27 million from consulting services. As Enron collapsed, so did Andersen. Within six months of the Enron bankruptcy filing, Andersen was found guilty of obstruction of justice but they also admitted failures in internal processes to ensure quality audits and professional integrity (Hecht, 2003). The tone at the top and culture in Andersen had parallels to the previously discussed corporate cultures. Andersen had placed great emphasis on growth with evidence suggesting that client satisfaction and growth may have been more important than ethical financial reporting (Byrne, 2002).

The remaining Big Four continue to have ethical and financial reporting problems. A critical question is, can the US and global economic systems afford to lose another major accounting firm? If not, can the Sarbanes-Oxley Act promote the ethical behav-

Table III. Sample of Recent CPA Firm Involvements in Financial Irregularities

Firm	Client	Charge	Outcome
Andersen (1997)	Waste management	SEC: False and misleading audit reports	Paid $256 million; three partners agreed to anti-fraud injunction, a civil penalty and a bar from appearing or practicing in front of the SEC as an accountant. Company settled class action for $457 million
Andersen (1996–1997)	Sunbeam	Shareholder suit: Concealing material adverse non-public information from the public	Paid $110 million. No admission of fraud or liability
Andersen (2002)	Enron	Destruction of documents, obstruction of justice	Paid $40 million in shareholder suit. Convicted of obstruction of justice. Firm dissolved
Andersen (2002)	WorldCom/MCI	Improper audit procedures	Court held Andersen would have uncovered fraud if it had done required review procedures, audit opinions materially misrepresented company financial position
Ernst and Young (2003–2004)	HealthSouth	Shareholder suit: Alleges auditors knew about the fraudulent accounting	Investigation in process
Ernst and Young (2003)	Private tax clients	Created and marketed alleged illegal tax shelters	Paid $15 million to settle a US Internal Revenue Service investigation into its sale of tax shelters
Ernst and Young (2003)	PeopleSoft	SEC's conflict of interest charges and lack of independence in software installations	SEC sought to bar E and Y from accepting new publicly traded clients, repay fees. Ongoing investigation
Ernst and Young (2003)	American Express, American Airlines, Continental Airlines	Conflict of interest and potential lack of independence resulting from "profit sharing" under exclusive travel contracts	Ongoing investigation
Ernst and Young (2003)	Nextcard Inc.	Obstruction of justice and alteration and destruction of documents	Civil and criminal charges against E and Y employees. Guilty plea by one employee
KPMG (1997)	Xerox	SEC charged four KPMG partners with fraud. Allege fraudulently allowed company to manipulate accounting practices to fill a $3 billion gap between actual and reported results	KPMG denies charges and rebutting in court
KPMG (2003)	Private tax clients	Created and marketed alleged illegal tax shelters	Ongoing investigation
PWC (2003)	SmarTalk Teleservices Inc.	SEC annual report contained materially false and misleading financial statements	Paid $1 million, neither admitted nor denied wrongdoing
PWC (2000)	Microstrategy	Fraudulent accounting	Three top executives fined. PWC not charged
Deloitte (2003–2004)	Parmalat	Fraudulent financial reporting	Ongoing
Deloitte (2003)	Reliance Insurance Company	Knew of company condition prior to signing audit, contributed to failure	Ongoing. Deloitte denies charges
Deloitte (2003)	Manhattan Investment Fund	Improper audit procedures	Paid $32 million in settlement

ior necessary for survival? The relevant provisions of Sarbanes are discussed in "Sarbanes-Oxley Act of 2002" Section.

Sarbanes-Oxley Act of 2002

> "Today I sign the most far-reaching reforms of American business practices since the time of Franklin Delano Roosevelt. This new law sends very clear messages that all concerned must heed. This law says to every dishonest corporate leader: you will be exposed and punished; the era of low standards and false profits is over; no boardroom in America is above or beyond the law." (Bush, 2002).

Almost two years have passed since the signing of the Sarbanes-Oxley Act (Sarbanes), and the scandals and restatements continue. We are still witnessing corporate misconduct and failure, as well as unethical actions in hedge funds, the stock exchanges, and mutual funds. Sarbanes takes a strong punitive approach to regulating public accountants, corporate management, and investment houses calling for an ethical tone at the top as well as an ethical corporate culture. Sarbanes is very inclusive and prescribes expected behaviors, ethical responsibilities, and certifications that carry heavy penalties if violated. Our discussion focuses on the provisions of Sarbanes that have direct implications for corporate and accounting firm ethical behavior. These provisions are outlined in Table IV and the major points are discussed next.

Corporate Ethical Provisions

Sarbanes primary focus is on regulating corporate conduct in an attempt to promote ethical behavior and prevent the fraudulent financial reporting failures of the past decade. The legislation applies to the Board of Directors, the Audit Committee, the CEO, the CFO, and all other management personnel that have influence over the accuracy and adequacy of external financial reports.

Table IV. Key Behavioral Provisions of Sarbanes-Oxley for Issuers and Auditors of Financial Statements

Title	Section	Subject	Content
I. Public Company Accounting Oversight Board	105	Investigations and disciplinary proceedings	Investigation procedures, disciplinary hearings, and sanctions of firms and associated persons
II. Auditor Independence	201	Prohibited services	Prohibits external auditor from engaging in nine specific non-audit services for the audit client
	203	Partner rotation	Mandates lead and reviewing partner rotation every five years, other audit partners must rotate every seven years
	206	Conflicts of interest	Prohibits employment of CEO, controller, Chief Accounting Officer or equivalent by firm's audit firm within one year of employment
III. Corporate Responsibility	302	Corporate responsibility for financial reports	CEO and CFO must certify "the appropriateness of the financial statements and disclosures" and that the "financial statements and disclosures fairly present (…) the operations and financial condition of the issuer."
	303	Improper influence on conduct of audits	Unlawful for officer or director of firm to take any action to influence, coerce, manipulate, or mislead any auditor engaged in performing the audit for the purpose of reporting materially misleading financial statements

Title	Section	Subject	Content
	304	Forfeiture of certain bonuses and profits	CEO and CFO shall "reimburse the issuer for any bonus or other incentive-based or equity-based compensation received" or "profits realized from sale of securities of the issuer" during the twelve months following the issue or filing of statements requiring later restatement
	305	Officer and director bars and penalties	SEC may prohibit any person violating section 10b of 1934 Act from acting as officer or director of any issuer if person engages in conduct which "demonstrates unfitness" to serve
	306	Insider trades during pension fund blackout dates	Prohibits purchase or sale of stock by officers, directors, or other insider during blackout periods
IV. Enhanced Financial Disclosures	402	Enhanced conflict of interest provisions	Includes prohibition of personal loans to directors or officers
	404	Internal control reporting	Management must issue an annual report with auditor attestation on the effectiveness of internal controls and procedures for financial reporting
	406	Code of ethics for senior financial officers	Requires issuer to disclose if it has adopted a code of ethics for its senior financial officers and the content of the code
V. Analyst Conflicts of Interest	501	Treatment of security analysts by registered securities associations and national security exchanges	Requires securities associations and securities exchanges to adopt conflict of interest rules
VIII. Corporate and Criminal Fraud Accountability	802	Criminal penalties for altering documents	Felony to knowingly destroy documents to "impede, obstruct or influence" existing or contemplated federal investigation. Requires retention of audit papers for five years. Extends statute of limitations to five years from fraud or two years from discovery
	806	Protection for employees of publicly traded companies who provide evidence of fraud	"Whistleblower protection" for employees of issuers and accounting firms who disclose employer information to parties in a judicial proceeding involving fraud claim
	807	Criminal penalties for defrauding shareholders of publicly traded companies	New crime for securities fraud with fines and up to 10 years imprisonment
IX. White Collar Crime Penalty	903	Criminal penalties for mail and wire fraud	Penalty increased from 5 years to 10 years
	906	Corporate responsibility for financial reports	Penalties for willfully and knowingly filing fraudulent financial reports include fine up to $5,000,000 and/or up to 20 years in prison
XI. Corporate Fraud and Accountability	1102	Tampering with a record or otherwise impeding an official proceeding	Establishes criminal penalty of up to 20 years and fine for destroying or tampering with documents with intent to impair use in official proceeding or otherwise impede official proceeding
	1105	Authority of the Commission to prohibit persons from serving as officers or directors	Amends SEC Acts of 1933 and 1934 to allow SEC to prohibit persons subject to a cease-and-desist proceeding from serving as an officer or director
	1106	Increase criminal penalties under Securities Exchange Act of 1934	Increases maximum penalties under SEC Act of 1934 to $25,000,000 fine and 25 years imprisonment
	1107	Retaliation against information	Provides criminal penalties for "whomever knowingly, with intent to retaliate, takes any action harmful to any person for Whistle blowing." Penalties up to 10 years and $250,000 fine

Section 301 addresses the responsibilities of the Board of Directors' Audit Committee. Corporate audit committee responsibilities have increased significantly. In some of the recent ethical failures, the audit committee was directly involved, perceived as too closely tied to the corporation, or oblivious to financial reporting situations (Lublin and Carms, 2003). Under Sarbanes, audit committees are directly responsible for appointment and compensation of the external auditor and must approve all non-audit services provided by the external auditor. Audit committee members must also be independent which means they may not receive fees from the company other than for board service and may not be affiliated in other ways. The audit committee must provide a mechanism for direct communication of unethical behavior within the organization by employees and the external auditor and must establish appropriate procedures to facilitate this communication.

Additionally Sarbanes requires all audit committees to have a financial expert on the committee or disclose why they do not have such an expert. One of the concerns was the ability of audit committees to understand fully the financial reporting issues and recognize unethical or fraudulent behavior. Thus, at least one member of the committee must have significant financial training and knowledge.

Much of the legislation is aimed directly at senior management. Section 302 is probably the most significant provision for CEOs and CFOs requiring certification of the financial statements. Both the CEO and CFO must sign and certify personally that the company's financial report does not contain any known untrue material statement(s) or omit a material fact(s). In addition, they must attest that they are responsible for establishing and maintaining internal controls, that disclosure is made of any changes in internal controls and they have evaluated the effectiveness of the internal controls within 90 days prior to the report. Certifications of financial statements were required beginning in August 2002 with management reporting on the effectiveness of

internal controls extended to year ends after November 20, 2004 for large companies (SEC, 2003b).

The consequences of failing to certify statements or signing false statements are severe. CEOs and CFOs are subject to a five million dollar fine and a 20-year prison term. Violation of the certification regulation falls under federal court jurisdiction without option for parole. As discussed earlier, HealthSouth's former CEO, Scrushy, was the object of the first major indictment under this legislation (National Accounting News, 2003).

Sarbanes provisions 303, 304, and 306 further promote ethical conduct by the board of directors, corporate executives and key employees. It is unlawful for an officer or director to take any action to influence or mislead the external auditor. CEOs and CFOs must forfeit bonuses and profits when earnings are restated due to fraud. Executives are prohibited from selling stock during blackout periods and are prevented from receiving company loans unavailable to outsiders. These provisions directly reflect the unethical and fraudulent activities witnessed at Enron that precipitated the legislation.

Sarbanes takes a much stronger consequences (jail-time) approach to legislating ethical behavior than the US has experienced in past regulation. Key provisions of the Act: raised the maximum penalty for securities fraud to 25 years, raised maximum penalties for mail and wire fraud to 20 years, created a 20-year crime for destroying, altering or fabricating records in federal investigations, and required preservation of key financial audit documents and e-mail for five years with a 10-year penalty for destroying such documents. As with CEO/CFO certification, these criminal charges fall under federal jurisdiction. Under the Sentencing Reform Act of 1984, parole for federal offenders was abolished (Murphy, 2002). In response to requirements of Sarbanes, the Federal Sentencing Commission promulgated emergency guidelines in November 2003 to ensure that corporate criminal sentences are sufficiently severe to "deter, prevent and punish such offenses" including longer sentences for larger dollar losses (Robinson and Lashway, 2003). Robinson and Lashway provide an example under the new guidelines: "assume the CFO of a Fortune 500 company is convicted after trial of participating in a complex accounting fraud that causes $150 million in losses. Further assume the CFO directed six members of the accounting staff in carrying out the fraud." The CFO now faces a sentencing range of at least 30 years to life with no possibility of parole, even if it is a first offense (Robinson and Lashway, 2003). The guidelines also require that anyone convicted of obstruction of justice serve a mandatory prison sentence.

Sarbanes not only legislates strong punishment for wrongdoers but also prescribes guidelines for corporations to establish an ethical culture in order to maintain a high level of integrity. The tone at the top is cited as key to an ethical corporate culture. Section 406 requires public corporations to have a code of ethics for senior executives or to state in their annual report that they do not have such a code as well as why they do not. The code must be available to the public. Under SEC rules, detailed guidance for the content of the code is provided including: promotion of honest and ethical conduct, full and fair disclosure, compliance with laws, internal reporting for violations, and accountability for adherence to the code (SEC, 2003b). Whistleblowers are protected under Section 1107, and individuals who retaliate against whistleblowers are personally liable and face penalties up to 10 years.

Accounting Firm Ethical Provisions of Sarbanes

Sarbanes has changed the basic structure of the US public accounting profession. The first section creates the Public Company Accounting Oversight Board (PCAOB) imposing external independent regulation on the profession and ends self-regulation under the AICPA. The Act applies to all CPAs serving US publicly traded clients. A majority of members of the five-member PCAOB board are not and can never have been CPAs. This Board now sets auditing standards and conducts inspections of CPA firms. The Board also is responsible for disciplinary actions against CPAs and for setting the ethical tone for the profession. A recent quote from the Board Chairman William McDonough makes their ethical expectations clear to the profession: "I expect that you, as members of a regulated profession, know what the rules are. I expect that you are following those rules, both in their letter and their spirit. If you depart from those expectations—that is, if you break the rules, if you ignore the spirit of the law even while meeting the letter—woe be unto you. There will be consequences, and they will be grave" (McDonough, 2003).

Section 201 of the Act is a direct response to the conflict of interest issues arising from the consulting and external audit services provided to Enron by Andersen. This section has a very significant impact on the CPA profession. Most other professional services auditors historically performed for their audit clients (Table V lists the restricted services) are prohibited. Board of directors approval is required for any services provided by the external auditor in addition to the external audit that are not specifically prohibited by Sarbanes. Evidence to date indicates that corporate boards are reluctant to approve even permissible tax services by their external auditors. Sam DiPiazza, CEO PricewaterhouseCoopers, testified that PWC had lost 20% of its US tax work since the passage of Sarbanes (DiPiazza, 2003). The prohibited services mirror the SEC proposal of 2000 with one significant addition: the PCAOB now has the authority to determine any other impermissible services. This gives the PCAOB complete control to regulate the independence and thereby conflicts of interest in the attest function.

To further strengthen independence, Section 203 mandates audit partner rotation. The lead auditor must rotate off an audit every five years with a five-year time out. Other audit partners must rotate after seven years with a two-year time out. The intent is to keep auditors from getting too close to their clients and to inhibit unethical or fraudulent collusion between auditors and clients. Prior to the Act, suggestions were made for mandatory audit firm rotation and Sarbanes required a study to further examine the feasibility of rotation of audit firms. The GAO concluded in November 2003 that mandatory firm rotation was not the most efficient way to strengthen auditor independence or improve audit quality considering additional costs and institutional knowledge (GAO, 2003).

Table V. Prohibited Services by External Auditors for Audit Clients under Sarbanes-Oxley Act

Bookkeeping

Financial information systems design and implementation

Appraisal or valuation services, fairness opinions

Actuarial services

Internal audit outsourcing services

Management functions or human resources

Broker or dealer, investment adviser or investment banking services

Legal services and expert services

Any other service the PCAOB determines impermissible

The final conflict of interest issue addressed by Section 206 is the well-known practice of corporations hiring their external auditor's staff as financial managers, controllers and CFOs. It has been a long-standing and common practice for auditors leaving public accounting to accept employment with an audit client. This was especially true at HealthSouth. Section 206 now prohibits such employment within a one-year period of the audit. SEC regulations are more restrictive. They prohibit employment in a management position overseeing financial reporting matters of the lead partner, the concurring partner, or any other member of the audit engagement team who provided more than ten hours of audit, review, or attest services within the one-year period preceding the start of the audit (SEC, 2003a).

Basic Premises for Ethical Financial Reporting

"We have learned the same thing again and again: financial fraud does not start with dishonesty, your boss doesn't come to you and say, 'Let's do some financial fraud.' Fraud occurs because the culture has become infected. It spreads like an unstoppable virus." (Young, 2003)

The preceding description and analysis of fraudulent financial reporting as well as regulatory responses suggests four premises.

Premise 1: History suggests that legislative attempts to impose ethical behavior in corporate financial management and reporting have failed.

As demonstrated in this paper, the almost one hundred year history of US legislation attempting to impose transparency, integrity, and honesty as underlying values in corporate management and financial reporting has failed to prevent periodic systemic ethical failure. They often have proven effective for a time. However, management and their external auditors have responded to legislated behaviors by finding new ways to obscure results; defraud shareholders, customers, or suppliers; and hide failure. In the latest wave of corporate fraudulent reporting, the SEC history of fines for offending corporations and civil proceedings against senior management evidently were not effective deterrents. Occasional US Department of Justice criminal proceedings resulting in light sentences in federal white-collar crime prisons also were not effective deterrents.

Premise 2: Corporate controls in an IT world cannot and will not prevent corporate fraud.

There is a tendency to believe that the advent of large, complex, sophisticated electronic information systems for financial reporting and operations can limit the potential for widespread unethical behavior in financial reporting. The financial reporting frauds, errors, and restatements including those identified in this paper raise serious doubts about the progress companies have made in using IT to improve the accuracy, reliability, and integrity of financial data and financial reporting. The failures chronicled in this paper can be traced to three IT weaknesses: internal control systems are built on a set of assumptions that have proven invalid; internal controls are difficult to design, implement, and document in today's complex business environment; and internal audit has assumed a much less significant role in many corporations at a time that systems have become more difficult to audit.

Assumptions underlying IT controls do not reflect the business environment existing in the previously discussed corporate failures. IT controls are designed to ensure the integrity of data assuming the data reflect actual transactions, are correctly captured, and are appropriately classified. Controls are designed into the systems to limit the potential for inappropriate access, guarantee the numerical integrity of data transmitted and processed, and prevent unauthorized modification of software, data or reports. The underlying assumption in control design is that fraud will be deterred by (Carmichael, 1970)[1]

- Threat of exposure;
- Independent individuals reporting irregularities;
- A low probability of collusion because asking is too risky;
- Records and documentation providing proof of actions and transactions;
- A lack of inherent conflict between performance goals and the production of reliable information;
- Senior management that will not override the system.

Simons (1999) argues that these behavioral assumptions still form the foundation for most internal control systems. The unethical and fraudulent behavior at WorldCom, Enron, HealthSouth, and Andersen as well as the other frauds in Table II question the veracity of IT assumptions. Senior management involvement, collusion, fraudulent documentation, and lack of individual reporting were evident in most cases. Thus IT controls based on these assumptions did not prevent failures and there is no reason to expect them to prevent future failures.

The complexities of today's business environments make high quality IT controls much more difficult to design, implement, and maintain. The average $1 billion company has 48 different financial systems and uses 2.7 different ERP systems (Hackett Group, 2004). Typically, these systems do not communicate electronically. Rather, companies still make widespread use of hand consolidation of disparate systems on electronic spreadsheets making entries difficult to document, control, and audit. Furthermore, the growth of off-balance sheet transactions has removed many transactions from the domain of the formal information systems. IT control systems are further complicated with attempted integration of financial reporting systems and tax systems.

In our current state, the IT controls may provide more opportunity for unethical and fraudulent behavior than they prevent and create the opportunity to make the fraud bigger through mechanization. For example, HealthSouth employees were able to enter a large number of small transactions for assets at a large number of widely disbursed facilities with each transaction small enough to be under the external auditor's dollar threshold for the asset. The magnitude of this fraud ($800 million) would have been difficult without IT (SEC, 2003c).

Finally, there has been less emphasis on the internal audit function. In the 1990s many corporations shrunk or disbanded internal audit groups and outsourced all or part of the internal audit function to their external auditors or other consultants. Even those who did not outsource internal audit and/or development of internal control systems struggled with the maintenance of internal control across business units and across geographic regions. The shrinking role of internal audit, less attention paid to internal controls, and the difficulties of auditing complex, disparate systems came at a time when the incentives for management to engage in fraudulent financial reporting had never been higher given the heavy reliance by corporations on performance-based pay at multiple layers in the organization.

Premise 3: A strong corporate culture as the context and imbedded corporate ethical values as the driver of behavior are a necessary condition for "fixing" financial management and reporting.

> "A corporation's culture is what determines how people behave when they are not being watched." (Tierney, 2002)

Solomon (1992) reminds us that business ethics is not a set of impositions and constraints but rather is the motivating force behind business behaviors and that virtues are social traits even though they are reflected in individual actions. In the business context, the set of social traits form a key component of the corporate culture. Schein (1999) describes corporate culture as the "sum total of all the shared, taken-for-granted assumptions that a group has learned throughout its history" from a mission and goals to deep underlying assumptions about the nature of truth, human nature, and human relationships. Kotter and Heskett (1992) emphasize that corporate culture should be built on "doing the right thing" on behalf of corporate constituencies including customers, employees, suppliers, and stockholders. Common to all is the need for the organization's leadership to nurture culture in ways that imbed virtue in the set of assumptions underlying the culture. Schein (1992) suggests that corporate leaders communicate the organizations values and ethics (and thereby the assumptions underlying the culture) by the focus of their attention and also by what they ignore.

Morris (2002) provides a discussion of three corporate trends that emerged with regard to the ethical behavior of both corporate leaders and their auditors that provide some insight into how unethical behavior has grown in the face of corporate codes of ethics and external penalties for fraud. First, there has been a growing attitude that ethics is just a matter of having rules and playing by the rules. It became a game to see who could most creatively stay within the letter of the law while bending the rules for personal gain. The acceptable practice was to do what was technically correct regardless of the moral correctness of the action. Second, people were more concerned about externals than internal matters. The drive for personal happiness became focused on external wealth and success rather than internal satisfaction. And third, the panic for quick results replaced patience and more modest expectations.

Kotter and Heskett (1992) emphasize that corporate culture should be built "doing the right thing" on behalf of corporate constituencies. Turner (2002) argues that "... we need a cultural change." The excesses of the 1990s have led to too many businesses, playing too close to the line. And, often the line has been crossed. Waters and Bird (1987) conclude that it is easier to influence ethical behavior through culture than through bureaucratic rules. Dobson (1990), arguing from a global perspective, suggests that when there are managers and employees that do not have the desired ethical attitude, the result is a weak set of beliefs and a non-ethical culture. He further argues that the resulting changes will result from economic needs rather than ethical ones. Thus, failure to build a strong culture, or building a culture that tolerates inappropriate behaviors, allows the inappropriate behaviors to spread across the organization in ways that make significant fraud not only possible but likely (Levitt, 1998). The failures at Enron, WorldCom, Tyco, HealthSouth, and many of the others reflect unethical values at the very top of organization accompanied by a culture accepting of unethical behavior. The results are well-chronicled here and elsewhere.

It is important to recognize the stark difference between a strong culture (usually characterized by a strong leader as in our examples) and a strong ethical culture. Kotter and Heskett (1992) conclude that there is a positive relationship between strong culture and economic performance but it is modest. Furthermore, "with much success, that strong culture can easily become arrogant, inwardly focused, and bureaucratic" (Kotter and Heskett, 1992, 24). The long-run successful corporation is characterized by norms and values that reflect caring deeply about their customers, employees, and stockholders, a deep commitment to leadership and other engines that can help firms adapt to a changing environment. At the same time, the culture must be intolerant of arrogance in others and in themselves (Kotter and Heskett, 1992). The firms we have reviewed reflect strong cultures exhibiting great success for a time, arrogance, and an inability to deal with changing economic circumstances in a positive, ethical, constructive manner. They reflected a strong but unethical tone at the top which reached through the organization. The end result was failure.

We have documented a variety of settings in which the very people who might be expected to establish a strong culture with strong ethical values reaching across the organization have been at best contributors and more frequently instigators of unethical or fraudulent behavior. Similarly, the Treadway Commission (1987) found that a significant portion of companies committing financial reporting fraud had founders and Board members who retained significant ownership. COSO (1999) found that 72 of the 200 fraud cases they examined appeared to involve the CEO and the companies' Boards were dominated by insiders. Thus, a strong culture is not the same as a strong ethical culture. Repeatedly, strong cultures emerged in the 1990s (Enron, WorldCom, HealthSouth) that were not built on doing the right thing so much as achieving the "right outcome." These cultures proved unable to support appropriate ethical behaviors when these organizations encountered difficult times. As we move forward, it is our conclusion that the responsibility for ensuring an ethical culture must rest not only with the CEO but also with an independent Board of Directors. The Board must be responsible for the values and ethics they seek in officers of the corporation to ensure a culture that supports, nurtures, fosters, and attracts individuals of high personal integrity. The Board must provide the oversight necessary to ensure that ethical behavior is noticed and rewarded. Similarly, the culture must encourage the departure of those who violate the ethical principles regardless of their other contributions to the organization.

The Board of Directors must also assume increased responsibility for the control environment. Virtually all frameworks posited for establishing and maintaining the integrity of financial reporting begin with the control environment (see COSO, 1992; COBIT, 2000; for examples). COSO (1992) identifies key indicators of the control environment including integrity, ethical values, Board of Directors participation, management philosophy, and human resource policies and practices. The indicators of significant deficiencies include insufficient oversight by senior management, a passive audit committee, no code of conduct or one that does not address conflicts of interest, related party transactions, illegal acts by the management and the Board, an ineffective whistleblower program, and an inadequate process for responding to allegations or suspicions of fraud. The financial frauds identified in Table II reflect some or all of the deficiencies identified in the COSO (Committee of Sponsoring Organizations of the Treadway Commission) framework and few of the key indicators of a good control environment.

Premise 4: Compliance with laws, internal controls, and corporate cultural norms must be built on both predictable rewards for "right" behaviors as well as swift delivery of significant sanctions for inappropriate behaviors supported by strong societal sanctions.

"No one should be entrusted to lead any business or institution unless he or she has impeccable personal integrity. Top rung executives have to ensure that the organizations they lead are committed to a strict code of conduct. This is not merely good corporate hygiene. It requires management discipline and putting in place checks and balances to ensure compliance." (Gerstner, 2002)

Solomon (1994) argues that the free market "requires protection from rule breakers, those who would take advantage of its freedoms and commit fraud or extortion." He argues, further, that such rules and sanctions are necessary for the protection of markets. In the 1990s, civil and criminal penalties for fraudulent financial reporting resulting from the Securities Acts of 1933 and 1934 proved to be ineffective deterrents. Arguably, the societal penalties for fraudulent financial reporting under the 1933 and 1934 Securities Acts were not severe enough to deter fraudulent behavior in the 1990s. HealthSouth's Mr. Scrushy is charged with telling employees in 1997 that earnings had to meet market expectations until he could sell his stock. He subsequently sold 7,782,130 shares of HealthSouth stock (SEC, 2003c). Potential personal sanctions were irrelevant in determining behavior at HealthSouth. Under the 1933 and 1934 Acts, the most likely outcome was a fine, a prohibition from serving as an officer or director of an SEC company, and, occasionally, a light sentence in a "white collar" jail. Just as clearly, Scrushy either believed he would not be caught or the potential penalty was insufficient to deter the action.

Corporate codes of conduct have been suggested or required for corporations since the Foreign Corrupt Practices Act of 1977. They also have proven to be a limited deterrent to unethical behavior. Whistleblower programs, with access to the Board of Directors for corporate wrongdoing, were recommended by the Treadway Commission as early

as 1987, yet few whistleblowers have come forward. Unethical behavior has continued with the magnitude and number of frauds growing throughout the 1990s (KPMG, 2003).

Despite codes of conduct and penalties, greed, personal gain, and pursuit of power prevailed in many of the cases of the 1990s. The financial frauds corresponded to an exponential growth in executive compensation. The Institute for Policy Studies 2003 CEO Compensation Survey compares CEO compensation in the late 1990s and early 2000s with compensation in the early 1980s. Results indicate a dramatic increase in absolute and relative CEO compensation during the period. They report that average CEO pay was 42 times average production-worker pay in 1982 but had grown to 530 times average production-worker pay by 2000. Further, stock options or other performance-based pay had grown to 80 per cent of CEO compensation (Anderson et al., 2003). Our premise is that legislation, controls, and cultural norms did not deter corporate unethical behavior by some because of the potential for enormous personal gain. In too many cases, senior management's greed overcame personal integrity and was unchecked by adequate penalties for unethical/illegal behavior. CEOs and CFOs, and in more limited cases corporate boards, did not have the personal integrity and companies did not have the ethical cultures in place to overcome the potential for personal gain in light of very limited potential external sanctions. Or, simply stated, for many CEOs the expected benefits from stock options, position, and power were greater than the expected cost of civil or criminal penalties if caught and if punished.

When otherwise good people do bad things in a financial reporting context, a more utilitarian approach may well be the way to control behavior (if not values). Where management is driven by ego or greed, deterrence must be focused on outcomes ... making the cost of unethical behavior exceed the potential gain from the behavior. Petrick and Scherer

(2003) make a similar argument for an interdependent moral and legal framework in their discussion of Enron. There are three required components. First, corporate cultures and codes of ethics must deliver swift and meaningful sanctions for unethical behavior including separation from the organization. Second, internal controls including effective whistleblower programs must make the probability of discovering unethical behavior high. Third, external penalties for unethical or illegal behavior must be greater than the rewards realized from engaging in the behavior.

Three changes in US laws for societal penalties have come together to potentially make the punishment exceed the payoff from fraudulent reporting. First, Sarbanes increases the penalties for fraudulent reporting including management certification of results and internal controls to a maximum of $25 million and 20 years, and imposes new sentencing penalties for other fraudulent actions (Table IV). Second, revised federal sentencing guidelines issued in 2001 substantially increase penalties for economic crimes, doubling penalties for crimes involving multi-million dollar losses. The effect is to remove judicial discretion in imposing sentences for white collar crimes. Sentencing guidelines were further strengthened in 2003 at the direction of the Sarbanes-Oxley Act (Robinson and Lashway, 2003). Third, 1984 legislation eliminated parole in the federal justice system (US Department of Justice, 1997). The maximum reduction in sentence for good behavior is 15 per cent of the sentence. For example, in March of 2004, a former senior director of tax planning at Dynegy Corporation was convicted of wire fraud, securities fraud, conspiracy, and mail fraud. He was sentenced to 24 years and four months of which he must serve a minimum of 20 years and 10 months. His crime—illegally disguising corporate debt in 2001 which the prosecution alleged caused $500 million in Dynegy stock losses. The judge in the case said, "I take no pleasure in sentencing you to 292 months. Sometimes good people

commit bad acts, and that's what happened in this case" (ABC News, 2004).

Having argued the necessity of appropriate sanctions for fraudulent behavior, Solomon (1994) suggests that laws, regulations, and associated penalties can only help prevent behaviors already viewed as inappropriate by those subject to the laws and regulations. Thus, they complement an ethical culture rather than replace the need for carefully nurturing a culture built on "doing the right thing."

Conclusion

This paper has documented the failures of laws, corporate internal controls, and corporate culture to deter unethical and fraudulent financial reporting. None, taken alone, have stood the test of time in guaranteeing appropriate corporate ethical behavior. Sarbanes broadens and deepens sanctions and penalties for unethical management behavior but does not address the relationship between management behavior and rewards. Sarbanes also calls for much greater focus on internal controls by senior management. Internal control systems, including IT controls, can help reduce the opportunity for fraudulent or unethical behavior but cannot eliminate it in a world where nearly 50 per cent of large corporations still use spreadsheets in some aspect of financial reporting (Hackett Group, 2004). Finally, corporate ethical failures arguably appear more likely to occur in very successful companies lacking a solid ethical foundation when economic conditions change as witnessed by our case studies and the work of Kotter and Heskett (1992). It is the combination of a strong ethical corporate culture (beginning with the Board of Directors), controls, laws, rewards, and penalties that provide a context for obtaining ethical and transparent financial reporting.

We believe research exploring the interactions between and among corporate culture, internal controls, societal controls, and rewards/sanctions will provide better answers than we now have for improving corporate financial reporting.

NOTE

1 Douglas Carmichael is now the Chief Auditor and Director of Financial Standards of the PCAOB (PCAOB, 2003).

REFERENCES

ABC News: (2004) "Judge Sentences Ex-Dynegy Exec for Fraud," *ABC News*, March 25, <http://www.wjla.com/news/stories/0304/134906.html> (accessed on May 21, 2004).

AICPA: (2002) "Consideration of Fraud in a Financial Statement Audit," SAS (Statements on Auditing Standards) 99, AICPA, *Professional Standards*, Vol. 1, AU sec. 316.

Anderson, S., J. Cavanagh, C. Hartman and S. Klinger: (2003) *Executive Excess in 2003* (Washington, DC: Institute for Policy Studies).

Arthur Andersen, Coopers and Lybrand, Deloitte and Touche, Ernst and Young, KPMG and Price Waterhouse: (1992) "The Liability Crisis in the United States: Impact on the Accounting Profession," White Paper, New York.

Bartlett, C.A. and M. Glinska: (2001) *Enron's Transformation: From Gas Pipeline to New Economy Powerhouse* (Boston, MA: Harvard Business School Press).

Bassing, T.: (2003) "HealthSouth's Scrushy Indicted on 85 Counts," *Birmingham Business Journal*, November 4, <http://baltimore.bizjournals.com/birmingham/stories/2003/11/03/daily9.html?page=1> (accessed on June 8, 2004).

Buchholz, R. and S. Rosenthal: (1998) *Business Ethics: The Pragmatic Path Beyond Principles to Process* (Upper Saddle River, NY: Prentice Hall).

Bush, G.W.: (2002) "President Bush Signs Corporate Corruption Bill," White House Press Release, July 30, <http://www.whitehouse.gov/news/releases/2003/07/20020730.html> (accessed on June 8, 2004).

Business Week: (2000) "Accounting Wars," *Business Week*, September 25, 157-72.

Byrne, J.A.: (2002) "Fall From Grace," *Business Week*, August 12, 51-56.

Carmichael, D.: (1970) "Behavioral Hypothesis of Internal Control," *The Accounting Review* Vol. 45, 235-45.

CBSNEWS: (2004) "Indicted CEO Turns TV Preacher," *CBSNEWS*, March 18, <http://www.cbsnews.com/stories/2004/03/18/eveningnews/main607222.shtml> (accessed on May 21, 2004).

CNN Money: (2004) "Enron Scorecard," *CNN Money*, January 14, <http://money.cnn.com/2004/01/14/news/companies/enron_scorecard/> (accessed on May 21, 2004).

COBIT Steering Committee: (2000) *Control Objectives for Information and Related Technology*, 3rd Edition (Chicago, IL: IT Governance Institute).

COSO (Committee of Sponsoring Organizations of the Treadway Commission): (1992) *Internal Control and Integrated Framework* (New York: Institute of Internal Auditors).

COSO (Committee of Sponsoring Organizations of the Treadway Commission): (1999) *COSO Study on Fraudulent Financial Reporting* (New York: Institute of Internal Auditors).

DiPiazza, S.A.: (2003) "Testimony Concerning the Implementation of the Sarbanes-Oxley Act and Restoring Investor Confidence," September 23, US Congress, Washington, DC.

Dobson, J.: (1990) "The Role of Ethics in Global Corporate Culture," *Journal of Business Ethics* Vol. 9, 441-48.

Flood, M.: (2004) "Enron's Skilling Charged with Fraud, Insider Trading, and More," *Houston Chronicle*, February 19, <http://www.chron.com/cs/CDA/ssistory.mpl/topstory2/2410325> (accessed on May 21, 2004).

Forbes: (2003) "UPDATE 3—Citigroup, JP Morgan Settle SEC Probe into Enron," *Forbes*,

July 28, <http://www.forbes.com/newswire/2003/07/28/rtr1040132.html> (accessed on May 21, 2004).

Fortune: (1999) "Lies, Damned Lies, and Managed Earnings," *Fortune*, August 2, 76-92.

GAO: (2002) "Financial Statement Restatements: Trends, Market Impact, Regulatory Responses and Remaining Challenges," Report to Chairman, Committee on Banking, Housing, and Urban Affairs, US Senate, ID GAO-03-138, GAO, Washington, DC.

GAO: (2003) "Public Accounting Firms: Required Study on the Effects of Mandatory Audit Firm Rotation," Report to the Senate Committee on Banking, Housing, and Urban Affairs and the House Committee on Financial Services, GAO-04-216, GAO, Washington, DC.

Gerstner, L.V.: (2002) *Who Says Elephants Can't Dance* (New York: HarperCollins).

Hackett Group: (2004) "Companies Ignore IT in Compliance Efforts," *DMReview.com*, February 10, <http://www.drnreview.com/article_sub.cfin?articleId=8101> (accessed on May 21, 2004).

Hecht, C.: (2003) "SEC Central: Who is Responsible?" *SmartPros*, August, <http://finance.pro2net.com/ x39848.xml> (accessed on May 21, 2004).

Huron Consulting Group: (2003) *Huron Consulting Group Releases 2003 Restatements Results*, <http://www.huronconsultinggroup.com/general01.asp?id=401&relatedResourceID=278> (accessed on May 21, 2004).

Kotter, J.P. and J.L. Heskett: (1992) *Corporate Culture and Performance* (New York: The Free Press).

KPMG: (2003) *Fraud Survey 2003* (New Jersey: KPMG).

Levitt, A.: (1998) "The Numbers Game," SEC speech, September 28, <http://www.sec.gov/news/speechl/speecharchive/1998/spch220.txt> (accessed on June 8, 2004).

Levitt, A.: (2000) "Renewing the Covenant with Investors," SEC speech, May 10, <http://www.sec.gov/news/speech/spch370.htm> (accessed on June 8, 2004).

Lublin, J. and A. Carms: (2003) "Directors Had Lucrative Links at HealthSouth," *Wall Street Journal*, April 11, B1.

McDonough, W.: (2003) "Speech Before the Foundation for Accounting Education: New York," September 9, Society of Certified Public Accountants, New York.

Morris, T.V.: (2002) *The Art of Achievement: Mastering the Seven C's of Success in Business and Life* (Kansas City, Missouri: Andrews McMeel Publishing).

Morse, J. and A. Bower: (2002) "The Party Crasher," *Time Magazine* 160, 27/1, 53-56.

MSNBC: (2004) "HealthSouth Fraud Larger than Estimated," *MSNBC*, January 21, <http://www.msnbc.msn.com/id/4016152> (accessed on June 8, 2004).

Murphy, D.E.: (2002) "The Federal Sentencing Guidelines for Organizations: A Decade of Promoting Compliance and Ethics," *Iowa Law Review* Vol. 87, 697-704.

National Accounting News: (2003) "Scrushy Attorneys to Seek Repeal of Sarbanes-Oxley," *National Accounting News*, December 12, <http://www.tscpa.org/welcome/AcctWeb/acctweb121203.asp#1> (accessed on May 21, 2004).

PCAOB: (2003) "Board Hires Chief Auditor," April 17, <http://www.pcaobus.org/pcaob_news_4-7-03_b.asp> (accessed on July 15, 2004).

Padgett, T.: (2002) "The Rise and Fall of Bernie Ebbers," *Time Magazine*, May 13, 42.

Pearlstein, S.: (2002) "In Blossoming Scandal, Culprits are Countless," *Washington Post*, June 28, Section A, 01.

Perrotta, T.: (2004) "Ex-CEO Ebbers is Charged in $11 Billion WorldCom Scandal Over Accounting," *New York Lawyer*, March 3, <http://www.

nylawyer.com/news/04/03/030304c.html> (accessed on May 21, 2004).

Petrick, J.A., and R.F. Scherer: (2003) "The Enron Scandal and the Neglect of Management Integrity Capacity," *Mid-American Journal of Business* Vol. 18(1), 37-50.

Pulliam, S.: (2003) "A Staffer Ordered to Commit Fraud Balked, Then Caved," *Wall Street Journal*, June 23, A 1.

Ripley, A.: (2002) "The Night Detective," *Time Magazine*, December 30, 45-50.

Robinson, J.K. and S.T. Lashway: (2003) "The New Sentencing Guidelines for Corporate Crime," *New York Law Journal* Vol. 229(20), 4.

Sarbanes-Oxley Act of 2002: (2002) One Hundred Seventh Congress of the United States of America, at the Second Session, Washington, DC.

Schein, E.: (1992) *Organizational Culture and Leadership*, 2nd Edition (San Francisco: Jossey-Bass Publishers).

Schein, E.: (1999) *The Corporate Culture Survival Guide* (San Francisco: Jossey-Bass Publishers).

SEC (Securities and Exchange Commission): (1933) *Securities Act of 1933* (Washington, DC: Government Printing Office).

SEC (Securities and Exchange Commission): (1934) *Securities Exchange Act of 1934* (Washington, DC: Government Printing Office).

SEC (Securities and Exchange Commission): (2003a) *Final Rule: Strengthening the Commission's Requirements Regarding Auditor Independence*, January 23 (Washington, DC: Government Printing Office).

SEC (Securities and Exchange Commission): (2003b) *Final Rule: Disclosure Required by Sections 406 and 407 of the Sarbanes-Oxley Act of 2002*, January 24 (Washington, DC: Government Printing Office).

SEC (Securities and Exchange Commission): (2003c) *Securities and Exchange Commission v. HealthSouth Corporation and Richard M. Scrushy*, Civil

Action No CV-03-J-0615-S, March 19 (Washington, DC: Government Printing Office).

SEC (Securities and Exchange Commission): (2004a) "Enron Related Enforcement Actions," <http://www.sec.gov/spotlight/enron.htm#enron_enforce> (accessed on June 8, 2004).

SEC (Securities and Exchange Commission): (2004b) "Spotlight on Enron," <http://www.sec.gov/spotlight/ enron.htm> (accessed on May 21, 2004).

Shearman and Sterling: (2001) *The Foreign Corrupt Practices Act* (New York: Shearman and Sterling Client Publications).

Simons and Robert: (1999) *Performance Measurement and Control Systems for Implementing Strategy* (New York: Prentice-Hall).

Sims, R.R., and J. Brinkmann: (2003) "Enron Ethics (or: Culture Matters More Than Codes)," *Journal of Business Ethics* Vol. 45, 243-56.

Solomon, R.: (1992) "Corporate Roles, Personal Virtues: An Aristotelean Approach to Business Ethics," *Business Ethics Quarterly* Vol. 2, 317-39.

Solomon, R.: (1994) *The New World of Business: Ethics and Free Enterprise in the Global Nineties* (Boston: Rowman and Littlefield Publishers).

Sweeney, P.: (2003) "What Starts Small Can Snowball," *Financial Executive*, December, <http://finance.pro2net.com/x41723.xml> (accessed on May 22, 2004).

Taub, S.: (2002) "Myers, I Knew It Was Wrong," *CFO.com*, <http://www.cfo.com/article/1,5309, 7762%7C%7CA%7C93%7C100,00.html> (accessed on June 8, 2004).

Tierney, T.: (2002) quoted in *The Economist* Vol. 364, Issue 8283, 61.

Tipgos, M.A.: (2002) "Why Management Fraud is Unstoppable," *The CPA Journal* Vol. 72, 34-42.

Treadway Commission (National Commission on Fraudulent Financial Reporting): (1987) *Report of the National Commission on Fraudulent Financial Reporting* (New York: Committee of Sponsoring Organizations of the Treadway Commission).

Turner, L.: (2002) "From Enron, Chance to Save Capitalism," *Rocky Mountain News*, April 27, <http://www.biz.colostate.edu/qfr/testimony4-27-02.htm> (accessed on June 15, 2004).

US Congress: (1991) *Federal Deposit Insurance Corporation Improvement Act* (Washington, DC: Government Publications Office).

US Congress: Senate: (1992) "Efforts to Combat Criminal Financial Institution Fraud," Committee on Banking, Housing, and Urban Affairs, 102nd Congress, 2nd Session (Washington, DC: Government Publications Office).

US Congress: (1995) *Private Securities Litigation Reform Act* (Washington, DC: Government Publications Office).

US Department of Justice: (1997) *An Overview of the United States Parole Commission* (Washington, DC: US Department of Justice).

Vickers, M. and M. France: (2002) "How Corrupt is Wall Street?" *Business Week*, May 13, 36.

Washington Post: (2004) "Ebbers Indicted on Federal Charges," *Washington Post*, March 2, <http://www.washingtonpost.com/wp-dyn/articles/A221922004Mar2.html> (accessed on June 8, 2004).

Waters, J.A., and F. Bird: (1987) "The Moral Dimensions of Organizational Culture," *Journal of Business Ethics* Vol. 6, 15-22.

Wyatt, A.R.: (2004) "Accounting Professionalism: They Just Don't Get It," *Accounting Horizons* Vol. 18, 45-54.

Young, M.: (2003) quoted in P. Sweeney: (2003) "Fraud, What Starts Small Can Snowball," *Financial Executive* Vol. 18(9), 18-20.

Zimring, F.E. and G. Hawkins: (1993) "Crime, Justice, and the Savings and Loan Crisis," in M.J. Tonry and A.J. Reiss (eds.), *Beyond the Law: Crime in Complex Organizations* (Chicago: The University of Chicago Press), 247-92.

◆ ◆ ◆ ◆ ◆

CATHERINE GOWTHORPE and ORIOL AMAT

Creative Accounting: Some Ethical Issues of Macro- and Micro-Manipulation

ABBREVIATIONS: APB, The Accounting Principles Board; ASRB, Accounting Standards Review Board; FASB, Financial Accounting Standards Board; IASB, International Accounting Standards Board; IASC, International Accounting Standards Committee; ICAC, Instituto de Contabilidad y Auditoria de Cuentas (Spanish Institute of Accounting and Auditing); IFRS, International Financial Reporting Standards; IOSCO, International Organization of Securities Commissions; PGC, Plan General de Contabilidad (Spanish Accounting Plan); SEC, Securities and Exchange Commission

Introduction

Financial statements provide information that is used by interested parties to assess the performance of managers and to make economic decisions. Users may assume that the financial information they receive is reliable and fit for its purpose. Accounting regulation attempts to ensure that information is produced on a consistent basis in accordance with a set of rules that make it reliable for users. However, communications between entities and shareholders may be deliberately distorted by the activities of financial statement preparers who wish to alter the content of the messages being transmitted. This type of distortion is often referred to as "creative accounting" or "earnings management." While opinions on the acceptability of accounting manipulation vary, it is often perceived as reprehensible.

This paper aims to identify some manipulative behaviour on the part of preparers of financial statements, taking into account some important ethical concerns. To achieve this, we will broaden out the usual definition of creativity in accounting to examine two principal categories of behaviour by the preparers of financial statements:

- *Macro-manipulation.* When preparers become aware of a proposal to alter accounting regulation in a way that they feel will be disadvantageous to them, they may engage in lobbying to attempt to prevent the change. They attempt to bring about an alternative depiction of economic reality which is more favourable to them. In this paper we identify this type of behaviour as macro-manipulation.
- *Micro-manipulation.* Creative accounting at an individual entity level involves preparers in altering accounting disclosures so as to create the view of reality that they wish to have communicated to users of the financial statements. This type of behaviour is described in this paper as micro-manipulation.

In both cases, preparers are interested in creating the financial statements to suit their own purposes. Of course, they may genuinely feel that their view of economic reality is preferable from all points of view. However, it is also possible that they seek to distort the picture to meet their own needs or desires. This paper identifies and discusses some significant ethical issues related to these manipulations of accounting reality.

The paper proceeds as follows: first, the principal features of the current accounting regulatory landscape are described. The purpose of regulation, and the objective of financial statements are explained, and then the paper goes on to discuss the ways in which preparers of financial statements may confound the intentions of the regulators. We then consider two cases of manipulation. The first concerns a case of lobbying over a significant accounting issue in the United States. The second examines some recent evidence from Spain on the manipulation of financial

statements that takes place at the entity level. The discussion then moves to consideration of ethical issues of respect, fairness, justice and personal morality.

The Accounting Regulatory Background

Accounting is regulated in most countries by two principal means: first, local laws relating to corporate and other bodies, and second, a system of accounting regulation in the form of standards. These are often promulgated by non-governmental organisations and foundations. Also, in recent years, a supra-national body, the International Accounting Standards Committee (IASC) has become more important in setting standards. The IASC came into being in 1973 via an agreement by several leading national professional accountancy bodies. In the period between 1973 and 2001 it grew in status, authority and membership. By 2001 it was poised to become the de facto supra-national standard setter for much of the world. A key point was gained with the agreement, in 1995, with the International Organization of Securities Commissions (IOSCO), that the IASC would be responsible for developing a set of "core standards." If these were agreed by IOSCO they would be endorsed for use in all global markets. This endorsement took place in 2000. In 2000, the IASC decided to alter its constitution: from 2001 the standard setting body was reconstituted as the International Accounting Standards Board (IASB), to be responsible for issuing International Financial Reporting Standards (IFRS).[1] The IASB is currently in the process of addressing some highly complex technical issues that will, in due course, result in the publication of further IFRS.

In 2001 the European Commission took the decision to present legislation that required the adoption of international standards by the listed companies of all member states from 2005 onwards. Similar arrangements will shortly come into operation in Australia and New Zealand.[2] It can be expected that several national standard setting bodies around the world will gradually become less important, and may even eventually cease to exist. However, a national standard setter that is likely to exist into the foreseeable future is the Financial Accounting Standards Board (FASB) in the USA. Until recently, it appeared quite possible that US standard setting might proceed autonomously without much regard to the activities of the IASB. However, a convergence project has been launched and it is likely that there will be some significant movement towards convergence over the next few years.

The "Infrastructure of Financial Reporting"

Schipper (2000) identifies four elements as forming part of "the infrastructure of financial reporting":

1. The effectiveness of mechanisms for identifying and resolving interpretative questions.
2. The structure, processes, independence, expertise, incentives and resource base of the standards setting organisation.
3. Auditing and auditors.
4. Enforcement of accounting standards and the supporting regulations.

In many national systems, one or more of these elements can be found to be relatively weak (for example, UK accounting regulation was relatively weak in respect of the first and second elements until the early 1990s when the national accounting regulatory system was overhauled).

Although international accounting regulation can claim to possess the first two of Schipper's (2000) four elements, it is vulnerable in respect of enforcement mechanisms and in respect of auditing and auditors. The IASB has to rely upon national systems and these are likely to be patchy and inconsistent. Fearnley and Macve (2001) identify some of the principal weaknesses prevalent in national systems of compliance: weak support mechanisms for

auditors, lack of effective sanctions against directors, and differences between the legal framework and practice. Cairns (2001), summarizing the findings of his International Accounting Standards Survey published in 2000, notes a substantial level of non-compliance with international standards amongst companies claiming to adopt them.

Current developments in accounting regulation are proceeding rapidly, and the movements towards convergence and even international standardisation are welcomed in many quarters as helping to break down the barriers that hamper the operations of the international capital markets. However, there are some structural weaknesses in accounting regulation, as we aim to show here.

The Purpose of Accounting Regulation

This paper is based in part upon the proposition that accounting regulation has an important function in society. It affects the allocation of economic resources, and so it has potentially wide-ranging effects upon social welfare and the balance of economic power between parties with often competing interests. Prior to the 1970s accounting regulatory bodies were not generally much concerned with the consequential effects of their actions on such matters as distribution and economic well-being. However, from the 1970s onwards, economic impact issues were recognised as being of increasing importance. For example, Zeff (1978) recounts several instances of behaviour on the part of lobbyists that made the Accounting Principles Board in the United States (the predecessor of the current [FASB]) increasingly aware of the impact of its actions. He identifies several factors leading to the recognition of economic consequences as an issue of primary importance, including the following:

• A general societal trend towards holding institutions accountable for their actions;

- The sheer scale of the potential economic impact of accounting regulation;
- Increasing awareness of the information economics and social choice literature.

The growing awareness of economic impact issues informed the debate that took place in the last 30 years or so of the twentieth century about the establishment of a conceptual framework for accounting. The impetus for the establishment of a conceptual framework started in the USA where the first serious work was done on this type of project. However, conceptual frameworks have subsequently been promulgated elsewhere (for example, in Australia and the United Kingdom and at an international level by the [IASC]). The frameworks define the fundamental purpose of financial statements, specify the parties who have a right to take an interest in the products of financial reporting and establish definitions of the key elements of financial accounting, such as assets and liabilities. The objective of financial statements is defined as follows in the *Framework for the Preparation and Presentation of Financial Statements* published by the IASC in 1989:

> The objective of financial statements is to provide information about the financial position, performance and changes in financial position of an enterprise that is useful to a wide range of users in making economic decisions. (paragraph 12)

Accounting regulation, in the form of accounting standards, is based upon this objective which is stated in terms of utility to broadly defined groups in society. It is worth observing, too, that the user groups described in the *Framework* statement (and the other conceptual framework statements) are extensive in nature, covering investors, employees, lenders, suppliers, customers, governments and the final catch-all of the public. However, priority is awarded to the information needs of investors as the providers of risk capital to business.

So, in summary, financial statements are geared towards decision-making by various different types of user, but the user group of most importance consists of the risk-taking investors. Accounting regulators are attuned to the needs of this group in particular, and are concerned with the economic consequences of the standards that they promulgate.

Confounding their Policies: Preparers vs. Regulators

As Zeff (1978) observed, an important factor in accounting regulation is the sheer scale of the economic impact of accounting rules. The choice of an accounting rule may have a very significant impact on, for example, reported profits. The level of profitability of a commercial entity potentially affects distributions to owners, wage and salary negotiations, levels of pensions funding, ability to borrow or to raise further risk capital, taxes paid and so on. The stakes are high, especially in the context of major national or multi-national corporations whose activities have consequential effects on the lives of many people. Regulators may attempt to take the economic consequences of their actions into account, but they are likely to be confounded in many ways. For one thing, the consequences of actions are not always predictable (this is a significant ethical problem in its own right that will be the subject of a separate paper). Another problem, however, and the one with which this paper is concerned, is that when the stakes are high there are considerable incentives for financial statement preparers to confound the work of the regulators.

There are two principal means by which the intentions of the regulators can be confounded by preparers. First, preparers may lobby against proposals for rules that will have an adverse effect upon the financial statements prepared by their entities. Second, where strict application of the rules does not produce an accounting result that meets the needs of preparers, there is an incentive to misapply or to ignore the rule. This condition can pertain only where regulation is weak and/or is inadequately enforced. Both of these means involve manipulation, but the first is at the macro level of policy, and the second at the micro level of the business entity.

The term "creative accounting" is generally applied to the type of manipulation that takes place at the level of individual business entity. However, we characterise both the macro- and micro-activities as creative processes: in both manifestations preparers are busily engaged in managing financial accounting disclosures to their own ends. In both cases preparers assert the primacy of their own views of the world and seek to dominate the reporting process with their partisan version of the truth.

In order to illustrate the nature of the problems identified so far, the next two sections of the paper provide detailed examples of accounting manipulation. The first examines a case of recent successful macro-manipulation in the United States where a highly significant policy decision by the principal accounting regulator was confounded by successful preparer lobbying.

The second case looks at micro-manipulation at the individual accounts level. The case selected for examination is that of Spain, where, as will be seen, quite overt manipulation of earnings figures takes place.

Goodwill Accounting in the USA: A Case of Macro-Manipulation

In July 2001 FASB, the US accounting regulator, issued two new standards: FAS Statement no 141 *Business combinations* and FAS Statement no 142 *Goodwill and other intangible assets*. FASB had devoted a great deal of time over a five year period to its project on business combinations. The principal concern was the status of pooling of interests (merger) accounting. This is a relatively complex area of accounting, but suffice it to note that pooling of interests generally produces combined statements that show the combination in much better light than under the alternative method of acquisition accounting. The Accounting Principles Board (APB), the predecessor body to FASB, had discussed the issue as early as 1968 with a view to eliminating the use of the pooling method of accounting for combinations. The initial result of the deliberations had been a preliminary recommendation to eliminate the pooling method altogether, but the APB was persuaded to retreat from this hard line position. According to Zeff (1978) the APB appeared "almost as a pawn in a game of political chess ... as it abandoned positions of principle in favor of an embarrassing series of pressure-induced compromises" (59). APB Statement no 16 instead established a set of 12 restrictive criteria to be met before the pooling method could be adopted. Although APB Statement no 16 restricted the use of the pooling method, according to Ayers et al. (2000), subsequent research suggested that "... managers prefer this accounting method and are willing to incur significant costs to avoid the recognition of additional assets and expenses associated with the purchase method" (2).

Pooling has been heavily used: one recent estimate is that in 1998 around 55% of new business combinations (out of a total of 11,400 transactions) were accounted for under the pooling method (Ayers et al., 2000). FASB's concerns about the issue included the following:

- The issue of comparability between groups of companies.
- The heavy utilisation of regulatory resources upon the results of this method of accounting (FASB and SEC staff were spending "considerable time" interpreting financial statements produced under the pooling method).
- The underlying substance of genuine pooling is rarely encountered in practice.

FASB therefore proposed, via an exposure draft issued in 1999, that the pooling method be completely outlawed, a proposal which was eventually to form a significant part of SFAS 141. Ayers et al.

(2000), writing before the issue of the standard itself, had estimated, based upon examination of many transactions accounted for by the pooling method, that the elimination of the pooling method in US accounting would have significant economic consequences in that, for example, earnings per share and return on equity would deteriorate.

The worsening of key ratios which results from recording combinations via the purchase method no doubt had much to do with corporate America's reluctance to accept the elimination of the pooling method. The technology company Cisco (2000), a significant lobbyist against FASB's proposals, provided the following list of dire consequences[3] which could follow FASB's standard:

- Impeding of innovation and investment in new technologies.
- Slowing of overall economic growth of high-tech companies.
- Significant reduction in merger and acquisition activity.
- Impact on shareholder value and artificial reduction in corporate earnings.
- Reduction in the number of small entrepreneurial companies able to develop or compete with established companies.

One of the technical accounting issues that arises where acquisition accounting is carried out is that, in most acquisitions, there is a difference between the price paid for the business and the value of the net assets acquired. This difference is known as goodwill, and accounting for it has occupied the minds of standard setters and preparers for decades. If it is treated as an asset and amortised, it can have a significant effect in depressing reported profits. An alternative accounting treatment involves treating goodwill as an asset, but not subjecting it to regular amortisation. Instead, the asset would be regularly tested for so-called "impairment," that is, tested to see if its value has reduced. Only if it can be proved that it has lost value, would there be any effect on profit.

Initially, FASB proposed to reduce the maximum acceptable period for amortisation of goodwill from 40 to 20 years (which would mean that many businesses would have to set higher amounts of amortisation against their profits, thus reducing reported earnings and earnings per share). Strange to relate, during the course of discussions and hearings FASB's view changed, and the Board decided to take a non-amortisation approach to goodwill. In FASB's annual report the chairman reported this highly significant change in neutral terms: "Rather than have companies write off goodwill against earnings for up to 20 years as originally proposed, after thorough analysis we concluded that it would be more appropriate to test goodwill for impairment" (Financial Accounting Foundation, 2000). This was clearly a politically motivated concession to its critics. One of the principal reasons for fearing curtailment to the use of pooling was the obligation under the purchase method to account for goodwill and to take an earnings hit (albeit over a period of up to 20 years under the new proposals).[4] Under the FASB concession earnings will be affected only if there is an impairment in the value of goodwill. Much therefore depends upon the de facto effectiveness of the impairment requirements, but, given that goodwill valuation is such a subjective and difficult area, it seems likely that American corporations will be able to use the requirement as quite an effective way to manage their earnings.

The story behind the issuing of standards 141 and 142 is interesting and instructive. It illustrates the intense political nature of standards setting in the USA (at one stage a bill was presented to Congress to place a moratorium on FASB's ability to eliminate the pooling method of accounting).[5] In order to be able to introduce the standard eliminating pooling FASB had to make a major concession by removing the requirement to amortise goodwill, thus creating an opportunity for some creative earnings management at the individual company level. It appears that the principal consequential outcome informing its action in this respect was the threat to its own survival as a standard setter.

Creative Accounting in Spain: A Case of Micro-Manipulation

As noted earlier in the paper, where strict application of the rules does not produce an accounting result that meets the needs of preparers, there is an incentive to misapply or to ignore the rule. Creative accounting (also known as income smoothing, earnings management, cosmetic accounting or financial engineering) has been variously defined as

> ... the deliberate dampening of fluctuations about some level of earning considered to be normal for the firm. (Barnea et al., 1976)

> ... any action on the part of management which affects reported income and which provides no true economic advantage to the organization and may, in fact, in the long-term, be detrimental. (Merchant and Rockness, 1994)

> ... [involving] the repetitive selection of accounting measurement or reporting rules in a particular pattern, the effect of which is to report a stream of income with a smaller variation from trend than would otherwise have appeared. (Copeland, 1968)

Many research studies have tended towards the conclusion that creative accounting does exist (e.g., Barnea et al., 1976; Dascher and Malcolm, 1970; Dempsey et al., 1993; McNichols and Wilson, 1988). However, there is also evidence to suggest that investors do not necessarily see through creative accounting (e.g., Healy and Wahlen, 1999, cite studies that find that creative accounting prior to equity issues does affect share prices). Also, there is some evidence that even quite clear signalling can be misinterpreted or ignored even by relatively sophisti-

cated users (Breton and Taffler, 1995). Furthermore, Dechow and Skinner (2000) argue that even if financial statements provide sufficient information to permit users to adjust for creative accounting, there would still be cause for concern because certain categories of investors have limited ability to process the information available in the notes to the financial statements.

Amat et al. (2003) report a study identifying a set of quite overt creative accounting practices in some of the IBEX-35, stockmarket index which includes the 35 largest listed companies in Spain. The following occurrences were classified for the purposes of the study as possible indicators of creative accounting (in that they alter the impression presented to users by the financial statements):

Table I. IBEX-35 Companies Adopting Practices Indicative of Creative Accounting 1999-2001

	1999	2000	2001
% of IBEX-35 companies adopting one or more of the three practices	40	45.7	25.7
Number of companies	14	16	9
Reported earnings > adjusted earnings	5	11	7
Reported earnings < adjusted earnings	9	5	2

- Auditor report qualifications (in Spain, there is no requirement to restate the financial statements to reflect the effects of qualifications, although the effect is noted in the auditor's report. This means that the view given by the financial statements can be, at least superficially, misleading).
- Special authorisations from regulatory agencies to adopt non-standard accounting policies (this is a peculiarity of the Spanish accounting environment).[6]
- Changes in accounting policy from one year to another (these are relatively common in Spain. The effects of such changes have to be quantified and explained in the auditor's report).

The impact of these factors was assessed for each of the three financial years in the 1999-2001 period. The aggregate impact on earnings of these practices amounted to 20% of total reported earnings. Table I summarises the findings.

It may be noted that in 1999, a year when the economy was in a relatively buoyant condition, the reported earnings of nine firms were less than adjusted earnings. However, in 2000 and 2001 when the Spanish economy was affected by an economic downturn, the position was reversed. This result suggests the possibility that creative presentation of results could be related to general economic conditions (a possibility flagged by Merchant, 1990).

This study has some important implications for the enforceability of international standards. Listed companies in Spain, in common with those in other European countries, will shortly adopt international standards.[7] It seems, however, that the peculiarly Spanish approach to implementing accounting regulation will cease. Currently, supervising agencies, notably in the banking sector, may permit companies to adopt an accounting policy that contravenes current accounting regulation. These authorisations are provided as the result of successful lobbying by either a company or representative companies within an industrial sector.[8] Successful lobbying of this type illustrates the power and influence that preparers may exert over regulators. It seems highly unlikely that such power relationships will suddenly cease in 2005, and we may expect that Spanish companies will continue with their existing practices as far as it is possible to do so. Because the international accounting regulation is extremely weak in respect of enforcement, any enforcement that exists will rely upon the same national authorities that currently permit relatively slack accounting disclosure in Spain.

Discussion

The two kinds of behaviours discussed above illustrate different manifestations of the power and influence of preparers of financial statements.

The first case illustrates the relative weakness of the US standard setting body in dealing with a powerful preparer lobby. The contretemps over accounting for goodwill was not the first time that the authority of FASB has been challenged but the lobbying efforts that took place on this occasion were perhaps the most serious challenge that has been made to the authority of a national standard setter. The second case demonstrates that lobbying against regulation can become institutionalised. It is also clear that some significant manipulation of the appearance of major corporations' income statements takes place in other ways too. Regulation in both cases becomes a negotiation between the regulator and the preparer of financial statements. The interests of the users of the statements are likely to be overlooked or ignored in such cases. The overt manipulation robs the regulating body and the regulatory process of respect and authority.

User needs are ignored in the processes of manipulation at both macro- and micro- level that we have analysed in the paper. The exercise of power of the preparers is both unjust and unfair to the supposed beneficiaries of the reporting process. The fundamental objective of financial statements is deemed to be the provision of useful information for decision-making, but it appears that accounting regulation is too compromised to fulfil this purpose properly.

Macro-manipulation is ethically questionable, since preparers engage in lobbying to attempt to prevent changes in regulations that they feel will be disadvantageous to them. Perhaps little would be wrong with this if their interests were not against the legitimate rights of those who are recipients of the financial information and will be taking decisions based upon deceiving reports. It is generally accepted that regulations have to be promulgated considering the common good of the whole society and not only the interests of a particular group.

Regarding both macro- and micro-manipulation, several ethical considerations arise. First, the system of accounting regulation shares many features with a system of law. We can look to values and ideas emanating from legal systems and systems of justice. Because such systems are societal constructs we can look behind them to fundamental moral values such as truthfulness. Lyons (1984) discusses the values that are exemplified in legal processes, and identifies respect for the law as an important ethical element. "For example, well-designed procedures might encourage respect for law, and thus obedience to law, which many believe is a good thing" (196). It may be argued that regulations that can be easily flouted, perhaps because they have been poorly drafted, or because enforcement mechanisms are inadequate, do not command respect. Lyons is discussing the rule of law, but the point applies perhaps with even more force to non-statutory regulation such as accounting regulation. If it fails to command respect from those who are called upon to apply it, then regulatory failure is likely to ensue. In the context of the macro- and micro-manipulation of financial statements that we have identified as problematic in the existing system of accounting regulation, regulation loses authority if it is open to manipulation by a powerful interested party and if it cannot, in any case, be enforced.

Second, accounting regulators, as we have seen, intend that financial statements should be useful to a wide range of users. The preparers of those financial statements act as intermediaries between the regulators and the users of the statements. They therefore occupy a powerful position as interpreters of the regulations, and, given the complexity of the business world, it is hard to see how some degree of interpretation can be avoided. Some, possibly many, preparers no doubt seek to interpret the regulation fairly and do not attempt to intervene in the regulatory process. However, it is clear that some preparers will adopt any means to hand to assert their own views. This can be seen as a misuse of the authority inherent in their position.

It is generally accepted that power implies responsibility and injustice is nothing other than abuse of power, as was pointed out 25 centuries ago (Plato, 1992). Similar ideas of justice, according rights to each person or group, have been held by many other moral philosophers throughout history. According to this conception of justice and others more recent, such as Rawls' well-known theory of justice (1972), there is no doubt that the preparers of financial statements who misuse the authority inherent in their position are committing injustices.

Empirical perceptions support these notions of justice. Fischer and Rosenzweig (1995) found accounting and MBA students to be critical of manipulated transactions and the abuse of accounting rules. Merchant and Rockness (1994) found that accountants were critical of such abuses, and Naser and Pendlebury (1992) discovered similar disapproval amongst UK auditors.

Moving from the general conceptions of injustice and unfairness, we can proceed to a more personal level where individuals make business decisions that may be more or less defensible. However, business life and decisions are not exempt from considerations of morality. As Solomon (1993) points out: "We can no longer accept the amoral idea that 'business is business' (not really a tautology but an excuse for being an unfeeling bastard)" (206). Any decisions to lobby from a partisan point of view, or to dress up financial statements, are made by a group of individuals who are themselves moral agents. An Aristotelian approach to business ethics requires virtue and good character in the individual.

It is helpful to bear in mind the idea of individual responsibility for wrong actions, and the notion of good character when examining the rather amoral arguments employed to excuse accounting manipulative behaviour. A defence of creative accounting behaviour can be made which rests upon agency and positive accounting theories. Revsine (1991) discusses the "selective financial misrepresentation hypothesis." He considers the problem in relation to both managers and shareholders, and argues that each can draw benefits from loosely drafted accounting standards that permit latitude in determining the timing of income. Shareholders can benefit from the fact that managers are able to manipulate earnings to "smooth" income since this may decrease the apparent volatility of earnings and so increase the value of their shares. The fact that this involves deliberate manipulation and deceit is to be overlooked. Shareholders in this view become unwitting accessories to manipulation, but the agency's theoretical supposition is that such behaviour is inevitable given the conflict inherent in agency relationships.

Fundamentally, however, it is reasonable to question the validity of activities involved in dressing up financial statements to present an appearance that is not fully justified by the underlying economic activity. This type of micro-level creative accounting is informed by an intention to deceive the recipients of financial statements, and can therefore be regarded as morally reprehensible.

Conclusion

This paper has identified some manipulative behaviour on the part of preparers of financial statements, taking into account some important ethical concerns. To achieve this, we have tried to broaden out the usual definition of creativity in accounting examining two principal categories of behaviour by the preparers of financial statements: macro-manipulation and micro-manipulation.

At the macro-manipulation level, some preparers of financial statements are willing to engage in lobbying in an attempt to sway accounting regulators to produce rules that are advantageous to the interests of preparers. In doing so, they are likely to shift the attention of regulators away from the interests of users of the financial statements.

At the micro-manipulation level, some preparers engage in manipulation at their entities in order to present a biased view of economic reality.

Both categories of behaviour are likely to result in financial statements that may suit the purposes of the preparer but which are less than satisfactory from a user's point of view. From an ethical perspective these manipulations can be regarded as morally reprehensible. They are not fair to users, they involve an unjust exercise of power, and they tend to weaken the authority of the regulators. Where regulation is breached with impunity a diminution of respect for it and its procedures is likely to ensue.

NOTES

1 The predecessor body, the IASC, issued forty-one standards over a period of almost thirty years. So far, the IASB has issued (at the time of writing) two IFRSs.

2 In the case of Australia, the Australian Financial Reporting Council (FRC) announced on July the third of 2002 that it would recommend that from January the first of 2005 the accounting standards applicable to companies would be those issued by the IASB (FRC, 2002). In New Zealand the Accounting Standards Review Board has recommended to the government that IFRSs should be adopted by entities in both the public and private sectors from January the first of 2007, with the option to adopt them as early as January the first of 2005 (ASRB, 2002).

3 Subsequent events in the new technology market proved that several of these predicted consequences could occur without the assistance of FASB.

4 A proposal which would have ensured convergence with the UK's FRS 10 and the IASE's IAS 22.

5 A bill introduced by Representatives Dooley and Cox in the 106th congress.

6 A peculiarity shared by France.

7 In addition, a decision has been taken by the Spanish government to extend the application of international standards to non-listed companies. In order to effect this change the Spanish *Instituto de Contabilidad y Auditoría de Cuentas*

(ICAC, Spanish Institute of Accounting and Auditing) plans to issue a new *Plan General de Contabilidad* (PGC, Spanish Accounting Plan) which will be adapted to IFRSs.

8 This provides an interesting example of an hybrid between macro- and micro-manipulation.

REFERENCES

Accounting Standards Review Board [New Zealand]: (2002) Press release, 19 December, <http://www.asrb.co.nz> (accessed on March 8, 2004).

Amat, O., C. Gowthorpe and J. Perramon: (2003) "Earnings Management in Spain: An Assessment of the Effect on Reported Earnings of Larger Listed Companies 1999-2001," *Economic Working Paper Series*, Universitat Pompeu Fabra, Barcelona.

Ayers, B.C., C.E. Lefanowicz and J.R. Robinson: (2000) "The Financial Statement Effects of Eliminating the Pooling-of-interests Method of Acquisition Accounting," *Accounting Horizons* Vol. 14(1), 1-19.

Barnea, A., J. Ronen and S. Sadan: (1976) "Classificatory Smoothing of Income with Extraordinary Items," *The Accounting Review* January, 110-22.

Breton, G. and R.J. Taffler: (1995) "Creative Accounting and Investment Analyst Response," *Accounting and Business Research* Vol. 25(98), 81-92.

Cairns, D.: (2001) "IAS Lite is Alive and Well," *Accountancy*, May, 88-89.

Cisco: (2000) "Eliminating the Pooling Method of Accounting Standards: A Threat to the Internet Economy," <http://www.cisco.com/warp/public /779/govtaffs/archive/fasb.html> (accessed January 18, 2002).

Copeland, R.M.: (1968) "Income Smoothing," *Journal of Accounting Research* VVI, Supplement, 101-16.

Dascher, P.E. and R.E. Malcom: (1970) "A Note on Income Smoothing in the Chemical Industry," *Journal of Accounting Research*, Autumn, 253-59.

Dechow, P.M. and D.J. Skinner: (2000) "Creative Accounting: Reconciling the Views of Accounting Academics, Practitioners and Regulators," *Accounting Horizons* Vol. 14(2), 235-51.

Dempsey, S.J., H.G. Hunt and N.W. Schroeder: (1993) "Creative Accounting and Corporate Ownership Structure: An Examination of Extraordinary Item Reporting," *Journal of Business Finance and Accounting* Vol. 20(4), 479-500.

Fearnley, S. and R. Macve: (2001) "Global Problems," *Accountancy*, October, 110.

Financial Accounting Foundation: (2000) *Annual Report* (Financial Accounting Foundation, Norwalk, CT), <http://www.fasb.org> (accessed on March 8, 2004).

Financial Reporting Council (Australia): (2002) Bulletin, July 3, <http://www.frc.gov.au> (accessed on March 8, 2004).

Fischer, M. and K. Rosenzweig: (1995) "Attitudes of Students and Accounting Practitioners Concerning the Ethical Acceptability of Earnings Management," *Journal of Business Ethics* Vol. 14, 433-44.

Healy, P.M. and J.M. Wahlen: (1999) "A Review of the Creative Accounting Literature and its Implications for Standard Setting," *Accounting Horizons* Vol. 13(4), 365-383.

Lyons, D.: (1984) *Ethics and the Rule of Law* (Cambridge: Cambridge University Press).

McNichols, M. and G.P. Wilson: (1988) "Evidence of Creative Accounting from the Provision for Bad Debts," *Journal of Accounting Research* Vol. 26, Supplement, 1-33.

Merchant, K.A.: (1990) "The Effects of Financial Controls on Data Manipulation and Management Myopia," *Accounting, Organizations and Society* Vol. 15(4), 297-313.

Merchant, K.A. and J. Rockness: (1994) "The Ethics of Managing Earnings: An Empirical Investigation," *Journal of Accounting and Public Policy* Vol. 13, 79-94.

Naser, K. and M. Pendlebury: (1992) "A Note on the Use of Creative Accounting," *British Accounting Review* Vol. 24, 111-18.

Plato: (1992) *Republic*, translated by G.M. Grube, revised by C.D. Reeve (Indianapolis, IN: Hackett Publishing).

Rawls, J.: (1972) *A Theory of Justice* (Oxford: Oxford University Press).

Revsine, L.: (1991) "The Selective Financial Misrepresentation Hypothesis," *Accounting Horizons*, December, 16-27.

Schipper, K.: (2000) "Accounting Research and the Potential use of International Accounting Standards for Cross-Border Securities Listings," *The British Accounting Review* Vol. 32, 243-56.

Solomon, R.C.: (1993) "Corporate Roles, Personal Virtues: An Aristotelian Approach to Business Ethics," in E.R. Winkler and J.R. Coombs (eds.), *Applied Ethics: A Reader* (Oxford: Blackwell), 201-21. Originally published in *Business Ethics Quarterly* Vol. 2(3), 1992, 317-30.

Zeff, S.A.: (1978) "The Rise of 'Economic Consequences,'" *The Journal of Accountancy* 56-63.

INSIDER TRADING

PATRICIA H. WERHANE

The Ethics of Insider Trading

Insider trading is the reverse of speculation. It is reward without risk, wealth-generated—and injury done to others by an unfair advantage in information.... [T]he core principle is clear: no one should profit from exploitation of important information not available to the public.[1]

Insider trading in the stock market is characterized as the buying or selling of shares of stock on the basis of information known only to the trader or to a few persons. In discussions of insider trading it is commonly assumed that the privileged information, if known to others, would affect their actions in the market as well, although in theory this need not be the case. The present guidelines of the Securities and Exchange Commission prohibit most forms of insider trading. Yet a number of economists and philosophers of late defend this kind of activity both as a viable and useful practice in a free market and as a practice that is not immoral. In response to these defenses I want to question the value of insider trading both from a moral and an economic point of view. I shall argue that insider trading both in its present illegal form and as a legalized market mechanism violates the privacy of concerned parties, destroys competition, and undermines the efficient and proper functioning of a free market, thereby bringing into question its own raison d'être [i.e., reason for being]. It does so and therefore is economically inefficient for the very reason that it is immoral.

That insider trading as an illegal activity interferes with the free market is pretty obvious. It is like a game where there are a number of players each of whom represents a constituency. In this sort of game there are two sets of rules—one ostensive set and another, implicit set, functioning for some of the players. In this analogy some of the implicit rules are outlawed, yet the big players manage to keep them operative and actually often in control of the game. But not all the players know all the rules being played or at least they are ignorant of the most important ones, ones that determine the big wins and big losses. So not all the players realize what rules actually manipulate the outcome. Moreover, partly because some of the most important functioning rules are illegal, some players who do know the implicit rules and could participate do not. Thus not everyone in a position to do so plays the trading game the same way. The game, then, like the manipulated market that is the outcome, is unfair—unfair to some of the players and those they represent—unfair not only because some of the players are not privy to the most important rules, but also because these "special" rules are illegal so that they are adopted only by a few of even the privileged players.

But suppose that insider trading was decriminalized or not prohibited by SEC regulations. Then, one might argue, insider trading would not be unfair because anyone could engage in it with impunity. Although one would be trading on privileged knowledge, others, too, could trade on their privileged information. The market would function more efficiently since the best-informed and those most able to gain information would be allowed to exercise their fiscal capabilities. The market itself would regulate the alleged excesses of insider trading. I use the term "alleged" excesses because according to this line of reasoning, if the market is functioning properly, whatever gains or losses are created as a result of open competition are a natural outcome of that competition. They are not excesses at all, and eventually the market will adjust the so-called unfair gains of speculators.

There are several other defenses of insider trading. First, insider information, e.g., information about a merger, acquisition, new stock issue, layoffs, etc., information known only to a few, *should* be and remain private. That information is the property of those engaged in the activity in question, and they should have the right to regulate its dissemination.

Second and conversely, even under ideal circumstances it is impossible either to disseminate information to all interested parties equally and fairly, or alternately, to preserve absolute secrecy. For example, in issuing a new stock or deciding on a stock split, a number of parties in the transaction from brokers to printers learn about that information in advance just because of their participation in making this activity a reality. And there are always shareholders and other interested parties who claim they did not receive information of such an activity or did not receive it at the same time as other shareholders even when the information was disseminated to everyone at the same time. Thus it is, at best, difficult to stop insider trading or to judge whether a certain kind of knowledge is "inside" or privileged. This is not a good reason to defend insider trading as economically or morally desirable, but it illustrates the difficulties of defining and controlling the phenomenon.

Third, those who become privy to inside information, even if they take advantage of that information before it becomes public, are trading on probabilities, not on certainties, since they are trading before the activity actually takes place. They are taking a gamble, and if they are wrong the market itself will "punish" them. It is even argued that brokers who do not use inside information for their clients' advantage are cheating their clients.

Finally, and more importantly, economists like Henry Manne argue that insider trading is beneficial to outsiders. Whether it is more beneficial than its absence is a question Manne admits he cannot answer. But Manne defends insider trading because, he argues, it reduces the factor of chance in trading both for insiders and outsiders. When shares are traded on information probabilities rather than on rumor or whim, the market reflects more accurately the actual economic status of that company or set of companies. Because of insider trading, stock prices more closely represent the worth of their company than shares not affected by insider trading. Insider trading, then, actually improves the fairness of the market, according to this argument, by reflecting in stock prices the fiscal realities of affected corporations thereby benefitting all traders of the stocks.[2]

These arguments for insider trading are persuasive. Because outsiders are allegedly not harmed from privileged information not available to them and may indeed benefit from insider trading, and because the market punishes rash speculators, insider trading cannot be criticized as exploitation. In fact, it makes the market more efficient. Strong as these arguments are, however, there is something amiss with these claims. The error, I think, rests at least in part with the faulty view of how free markets work, a view which stems from a misinterpretation that derives from a misreading of Adam Smith and specifically a misreading of Smith's notions of self-interest and the Invisible Hand.

The misinterpretation is this. It is sometimes assumed that the unregulated free market, driven by competition and self-interest, will function autonomously. The idea is that the free market works something like the law of gravity—autonomously and anonymously in what I would call a no-blooded fashion. The interrelationships created by free market activities based on self-interested competition are similar to the gravitational relationships between the planets and the sun: impersonal, automatic interactions determined by a number of factors including the distance and competitive self-interest of each of the market components. The free market functions, then, despite the selfish peculiarities of the players just as the planets circle the sun despite their best intentions to do otherwise. Given that picture of the free market, so-called insider trading, driven by self-interest but restrained by competitive forces, that is, the Invisible Hand, is merely one gravitational mechanism—a complication but not an oddity or an aberration in the market.

This is a crude and exaggerated picture of the market, but I think it accounts for talk about the market *as if* it functioned in this independent yet forceful way, and it accounts for defenses of un-restrained self-interested actions in the market place. It allows one to defend insider trading because of the positive market fall-out from this activity, and because the market allegedly will control the excesses of self-interested economic activities.

The difficulty with this analysis is not so much with the view of insider trading as a legitimate activity but rather with the picture of economic actors in a free market. Adam Smith himself, despite his seventeenth-century Newtonian background, did not have such a mechanical view of a laissez-faire [i.e., to let do. In the present context it refers to the principle of non-interference by government in commercial enterprise.] economy. Again and again in the *Wealth of Nations* Smith extols the virtues of unrestrained competition as being to the advantage of the producer and the consumer.[3] A system of perfect liberty he argues, creates a situation where "[t]he whole of the advantages and disadvantages of the different employments of labour and stock ... be either perfectly equal or continually tending to equality."[4] Yet for Smith the greatest cause of inequalities of advantage is any restrictive policy or activity that deliberately gives privileges to certain kinds of businesses, trades, or professions.[5] The point is that Smith sees perfect liberty as the necessary condition for competition, but perfect competition occurs only when both parties in the exchange are on more or less equal grounds, whether it be competition for labor, jobs, consumers, or capital. This is not to imply that Smith favors equality of outcomes. Clearly he does not. But the market is most efficient and most fair when there is competition between equally matched parties.

Moreover, Smith's thesis was that the Invisible Hand works because, and only when, people operate with restrained self-interest, self-interest restrained by reason, moral sentiments, and sympathy, in Smith's case the reason, moral sentiments, and sympathies of British gentlemen. To operate otherwise, that is, with unrestrained self-interest, where that self-interest causes harm to others would "violate the laws of justice"[6] or be a "violation of fair play,"[7] according to Smith. This interferes with free competition just as government regulation would because the character of competition, and thus the direction of the Invisible Hand, depends on the manner in which actors exploit or control their own self-interests. The Invisible Hand, then, that "masterminds" the free market is not like an autonomous gravitational force. It depends on the good will, decency, self-restraint, and fair play of those parties engaging in market activities.[8] When self-interests get out of hand, Smith contends, they must be regulated by laws of justice.[9]

Similarly, the current market, albeit not Smith's ideal of laissez-faire, is affected by how people operate in the marketplace. It does not operate autonomously. Unrestrained activities of insider traders affect competition differently than Smithian exchanges which are more or less equal exchanges between self-interested but restrained parties. The term "insider trading" implies that some traders know more than others, that information affects their decision-making and would similarly affect the trading behavior of others should they become privy to that information. Because of this, the resulting market is different than one unaffected by insider trading. This, in itself, is not a good reason to question insider trading. Henry Manne, for example, recognizes the role of insider trading in influencing the market and finds that, on balance, this is beneficial.

Insider trading, however, is not merely a complication in the free market mechanism. Insider trading, whether it is legal or illegal, affects negatively the ideal of laissez-faire of *any* market, because it thwarts the very basis of the market: competition, just as "insider" rules affect the fairness of the trader even if that activity is not illegal and even if one could, in theory, obtain inside information oneself. This is because the same information, or equal information, is not available to everyone. So competition, which depends on the availability of equal advantage by all parties, is precluded. Insider trading allows the insider to indulge in greed (even though she may not) and that, by eschewing stock prices, works against the very kind of market in which insider trading might be allowed to function.

If it is true, as Manne argues, that insider trading produces a more efficient stock market because stock prices as a result of insider trading better reflect the underlying economic conditions of those companies involved in the trade, he would also have to argue that competition does not always produce the best results in the marketplace. Conversely, if competition creates the most efficient market, insider trading cannot, because competition is "regulated" by insiders. While it is not clear whether outsiders benefit more from insider trading than without that activity, equal access to information would allow (although not determine) every trader to compete from an equal advantage. Thus pure competition, a supposed goal of the free market and an aim of most persons who defend insider trading, is more nearly obtained without insider trading.

Insider trading has other ethical problems. Insider trading does not protect the privacy of information it is supposed to protect. To illustrate, let us consider a case of a friendly merger between Company *X* and Company *Y*. Suppose this merger is in the planning stages and is not to be made public even to the shareholders for a number of months. There may be good or bad reasons for this secrecy, e.g., labor problems, price of shares of acquired company, management changes, unfriendly raiders, competition in certain markets, etc. By law, management and others privy to knowledge about the possible merger cannot trade shares of either company during the negotiating period. On the other hand, if that information is "leaked" to a trader (or if she finds out by some other means), then information that might affect the merger is now in the hands of persons not part of the negotiation. The alleged privacy of information, privacy supposedly protected by insider traders, is now in the hands of not disinterested parties. While they may keep this information a secret, they had no right to it in the first place. Moreover, their possession of the information has three possible negative effects.

First, they or their clients in fact may be interested parties to the merger, e.g., labor union leaders, stockholders in competing companies, etc., the very persons for whom the information makes a difference and therefore are the objects of Company X and Y's secrecy. Second, insider trading on privileged information gives unfair advantages to these traders. Even if outsiders benefit from insider trading, they are less likely to benefit as much nor as soon as insider traders for the very reason of their lack of proximity to the activity. Insider traders can use information to their advantage in the market, an advantage neither the management of X or Y nor other traders can enjoy. Even if the use of such information in the market makes the market more efficient, this is unfair competition since those without this information will not gain as much as those who have such knowledge. Even if insider trading does contribute to market stabilization based on information, nevertheless, one has also to justify the fact that insider traders profit more on their knowledge than outsiders, when their information becomes an actuality simply by being "first" in the trading of the stock. Do insider traders deserve this added profit because their trading creates a more propitious market share knowledge for outsiders? That is a difficult position to defend, because allowing insider trading also allows for the very Boeskyian greed that is damaging in any market.

Third, while trading X and Y on inside information may bring their share prices to the value most closely reflecting their real price-earnings ratio, this is not always the case. Such trading may reflect undue optimism or pessimism about the possible outcome of the merger, an event that has not yet occurred. So the prices of X and Y may be overvalued or undervalued on the basis of a probability, or, because insider traders seldom have all the facts, on guesswork. In these cases insider trading deliberately creates more risk in the market since the stock prices for X or Y are manipulated for not altogether solid reasons. So market efficiency, the end which allegedly justifies insider trading, is not guaranteed.

What Henry Manne's defenses of insider trading do show is what Adam Smith well knew, that the market is neither independent nor self-regulatory. What traders do in the market and how they behave affects the direction and kind of restraint the market will exert on other traders. The character of the market is a product of those who operate within it, as Manne has demonstrated in his defense of insider trading. Restrained self-interest creates an approximation of a self-regulatory market, because it is that that allows self-interested individuals and companies to function as competitively as possible. In the long run the market will operate more efficiently too, because it precludes aberrations such as those exhibited by Ivan Boesky's and David Levine's behavior, behavior that created market conditions favorable to no one except themselves and their clients.

NOTES

1 George Will, "Keep Your Eye on Guiliani," *Newsweek*, March 2, 1987, 84.

2 See Henry Manne, *Insider Trading and the Stock Market* (New York: The Free Press, 1966), especially Chapters X and XI.

3 Adam Smith, *The Wealth of Nations*, ed. R.A. Campbell and A.S. Skinner (Oxford: Oxford University Press, 1976), I.x.c, II.v.8-12.

4 *Wealth of Nations*, I.x.a.1.

5 *Wealth of Nations*, I.x.c.

6 *Wealth of Nations*, IV.ix.51.

7 Adam Smith, *The Theory of Moral Sentiments*, ed. D.D. Raphael and A.L. Macfie (Oxford: Oxford University Press, 1976), II.ii.2.1.

8 See Andrew Skinner, *A System of Social Science* (Oxford: Clarendon Press, 1979), especially 237ff.

9 See, for example, *The Wealth of Nations*, II.ii.94, IV, v.16.

◆ ◆ ◆ ◆ ◆

TIBOR R. MACHAN

What Is Morally Right with Insider Trading

Introduction

Insider trading per se is obtaining information from non-public sources—private acquaintances, friends, colleagues—and using it for purposes of enhancing one's financial advantage. As Vincent Barry explains, "Insider dealings refers to the ability of key employees to profit from knowledge or information that has not yet become public."[1] Sometimes such a practice can be conducted fraudulently, as when one who has obtained the information has a fiduciary duty to share it with clients but fails to exercise it, or in some other criminal fashion, as when the information is itself stolen. These are not, however, features of insider trading as such, as understood in the context of the discussion of business ethics. Never mind that in the enforcement of government regulations it is in fact fraud that is cited that makes the conduct illegal when referred to as insider trading.[2] (This suggests that the bulk of the relevant law does not concern itself so much with what many in the business ethics community worry about, namely, "justice as fairness," but with "justice as honoring of contracts.")

What makes the insider trading business ethics discussions focus upon distinctive is that the information on which trade is based is not known to others within the interested trading community aside from the insider. Insider trading is dealing with the aid of what is not so-called "public knowledge" and, thus, it gives the trader an advantage over the rest of the market participants who are on the outside.

Against the common view of insider trading presented in business ethics discussions, I want to argue that it may be one's achievement or good fortune to learn of opportunities ahead of others and there is nothing morally wrong with this. In fact, acting on such information can be prudent, exhibiting good business acumen, whenever it does not involve the violation of others' rights. The conventional view rests on the belief that others have a right to one's revealing to them information one has honestly obtained ahead of them. But there is no sound general moral principle that requires this.

We clearly make morally unobjectionable use of special information for our own benefit, despite the fact that others might also benefit were it available to them: as when we are first to learn of the presence of a potential dating partner, a good buy on a used car, or a house coming up for sale in a highly preferred neighborhood. To take advantage of such special opportunities is a sign of good judgment, not of unfairness or deception.

Those who claim otherwise as regard insider trading confuse the marketplace with a game in which rules are devised or set down with the special purpose of giving everyone an even chance—e.g., when in golf or steeple chasing handicaps are assigned, or when in pro football the lowest ranked team gains first choice in the player drafts. The market is more akin to life itself, in which different persons enter with different assets—talents, looks, genetic make up, economic and climatic circumstances—and they must do their best with what they have. In life, apart from occasionally benefiting from the generosity or charity of others, all one has is a fighting chance. Children of musically proficient parents will probably benefit "unfairly" as far as obtaining musical opportunities are concerned. Those born in Bombay, to poor parents, will face harder times than those born in Beverly Hills to movie star parents. No general moral requirement exists for strangers to even this out, only to abstain from imposing obstacles on others, from violating their rights to liberty. The marketplace, too, is a setting wherein different persons face different circumstances. People do not have a natural obligation to perform involuntary service to strangers. In competing with others for opportunities that the market provides by way of demands one can fulfill in return for voluntary compensation, one is treating all other agents with the respect they deserve as the potential traders they mostly are in such a context. Exceptions exist, of course, as when one trades with friends or family, which raises some moral complications. But the norm is where people treat each other as seeking to find opportunities for trade, nothing more. Other human relationships can obtain side by side, of course, but we can keep the commercial ones distinct enough to understand the ethics that ought to govern us as we embark upon trade. Let me now develop some of these points.

What Is Insider Trading?

The concept "insider trading" employed in business ethics discussions has a broader meaning: it includes anyone's ability to make deals based on not yet publicized knowledge of business opportunities. Insider trading as such, apart from what it may be related to in some cases (such as fraud or the violation of fiduciary duty), involves making financial investments on the basis of knowledge others do not have and may not be able to obtain in ordinary ways. A knows the president of a firm who tells A that they are thinking of expanding one of their divisions or have struck oil in a new field, so A buys a block of stock in anticipation of the increase of value once the deal is done or the knowledge becomes public. A is not deceiving anyone, nor is A defrauding anyone. A is not taking anything from others that A wasn't freely given. A is acting on special, "insider," information, that is all.

It is conventional wisdom to treat this version of insider trading as morally wrong because it is supposed to affect others adversely by being unfair. As one critic has put it, "What causes injury or loss to outsiders is not what the insider knew or did, rather it is what they themselves [the outsiders] did not know. It is their own lack of knowledge which exposes

them to risk of loss or denies them an opportunity to make a profit."[3] By the fact that these others do not know what the insider does know, they are harmed since they are not able to make use of opportunities that are in fact available, knowable to us.

But what kind of causation is it that fails to make a difference when it does not exist? If someone's knowing a good deal has no impact on what another does, it cannot be said that any harm upon another had been caused by that someone. Certainly, had the other known what the insider knew, he or she could have acted differently. By not acting differently, he or she could easily have failed to reap advantages the insider did reap. But nothing here shows that the insider caused any harm, only that he or she had a better set of opportunities. Unless we assume that valuable information known by one person ought, morally—and perhaps legally—be distributed to all interested parties—something that would beg the most important question—there is no moral fault involved in insider trading nor any causation of harm.[4]

Because of the widespread but mistaken view that insider trading is morally wrong, it is conventional wisdom to support its legal prohibition. Of course, even if morally wrong, it may not follow that it should be morally prohibited. Yet there is reason to think that the moral objections are wrongheaded. Because of this we may suspect that the opposition to insider trading is more likely the result of widespread, strong prejudice against gaining economic prosperity without sharing it. Clearly there is a lot of thinking afoot in our era to the effect that a level playing field is morally mandatory when people embark upon commercial or business endeavors.[5]

Why Insider Trading Is Right

Certainly I am at an advantage when I possess information others lack. Nearly everyone in the marketplace is in that position to a certain extent. One might even wish to call this "unfair" in the sense in which any kind of good fortune may be to some people's but not to others' advantage. More precisely, though, the concept of fairness does not apply in this context, even though many believe otherwise. For someone to act fairly requires some prior obligation to distribute burdens or benefits among a given number of people in some suitable proportion or in line with certain specified procedures. But to act fairly does not amount to a primary moral duty—for example, thieves can fairly enough distribute their loot and yet are morally delinquent. Only when one ought to treat others alike, which may occur in special circumstances such as paying attention to all the students in one's class or feeding all of one's children equally well, does fairness count for something morally important.

As this applies to insider trading, if I have a prior obligation to share my information with others, that is, a fiduciary duty to clients or associates, then it is not that the information is "from the inside" but that it is owed to others that makes my dealings morally and possibly legally objectionable. It is only in such cases that fairness is obligatory, as a matter of one's professional relationship to others, one established by the promise made or contract one has entered into prior to the ensuing duty to be fair. It is only then that one can cause injury by refusing to do what one has agreed to do, namely, divulge information prior to using it for oneself. Accordingly, Hetherington's objection to insider trading is without moral force. What he should have objected to is the breaching of fiduciary duty, which may occur on occasion by means of failing to divulge information (possibly gained "from the inside") that has been—perhaps even contractually—promised to a client.

Furthermore, if I have stolen the information—spied or bribed for or extorted it—again the moral deficiency comes not from its being inside information but from its having been ill gotten.

What if the information was come by accidentally? I overhear some people talking in the lavatory or at a bar after they've had too much to drink and have loose tongues. Am I wrong to make use of it?

Here again the issue is just what I owe others. Do I have a natural obligation to share my good fortune with other people?

In emergency situations, when others are in dire need or have met with some natural disaster, virtues such as generosity and charity are usually binding on those who are able to assist. Yet these are not obligations in the sense of something the law must enforce. Indeed, enforcing generosity or charity is impossible—the moral significance of a virtue is destroyed if it is practiced at the point of a gun! Furthermore, in the context of the normal hustle and bustle of life, no such virtues are called for toward strangers, only toward those one is related to by prior commitments, intimacy, and love. Instead, in the ordinary course of life one ought to strive to live successfully, to prosper, to make headway with one's legitimate projects, not embark upon the tasks of emergency crews during an earthquake. Unless one is specifically suited for those professions that address those in special need, one has no business to meddle in the lives of others and ought to carry forth without compunction in those tasks that advance the lives of those one has freely embarked upon to promote.

From the viewpoint of common sense ethics, the idea that there is something morally amiss with insider trading has little to support it. One clearly has no moral, let alone legal, obligation to share information with strangers that may benefit one in other familiar circumstances.

Imagine, for example, that an appealing eligible single woman moves into a neighborhood in which several eligible men would like to meet her. I, one of these men, obtain (insider) information about her impending arrival before others and approach her before other men in my position learn of the fact that she will be part of the community. Have I done wrong? Isn't the prospect of successful romance even more important to people than the prospect of successful investment? Suppose, again, that I learn of a very good violin teacher who is moving to our town and I am first in line to take lessons from him. Am I doing something morally wrong? Nothing supports such a view.

Of course, were I someone who is in no great hurry with finding a mate and had a friend who is, I might generously tell him about the impending arrival of the lady. This would be generous but not obligatory. The same would hold if I had a friend of whose musical ambitions with the violin I am well aware and I learned of the opportunity for taking lessons from a new master in our neighborhood. Were I to forget about my friends in these cases, this might well be justly held against me. But the same does not apply when it comes to strangers.

In fact, there are areas of commerce in the USA not to mention in other societies where insider trading is not prohibited (e.g., Japan), where the type of conduct insider trading exhibits is not only accepted but praised. Consider news reporting. When a news reporter scoops the competition, no one considers this legally actionable, nor, indeed, morally insidious. On the contrary, it is a mark of professional savvy and achievement. Why does this not apply in the case of insider trading? I'll turn to this next.

The Bad Reputation of Commerce

The reason these situations, as distinct from insider trading, do not invite widespread moral rebuke is that we tend to consider objectives such as finding the right mate or learning a musical instrument something benign, morally untainted. When it comes to making economic or financial gains, in many quarters there is an initial moral discomfort about it. The shadow of greed looms very large and tends even to overwhelm prudence, which is, after all, the first of the cardinal virtues.

Why Insider Trading Seems Wrong

Indeed, the intellectual source of moral disdain for insider trading is the more general disdain for economic or commercial self-enhancement, at least

among moral philosophers and others in the humanities. There seems to be no end to how fiercely commercial success is demeaned among many of those who preach and reflect upon morality. Yet this seems to me to be utterly misguided.

Becoming prosperous can be a means toward the attainment of numerous worthy goals and should, thus, itself be deemed to be a worthy goal. Not that riches cannot be pursued obsessively, but it need not be done so at all. Any other goal can also be pursued *to a fault*. An artist can be over ambitious vis-à-vis being an artist and, thereby, neglect family, friends, polity. Even truth can be pursued too fanatically. The chances for corruption through the pursuit of economic advantage are no greater than through other pursuits. The disdainful attitude toward commercial professionals is entirely unjustified, a prejudice that deserves as much study as prejudices toward racial, religious or ethnic groups.

What about the fact that we encourage fairness in athletic competition, such as imposing handicaps in golf and horse racing? What about the way baseball and football leagues utilize the player draft to even out the advantages of teams? Does this not indicate that we stress fairness more than I have allowed? Don't we find fairness heavily stressed in the allocation of chores in families and fraternities, not to mention teams?

Bad Analogies

These examples are misleading. It isn't fairness *per se* that's stressed in golf and horse racing; what appears as such is actually an effort to foster games and races that capture and keep the interest of spectators. The same holds for the policy on player drafts. If a team wins repeatedly, interest will begin to wane and the sport will lose its fans.

As to families, there exists a prior obligation to share burdens and benefits among the members, if not equally then at least proportionately. Parents have invited their children into the family, as it were, and when benefits (or burdens) are reaped, all those invited should share them.

Among people who are not in such relationships no fairness principle operates. No doubt, sometimes we make a mistake and transfer the attitudes we have acquired for how to handle matters in the family to other areas of our lives, but that is an illogical extrapolation. And this is evident enough by considering that if I am born to a family with musical talents or good genes, it is not my duty to make sure that those born to families without them somehow share my advantages. Nor am I doing the right thing in imposing my burdens on members of families who do not suffer as mine does. That sort of policy would be more appropriately associated with envy and resentment, not with moral decency.

The Moral Merit of Insider Trading

Accordingly, seeking to benefit through ingenuity and shrewdness is good business, and good business is as important a professional trait as good medicine, good law, good education, etc. Professional ethics, in turn, cannot condemn that which is in accord with ethics in general, such as fortitude and prudence. Competence and skill, even excellence, at managing the material progress one might be able to make in life ought not to be treated as less important than competence and skill at managing artistic, scientific, educational or other types of progress.

There are those who defend insider trading because it contributes to the overall efficiency of market transactions. They argue that those trading from the inside send signals to others whose reactions then help propel the market to its new level of efficiency.

There may be something to this line of defense, although it comes perilously close to arguing that the end justifies the means. Unless the actions of the individuals who engage in insider trading can themselves be shown to be justified, such arguments do not do much good. One can show benefits to society

at large based on theft, even murder, yet these are by no means justified based on such reasoning.

Insider trading, moreover, is held to be morally suspect not because its overall value to the society is denied but because many regard fairness, equality, a level playing field, the most important criteria for a morally decent marketplace. The fact is that those are actually not what counts most for the morality of trade. That place is occupied by the respect for individual rights. Within the framework of such respect, insider trading is entirely unobjectionable. In addition, it can be perfectly ethically commendable to act based on such information; it is a matter of prudence and commercial savvy, both of which should be encouraged from those who work for a living.[6]

NOTES

1 Vincent Barry, *Moral Issues in Business* (Belmont, CA: Wadsworth Publishing Company, 1983), 242.
2 Rule 106-5 of Securities Exchange Act of 1934. See, also, SEC v. Texas Gulf Sulpher (1968); U.S. v. Chiarella (1980), and U.S. v. Newman (1981). Both definitions and sanctions vary somewhat from state to state and case to case. *Black's Law Dictionary* states that "Insider trading ... refers to transactions in shares of publicly held corporations by persons with insider or advance information on which the trading is based. Usually the trader himself is an insider with an employment or other relation of trust and confidence with the corporation" (St. Paul, MN: West Publishing Company, 1991), 547. Pub. L. 100-704. Sec. 7, Nov. 19, 1988, 102 Stat. 4682, provides that there be a study and investigation of, among other things, "impediments to the fairness and orderliness of the securities markets...."

While the language of securities law does mention the fairness that is most often the concern of those discussing insider trading in the field of business ethics, it seems that the main focus of the law and the regulatory bodies fine tuning and enforcing it has to do with fraudulent trading in insider information or its misuse by those who have fiduciary duties not to disclose and use it until it is made available to the general trading public.

3 John A.C. Hetherington, "Corporate Social Responsibility, Stockholders, and the Law," *Journal of Contemporary Business*, Winter (1973), 51; quoted in *op. cit.*, Barry, *Moral Issues*, 242-43. One feature of the business ethics discussions of insider trading and other normative topics is that there is hardly any attention paid to the distinction between ethics and public policy. Thus, even if there were something ethically objectionable about some business practice, this does not ipso facto warrant rendering it illegal or subject to government regulation. An analogy might help here: when we discuss journalistic ethics, it is clear enough that journalists may engage in unethical behavior that should not be made illegal. This same distinction is not generally observed when it comes to the profession of business. For an exception, see Tibor R. Machan, ed., *Commerce and Morality* (Lanham, MD: Rowman & Littlefield, 1988), especially "Ethics and Its Uses." For a business ethics perspective hospitable to viewing business as a morally honorable profession, see Tibor R. Machan, "Professional Responsibilities of Corporate Managers," *Business and Professional Ethics Journal*, Vol. 13 (1994).

4 If someone does not do what he or she ought to do, the causation involved may be the kind that consists in taking away a supporting feature of an action: Someone who steals a part of my car engine causes it to fail to operate properly by removing what such operation needs. That is how stealing can cause the ensuing harm. Fraud produces harm similarly: something one owns, namely, what another has legally committed to one, is in fact withheld. But without such commitment, nor even a moral duty to provide, no causation of the lack of desired advantage can be identified. For more on this, see Eric Mack, "Bad Samaritarianism and the Causation of Harm," *Philosophy and Public Affairs*, Vol. 9 (1980).

5 The most prominent is, of course, John Rawls, *A Theory of Justice* (Cambridge, MA: Harvard University Press, 1971). One main problem in Rawls' defense of "justice as fairness" is that Rawls believes that no one can deserve his or her advantages or assets in life—it's all a matter of luck. As he puts it, "No one deserves his greater natural capacity nor merits a more favorable starting point in society." The reason? Because even a person's character (i.e., the virtues he or she practices that may provide him with ways of getting ahead of others) "depends in large part upon fortunate family and social circumstances for which he can claim no credit" (104). If one rejects this deterministic account of virtues, than a trader's prudence cannot be discounted as one assesses whether he or she deserves to gain from how trade is conducted.

6 I wish to thank Professor Clif Perry, the editors of *Public Affairs Quarterly*, and George Childress for the help I received from them in the preparation of this paper. I am, of course, fully responsible for the use I made of this help.

◆ ◆ ◆ ◆ ◆

RICHARD L. LIPPKE

Justice and Insider Trading

Long illegal in the United States, insider trading in securities markets is increasingly being legally proscribed in European and Asian countries. France led the way in prohibiting insider trading, outlawing it in 1970, but the United Kingdom, Italy, Sweden,

Norway, Spain, Greece, and others have since followed suit.[1] Pressure from the European Community has recently forced Germany to enact laws against such trading, and even Japan and Hong Kong have taken steps to limit its occurrence in their formerly wide-open securities markets.[2]

Meanwhile, the morality of insider trading remains a hotly contested topic in a variety of scholarly journals. Many scholars enthusiastically defend it, and some, while not wholeheartedly defending it, seek to debunk the many arguments against it. The focus of this paper will be on the fairness arguments against insider trading. The underlying idea behind these arguments is that to permit insider trading would be to set up stock market trading rules that are unfair to non-insiders, individuals who do not possess or have access to the sorts of materials, non-public information that insiders do. These arguments have been widely discussed. I will lay bare the largely unstated assumptions about fairness behind these discussions and then attempt to show that these assumptions yield, at best, a truncated conception of justice. At worst, these assumptions legitimise, without argument, the political and economic *status quo* in countries with large inequalities. I argue that a defensible treatment of the fairness of insider trading requires both a complete conception of justice and its thoughtful application to existing political and economic institutions.

The discussion is in three main sections. In the first, I summarise the fairness debate about insider trading as that debate has been presented in the recent scholarly literature. In the second section, I reveal the assumptions about fairness implicit in that debate and argue that these assumptions cannot be defended independently of a larger conception of justice. In the third section, I briefly summarise and then use an egalitarian conception of justice to analyse insider trading. By doing so, I hope to illustrate how a more systematic approach to the analysis of insider trading one that invokes a complete theory of justice, transforms the debate about the fairness

of insider trading. I should add that the conception I employ is one that most commentators would find unappealing. However, one of the points I wish to make is that their discussions do little more than beg the question against such a conception.

Before proceeding farther, let me clarify two matters. First, the insiders with which I will most concern myself throughout the paper are corporate managers. They are the individuals most likely to have inside information, and as such, their actions are the principal focus of most discussions of the fairness of insider trading. I won't say much about the other individuals who might come to possess inside information, referred to in the literature as tippees and misappropriators.[3] Second, I will use the term "non-insiders" to refer to those individuals who do not possess any inside information relevant to a particular stock purchase or sale. Non-insiders might be insiders with regard to some stock transactions. And, of course, non-insiders might be and often are corporate employees.

I

As long as insider trading is legally proscribed, there is a fairly simple argument that shows how its existence is unfair to non-insiders.[4] Insiders who trade on material, non-public information, rather than disclosing the information or abstaining from trading as the rules typically prescribe, will be doing little more than cheating. They will be acting in a manner that violates the social expectations fostered by the rules. It is not convincing to argue, as some do, that since non-insiders "know" insider trading takes place, they realise that the official (legal) rules are not the actual rules; therefore their participation in the investing game must condone insider actions. First, it is likely that not all non-insiders know that insider trading takes place or how frequently it occurs. Second, the fact that insider trading is legally prohibited and socially disapproved surely muddies the waters for those who maintain that non-insiders "know" it occurs. At best, non-insiders may be confused about how insiders actually behave. At worst, they may assume that most insiders will abstain from trading or disclose material information.

The more interesting question is whether, morally speaking, insider trading should be legally proscribed. In particular, is there something unfair about such trading such that it ought to be a legitimate target of state action? Now the debate begins in earnest.

The most plausible case to be made that there is something unfair about insider trading emphasises the notion of "equal access to information."[5] It seems a mistake to hold that all parties to a market transaction must have equal information. To require this would be, in effect, to deprive persons of informational advantages they may have acquired through diligent effort. What seems bothersome about insider trading is that non-insiders lack *access* to the information on which insiders are trading. The informational advantage that insiders have is not "erodable" by the diligence or effort of non-insiders. No matter how carefully or exhaustively non-insiders study the available public information about firms in which they invest, they cannot really compete against those insiders who have access to material non-public information.[6]

A typical scenario described by opponents of insider trading is as follows: insiders know of an impending takeover bid for another firm by their firm. In anticipation of the rise in stock prices that usually results from such bids, they purchase shares of the target firm's stock. Often, such insider trading activity will send the target firm's stock price up slightly. Non-insiders who hold stock in the target firm, believing there is no plausible reason for the rise in the share price, may decide to cash in by selling their stock. Though the non-insiders were able to sell their stock at a higher price than they would have received had the insiders not been active, opponents of insider trading argue that the non-insiders lose out on the further gains that typically result once a takeover bid

is publicly announced. Non-insiders, because they lacked access to the information about the takeover bid prior to the public announcement, lose out on the opportunity to receive the additional gain.[7] Instead, the gain goes to insiders and this, opponents argue, is unfair to the non-insider.

Some commentators argue that insider trading is not likely to result in such losses (or unrealised gains) for non-insiders.[8] Yet none of these arguments seems to address the equal access objection head on. It seems likely that there will be some occasions where non-insiders do sell in response to a price rise caused by insider trading activity. The fact that this may not necessarily happen or happen often seems beside the point. If insider trading is legally permitted, non-insiders can reasonably complain that the rules are set up in ways that are unjustifiably advantageous to insiders and so likely to the disadvantage of non-insiders. The possibility that the informational advantages insiders have and might use work out to the advantage of non-insiders does not explain why insiders should be allowed to have and use those advantages.[9]

Frank Easterbrook and Jennifer Moore contend that non-insiders really cannot justifiably complain that they do (or did) not have equal access to this information.[10] Non-insiders could have made career choices to become corporate executives, choices that would have given them access to inside information. Such information is, on this view, one of the perquisites of being a corporate insider. Moore draws an analogy. Plumbers have access to certain kinds of information that non-plumbers do not have (or to which they have more difficult access). Yet, no one complains when plumbers use their informational advantages to their own benefit by charging non-plumbers for their services. Similarly, non-insiders should not complain when insiders use informational advantages to their benefit. Easterbrook maintains that the different costs of access to information are simply a function of the division of labour: "A manager (or a physician) always knows more than a shareholder (or patient) in some respects, but unless there is something unethical about the division of labour, the difference is not unfair."[11]

This is a dubious argument for a number of reasons. Critics of insider trading who rely on the equal access argument clearly have in mind a different point of equal access than the one proffered by Moore and Easterbrook. The critics have in mind equal access via the typical ways in which corporations make information about themselves matters of public record—press releases, trade journals, reports to shareholders, etc. They might argue that there is a great deal of difference between saying that non-insiders should have researched their investment decisions more carefully and saying that non-insiders should have made different career choices.

Still, Easterbrook and Moore may simply be challenging the critics' conception of equal access and offering a substitute. However, there are problems with this substitute. What the non-insiders need is not simply the sort of knowledge that comes with the career choice of becoming a corporate manager. After all, some non-insiders (with respect to particular trades) might indeed be corporate managers and so they presumably have that kind of knowledge. Non-insiders need the specific information insiders have enabling them to deal on the stock market with an advantage over others. The claim that non-insiders cannot reasonably complain about the fairness of particular transactions because they too "could" have chosen to become corporate managers is not to the point. It is not insiders' career skills that non-insiders need but the insiders' information about particular business events.[12]

Also, the informational advantages insiders have over non-insiders have no clear analogue in the case of plumbers and non-plumbers. What non-plumbers pay plumbers for is plumbers' knowledge about plumbing. What shareholders pay managers for is managers' knowledge about managing. But plumbers do not seem to have an additional way of gaining an advantage over non-plumbers as do insiders in

relation to non-insiders if insider trading is permitted. Insiders are already being compensated for their labour by the shareholders. Insider trading would give them something extra. If that something extra is "taken" without the shareholders' knowledge and consent, then it seems that the shareholders would have two different grounds for complaint. They could complain about their lack of equal access to information, or they could complain that the managers who take advantage of them via insider trades are failing to live up to their fiduciary responsibilities, which are to promote shareholder interests.

Still, both grounds for complaint can be undermined *if* insider trading is authorised by the shareholders. In effect, the shareholders would give their consent to an arrangement whereby corporate managers would be allowed, under certain conditions, to take advantage of their superior access to information.[13] Remember, we are no longer assuming that insider trading is illegal. Instead, we are trying to determine what set of rules regarding insider trading would be fair to all interested parties. Advocates of insider trading contend that it should be up to the shareholders to decide whether insider trading is to be permitted. After all, the information that is being traded on is their property. They should be allowed to determine how this information will best be put to use.

This leads to the question of why the shareholders would ever agree to permit managers to take advantage of the information to which they are privy, especially when the resultant trades might lead to losses (or failures to gain) by shareholders. Also, why would potential investors in a company purchase shares if they knew that the company permitted insider trading? Wouldn't investors be inclined to steer clear of such firms?

The boldest response to these questions is provided by Henry Manne and his followers.[14] Manne argues that if firms allowed insider trading as part of the management compensation package, this would enable them to attract managers who are likely to be more creative, productive, risk-takers. Allowing managers to trade on inside information would provide them the incentive to undertake riskier ventures, try out innovative production techniques, develop new products or services—in general, to engage in those activities that would create more value, in the long run, for the shareholders. Insider trading would allow these managers to reap the benefits of the new information they create and firms would save money by having to pay managers less base compensation. Of course, shareholders would not know precisely when insiders of their own firm were trading based on material non-public information, so shareholders might occasionally lose out in trades where insiders are involved. However, this is something the shareholders might consent to in the hopes of finding managers who will increase the long-term value of their shares.[15]

Consistent with Manne's argument, others have suggested that as long as a firm's rules about insider trading are a matter of public record, individuals who invest in such firms will have voluntarily assumed the risk of trading in situations where insiders may be operating. Indeed, some argue that investors will react to this prospect by altering their own behaviour. They may try to compensate for the possibility of future losses to insiders by paying less for stocks initially.[16] Or, when they see a stock's price rising, anticipating that insiders may know something, they may demand a higher price to induce them to sell. Moreover, most investors seek to reduce their risks by diversifying their stock portfolios. As Kenneth Scott points out, such investors will be less interested in the details of the buying and selling of particular stocks than in the overall performance of their portfolios.[17]

This general line of argument is both limited in its scope and has been subjected to withering criticism by various commentators. Its scope is limited because it seems to justify insider trading only by those employees who have a role in creating the information. It would not justify such trading by tip-

pees or misappropriators. Also, some have suggested that since insiders can profitably trade on negative information, the shareholders would have to be careful to limit any incentives for managers to create such information.[18] Criticisms of the argument have focused on whether there are not other, more effective ways shareholders might use to provide incentives to managers to create value; on whether there are ways to ensure that managers do not derive "too much" compensation from insider trading; and on whether managers themselves are likely to find the prospect of cashing in on inside information attractive enough to agree to compensation packages that permit such trading.[19]

As Easterbrook and Shaw both note, it is no easy task to weigh all of the pros and cons that have been unearthed by the various commentators.[20] In large part, this is due to the debate turning on the answers to a variety of empirical questions about the effects of firms permitting insider trading versus the effects of their not doing so—questions about which we have little evidence to go on. In any case, there seems a great deal to be said at this point for allowing shareholders to experiment with permitting insider trading if that is what they so desire. After all, it is their property, and the costs and benefits to third parties seem pretty speculative at this point. Investors who wish to steer clear of firms that permit forms of insider trading will presumably be able to do so, at least as long as corporate policies on the subject are made clear. In short, the debate about whether insider trading is fair seems to have been transformed into one about what it is reasonable for shareholders and their hired managers to negotiate amongst themselves.

II

In the preceding section, I explicated the logic of the fairness debate about insider trading as that debate has been recently carried on by scholars in various fields. In this section, I will highlight the assumptions about fairness that seem implicit in that debate and show how they are, if not problematic, at least controversial.

The place to begin is by noting that none of the commentators referred to in the previous section raises any questions about the fairness of the distribution of wealth, income, opportunities, and power that is the broader social context for decisions about what the rules regarding insider trading will be. Their discussions are simply divorced from the larger and more difficult questions that have been raised by moral and political theorists about the nature of social justice. They are also divorced from the implications the various theories offered have for an analysis of existing political and economic institutions. The existing distribution of property and other goods is taken as given and so, implicitly at least, legitimised.

One point at which this assumption of the legitimacy of the *status quo* is most clearly revealed is in Moore and Easterbrook's contention that non-insiders do have access to inside information at the point when they make their career choices. As we saw, this is a poor argument as a response to the equal access objection to insider trading. It is also an argument that seems rife with assumptions about the justice of the political and economic system in which people in countries like the United States live. I say "seems rife" because it is not altogether clear what Moore or Easterbrook are assuming. Are they assuming, for instance, that no questions of fairness can be raised about the existing division of labour which distributes income, wealth, opportunities, and prestige in certain ways? Or, are they assuming that all people's career paths are, in a meaningful sense, matters of choice, such that coal miners could just as easily have "chosen" to be lawyers or investment bankers? Are they assuming that everyone in society has equal access to insider information, at least at the point at which they "choose" their careers?

Again, it is not apparent which, if any, of these assumptions Moore or Easterbrook are making,

though their willingness to defend insider trading by invoking the division of labour and the career choices with which it presents individuals certainly suggests that they do not see anything problematic about either notion. If so, their assumptions are obviously at odds with the views of welfare liberals and radical egalitarians about the justice of institutions that tolerate significant disparities in people's income, wealth, and life-prospects. Moore and Easterbrook's underlying assumptions about justice or fairness seem quite controversial given the current state of discussion of these matters by moral and political theorists.

However, since their argument is of scant value in the debate about insider trading perhaps we should turn our attention to the argument that seems to command more respect. That argument holds that as long as insider trading is consented to by the shareholders, there is nothing unfair about the unequal access to information had by insiders. It might seem that such a notion is not in the least controversial, that regardless of one's theory of justice, one will endorse the idea that these sorts of transactions between people are paradigms of fairness. What could be more fair than an informed exchange between parties none of whom is in any way forced to participate in the exchange or accept terms they find unreasonable? Doesn't this show that we can separate the debate about insider trading from the larger, more contentious debates about social justice?

Not really. I suspect that the notion of "voluntary informed consent" will play some important role in almost any plausible theory of justice. However, part of what distinguishes theories of justice is that they say very different things about the conditions that must be satisfied if a voluntary exchange is to be regarded as fully fair. Judgments about the fairness of particular transactions between or among persons are, I would argue, always defeasible in light of judgments about the extent to which the relevant conditions are satisfied. For moderate egalitarians like John Rawls, the focus will be on the extent to which the basic structure of the society in question satisfies his two principles of justice, especially the Difference Principle.[21] To the extent that the two principles are not satisfied, judgments about the fairness of particular transactions between or among persons are problematic. Moderate egalitarians like Rawls will emphasise that exchanges between parties vastly unequal in bargaining power (owing to wealth or social status) are likely to be fair in only a qualified sense even if they involve no overt deception or force.

In contrast, for libertarians, the conditions that must be satisfied if a voluntary informed exchange between persons is to be deemed just are less structural and more historical in character.[22] To the extent that a particular distribution of property holdings came about in ways that violate libertarian principles of property acquisition and transfer, reference to the fairness of voluntary informed exchanges among individuals whose holdings depend on that distribution is problematic. For instance, suppose that recently released slaves, individuals who have been forcibly deprived of the fruits of their labour, reach wage-labour agreements with their comparatively wealthy former owners, the terms of which greatly favour the former owners. Even libertarians might acknowledge that because of the historical conditions leading up to them, these wage-labour agreements are not paradigms of fairness.

Now, if it is true that judgments about the fairness of voluntary informed exchanges amongst persons cannot meaningfully be separated from theory-dependent judgments about the extent to which certain other conditions are satisfied, what implications does this have for the debate about the fairness of insider trading? It is not that those who have written about insider trading all seem to favour one larger theory of justice over another, or that they do so without really arguing for their preferred theory. It is rather that none of them appears to be operating with any such theory at all—or if they are, it is one that rather simply implies that the social and economic *status quo*

in countries like the United States is unproblematically just. I know of no plausible theory that implies this. My hunch is that the commentators wish to avoid delving into the difficulties that discussions of these larger theories of justice inevitably raise. Yet, by avoiding these difficulties, they deprive themselves of the sort of theoretical framework which can alone make an analysis and evaluation of insider trading maximally well-grounded and coherent.[23]

In the next section, I will show how an analysis of insider trading grounded in a larger theory of justice might look. I hope this will further develop and illuminate the points I have made in this section.

III

Egalitarian theories of justice are a diverse lot, ranging from the moderate types like that of Rawls to the more radical types like that of Kai Nielsen.[24] All however, share certain features, the most important of which for our purposes I will briefly summarise.

First, egalitarian theories generally hold that inequalities in things like income, wealth, power, opportunities, the social conditions for self-respect, etc., ought to be limited. Egalitarians are concerned that people's life-prospects should not differ too significantly along these dimensions affected by humanly alterable institutions and practices. Inequalities can be constrained by the designing of political and economic institutions that maintain certain structural features in society. For instance, while egalitarians may believe competitive markets can play important roles in a just society, they are reluctant to let markets wholly determine the distribution of goods like income and opportunities. Hence, they will favour state involvement in ensuring for all persons not only traditional civil liberties but also goods like subsistence, education and medical care. Or, to take another example, egalitarians are likely to be concerned about the ways in which social and economic power can be exercised to the detriment of some people's interests. Thus, they are likely to favour rather strict limits on the extent to which wealth can be transferred between generations and on the extent to influence democratic political decisions. Also, some egalitarians favour extending democratic decision-making structures into the economic sphere. This would entail the institutionalisation of schemes of worker participation, if not control.

Obviously, the preceding depiction of egalitarianism rather brutally oversimplifies it and leaves a great deal of the conception unexplained and undefended. However, I think it will serve to introduce an egalitarian analysis of insider trading.

First, egalitarians would attempt to gauge the extent to which the basic institutional structures of societies accord with their favoured principles of justice. Obviously, different egalitarians will employ slightly different principles, and even among egalitarians who are in rough agreement about principles of justice, there will be room for disagreement about what these principles imply about the justice of actual societies. In any case, I think it is fair to say that most egalitarians would be greatly dismayed by the distribution of income, wealth, opportunities, and power in many advanced capitalist societies.[25]

Consider the United States, for instance. The existence of significant segments of the population that cannot satisfy their basic needs for subsistence and health care; of large disparities in access to quality education and meaningful work; the ability of those with wealth and economic power to exercise inordinate political and cultural power; and the evidence that the gap between rich and poor is growing, with many in the middle class slipping into poverty, would, for egalitarians, be among the most disturbing features of US society.[26]

Second, egalitarians might note that both corporate insiders and shareholders are likely to be among the most advantaged members of advanced capitalist societies. Corporate executives, those most likely to be in a position to have access to inside information, are handsomely paid and enjoy other perquisites such as prestigious work, power over others, and access to political influence. Those who invest in stocks, corporate executives among them, are also likely to be quite well off. Recent studies of wealth in the US, for instance, suggest that approximately 80% of families own no stocks.[27] These studies also suggest that about 95% of all stocks are owned by families with incomes of more than $96,000 per year—that is, by about 3% of all families. Thus, those who are in the top income-bracket are also those able to invest in stocks and accumulate even more wealth.

Egalitarians will note the many attendant effects of this concentration of stock ownership, and with it, legal control of corporations. Though actual control over the day-to-day operations of corporations is typically ceded to hired managers, these managers will generally seek to advance the shareholders' interests. Historically, managements' attempts to do this have resulted in "costs" being passed onto other members of society. For instance, corporations have often sought to evade or weaken environmental regulations with the result that the costs of pollution, hazardous wastes, and the depletion of scarce resources fall on those with less economic power and influence (including members of future generations). Or, to take another example, corporations have often resisted attempts to provide employees with clear and safer working environments because doing so would increase costs of production. The result, however, is that employees then bear greater costs owing to the resulting injuries and illnesses.

Supporters of the current scheme of property rights might respond by saying that corporations are answerable to a much broader constituency than the shareholders. First, they must conform to laws and regulations that are directly or indirectly, democratically enacted. These laws and regulations constrain corporate decision-making in ways that make it more conducive to the interests of all in society. Second, corporations are answerable to the public in other ways. They must produce goods and services that the public is willing to buy—that is, they must be responsive to consumer "votes." Also, corporations are vulnerable to consumer boycotts if their actions are perceived by many as socially irresponsible. The fact that such boycotts are rare suggests that corporations are generally perceived as acting in the interests of all members of society. Finally, supporters of the *status quo* will argue that the stock market performs an invaluable service to society, generating capital funds for businesses that provide jobs and goods and services for many people.

Let me indicate, briefly, what I believe would be the egalitarian response to this line of argument. First, they would repeat their concerns about the extent to which wealth and economic power influence democratic decision-making in advanced capitalist societies. This influence significantly dilutes the actual democratic control that ordinary citizens have over large corporations, arguably to the detriment of those citizens. Second, they will argue that it is naive to think that corporations simply respond to consumer "votes." Instead, they actively seek to shape consumer attitudes, preferences, and values through massive persuasive advertising. It is at least an open question whether the resulting consumer "votes" reflect consumers' autonomous beliefs and preferences (those they would have if the conditions for critical reflection on them were not undermined by massive persuasive advertising) or whether they reflect the economic interests of large corporations. Also, corporations are very active in their efforts to shape public perceptions about their character and conduct as economic enterprises. It is no easy matter for the average consumer to get accurate information about the actual conduct of large corporations, even assuming that the average consumer had the time or inclination to engage in the monitoring of corporate conduct. Last, while the current scheme of stock ownership does generate investment funds for economic enterprises, the point of the egalitarian critique of that scheme is to raise the question whether there might be a more desirable alternative scheme. In particular, might there be a scheme that does not rest on and so reflect the influence of con-

siderable inequality, one that would generate investment funds in ways that better advance the interests of *all* members of society?

In the light of the preceding discussion, it might be suggested that egalitarians would view the debate over insider trading as one of little significance—that the "negotiations" between management and shareholders that proponents of insider trading favour are little more than ways for unjustly advantaged members of society to determine how best to divide, or perhaps increase, the spoils of their advantages.

However, it seems to me that egalitarians could offer more than this to the insider trading debate. They could point out that most who have written about insider trading simply presuppose that those most directly affected by the rules about insider trading are managers and shareholders. Occasionally, in discussions of insider trading, reference is made to its broader effects on the efficiency of the market. But typically, the focus of most analyses is on the motivations, interests, expectations, and behaviour of managers and shareholders. Yet this leaves out of the reckoning how other interests are potentially affected by whatever agreements are reached by managers and shareholders. In particular, employees of corporations, especially those not in the top managerial classes, may be affected by those agreements.

For instance, suppose that the shareholders are convinced by Manne's arguments that insider trading will offer valuable incentives to managers to be less risk-averse and so they agree to allow managers to take advantage of the information they "create" through their activities by engaging in insider trading. There are risks here, to be sure, for the shareholders, for their less risk-averse managers may undertake ventures that ultimately cost the shareholders money. Still, the shareholders, at least, take this chance with their eyes open. But what of the other employees of the corporation who lose their jobs or have their wages and benefits cut when the inevitable belt-tightening occurs as a result of failed ventures? Or, to take another possible scenario, what of the employees who lose their jobs or have them downgraded when top management decides to "create value" by taking over another company only then to cut the target's labour costs by eliminating mid-level management positions? These examples make clear that what top managers and shareholders negotiate with regard to insider trading can affect other members of the organisation, not to mention members of the surrounding communities. Less risk-averse managers may be a boon to the shareholders, but not necessarily to other employees or members of society.

Perhaps the interests of other employees are ignored in the debate over insider trading because analysts simply assume that another, independent set of negotiations takes place between corporations and their non-executive employees. Corporations that permit insider trading by their top-level managers could make this clear to other prospective employees, and the latter could be understood to give their consent to the risks involved by agreeing to work for the corporation. Or perhaps most analysts are simply assuming that whatever the negative effects on employees due to the incentives created by insider trading, they are, in principle, no different from the ones that might occur because of other ways of compensating top-level managers. All compensation schemes for top-level managers may contain incentives that lead to decisions that adversely affect certain other employees. What is the difference, it might be asked, between top-level decisions to close plants based on the usual profit-considerations and decisions to lay off employees due to risky ventures (spurred by the lure of insider trading profits) gone sour?

Neither assumption is likely to be seen as defensible from an egalitarian perspective. Egalitarians will regard the claim that employees "consent" to whatever rules corporations have about insider trading (and so to the decision that may adversely affect them resulting from those rules) as insensitive to the lack of bargaining power most employees find themselves with in relation to large corporations. The inability of prospective employees to do any-

thing but simply accept what the shareholders and managers have negotiated will be seen as especially severe where the alternatives to gainful employment are few and unattractive. Most workers are not as mobile as shareholders who can easily take their investments elsewhere if they do not like the rules regarding insider trading that corporations adopt. Also, if many corporations decide to permit insider trading, the options open to many workers will be greatly limited.

Moreover, it seems that most analysts are simply assuming that employees are to have no say in whether the businesses for which they work permit insider trading. The claim that the possible negative effects of corporate policies permitting insider trading are no different from other policies designed to keep businesses operating efficiently, and at a profit, rests on this assumption. The traditional powers and prerogatives that go with the ownership of property in many advanced capitalist societies are thereby simply reaffirmed. Yet many egalitarians regard the current distribution of power in the workplace as deeply suspect morally because it fails to affirm the autonomy of workers and results in business decisions that fail to advance impartially the interests of all affected. To assume the legitimacy of this distribution without argument is simply question-begging.[28]

It may seem that discussion in the preceding section strays quite a way from the simpler question about the fairness of insider trading with which we began this paper. However, the point I have attempted to make throughout this paper, illustrated in the preceding section, is precisely that the simpler question is too simple. It presupposes that we can intelligently discuss what the rules for insider trading should be independent of a discussion of the broader principles of justice that should be adopted and the extent to which existing institutions realise those principles. If my argument is correct, it points the discussion away from the simple question about the fairness of insider trading to the more complex and contested questions discussed by theorists of social justice. Current analysis of the fairness of insider trading simply begs all of these questions, and to that extent are philosophically facile.

NOTES

1 Pierre Lemieux, "Exporting the Insider Trading Scandal," *The Wall Street Journal*, October 13, 1992.

2 For developments in Germany, see "Behind the Times," *The Economist*, July 13, 1991, 86; for developments in Japan, see "Over to the Men in Uniform," *The Economist*, May 19, 1990, 91-92; for developments in Hong Kong, see Michael Taylor, "Lifting the Veil," *Far Eastern Economic Review*, November 28, 1991, 634.

3 Tippees are individuals who are typically not corporate employees but who are given inside information by corporate employees. Misappropriators are individuals who are typically not corporate managers but who come across inside information (e.g., financial printers temporarily employed by corporations).

4 For a useful summary of the legal status of insider trading in the United States, see Bill Shaw, "Shareholder Authorized Inside Trading: A Legal and Moral Analysis," *Journal of Business Ethics* Vol. 9.12 (1990): 913-28.

5 Victor Brudney was one of the first to articulate the equal access argument. See his "Insiders, Outsiders and Informational Advantages under the Federal Securities Laws," *Harvard Law Review*, Vol. 93 (1979): 322-76.

6 Also, Patricia Werhane argues that if we value competition on the assumption that it will lead to the most socially beneficial results, then we should favour those rules which promote more vigorous competition. If we allow insiders to trade on their informational edge, competition will be systematically diminished because non-insiders will predictably lose out to insiders. See her "The Ethics of Insider Trading," in this volume.

7 Cf. Richard DeGeorge, "Ethics and the Financial Community," in Oliver Williams, Frank Reilly, and John Houck, *Ethics and the Investment Industry* (Savage, MD: Rowman and Littlefield, 1989), 203.

8 For instance, Jennifer Moore argues that insider trading can sometimes actually benefit non-insiders by enabling them to avoid losses, and so is not systematically harmful to non-insiders. See her "What is Really Unethical about Insider Trading?" *Journal of Business Ethics*, Vol. 9 (1990): 171-82. For arguments that insider trading is not likely to harm non-insiders, see Deryl W. Martin and Jeffrey H. Peterson, "Insider Trading Revisited," *Journal of Business Ethics*, Vol. 10 (1991): 57-61.

9 Bill Shaw points out that the current rules with regard to insider trading already give insiders an edge in relation to non-insiders. If nothing else, insiders with material, non-public information know when not to trade, and the disclose-or-abstain rule permits this. See his "Shareholder Authorized Inside Trading: A Legal and Moral Analysis," 916. Still, allowing insiders to trade on such information might tilt things even more in their favour, so the equal access argument could be modified to say that insiders should not be given any more advantages than they already have.

10 Frank H. Easterbrook, "Insider Trading, Secret Agents, Evidentiary Privileges, and the Production of Information," *Supreme Court Review* (1981): 309-65, especially 323-30. Moore, "What Is Unethical About Insider Trading?" 172-74.

11 Easterbrook, "Insider Trading, Secret Agents, Evidentiary Privileges, and the Production of Information," 330.

12 Indeed, the reason why tippees, free riders, and misappropriators can make use of inside information to their advantage is precisely that its usefulness has little to do with having made the

career choice to become a corporate manager. Such information is thoroughly "detachable" from the division of labour.

13 For the most explicit presentation of the shareholder authorisation argument, see Shaw, "Shareholder Authorized Inside Trading: A Legal and Moral Analysis," 920-21.

14 Henry G. Manne, *Insider Trading and the Stock Market* (New York: The Free Press, 1966); see also Dennis W. Carlton and Daniel R. Fischel, "The Regulation of Insider Trading," *Stanford Law Review*, Vol. 35 (May 1983): 857-95.

15 In response to Werhane's argument that insider trading undermines competition (*supra* note 6), Manne might argue that permitting it may reduce competitiveness in one area but heighten it in others. The market for corporate managers will heat up as firms that permit insider trading compete for those individuals who will take more risks and be more innovative. Also, within firms, allowing managers to profit from insider trading may spur them to try to outdo one another so that they can trade on any information "created."

16 See Kenneth E. Scott, "Insider Trading: Rule 10b-50. Disclosure and Corporate Privacy," *The Journal of Legal Studies*, Vol. 9 (1980): 801-18.

17 Ibid., 809.

18 Negative information might include such things as news of an impending major lawsuit against the corporation, news of poor earnings, or news of a product failure.

19 There is also considerable speculation about the effects of insider trading on the efficiency of the stock market. However, the concern with efficiency is different from the concern with fairness.

20 Easterbrook, "Insider Trading, Secret Agents, Evidentiary Privileges, and the Production of Information," 338, see also his "Insider Trading as an Agency Problem," in John W. Pratt and Richard J. Zeckhauser, *Principals and Agents:*

The Structure of Business (Boston Harvard Business School Press, 1985) 81-100; Shaw, "Shareholder Authorized Inside Trading: A Legal and Moral Analysis," 921-22.

21 John Rawls, *A Theory of Justice* (Cambridge, MA: Harvard University Press, 1971). See also his essay "The Basic Structure as Subject," in Alvin I. Goldman and Jaegwon Kim, *Values and Morals* (Boston: D. Reidel, 1978): 47-71.

22 Cf. Robert Nozick, *Anarchy, State and Utopia* (New Basic Books, 1974).

23 For more on the tendency of those who write about business ethics to avoid the problems raised by competing theories of justice, see my "A Critique of Business Ethics," *Business Ethics Quarterly*, Vol. 1 (October 1991): 367-84.

24 Rawls, *A Theory of Justice*; Kai Nielson, *Equality and Liberty: A Defense of Radical Egalitarianism* (Totowa, NJ: Rowman and Allanheld, 1984).

25 Of course advanced capitalist societies differ from one another in some of their structural features. Any egalitarian analysis will have to take these differences into account in assessing the impact of various insider trading rules.

26 On the last point, in particular, see Denny Braun, *The Rich Get Richer* (Chicago: Nelson-Hall Publishers, 1991), 137-97.

27 See the three wealth studies analysed by Richard T. Curtin, F. Thomas Juste and James N. Morgan, "Survey Estimates of Wealth: An Assessment of Quality," in Robert E. Lipsey and Helen Stone Tice, *The Measurement of Saving Investment, and Wealth* (Chicago: The University of Chicago Press, 1989): 473-548.

28 Of course, this extension of democratic decision-making into the economic sphere that many egalitarians favour may seem unattractive if divorced from the other collateral changes urged by egalitarians. These changes will include better education for many workers, along with the enforcement of due process and the protection of free speech in the workplace.

EARNINGS AND ETHICS: THINKING ABOUT ENRON

DANIEL J. WIRTH

Case Description

In 1985, Kenneth Lay founded Enron Corporation in Omaha, Nebraska. At a later date, its corporate headquarters was relocated to Houston, Texas. As a public corporation in the energy industry Enron employed approximately 21,000 workers by the end of 2001, and was the seventh largest company in the United States. It claimed to have earned $101 billion in profits in 2000, and enjoyed a reputation of stability and financial success in the business sector.

Such a reputation included earning the title of "America's Most Innovative Company" by Fortune magazine from 1996 to 2001, and a place on the magazine's list of "100 Best Companies to Work for in America" in 2000. Enron's profits in the stock market also enhanced this reputation. The corporation repeatedly garnered substantial financial earnings, and in 2000 its stock soared to a selling price of $85 per share. By all appearances Enron was a thriving business, and its future prospects looked promising in the eyes of its investors and employees.

Enron stunned the global market by filing for bankruptcy in the end of 2001, however, amid controversy of its accounting practices. Investigations into the matter led to allegations of fraud, where Enron exaggerated its earnings in reports, and simultaneously buried its debts and losses in an assortment of subsidiary partnerships known as the Raptors. Until this time the general public had little reason to doubt Enron's reported financial transactions and success. Now, however, questions are being asked regarding the appropriateness of removing expenses from a parent company's ledgers to that of its subsidiary to generate a more optimistic picture of the parent company's success. Enron's chief executive officers Kenneth Lay and Jeffrey Skilling went to trial in answer to the above charge in January 2006. The trial is still underway at the time of this study.

Enron's actual financial performance in 2000 was poor, in contrast to what was reported. This was due, in part, to high risk ventures that did not perform as well as expected. Such monetary losses amounted to millions of dollars in US currency, and affected investors and Enron employees alike. Company executives are paying back investors, but Enron's employees are not as fortunate. Since Enron stock was hit hard by the controversy, Enron employee benefits dependent on the company's stock were completely exhausted. Thus all employee retirement savings via the company's 401k program were lost, and apart from litigation such monies will not be restored.

Enron still manages some of its accounts until the company can be divided into smaller organizations in the industry. About 300 people are in its current employ.

Ethical Analysis

One feature that is essential to understanding what is at stake in the Enron case is to recognize what a subsidiary partnership is and how these are typically used by corporations. Subsidiary partnerships, or Special Purpose Entities (SPEs), are a type of fund or trust that is created by a parent company with an aim toward starting a new type of business venture. Such trusts allow the company to pursue these new business ventures with minimal risk attached. That is, if the new project does not work out financially, and the trust is drained, this will not jeopardize the parent company's financial status, because the very nature of SPEs prevents this. One advantage of such a financial entity, then, is to encourage a business's growth and development into new areas of industry.

Such financial ingenuity has other benefits as well. By creating a SPE, the parent company can gain a loan at a lower interest rate from a lender via a SPE, than the parent company could obtain through the lender otherwise. For the newly created SPE will have no debt from the parent company, enabling it to secure the loan. SPEs also afford a parent corporation the option of legitimately removing its debts and losses from its reports to its subsidiary accounts, and avoid reports that would show a decrease in earnings. Such moves appear to be in accordance with Generally Accepted Accounting Principles, (GAAP), which are a standard set of reporting rules for companies to follow.[1]

Enron used SPEs to both boost earnings in reports and remove its debts and losses, making the crux of the issue whether or not ailing financial corporations should be able to use such accounting methods to make their numbers appear more attractive to investors than they might actually be. One element worth noting is that by using SPEs in this manner a company like Enron acquires an unfair market advantage over that of its competitors. This lack of candour in not reporting its earnings and losses in a more straightforward fashion gives a false impression of the company's performance, by making it appear more successful than it actually is. Considering that investors are interested in thriving companies that generate profit, Enron would draw out more hopeful investors with money to spend and gain more earnings than its competitors through this technique.

Also instructive is considering the other side of the issue. One of the commonly touted reasons for entering business is to make a profit. Surely there are times when a lack of candour is called for in such an industry. This is not uncommon. For example, one's resume will often include achievements and highlight one's skills. No one would seriously consider mentioning one's weaknesses and failures on such a document. The expectation is to advertise in a fashion that would aid your objective: in this case getting the applied-for position. It may be that Enron's use of SPEs is not much different than another company's sale pitch, but simply uses its numbers to make its point.

Study Questions

1. Imagine that the public never discovered Enron's reporting technique. Let's also say that Enron was able to pay off all its losses and debts through this strategy, and make a substantial profit. Would such a strategy be a moral course of action? Why or why not?

2. When is candour expected in the business world, and when is it not? Are there other occasions outside of one's job when one would not want to be candid with others? When? How does this dynamic change in relation to those closest to you?

3. Would your opinion of Enron change if it retracted its earlier reports and fully disclosed its financial gains and losses while at the height of its popularity and purported earnings? Does changing the timing of this disclosure change the morality of the situation? If so, how?

4. In what ways is Enron's use of SPEs similar to forms of advertising? In what ways is it not? Why or why not?

NOTE

1 Holtzman, Mark P., Elizabeth Venuti, and Robert Fonfeder, "Enron and the Raptors," *CPA Journal* (2006). April 19, 2006 <http://www.nysscpa.org/cpajournal/2003/0403/features/fo42403.htm>. See also Byrnes, Tracy, "Special-Purpose Entities Are Often a Clever Way to Raise Debt Levels," (February 21, 2002.) April 19, 2006 <http://pages.stern.nyu.edu/~adamodar/New_Home_Page/articles/specpurpentity.htm>. Note also that these sources differ as to the appropriateness of Enron's actions in light of GAAP standards.

UNIT 2

Engineering Ethics

BRENNAN JACOBY

Engineering Ethics

The primary role of an engineer is to design and build mechanical and stationary products. Because these products will be used by many people, his work affects the health, safety and welfare of the public at large. This can be seen in the engineering of airplanes, elevators, cars and other products that, in the event of a malfunction, may be detrimental to those making use of them. Due to the important role of the engineer in society there is a level of trust that the public must have in an engineer. Like physicians, engineers possess expert knowledge not easily critiqued by laypersons.

Unlike doctors, however, not all engineers are required to be certified, or belong to an engineering society with a code of ethics in order to practice engineering. Even in those situations where engineering work does in fact require proper licensing, unlicensed non-professional engineers may still work on those projects. As a result, the public may be left to trust not only the soundness of a professional engineer's work, but also the integrity of the non-professional engineers associated with him.

If employers, clients, and the public are to trust the work of an engineer, on what grounds are they to base such trust? A code of ethics for engineers might suffice as a foundation for trust, but what might such a code look like? One possibility is to rely on the National Society of Professional Engineers (NSPE), which has its own code of ethics. Two concerns arise regarding such codes.

First, as stated above, an engineer is not obligated to be a member of a society like NSPE in order to practice engineering. As a result, any guidance given by a society like the NSPE may not be heeded by all engineers. Second, most codes of ethics held by such societies are limited. In many cases, since these codes are based on consensus, the resulting code ends up being only that to which everyone would

agree. While such agreement can be beneficial, in many cases the result is only a general (as opposed to extremely specific) rule. General rules can only offer guidance, so engineers are often left without mandates in particular cases. In addition, many codes of this sort do not impose sanctions on those who violate their terms.

A broad code also fails frequently to take account of new issues as they arise. For example, current codes of ethics for engineers offer little guidance regarding issues of environmental concern. A beneficial ethical code would be one that is not only broad, and agreed upon by most engineers, but is also capable of accommodating evolving concerns.

It is also the case that principles gleaned from multiple codes may conflict. What is an engineer to do in a case where his responsibility to his client and his responsibility to the health and well-being of the individuals that will use his product conflict? As an illustration, consider the case of the space shuttle *Challenger*.

The night before the January 28, 1986 launch, engineers from engineering firm Morton Thiokol held a teleconference with the Marshall Space Center. Concern was expressed regarding the ability of O-rings to seal properly. Failure of the O-rings to seal would mean a leakage of hot gases resulting in a fatal explosion. A no-launch recommendation was given.[1]

Roger Boisjoly, the chief engineer of the O-rings used on the Challenger, had warned of potential problems more than a year previous, and continued to warn. But safety was not the only concern. If the launch was delayed it would not bode well for the relationship between Morton Thiokol and the National Aeronautics and Space Administration (NASA).

While there was a break in the teleconference, senior vice-president of Morton Thiokol, Gerald Mason, told the supervising engineer Robert Lund, "Take off your engineering hat and put on your management hat."[2] The no-launch recommendation was reversed and, despite Boisjoly's best attempts to stop the launch, on January 27, 1986, the space shuttle *Challenger* launched. Seventy-three seconds into launch the shuttle exploded taking the lives of all on board.[3] Situations like those presented in the case of the *Challenger* raise many questions: when is one justified in blowing the whistle? how is one's role as an engineer related to one's role as a manager? to whom is one primarily responsible: one's company, the company's clients, the end users, or the public in general? to name a few.

In the series of essays that follow, issues concerning the role of engineers as professionals and responsible members of society, as well as the situations that confront them—such as whistle blowing and conflicts of interest—will be assessed.

NOTES

1 Harris, Charles E. Jr., Michael S. Pritchard, and Michael J. Robins. *Engineering Ethics: Concepts and Cases*, 3rd ed. (Belmont, CA: Wadsworth, 2005) 1-3.

2 Rogers Commission, Report to the President by the Presidential Commission on the Space Shuttle Challenger Accident, June 6, 1986 (Washington, DC), 772-73.

3 Harris et al., 1-3.

THE MORAL FOUNDATIONS OF ENGINEERING

MICHAEL DAVIS

Is There a Profession of Engineering?

I do not take up the question of engineering's status as a profession because I doubt there is a profession of engineering. Instead, I take up the question because those who have maintained that engineering is not a profession seem to rely on one of two methods of defining "profession"—"conceptualism" and "sociology"—causing unnecessary confusion among those who do practical ethics. Doubt about the professional status of engineering has more to do with these methods than with any important difference between engineering and the "traditional," "classic," or "true" professions (law, medicine, and so on). The way to dispose of doubts about engineering's status as a profession is to describe, defend, and apply a better method of defining profession. I shall do that here—after explaining what is wrong with the other two methods.

We may distinguish three reasons often given for saying that engineering falls short of a "true profession": 1) that engineering lacks an ideal internal to its practice; 2) that engineering's ideal, whether internal or not, is merely technical (rather than intrinsically good or rational); and 3) that engineering lacks the social arrangements characteristic of a true profession (such as universal licensure). I shall consider these three in order. A fourth reason often given for denying that engineering is a profession is that engineers generally lack the control of work or occupational autonomy characteristic of true professionals. I shall not address that fourth reason here in part because it falls outside the scope of this paper, but in part too because I have, I think, already shown that the empirical evidence so far leaves open the question whether engineers have more, less, or the same control or autonomy as such true professions as law or medicine.[1]

I. Engineering as a "Pseudo-Profession"

Timo Airaksinen, a Finnish philosopher, offers a good example of the first argument I want to consider: Medicine, which everyone agrees is a profession, clearly has a distinctive aim, health. This aim is, he claims, distinctive not because other occupations (such as politics or engineering) are not also concerned with it, but for two other reasons. First, medicine *defines* health: "without medicine, we are not ill. We just suffer and die."[2] Second, medicine itself is inconceivable without health as its object. So, for example, "if a doctor works to undermine health, she does not work as a doctor but as an impostor and charlatan."[3] In these two respects, medicine's aim, the ideal it serves, is internal to its practice. The connection between health and doctoring is not a mere consequence of social decision or historical accident but of relations among concepts.

Engineering's ideal of service, Airaksinen continues, lacks this conceptual relation to engineering. Suppose, for example, that the engineers' ideal of service is "using their knowledge and skill for the enhancement of human welfare," a description of their work common to many codes of engineering ethics. Such an ideal fails to be internal to engineering in either way in which health, according to Airaksinen, is internal to medicine. First, engineering does not define human welfare in the way medicine defines health. To some degree, each of us defines human welfare for himself; to a large degree, we do it together through public debate, legislation, judicial decision, and administrative ruling, processes in which engineers have only a small part. Second, even if engineering did define human welfare for its own practice in the way medicine defines health, we could point to engineers who ignore human welfare in their work, for example, the engineers who designed the Nazis' gas chambers.[4] Unlike the doctor who pays no attention to health, such an engineer, however reprehensible, is not obviously an impostor or charlatan. To any charge that he is an impostor or charlatan, he could answer that his work embodies the knowledge and skill characteristic of engineering. He has served his client well—and that is enough to be a good engineer, if not a good person. So, Airaksinen concludes:

> any attempt to introduce internal values and ideals into engineering is bound to fail. Engineering and similar pseudo-professions are technical by nature. They deal with methods by means of which the client/employer can realize his own values [rather than with methods designed to achieve values—like health—internal to the profession itself].[5]

What is wrong with this argument? Every discussion of what constitutes a profession begins—at least implicitly but often explicitly—with a list of clear cases, the "traditional," "classic," or "true" professions. Naturally, which professions make it onto the initial list can affect the analysis of professions and, in consequence, which occupations will be recognized as professions (strictly so called). The initial list can vary a good deal. For example, while Michael Bayles lists lawyers, physicians, engineers, and accountants,[6] Daryl Koehn lists medicine, law, and the clergy.[7] Airaksinen's list differs from both: along with the perennials, law and medicine, his includes two rather controversial items, teaching and social work.[8] We need not now ask why teaching and social work are on his list: the reason will appear soon enough. For now, what is important is that Airaksinen's list includes "law"—by which, I assume, he means lawyering.[9]

The reason Airaksinen's inclusion of law among the traditional professions is important is that lawyers do not, as far as I can see, stand in the same relation to justice, even to legal justice, as (according to Airaksinen) doctors stand to health. First, in no country does the legal profession as such define legal justice, much less justice as such. Legislatures, courts, and administrative bodies have a large part. Most of what lawyers do is present evidence and arguments to such bodies, prepare documents for use in such bodies, advise clients what to expect of such bodies, and so on. Second, a lawyer who, without breaking the law herself, gets her clients what they want, ignoring considerations of (legal) justice, seems no more an impostor or charlatan than do the engineers who designed the Nazis' gas chambers. Generally, we reserve the terms "impostor" and "charlatan" for those whose practice routinely falls well short of what they promise, whether through incompetence or malice. That is not our objection to either the Nazi engineer or the lawyer indifferent to justice.

To admit that law is only a pseudo-profession would reduce Airaksinen's list of traditional professions to medicine, teaching, and social work, a sufficiently eccentric ensemble to put in doubt any analysis relying on it.

To save the status of law as a profession, Airaksinen would, it seems, have to revise the profession of law to include judges, administrators, and others who help to define legal justice. Such a revision seems hard to justify. Even in the United States, not all judges or administrators are lawyers. In some countries, such as Switzerland, most are not. To combine into one legal profession those learned in the law and those who are not, simply because all have a part in defining legal justice, would be to give theoretical passion precedence over common sense. It would certainly ignore the almost universal view that part of what distinguishes lawyers from non-lawyers is being learned in the law.

Of course, we can see at least two related reasons why Airaksinen might want to combine lawyering with judicial and administrative adjudication to form one omnibus profession of law. First, judges do seem to stand in the appropriate relationship to justice. A judge who ignores legal justice certainly does seem an impostor or charlatan—in part, no doubt, because claiming to be a judge invites others to expect (legal) justice to be the guiding concern. So, if each profession must have its own distinctive

rational ideal, one different from all others, lawyers can have justice as their ideal only if they belong to the same profession as judges. Second, the separation of lawyering and adjudication is what makes it possible for a lawyer to ignore legal justice without seeming an impostor or charlatan. If every lawyer were as such also a judge, an "officer of the court" in an extraordinary sense, a lawyer who ignored considerations of justice would also seem an impostor or charlatan. The problem for Airaksinen is that we do not seem to understand lawyering in this way. If we do not understand lawyering in this way, lawyering cannot be the profession seeking justice or defining it.

Behind Airaksinen's claim that engineering is only a pseudo-profession seems to be a methodological assumption concerning what professions must be, their essence or defining concept. We may state it:

> *Conceptualist Assumption 1*: A profession is defined by its end. Each profession must have a single distinct end, one internal to its practice. Any other relation to its end would make the "profession" (as a matter of logical truth) a mere pseudo-profession. The number of such ends is the same as the number of professions.

This assumption cannot derive from any list of traditional professions—or, at least, any list that, for the sake of plausibility, includes law. What then can it derive from?

Something like it has a long history, one going back at least to Plato. Its appeal has, I think, always been theoretical. Indeed, only the blinding light of theory could make plausible Airaksinen's treatment even of medicine (which, of course, is the foundation of his treatment of engineering). Airaksinen can claim that medicine defines health only by collapsing a great many actual professions (kinds of "doctors") into one omnibus profession of medicine. Such collapsing cannot rest on observation. In the United

States, for example, the term "medical profession" (or "profession of medicine") refers to medical doctors, that is, physicians (and surgeons), those who, holding an M.D., are eligible for full membership in the American Medical Association (AMA). In addition to such doctors, we have dentists (D.D.S.), podiatrists (D.P.M.), osteopaths (D.O.), optometrists (D.O.), naprapaths (D.N.), chiropractors (D.C.), public health officers (D.P.H.), and psychologists (Ph.D.)—not to mention nurses, physical therapists, occupational therapists, acupuncturists, homeopaths, Christian Science practitioners, and other healers who do not claim the title "doctor." Health remains a contested concept over which physicians have nothing approaching a monopoly.

Once we descend from the heaven of concepts to the hurly-burly of practice, we will also notice "doctors" who, though not serving "health," do not seem to be impostors or charlatans. Consider, for example, those (medical) doctors who do cosmetic surgery. They may, for example, reconstruct a face not because it is broken but because, though healthy, it can be made "more beautiful." Such beautification may weaken the underlying bone, rendering it more susceptible to fracture and so, it seems, less healthy; yet, we do not consider doctors doing such surgery to be impostors or charlatans. We recognize them as skilled doctors working in a recognized medical specialty, doing more or less what they advertise.[10]

I have more to say about "conceptualism." But I must first consider another argument against engineering's status as a profession.

II. Lack of a Rational Ideal

By "rational ideal," I mean an end that, all else equal, we may rationally pursue for its own sake, that is, without anything more in view. Among rational ideals are health, justice, and knowledge. So, for example, to tell me truthfully that if I do X, I will become more healthy, knowledgeable, or just is to give me a (good) reason to do X. I may

rationally do X for that reason—unless other reasons weigh against it. Health, knowledge, or justice is "reason enough" to do what otherwise I would have no reason to do.

Each of Airaksinen's "traditional professions" seeks to serve a rational ideal: medicine serves health, law serves justice, teaching serves knowledge, and social work serves welfare (where "welfare" means something like "happiness" or "prosperity"). Since social work is too new an occupation to count as a "traditional profession" on any historically informed account of professions, what seems to explain its presence on Airaksinen's list is the ideal served. That ideal, welfare, certainly belongs on any list of traditional rational ideals.[11] For Airaksinen, then, social work's status as a "traditional profession" must be a matter of logic, not history or social fact, a deduction from the ideal served.[12]

What about engineering? One might, according to Airaksinen, restate engineering's ideal of service as "good control over the artificial environment, where 'good' means safe, healthy, and welfare promoting."[13] Though engineers will probably want to tinker a bit with this characterization of their ideal to emphasize positive human benefit, we may accept it now for purposes of argument.

Good control of the artificial environment is not, according to Airaksinen, a rational ideal in the way health, justice, knowledge, and welfare are. To see why, he asks us to consider two practical syllogisms. The first concerns medicine:

1. I believe the only way to stay healthy is to do X.
2. I want to stay healthy.
3. So, I do X.

The other concerns engineering:

1. I believe that the only way to build a bridge is to do Y.
2. I want to build a bridge.
3. So, I do Y.

Airaksinen observes:

> The second syllogism is different [from the first]. One can easily deny the second premise, since there is nothing compelling in it, simply because neither a bridge nor bridge building are value notions [sic].... Though we need a reason to build a bridge, we need no reason for being healthy.[14]

The fallacy in this argument is stunning. The second syllogism is not the closest engineering analogue of the first. While health is the aim of medicine, bridge building is not—even on Airaksinen's own account—the aim of engineering. Good control over the artificial environment is. So, the closest engineering analogue of the first syllogism is:

1. I believe that the only way to have good control over the artificial environment is to do Y.
2. I want to have good control over the artificial environment.
3. So, I do Y.

Rewritten in this way, the second syllogism is no longer so different from the first. We can no longer "easily deny the second premise." "Good control over the artificial environment" *is* a "value notion," that is, a rational ideal.

That disposes of Airaksinen's argument as stated but not of the underlying insight. Control over the artificial environment is *not* a rational ideal in the way health, justice, knowledge, and even welfare are. Control as such can be rationally undesirable. Think, for example, of the undisciplined control of the Sorcerer's apprentice. Health, justice, knowledge, and perhaps welfare, in contrast, cannot be bad in that way. So, for example, bad health is not health at all. Control over the artificial environment becomes a rational ideal only when it is "good," that is, when it serves safety, health, welfare, or some other rational ideal. In this respect, engineering's ideal, even if rational, is *technical* (that is, necessarily a means to another rational ideal) rather than *in-trinsically* rational (that is, rational without reference to another rational ideal). That much seems plain. What follows?

The technical nature of engineering's ideal of service does distinguish engineering from medicine, teaching, and social work—but not from law. What lawyers aim at is, it seems, not legal justice but (something like) providing clients with good control over their legal environment—where "good" implies taking reasonable account of the safety, health, and welfare of others. Law's ideal of service is as much a technical ideal as engineering's. So, the question is not whether engineering differs from medicine in this respect, but what that difference has to do with engineering's status as a true profession. Again, it seems to me, Airaksinen must fall back on a conceptualist assumption, though not the same one as before. The new assumption is:

> *Conceptualist Assumption 2*: Professions serve a rational ideal directly, not by serving some ideal having only an instrumental connection with a rational ideal.

Why accept this assumption? Although he does not say, I think we know what Airaksinen would or, at least, should say: The point of any definition of profession is to distinguish those occupations that are professions from those that are not. If we limit professions to those occupations defined by an intrinsic (rational) ideal, we get a relatively short list corresponding roughly to what we would expect. But, once we let in technical ideals, the list becomes unduly long. So, for example, insofar as the aim of barbers is to provide good haircuts, where "good" takes into account safety, health, and welfare, barbering would be a profession—by definition. The same would be true of almost any other honest occupation from plumbing to garbage collection, from sales to salad-making. Better to exclude engineering from the list of professions than to destroy the utility of the term "profession" by admitting every honest occupation.

That, it seems to me, is a good reason to accept Assumption 2—if one adopts the method of conceptualism. But why adopt that method?

III. Conceptualism's Appeal

Airaksinen's conceptualism rests on a certain understanding of the relation of philosophy to professional ethics. Airaksinen distinguishes three approaches to professional ethics (and related social policy). One, the sociological, I shall take up in the next section. The second, "the textbook approach," focuses on specific questions of professional ethics, for example: should the doctor perform an abortion in the case of a very young girl who has been raped? The textbook approach attempts to answer such questions using moral theories: utilitarianism, Kantianism, and so on. Moral theories can, according to the textbook approach, be applied to professional decisions and policies just as we apply them to human action generally. Such theories provide the foundation of professional ethics, though at the cost of making professional ethics a theoretically uninteresting corner of ordinary morality. For the textbook approach, membership in a profession is not an important ingredient in professional ethics.[15]

The third approach, Airaksinen's own, is a "broader philosophical view" that opens up the possibility of "criticizing the professions in a non-foundationalist manner."[16] What is that broader approach? It consists in recognizing that:

> professions serve values which are simple and objective and possess scientific expertise. Of such values one wants to say only that they are as objective as socially possible. This much one must say because professions are justifiable in social life. It is part and parcel of their social existence that their service ideals cannot be questioned. Their life is a good one by definition.[17]

In other words, to describe an occupation as a profession is to compliment it, to say that it is "good," on at least one of two dimensions. One dimension is competence ("scientific expertise"). To describe anyone as, for example, a "true professional" is at least to say that she is not only learned but skilled in the appropriate respect—and likely to exercise that skill effectively. That is certainly a compliment. The other dimension of compliment is moral (or, at least, normative).[18] To describe someone as a "true professional" may as well, or instead, compliment her for serving some good which, being "simple and objective," virtually everyone recognizes as worthy of pursuit—"ideals [the serving of which] cannot be questioned." According to Airaksinen, professions are, by definition, the pursuit of an ideal worthy of pursuit. Hence, professions are "justifiable in social life" (as much so as any social activity can be); justification is part of the very concept of profession. A social arrangement that cannot be justified cannot be a profession.

Understanding professions in this way, a philosopher can, Airaksinen claims, deal with textbook problems—like the propriety of a doctor's giving an abortion to a young girl who has been raped—without recourse to moral theory. One need only compare the particular act or practice in question with the rational ideal embodied in the profession. So, presumably, if the abortion serves health, it is professionally proper for a doctor to do the abortion. If not, it is not. Of course, difficulties may arise in working out the concept of health enough to decide whether the pregnancy as such, or its connection with rape, threatens health, and whether the fetus constitutes an independent entity whose health can be injured by abortion and must therefore be brought into the analysis.[19] But such difficulties will not daunt philosophers. Philosophers can, Airaksinen believes, do the required *conceptual* analysis without going into *moral* theory, though they may have to bring in a good deal of empirical science.

The textbook approach begins with moral theory, a nest of controversies from which few practical questions have ever emerged resolved. The advantage conceptualism has over the textbook approach is that it offers a relatively uncontroversial starting point, that is, the rational ideal integral to the profession in question. The ultimate appeal of conceptualism, then, is that, without recourse to moral theory, it gives philosophers an "Archimedean point" from which to study professional ethics, to advise concerning particular ethical problems of professionals, and to offer arguments for revising professional practice.

IV. Sociological Approach

My criticism of Airaksinen's argument has, at several crucial points, relied on the sort of information sociologists provide, for example, information about the various kinds of "doctor." That reliance may seem to commit me to sociology as the alternative to Airaksinen's conceptualism. It does not, for two reasons.

The first reason I share with Airaksinen. As he says, sociology "as an empirical social science is not well equipped to handle ... normative problems."[20] Sociology can tell us what people think and do, indeed, even what they think they should think or do, but *not* what they *should* think or *should* do. If, as Airaksinen and I agree, "profession" is a normative concept, one defining in part what certain people, members of the professions, should do, sociology is not likely to tell us what a profession is (though it certainly can tell us what people think it is or should be).

The other reason to reject the sociological approach is that it leads to the same conclusion conceptualism does—that engineering is not a profession—though by a somewhat different, if equally dubious, route. Consider a typical sociological treatment of engineering's status as a profession. Robert Zussman, an American social scientist, begins a discussion of engineering's professional status—much as Airaksinen does—by noting that "the most prominent and fully developed examples of professional-

ization are medicine and law."[21] Zussman's reason for considering these two "the most fully developed" professions nonetheless differs from Airaksinen's. Instead of pointing to the ideals law and medicine serve, Zussman points to ends lawyers and physicians seek. Lawyers and physicians have sought "the right to practice in specified areas ... limited by statute to graduates of certain schools, [they have also sought] the monopolistic right to offer medical or legal services for a fee ... and even the right to use occupational titles [restricted to those who are] full members."[22] Seeking these ends is part of a "collective mobility project"—a way to raise income and status—which has gone by the name "professionalization." Hence, achieving these ends is part of becoming a profession. Law and medicine are professions because they have been largely successful at achieving these ends. Engineering has not been nearly so successful at that. Hence, Zussman concludes, "[engineering] is not a profession, at least not in the sense of medicine and law."[23]

Zussman never asks why a monopoly on providing services for a fee should make an occupation a profession—or even how it could contribute to the "process of professionalization." He does not fail to ask that because the answer is obvious. After all, barbers have such a monopoly on barbering, but no one supposes barbering a profession (in the sense medicine and law are) or pointing to its monopoly a compliment. Only sociologists and those relying on them even think a barbers' monopoly, where it exists, to be evidence of their approach to professional status.

There are two other oddities of Zussman's approach to professions worth noting. First, Zussman has nothing to say about the service ideal of which both Airaksinen and members of professions make so much (and which does seem to invite compliment). He seems to observe professions much as entomologists observe bugs, working as if the professions' own understanding of what professions are did not exist. Second, Zussman does not consider the significance of his own hedge "at least … in the sense of medicine and law." What other senses are there? Might any of them be better for determining professional status, even for medicine and law?[24] These are important questions for at least two reasons.

First, in Canada, Mexico, most of Europe, and indeed much of the rest of the world, engineers do have a monopoly much like that lawyers (and barbers) have in the United States. Though Zussman never says so explicitly, except in the title of his book, his description of engineering's professional status is almost entirely a description of engineers in the US—as Airaksinen's is not.

Second, if monopoly is necessary for an occupation to be a profession, then—in the United States—lawyers are much closer to having a profession than physicians are. Except for a few specialized areas such as patent law, lawyers really do have a monopoly on doing legal work for pay. Not only do physicians have no monopoly on calling themselves "doctor" (though, not surprisingly, they do have a monopoly on "medical doctor" just as engineers have on "professional engineer"), they also have no monopoly on performing surgery or prescribing medicine. Physicians must share the entire domain of their practice with osteopaths and parts of it with podiatrists, nurse practitioners, occupational therapists, midwives, and other "health-care professionals." How odd that sociology's treatment of medicine as an exemplary profession should ignore such facts, facts tending to undercut its own judgment that engineering is not a profession "in the sense of medicine"![25]

A sociological definition tends to be a list of factors brought together by historical accident or social prejudice, a heap without any internal order. The finding of sociology that engineering is not a profession is simply the result of poking about in such a heap. Forced to choose between Airaksinen's conceptualism and the sociological approach to professions, many philosophers (and engineers) might choose conceptualism without a second thought. To dispose of conceptualism, we must have an alternative, one clearly better than the three—textbookism, conceptualism, and sociology—among which Airaksinen chooses. It is to such an alternative I now turn.

V. Professions without an Archimedean Point

Archimedes is supposed to have said that, with a bar long enough and strong enough and a place to stand, he could move the earth. He understood that finding "the Archimedean point," the appropriate place to stand, is not all there is to making practical the theoretician's dream of moving the earth. One must also have a bar long enough and strong enough (and a suitable fulcrum on which to set it).

In practice, we could not move the earth even if we could find a place to stand. We would still need a bar many times longer than the earth's diameter—and, given the strength of materials, many times the earth's mass. In practice, we must restrict our leveraging to relatively small objects with relatively short bars. Those who, like Airaksinen, hope to find in conceptualism's heaven of concepts an "Archimedean point" from which to move mundane ethical problems closer to solution seem to have overlooked the problem of finding a philosophical lever long enough to reach the earth of practice and strong enough to bear the weight of argument. The approach I shall now sketch and sketchily defend avoids this problem of conceptualism by working much closer to practice. The concept of profession it develops is, like sociology's, historically conditioned, but not, as sociology's is supposed to be, historically given.

My approach should be familiar to philosophers. I carry on a "conversation" in which I offer a definition to those who know a profession first hand, "practitioners." In part, I carry on this "conversation" metaphorically, that is, by examining what professionals write about themselves. In part, though, I do it more or less literally by, for example, presenting the definition to colleagues in professional schools in engineering, law, and so on, by reading papers at meetings of professionals to see how they react, and by giving invited talks where members of one profession or another predominate. The practitioners may reject the definition but they must state their reasons. I revise the definition trying to take those reasons into account. I offer the revised definition. The process continues until we get a definition there is no good reason to reject. The definition must meet my (philosopher's) standards of clarity, precision, informativeness, comportment with common sense, fitness for use, and so on, as well as theirs. Here is the definition of profession that this approach has so far yielded:

> A profession is a number of individuals in the same occupation voluntarily organized to earn a living by openly serving a certain moral ideal in a morally-permissible way beyond what law, market, and morality would otherwise require.[26]

This definition has, I believe, at least five advantages over definitions that sociology or conceptualism have so far produced. First, it seems to fit what most professionals (or, at least, my sample of them) now think about their own profession. Second, this definition helps us to understand the relatively high opinion we have of professions as such, as the sociological definition does not. Third, it can help us understand the criticism we make of actual professions, and of particular members of a profession as members of that profession. Fourth, it provides a plausible framework for explaining the empirical relationship between profession and professional monopoly—without making monopoly a criterion of profession. And last, and most important here, the definition will allow us to explain why engineering is plainly a profession in just the sense law and medicine are. I shall now show that the definition does all that, taking up its interrelated elements more or less in order.

Professions have a number of members. There is no profession of one. Though this may seem a small point, it is one with which conceptualists have trouble.[27] For them, a member of a profession, a professional, is the historical actualization of a concept, an agent serving a certain rational ideal. Nothing in the concept guarantees that there will ever be more than one actualization of the ideal.[28]

Each profession engages in an occupation. An occupation is a "full time" activity, one typically taking up (most of) the working day. Each occupation is distinguished from all others by exercise of a certain more or less coherent body of knowledge, skill, and judgment maintained through use. For me, an occupation is, as such, a morally permissible activity—though a few occupations, such as theft or smuggling, are not. For conceptualism, many seemingly morally permissible occupations are mere charlatanism unless professionalized.

Conceptualism can distinguish between profession and underlying occupation, but only in a way leading to a distinctly different judgment of the moral status of the unprofessionalized part of many occupations. For conceptualism, what a profession and the underlying occupation can share is knowledge, skill, and judgment applied to the same range of services. What distinguishes a profession from the underlying occupation is that the profession serves the appropriate rational ideal while others in the same occupation do not. But, according to conceptualism (or, at least, Airaksinen's version of it), a member of a certain occupation (say, a doctor) who does not try to serve the profession's rational ideal (health) is a charlatan or impostor. Conceptualism seems to rule out the possibility that one may honestly engage in an occupation capable of professionalization without being a professional. On my analysis, in contrast, there need be nothing wrong with an occupation capable of professionalization declining to professionalize.

Professions are voluntary in two respects. First, there is no requirement that any occupation be a profession. Becoming a profession is one morally permissible option; doing no more than what law, market, and morality demand is another. Second, individual members of a profession both join and remain in the profession voluntarily. Indeed, one must claim membership—whether by seeking a license to practice the profession, by applying for a job calling for a member of that profession (for example, "engineer"), or just by declaring oneself a member of that profession (for example, "I am an engineer"). One can also leave a profession simply by giving up the license if there is one, withdrawing from practice, and ceasing to claim membership. (The voluntariness of professions is, as we shall see, crucial for explaining the special moral obligations—the ethics—of professionals.)

Professions are organizations. One is not a member of a profession, "a professional," just because one claims to be. One must also meet certain minimum standards of competence and conduct that the group treats as a condition of membership. Professions vary in degree of organization. Some have formal tests for admission, licensing bodies, disciplinary committees, and the like. Most have schools from which would-be members should graduate, a written code of ethics, and various associations speaking for the profession in certain contexts. All recognize a distinction between those who, in virtue of competence and conduct, belong to the profession and those who, falling short in some important way, do not belong though they claim to ("charlatans," "impostors," "quacks," "shysters," "frauds," "pettifoggers," and so on).

Professions are a way to earn a living. There is no profession of amateurs.[29] A profession differs from an ordinary business in being for persons in a single occupation (or, at least, in a family of occupations sharing much the same knowledge, skill, and judgment). A profession differs from a trade association, union, or other occupational organization in having as its (primary) purpose something beyond benefiting its members.[30] A profession differs from both

businesses and occupational organizations in being designed (primarily) to serve a certain moral ideal. Physicians, for example, have organized to serve health (or, at least, to cure the sick, comfort the dying, and help preserve the health of those who are well). Professions differ from charities, mutual assistance societies, and other altruistic organizations that also serve a moral ideal in being concerned with how members earn their living. In this respect, professions do resemble mere business or occupational organizations.[31]

What is a *moral ideal?* A moral ideal may be simple (health) or complex (cure the sick, comfort the dying, and preserve the health of those who are well). The "moral" in "moral ideal" is meant to exclude both such immoral ideals as the perfect crime and such non-moral ideals as art for art's sake. A moral ideal is moral both in the minimal sense of being morally permissible to pursue—as, for example, the perfect crime is not—and in the stronger sense of being morally good to pursue, that is, its pursuit tends to support morally right conduct—as art for art's sake does not. But a moral ideal is also moral in a stronger sense. A moral ideal is a state of affairs which, though not morally required, is one that everyone (that is, every rational person at his rational best) wants pursued, wanting that so much as to be willing to reward, assist, or at least praise its pursuit if that were the price for others to do the same. If we think of morality as consisting of those standards of conduct everyone wants everyone else to follow even if that means having to do the same, then morality gives us a reason to support by reward, assistance, or at least praise anyone pursuing a moral ideal.

Because moral ideals have this moral claim on us and each profession, by definition, serves a moral ideal, professions are, by definition, morally praiseworthy, that is, activities we always have good moral reason to praise. The relationship between moral ideals and (what we have called) rational ideals is therefore tricky. On the one hand, a moral ideal is necessarily a rational ideal, whether intrinsic or technical. We always have good reason to pursue a moral ideal because achieving it would be morally good. That cannot be said of all rational ideals. Prudence is an example of a rational ideal of which this cannot be said. Prudence certainly is a rational ideal. That an act is prudent is, all else equal, reason enough to do it.[32] But a prudent act does not deserve the reward, assistance, or even praise an act in pursuit of a moral ideal does. It does not, in part, because we do not have the same pressing reasons to encourage prudence in our enemies that we have to encourage morality in them.[33] Because rational ideals are not necessarily moral ideals, there can be no profession serving a mere rational ideal.

How Airaksinen formulates a rational ideal is therefore quite important to whether what he calls a profession can be one in the sense I have given "profession." For example, health understood merely as one's own health is a rational ideal but not a moral one. To be a moral ideal, health must be understood as a state of affairs we all share in, "public health." So, if there is to be a profession serving health, it will have to aim at everyone's health, not just at the health of some individuals, its patients. Insofar as it in fact focuses its efforts on individual patients, as medicine does, a profession of health will have to do that as part of a strategy for serving everyone's health, that is, as a "public service." Only seeking to serve everyone's health will deserve the moral praise, assistance, and rewards appropriate to a profession. For this reason. I think, the Preamble to the AMA's Principles of Medical Ethics explicitly recognizes a "responsibility not only to patients, but also to society," a recognition that led the AMA to call for legislation restricting handguns, to condemn smoking, and to take other stands for public health.[34]

Each profession has a certain way of carrying on its occupation, one defined in part by standards beyond what law, market, and morality would otherwise demand. Physicians, for example, have special standards governing everything from how to make an incision to how to deal with a conflict of interest. The primary purpose of these standards (considered as a unit) is to offer the public some benefit or protection beyond what law, market, and morality ordinarily require.[35] These standards differ from profession to profession. So, for example, while engineers have undertaken to use their distinctive knowledge, skill, and judgment in ways that hold the public health, safety, and welfare paramount, lawyers have not. Lawyers give something like that priority to client and court.

Professional standards are always morally permissible. Morality rules out professionalizing certain occupations. A "profession of thieves" is no more a profession than play-money is money.[36] Insofar as moral theories differ concerning what is morally permissible, they will differ concerning what can be a profession. Indeed, the relation between moral theory and profession is closer than that. A profession must set standards beyond what law, market, and (ordinary) morality require. Any moral theory that makes (ordinary) morality too demanding, leaving few, if any, acts optional, will make professions, in my sense, impossible.[37] That a moral theory did that would, I believe, be a good reason to reject the theory, not a good reason to reject either my definition or the possibility of (true) professions.

Professions may, then, be distinguished from one another in at least one of three ways. They may differ in underlying occupation, as engineering and medicine do; in moral ideal, as medicine and osteopathy do, osteopaths claiming to be "more wholistic" in their approach to health; or in the way they seek to achieve the same ideal, as psychiatry and clinical psychology do, for example, by requiring different training.

If "ethics" is understood as special, morally-binding standards of conduct, then a profession's distinctive way of carrying on its occupation, or at least the standards articulating it, constitute the profession's ethics.[38] But why should the standards of a profession be morally binding when, by definition, they go beyond what morality ordinarily requires, that is, beyond what morality requires of those who do not voluntarily join a profession? The standards may be morally binding (in part) because the members of the profession take an oath (as lawyers do). An oath can convert acts otherwise morally optional into acts morally required.

In general, however, a profession's standards are morally binding, when they are, for another reason. They constitute a practice benefiting those who participate in it, the members of the profession. The benefit consists in part at least in being able to carry on one's occupation in a way not possible at all, or not possible at so low a cost, without the cooperation of other members of the profession. The benefit may come to each member insofar as, for example, other members of the profession build the profession's reputation by meeting the profession's standards. Because one is a member of that profession, each can count on an initial level of trust beyond what law, market, and morality would otherwise grant. Who would claim to be an engineer if engineers were thought to be no better at what they do, or no more to be trusted, than a mere technician, scientist, or manager? Those who *voluntarily* claim such benefits without satisfying the standards that generate them, act unfairly. They take advantage of those who do their share of helping to maintain the public trust in the profession's "brand name." Their conduct is therefore (at least prima facie) morally wrong in much the way cheating at cards is.[39]

So, ethics, that is, moral obligations beyond the ordinary, though not explicit in my definition of profession, is implicit in it, deducible from certain elements of the definition together with certain ordinary moral rules. We may, then, divide the third way of distinguishing one profession from another in two. One, the technical, would distinguish professions sharing a moral ideal by differences in standards of training, theories of treatment, specific methods, and other matters of mere competence. So, for example, if one organization of doctors considered "medically indicated" some important treat-

ments another considered "quackery," the two would be different professions. The other way to distinguish professions sharing a common ideal is ethical: they have different codes of ethics. So, for example, Canadian lawyers belong to a different profession than American lawyers insofar as they are subject to a different code of ethics.

To be a member of a profession is to be subject to a set of special, morally-binding standards beyond what law, market, and morality (otherwise) demand. To act as a member of a profession is openly to carry on one's occupation according to those higher standards—for example, to declare by word and deed, "I work as an engineer [that is, as engineers are supposed to work]." There is no "profession" without such professing.

To declare that one will carry on one's occupation by a higher standard than law, market, and morality otherwise demand is, of course, morally praiseworthy, in the way any morally good resolution is. Actually to carry on one's occupation in accordance with one's declaration is morally praiseworthy too, in the way doing one's duty is. But such potential praise has its price. The professional whose deeds fall short of her profession's standards is open to moral criticism she would not be open to had she not declared her commitment to those standards. To be a professional is to be open to a range of moral criticism to which a non-professional doing identical work is not. A member of a profession must satisfy a higher standard than a mere practitioner of the underlying occupation just to do what she is supposed to do.

Having compared members of a profession and mere practitioners of the underlying occupation, a society may conclude that it will be better off if practice of that occupation is restricted to members of the profession. Members of a profession may also properly urge that practice of their occupation be so restricted if they believe that the public will be better off if practice is so restricted. Whether the public will be better off depends on a number of

considerations, not least of which is the sophistication and bargaining power of those who must hire
or otherwise choose practitioners of that sort. So, for
example, the large companies that employ most engineers seem in a much better position to protect
themselves from the incompetent, the indifferent,
and the dishonest than the lawyer's client or doctor's
patient typically is. Because licensing as such is a social expense—that is, an administrative burden and
a restriction of liberty—there is always a presumption against it. Licensing is justified, when it is, because the society benefits overall from imposing its
own controls on practice. Such benefits have little
bearing on what is or is not a profession.[40]

If we re-examine what Airaksinen and Zussman
said, we shall find nothing suggesting that engineering fails to satisfy the definition of profession offered
here. Engineers constitute a number of individuals
in a single occupation (engineering) voluntarily
organized to earn their living by openly serving a
certain moral ideal—in Airaksinen's formulation,
"good control of the artificial environment"—in a
morally-permissible way beyond what law, market,
and morality would otherwise demand, that is, according to engineering's special standards, including
its code of ethics.[41]

VI. Nazi Engineers?

We can now test our definition against that apparent
counter-example to engineering's status as a profession, the Nazi engineer. Our definition suggests five
versions of the example. On none is the existence
of such an engineer inconsistent with there being a
profession of engineering.

First, the Nazi engineer, though undoubtedly
sharing an occupation with other engineers, may not
be a member of their profession. He may belong to
a time or place where there is no profession of engineering. Where that is so (Germany, 1942), those
having the characteristic knowledge, skill, and judgment of engineers may simply work as individuals

subject only to law, market, and ordinary morality.
Our definition of profession makes the existence of
a profession a matter of history, one depending on
whether members of an occupation voluntarily organized themselves in a specific way. That engineers
sometimes somewhere do not so organize themselves
does not mean engineering cannot be a profession,
only that it is not then and there a profession. Professionalism is relative to time and place, even if ordinary morality is not.

Second, the Nazi engineer may belong to an
organization of engineers committed to carrying
on their common occupation by standards beyond
what law, market, and morality would otherwise demand. The problem may be that those standards require conduct which is morally impermissible, for
example, following government orders even if that
means contributing relatively directly to murder of
large numbers of innocent people. A "profession" that
requires morally impermissible conduct is no more
a profession (strictly speaking) than play-money is
money. The existence of such a "profession" would
show only that an organized occupation can claim to
be a profession and yet not be. It does not show that
engineering cannot be a profession.

Third, the organization of engineers to which the
Nazi engineer belongs may have morally permissible
standards of conduct but standards silent concerning the conduct of concern here. In that case, the
engineer will be a member of an engineering profession.[42] That the profession's code of ethics does not
forbid such a serious misuse of engineering reveals
a substantial hole in the code. But the existence of
such a hole does not turn what would otherwise be a
profession into a "pseudo-profession." All codes have
holes; many have substantial holes. Such holes are
consistent with profession (as I have defined it)—in
part at least because the existence of such a hole provides no moral justification for the engineer's conduct. The engineer's conduct is morally wrong, code
or no code; morality is not relative, even though professional ethics is. All the hole does is protect the en-

gineer from having his conduct also condemned as unprofessional, a violation of his profession's ethics.

Fourth, the Nazi engineer may belong to a profession having standards that forbid his conduct. He would, then, have acted unprofessionally. He might, however, disagree with the official interpretation of the code.[43] He might, for example, defend his work on the gas chambers as serving human welfare, that is, human welfare as Nazis define it. Such disagreement is always possible. A profession is, among other things, a continuing discussion of how its standards should be interpreted. Sometimes an individual member of the profession must act on her own interpretation of a standard, her act itself being the only way effectively to put forward a certain interpretation of the code (much as a "test case" is sometimes the only way to settle a legal question). That the Nazi engineer was in fact acting on his good-faith (but mistaken) interpretation of the code does not protect his act from being condemned as unprofessional (as well as immoral); it does not even protect him from being judged to have committed an error sufficiently grave to raise doubts about whether he has the character to be a good engineer. Indeed, some errors of judgment may be so gross that, even standing alone, they seem decisive proof of technical or moral incompetence. But, however that may be, nothing we have assumed in our fourth interpretation of the Nazi engineer in question, prevents us from judging him as a member of an engineering profession, indeed, in principle, of a profession he might share with American engineers as well as German. He is not, on this interpretation, evidence against the existence of such a profession.

Fifth, and last, the Nazi engineer may recognize the existence of a profession of engineering but declare independence of it: "I am an engineer, but I am not that kind of engineer; I am not a member of their profession; I make my own rules." The Nazis may be glad to have the knowledge, skill, and judgment of such an engineer, especially after he has gained their trust. But they will not have an engineer in what is now the ordinary sense, that is, a member of the profession of engineering. They will not have someone whom they can trust to work as ordinary engineers do. But they will not have an impostor or charlatan either. Only if the Nazi engineer had failed to make clear that he is a mere individual with certain skills, not a member of the engineering profession working as members of that profession do, would he be an impostor. And, even then, he would not be a charlatan, that is, someone incompetent to do what he invites clients to expect.

So, on this fifth version of the counter-example, the Nazi engineer can honestly use the title "engineer," but only with scare quotes, that is, with an explanation of how he differs from the ordinary engineer. History, that is, public appreciation of the overwhelming predominance of the engineering profession among those doing engineering, has settled what the standard use of "engineer" is. The Nazi engineer's variant, though linguistically legitimate, is still secondary and therefore potentially misleading. It takes its meaning by analogy with members of the profession, an analogy which is less than complete in an important respect. Honesty requires the Nazi engineer to make the disanalogy clear to those seeking his help in their dreadful crimes.

VII. Professional Ethics and Moral Theory

I have, it will be noted, been able to decide whether the Nazi engineer acted unethically, that is, in violation of his profession's special standards, without direct appeal to moral theory. My approach to professional ethics thus resembles Airaksinen's conceptualism in being relatively independent of "moral foundations." It nonetheless differs from Airaksinen's in two respects, both of which I consider to be advantages.

First, my approach is not as independent of moral theory as Airaksinen's. I have explicitly understood professions in a way recognizing moral constraints on the pursuit of a professional ideal. I have also understood professional standards in a way making them morally binding (in the sense that promises bind). I have therefore left room for moral theory insofar as moral theory can enlighten us concerning how morality makes professional ethics binding and what professional ethics can bind us to.

Second, my approach is not as independent of the social sciences as Airaksinen's. As I understand professions, the social sciences may help us to distinguish "true professions" from "pseudo-professions." True professions are those organized occupations that largely live up to the special standards they profess; pseudo-professions, those organized occupations that, though having professional standards, fall too far short of them, whether by incompetence, indifference, or venality, to count as professions. I have, however, not understood professions in a way making the social sciences the arbiter of what is a profession. My approach allows us to conclude, for example, that engineering is a profession even if social scientists say it is not. Indeed, I have provided a definition that might help the social sciences to understand the professions better and so help the rest of us to do the same.

Acknowledgements

Thanks to Vivian Weil and Mike Rabins for comments on the first draft of this article; to those who participated in the Philosophy Colloquium, Illinois Institute of Technology, February 26, 1997, for many helpful comments on the second draft; to the Center for Professional Ethics, Case Western Reserve University, March 20, 1997, for their comments on the third draft; and to two anonymous referees of this journal for comments on the fourth.

NOTES AND REFERENCES

1 See Davis, Michael (1996) "Professional Autonomy: A Framework for Empirical Research," *Business Ethics Quarterly* Vol. 6: 441-60.

2 Airaksinen, Timo (1994) "Service and Science in Professional Life," in Chadwick, Ruth F. (ed) *Ethics and the Professions* (Aldershot, England: Avebury), 9.

3 Airaksinen (1994) 9.

4 Harris, Nigel G.E. (1994) "Professional Codes and Kantian Duties," in Chadwick, 107.

5 Airaksinen (1994) 10.

6 Bayles, Michael D. (1981) *Professional Ethics* (Belmont, California: Wadsworth Publishing), ix (but then admits to "emphasizing law and medicine").

7 Koehn, Daryl (1994) *The Ground of Professional Ethics* (London: Routledge), 12.

8 Airaksinen (1994) 1.

9 I make this assumption because most of those whom I have read on the subject who list law as a "traditional profession," that is, those writing in English, seem to mean lawyering. For Americans, this is natural enough, since we have only one profession of law (judges generally not being counted at all). But for Europeans, it may not be so clear. The English have two professions of law, solicitors (legal agents) and barristers (advocates), with judges being drawn (mostly) from the barristers. Civil law countries have a third legal profession, notaries (only the distant cousins of our poor notaries public). Civil law countries may also divide advocates into prosecutors, trial advocates, and appellate advocates, and train judges separately. We may ignore these complexities here.

10 Or, at least, we will so recognize them unless we have a theoretical ax to grind. Note that Koehn (1994) 26-27, considers cosmetic surgery foreign to medicine.

11 The one profession on Daryl Koehn's list but not on Airaksinen's also meets this criterion: the clergy helps its flock live in harmony with the ultimate order of things (or, as Koehn puts it, "find salvation"). Living in harmony with the

ultimate order of things is as much a rational ideal as health is.

12 Query: is social work's ideal of service, welfare, internal to its practice in the two-fold way Airaksinen claims medicine's is? Certainly welfare understood as prosperity or happiness is not something social work defines (any more than it is something engineering defines). Would a social worker be an imposter if he sought some good other than his client's prosperity or happiness?

13 Airaksinen (1994) 10.

14 Airaksinen (1994) 10.

15 Airaksinen (1994) 3. The "textbook" approach is exactly what is suggested by the arrangement of those textbooks in professional (and business) ethics, perhaps still the majority, that begin with a chapter or two on moral theory.

16 Airaksinen (1994) 2.

17 Airaksinen (1994) 3.

18 I have hedged here because conceptualism as such seems to be completely silent about moral constraints on pursuit of good aims. Some of these constraints may, I grant, be made to appear internal to the practice, but others may not. The pursuit of health, for example, seems to have nothing to say about racial, sexual, or class discrimination in admission to the profession. Hence, it seems, according to conceptualism, that treating one's colleagues unfairly would raise no issue of professional ethics.

19 For an example of what a conceptualist treatment of this question might look like, see Koehn, 123-25.

20 Airaksinen (1994) 1.

21 Zussman, Robert (1995) *Mechanics of the Middle Class: Work and Politics Among American Engineers* (Berkeley: University of California Press), 222. I do not want my criticism of Zussman's treatment of engineering's status as a profession to give the impression that I dislike his study as a whole. On the contrary, I consider it among the two or three best studies of engineers at work I have seen. I don't think any sociologist who has discussed engineering's status as a profession has done better.

22 Zussman (1995) 222.

23 Zussman (1995) 222.

24 Since Zussman's analysis seems to rely on degrees, not kinds, of professionalization, he seems to have only one sense of profession. His claim must, then, actually be that medicine and law are professionalized enough to count as true professions while engineering is not. He does not, however, give any hint of why the line between professionalized enough and not professionalized enough should be drawn where he draws it.

25 One of this journal's referees suggested that I should consider a different sociological explanation of why engineering is not a profession: "while physicians [and] lawyers tend to remain as such throughout their careers, many engineers go into management—a new career?" Hence, engineers are not professionals in the sense that physicians and lawyers are, because they lack "life-long commitment" to their line of work. This explanation rests, in part, on an important mistake about engineering. Engineers who "enter management" do not generally leave engineering. The line most employers draw between "bench engineers" and "managers" does not correspond to any distinction between those employees concerned only with things and those employees who order people's work. All engineering is technical management; even the lowest "bench engineer" helps to prepare instructions for how people will work with things; engineers "in management" do much the same, though they have assistants whose work they must oversee. The difference between "bench engineers" and "engineers in management" is like the military's distinction between lieutenants and captains, majors, and

so on, not like that between privates and officers. The suggested explanation also rests on a mistake about professions. Life-long commitment is a tendency in professions, but not a prerequisite of profession. What is prerequisite, as we shall see, is a commitment to carry on the profession according to its special standard while one engages in the underlying occupation. For empirical evidence that engineers in management generally see themselves as engineers, see Davis, Michael (1997) "Better Communications Between Engineers and Managers: Some Ways to Prevent Ethically Hard Choice," *Science and Engineering Ethics* Vol. 3: 171-213.

26 For defense of this analysis of profession against some criticisms ignored here, see my other attempts to explain and defend it, especially, Davis, Michael: (1987) "The Moral Authority of a Professional Code," *NOMOS* Vol. 29: 302-37; (1987) "The Use of Professions," *Business Economics* Vol. 22: 5-10; (1988) "Vocational Teachers, Confidentiality, and Professional Ethics," *International Journal of Applied Philosophy* Vol. 4: 11-20; (1988) "Professionalism Means Putting Your Profession First," *Georgetown Journal of Legal Ethics*: 352-66; (1991) "Thinking Like an Engineer: The Place of a Code of Ethics in the Practice of a Profession," *Philosophy and Public Affairs* Vol. 20: 150-67; (1991) "Do Cops Need a Code of Ethics?" *Criminal Justice Ethics* Vol. 10: 14-28; (1993) "Treating Patients with Infectious Diseases: An Essay in the Ethics of Dentistry," *Professional Ethics* Vol. 2: 51-65; (1995) "The State's Dr. Death: What's Unethical about Physicians Helping at Executions?" *Social Theory and Practice* Vol. 21: 31-60; and (1995) "Science: After Such Knowledge, What Responsibility?" *Professional Ethics* Vol. 4: 49-74.

27 Even Koehn (1994) 111-12, a conceptualist unusually careful about practice, seems to admit at least the possibility of a one-member profession.

28 On my analysis, there is a temporal asymmetry worth pointing out. While no one can be the first member of a profession, since there must be more than one member of the profession for there to be an organization, there can be a last member of a profession, all the other members of which have died or quit. The status of this last member is, however, equivocal. He is still a member of the profession in question only if we recognize him as belonging to an organization that, in one plain sense, no longer exists.

29 In the United States, the notary public is an interesting test case. Notaries public are licensed by the state to attest to the validity of signatures on certain legal documents (wills, deeds, passport applications, and so on). They have a monopoly on such attestation. They must meet certain (minimal) educational requirements and pass a test to be licensed. They have clients (those who seek them to have a signature put under seal) and receive a fee for the service rendered. But the fee, set by statute, is always so small ($2 the last time I used a notary) that few can make a living as a notary. (In my experience, the time most notaries take to explain what to do, to watch it done, and to seal the document, would make it hard even for a notary with clients lined up at the door to earn much more than $8 an hour.) Notaries are nonetheless so common that few notaries have much business. People in some occupations, for example, secretaries or receptionists, become notaries to assure their organization has one when needed; other people become notaries just to attract potential customers into their main business, to be of service to their neighbors, to earn a little money on the side, or as a hobby. Though American notaries have organized in much the way professions have (with a national society, code of ethics, and so on), they are, on my view, not a profession (strictly so called), because there

is no underlying occupation (no way to make a living at it). What then are they? Holders of a public office? A hybrid between a profession and a charity? They certainly constitute an exception to test any rule. I would count my definition a complete success if they constitute the only counter-example to which it is open.

30 So, insofar as the sociological definition emphasizes income and social status as the objects of professionalization, it reduces profession to another category, trade union or trade association.

31 That is not to say that members of a profession cannot join a union, or even that a professional organization cannot share its membership with a union. It is simply to point out that the logic of unionism and professionalism are different—and, indeed, in tension. For a profession, the material welfare of its members is a mere side constraint limiting the pursuit of its moral ideal. For a union, the profession's pursuit of a moral ideal is the side constraint; the union's purpose is (among other things) cultivating the material welfare of its members. While it is possible for the same people both to pursue a certain moral ideal (through their profession) and to pursue their material well-being (through their union), combining the two pursuits into one (unitary) organization may be problematic.

32 By "prudence" I mean those standards of conduct everyone (every rational person at his rational best) wants to follow whatever anyone else is doing. Prudence resembles morality in being a standard of conduct, but differs from morality in the reasons for the standard. Because one can be both prudent and moral, indeed must be prudent to be morally effective, prudence is more like the converse of morality than its exact contrary (as, perhaps, acting selfishly is).

33 Prudence is, of course, praiseworthy, but not morally praiseworthy. To describe someone as prudent is to compliment her, but only in the way describing her as clever, unflappable, or healthy is. Contrast such praise with the praise of morally good conduct or character, for example, kind, just, or candid.

34 Gorlin, Rena A. (ed) (1986). *Codes of Professional Responsibility* (Washington, DC: Bureau of National Affairs), 101. The American Dental Association's early advocacy of fluoridation of the public water supply is another example of the public service a profession feels compelled to provide, even when its primary activity is serving individual patients.

35 I say "ordinarily" because a profession can have an impersonal ideal. For example, science, at least on some conceptions, serves no client, employer, or public but only knowledge. What distinguishes professions from other occupations is not service to others as such but a moral ideal, defensible in part by the way serving it benefits others. The knowledge of science, though an impersonal object of service, remains a morally good object of service (just as justice, health, and welfare are) because scientific knowledge serves us all, whether practically (as much of physics, chemistry, and biology do) or just intellectually (as much of astronomy, etymology, and anthropology do). But if the ideal that science serves is knowledge, then Airaksinen seems to have a problem distinguishing science from teaching (which, presumably, is a different profession). Knowledge is, according to Airaksinen, the rational ideal that teaching serves; hence, according to Conceptualist Assumption 1, it cannot also be the ideal that science serves. Airaksinen also has a problem with who defines knowledge. Presumably science, not teaching, does that (at least for scientific knowledge). So, another of Airaksinen's "traditional professions," teaching, seems to fail his

own test of a true profession. For me, there is no problem, even if I admit that science and teaching share the same moral ideal, because it is clear that scientists and teachers serve knowledge in different ways: scientists serve knowledge by adding to what we collectively know while teachers serve knowledge by helping us all share in that collective good.

36 This is a point about the division of labor among concepts, one to be defended by considering which usage provides the most information, avoids the most odd results, helps identify important considerations other ways of using the word do not, and so on. For someone who rejects "moral permissibility" as a part of the definition of "profession" (reducing profession to mere "competence"), see, Sanders, John T. (1993) "Honor Among Thieves: Some Reflections on Professional Codes of Ethics," *Professional Ethics* Vol. 2: 83-103. If the article's title is not itself a decisive argument against equating mere competence with profession, the article's suggestion that we consider the mafia to be a proto-typical profession should be. Sanders has, I think, provided another example of what is wrong with conceptualism (though one relying on a different conception).

37 Consider, for example, act utilitarianism. Insofar as one is, according to that moral theory, obliged to choose that act, among those available, maximizing overall utility (or human happiness), ordinary morality would leave one free to choose among several alternatives only on those rare occasions when two or more options generate the same utility. Ordinary morality would leave no room for professions, as I have defined them.

38 There are, of course, at least two other common (and proper) ways to understand "ethics": a) as a synonym for morality; and b) as the name of a field of philosophy (moral theory). Nonetheless, the way I propose to understand "ethics" here seems to me the most useful when trying to understand professional ethics. For defense of this usage, see Davis, Michael (1990) "The Ethics Boom: What and Why," *Centennial Review* Vol. 34: 163-86.

39 I believe this voluntary version of the principle of fairness is now relatively uncontroversial. But, for those who think otherwise, I recommend two papers defending the involuntary version against the standard criticisms: Davis, Michael (1987) "Nozick's Argument FOR the Legitimacy of the Welfare State," *Ethics* Vol. 97: 576-94; and Arneson, Richard (1982) "The Principle of Fairness and Free-Rider Problems," *Ethics* Vol. 92: 616-33.

40 These considerations are almost identical with those determining whether trades such as barbering should be restricted to those having a license and whether those granted a license should have to have certain training, experience, and character, another reason to believe that licensure has no direct bearing on profession.

41 What about barbers? Are they forever banned from forming a profession? Not on my analysis. If they organized as engineers have, that is, if they set for themselves a standard of conduct beyond what law, market, and morality demand and then held themselves to it, they too could form a profession, one serving the moral ideal of "good barbering" defined by that standard. The claim that professions, as such, require a college degree ("higher education") seems to me unnecessary for any morally interesting conception of profession. Requiring a higher education for practice of a profession does set a higher standard, but that higher standard may not be appropriate for every would-be profession; it may, for example, simply drive up the cost of service without improving it. That is an empirical question to be decided profession by profession. That, anyway, is how I would an-

swer the question. Any adequate defense of that answer would require another paper.

42 Note that I say "an engineering profession," not "the engineering profession," recognizing the possibility of more than one. Is there one engineering profession or many? That, I think, is a practical question before it is an empirical one. If I ignore the exact wording of standards, especially, ethical standards, I am inclined to say there is only one profession of engineering, the same in Cairo as in Chicago, the same in Riga as in Rangoon. If, however, I pay close attention to standards, I am inclined to distinguish between professions not only by country but also by field (for example, between civil and chemical engineering). In general, I think, the differences in engineering standards across borders and between fields is small enough today that engineers are not unreasonable in thinking of themselves as all sharing one world-wide profession. But I must admit that how many engineering professions we recognize is, as I understand profession, a function of our purpose in asking.

43 Debate is, of course, seldom limited to interpreting the code. Professions seem always to be considering amendments of the code as well, generally to "clarify" but sometimes to add new requirements or subtract old ones. For our purposes, the two processes, re-interpreting and amending, are equivalent.

◆ ◆ ◆ ◆ ◆

MICHAEL S. PRITCHARD
Responsible Engineering: The Importance of Character and Imagination

Introduction

Discussions of ethics in engineering practice typically have two common features. First, understandably, they tend to focus on specific events, typically events that are newsworthy because of their unfortunate, if not tragic, consequences. Second, they usually focus on questions about alleged *wrongdoing*, its avoidance, or its prevention. Important as such discussions are, this paper will focus on a different, though related, aspect of engineering ethics—namely, *responsible* engineering practice. Given the importance of responsible professional practice, it is perhaps surprising how little attention has been directed to this more positive side of ethics in the literature.

In this paper I will explore the role that character and imagination might play in determining how engineers understand and deal with their responsibilities as engineers. I will offer only preliminary reflections on this relatively unexplored topic, inviting others to join in both widening and deepening the inquiry. In illustrating what I have in mind, I will limit my primary focus to the responsibilities of engineers to protect public safety, health and welfare. These are by no means the only sorts of responsibilities engineers have, but I will say little about them here. My basic thesis is that fulfilling an engineer's responsibilities to protect public safety, health, and welfare calls as much for *settled dispositions*, or *virtues*, as it does for performing this or that specific action.

My reflections take their cue from William F. May's observation that it is particularly important for professional ethics to pay attention to moral character and virtue, as these dispositions shape professionals' approach to their work.[1] He notes that professionals typically work in institutional settings, often making it difficult to determine just where things have gone wrong and who should bear the responsibility. Also, professional expertise, particularly in large organizations, is not widely shared, even by fellow professionals. So, May concludes, we need professionals to have virtues that warrant their being trusted: "Few may be in a position to discredit [them]. The knowledge explosion is also an ignorance explosion; if knowledge is power, then ignorance is powerlessness." He adds, "One test of character and virtue is what a person does when no one else is watching. A society that rests on expertise needs more people who can pass that test."[2]

What counts as "passing" this test of character? Especially when bad consequences become apparent only after the passage of considerable time, it can be very difficult to discredit specific professionals. This suggests that, when no one is watching (which is much of the time), professionals may be able to get away with shoddy, if not deliberately wrongful, behavior. So, "passing" the test seems to require avoiding such behavior even when no one will notice. But this is essentially negative— the avoidance of behavior that would be to one's *discredit* if noticed by others. Although this is the dominant emphasis in literature on professional responsibility, we should also want to know what contributions professionals make to *desirable* outcomes when no one is looking. This can be equally difficult to notice and to assess. We typically take for granted the reliability of the work of engineers. For example, we assume that the elevator will work, that the bridge will bear the weight of traffic, that the building will not fall, and so on, even though we have little understanding of the work that is required to make this so—let alone the special engineering efforts that may have prevented failures or improved reliability.

When we shift our attention in this more positive direction, it quickly becomes apparent that what might count as responsible (as distinct from irresponsible) professional practice can vary widely. Followers of the now retired comic strip *Calvin and Hobbes* may recall the episode in which six-year-old Calvin has finally made his bed. His pal, Hobbes the stuffed tiger, says, "Gee, your mom sure was impressed when you made your bed." Calvin replies, "Right. That's how I like it—to impress her by fulfilling the *least* of my obligations."[3] We can think of Calvin as occupying one end of a spectrum of responsibility that ranges from the minimal to the supererogatory ("above and beyond the call of duty"). Somewhere between these two ends of the spectrum is where most of us spend most of our time.

It is interesting that, like the work of professionals, Calvin's bed-making requires certain skills—skills that may be well developed or poorly developed, conscientiously employed or lackadaisically employed, and so on. Of course, we would prefer the services of conscientious professionals who have well developed skills, good judgment, and the like. However, we may end up with a clever Calvin who is content to stay out of trouble and to exert the least effort necessary for "success"; and if May is right, we may not be in a good position to know just how marginal the services are. By the same token, we may not be in a good position to know just how competent and conscientious other professionals are.

Whether or not we are in a good position to determine these things, our well-being, both as individuals and as a society, is at stake. As we reflect on the extent to which our well-being is dependent on the performance of professionals whose expertise and organizational workplace we do not understand, we can see why it is not only moral dispositions such as honesty, fairmindedness, and benevolence that are important to professional ethics; equally important are those dispositions that relate to professional competence. Professional ethics calls for a level of performance, not just good moral purpose and intention. Competence needs to be linked with commitment to ethical values that are basic in a given profession—for example, public safety, health and welfare in engineering. But commitment, like competence, can range from the minimal to the exemplary. Unfortunately, by emphasizing wrongdoing and its avoidance, most of the engineering ethics literature slights the more positive end of the responsibility spectrum. Even if falling short of the exemplary does not warrant discredit or blame, our needs exceed what merely avoiding discredit or blame provides. In what follows, I will expand May's concern about what professionals do when no one is watching to include the exemplary as well.

Although May intends his remarks to apply to all the professions, they are especially apt for engineers. Clearly, the public depends heavily on, but is not privy to, the expertise of engineers. Furthermore, from the public's perspective, the work of engineers is largely anonymous; few members of the public ever meet the engineers whose work they depend on. But even engineers who work in the same organization, or even on the same projects, may not be in a good position to check on each other's work. Insofar as engineers do not share each others' expertise, or do not have time to check up on each other, there is an important sense in which engineers are not being watched by each other either. In short, largely unwatched by those who depend on them, engineers are expected to conduct themselves responsibly. Hence the special pertinence of May's question: "What do professionals do when no one is watching?"

Dedication to Safety

As a glance at engineering codes of ethics reveals, many of their most important provisions are stated in such a way that what might count as satisfying them is open to considerable interpretation. The National Society for Professional Engineers code of ethics, like most other engineering codes, identifies protecting public safety, health, and welfare as the engineer's paramount obligation. It is interesting to notice how little assistance the NSPE code provides in interpreting what this responsibility entails. The Preamble says that, because engineering work has a direct and vital impact on everyone's quality of life, engineers must be dedicated to the protection of the public health, safety and welfare. The first of the Fundamental Canons says that engineers shall *hold paramount* the safety, health and welfare of the public. Under Rules of Practice this same language is used. But just what does this come to? And what is implied by being *dedicated* to protecting the public?

At its best, a code of engineering ethics prescribes the highest *common* denominator for members of its society. This means that individual professionals may have higher aspirations than the code requires. Much is left for individual interpretation. For example, under the Rules of Practice, the NSPE code offers guidance for only two kinds of circumstance that have to do specifically with protecting public safety, health, and welfare: 1) an engineer should inform appropriate persons if his or her engineering judgment is overruled when the public is endangered; and 2) an engineer should approve only those engineering documents that protect the public safety, health, and welfare. Can this be all that the framers of the code had in mind in saying that the engineer's paramount responsibility is to protect public safety, health and welfare? Clearly the answer is, no. However, this may be all that can be identified in terms of specific courses of action that are required (and even "appropriate persons" is left open to interpretation). In any case, being *dedicated* to protecting the public and *holding paramount* public safety, health, and welfare seem to be more enduring requirements; they refer to dispositions engineers are expected to have. They mark a *readiness* to take safety, health, and welfare into appropriate account. Sometimes we can see this exemplified in particular actions. But there does not seem to be any way to prescribe a certain set of required courses of action.

The Importance of Dispositions

What I hope to show is that both character and imagination can assist the end of protecting the public in ways that no list of required courses of action can specify. Here there are no algorithms. Despite this, we should be able to list a number of dispositions that, by framing an engineer's approach to his or her work, can importantly contribute to protecting public safety, health, and welfare.

Several years ago, my colleague James Jaksa and I undertook a project to develop educational materials that illustrate responsible, if not exemplary engineering practice.[4] We sought stories from engineers and their managers. To give them some idea of what we were interested in, we first asked them what characteristics they would look for if they were trying to hire a highly responsible engineer. Then we asked them if they could provide illustrations of engineers who exemplified these characteristics in their engineering practice. Although hardly a scientific survey, a list of commonly mentioned dispositions emerged. Many items on the list seem to have an inherent connection with ethics and would be expected to appear in one form or another on virtually anyone's list of virtues. For example:

- integrity
- honesty (even candor)
- civic-mindedness
- courage (to speak up, to "stick to one's guns")
- willingness to make self-sacrifice (including willingness to assume some personal risk)
- not being too personally ambitious

Virtues such as these are quite generic, not only in regard to the professions, but in regard to ordinary, non-professional life as well. How they might manifest themselves in engineering practice requires special attention to the working environment of engineers.

As attention shifts to the context of engineering practice, other items show up on the list. However, these items are less obviously connected with ethics, and several can readily be associated with undesirable behavior as well:

- competence
- ability to communicate clearly and informatively
- cooperativeness (being a good "team player")
- willingness to compromise
- perseverance
- habit of documenting work thoroughly and clearly
- commitment to objectivity
- openness to correction (admitting mistakes, acknowledging oversight)
- commitment to quality
- being imaginative
- seeing the "big picture" as well as the details of smaller domains

As with the first group of virtues, when listed abstractly, they are not engineering-specific. To understand how they might manifest themselves in the lives of engineers, they must be seen in the context of engineering practice. However, it is conceivable that an engineer could have all of the dispositions in this second group and still be dedicated to any number of morally reprehensible engineering projects.

This may suggest to some that items in this second group of dispositions should not be included in an account of the virtues of responsible engineers. Admittedly, *having* these dispositions is not sufficient for responsible engineering practice. However, *lacking* them detracts from responsible engineering practice in general, and exemplary practice in particular. Furthermore, having these dispositions is a fundamental part of what we admire in those engineers who are likely to be identified as morally commendable. It is fundamental because, without these dispositions in addition to the more obvious virtues of honesty, justice, and benevolence (to take three traditional moral virtues), there is little reason to expect even competent engineering practice. In short, having the virtues of honesty, justice, and benevolence does not qualify one as a competent engineer. In fact, many who have these virtues might correctly conclude that they should not try to become engineers—they might be better suited for other kinds of work.

Given their fundamental role in responsible engineering practice, it is no accident that this second group of dispositions show up on the list of characteristics engineers and their managers would look for if they were trying to hire a highly responsible engineer. What still needs to be explained, however, is the specific fit these dispositions might have in engineering practice. Simply listing a set of desirable dispositions, or virtues, does not tell us how they might play themselves out in responsible engineering practice. A good place to begin is with examples that show concretely that the presence or absence of some of these dispositions can have an important impact on ethical values in engineering.

An Illustration

To illustrate more concretely what I have in mind regarding the role of character and imagination in responsible engineering practice, I will turn to the much celebrated story of William LeMessurier and the Citicorp Center in Manhattan.[5] This story centers around the engineer's responsibility to protect public safety. Engineer William LeMessurier designed the structural frame of the Citicorp Center, built in 1977. In 1978 he discovered a structural problem that, because of the building's unusual features, rendered the building vulnerable to 16 year storms. He knew how to correct the problem, but only at the cost of millions of dollars and at the risk of his career if he were to tell others about the problem. Nevertheless, he promptly notified lawyers, insurers, the chief architect of the building, and Citicorp executives. Corrections were made, all parties were cooperative, and LeMessurier's career was not adversely affected.

In response to Joe Morgenstern's *New Yorker* article recounting the Citicorp story, LeMessurier received phone calls and letters of praise from engineers around the country acknowledging that they, too, had faced similar challenges. Some asked whether, faced with a similar situation, "Would I be this good?" This is an interesting question, since once he discovered the problem, it seems clear that LeMessurier had a duty to take some sort of action; this was not an instance of going "above and beyond the call of duty." In fact, this is explicitly acknowledged by LeMessurier himself. After mentioning LeMessurier's brief consideration of two unacceptable options (keeping silent or committing suicide, Morgenstern writes:

> What seized him an instant later was entirely convincing, because it was so unexpected—an almost giddy sense of power. "I had information that nobody else in the world had," LeMessurier recalls. "I had the power in my hands to effect extraordinary events that only I could initiate. I mean, sixteen years to failure—that was very simple, very clearcut. I almost said, 'Thank you, dear Lord, for making this problem so sharply defined that there's no choice to make.'"[6]

That is, although it would still take courage to take constructive steps to protect public safety, there was no ambiguity or unclarity about having this duty in these circumstances. However, to focus primarily on this moment is to miss an important dimension of the story. This moment of truth for LeMessurier was of a piece with what led him to the discovery in the first place. But when we look at that trail of discovery, it is somewhat less clear what his responsibilities were.

When he first learned that Citicorp braces had bolted rather than welded joints, apparently LeMessurier had no special reason to be concerned. Morgenstern says:

The choice of bolted joints was technically sound and professionally correct. Even if the failure of his associates to flag him on the design change was justifiable; had every decision on the site in Manhattan waited for approval from Cambridge, the building would never have been finished. Most important, modern skyscrapers are so strong that catastrophic collapse is not considered a realistic prospect; when engineers seek to limit a building's sway [the purpose for having welded joints], they do so for the tenants' comfort.[7]

Instead, what initially aroused LeMessurier's interest was a phone call from an engineering student whose professor told him that the building was poorly designed (with supporting pillars being at the center of each side rather than at the four corners). He explained to the student that his design could handle quartering winds more effectively than more standard structures, and he referred him to a technical article on the matter written by one of his engineering partners. Next he decided to share technical aspects of his design with students in one of his own classes. It was determined, he told his class, that the building would be vulnerable only to 100 year storms, well beyond the minimally acceptable requirements.

As already noted, even after learning that the joints were bolted rather than welded, LeMessurier remained confident that the building would still more than satisfy the New York building code, which required wind resistance tests only at a 90 degree angle. However, Morgenstern comments, "in the spirit of intellectual play, he wanted to see if they were just as strong in winds hitting from 45 degrees." It is this that ultimately led LeMessurier to his shocking conclusion that the building was much less safe than he had thought.

What I would like to suggest is that this "intellectual play," this exercise of engineering imagination,

manifests LeMessurier's abiding concern for public safety. However confident he may have been that his calculations would show that the building was as safe as he initially thought, without a firm commitment to safety, it is not clear why he would have been interested in undertaking the calculations. Further evidence of this commitment is LeMessurier's persistence in working out the calculations to their disturbing conclusion.

We could imagine different scenarios. He could have simply dismissed the student's challenge. Confident that everything was according to code, LeMessurier might have decided he had other things to do with his time. Instead, he seemed to take particular pride in trying to show the student that the building was first rate in every respect, but especially in regard to safety. Confident that the structure was in compliance with code, other engineers might well have simply turned their attention to other matters. Even in the remote chance that something bad would happen to the structure, how could they be faulted for this?

It seems plausible to say that what LeMessurier did from the moment he learned that bolted rather than welded joints were used expressed his character and imagination as an engineer. Despite his self-confidence (or perhaps even because of it), LeMessurier is the sort of engineer who is prepared to acknowledge mistakes and take necessary action, even at his own expense. Getting it right, we might say, is more important than preserving his reputation—particularly when public safety is at stake. Aiding him in this is his very active engineering imagination. As an illustration of LeMessurier's imagination at work, Morgenstern points out that the building's wind braces were "first sketched out, in a burst of almost ecstatic invention, on a napkin in a Greek restaurant in Cambridge: forty-eight braces, in six tiers of eight, arrayed like giant chevrons behind the building's curtain of aluminum and glass."[8]

In some respects, we could say William LeMessurier was just doing his job. However, I think this understates matters a great deal. Calvin, too, was just doing his job—minimally. Engineers like LeMessurier bring something more to their work. They exemplify what it means to *dedicate* oneself fully to the protection of public safety, health, and welfare. The recognition of such dedication evokes praise from others.

Calvin thinks he deserves praise, too. He wants Santa Claus to reward him for being good: "How good do you have to be to qualify as good?" he asks. "I haven't *killed* anybody. See, that's good, right? I haven't committed any felonies. I didn't start any wars. I don't practice cannibalism. Wouldn't you say I should get lots of presents?" Pausing for a moment of reflection, Hobbes wisely replies: "But maybe good is more than the absence of bad."[9]

However, even granting that Hobbes has a point, some might question whether it actually applies to William LeMessurier's handling of the Citicorp problem. In response to a talk I once gave on this story, a member of the audience posed the following challenge. Why, he asked, should LeMessurier be lauded for his handling of the Citicorp problem? After all, once he discovered the problem, it was, as he himself acknowledges, his duty to report it to the appropriate authorities. Furthermore, the questioner continued, wasn't it just a matter of *luck* that LeMessurier made the discovery at all? An unexpected phone call from a student, a fortuitous conversation about welded joints in Pittsburgh, and so on.

My response about LeMessurier's duty to report the problem is twofold. First, although acting on his duty may not be "going above and beyond the call of duty," a reason for lauding LeMessurier is that it did take a fair amount of courage to do this. Admittedly, failure to report the problem would have been blameworthy, but doing what is right under such challenging circumstances can nevertheless merit praise. Second, *how* LeMessurier handled this duty also seems to warrant praise. He not only reported the existence of the problem, he also proposed a solution; and his ability to do so, especially in such

circumstances, reflects his character and imagination as an engineer. There can be, we might say, better and worse ways of fulfilling one's duty; and LeMessurier's was exemplary.

My response to the comment about luck is that it is precisely LeMessurier's character and imagination as an engineer that explains why he made something of the crucial moments that ultimately led to his discovery of the problem. Many, perhaps most, other engineers would not have capitalized on these events in the way he did. They could not fairly be faulted for this. But LeMessurier can praised for his perceptiveness, persistence, and imagination—and his unqualified commitment to safety and quality. Engineers like LeMessurier seem to be somehow *prepared to be lucky*. That is, because of their skills and commitment, they are prepared to pick up cues and run with them, to notice what others fail to notice, and so on.

In the end, ethical values appropriate to a profession must be joined with professional commitment, competence, and imagination in order to provide a complete picture of the virtues in professional life. It is important for professionals to be prepared to be lucky. This requires a blending of moral dispositions and professional expertise; and this is not primarily a matter of making this or that momentous, ethical decision. It is a way of (professional) life.

Where to Go from Here

I have offered but a sketch of the fundamental role of character and imagination in William LeMessurier's handling of the Citicorp problem. If this sketch is on the right track, there should be many other stories of how character and imagination have played themselves out in his professional career. Lacking the drama of the Citicorp story, most of these stories will probably never be told. The Citicorp story was told only after 17 years had passed by, and it might well never have been told. Furthermore, it is as much a story of what did *not* occur as what did occur. There was no disaster. Would there have been a disaster had LeMessurier not intervened as he did? We will never know. All we can know is that his intervention significantly reduced the odds. That is, safety was significantly enhanced. So, it is overly dramatic to say that he actually prevented a disaster.

Nevertheless, we certainly hope that engineers will approach their work with the sorts of dispositions and skills that will reduce the chances of bad things happening—and that will enhance the chances of good things happening. We also hope that these same dispositions and skills will anticipate safety concerns at the earliest possible stages of design development so that later corrections will not be necessary, or too late.

Important as all of this is to responsible engineering, remarkably little attention has been paid to it in engineering ethics literature. This may be partly due to our general tendency to take for granted the good work of engineers and take special note only of failures. But it may also be because failures are more readily observable. As already noted, had LeMessurier kept silent, we might never have been the wiser; both the diagnosis and the correction were made without public knowledge, including the wider circle of engineers, lawyers, insurance agents, and public officials. Furthermore, even though he reduced the odds, we cannot know whether LeMessurier actually prevented a disaster. This poses a special problem of counterfactuals. We need to ask, "What *might* have happened if ...?," rather than "What *would* have happened if ...?" Either question is especially challenging. In contrast, actual failures are harder to hide; and once we are alerted to them, the search for causes begins. This search may itself fail or involve a great deal of frustration, but the motivation and desired outcome of the search are much more transparent.

The William LeMessurier story is barely a beginning; and in many respects it is not a representative story. First, most practicing engineers will not find themselves in such high drama, high stakes circumstances. Yet, they will have opportunities to exercise their dispositions and skills in responsible, if not exemplary, ways. So, we need stories of more ordinary, less dramatic, ways in which character and imagination come into play in engineering practice.

Second, the LeMessurier story focuses almost exclusively on a high profile, high level engineer. Stories of engineers operating at various levels need to be told. Relatively few will ever reach the level of responsibility, authority, power, and influence of internationally renowned engineers such as William LeMessurier. Of course, stories from the top are inspiring, but students will not begin their careers in leadership positions, and most will never end up occupying leadership roles comparable to LeMessurier's. So, there is a need for examples that are more representative of the kinds of work situations they will be in for most, if not all, of their careers.

Third, as told, the Citicorp story is mainly about one individual, William LeMessurier. Although the roles of others are either mentioned or implied in Morgenstern's story, they remain in the background. A fuller story would talk about other major players as well, ranging from skyscraper designer Leslie Stevenson, who conducted the external review of the problem, to all the other engineers involved in repairing the structure.[10]

Fourth, most of the engineers and managers that James Jaksa and I interviewed stressed the importance of being a good team player. By this they did not mean being an uncritical, "yes" person. They meant that good engineers need to be able to work well with others. Especially in large organizations, engineers work in teams. We had the privilege of interviewing William Bolander, who in 1995 was the first winner of the $500,000 Lemelson/MIT award for invention and innovation. Prior to the interview Jaksa and I were struck by the fact that the majority of accomplishments credited to Bolander involved cost effective safety improvements in the Saturn automobile. However, when we talked with him he expressed some embarrassment at having been singled out for the award. Although he was obviously proud to have worked on these improvements, he continually insisted that he regards himself as a team player who enjoys working with others—and who thinks that his fellow team players deserve recognition as well.

Unfortunately, we did not ask Bolander what he thinks made his teams work so well together, let alone how the dispositions and skills of the individual engineers on his teams combined to come up with such impressive results. Shifting attention to what responsible engineering requires of those on engineering teams does not really diminish the importance of the individual engineer. After all, engineering teams are made up of individual engineers. However, it does require thinking of responsible engineering more in terms of collaborative work than of individuals working alone.

Fifth, attention in the LeMessurier story is, understandably, focused primarily on public safety. However, engineering responsibilities extend to many areas other than safety—responsibilities regarding the interests of employers and clients, the quality of products, the handling of actual or potential conflicts of interest, the handling of confidential information, and so on. Many of the virtues listed earlier are relevant to fulfilling these responsibilities, too; but stories of just how they might be relevant remain to be told.

So, there is much work to be done. The sort of work that is needed is best undertaken collaboratively, combining the skills, experiences, and insights of ethicists, managers, communication specialists, psychologists, organizational theorists, and, most importantly, engineers themselves.

Although ethicists are needed because of their knack for clarifying and thinking through conceptual and normative issues, they are unlikely to be successful going it alone—at least not unless they, at least to some extent, wear the hats of several other disciplines as well. Underlying the conceptual and normative issues surrounding, for example, what should count as ethically desirable commitment to honesty, objectivity, or quality in engineering practice are major empirical issues as well—issues regarding the details of engineering work itself, the organizational structures within which engineers work, the conditions that foster or inhibit effective communication, the individual characteristics and social environment that are conducive to (or interfere with) the sorts of cooperative endeavors that are essential to responsible practice, and so on.

In his recent book, *Meaningful Work: Rethinking Professional Ethics*, Mike Martin identifies two kinds of explanations of wrongdoing.[11] First, there are *character explanations*, which are cast in terms of features of persons, flaws of character, that play a significant role in wrongdoing. Second, there are *social explanations*, which are cast in terms of "outside structures and pressures that contribute to misconduct, including influences within professions, corporations, and the wider society."[12] Martin distinguishes these two types of explanations in the context of wrongdoing. However, the same distinctions can be applied in the context of explaining responsible practice. Social explanations, Martin observes, are dominant in the social sciences. Character explanations, he says, typically are viewed as "naive, superficial, subjective, and even incompatible with scientifically rigorous social explanations."[13] Even if Martin overstates the case, some resistance to the sort of collaborative work I am recommending can be expected.

However, like Martin, I believe that it is a mistake to think that character and social explanations must be opposed to one another. As Martin says, "Professionals are not merely hapless victims of external forces (although occasionally they are). They are responsible moral agents who make choices in response to outside influences."[14] Thus, it seems that *some* space should be allowed for character in explaining wrongdoing and in explaining responsible practice. At the same time, the influence of external social forces, institutional structures, and specific working environments is undeniable. This influence may extend not only to the range of choices available to engineers in their workplace, but also to the attitudes they bring to their work. How, we might ask, are engineers' attitudes affected by working environments that encourage or discourage imaginative thinking, cooperation with others, careful work, honesty, and so on?

For example, the workplace portrayed in the fictional video *Gilbane Gold* does not encourage proactive approaches to controlling environmental pollution, cooperative problem-solving, or full honesty in communicating with city environmental officials.[15] Z-Corps' young environmental engineer, David Jackson, is deeply troubled ethically in this setting, and he ends up blowing the whistle on his company. However, he does not seem terribly imaginative in coming up with alternative ways of dealing with the company's environmental problems.[16] Phil Port, manager of environmental affairs, seems not to be ethically troubled by how the company is operating—nor does he seem to be much concerned about the environmental damage his company may be causing. To what extent are David Jackson's lack of imagination and Phil Port's relative indifference to environmental concerns a function of the general working atmosphere at Z-Corp?

Imagine a rather different sort of company, such as 3M, that adopts a strong pollution prevention program, with a corresponding reward system for success.[17] 3M claims that its 3P program has saved the company $810 million since 1975. Prior to adopting its aggressive pollution control program, 3M was regarded as a major polluter. Did the new program stir up the imagination of the Phil Ports and David Jacksons in their employ? Or did 3M have to go out and hire new engineers because too few at 3M cared enough, or were imaginative enough, about pollution prevention to meet the challenge? I do not have answers to these questions. I also do not have satisfying answers to the following two questions: To what extent, if any, can a social explanation alone account for whatever attitudes and behavior we might find among engineers at a Z-Corp or a 3M? To what extent, if any, can a character explanation alone account for whatever attitudes and behavior we might find among engineers at a Z-Corp or a 3M? Martin's suggestion, I think, would be that neither kind of explanation by itself is likely to take us far enough. Instead, what is needed are much more complicated kinds of explanations that take advantage of what each has to offer.

This seems to me to be right, which makes the task of articulating the role of character and imagination in responsible engineering practice quite challenging. But if Martin is right in insisting that individual engineers are to some significant extent responsible for the work they do, and that character and imagination have *some* real bearing on how they approach their work, recognizing the difficulty of the task is no excuse for avoiding beginning to chip away at it.

Ethics in the Education of Engineering Students

There are ABET 2000 incentives for shifting the focus of engineering ethics from the negative to the positive. In addition to requiring accredited engineering programs to attempt to foster in their students "an understanding of the ethical characteristics of the engineering profession and practice," it requires that students have a major design experience that includes ethical as well as economic, environmental, social, and political factors.[18] Dwelling mainly on wrongdoing and its avoidance or prevention shortchanges students in helping them understand what the full range of ethical opportunities in engineering design and practice are. Ample room should also be provided for discussing the importance of the sorts of dispositions and skills that are fundamental to responsible, if not exemplary, engineering practice.

REFERENCES

1   William F. May (1988) "Professional Virtue and Self-Regulation," in Callahan, Joan (ed.) *Ethical Issues in Professional Life* (New York, NY: Oxford University Press), 408.

2   Ibid.

3 Waterson, Bill (1990) *Calvin and Hobbes.*

4 For a discussion of some of the results of this project, see Michael S. Pritchard (1988) "Professional Responsibility: Focusing on the Exemplary," *Science and Engineering Ethics* Vol. 4 (2): 215-33. This was supported by National Science Foundation Grant #SBR-930257.

5 My account is based on Joseph Morgenstern's excellent, "The Fifty-Nine Story Crisis," *The New Yorker*, May 29, 1995.

6 Ibid., 48.

7 Ibid.

8 Ibid.

9 Waterson, Bill (Dec. 23, 1990) *Calvin and Hobbes.*

10 Many non-engineers were involved, as well: Citicorp bank officials, insurance agents, New York police, the mayor of New York, and others involved in developing a contingency plan for evacuation of the area if necessary. All of this was done without the public's knowledge. Some might question this "ethics of silence," but the full story of how all these efforts were successfully coordinated is no doubt fascinating in itself.

11 Martin, M. (2000) *Meaningful Work: Rethinking Professional Ethics* (Lawrence, KS: University Press of Kansas), 173.

12 Ibid. Social psychologist Irving Janis's important work on group dynamics seems to focus primarily on social explanations of wrongdoing. However, his more positive account of how groups can resist the shortcomings of "groupthink" seems to presuppose that certain qualities of character on the part of individual members of groups can make a crucial difference (e.g., the commitment to developing and sustaining independent, critical judgment even in the face of pressure to go along with others, and the courage to speak up in opposition to apparent consensus). See Janis, Irving (1982) *Groupthink*, 2nd ed. (Boston: Houghton Mifflin).

13 Ibid.

14 Ibid.

15 For a discussion of the exercise of imagination in addressing Z-Corp's problems, see Michael Pritchard and Mark Holtzapple's (1997) "Responsible Engineering: *Gilbane Gold* Revisited," *Science and Engineering Ethics* Vol. 3(2): 217-30.

16 *Gilbane Gold* (1989), National Society for Professional Engineers, 1420 King Street, Alexandria, VA 22314.

17 For 3M's own account of its Pollution Prevention Pays (3P) program, see its website at <http://www.mmm.com/profile/envt/3p.html>.

18 ABET is the Accreditation Board for Engineering and Technology. For the precise wording of ABET 2000 requirements, see <http://www.abet.org/EAC/each2000.html>.

THE ROLE OF THE ENGINEER

RICHARD T. DE GEORGE

Ethical Responsibilities of Engineers in Large Organizations: The Pinto Case

The myth that ethics has no place in engineering has been attacked, and at least in some corners of the engineering profession has been put to rest.[1] Another myth, however, is emerging to take its place—the myth of the engineer as moral hero. A litany of engineering saints is slowly taking form. The saints of the field are whistle blowers, especially those who have sacrificed all for their moral convictions. The zeal of some preachers, however, has gone too far, piling moral responsibility upon moral responsibility on the shoulders of the engineer. This emphasis, I believe, is misplaced. Though engineers are members of a profession that holds public safety paramount,[2] we cannot reasonably expect engineers to be willing to sacrifice their jobs each day for principle and to have a whistle ever by their sides ready to blow if their firm strays from what they perceive to be the morally right course of action. If this is too much to ask, however, what then is the actual ethical responsibility of engineers in a large organization?

I shall approach this question through a discussion of what has become known as the Pinto case, i.e., the trial that took place in Winamac, Indiana, and that was decided by a jury on March 16, 1980.

In August 1978 near Goshen, Indiana, three girls died of burns in a 1973 Pinto that was rammed in traffic by a van. The rear-end collapsed "like an accordion,"[3] and the gas tank erupted in flames. It was not the first such accident with the Pinto. The Pinto was introduced in 1971 and its gas tank housing was not changed until the 1977 model. Between 1971 and 1978 about fifty suits were brought against Ford in connection with rear-end accidents in the Pinto.

What made the Winamac case different from the fifty others was the fact that the State prosecutor charged Ford with three (originally four, but one was dropped) counts of reckless homicide, a *criminal* offense, under a 1977 Indiana law that made it possible to bring such criminal charges against a corporation. The penalty, if found guilty, was a maximum fine of $10,000 for each count, for a total of $30,000. The case was closely watched, since it was the first time in recent history that a corporation was charged with this criminal offense. Ford spent almost a million dollars in its defense.

With the advantage of hindsight I believe the case raised the right issue at the wrong time.

The prosecution had to show that Ford was reckless in placing the gas tank where and how it did. In order to show this the prosecution had to prove that Ford consciously disregarded harm it might cause and the disregard, according to the statutory definition of "reckless," had to involve "substantial deviation from acceptable standards of conduct."[4]

The prosecution produced seven witnesses who testified that the Pinto was moving at speeds judged to be between 15 and 35 mph when it was hit. Harly Copp, once a high ranking Ford engineer, claimed that the Pinto did not have a balanced design and that for cost reasons the gas tank could withstand only a 20 mph impact without leaking and exploding. The prosecutor, Michael Cosentino, tried to introduce evidence that Ford knew the defects of the gas tank, that its executives knew that a $6.65 part would have made the car considerably safer, and that they decided against the change in order to increase their profits.

Federal safety standards for gas tanks were not introduced until 1977. Once introduced, the National Highway Traffic Safety Administration (NHTSA) claimed a safety defect existed in the gas tanks of Pintos produced from 1971 to 1976. It ordered that Ford recall 1.9 million Pintos. Ford contested the order. Then, without ever admitting that the fuel tank was unsafe, it "voluntarily" ordered a recall. It claimed the recall was not for safety but for "reputational" reasons.[5] Agreeing to a recall in June, its first proposed modifications failed the safety standards tests, and it added a second protective shield to meet safety standards. It did not send out recall notices until August 22. The accident in question took place on August 10. The prosecutor claimed that Ford knew its fuel tank was dangerous as early as 1971 and that it did not make any changes until the 1977 model. It also knew in June of 1978 that its fuel tank did not meet federal safety standards; yet it did nothing to warn owners of this fact. Hence, the prosecution contended, Ford was guilty of reckless homicide.

The defense was led by James F. Neal who had achieved national prominence in the Watergate hearings. He produced testimony from two witnesses who were crucial to the case. They were hospital attendants who had spoken with the driver of the Pinto at the hospital before she died. They claimed she had stated that she had just had her car filled with gas. She had been in a hurry and had left the gas station without replacing the cap on her gas tank. It fell off the top of her car as she drove down the highway. She noticed this and stopped to turn around to pick it up. While stopped, her car was hit by the van. The testimony indicated that the car was stopped. If the car was hit by a van going 50 mph, then the rupture of the gas tank was to be expected. If the cap was off the fuel tank, leakage would be more than otherwise. No small vehicle was made to withstand such impact. Hence, Ford claimed, there was no recklessness involved. Neal went on to produce films of tests that indicated that the amount of damage

the Pinto suffered meant that the impact must have been caused by the van's going at least 50 mph. He further argued that the Pinto gas tank was at least as safe as the gas tanks on the 1973 American Motors Gremlin, the Chevrolet Vega, the Dodge Colt, and the Toyota Corolla, all of which suffered comparable damage when hit from the rear at 50 mph. Since no federal safety standards were in effect in 1973, Ford was not reckless if its safety standards were comparable to those of similar cars made by competitors; that standard represented the state of the art at that time, and it would be inappropriate to apply 1977 standards to a 1973 car.[6]

The jury deliberated for four days and finally came up with a verdict of not guilty. When the verdict was announced at a meeting of the Ford Board of Directors then taking place, the members broke out in a cheer.[7]

These are the facts of the case. I do not wish to second-guess the jury. Based on my reading of the case, I think they arrived at a proper decision, given the evidence. Nor do I wish to comment adversely on the judge's ruling that prevented the prosecution from introducing about 40% of his case because the evidence referred to 1971 and 1972 models of the Pinto and not the 1973 model.[8]

The issue of Ford's being guilty of acting recklessly can, I think, be made plausible, as I shall indicate shortly. But the successful strategy argued by the defense in this case hinged on the Pinto in question being hit by a van at 50 mph. At that speed, the defense successfully argued, the gas tank of any subcompact would rupture. Hence that accident did not show that the Pinto was less safe than other subcompacts or that Ford acted recklessly. To show that would require an accident that took place at no more than 20 mph.

The contents of the Ford documents that Prosecutor Cosentino was not allowed to present in court were published in the *Chicago Tribune* on October 13, 1979. If they are accurate, they tend to show grounds for the charge of recklessness.

Ford had produced a safe gas tank mounted over the rear axle in its 1969 Capri in Europe. It tested that tank in the Capri. In its over-the-axle position, it withstood impacts of up to 30 mph. Mounted behind the axle, it was punctured by projecting bolts when hit from the rear at 20 mph. A $6.65 part would help make the tank safer. In its 1971 Pinto, Ford chose to place the gas tank behind the rear axle without the extra part. A Ford memo indicates that in this position the Pinto has more trunk space, and that production costs would be less than in the over-the-axle position. These considerations won out.9

The Pinto was first tested it seems in 1971, after the 1971 model was produced, for rear-end crash tolerance. It was found that the tank ruptured when hit from the rear at 20 mph. This should have been no surprise, since the Capri tank in that position had ruptured at 20 mph. A memo recommends that rather than making any changes Ford should wait until 1976 when the government was expected to introduce fuel tank standards. By delaying making any change, Ford could save $20.9 million, since the change would average about $10 per car.10

In the Winamac case Ford claimed correctly that there were no federal safety standards in 1973. But it defended itself against recklessness by claiming its car was comparable to other subcompacts at that time. All the defense showed, however, was that all the subcompacts were unsafe when hit at 50 mph. Since the other subcompacts were not forced to recall their cars in 1978, there is *prima facie* evidence that Ford's Pinto gas tank mounting was substandard. The Ford documents tend to show Ford knew the danger it was inflicting on Ford owners; yet it did nothing, for profit reasons. How short-sighted those reasons were is demonstrated by the fact that the Pinto thus far in litigation and recalls alone has cost Ford $50 million. Some forty suits are still to be settled. And these figures do not take into account the loss of sales due to bad publicity.

Given these facts, what are we to say about the Ford engineers? Where were they when all this was going on, and what is their responsibility for the Pinto? The answer, I suggest, is that they were where they were supposed to be, doing what they were supposed to be doing. They were performing tests, designing the Pinto, making reports. But do they have no moral responsibility for the products they design? What after all is the moral responsibility of engineers in a large corporation? By way of reply, let me emphasize that no engineer can morally do what is immoral. If commanded to do what he should not morally do, he must resist and refuse. But in the Ford Pinto situation no engineer was told to produce a gas tank that would explode and kill people. The engineers were not instructed to make an unsafe car. They were morally responsible for knowing the state of the art, including that connected with placing and mounting gas tanks. We can assume that the Ford engineers were cognizant of the state of the art in producing the model they did. When tests were made in 1970 and 1971, and a memo was written stating that a $6.65 modification could make the gas tank safer,11 that was an engineering assessment. Whichever engineer proposed the modification and initiated the memo acted ethically in doing so. The next step, the administrative decision not to make the modification, was, with hindsight, a poor one in almost every way. It ended up costing Ford a great deal more not to put in the part than it would have cost to put it in. Ford still claims today that its gas tank was as safe as the accepted standards of the industry at that time.12 It must say so, otherwise the suits pending against it will skyrocket. That it was not as safe seems borne out by the fact that only the Pinto of all the subcompacts failed to pass the 30 mph rear impact NHTSA test.

But the question of wrongdoing or of malicious intent or of recklessness is not so easily solved. Suppose the ordinary person were told when buying a Pinto that if he paid an extra $6.65 he could increase the safety of the vehicle so that it could withstand a 30 mph rear-end impact rather than a 20 mph impact, and that the odds of suffering a rear-end impact of between 20 and 30 mph was 1 in 250,000. Would we call him or her reckless if he or she declined to pay the extra $6.65? I am not sure how to answer that question. Was it reckless of Ford to wish to save the $6.65 per car and increase the risk for the consumer? Here I am inclined to be clearer in my own mind. If I choose to take a risk to save $6.65, it is my risk and my $6.65. But if Ford saves the $6.65 and I take the risk, then I clearly lose. Does Ford have the right to do that without informing me, if the going standard of safety of subcompacts is safety in a rear-end collision up to 30 mph? I think not. I admit, however, that the case is not clear-cut, even if we add that during 1976 and 1977 Pintos suffered 13 fiery fatal rear-end collisions, more than double that of other US comparable cars. The VW Rabbit and Toyota Corolla suffered none.[13]

Yet, if we are to morally fault anyone for the decision not to add the part, we would censure not the Ford engineers but the Ford executives, because it was not an engineering but an executive decision.

My reason for taking this view is that an engineer cannot be expected and cannot have the responsibility to second-guess managerial decisions. He is responsible for bringing the facts to the attention of those who need them to make decisions. But the input of engineers is only one of many factors that go to make up managerial decisions. During the trial, the defense called as a witness Francis Olsen, the assistant chief engineer in charge of design at Ford, who testified that he bought a 1973 Pinto for his eighteen-year-old daughter, kept it a year, and then traded it in for a 1974 Pinto which he kept two years.[14] His testimony and his actions were presented as an indication that the Ford engineers had confidence in the Pinto's safety. At least this one had enough confidence in it to give it to his daughter. Some engineers at Ford may have felt that the car could have been safer. But this is true of almost every automobile. Engineers in large firms have an ethical responsibility to do their jobs as best they can, to report their observations about safety and improve-

ment of safety to management. But they do not have the obligation to insist that their perceptions or their standards be accepted. They are not paid to do that, they are not expected to do that, and they have no moral or ethical obligation to do that.

In addition to doing their jobs, engineers can plausibly be said to have an obligation of loyalty to their employers, and firms have a right to a certain amount of confidentiality concerning their internal operations. At the same time engineers are required by their professional ethical codes to hold the safety of the public paramount. Where these obligations conflict, the need for and justification of whistle blowing arises.[15] If we admit the obligations on both sides, I would suggest as a rule of thumb that engineers and other workers in a large corporation are morally *permitted* to go public with information about the safety of a product if the following conditions are met:

1. if the harm that will be done by the product to the public is serious and considerable;
2. if they make their concerns known to their superiors; and
3. if, getting no satisfaction from their immediate superiors, they exhaust the channels available within the corporation, including going to the board of directors.

If they still get no action, I believe they are morally *permitted* to make public their views; but they are not morally *obliged* to do so. Harly Copp, a former Ford executive and engineer, in fact did criticize the Pinto from the start and testified for the prosecution against Ford at the Winamac trial.[16] He left the company and voiced his criticism. The criticism was taken up by Ralph Nader and others. In the long run it led to the Winamac trial and probably helped in a number of other suits filed against Ford. Though I admire Mr. Copp for his actions, assuming they were done from moral motives, I do not think such action was morally required, nor do I think the other engineers at Ford were morally deficient in not doing likewise.

For an engineer to have a moral *obligation* to bring his case for safety to the public, I think two other conditions have to be fulfilled, in addition to the three mentioned above.[17]

4. He must have documented evidence that would convince a reasonable, impartial observer that his view of the situation is correct and the company policy wrong.

Such evidence is obviously very difficult to obtain and produce. Such evidence, however, takes an engineer's concern out of the realm of the subjective and precludes that concern from being simply one person's opinion based on a limited point of view. Unless such evidence is available, there is little likelihood that the concerned engineer's view will win the day simply by public exposure. If the testimony of Francis Olsen is accurate, then even among the engineers at Ford there was disagreement about the safety of the Pinto.

5. There must be strong evidence that making the information public will in fact prevent the threatened serious harm.

This means both that before going public the engineer should know what source (government, newspaper, columnist, TV reporter) will make use of his evidence and how it will be handled. He should also have good reason to believe that it will result in the kind of change or result that he believes is morally appropriate. None of this was the case in the Pinto situation. After much public discussion, five model years, and failure to pass national safety standards tests, Ford plausibly defends its original claim that the gas tank was acceptably safe. If there is little likelihood of his success, there is no moral obligation for the engineer to go public. For the harm he or she personally incurs is not offset by the good such action achieves.[18]

My first substantive conclusion is that Ford engineers had no moral *obligation* to do more than they did in this case.

My second claim is that though engineers in large organizations should have a say in setting safety standards and producing cost-benefit analyses, they need not have the last word. My reasons are two. First, while the degree of risk, e.g., in a car, is an engineering problem, the acceptability of risk is not. Second, an engineering cost-benefit analysis does not include all the factors appropriate in making a policy decision, either on the corporate or the social level. Safety is one factor in an engineering design. Yet clearly it is only one factor. A Mercedes-Benz 280 is presumably safer than a Ford Pinto. But the difference in price is considerable. To make a Pinto as safe as a Mercedes it would probably have to cost a comparable amount. In making cars as in making many other objects some balance has to be reached between safety and cost. The final decision on where to draw the balance is not only an engineering decision. It is also a managerial decision, and probably even more appropriately a social decision.

The difficulty of setting standards raises two pertinent issues. The first concerns federal safety standards. The second concerns cost-benefit analyses. The state of the art of engineering technology determines a floor below which no manufacturer should ethically go. Whether the Pinto fell below that floor, we have already seen, is a controverted question. If the cost of achieving greater safety is considerable—and I do not think $6.65 is considerable—there is a built-in temptation for a producer to skimp more than he should and more than he might like. The best way to remove that temptation is for there to be a national set of standards. Engineers can determine what the state of the art is, what is possible, and what the cost of producing safety is. A panel of informed people, not necessarily engineers, should decide what is acceptable risk and hence what acceptable minimum standards are. Both the minimum standards and the standards attained by a given car should be a matter of record that goes with each car. A safer car may well cost more. But unless a customer knows how much safety he is buying for his money, he may not know which car he wants to buy. This information, I believe, is information a car buyer is entitled to have.

In 1978, after the publicity that Ford received with the Pinto and the controversy surrounding it, the sales of Pintos fell dramatically. This was an indication that consumers preferred a safer car for comparable money, and they went to the competition. The state of Oregon took all its Pintos out of its fleet and sold them off. To the surprise of one dealer involved in selling turned-in Pintos, they went for between $1000 and $1800.[19] The conclusion we correctly draw is that there was a market for a car with a dubious safety record even though the price was much lower than for safer cars and lower than Ford's manufacturing price.

The second issue is the way cost-benefit analyses are produced and used. I have already mentioned one cost-benefit analysis used by Ford, namely, the projection that by not adding a part and by placing the gas tank in the rear the company could save $20.9 million. The projection, I noted, was grossly mistaken for it did not consider litigation, recalls, and bad publicity which have already cost Ford over $50 million. A second type of cost-benefit analysis sometimes estimates the number and costs of suits that will have to be paid, adds to it fines, and deducts that total amount from the total saved by a particular practice. If the figure is positive, it is more profitable not to make a safety change than to make it.

A third type of cost-benefit analysis, which Ford and other auto companies produce, estimates the cost and benefits of specific changes in their automobiles. One study, for instance, deals with the cost-benefit analysis relating to fuel leakage associated with static rollover. The unit cost of the part is $11. If that is included in 12.5 million cars, the total cost is $137 million. That part will prevent 180 burn deaths, 180 serious burn injuries and 2100 burned vehicles. Assigning a cost of $200,000 per death, $67,000 per major injury, and $700 per vehicle, the

benefit is $49.5 million. The cost-benefit ratio is slightly over 3-1.[20]

If this analysis is compared with a similar cost-benefit analysis for a rear-end collision, it is possible to see how much safety is achieved per dollar spent. This use is legitimate and helpful. But the procedure is open to very serious criticism if used not in a comparative but in an absolute manner.

The analysis ignores many factors, such as the human suffering of the victim and of his or her family. It equates human life to $200,000, which is based on average lost future wages. Any figure here is questionable, except for comparative purposes, in which case as long as the same figure is used it does not change the information as to relative benefit per dollar. The ratio, however, has no *absolute* meaning, and no decision can properly be based on the fact that the resulting ratio of cost to benefit in the above example is 3 to 1. Even more important, how can this figure or ratio be compared with the cost of styling? Should the $11 per unit to reduce death and injury from rollover be weighed against a comparable $11 in rear-end collision or $11 in changed styling? Who decides how much more to put into safety and how much more to put into styling? What is the rationale for the decision?

In the past consumers have not been given an opportunity to vote on the matter. The automobile industry has decided what will sell and what will not, and has decided how much to put on safety. American car dealers have not typically put much emphasis on safety features in selling their cars. The assumption that American drivers are more interested in styling than safety is a decision that has been made for them, not by them. Engineers can and do play an important role in making cost-benefit analyses. They are better equipped than anyone else to figure risks and cost. But they are not better equipped to figure the acceptability of risk, or the amount that people should be willing to pay to eliminate such risk. Neither, however, are the managers of automobile corporations. The amount of acceptable risk is a public decision that can and should be made by representatives of the public or by the public itself.

Since cost-benefit analyses of the types I have mentioned are typical of those used in the auto industry, and since they are inadequate ways of judging the safety a car should have, given the state of the art, it is clear that the automobile companies should not have the last word or the exclusive word in how much safety to provide. There must be national standards set and enforced. The National Highway Traffic Administration was established in 1966 to set standards. Thus far only two major standards have been established and implemented: the 1972 side impact standard and the 1977 gasoline tank safety standard. Rather than dictate standards, however, in which process it is subject to lobbying, it can mandate minimum standards and also require auto manufacturers to inform the public about the safety quotient of each car, just as it now requires each car to specify the miles per gallon it is capable of achieving. Such an approach would put the onus for basic safety on the manufacturers, but it would also make additional safety a feature of consumer interest and competition.

Engineers in large corporations have an important role to play. That role, however, is not usually to set policy or to decide on the acceptability of risk. Their knowledge and expertise are important both to the companies for which they work and to the public. But they are not morally responsible for policies and decisions beyond their competence and control. Does this view, however, let engineers off the moral hook too easily?

To return briefly to the Pinto story once more, Ford wanted a subcompact to fend off the competition of Japanese imports. The order came down to produce a car of 2,000 pounds or less that would cost $2000 or less in time for the 1971 model. This allowed only 25 months instead of the usual 43 months for design and production of a new car.[21] The engineers were squeezed from the start. Perhaps this is why they did not test the gas tank for rear-end collision impact until the car was produced.

Should the engineers have refused the order to produce the car in 25 months? Should they have resigned, or leaked the story to the newspapers? Should they have refused to speed up their usual routine? Should they have complained to their professional society that they were being asked to do the impossible—if it were to be done right? I am not in a position to say what they should have done. But with the advantage of hindsight, I suggest we should ask not only what they should have done. We should especially ask what changes can be made to prevent engineers from being squeezed in this way in the future.

Engineering ethics should not take as its goal the producing of moral heroes. Rather it should consider what forces operate to encourage engineers to act as they feel they should not; what structural or other features of a large corporation squeeze them until their consciences hurt? Those features should then be examined, evaluated, and changes proposed and made. Lobbying by engineering organizations would be appropriate, and legislation should be passed if necessary. In general I tend to favor voluntary means where possible. But where that is utopian, then legislation is a necessary alternative.

The need for whistle blowing in a firm indicates that a change is necessary. How can we preclude the necessity for blowing the whistle?

The Winamac Pinto case suggests some external and internal modifications. It was the first case to be tried under a 1977 Indiana law making it possible to try corporations as well as individuals for the criminal offenses of reckless homicide. In bringing the charges against Ford, Prosecutor Michael Cosentino acted courageously, even if it turned out to have been a poor case for such a precedent-setting trial. But the law concerning reckless homicide, for instance, which was the charge in question, had not been rewritten with the corporation in mind. The penalty, since corporations cannot go to jail, was the maximum fine of $10,000 per count—hardly a significant amount when contrasted with the 1977 income of Ford International which was $11.1 billion in revenues and $750 million in profits. What Mr. Cosentino did *not* do was file charges against individuals in the Ford Company who were responsible for the decisions he claimed were reckless. Had highly placed officials been charged, the message would have gotten through to management across the country that individuals cannot hide behind corporate shields in their decisions if they are indeed reckless, put too low a price on life and human suffering, and sacrifice it too cheaply for profits.

A bill was recently proposed in Congress requiring managers to disclose the existence of life-threatening defects to the appropriate Federal agency.[22] Failure to do so and attempts to conceal defects could result in fines of $50,000 or imprisonment for a minimum of two years, or both. The fine in corporate terms is negligible. But imprisonment for members of management is not.

Some argue that increased litigation for product liability is the way to get results in safety. Heavy damages yield quicker changes than criminal proceedings. Ford agreed to the Pinto recall shortly after a California jury awarded damages of $127.8 million after a youth was burned over 95% of his body. Later the sum was reduced, on appeal, to $6.3 million.[23] But criminal proceedings make the litigation easier, which is why Ford spent $1,000,000 in its defense to avoid paying $30,000 in fines.[24] The possibility of going to jail for one's actions, however, should have a salutary effect. If someone, the president of a company in default of anyone else, were to be charged in criminal suit, presidents would soon know whom they can and should hold responsible below them. One of the difficulties in a large corporation is knowing who is responsible for particular decisions. If the president were held responsible, outside pressure would build to reorganize the corporation so that responsibility was assigned and assumed.

If a corporation wishes to be moral or if society or engineers wish to apply pressure for organizational changes such that the corporation acts morally and responds to the moral conscience of engineers and others within the organization, then changes must be made. Unless those at the top set a moral tone, unless they insist on moral conduct, unless they punish immoral conduct and reward moral conduct, the corporation will function without considering the morality of questions and of corporate actions. It may by accident rather than by intent avoid immoral actions, though in the long run this is unlikely.

Ford's management was interested only in meeting federal standards and having these as low as possible. Individual federal standards should be both developed and enforced. Federal fines for violations should not be token but comparable to damages paid in civil suits and should be paid to all those suffering damage from violations.[25]

Independent engineers or engineering societies—if the latter are not co-opted by auto manufacturers—can play a significant role in supplying information on the state of the art and the level of technical feasibility available. They can also develop the safety index I suggested earlier, which would represent the relative and comparative safety of an automobile. Competition has worked successfully in many areas. Why not in the area of safety? Engineers who work for auto manufacturers will then have to make and report the results of standard tests such as the ability to withstand rear-end impact. If such information is required data for a safety index to be affixed to the windshield of each new car, engineers will not be squeezed by management in the area of safety.

The means by which engineers with ethical concerns can get a fair hearing without endangering their jobs or blowing the whistle must be made part of a corporation's organizational structure. An outside board member with primary responsibility for investigating and responding to such ethical concerns might be legally required. When this is joined with the legislation pending in Congress which I mentioned, the dynamics for ethics in the organization will be significantly improved. Another way of achieving a similar end is by providing an inspector general for all corporations with an annual net income of over $1 billion. An independent committee of an engineering association might be formed to investigate charges made by engineers concerning the safety of a product on which they are working;[26] a company that did not allow an appropriate investigation of employee charges would become subject to cover-up proceedings. Those in the engineering industry can suggest and work to implement other ideas. I have elsewhere outlined a set of ten such changes for the ethical corporation.[27]

In addition to asking how an engineer should respond to moral quandaries and dilemmas, and rather than asking how to educate or train engineers to be moral heroes, those in engineering ethics should ask how large organizations can be changed so that they do not squeeze engineers in moral dilemmas, place them in the position of facing moral quandaries, and make them feel that they must blow the whistle.

The time has come to go beyond sensitizing students to moral issues and solving and resolving the old, standard cases. The next and very important questions to be asked as we discuss each case is how organizational structures can be changed so that no engineer will ever again have to face *that* case.

Many of the issues of engineering ethics within a corporate setting concern the ethics of organizational structure, questions of public policy, and so questions that frequently are amenable to solution only on a scale larger than the individual—on the scale of organization and law. The ethical responsibilities of the engineer in a large organization have as much to do with the organization as with the engineer. They can be most fruitfully approached by considering from a moral point of view not only the individual engineer but the framework within which he or she works. We not only need moral people. Even more importantly we need moral structures and organizations. Only by paying more attention to these can we adequately resolve the questions of the ethical responsibility of engineers in large organizations.

NOTES

1   The body of literature on engineering ethics is now substantive and impressive. See, *A Selected Annotated Bibliography of Professional Ethics and Social Responsibility in Engineering*, compiled by Robert F. Ladenson, James Choromokos, Ernest d'Anjou, Martin Pimsler, and Howard Rosen (Chicago: Center for the Study of Ethics in the Professions, Illinois Institute of Technology, 1980). A useful two-volume collection of readings and cases is also available: Robert J. Baum and Albert Flores, *Ethical Problems in Engineering*, 2nd edition (Troy, NY: Rensselaer Polytechnic Institute, Center for the Study of the Human Dimensions of Science and Technology, 1980). See also Robert J. Baum's *Ethics and Engineering Curricula* (Hastings-on-Hudson, NY: Hastings Center, 1980).

2   See, for example, the first canon of the 1974 Engineers Council for Professional Development Code, the first canon of the National Council of Engineering Examiners Code, and the draft (by A. Oldenquist and E. Slowter) of a "Code of Ethics for the Engineering Profession" (all reprinted in Baum and Flores, *Ethical Problems in Engineering*).

3   Details of the incident presented in this paper are based on testimony at the trial. Accounts of the trial as well as background reports were carried by both the *New York Times* and the *Chicago Tribune*.

4   *New York Times*, February 17, 1980, IV, 9.

5   *New York Times*, February 21, 1980, A6. *Fortune*, September 11, 1978, 42.

6   *New York Times*, March 14, 1980, 1.

7   *Time*, March 24, 1980, 24.

8 *New York Times*, January 16, 1980, 16; February 7, 1980, 16.

9 *Chicago Tribune*, October 13, 1979, 1, and Section 2, 12.

10 *Chicago Tribune*, October 13, 1979, 1; *New York Times*, October 14, 1979, 26.

11 *New York Times*, February 4, 1980, 12.

12 *New York Times*, June 10, 1978, 1; *Chicago Tribune*, October 13, 1979, 1, and Section 2, 12. The continuous claim has been that the Pinto poses "No serious hazards."

13 *New York Times*, October 26, 1978, 103.

14 *New York Times*, February 20, 1980, A16.

15 For a discussion of the conflict, see, Sissela Bok, "Whistleblowing and Professional Responsibility," *New York University Educational Quarterly*, 2-10. For detailed case studies see, Ralph Nader, Peter J. Petkas, and Kate Blackwell, *Whistle Blowing* (New York: Grossman Publishers, 1972); Charles Peters and Taylor Branch, *Blowing the Whistle: Dissent in the Public Interest* (New York: Praeger Publishers, 1972); and Robert M. Anderson, Robert Perrucci, Dan E. Schendel and Leon E. Trachtman, *Divided Loyalties: Whistle-Blowing at BART* (West Lafayette, IN: Purdue University, 1980).

16 *New York Times*, February 4, 1980, 12.

17 The position I present here is developed more fully in my book *Business Ethics* (New York: Macmillan, 1981). It differs somewhat from the dominant view expressed in the existing literature in that I consider whistle blowing an extreme measure that is morally obligatory only if the stringent conditions set forth are satisfied. Cf. Kenneth D. Walters, "Your Employees' Right to Blow the Whistle," *Harvard Business Review*, July-August, 1975.

18 On the dangers incurred by whistle blowers, see Gene James, "Whistle-Blowing: Its Nature and Justification," *Philosophy in Context*, 10 (1980), 99-117, which examines the legal context of whistle blowing; Peter Raven-Hansen, "Dos and Don'ts for Whistleblowers: Planning for Trouble," *Technology Review*, May 1980, 34-44, which suggests how to blow the whistle; Helen Dudar, "The Price of Blowing the Whistle," *The New York Times Magazine*, 30 October, 1977, which examines the results for whistleblowers; David W. Ewing, "Canning Directions," *Harpers*, August, 1979, 17-22, which indicates "how the government rids itself of troublemakers" and how legislation protecting whistleblowers can be circumvented; and Report by the US General Accounting Office, "The Office of the Special Counsel Can Improve Its Management of Whistleblower Cases," December 30, 1980 (FPCD-81-10).

19 *New York Times*, April 21, 1978, IV, 1, 18.

20 See Mark Dowie, "Pinto Madness," *Mother Jones*, September/October, 1977, 24-28.

21 *Chicago Tribune*, October 13, 1979, Section 2, 12.

22 *New York Times*, March 16, 1980, IV, 20.

23 *New York Times*, February 8, 1978, 8.

24 *New York Times*, February 17, 1980, IV, 9; January 6, 1980, 24; *Time*, March 24, 1980, 24.

25 *The Wall Street Journal*, August 7, 1980, 7, reported that the Ford Motor Company "agreed to pay a total of $22,500 to the families of three Indiana teen-age girls killed in the crash of a Ford Pinto nearly two years ago.... A Ford spokesman said the settlement was made without any admission of liability. He speculated that the relatively small settlement may have been influenced by certain Indiana laws which severely restrict the amount of damages victims or their families can recover in civil cases alleging wrongful death."

26 A number of engineers have been arguing for a more active role by engineering societies in backing up individual engineers in their attempts to act responsibly. See, Edwin Layton, *Revolt of the Engineers* (Cleveland: Case West-

ern Reserve, 1971); Stephen H. Unger, "Engineering Societies and the Responsible Engineer," *Annals of the New York Academy of Sciences*, 196 (1973), 433-37 (reprinted in Baum and Flores, *Ethical Problems in Engineering*, 56-59; and Robert Perrucci and Joel Gerstl, *Profession Without Community: Engineers in American Society* (New York: Random House, 1969).

27 Richard T. De George, "Responding to the Mandate for Social Responsibility," *Guidelines for Business When Societal Demands Conflict* (Washington, DC: Council for Better Business Bureaus, 1978), 60-80.

◆ ◆ ◆ ◆ ◆

LINDA RUSH FRANTZ

Engineering Ethics: The Responsibility of the Manager

1. Introduction

In early centuries and in small self-sufficient clans, it was possible to generate a fierce family loyalty in the spirit of D'Artagnan's "one for all and all for one," thus assuring maximum effort and internal harmony. In the large organizations of the present day, carrying on technically complex and far-flung enterprises, it is far more difficult to inspire wholehearted devotion. Hence, strict rules with penalties for lack of effort are generally employed to supplement the normal incentives (Alger, 1965). Most professional societies have adopted "Codes of Ethics" to deal with these problems.

This paper looks at the ethical responsibilities of the engineering manager not only as an engineer but to his employees and to society as well. The importance of this responsibility to the individual as well as the engineering profession will be highlighted.

All of the recognized professions, including engineering, have developed codes of ethics for the guidance of their members. The purpose of these codes is twofold: (1) to emphasize the broad general principles by which all members of the profession should be guided, and (2) to indicate how these principles apply in specific circumstances. What gives the professional code of ethics its peculiar significance is that it prescribes not only the duties of the members of the profession to each other, but also the duties of the members towards those outside the group (MacIver, 1955). The codes were developed to establish ideals and form general patterns of conduct which help to improve the performance and the public standing of the profession as a whole.

2. History of "The Codes"

An ethical code for a profession should not be a statement of general morality. Neither should it be a mere listing of established customs prevailing among a certain group of people. Rather, it should be a statement of ethical principles applied to the daily performance of a particular profession.

Objectively, a code is developed to establish publicly certain approved standards of practice, to support the well-intentioned individual, and to discourage those who should disregard these approved standards. In this undertaking, it should not attempt the impossible by upholding standards beyond the potential of human achievement. "By association with the rules that cannot be obeyed, rules that can be obeyed lose their authority" (Spencer, 1905). A code of ethics, if it is to accomplish anything must restrict itself to that which is in the realm of possibility.

In 1932, representing nine individual societies, the Engineers Council for Professional Development (ECPD) formed with the purpose "to coordinate and promote efforts to attain higher professional standards of education and practice, greater solidarity of the engineering profession, and greater effectiveness in dealing with technical, economic and social problems" (Alger, 1965).

By 1941, ECPD developed several versions of a statement on "Canons of Ethics" which were presented to the various societies involved for discussion and debate. As with most organizations, numerous differences of opinion arose and the Canons were not adopted by all the societies of ECPD until 1947. However, before this, the National Society of Professional Engineers, not an ECPD member, had already accepted them.

From 1960 to 1963 the ethics committee undertook a revision of the original Canons to embody numerous suggested changes and to give greater recognition to the needs of practicing engineers. The revised Canons include a short statement of the fundamental ethical principles of the engineering profession.

> The Engineer, to uphold and advance the honor and dignity of the engineering profession and in keeping with high standards of ethical conduct:
>
> I. Will be honest and impartial, and will serve with devotion his employer, his clients, and the public;
> II. Will strive to increase the competence and prestige of the engineering profession;
> III. Will use his knowledge and skill for the advancement of human welfare.

The entire ECPD Canons of Ethics of Engineering were approved by the Engineers Council for Professional Development on September 30, 1968.

Later, in 1973, NSPE endorsed a set of guidelines to professional employment for engineers and scientists. These guidelines were set up by the Intersociety Committee for Professional Employment Guidelines. The second edition was presented in 1978 and accepted by 31 professional societies.

3. Responsibilities to the Organization

Typically, one of the manager's first duties is to formalize a new employee's responsibility to the organization by signing an employment contract or agreement. Employers are allowed to require this as a condition of employment and many do. It usually includes statements that waive the employee's rights to patents developed at the company's expense and give to the company exclusive ownership of the patents as well as prohibiting the disclosure of any company confidential information which the employee may have acquired.

In their book, *Entering Industry: A Guide for Young Professionals*, Billmeyer and Kelley (1975) give the following description of employment agreements.

> "A typical employment agreement also contains a clause providing for the return of all confidential information when employment terminates. The concern over patents is justified, for they provide the major mechanism by which the employer can protect his investment in research and development. In the United States and many other countries, patents are granted only to individual inventors and must subsequently be assigned by the individual to his company.
>
> Some employment agreements specify further obligations of the employee. It is often agreed that he will not, while employed, enter into any additional jobs or activities that would conflict with his employment or impair his performance. More controversial are the post-employment contracts required by some employers, which preclude the employee from working for competitors for a specified time after termination of the job covered by the contract. Such an agreement is needed only when the

employee will be involved in an unusually important confidential development."

Once an employment agreement is signed, the manager may wish to discuss those policies dealing with confidential information commonly referred to as "trade secrets." Legally, a trade secret may be defined as "any formula, pattern, device, or compilation of information which is advantageous to the business and not available to a competitor." It may be a chemical formula, a process for manufacturing or formulating, a blueprint for a machine, or a list of customers, and the manager must define these secrets clearly. In deciding what is a trade secret, one should consider the cost to the company (in money and effort) to get the information through his own research efforts, the extent to which the secret is known to the employees, and what protective measures are taken to safeguard its secrecy (O'Meara, 1971).

Other trade secrets may include: customer lists, discount schedules, marketing plans, or purchasing specifications; specific formulas and formulation procedures; design drawings; analytical test methods developed within the company, information on production costs, process rates and the like; patentable ideas, patent applications and preliminary reports or inventions; lists of research and development programs under way; figures on production capacity, waste, manpower requirements, sales, costs or profits, computer programs; and lists of suppliers and quantities of materials purchased.

Alger (1965) compared a trade secret to a bottle of perfume. "If it is permitted to leak out, its value to the owner is gone."

How are trade secrets protected? The following is a list of common practices used by companies.

- Employment Contracts
- Precautions to avoid conflict of interest
- Release of information only on a "need to know" basis where it is not possible to get patent protection (generally, companies prefer to seek patent protection where possible)

- Internal communications on secrecy, reminding employees of their obligations to protect company secrets at all times
- Termination interviews to remind the departing employees of their obligations, which in some cases include restrictions against working for competitors in the same area for specified periods of time
- Precautions to ensure that visitors do not gain access to company secret information

It is clear from the foregoing that one critical period with respect to trade secrets arises when an employee plans to change jobs. Most companies rely on his professional ethics and honesty to avoid disclosure of company confidential information, but frequently he is asked to sign an agreement not to work for competitors for a specific period of time. In many cases, he is provided compensation if he cannot get another job of his specialized training. Billmeyer and Kelley (1975) have noted many managers, wanting to avoid controversy, will not hire an applicant for work in a sensitive area identical to that in which he was previously employed.

Still, the question remains whether an employee exposed to trade secrets can ethically and honestly work for a competing company in a similar field. The following case is an example of what happens when this touchy subject arises.

Dr. Hirsch, an employee of the DuPont Company for twelve years, had spent six years on research and development of a new chloride process for making TiO_2. Increasingly dissatisfied with the lack of job openings in management, he began to look for new job opportunities. He applied to some ten companies over a three-year period, but without success.

In 1962, the American Potash and Chemical Corporation (Ampot) began recruiting personnel for a new TiO_2 plant to use a chloride process developed by a third company, taking full precautions to prevent disclosure of confidential information by job applicants. Hirsch applied and, concluding that Ampot wanted his skills and general knowledge rather than DuPont's proprietary knowledge, accepted the position of manager of technical services for the new plant then being planned. Fifteen years earlier, he had signed an employment agreement with DuPont containing the usual disclosure clause. As a condition for employment at Ampot, he had signed an agreement with them that he would neither disclose to nor employ for Ampot any confidential information or trade secrets learned on his earlier job.

DuPont immediately obtained a court order preventing Hirsch from working on the TiO$_2$ project at Ampot, contending that it would be impossible for him to do so without divulging or employing the confidential knowledge received at DuPont. Ampot was forced to assign Hirsch to a position elsewhere. The case came to trial two years later, and was finally dismissed some three years after that. The legal arguments were far too involved to review here, but it is clear that the court was fully aware of the conflict between the protection of trade secrets and the protection of the individual's right to use his knowledge and skills in gainful employment. (Billmeyer and Kelley, 1975)

Although each case involves differing circumstances, it is obvious that the best practice for an employee is simply to avoid changing jobs within the same field in which trade secrets are known. Similarly, most companies and managers take great precautions against hiring someone into such a position.

Billmeyer and Kelley continued that to many people the idea of espionage exists only in the tele-

vision spy movie, and most take an attitude of "it can't happen here" toward espionage in relation to industrial trade secrets. Yet it does happen at an estimated cost of $4 billion each year. As professionals, engineering managers have the responsibility of guarding against loss by espionage of shared trade secrets.

Occasionally a spectacular espionage case brings home the fact that "it can happen here." One such involved Dr. Robert S. Aries, a chemical engineer. A naturalized citizen, educated in the United States, Aries was highly respected for his technical articles and patents. But he took every opportunity to "pump" his associates for proprietary information, and sold these pirated trade secrets.

This espionage was uncovered by chance. As Merck and Company was about to market a new articoccidial agent for destroying poultry parasites, Aries presented a technical paper in Canada describing a similar drug he had developed. Considering the time and effort Merck had invested, it seemed highly unlikely that Aries could have developed such an agent independently. By chance, Merck was then completing negotiations to purchase a French chemical company, whose management reported to Merck that Aries had licensed them to manufacture and market his agent. Further investigation showed that he had also licensed companies in the United States, Great Britain, and Switzerland, for sizeable sums of money. The formulas for the two drugs were identical.

It was discovered that a former student of Aries, employed by Merck but not on the same project, had stolen and copied documents and provided them, together with samples, to Aries. In some cases Aries transmitted the documents to his licensees without recopying them, so the case was easy to follow. Subsequently it was found that secrets regarding a lubricating oil additive and electrical components for computers had been obtained by Aries from other former students.

Prosecution followed, and judgements of more than $21 million were awarded to Merck and the other two companies whose secrets had been pirated. But Aries had fled to Europe and his American companies were insolvent. Despite civil and criminal actions pending against him here and abroad, he has not been brought to trial. (Walsh, 1973)

As I mentioned earlier, professional ethics in engineering is so broad a subject that it would be impossible to discuss everything in a research paper such as this one. As a Manufacturing Engineer, I have seen many other problems that can arise other than the ones I have previously discussed. Pilferage, expense accounts, drug abuse and alcoholism, theft, vacation pay allowances, and false advertising are only a few more topics that should be considered and dealt with in an ethical manner by any professional.

4. Responsibilities to the Public

Only in the past few years have companies, professional societies, and managers become increasingly aware that they have a responsibility to the public. A number of well-known professionals have expressed this in the following statements:

"The cry for social responsibility demands that scientists consider society their client and the public interest their paramount concern ..." (Jacobson, 1972)

"In a word, we should work toward a more perceptive and participatory social con-

science for chemistry and chemists." (Long, 1972)

"We must change from an attitude of exploitive chemistry to a new humanistic chemistry." (Linnell, 1971) "Scientific and educational societies should take an active interest in public and political affairs ... not only because the work of their members is affected ... but because the influence of that work on society is affected." (Kenyon, 1967a)

"The apparent direction of evolution of our society suggests that public position may become almost as important to an industrial corporation ... as economic condition." (Kenyon, 1967b)

Clearly, the call has been made for recognition of responsibility to the public and action to implement it. A recent series of articles by Herbert Popper supplies some of the answers and includes specific suggestions for the professional's action in response to it. Among these courses of responsible action are running for public office, working for local civic groups, writing to legislators, becoming active in a professional society's environmental or other public service group, providing tutoring or career guidance to students (especially the underprivileged), serving on school or hospital boards, and many more. In this wide spectrum of opportunities there should be some to interest and challenge any self-respecting engineer or scientist. By accepting this responsibility, the manager can become a better citizen as well as a better professional and perhaps influence his subordinates to accept this responsibility as well.

5. Recommendations and Conclusions

Our entire way of life is based on ethical concepts which have evolved over the centuries. Part of the responsibilities of a profession and a professional individual is adherence to sets of principles of professional ethics. "Ideally, the mutual benefits of an open and honest relationship between manager and employee ought to be obvious. But in the real world, with all its complexities, this isn't always so, and the professional manager must constantly review his motivations, off as well as on the job. Unfortunately, the difference between right and wrong may not be clear, and decisions must be based on previous experience and personal values" (Billmeyer and Kelley, 1975).

"So," you say, "this sounds well and good, but how can professional engineering ethics become more widely accepted and supported?" That is the job of the engineering manager. In most organizations, the leader acts as a role model. If an engineer wants to grow and advance with a company, he must follow in the footsteps of his manager. When a manager behaves in a manner seen as unethical, his subordinates will more than likely behave in a similar fashion.

Yet, the manager may eventually feel pressured by the organization to compromise his beliefs in what is right and wrong "for the good of the company." Ethical standards must be supported by top management to be effective, but until that day comes, the manager will continually be forced to make ethical decisions—some of which could possibly cost him his position and perhaps his job.

It is this Engineer's opinion that the engineering profession is one of great dignity and honor. With the acceptance of such a respected career, one should apply himself (or, in this case, herself) to the improvement of technology but not at the expense of others.

A good manager will ensure subordinates that the ethical decision is always the right decision. An employee should be able to trust a manager and feel free to go to him when faced with an ethical decision.

How does a manager go about supporting ethical standards? There really is no simple solution. However, the best way is to simply provide a good example. Another suggestion is to provide engineers with information and strive to have all engineering employees register as Professional Engineers. Once an engineer becomes registered, a sense of duty and obligation will follow.

Due to the generality of ethical codes, Baling suggests that ethical standards can become more meaningful if there is participation among an organization's membership in setting those standards. Managers can direct groups of employees in setting up their own sets of guidelines. In this way, the guidelines will have more meaning because there is not the feeling of having a set of rules "handed down from the top."

The task of supporting ethical decisions and ensuring employees work in an ethical environment is no small job for an engineering manager. This job is made doubly difficult when the manager carries a reputation of not working in a similar manner. This is a big responsibility to place on a manager, but the rewards of a job well done not only benefit the organization, but other engineers and the public as well.

REFERENCES

Alger, P.L., 1965. In Alger et al. (eds.), *Ethical Problems in Engineering*, New York, NY: John Wiley and Sons.

Billmeyer, F.W. and Kelley, R.N., 1975. *Entering Industry: A Guide for Young Professionals*, New York, NY: John Wiley and Sons.

Hicks, H.G., 1981. *Management*, New York, NY: McGraw-Hill.

Jacobson, M., 1972. "Science in the Public Interest," *Chem. Eng. News*, Vol. 3(5).

Kenyon, R.L., 1967a. "Industry and the Pecking Order," *Chem. Eng. News*, Vol. 3(5).

Kenyon, R.L., 1967b. "Scientific Societies and Public Order," *Chem. Eng. News*, Vol. 8(5).

Linnell, R.H., 1971. "Humanistic Chemistry," *Chem. Eng. News*, Vol. 47(3).

Long, F.A., 1972. "Social Conscience of Chemists," *Chem. Eng. News*, Vol. 14(3).

MacIver, R. (1995). "The Social Significance of Professional Ethics," *The Annals of the American Academy of Political and Social Science*, January, 118-24.

O'Meara, J.R., 1971. "How Smaller Companies Protect their Trade Secrets," in *Report Number 530*, New York, NY: The Conference Board.

Spencer, H., 1905. *The Data of Ethics*, New York, NY: John Wiley and Sons.

Walsh, T.F., 1973. *Protecting Your Business Against Espionage*, New York, NY: American Management Association.

◆ ◆ ◆ ◆ ◆

JOHN LADD

Bhopal: An Essay on Moral Responsibility and Civic Virtue

I.

On December 3, 1984 the greatest industrial accident ever recorded took place in Bhopal, India. The accidental release of deadly methyl isocyanate gas in a Union Carbide chemical plant resulted in the deaths of enormous numbers of people, variously estimated from 2000 to 5000, and in injuries to many others, estimated at 100,000 to 200,000, as well as the deaths of large numbers of cattle and other animals (See Bowonder, Castleman, *NY Times*).

The tragedy at Bhopal provides a concrete, spectacular and instructive illustration of a particular set of moral problems that are a peculiar product of our time, namely, problems relating to individual and social responsibility for catastrophic accidents connected with high technology. In fact, Bhopal may provide the model for analyzing our responsibilities for preventing an even greater catastrophe, an accidental nuclear explosion.

My theme in this essay is that not only is our society, along with its various social institutions, ill prepared to cope with this new kind of problem, but philosophy also has failed to provide any kind of satisfactory framework for conceptualizing the moral issues arising out of high-risk technology. In particular, I contend that the adherence by most philosophers to a narrow, legalistic notion of responsibility, henceforth called the "standard concept of responsibility," has rendered meaningful discourse about moral responsibility in contexts like the Bhopal disaster impossible, if not incoherent. Philosophically, I shall argue, what is required is a broader and deeper notion of moral responsibility. In the brief compass of this essay, I shall try to identify some of the reasons why standard notions of responsibility are unsatisfactory and shall suggest ways in which they can be emended to make them more satisfactory. My conclusion will be that any kind of satisfactory analysis of moral responsibility must tie it to the virtues and, in particular, in cases like Bhopal, it must be tied to what I shall call "civic virtue."

When disasters like Bhopal occur, it is natural to ask: why did it happen? Who or what is to blame for this calamity? Who, if anyone, is responsible? Or, as the *New York Times* succinctly put it: "Where does the main responsibility for Bhopal lie?" (*NYT* headline 1/31/1985).

Responsibility, Litigation and Blame

Ever since the disaster took place there has been a great deal of soul-searching as well as a flood of "blame rhetoric" in newspapers and magazines: charges and countercharges, the Americans blaming the Indians and the Indians blaming the Americans; the company blaming the government and the government blaming the company, groups with vested interests and ideologies blaming other groups with vested interests and ideologies, and so on. All this blame rhetoric has been accompanied by wholesale denials of responsibility and attempts to shift responsibility onto others; for these purposes, there have also been cover-ups and suppression of information. In addition to those more directly involved in the accident itself, lawyers, politicians, editorial writers and pundits like William F. Buckley (q.v.) have jumped into the game of placing responsibility and blame.

On reflection, it is obvious that the adversarial approach to questions about responsibility blinds us to the serious and deep underlying moral issues and makes a forthright and thoroughgoing discussion of these issues, general as well as particular, difficult if not impossible. Furthermore, the approach itself is founded on what I shall argue is a basic misconception: first, that it is both necessary and possible to identify one specific person or set of persons as morally responsible for the accident and, second, that those so identified can or should be *blamed* for it. It will become evident very soon that this two-fold assumption, which underlies what I shall call *blame-responsibility*, raises more questions than it answers. This entire essay might be regarded as an attack on the notion of blame-responsibility.

The blame approach towards responsibility, along with its adversarial posture, is part and parcel of what I call *legalism*, an approach reflected in the American fondness for turning moral problems into legal ones. "Legalism" may be defined as the wholesale use of legal or quasi-legal concepts, arguments and models as a framework for the analysis of moral issues (See Ladd 1979). Legalism reduces questions of moral responsibility to questions of legal liability, which themselves amount in the end, in crass terms, to questions of who is to pay for the damages and for the costs. (Being blamed or punished might be regarded as a kind of payment.) I shall try to show as we go along that nothing but moral confusion results from the reduction of responsibility as a moral category to the legal concepts of responsibility and liability.

The simple point about legal responsibility is that it would be a mistake to conclude that if and when it is decided by the courts after litigation that, say, UC as a corporate entity is legally responsible, i.e., liable, that is the end to the matter of moral responsibility. To put it bluntly, moral issues about responsibility cannot be resolved through litigation. I shall return to the distinction between legal and moral responsibility later in this essay when I discuss different uses of the concept of responsibility.

The general theoretical question that this essay will be concerned with is a moral one, namely, whether or not the concept of responsibility *in a moral sense* has any pertinence at all to cases like the Bhopal catastrophe and, granted that it is pertinent, how it is to be applied. The problem arises, of course, from the fact that the accident itself and its disastrous consequences were due to such a complicated combination of factors that it is virtually impossible to assign moral responsibility to particular nameable individuals or set of individuals—as ordinarily required by the standard concept of responsibility. In addition, perhaps the notion of blaming particular individuals or groups of individuals does not make any sense in this context. How is it possible, then, to apply the concept of responsibility to Bhopal-like disasters?

Normal Accidents and the Problem of Responsibility

The moral problem posed by Bhopal presents a challenge of some urgency because the accident is a typical example of a new kind of catastrophe due to high technology that Charles Perrow calls *normal accidents* (Perrow 1984). Perrow's important book on the subject brings up a whole set of issues that need to be addressed by moral philosophers. He describes in detail a number of accidents of this type, including Three Mile Island. Drawing on many examples from different kinds of high technology, he shows how normal accidents are characteristically catastrophic, unpredictable and, in a sense, unavoidable. The theme of Perrow's book is that these accidents take place where there are complex inter-active systems and where the systems are also tight-ly coupled, "that is, processes happen very fast and can't be turned off, the failed parts cannot be iso-lated from other parts, or there is no other way to keep the production going safely ... recovery from the initial disturbance is not possible; it will spread quickly and irretrievably for at least some time, etc" (4). The coincidence of a number of small and in themselves insignificant failures lead to breakdowns with enormous ramifications, where no one at the time understands what is happening, partly because the antecedent probability of these failures occur-ring together is so low. His conclusion is that high technology is statistically bound to produce more normal accidents, unpredictable catastrophes due to technological complexities and the tight coupling of complex systems.

Bhopal has all the characteristics of a normal ac-cident just described. As of this date, no one has de-termined what "*really* caused it"; indeed, there is the much deeper question of what we might mean by "the cause" of a normal accident. I shall discuss this question later. In the meantime, it should be point-ed out that the hypothesis, offered by UC officials, that the accident was "caused" by a deliberate act of sabotage, even if it could be established that there was a saboteur, would still be insufficient to explain the dimensions of the tragedy and to answer in a satisfactory way the question: "who was ultimately responsible?" It is obviously fallacious in accidents of this kind to assume that there must have been a single cause embodied in a chain of simple linear causation. In Aristotelian terms, the accident was the chance result of the intersection of many causal lines.

If there is no single cause, then, as I have already pointed out, it seems patently insufficient ethically, if not downright foolish, to try to fix the blame on one or more individuals and even sillier to put one such an individual in prison, as the Indian authorities did to Mr. Warren Anderson, the CEO of Union Car-bide, when he arrived from the US to make an on the spot survey of the situation. The point should be obvious: that simple blame fixing of this kind, whether it be by the Indian government or by Union Carbide, is ethical nonsense. (This will be more ob-vious after I have given more details about Bhopal in Part II.)

Because of the patent absurdities, theoretical, practical, and moral, of holding any single indi-vidual or set of individuals "ultimately responsible" for the disaster, as would be required by the stan-dard concept of responsibility, one might draw the conclusion that the concept of moral responsibility has no pertinence at all to normal accidents. If it is impossible to blame particular individuals, is it not quite pointless to look for moral responsibility in disasters of this kind?

If the answer to this question is *Yes*, there are still a number of ways left open for dealing with the moral quandary created by Bhopal-like accidents, that is, without surrendering to fatalism or Stoicism and simply saying that "it just had to happen and there is nothing that can be done about it." A few of these ethical alternatives to conceptions of respon-sibility might be briefly mentioned.

First, there is the extreme position that places the blame on the technology itself and concludes therefrom that high technology is almost always too dangerous to be developed at all. This kind of anti-technology attitude seems to be what lies behind Hans Jonas's proposal for what he calls the "heur-istics of fear" (See Jonas). A variant of this limita-tion on technology is found in the view that high technology should not be exported to Third World countries, because the indigent populations are un-able to cope with dangerous technologies, or, if it is exported to them, then it should remain under the close and constant surveillance of Western techni-cians. We should export only what has come to be known as "appropriate technology."

Against these negative evaluations of high tech-nology, we have to weigh the general feeling in governments and among the people in countries like India, that high technology, including Union Carbide, is a godsend in that it has already brought and promises even more in the future to bring relief from suffering to millions of people. The pesticides manufactured by Union Carbide are referred to by the Indian people as "medicine for plants." It would seem that only a callous indifference to the plight of the multitudes of poor and hungry in other parts of the world could lead to the categorical dismissal of the benefits of high technology and the casual denial of the good that has been achieved by the so-called "Green Revolution." Simple negativistic answers are not the solution to complicated ethical problems like those we are concerned with here. We must resist the temptation to throw out the baby with the bath!

On the other side, we find pro-technology answers in theories like utilitarianism. Utilitarianism, for example, typically approaches accidents like Bhopal through a cost-benefit analysis, which leads to the conclusion that such accidents are one of the costs of high technology, costs that in the long run are outweighed by the overall benefits it brings about. Apart from questions about the factual basis of such "rationalizations of accidents" as "acceptable risks," there are other philosophical and ethical difficulties with utilitarianism that need not be discussed here, including the question of whether human suffering should simply be regarded as a cost.

In the context of the Bhopal tragedy, the chief objection to utilitarianism as a tool of analysis is that it has no clear way of pinning down specific sorts of moral requirements to specific individuals or set of individuals. The difficulty arises from the fact that utilitarianism, as some contemporary writers express it, is "agent-neutral," that is, the obligation to promote utility or to prevent harm, not to mention to repair harm, is not relative to particular agents, but rests on anyone and everyone who has the ability to do so (Nagel 1980). Agent-neutrality means that every moral agent as such has the "responsibility" for promoting utility in general as distinct from a specif-

ic responsibility of a specific agent to specific recipients on account of something specific about them. Instead of the terms "agent-neutral" and "agent-relativity," I think that terms like "agent-specific" and "recipient-specific," are more apposite. Accordingly, I prefer to say that utilitarianism lacks agent- and recipient-specificity.

The difficulty with utilitarianism is that it has no place in its ethics for specific social contexts, that is, for moral requirements based on specific roles, relationships and commitments, considerations that bind specific individuals to each other and that furnish the framework and specificity of our social obligations and responsibilities. In sum, utilitarianism cannot explain why one specific individual or set of individuals is more responsible than others for the welfare of other specific individuals to which they are committed by virtue of, say, some prior relationship.

Instead of using an abstract theoretical approach such as utilitarianism or cost-benefit analysis to sort out the moral problems connected with Bhopal, we will find that the concept of moral responsibility is a much more appropriate tool of analysis for this purpose. To begin with, it provides the specificity lacking in utilitarianism and explains why there is a greater moral burden on certain individuals and sets of individuals like Mr. Warren Anderson, CEO of Union Carbide, to concern themselves with the misfortunes of the victims of Bhopal than there is on others, say, ordinary American citizens who have no special personal relationship to the people in Bhopal or to the disaster. It also explains why the lack of solicitude on the part of the chief actors for the health and safety of the people in Bhopal, both prior to the accident and subsequent to it, is morally so outrageous. I shall argue that the advantage of the concept of moral responsibility as a moral category for analyzing moral aspects of tragedies like Bhopal is that it is at once consequentialist, person-specific (= agent-relative) and, as a moral virtue, intrinsically motivational. (All this will be explained later.)

The rest of this essay will be concerned with the concept of moral responsibility as a moral category and with the problem of how to apply it to complex disasters, normal accidents, where many different individuals are involved at many different levels and in many different capacities. As we proceed, I shall try to show how and in what ways in such complicated cases, it might make sense to blame the "system" or to introduce some concept or other of "collective responsibility," instead of laying the entire blame on particular individuals, as would be required by the standard concept of responsibility.

Normal Accidents Compared and Contrasted Ethically with Two Other Kinds of Disaster

Let us begin our inquiry into the concept of moral responsibility by comparing and contrasting normal accidents like Bhopal with two other sorts of disaster: first, humanly initiated calamities, and, second, natural disasters.

By *humanly initiated calamities*, I mean calamities that are deliberately started by human beings for their own nefarious purposes, for example, wars and massacres. Typical instances are the Nazi holocaust and the massacre at My Lai. It should be observed first of all that like normal accidents, the etiology of these calamities is more complicated than it would first appear to be. Both kinds of disaster have background causes more basic than the acts or omissions of individual agents. Through their acts or omissions, particular individuals may be proximate causes or triggers of, say, a war or a massacre, but there are deeper historical, social and cultural factors behind them that it would be foolish to ignore: racism, for example, is a frequent underlying cause of massacres. In this regard, no one could seriously maintain that the (chief) cause of World War I was the assassination of the Austrian archduke at Sarajevo, or that the Nazi holocaust was caused by the actions of a few individual Nazis, such as Hitler,

Himmler or Eichmann. A speculative philosopher of history like Hegel might prefer to say that these individuals were simply instruments for carrying out the Will of the *Volksgeist* or *Zeitgeist*, the spirit of the nation or of the times.

Less picturesque and more to the point is the unhappy fact that behind the scenes in these massacres and wars there is the passive acquiescence of a large silent minority, whose failure to intervene plays a significant role in making the horrendous outcome possible; had there been a loud public outcry within Germany against the Nazis or within the United States against the conduct of the military in Viet Nam, an outcry expressing a broad consensus of disapproval in advance of any of their operations, neither the holocaust nor My Lai would have taken place. Considerations such as these lend plausibility to the notion of collective responsibility (See French).

Although for reasons just stated it is implausible to assign moral responsibility *exclusively* to particular individuals, either for normal accidents or for humanly initiated disasters, that is not the whole story as far as humanly initiated calamities are concerned. For it is still possible in regard to the latter to hold specific nameable individuals especially responsible or "guilty" (e.g., Eichmann or Calley)—more so than others. They are so not simply because their actions contributed significantly to bringing about the outcome, but on account of their *mens rea*, their evil intentions. Their *mens rea* makes it easier to blame specific people, i.e., to hold them responsible, in the case of humanly initiated calamities, than it does in the case of normal accidents, where blame may be less appropriate because none of the actors could be accused of comparable evil intentions.

Thus, there are significant ethical differences between the two kinds of calamities. Generally speaking, humanly initiated calamities like the Nazi holocaust and My Lai, and, of course, wars, are causally linked to human purposes, motives and goals of one sort or another, which, however objectionable, provide at least a partial explanation of their occurrence or at least their "initiation." Normal accidents, on the other hand, have no such link, at least, no direct link. It is inconceivable, for example that anyone, however evil, would intentionally and deliberately initiate a disaster like Bhopal, Chernobyl or the explosion of Challenger, in the way that SS guards intentionally and deliberately participated in bringing about the deaths in the gas chambers and Calley and other soldiers engaged in the massacres of My Lai (See Hersh, French). The participation and *mens rea* of the latter raises the frightful question of complicity that does not exist in normal accidents. In some ways, from the moral point of view, the unquestioned complicity of individuals and groups in these enterprises and the condoning of them by others makes it easier to accept the attribution of responsibility than where there is no complicity or condonation. Complicity and condonation, then, provide us with a useful way of distinguishing morally between humanly initiated calamities and accidental catastrophes due to the failures of high technology.

The lack of complicity and condonation as well as the accompanying sense of helplessness on the part of the people involved, suggests that industrial catastrophes might be fruitfully compared to natural disasters such as earthquakes, floods and hurricanes. For like natural disasters, industrial accidents are calamities for everyone and are wanted by no one. They are simply misfortunes and as such might even, in the quaint expression, be called "acts of God." Does it not make sense to place normal accidents in the same moral category as natural disasters?

Somehow, however, it is difficult to escape the feeling that there *is* a moral difference between industrial accidents due to high technology and natural disasters. We seem to feel that the fact that such accidents are a by-product, albeit an unintended one, of human designs and of human endeavors places them in a different category. There is a time-honored assumption that if human beings create machines then they are responsible for them and for what they do, even if the machines get out of hand—as in the case of Frankenstein and his monster.

Perhaps the key to the difference is this. The occurrence of natural disasters is *completely* beyond human control and in that sense such disasters are absolutely unpreventable. Large-scale industrial disasters, on the other hand, are preventable in the sense that they might have been prevented by human intervention, "if only X had done Y"—although perhaps how they might have been prevented could only be known in hindsight. When, in retrospect, we say: "if only ...," we introduce counterfactuals of the type: "if P, Q, and R had done X, Y, and Z, then the accident would not have occurred," e.g., if the valve from tank A to tank B had been closed, etc., then there would have been no leak, etc., and no accident. Hence, normal accidents are preventable by human action in a counterfactual sense and in this way they differ in an important respect from, say, earthquakes.

The counterfactual "if ..." in normal accidents like Bhopal includes such things as taking greater pains to be informed and to give information to others, being more careful, being better organized, paying more attention to safety, and so on. All of these counterfactual conditions imply that human deficiencies of some kind or other lie at the bottom of an industrial disaster. Considerations such as these lead us to say that a normal accident is a case, not where there is no human control, but where *human control has broken down*. That, in turn, simply means that there was no control where there ought to have been control.

The point about preventability and technology is worth pursuing further. One notable fact about normal technological accidents like the Challenger disaster, Chernobyl, and Bhopal, is that they are unlikely to be repeated—at least in precisely the same form as they first occurred. For as *homo faber*, man usually learns or is expected to learn from past mistakes; after an accident of large proportions, we know what to look for and look out for next time, and with this new knowledge we are in a position to avoid making the same mistake. If we know better and still make the mistake, the situation changes and becomes a case of criminal negligence, say, carelessness approaching *mens rea*.

The point is that it is of the nature of technological knowledge that, on the basis of information obtained from a *post mortem* after a breakdown occurs, new knowledge is acquired that can be used to prevent a repetition. For quite practical reasons, simply the cost of disastrous technological accidents, if only in economic terms, is usually enough to prompt an extensive investigation of an accident and the adoption of measures to avoid a recurrence. The remarkable progress in aircraft safety over the years attests to this fact. (On the other hand, where the costs of an accident are not so great and where they can be imposed on an outside party as an externality, this kind of progressive handling of accidents may be less frequent. The shipping industry is a case in point. See Perrow.)

Logically and epistemologically what happens in the case of an industrial accident is that it plays the role of a test—an experiment, which in engineering is the key to knowledge. In engineering, we learn as much or more from a negative result, e.g., a breakdown, as we do from a successful one. Good engineering, and consequently good technological practice, requires constant testing. In that regard, engineering is perhaps significantly different from more theoretical sciences, where consistency with accepted theories is more often than not the hallmark of acceptability. Engineering, by its very nature, builds on assumptions that eventually may turn out not to be valid. That is why one engineering textbook says that the purpose of testing is to check "the validity of the assumptions" (Beakley and Leach, 455).

As far as normal accidents are concerned, the situation is more complicated, because they involve complex interlocking systems, where only the component parts of the various systems can be adequately tested. By their very nature, complex systems, such as an industrial plant or a space project, are based on "one-of-a-kind" designs that cannot be tested as a whole. Logically, the confirmed safety of the parts, does not guarantee the safety of the whole, which involves the interaction and interlocking of the parts. For that reason, the conditions of safety of a large scale one-of-a-kind design are difficult to ascertain and can be established more easily *after* a breakdown than before. In such cases, the testing of this kind of complex technology is carried on in real life, as it were, instead of in the laboratory. Hence, one writer has aptly said that "the problem of the nuclear-power industry is that we have had too few accidents ... it's expensive, but that's how you gain experience" (Ford). Similarly, it has been alleged that the only way to know that the Star Wars plan will work is to have the Russians launch a few missiles to test it.

In any case, the fact that the conditions giving rise to normal accidents are correctable, if only after the fact (like a test), provides us with a possible criterion for differentiating between technological accidents and natural disasters. Because human interventions of one sort or another at various places in the causal network leading to a normal accident are possible, at least theoretically, it is a mistake to conclude that normal accidents belong in the same moral category as natural disasters. Therefore it is fallacious to dismiss the concept of moral responsibility for these accidents on the grounds that just like natural disasters "accidents are inevitable." It is also a moral cop-out. Thus, when Buckley writes cynically with regard to Bhopal: "human error is something the world will always be afflicted with," one wonders if he means to include a nuclear holocaust along with Bhopal, Challenger and Chernobyl.

We can see from this brief discussion of three different kinds of disasters that moral problems connected with responsibility for technologically related disasters like Bhopal, i.e., normal accidents, are quite unlike those connected with the other two kinds of disaster, although there are certain similarities between them that distinguish them from simple accidents where the standard concept of responsibility is used. What should emerge clearly from these comparisons is that the concept of responsibility when applied to normal accidents is indeed very complicated.

Different Uses of the Concept of Responsibility: Some Logical Considerations

It should be clear by now that the concept of moral responsibility is a complex, multifaceted concept with many different uses. Therefore, before we can proceed any further in our inquiry concerning the applicability of the concept to disasters like Bhopal, we need to sort out some of the different meanings and uses of the concept. In doing so, I shall focus on what might be called the "logical differences" between various uses of the concept of responsibility, that is, the different logical implications and consequences that are entailed by the different purposes for which the concept is used.

My main thesis in this section will be that the specific logical features of the standard concept of responsibility that stand in the way of its use in connection with normal accidents like Bhopal are derived from a narrow and specialized use of the concept that for the most part reflects a kind of legalism. I shall argue, then, that if the logical implications and consequences of this specialized use are rejected, then it will be possible to develop a broader and more encompassing concept of responsibility that can be applied in a meaningful and cogent way to Bhopal-like kinds of disaster. In the discussion that follows I shall draw on more detailed analyses of the concept of responsibility that I have presented elsewhere (See Ladd 1975, 1979, 1982, 1984).

Legal v. moral responsibility. I have already mentioned some of the morally objectionable consequences of confusing moral responsibility with legal responsibility. Here, I shall concentrate more par-ticularly on the "logic of the law," that is, on the distinctive logical implications and consequences of the concept of responsibility when it is used as a legal concept. As a legal concept, it differs from moral concepts in general inasmuch as it reflects certain special logical peculiarities of the law, which arise from the fact that law is a public institutional mechanism for authoritatively settling conflicts of interests. As a social institution of this kind, law has its own distinctive procedures, methods and authority. For example, in our own Anglo-American legal system, the procedure is adversarial and the method consists of appeals to authoritatively established local rules embodied in statutes and precedents. These general considerations concerning the law must be kept in mind by anyone tempted to assimilate moral responsibility to legal responsibility.

More particularly, the legal concept of responsibility is used in the law for a specific purpose, namely, to establish liability or non-liability. Thus, for example, the object of deciding, e.g., in a court of law, which party in a particular dispute is legally responsible for an accident is to determine who has the legal liability, e.g., of paying for the injuries and repairing the damages. (Under liability we should include criminal liability, i.e., liability to punishment.) Thus, the final outcome of a legal proceeding of this kind is an authoritative decision about the allocation of the costs, say, of an accident.

Legal ways of allocating costs are often not determined by straightforward moral considerations, whatever they might be, but by other considerations such as the ability to pay or public policy considerations. Thus, in our society, costs of reparation are often passed off onto large bodies, e.g., corporations or insurance companies, on the "deep pockets" principle, i.e., "their (relative) capacity to avoid the loss, or to absorb it, or to pass it along and distribute it in smaller proportions among a larger group" (Prosser, 24). Under the doctrine of strict liability, costs may be assigned without regard to responsibility (in the sense of fault).

Another important respect in which legal and moral responsibility differ is that legal responsibility applies to corporations, moral responsibility does not. Thus, although corporations can have legal responsibilities (liabilities), legal rights and obligations, they cannot as such have moral responsibilities, moral rights or obligations; for, as I have argued elsewhere, corporations are not persons in the moral sense and only persons can have moral responsibilities. Corporations like UC are simply creations of the law; they have no independent moral status (For arguments, see Ladd 1970, 1984).

To make a long story short, the occasions in which issues of legal responsibility (liability) arise, e.g., conflicts over who is to pay the costs of an accident, as well the way they are settled, e.g., by courts, and the methods used in settling them, e.g., the application of local legal rules, and the practical consequences of one particular settlement over another, e.g., costs and fines, show that legal responsibility and moral responsibility belong in entirely different categories (See Hart, Ladd 1982).

Negative responsibility and exclusivity. Another important distinction to note in our sorting out of concepts of responsibility is the distinction between what may be called "negative" and "positive" conceptions of responsibility. A negative conception of responsibility implies exclusivity in the sense that it assigns responsibility *exclusively* to one person or set of persons and, by implication, to no one else. Thus, its use is, at least partly, negative since in determining that one party (e.g., a person or set of persons) is responsible for X it *eo ipso* determines that other parties are *not* responsible. Responsibility of this kind (negative) is thus circumscribed and exclusive. For example, responsibility is used negatively when it is assumed that finding a hypothetical saboteur responsible for the accident at Bhopal implies that no one else besides him is responsible for it, i.e., he and possible co-conspirators are exclusively responsible.

Since for certain purposes involving the negative concept of responsibility it is often as desirable to establish non-responsibility as to establish responsibility, theories of negative responsibility are apt to focus on conditions that establish non-responsibility, such as absence of intent, mistake or coercion, in other words, excuses. A typical use of the negative concept of responsibility can be seen in the common practice known colloquially as "passing the buck": "I am not responsible, *he* is!"

An analogous negative use of responsibility is to be found in connection with what is generally known as "job-" or "task-responsibility." For in one of its many senses "responsibility" refers to the duties or requirements (= responsibilities) that go with an assigned task, job or office. Responsibilities in this sense are usually part of a "job-description." If we add to this some version or other of the division of labor principle, according to which jobs are demarcated and divided from each other according to some rigorous scheme, then we need to introduce the notion of not being responsible as part of the concept of responsibility. Thus, if it is A's responsibility to care for X, e.g., tending a machine, then it is not B's responsibility. Each person should mind his own business, as the saying goes. We hear claims of responsibility voiced in hearing "It's my job, not his" as well as disclaimers of responsibility in hearing "It's his job, not mine." In any case, the negative or exclusive aspect of responsibility is a significant side of this use of responsibility.

It is easy to see why the law operates almost exclusively with the negative conception of responsibility, for in allocating liability to one party in a litigation it implies that other parties are not liable. That is why legal rules for, say, tort liability, are as much concerned with establishing who is *not* liable as they are with establishing who is. Foisting responsibility onto others is part of the legal game.

Again, bearing in mind the purpose they serve in the law and the need to draw a sharp line between those who do and those who do not have responsibility for something, legal rules relating to responsibility are black or white. There are, in principle, no gray areas in between (except for uncertainty concerning the rules or the facts) and in that sense they are absolute.

Positive responsibility and moral responsibility. According to what I call the "positive conception" of responsibility, the ascription of responsibility to one party has no implications one way or another about the responsibility of others. One person's being responsible does not exclude others also from being responsible. Hence, in this sense of responsibility, many people, even an indefinitely large number, can be responsible for something. If a large part of the population is responsible we call it "collective responsibility." Again, positive responsibility is not only the kind of responsibility that can be shared by a lot of people, but it cannot be passed off onto others (as in "passing the buck"). Indeed, it cannot be alienated, e.g., given away. Positive responsibility is moral responsibility in the full sense.

Besides being non-exclusive and open-ended, positive responsibility is unlike negative responsibility in that it can also be a matter of varying degrees and stringency. Individuals can be more or less responsible for, say, a certain person's safety or welfare; those closer to a person are more responsible than those further away. This point can be illustrated by what was said earlier about Nazism and collective responsibility, namely, the fact that Eichmann was especially responsible for the deaths in the concentration camps does not mean that others in Germany were not also "collectively" responsible, although perhaps to a lesser degree. When I come to discuss the disaster at Bhopal, I shall argue that many different people are in one way or other responsible—perhaps indefinitely many people and that they are so to greater and lesser degrees. Granted that this is so, then the idea of exclusive responsibility in relation to Bhopal really makes no sense—except perhaps legally.

In sum, then, in identifying positive responsibility, i.e., non-exclusive responsibility, as moral responsibility in the full sense, we are in a position to block attempts by individuals or groups to escape responsibility for something by shifting it onto others, i.e., passing the buck, as everyone has tried to do in the case of Bhopal (and Nazism, for that matter). Furthermore, the angry accusations, legal infighting and self-serving rhetoric that has marked the debate over the Bhopal tragedy can be shown to be absurd and beside the point.

Not only does due recognition of the positive sense of responsibility render denials of responsibility pointless, but it also makes moral responsibility into something positively good, that is, something to be sought after. It becomes something that good people are ready and willing to acknowledge and to embrace. The reason for this is that moral responsibility in the positive sense is also a virtue, a point that will be explained towards the end of this essay.

Primary v. secondary consequences of being responsible. One important theoretical question relating to responsibility concerns what might be called its "cash value" (William James). What follows from saying that someone is responsible for something? What is the moral point of using terms like "responsible" and "responsibility"? As we have seen, in the case of legal responsibility (= liability), what follows is that the person who is found responsible has to pay. By the same token, it is often assumed that a person's being morally responsible for, say, an untoward state of affairs, means that he also has to "pay" something, for example, he may be blamed or censured for it. This, I hold, is a rather naive view of moral responsibility. The issue is really not that simple as far as moral responsibility is concerned.

To begin with, we need to distinguish between the primary and the secondary consequences of responsibility. By "primary consequences" I mean the direct ethical consequences (or implications) for the conduct of the agent himself, i.e., what he ought or ought not to do (or to have done), say, to prevent an untoward outcome. Primary consequences are the agent's *oughts*. I call them "primary" because they are a *sine qua non* of the other uses of responsibility;

any judgment whatsoever of responsibility implies an ought.

The secondary consequences relate almost entirely to what *third parties* should or should not do or are permitted or authorized to do to an individual by virtue of his being responsible for an untoward outcome. Thus, third parties may be authorized (or obligated) to blame or condemn the individual, to punish or reprimand him, to require him to apologize or to make reparations, or simply to make a moral assessment by placing "charges and credits on some ideal record" (Feinberg, 30). In a loose sense, these secondary consequences could be called the "retributive consequences" of finding someone responsible for something. Third parties involved here might be bystanders, the public at large, society, impartial spectators, moral judges, moral assessors and other godlike constructions.

On reflection, it should be clear that it is a mistake to confuse the secondary or retributive consequences of responsibility with its primary consequences. They are not only distinguishable, but separable. For, although responsibility may be necessary for, say, blaming or punishing a person, it is not sufficient. Blaming or punishing may be quite inappropriate or even wrong where there are excuses or other mitigating factors.

More generally, the separability of the secondary consequences of responsibility from responsibility in the primary sense means that in order to derive such things as blamability or punishability from responsibility (i.e., secondary consequences), additional premises are required. These additional premises might come, for example, from a separate theory of blaming or of punishment. In this regard, different moral theories can come up with different secondary consequences. Thus, Kant for one, has a theory of punishment but not one for blaming, which he disapproves on moral grounds. Since retributive responses like those just mentioned must be selective in order to have any point at all, i.e., not everyone can be punished or condemned morally, theories of responsibility that stress retribution as a secondary consequence are naturally negative or exclusivist (See above). The same considerations apply *mutatis mutandis* to theories of legal liability, including criminal liability, which need a theory of liability of some kind to make the connection between responsibility and liability. (Theories of strict liability, of course, deny the connection altogether.) (Prosser 1984)

Retrospective v. prospective uses of responsibility. At first look, there seems to be a puzzling asymmetry between the use of the concept of responsibility to apply to past conduct and its use to apply to future conduct (Ladd 1975). With respect to the past, the import is usually negative, that is, the focus is on untoward conduct resulting in untoward outcomes. Its concern is with something bad, i.e., things that ought not to have happened and that ought not to have been done, e.g., Eichmann was responsible for the deaths of millions of Jews. Future responsibility, on the other hand, is usually positive and relates to what ought to happen or ought to be done, that is, to something good. Are we dealing with two entirely different concepts here or are they basically the same concept used in different ways?

On first thought, the reason for the asymmetry is a difference of use: retrospective attributions of responsibility are generally used to justify retributions (blame, punishment, etc.), whereas prospective attributions are used to prescribe, advise, exhort, or perhaps warn.

On second thought, however, it becomes evident that the asymmetry is due to the secondary consequences (or uses) of responsibility, rather than to the primary consequences. For obvious reasons, retribution (blame or punishment) has to be directed at what happened in the past; but retribution is a secondary consequence. Other secondary consequences such as exhortation or warning, on the other hand, necessarily refer to the future. But in the ultimate analysis, when only the primary consequences of responsibility are taken into account, it is clear that there is no significant difference between responsibility as it relates to past or to future conduct. For our purposes, then, the distinction can safely be disregarded. If someone was responsible in the primary sense for events leading up to the Bhopal disaster, i.e., ought to have done X, then he would be responsible in the same sense for what happens in a similar situation in the future, i.e., ought to do X in the future.

Let us turn now to Bhopal.

II. Bhopal

In this part, I shall give a brief synopsis of salient facts about the Bhopal tragedy that bear on to the issue of moral responsibility. Since more detailed accounts of the accident are available in writings by others, I shall simply summarize a few of the principal items that might be regarded as significant factors in the causation of the accident; each one of these factors could be and has been blamed for the disaster (Bowonder, Castleman, *NYT*, Kurzman).

What I want to emphasize here is the complex causal structure that is typical of normal accidents like Bhopal (Perrow). The complexity is due not only to the multiplicity of causal factors, but to the fact that the causation is multidimensional and operates at many different levels. If attributions of responsibility are to have a causal basis, then we must be able to show how responsibility correlates with the causal complexity just mentioned.

Background

(1) *MIC:* The chemical agent that was the source of the devastation was methyl isocyanate (MIC), an unusually dangerous substance, both to store and to handle. It is reactive, toxic, volatile and flammable.

Absence of information about MIC: Very little information was given by the UCC to the Indian managers, operators and employees about the chemical properties of MIC. The company to advance its own interests appears to have exploited the fact that the

Indian government and the Indian populace were ignorant of the hazardous character of the technology. As a result of this lack of information, measures that might have been taken to avoid or to mitigate the disaster were unknown to those involved, including the doctors.

(2) *Economic:* The plant was not making money. For that reason, the company had cut back on personnel, including managers and operators. Safety and modernization of equipment were sacrificed to save money. Managers were untrained and unfamiliar with the technology and its hazards.

(3) *Demographic:* Contrary to official governmental policy, the UCI was permitted to locate in a highly populated area near the railway station, bus station, hospitals, etc. Consequently, the dimensions of the disaster were much greater than they would have been in a less densely populated area.

(4) *Organizational and political:* The organizational structure consisted of a complicated relationship between the UCC of Danbury, CT and the Indian unit, UCI, which was mostly under the supervision of Indian managers carrying out general directives issued from the parent company. The Indian governmental inspection agencies were themselves badly understaffed and uninformed about the safety problems relating to MIC. Safety was given a low priority by all the parties involved.

(5) *Educational:* There is no question that the operators and minor managers were not well educated nor adequately trained to deal with complicated technology. In this regard, blame has often been placed on *indigenization* by writers who claim that only those technologies that can be safely handled ought to be exported to Third World countries and that multinationals should not turn over control to local units (Buckley).

To be fair to the Indians, however, the use of untrained personnel is not limited to Third World operation of high technology. Accidents at Browns Ferry and Three Mile Island also involved untrained personnel (Ford 44, 16).

The Accident

The immediate cause of the accident has not yet been determined, but apparently water leaked into the MIC storage tank, causing a buildup of temperature and pressure leading to an explosion that could not be contained or controlled. It was ascertained that the MIC had already been in a dangerous state, long before the accident.

Failure of Safety Procedures

There is a long list of failures in the safety system including such items as the following: (a) The refrigeration unit had been out of operation for several months. (b) The scrubber did not have enough caustic soda to neutralize the MIC; its capacity was too small. (c) The spare tank was not empty. (d) The flare for burning off escaping gas was too short, and so on.

Operating Personnel

Essentially the operators did not realize what was going on when the leak first started. Either the instrumental temperature and pressure gauges were not working or else the operators did not trust them, owing to previous failures. The narrative of the discovery by the operators of the pressure buildup and of the subsequent events reveals that it began with nonchalance, then bewilderment, and finally panic.

No Preparation for Emergencies

There was lack of preparation for an emergency, a lack of information about the properties of MIC and little training in the handling of MIC of the local management, operators, medical staff, and the populace, a lack of reliable instrumentation and a lack of trained personnel to operate a plant that was technologically sophisticated and complex.

When the accident occurred, it was discovered that there was a shortage of oxygen masks. The siren was not turned on at once nor were the police notified, because it was company policy not to report minor accidents or leaks. If the surrounding population had been alerted and provided with information and equipment to deal with the emergency, many lives would have been saved.

General Factors

Other more general factors might be mentioned as contributory to the disaster. First, there was a striking discrepancy between directives and policies issued from on high by the UCC and even by the Indian government and the actual practices and everyday operations of plant operators, managers and governmental bureaucrats. This fact raises interesting questions about control and responsibility within a bureaucratic structure. The same sort of discrepancy has been noted in Three Mile Island (Ford 60-61).

Another general factor that needs to be mentioned is the *bureaucratic mentality*. The bureaucratic role often requires officials to be devious and irresponsible. Bureaucrats tend to sacrifice long-term considerations for short-term goals. There are numerous instances in Bhopal (as in the US Nuclear Power industry) of withholding information and of cover-ups, both before and after the accident. (A number of these have already been mentioned.)

Finally, one factor that should be mentioned is the functional racism among the Americans who conducted the operations and who commented on the accident after it happened. Many agreed implicitly with what one distinguished gentleman said to me in discussing Bhopal: "After all, the Indians do not place as much value on life as we do!" Q.E.D.

Who Was to Blame?

After the survey of a number of different kinds of factors contributing to the disaster of Bhopal, it is clear that any and all of them, as well as many others not mentioned, could with some plausibility be used as a reason for blaming or for ascribing responsibility for the outcome to someone or other or to something (e.g., the system). With so many candidates and of such different kinds it seems pointless if not arbitrary to identify any single one of them as "ultimate" in the sense assumed in the question posed by the *NY Times*: "Who was ultimately responsible for the tragedy?" Anyone who tries to offer a simple answer to this ambiguous question must have an axe to grind, such as the defense of an ideological position or narrow self-interest.

The obvious lesson is that where normal accidents are concerned the kind of unilinear causation presupposed by most common conceptions of responsibility is inappropriate if not meaningless. If we reject this presupposition, which is a presupposition of what I call the standard concept of responsibility, then we have one more reason for rejecting the standard concept of responsibility and the negative concept of responsibility that it implies.

I shall now turn to a further set of arguments for a broader, more positive concept of moral responsibility.

III. Moral Responsibility: A Larger View

The general ethical position underlying the enlarged conception of moral responsibility that I propose here is that moral responsibility is a matter of relationship between persons, where one party does (or ought or ought not to do) something that affects the welfare of the other party in some significant respect. The two parties may be called respectively the *agent* and the *victim* (or recipient). I use the word "party" to indicate that more than one individual may be involved on each side. Thus, as far as individuals are concerned, the relationship may be one-many, many-one or many-many. The structure of the relationship itself is complex in ways that I shall try to explain.

To begin with, the relationship between persons is both the *terminus a quo* and the *terminus ad quem*

of moral responsibility. It centers on the causal connection between something done (or not done) by the agent and something that happens to the victim (recipient). The relationship is basically a moral relationship in the sense that under the best of circumstances, it reflects an attitude of caring on the part of the agent for what happens to the recipient and, on the other hand, under the worst of circumstances, it represents an absence of caring for what happens to him, perhaps even malice. The relationship describes both how things are and how they should be or should have been, and so on. Thus, the analysis applies not only to actualities but also to possibilities, past and future, always in a framework, however, of what ought or ought not to be done.

The Three Components of Responsibility

The easiest way to describe the structure of moral responsibility is to compare and contrast it with the standard concept of responsibility. According to that concept, when applied, for example, to past conduct (as in tort liability), responsibility consists of three basic components: (a) an untoward outcome (harm or injury) to the victim, (b) an agent at fault, and (c) a causal relation of some kind between the agent's conduct and the outcome (See Prosser). Although we must be circumspect in arguing from the legal concept of responsibility, since it is in many respects a misleading model of moral responsibility, the threefold breakdown that it suggests can be used to bring out the principal features of the enlarged concept of moral responsibility. In using this schema, we must, of course, bear in mind the qualifications that have already been mentioned earlier in the critical discussions of the standard concept of responsibility, such as the rejection of exclusivity and of secondary consequences, e.g., blame, as essential ingredients in the concept of moral responsibility.

For purposes of exposition and argument, I shall assume, then, that moral responsibility consists of three different kinds of basic components, roughly as I have described them. Components (a) and (c) might be called the "objective side" and (b) the "subjective side" of responsibility. Since I have already discussed the objective side in some detail earlier in the essay, I shall comment only very briefly on (a) and (c). This section will be primarily concerned with the subjective component, e.g., fault.

First, with respect to (a), the outcome, many people are tempted to downplay the enormity of the disaster at Bhopal (or anywhere else, for that matter). Even Mother Teresa said that she found the disaster "to be a beautiful thing because it brought out the best in everybody," and Mr. Warren Anderson said that he regretted having "overreacted" when he first heard of the tragedy. In reply, I hope that it suffices to point out that Stoicism over the misery of others is hardly a moral virtue!

Second, as far as causality (c) is concerned, it must be recognized that moral responsibility for an accident like Bhopal involves many different kinds of causal complexities, complexities that may be due, for example, to multiple causes, to multiple causal levels, to multiple dimensions of causality, as well as to multiple agents acting in multiple capacities and, of course, to the multiplicity of victims. Where the causation embraces large numbers of agents, we find some sense in the notion of "collective responsibility," and where an untoward outcome is ostensibly due to complex technological and social structures, we feel that we can blame the "system" and say that it is responsible. In the final analysis, however, moral responsibility always boils down to a relationship of individuals to other individuals. Neither collective responsibility nor system responsibility provides an excuse relieving specific individuals from their responsibility for outcomes.

With regard to causality, it must also be pointed out that responsibility like causality can be indirect as well as direct. Accordingly, a large number of individuals can be held indirectly responsible for Bhopal. More important, the causality involved comprises negative causes (e.g., omissions) as well as positive causes (e.g., actions). For our purposes negative causes are important, for most technological accidents are breakdowns that are due to negative causes, such as the failure of a piece of machinery to operate properly or the failure of personnel to do something like closing or opening a valve or warning others about a danger. The fallacy of supposing one is responsible only for one's positive actions and not for omissions is nicely illustrated by Mr. Warren Anderson's smug comment that "The corporation (i.e., UC) did nothing that either caused or contributed to the accident...." (C&EN Apr 29, 7). Since omissions are, according to my analysis, also actions, the term "action" will henceforth be used to refer to both.

Fault and Moral Deficiency

Let us now turn to (b), the subjective side of responsibility, and to the question of fault. According to most versions of the standard concept of responsibility, in order to be responsible for an untoward outcome, the agent must have had what is variously described as a culpable intention, a blameworthy mental set, a fault of character, or a "weak or defective will," which explains or gives rise to his action (or non-action) (Glover).

For present purposes, we may dismiss the legal doctrine of strict liability, which denies that there must be fault for there to be liability. For this doctrine conflicts with the common view that, from the moral point of view, fault is a necessary condition for blame or punishment and hence is a necessary part of responsibility, specifically, retrospective responsibility. On the other hand, the mere fact that the notion of strict liability, liability without fault, has been incorporated into our legal system, can be taken as further evidence that legal liability has a different rationale and function from moral responsibility.

The requirement of fault, a blameworthy mental set or bad intention, appears to provide a stumbling block to the use of the concept of responsibility for accidents like Bhopal. For it is indeed difficult to pinpoint any single person or set of persons who was clearly at fault in the strict sense, e.g., a person who was careless or grossly negligent. A closer look at the notion of fault will show why it is inappropriate in this context. The fault requirement (*culpability*) is easily satisfied where there is manifest malice or gross negligence, and perhaps even where there is simply carelessness or heedlessness. As such, these mental qualities might be said to be reprovable in themselves, in the sense that their evil does not depend on the context. In other words, those subjective qualities subsumed under terms like *mens rea* or *culpa* are positively objectionable quite apart from any actual effect they may have on the welfare of others.

For this reason some theorists claim (mistakenly) that responsibility and blame can be attached to agents simply on the basis of their morally evil or morally deficient intentions without regard to whether or not these intentions result in actions causing evils in the real world. According to them, a person who intends to do evil but is unsuccessful is as culpable as a person who succeeds. Intention is enough to damn! Although for a number of reasons I find this position morally objectionable, e.g., in crucial cases it forgets about the victims, at least it shows clearly how fault can be conceived as a strong and stringent condition and an evil in its own right, so to speak.

It is clearly absurd, however, to attribute fault (*culpa*) in the sense of a reprovable mental quality to any of the people that were involved in the Bhopal case: operators, managers and officials. They were just ordinary people doing their job and trying to earn a living. Furthermore, the actual failures on the part of specific individuals or groups to act were in themselves relatively insignificant and commonplace. The accident was not due *per se* to the individual acts or omissions of a few persons but to the accidental coincidence of large number of failures, no one of which would have been fatal by itself. This is the typical configuration of a normal accident.

For this reason, to say that any or all of those involved were negligent, except after the fact, is to make a claim that under different circumstances would be unjustified. It is true that we can say that the managers ought to have instructed their employees more adequately about safety conditions and safety measures and that the operators ought to have taken the rise in pressure in the MIC tank more seriously and should not have gone off for tea. There are lots of *ought to haves*, but none of them amount to negligence, much less criminal negligence. If we insist on a strict and narrow interpretation of the fault requirement in our analysis of responsibility, then no one was responsible for Bhopal (and, by analogy, hardly any Germans were responsible for Hitler).

The root of the problem we face here comes from the implicit and unquestioned assumption that blame and blameworthiness are essential ingredients in the concept of responsibility. Therefore, in order to save the concept of moral responsibility for application, e.g., to Bhopal, we need to break the connection between responsibility and blame. If we do that we can hold a large number of individuals responsible without holding any of them blamable. Earlier in this essay, I tried to show how the connection can be broken by distinguishing between the primary and the secondary consequences of responsibility. I argued that blame and blameworthiness, blamability, are only secondary consequences of responsibility. The primary consequences, the oughts still remain, however, and pertain to the conduct of all the various individuals whose acts or omissions made the accident at Bhopal possible: there are lots of things that they ought to have done, but did not do.

Reflecting further on what lies behind the subjective requirement of fault, we find that we cannot help feeling that there is something missing in the attitudes of persons whose actions have or might have a calamitous effect on the safety, health and welfare of others, and yet who have no prior or subsequent concern for the actual or possible effect of their actions on others. After all, people are supposed to care about these things; an attitude of nonchalance or indifference may not be blameworthy, but surely it is deplorable.

In the case of Bhopal we note a general lack of concern, especially on the part of the management and the government, for the safety of those around them. Safety was a low priority for almost everyone who was in any way connected with the disaster in Bhopal; other things came first, notably, jobs, positions, and careers. This lack of concern, almost indifference, for safety was manifested at all levels: the publication of and compliance with safety regulations relating to MIC from UC on down was pro forma rather than realistic and in day to day plant operations safety was sacrificed for the sake of cutting costs. Even at the lowest level, among the workers, concern for safety was less important than holding down a job.

If, in the place of *mens rea* or *culpa*, which represent an excessively stringent and unrealistic notion of fault, we substitute as a subjective condition of responsibility for an untoward outcome some such notion as that of a moral deficiency, e.g., the lack of an appropriate attitude of concern or caring, then we will be able to accommodate a much more encompassing and realistic concept of responsibility. Substituting moral deficiency for fault makes it impossible to cut the tie between responsibility and blame and at the same time redirects our attention to the role of caring and of not-caring in the moral life and in our relations with each other. In contrast to fault, which in all of its ramifications and connotations suggests a positive evil for which blame may be the appropriate response (of third parties), moral deficiency calls our attention to a privation, something missing that ought to be there. Here it seems more appropriate simply to deplore the absence of a positive quality, something good. That good quality has usually been known in the Western philosophical tradition as "humanity" (e.g., in the works of Hume and Kant).

The move from fault to deficiency, from *mens rea* to what I shall call *mens deficiens humanitati*, from the presence of an evil to the absence of a good, and, in general, to an orientation towards humanity or lack thereof, broadens our perspective on the role of responsibility in our interpersonal and public life by bringing in a subjective condition of larger dimensions than blameworthiness. At the same time, it extends the scope of responsibility by reaching out to a wider range of people and to many more different sorts of causal contributions of individual conduct to outcomes affecting the welfare of others.

Moral Responsibility and Moral Virtue

We now come to the final point of the essay, namely, that responsibility is basically a virtue. As such it is to be contrasted with irresponsibility rather than with non-responsibility. (Non-responsibility is important only as part of the negative concept of responsibility discussed earlier.) As a virtue, the subjective side of responsibility, namely, an attitude of concern for the welfare of others, humanity, is an essential ingredient. The primary consequence of responsibility in the sense of virtue is that people ought to order their actions taking into consideration their possible effects on the welfare of others. Responsible action, as such, aims caringly at the prevention of harm to others with whom one has a relationship of one sort or another; irresponsible action, on the other hand, implies not caring.

Without entering into a full-fledged discussion of moral virtue, which I have discussed elsewhere, it suffices here to explain that I consider responsibility to be a virtue, because, like other virtues, it is other-regarding, it is intrinsically motivational and it binds persons to each other. The important thing about virtue, on my view, is that it is not just for saints and heroes, but it is for all of us. It is good for anyone and for everyone to be virtuous and, since responsibility is a virtue, it is good for anyone and for everyone to be responsible. In that regard, it is like kindness. Responsibility can be a virtue even though it is also agent and victim specific and context-specific in ways that have already been explained (Ladd 1989).

Civic Virtue and the Banality of Evil

I borrow the phrase "banality of evil" from Hannah Arendt, who uses it to describe the crimes of Eichmann (Arendt). The paradox of Eichmann is that he was in almost every respect entirely "normal" and yet had no appreciation of the fact that what he had done was wrong; he portrayed himself as an idealistic bureaucrat who just did his duty. The point of the reference in the present context is that the evil of irresponsibility, the nonchalance that we observe in Bhopal, both before and after the accident, is not due to some egregiously neglectful attitude on the part of various people whose actions or omissions contributed causally in one way or another to the outcome or on the part of the general public, including the stockholders of UC, who failed to concern themselves with safety. Instead, the moral deficiency of everyone who was or might have been involved was banal; it reflected a perfectly commonplace and "normal" preoccupation with matters of self-interest and of self-advancement to the exclusion of any consideration of the wider implications of their actions or non-actions and of their absence of concern for the safety and the welfare of others.

It should be obvious to all of us that the moral deficiency I have pointed out is not uncommon in our culture; it is not limited to a few miscreants. Rather it is something that we observe everywhere in our society, everywhere where a concern for the welfare of others, including particularly a concern for their safety, takes second place to other concerns, such as material self-advancement. This is part of our culture. It is reflected in our institutions and fostered by them. The effect is aggravated by the dangerous technology that we have accepted unreflectively and by the bureaucratic machinery that organizes how we use the technology and that determines how we treat each other. At the bottom of these institutions is the prevailing ideology that has aptly been called "utilitarian individualism" (Bellah). This ideology gives legitimacy to the priority given to self over others and to the material social values of self-advancement. It also teaches that commitment and concern for others is supererogatory, that is, it is a matter of individual preference ("expressive individualism") (Bellah). Virtue, according to the ideology, is optional; it is reserved for "saints and heroes" (Ladd 1989).

Our attitude towards whistleblowing illustrates how far we have gone in turning our values upside down: the concern for safety, which should motivate all of us, has been relegated to the private realm of heroes, troublemakers and nuts. Our society assumes that it is a matter of individual choice (and risk) to decide whether or not to call attention to hazards and risks instead of being, as it should be, a duty incumbent on all citizens as responsible members of society.

This is where virtue comes in, or what in the present context I shall call *civic virtue*. Civic virtue is a virtue required of all citizens as citizens. It is not just something optional—for saints and heroes. A virtuous citizen, and that should include everybody, should have a concern for the common good and for the long-range welfare of other people in the society, even where this concern demands individual sacrifices of one sort or another or simply giving less priority to one's own private interests and to one's advancement on the escalator to worldly success.

Civic virtue on the part of its citizens is what holds a society together (Bellah). Once it is lost, a society rapidly degenerates into violence and, in Hobbes's terms, into a war of all against all. Only a resurgence of civic virtue or of what Bellah calls the "republican virtues," among the citizenry can save our society from self-destruction, brought on, say, through the irresponsible use of dangerous technology (nuclear armaments) and the irresponsible exploitation by bureaucracies of fellow citizens for the sake of various narrow short-term goals (Ladd 1970, 1982, 1984).

REFERENCES

Arendt, Hannah. 1963. *Eichmann in Jerusalem: a Report on the Banality of Evil*. New York: Viking Press.

Beakley, George C. and H.W. Leach. 1972. *Engineering*. New York: Macmillan.

Bellah, Robert N., Richard Madsen, William M. Sullivan, Ann Swidler and Steven M. Tipton. 1985. *Habits of the Heart: Individualism and Commitment in American Life*. New York: Harper and Row.

Bowonder, B. 1985(a). "The Bhopal Incident: Implications for Developing Countries," *Environmentalist* Vol. 5:2, 89-103.

——. 1985(b) "Avoiding Future Bhopals," *Environment* Vol. 27:7.

Bracken, Paul. 1983. *The Command and Control of Nuclear Forces*. New Haven: Yale University Press.

Buckley, William F. 1985. "The Year of Bhopal," *National Review* Vol. 37:63.

Castleman, Barry I. and Prabir Purkavastha. 1985. "The Bhopal Disaster as a Case Study in Double Standards," in Jane H. Ives, ed. *The Export of Hazard*. Boston: Routledge & Kegan Paul.

Chemical and Engineering News. 1985. Articles on Bhopal: especially Jan. 21, Feb. 12, March 25 and April 7 and 29.

Feinberg, Joel. 1970. *Doing and Deserving*. Princeton: Princeton University Press.

Ford, Daniel F. 1982. *Three-Mile Island: Thirty Minutes to Meltdown*. New York: Viking Press.

French, Peter, ed. 1972. *Individual and Collective Responsibility*. Cambridge, MA: Schenkman Publishing Co.

Glover, Jonathan. 1970. *Responsibility*. London: Routledge & Kegan Paul.

Hart, H.L.A. and A.M. Honore. 1959. *Causation in the Law*. Oxford: Clarendon Press.

Hart, H.L.A. 1968. *Punishment and Responsibility*. New York: Oxford University Press.

Hersh, Seymour. 1970. *My Lai: A Report on the Massacre and its Aftermath*. New York: Random House.

Jonas, Hans. 1984. *The Imperative of Responsibility*. Chicago: Chicago University Press.

Kurzman, Dan. 1987. *A Killing Wind: Inside Union Carbide and the Bhopal Catastrophe*. New York: McGraw-Hill.

Ladd, John. 1965. "The Ethical Dimensions of the Concept of Action," *Journal of Philosophy* Vol. 62:21.

——. 1970. "Morality and the Ideal of Rationality in Formal Organizations," *Monist* Vol. 54:4.

——. 1975. "The Ethics of Participation," in J. Roland Pennock and John Chapman, eds. *Nomos XVI: Participation in Politics*. New York: Atherton-Lieber.

——. 1979. "Legalism and Medical Ethics," *Journal of Medicine and Philosophy* Vol. 4:1.

——. 1982. "Philosophical Remarks on Professional Responsibility in Organizations," *International Journal of Applied Philosophy* Vol. 1:2.

——. 1984. "Corporate Mythology and Individual Responsibility," *International Journal of Applied Philosophy* Vol. 2:1.

——. 1989. "The Good Doctor and the Rights of Children," in Loretta M. Kopelman and John C. Moskop, eds., *Children and Health Care*. Dordrecht: Kluwer.

Nagel, Thomas. 1980. "The Limits of Objectivity." *The Tanner Lectures on Human Values*, Vol. 1, ed. S.M. McMurrin.

New York Times. 1985. Jan 28, 30, 31, Feb. 3.

Perrow, Charles. 1984. *Normal Accidents*. New York: Basic Books.

Prosser and Keaton. 1984. *The Law of Torts*, fifth edition. St. Paul: West Publishing Co.

Shrivastava, Paul. 1987. *Bhopal: Anatomy of a Crisis*. Cambridge, MA: Ballinger Publishing Co.

Wallace, James D. 1978. *Virtues and Vices*. Ithaca, NY: Cornell University Press.

Weber, Max. 1946. "Politics as a Vocation." tr. H.H. Gerth and C. Wright Mills. *From Max Weber: Essays in Sociology*. New York: Oxford University Press.

A short summary of facts and a bibliography relating to the Bhopal disaster may be found in Castleman and Purkavastha (1985) and Kurzman (1987).

An earlier draft of this essay was read to the Department of Philosophy, Dartmouth College. I am indebted to my friends at Dartmouth for their helpful comments. I am also indebted to Dr. Bowonder for providing me with information about Bhopal and for his encouragement. Many friends and colleagues have provided useful comments for which I owe a debt of gratitude. I particularly want to thank Philip Quinn and Freeman Keith. After drafting this paper, the Wayland Collegium of Brown University generously provided funds for a trip to India, including a stay in Bhopal, where I had the opportunity to confer first-hand with victims, officials, reporters and scholars about the Bhopal tragedy and its aftermath.

ETHICAL DILEMMAS IN ENGINEERING

MIKE W. MARTIN

Whistleblowing: Professionalism, Personal Life, and Shared Responsibility for Safety in Engineering

More than most issues, life and death issues in the professions rivet our attention. Medicine presents us with questions about whether to remove life-support systems and whether to assist the suicide of patients who could live, but with a dubious quality of life. Law disturbs us with the need for defense attorneys to defend clients who they know are morally guilty of murder or rape and who may engage in those crimes again if released. And engineering confronts us with agonizing decisions about whether to whistleblow in order to warn the public of deadly hazards known only to those inside technological corporations.

Right off, this interest in whistleblowing tells us something important about engineering. Whistleblowing occurs in all professions, and most of what I say will have general relevance to professional ethics. Only in engineering ethics, however, has whistleblowing been something of a preoccupation. The reason is clear. Engineers work on projects that affect the safety of large numbers of people. As professionals, they live by codes of ethics which ascribe to them a paramount obligation to protect the safety, health, and welfare of the public, an obligation that sometimes implies whistleblowing. As employees of corporations, however, their obligation is to respect the authority of managers who sometimes give insufficient attention to safety matters, and who also severely punish whistleblowers. As a result, there are inevitable conflicts between professional obligations to employers and the public, as well as conflicts between professional and personal life.

I want to take a fresh look at whistleblowing in order to draw attention to some neglected issues concerning the moral relevance of personal life to understanding professional responsibilities. Specifically, the issues concern: personal rights and responsibilities in deciding how to meet professional obligations; increased personal burdens when others involved in collective endeavors fail to meet their responsibilities; the role of the virtues, especially personal integrity, as they bear on "living with oneself" and personal commitments to moral ideals beyond minimum requirements.

1. Definition and Cases

By "whistleblowing" I have in mind the actions of employees (or former employees) who identify what they believe to be a significant moral problem concerning their corporation (or corporations they deal with), who convey information about the problem outside approved organizational channels or against pressure from supervisors or colleagues not to do so, with the intention of drawing attention to the problem (whatever further motives they may have).[1] Examples of serious moral problems include felonies, immoral treatment of clients or employees (such as sexual harassment), misuse of public funds, and—my focus here—technological products that are unacceptably dangerous to the public.

I will focus on cases where whistleblowers identify themselves. While anonymous whistleblowing is a legitimate option in some situations, acknowledging one's identity and credentials is usually necessary in order to be taken seriously; in any case, corporations typically have resources to hunt down "leaks" in order to identify whistleblowers.[2] I will discuss both external whistleblowing, where information is passed outside the corporation (for example, to government officials, the press, professional societies), and internal whistleblowing, where information is passed to higher management against corporate policy or one's supervisor's directives. Let me bring to mind three well-known cases.

(1) In 1972 Dan Applegate wrote a memo to his supervisor, the vice-president of Convair Corporation, telling him in no uncertain terms that the cargo door for the DC-10 airplane was unsafe, making it "inevitable that, in the twenty years ahead of us, DC-10 cargo doors will come open and I would expect this to usually result in the loss of the airplane."[3] As a subcontractor for McDonnell Douglas, Convair had designed the cargo door and the DC-10 fuselage. Applegate was Director of Product Engineering at Convair and the senior engineer in charge of the design. His supervisor did not challenge his technical judgment in the matter, but told him that nothing could be done because of the likely costs to Convair in admitting responsibility for a design error that would need to be fixed by grounding DC-10s. Two years later, the cargo door on a Turkish DC-10 flying near Paris opened in flight, decompressurizing the cargo area so as to collapse the passenger floor—along which run the controls for the aircraft. All 346 people on board died, a record casualty figure at that time for a single-plane crash. Tens of millions of dollars were paid out in civil suits, but no one was charged with criminal or even unprofessional conduct.

(2) Frank Camps was a principal design engineer for the Pinto.[4] Under pressure from management he participated in coaxing the Pinto windshield through government tests by reporting only the rare successful test and by using a Band-Aid fix design that resulted in increased hazard to the gas tank. In 1973, undergoing a crisis of conscience in response to reports of exploding gas tanks, he engaged in internal whistleblowing, writing the first of many memos to top management stating his view that Ford was violating federal safety standards. It took six years before his concerns were finally incorporated into the 1979 model Pinto, after nearly a million Pintos with unsafe windshields and gas tanks were put on the road. Shortly after writing his memos he was given lowered performance evaluations, then demoted several times. He resigned in 1978 when it became clear his prospects for advancement at Ford were ended. He filed a law suit based in part on age discrimination, in part on trying to prevent Ford from making

him a scapegoat for problems with the Pinto, and in part on trying to draw further attention to the dangers in the Pinto.

(3) On January 27, 1986, Roger Boisjoly and other senior engineers at Morton Thiokol firmly recommended that space shuttle *Challenger* not be launched.[5] The temperature at the launch site was substantially below the known safety range for the O-ring seals in the joints of the solid rocket boosters. Top management overrode the recommendation. Early in the launch, the *Challenger* boosters exploded, killing the seven crew members, to the terrified eyes of millions who watched because schoolteacher Christa McAuliffe was aboard. A month later Boisjoly was called to testify before the Rogers Commission. Against the wishes of management, he offered documents to support his interpretation of the events leading to the disaster—and to rebut the interpretation given by his boss. Over the next months Boisjoly was made to feel increasingly alienated from his coworkers until finally he had to take an extended sick leave. Later, when he desired to find a new job he found himself confronted with companies unwilling to take a chance on a known whistleblower.

As the last two cases suggest, there can be double horrors surrounding whistleblowing: the public horror of lost lives, and the personal horror of responsible whistleblowers who lose their careers. Most whistleblowers undergo serious penalties for "committing the truth." One recent study suggests that two out of three of them suffer harassment, lowered performance evaluations, demotions, punitive transfers, loss of jobs, or blacklisting that can effectively end a career.[6] Horror stories about whistleblowers are not the exception; they are the rule.

2. Three Approaches to Whistleblowing Ethics

The literature on whistleblowing is large and growing. Here I mention three general approaches.

The first is to condemn whistleblowers as disloyal troublemakers who "rat" on their companies and undermine teamwork based on the hierarchy of authority within the corporation. Admittedly, whistleblowers' views about safety concerns are sometimes correct, but final decisions about safety belong to management, not engineers. When management errs, the corporation will eventually pick up the costs in law suits and adverse publicity. Members of the public are part of the technological enterprise which both benefits them and exposes them to risks; when things go wrong they (or their surviving family) can always sue.

I once dismissed this attitude as callous, as sheer corporate egoism that misconstrues loyalty to a corporation as an absolute (unexceptionless) moral principle. *If*, however—and it is a big "if"—the public accepts this attitude, as revealed in how it expresses its will through legitimate political processes, then so be it. As will become clear later, I take public responsibilities seriously. If the public refuses to protect whistleblowers, it tacitly accepts the added risks from not having available important safety information. I hope the public will protect the jobs of whistleblowers; more on this later.

A second approach, insightfully defended by Michael Davis,[7] is to regard whistleblowing as a tragedy to be avoided. On occasion whistleblowing may be a necessary evil or even admirable, but it is always bad news all around. It is proof of organizational trouble and management failure; it threatens the careers of managers on whom the whistle is blown; it disrupts collegiality by making colleagues feel resentment toward the whistleblower, and it damages the important informal network of friends at the workplace; it shows the whistleblower lost faith in the organization and its authority, and hence is more likely to be a troublemaker in the future; and it almost always brings severe penalties to whistleblowers who are viewed by employers and colleagues as unfit employees.

I wholeheartedly support efforts to avoid the need for whistleblowing. There are many things that can be done to improve organizations to make whistleblowing unnecessary. Top management can—and must—set a moral tone, and then implement policies that encourage safety concerns (and other bad news) to be communicated freely. Specifically, managers can keep doors open, allowing engineers to convey their concerns without retribution. Corporations can have in-house ombudspersons and appeal boards, and even a vice-president for corporate ethics. For their part, engineers can learn to be more assertive and effective in making their safety concerns known, learning how to build support from their colleagues. (Could Dan Applegate have pushed harder than he did, or did he just write a memo and drop the matter?) Professional societies should explore the possibility of creating confidential appeal groups where engineers can have their claims heard.

Nevertheless, this second approach is not enough. There will always be corporations and managers willing to cut corners on safety in the pursuit of short-term profit, and there will always be a need for justified whistleblowing. Labelling whistleblowing as a tragedy to be avoided whenever possible should not deflect attention from issues concerning justified whistleblowing.

We need to remind ourselves that responsible whistleblowing is *not* bad news all around. It is very good news for the public which is protected by it. The good news is both episodic and systematic. Episodically, lives are saved directly when professionals speak out, and lives are lost when professionals like Dan Applegate feel they must remain silent in order to keep their jobs. Systematically, lives are saved indirectly by sending a strong message to industry that legally protected whistleblowing is always available as a last resort when managers too casually override safety concerns for short-term profits. Helpful pressure is put on management to take a more farsighted view of safety, thereby providing a further impetus for unifying corporate self-interest with the production of safe products. (In the DC-10, Pinto, and *Challenger* cases, management made shortsight-

ed decisions that resulted in enormous costs in law suits and damaged company reputations.)

In this day of (sometimes justified) outcry over excessive government regulation, we should not forget the symbolic importance of clear, effective, and enforced laws as a way for society to express its collective vision of a good society.[8] Laws protecting responsible whistleblowing express the community's resolve to support professionals who act responsibly for public safety. Those laws are also required if the public is to meet its responsibilities in the creation of safe technological products, as I will suggest in a moment.

A third approach is to affirm unequivocally the obligation of engineers (and other professionals) to whistleblow in certain circumstances, and to treat this obligation as paramount—as overriding all other considerations, whatever the sacrifice involved in meeting it. Richard De George gave the classical statement of this view.[9] External whistleblowing, he argued, is obligatory when five conditions are met (by an engineer or other corporate employee):

1. "Serious and considerable harm to the public" is involved;
2. one reports the harm and expresses moral concern to one's immediate superior;
3. one exhausts other channels within the corporation;
4. one has available "documented evidence that would convince a reasonable, impartial observer that one's view of the situation is correct"; and
5. one has "good reasons to believe that by going public the necessary changes will be brought about" to prevent the harm.

De George says that whistleblowing is morally *permissible* when conditions 1-3 are met, and is morally *obligatory* when 1-5 are met.

As critics have pointed out, conditions (4) and (5) seem far too strong. Where serious safety is at stake, there is some obligation to whistleblow even when there are only grounds for hope (not necessarily belief) that whistleblowing will significantly improve matters, and even when one's documentation is substantial but less than convincing to every rational person.[10] Indeed, often whistleblowing is intended to prompt authorities to garner otherwise-unavailable evidence through investigations.

Moreover, having a reasonable degree of documentation is a requirement even for permissible whistleblowing—lest one make insupportable allegations that unjustifiably harm the reputations of individuals and corporations. So too is having a reasonable hope for success—lest one waste everyone's time and energy.[11] Hence, De George's sharp separation of requirements for permissibility and obligation begins to collapse. There may be an obligation to whistleblow when 1-3 are met and the person has some reasonable degree of documentation and reasonable hope for success in bringing about necessary changes.

My main criticism of this third approach, however, is more fundamental. I want to call into question the whole attempt to offer a general rule that tells us when whistleblowing is mandatory, *tout court*. Final judgments about obligations to whistleblow must be made contextually, not as a matter of general rule. And they must take into account the burdens imposed on whistleblowers.[12]

3. The Moral Relevance of Personal Life to Professional Duty

In my view, there is a strong *prima facie* obligation to whistleblow when one has good reason to believe there is a serious moral problem, has exhausted normal organizational channels (except in emergencies when time precludes that), has available a reasonable amount of documentation, and has reasonable hope of solving the problem by blowing the whistle. Nevertheless, however strong, the obligation is only *prima facie*: It can sometimes have exceptions when it conflicts with other important considerations. Moreover, the considerations which need to be

weighed include not only *prima facie* obligations to one's employer, but also considerations about one's personal life. Before they make all-things-considered judgments about whether to whistleblow, engineers may and should consider their responsibilities to their family, other personal obligations which depend on having an income, and their rights to pursue their careers.

Engineers are people, as well as professionals. They have personal obligations to their families, as well as sundry other obligations in personal life which can be met only if they have an income. They also have personal rights to pursue careers. These personal obligations and rights are moral ones, and they legitimately interact with professional obligations in ways that sometimes make it permissible for engineers not to whistleblow, even when they have a *prima facie* obligation to do so. Precisely how these considerations are weighed depends on the particular situation. And here as elsewhere, we must allow room for morally reasonable people to weigh moral factors differently.

In adopting this contextual approach to balancing personal and professional obligations, I am being heretical. Few discussions of whistleblowing take personal considerations seriously, as being morally significant, rather than a matter of nonmoral, prudential concern for self-interest. But responsibilities to family and to others outside the workplace, as well as the right to pursue one's career, are moral considerations, not just prudential ones. Hence further argument is needed to dismiss them as irrelevant or always secondary in this context. I will consider three such arguments.

(i) The *Prevent-Harm Argument* says that morality requires us to prevent harm and in doing so to treat others' interests equally and impartially with our own. This assumption is often associated with utilitarianism, the view that we should always produce the most good for the people. Strictly, at issue here is "negative utilitarianism," which says we should always act to minimize total harm, treating everyone's interests as equally important with our own. The idea is that even though engineers and their families must suffer, their suffering is outweighed by the lives saved through whistleblowing. Without committing himself to utilitarianism, De George uses a variation of the impartiality requirement to defend his criteria for obligatory whistleblowing: "It is not implausible to claim both that we are morally obliged to prevent harm to others at relatively little expense to ourselves, and that we are morally obliged to prevent great harm to a great many others, even at considerable expense to ourselves."[13]

The demand for strict impartiality in ethics has been under sustained attack during the past two decades, and from many directions.[14] Without attempting to review all of those arguments, I can indicate how they block any straightforward move from impartiality to absolute (exceptionless) whistleblowing obligations, thereby undermining the Prevent-Harm Argument. One argument is that a universal requirement of strict impartiality (as opposed to a limited requirement restricted to certain contexts) is self-demeaning. It undermines our ability to give our lives meaning through special projects, careers, and relationships that require the resources which strict impartiality would demand we give away to others. The general moral right to autonomy—the right to pursue our lives in a search for meaning and happiness—implies a right to give considerable emphasis to our personal needs and those of our family.

As an analogy, consider the life-and-death issues surrounding world hunger and scarce medical resources.[15] It can be argued that all of us share a general responsibility (of mutual aid) for dealing with the tragedy of tens of thousands of people who die each day from malnutrition and lack of medical care. As citizens paying taxes that can be used toward this end, and also as philanthropists who voluntarily recognize a responsibility to give to relief organizations, each of us has a *prima facie* obligation to help. But there are limits. Right now, you and I could dramatically lower our lifestyles in order to

help save lives by making greater sacrifices. We could even donate one of our kidneys to save a life. Yet we have a right not to do that, a right to give ourselves and our families considerable priority in how we use our resources. Similarly, engineers' rights to pursue their meaning-giving careers, and the projects and relationships made possible by those careers, have relevance in understanding the degree of sacrifice required by a *prima facie* whistleblowing obligation.

(ii) The *Avoid-Harm Argument* proceeds from the obligation not to cause harm to others. It then points out that engineers are in a position to cause or avoid harm on an unusual scale. As a result, according to Kenneth Alpern, the ordinary moral obligation of due care in avoiding harm to others implies that engineers must "be ready to make greater personal sacrifices than can normally be demanded of other individuals."[16] In particular, according to Gene James, whistleblowing is required when it falls under the general obligation to "prevent unnecessary harm to others" and "to not cause avoidable harm to others"; where "harm" means violating their rights.[17]

Of course there is a general obligation not to cause harm. That obligation, however, is so abstract that it tells us little about exactly how much effort and sacrifice is required of us, especially where many people share responsibility for avoiding harm. I have an obligation not to harm others by polluting the environment, but it does not follow that I must stop driving my car at the cost of my job and the opportunities it makes possible for my family. That would be an unfair burden. These abstract difficulties multiply as we turn to the context of engineering practice which involves collective responsibility for technological products.

Engineers work as members of authority-structured teams which sometimes involve hundreds of other professionals who share responsibility for inherently risky technological projects.[18] Engineers are not the only team-members who have responsibilities to create safe products. Their managers have exactly the same general responsibilities. In fact, they have greater accountability insofar as they are charged with the authority to make final decisions about projects. True, engineers have greater expertise in safety matters and hence have greater responsibilities to identify dangers and convey that information to management. But whatever justifications can be given for engineers to zealously protect public safety also apply to managers. In making the decision to launch the *Challenger*, Jerald Mason, Senior Vice President for Morton Thiokol, is said to have told Robert Lund, "Take off your engineering hat and put on your management hat." Surely this change in headgear did not alter his moral responsibilities for safety.

Dan Applegate and Roger Boisjoly acted responsibly in making unequivocal safety recommendations; their managers failed to act responsibly. Hence their moral dilemmas about whether to whistleblow arose because of unjustified decisions by their superiors. It is fair to ask engineers to pick up the moral slack for managers' irresponsible decisions—as long as we afford them legal protection to prevent their being harassed, fired, and blacklisted. Otherwise, we impose an unfair burden. Government and the general public share responsibility for safety in engineering. They set the rules that business plays by. It is hypocrisy for us to insist that engineers have an obligation to whistleblow to protect us, and then to fail to protect them when they act on the obligation.

(iii) The *Professional-Status Argument* asserts that engineers have special responsibilities as professionals, specified in codes of ethics, which go beyond the general responsibilities incumbent on everyone to prevent and avoid harm, and which override all personal considerations. Most engineering codes hint at a whistleblowing obligation with wording similar to that of the code of the National Society of Professional Engineers (NSPE):

> Engineers shall at all times recognize that their primary obligation is to protect the safety, health, property and welfare of the public. If their professional judgment is over-ruled under circumstances where the safety, health, property or welfare of the public are endangered, they shall notify their employer or client and such other authority as may be appropriate.[19]

The phrase "as may be appropriate" is ambiguous. Does it mean "when morally justified"; or does it mean "as necessary in order to protect the public safety, health, and welfare": The latter interpretation is the most common one, and it clearly implies whistleblowing in some situations, no matter what the personal cost.

I agree that the obligation to protect public safety is an essential professional obligation that deserves emphasis in engineers' work. It is not clear, however, that it is paramount in the technical philosophical sense of overriding all other professional obligations in all situations. In any case, I reject the general assumption that codified professional duties are all that are morally relevant in making whistleblowing decisions. It is quite true that professional considerations require setting aside personal interests in many situations. But it is also true that personal considerations have enormous and legitimate importance in professional life, such as in choosing careers and areas of specialization, choosing and changing jobs, and deciding how far to go in sacrificing family life in pursuing a job and a career.

Spouses have a right to participate in professional decisions such as those involving whistleblowing.[20] At the very least, I would be worried about professionals who do not see the moral importance of consulting their spouses before deciding to engage in acts of whistleblowing that will seriously affect them and their children. I would be equally worried about critics who condemn engineers for failing to whistleblow without knowing anything about their personal situation.[21]

Where does all this leave us on the issue of engineers' obligations? It is clear there is a minimum standard which engineers must meet. They have strong obligations not to break the law and not to approve projects which are immoral according to standard practice. They also have a *prima facie* obligation to whistleblow in certain situations. Just how strong the whistleblowing responsibility is, all things considered, remains unclear—as long as there are inadequate legal protections.

What is clear is that whistleblowing responsibilities must be understood contextually, weighed against personal rights and responsibilities, and assessed in light of the public's responsibilities to protect whistleblowers. We must look at each situation. Sometimes the penalties for whistleblowing may not be as great as is usually the case, perhaps because some protective laws have been passed, and sometimes family responsibilities and rights to pursue a career may not be seriously affected. But our all-things-considered judgments about whistleblowing are not a matter of a general absolute principle that always overrides every other consideration.

Yes, the public has a right to be warned by whistleblowers of dangers—assuming the public is willing to bear its responsibility for passing laws protecting whistleblowers. In order to play their role in respecting that right, engineers should have a legally backed *right of conscience* to take responsible action in safety matters beyond the corporate walls.[22] As legal protections are increased, as has begun to happen during the past decade,[23] then the relative weight of personal life to professional duty changes. Engineers will be able to whistleblow more often without the kind of suffering to which they have been exposed, and thus the *prima facie* obligation to whistleblow will be less frequently overridden by personal responsibilities.

4. Character, Integrity, and Personal Ideals

Isn't there a danger that denying the existence of absolute, all-things-considered, principles for whistleblowers will further discourage whistleblowing in the public interest? After all, even if we grant my claims about the moral relevance of personal rights and responsibilities, there remains the general tendency for self-interest to unduly bias moral decisions. Until adequate legal protection is secured, won't this contextual approach result in fewer whistleblowers who act from a sense of responsibility? I think not.

If all-things-considered judgments about whistleblowing are not a matter of general rule, they are still a matter of good moral judgment. Good judgment takes into account rules whenever they provide helpful guidance, but essentially it is a product of good character—a character defined by virtues. Character is a further area in which personal aspects of morality bear on engineering ethics, and in the space remaining I want to comment on it.

Virtues are those desirable traits that reveal themselves in all aspects of personality—in attitudes, emotions, desires, and conduct. They are not private merit badges. (To view them as such is the egoistic distortion of self-righteousness.)[24] Instead, virtues are desirable ways of relating to other people, to communities, and to social practices such as engineering. Which virtues are most important for engineers to cultivate?

Here are some of the most significant virtues, sorted into three general categories.[25]

(1) *Virtues of self-direction* are those which enable us to guide our lives. They include the *intellectual virtues* which characterize technical expertise: mastery of one's discipline, ability to communicate, skills in reasoning, imagination, ability to discern dangers, a disposition to minimize risk, and humility (understood as a reasonable perspective on one's abilities). They also include *integrity virtues* which promote coherence among one's attitudes, commitments, and conduct based on a core of moral concern. They include honesty, courage, conscientiousness, self-respect, and fidelity to promises and commitments—those in both personal and professional life. And *wisdom* is practical good judgment in making responsible decisions. This good moral judgment, grounded in the

experience of concerned and accountable engineers, is essential in balancing the aspirations embedded in the next two sets of virtues.

(2) *Team-work virtues* include (a) loyalty: concern for the good of the organization for which one works; (b) collegiality: respect for one's colleagues and a commitment to work with them in shared projects; and (c) cooperativeness: the willingness to make reasonable compromises. Reasonable compromises can be integrity-preserving in that they enable us to meet our responsibilities to maintain relationships in circumstances where there is moral complexity and disagreement, factual uncertainty, and the need to maintain ongoing cooperative activities—exactly the circumstances of engineering practice.[26] Unreasonable compromises are compromising in the pejorative sense: they betray our moral principles and violate our integrity. Only good judgment, not general rules, enables engineers to draw a reasonable line between these two types of compromise.

(3) *Public-spirited virtues* are those aimed at the good of others, both clients and the general public affected by one's work. *Justice virtues* concern fair play. One is respect for persons: the disposition to respect people's rights and autonomy, in particular, the rights not to be injured in ways one does not consent to.

Public-spiritedness can be shown in different degrees, as can all the virtues. This helps us understand the sense of responsibility to protect the public that often motivates whistleblowers. Just as professional ethics has tended to ignore the moral relevance of personal life to professional responsibilities, it has tended to think of professional responsibilities solely in terms of *role responsibilities*—those minimal obligations which all practitioners take on when they enter a given profession. While role responsibilities are sufficiently important to deserve this emphasis, they are not the whole of professional ethics. There are also *ideals* which evoke higher aspirations than the minimum responsibilities.[27] These ideals are important to understanding the committed conduct of whistleblowers.

Depth of commitment to the public good is a familiar theme in whistleblowers' accounts of their ordeals. The depth is manifested in how they connect their self-respect and personal integrity to their commitments to the good of others. Roger Boisjoly, for example, has said that if he had it all to do over again he would make the same decisions because otherwise he "couldn't live with any self respect."[28] Similarly, Frank Camps says he acted from a sense of personal integrity.[29]

Boisjoly, Camps, and whistleblowers like them also report that they acted from a sense of responsibility. In my view, they probably acted beyond the minimum standard that all engineers are required to meet, given the absence of protective laws and the severity of the personal suffering they had to undergo. Does it follow that they are simply confused about how much was required of them? J.O. Urmson once suggested that moral heroes who claim to be meeting their duties are either muddled in their thinking or excessively modest about their moral zealousness, which has carried them beyond the call of duty.[30]

Urmson, like most post-Kantian philosophers, assumed that obligations are universal, and hence that there could not be personal obligations that only certain individuals have. I hold a different view.[31] There is such a thing as voluntarily assuming a responsibility and doing so because of commitments to (valid) ideals, to a degree beyond what is required of everyone. Sometimes the commitment is shown in career choice and guided by religious ideals: think of Albert Schweitzer or Mother Teresa of Calcutta. Sometimes it is shown in professional life in an unusual degree of *pro bono publico* work. And sometimes it is shown in whistleblowing decisions.

According to this line of thought, whistleblowing done at enormous personal cost, motivated by moral concern for the public good, and exercising good moral judgment is both (a) supererogatory—beyond the general call of duty incumbent on everyone, and (b) appropriately motivated by a sense of responsibility. Such whistleblowers act from a sense that they *must* do what they are doing.[32] Failure to act would constitute a betrayal of the ideal to which they are committed, and also a betrayal of their integrity as a person committed to that ideal.

Here, then, is a further way in which personal life is relevant to professional life. Earlier I drew attention to the importance of personal rights and responsibilities, and to the unfair personal burdens when others involved in collective enterprises fail to meet their responsibilities. Equally important, we need to appreciate the role of personal integrity grounded in supererogatory commitments to ideals. The topic of being able to live with oneself should not be dismissed as a vagary of individual psychology. It concerns the ideals to which we commit ourselves, beyond the minimum standard incumbent on everyone. This appreciation of personal integrity and commitments to ideals is compatible with a primary emphasis on laws that make it possible for professionals to serve the public good without having to make heroic self-sacrifices.[33]

NOTES

1 Cf. Mike W. Martin and Roland Schinzinger, *Ethics in Engineering*, 2nd ed. (New York: McGraw-Hill, 1989), 213 ff.

2 See Frederick Elliston, "Anonymous Whistleblowing," *Business & Professional Ethics Journal* Vol. 1, No. 2 (Winter 1982): 39-58.

3 Paul Eddy, Elaine Potter, Bruce Page, *Destination Disaster* (New York: Quandrangle, 1976), 185.

4 Frank Camps, "Warning an Auto Company About an Unsafe Design," in Alan F. Westin (ed.), *Whistle-Blowing!* (New York: McGraw-Hill, 1981), 119-29.

5 Roger M. Boisjoly, "The Challenger Disaster: Moral Responsibility and the Working Engineer," in Deborah G. Johnson (ed.), *Ethical Issues in Engineering* (Englewood Cliffs, NJ: Prentice Hall, 1991), 6-14.

6 See, e.g., Myron P. Glazer and Penina Migdal Glazer, *The Whistleblowers* (New York: Basic Books, 1989).

7 Michael Davis, "Avoiding the Tragedy of Whistleblowing," *Business & Professional Ethics Journal* Vol. 8, No. 4, (Winter 1989): 3-19. Davis also draws attention to the potentially negative aspects of laws, as does Sissela Bok in "Whistleblowing and Professional Responsibilities," in D. Callahan and S. Bok (eds.), *Ethics Teaching in Higher Education* (New York: Plenum), 277-95. Those aspects, which include violating corporate privacy, undermining trust and collegiality, and lowering economic efficiency, are serious. But I am convinced that well-framed laws to protect whistleblowers can take them into account. The laws should protect only whistleblowing that meets the conditions for the *prima facie* obligation I state at the beginning of section 3.

8 Robert Nozick drew attention to the symbolic importance of government action in general when he recently abjured the libertarian position he once defended vigorously. *The Examined Life* (New York: Simon and Schuster, 1989), 286-88.

9 The quotes are from Richard T. De George's most recent statement of his view in *Business Ethics*, 3rd ed. (New York: Macmillan Publishing, 1990), 208-12. They parallel his view as first stated in "Ethical Responsibilities of Engineers in Large Organizations," *Business & Professional Ethics Journal* Vol. 1, No. 1 (Fall 1981): 1-14. As an example of a far higher demand on engineers see Kenneth D. Alpern, "Moral Responsibility for Engineers," *Business & Professional Ethics Journal* Vol. 2, No. 2 (Winter 1983): 39-47.

10 Gene G. James, "Whistle Blowing: Its Moral Justification," in W. Michael Hoffman and Jennifer Mills Moore (eds.), *Business Ethics*, 2nd ed. (New York: McGraw-Hill, 1990), 332-44.

11 David Theo Goldberg, "Tuning in to Whistle Blowing," *Business & Professional Ethics Journal* Vol. 7, No. 2 (Summer 1988): 85-94.

12 As his reason for conditions (4) and (5), De George cites the fate of whistleblowers who put themselves at great risk: "If there is little likelihood of his success, there is no moral obligation for the engineer to go public. For the harm he or she personally incurs is not offset by the good such action achieves" ("Ethical Responsibilities of Engineers in Large Organizations," 7). Like myself, then, he sees the personal suffering of whistleblowers as morally relevant to understanding professional responsibilities, even though, as I go on to argue, he invokes that relevance in the wrong way.

13 De George, *Business Ethics*, 214.

14 See especially Bernard Williams, "A Critique of Utilitarianism" in *Utilitarianism for and Against* (Cambridge: Cambridge University Press, 1973) and "Persons, Character, and Morality," in *Moral Luck* (New York: Cambridge University Press, 1981). For samples of more recent discussions see the special edition of *Ethics* Vol. 101 (July 1991), devoted to "Impartiality and Ethical Theory."

15 Cf. John Arthur, "Rights and Duty to Bring Aid," in William Aiken and Hugh La Follette (eds.) *World Hunger and Moral Obligation* (Englewood Cliffs, NJ: Prentice-Hall, 1977).

16 Alpern, "Moral Responsibilities for Engineers," 39.

17 James, "Whistle Blowing: Its Moral Justification," 334-35.

18 See Martin and Schinzinger, *Ethics in Engineering*, chapter 3. The emphasis on engineers adopting a wide view of their activities does not imply that they are culpable for all the moral failures of colleagues and managers.

19 National Society of Professional Engineers, Code of Ethics.

20 Cf. Thomas M. Devine and Donald G. Aplin, "Whistleblower Protection—The Gap Between the Law and Reality," *Howard Law Journal* 31 (1988), 236.

21 I am glad that the NSPE and other professional codes say what they do in support of responsible whistleblowing, as long as it is understood that professional codes only state professional, not personal and all-things-considered obligations. Codes provide a backing for morally concerned engineers, and they make available to engineers the moral support of an entire profession. At the same time, professional societies need to do far more than most of them have done to support the efforts of conscientious whistleblowers. Beyond moral and political support, and beyond recognition awards, they need to provide economic support, in the form of legal funds and job-placement.

22 I defend this right in "Rights of Conscience Inside the Technological Corporation," *Conceptus-Studien*, 4: *Wissell and Gewissen* (Vienna: VWGO, 1986): 179-91.

23 Alan F. Westin offers helpful suggestions about laws protecting whistleblowers in *Whistle-Blowing!* For a recent overview of the still fragmented and insufficient legal protection of whistleblowers see Rosemary Chalk, "Making the World Safe for Whistle-Blowers," *Technology Review* 91 (January 1988): 48-57; and James C. Petersen and Dan Farrell, *Whistleblowing: Ethical and Legal Issues in Expressing Dissent* (Dubuque; Iowa: Kendall/Hunt, 1986).

24 Cf. Edmund L. Pincoffs, *Quandaries and Virtues* (Lawrence, KS: University Press of Kansas, 1986), 112-14.

25 Important discussions of the role of virtues in professional ethics include: John Kultgen, *Ethics and Professionalism* (Philadelphia: University of Pennsylvania Press, 1988); Albert Flores (ed.), *Professional Ideals* (Belmont, CA: Wadsworth, 1988); and Michael D. Bayles, *Professional Eth-*

ics, 2nd edition (Belmont, CA: Wadsworth, 1989). John Kekes insight fully discusses the virtues of self-direction in *The Examined Life* (Lewisburg: Bucknell University Press, 1988).

26 Martin Benjamin, *Splitting the Difference* (Lawrence, KS: University Press of Kansas), 1990.

27 On the distinction between moral rules and ideals see Bernard Gert, *Morality* (New York: Oxford University Press, 1988), 160-78.

28 Roger Boisjoly, ibid., 14.

29 Frank Camps, ibid., 128.

30 J.O. Urmson, "Saints and Heroes," in A.I. Melden (ed.), *Essays in Moral Philosophy* (Seattle: University of Washington Press, 1958), 198-216.

31 Cf. A.I. Melden, "Saints and Supererogation," in *Philosophy and Life: Essays on John Wisdom* (The Hague: Martinus Nijhoff, 1984), 61-81.

32 Harry Frankfurt insightfully discusses this felt "must" as a sign of deep caring and commitment in *The Importance of What We Care About* (New York: Cambridge University Press, 1988), 86-88.

33 An earlier version of this paper was read in a lecture series sponsored by the Committee on Ethics in Research at the University of California, Santa Barbara (January 1992). I am grateful for the helpful comments of Jacqueline Hynes and Larry Badash, and also for conversations with Roland Schinzinger on this topic. I am especially grateful for the comments I received from the editor of this journal.

◆ ◆ ◆ ◆ ◆

RICHARD H. McCUEN

Engineering Research: Potential for Fraud

Introduction

The front page story was entitled, "Jimmy's World: 8-year old Heroin Addict Lives for a Fix" (9). The story described a reporter's eyewitness account of an eight-year old boy receiving an injection of heroin from his mother's boyfriend. The story caused considerable concern within the community and a month-long police investigation. This led Washington, DC Mayor Marion S. Barry, Jr., to describe the story as part myth. Despite the lack of corroborating evidence, the story was submitted by the *Washington Post*'s editors for consideration for a Pulitzer Prize. The author of the story listed college degrees on her resume that she had not actually received. The story was awarded the Pulitzer Prize in the feature-writing category. The publicity from the award led to the exposure of the author's hoax that she did not have the two degrees that were listed on her resume. This and other evidence, or lack of it, led the editors to press for more details. Under pressure, the author admitted the story was not totally true. She then resigned. With considerable embarrassment to the *Washington Post*, the Pulitzer Prize was returned. The following day the editors of the *Post* apologized to their readers in a feature editorial. Osborn Elliot, Dean of the Columbia School of Journalism, which administers the Pulitzers, said, "Anything like this damages the credibility of the press and wounds us all" (11).

While the journalistic hoax had nothing to do with engineering, a similar instance in engineering research could damage the credibility of a research institution and possibly the engineering profession. The hoax was the first time the *Washington Post* had been accused of any wrongdoing and poor journalistic practice; yet it cast a shadow on the Post's credibility. Additionally, the journalistic misdemeanor carried a cost to Washington, DC, in both wages to police officers who were investigating the story and the adverse impact to the image of the city. What would be the possible consequences of a similar hoax if one were carried out in a field of engineering research?

There is a considerable cost and effort involved in engineering research. The National Science Foundation reported funding for fiscal year 1981 in the area of engineering research of over $80 million. The American Society for Engineering Education reported expenditures of $834 million for the 1979-80 academic year; this involved over 48,000 personnel, including over 10,000 professorial positions (10). Expenditures for research within engineering practice are also substantial.

Recognizing the potential loss of credibility to the engineering profession, the magnitude of expenditures for engineering research, and the potential impact of engineering research on human welfare, it may be of interest to examine various facets of engineering research and the potential for fraud. The objective of this study is to examine the potential and make recommendations for minimizing the possibility of fraudulent behavior in engineering research.

Cases of Fraud in Biomedical Research

In layman's terms, fraud is a deception that is practiced deliberately to gain an unfair or unlawful advantage. It is somewhat more difficult to provide a legal definition because the exact definition varies from one state to the next. For example, in Maryland fraud is defined as an intentional perversion of the truth for the purpose of inducing another to part with something of value belonging to him or surrender a legal right. The difficulty in proving fraudulent behavior lies in the necessity to prove intent. This is compounded because of the precise way in which the definition is used in prosecuting a case. Lying is not fraud unless the person is made to surrender something of value or a legal right. However, when fraud cannot be proven, it may be possible to prosecute on a lesser charge, such as misconduct.

Biomedical research has recently been the subject of considerable scrutiny, including hearings by the House Science and Technology subcommittee on investigations and oversight, because of recent instances of fraudulent research. Four major cases of unethical, and possibly illegal, behavior in biomedical research were exposed in 1980 alone (5):

1. Vijay Soman, an assistant professor at Yale medical school, plagiarized a paper from another researcher who was involved in similar research, and fabricated data. As a result, 11 papers had to be retracted and his mentor and coauthor had to resign his new position as a department chairman at Columbia University because of the ethical questions involved (3,4).

2. Marc Strauss, a Boston University researcher who received nearly $1 million in cancer research grants over a period of three years, submitted reports containing repeated falsifications.

3. John Long, a researcher at Massachusetts General Hospital, forged data in a study of Hodgkin's disease after obtaining $750,000 in federal funds (15).

4. Elias A.K. Alsabti, a researcher from Jordan, had at least seven papers published in obscure journals that were almost a word-for-word copy of papers previously authored by a colleague.

Falsification of data in medical research, which was practiced in three of these four cases, could have public health consequences. Furthermore, fraudulent research is used as evidence that additional funding is justified and should be provided, often from public funds. This represents an intent to use false information to induce agencies to provide funds, which is clearly within the definition of fraud. Since publications are used to indicate that a researcher is qualified to perform research, and is thus an acceptable candidate for research funding, plagiarism, like data falsification, is fraudulent. Two of the previous four cases, in fact, involved plagiarism.

These cases of fraud in biomedical research are of interest here because there are many similarities between engineering and biomedical research. Both receive a significant amount of support from the public, involve university and private research institutes, and include research that has important implications to human welfare.

The Potential for Fraud in Engineering Research

With respect to engineering research the first question that surfaces is, should the potential for fraud be of concern to the engineering profession? Setting aside for a moment both the costs involved and the potential effect on human welfare, it is only necessary to recall the words of Dean Elliot with reference to the case involving the Pulitzer Prize; he indicated that one case can have a significant, adverse effect on the profession of journalism. The same can be said for the engineering profession. A major case of fraud in engineering research could adversely affect the engineering profession: both its credibility and the willingness of society to allow public funds to support it. When one also considers the cost involved, there is reason for concern. But, the most important consideration is the potential negative impact on human welfare. Thus, it is apparent that it is important for the engineering profession to take the steps that are necessary to minimize the risk of fraud in engineering research.

It is best to dispense with the obvious cases of fraud by researchers. University faculty, who do a large part of engineering research, are given examination copies of textbooks. It is obviously unethical to sell a book; if the person were to request a free examination copy from a publisher with the intent of selling the book, it is fraud. Computer usage offers

a second opportunity for researchers, and not just those in engineering, to act fraudulently. It would be both illegal and unethical to use the university or company computer system for personal consulting work. A third case deals with recruitment. Given the demand for qualified researchers, there are many opportunities for recruitment trips to places that they have never visited. An individual who would accept an expense paid trip to visit the potential employer, when the individual knows that he or she will not accept a job offer, is acting unethically, possibly fraudulently. Also, an individual who uses one field trip to visit two potential employers and then accepts reimbursement from both companies is obviously acting fraudulently. The writer would like to believe these incidents rarely occur; statistics and experience indicate they occur more often than anyone would like to admit. While the social costs of these cases may be minimal they suggest there is a potential for fraud; the potential being that a few individuals are willing to engage in unethical conduct.

Fraud in Proposal Writing

Writing a proposal is often the first formal step in obtaining research funding. The proposal is a prospectus of the research to be performed. With the exception of research initiation proposals, most proposals are an extension of a researcher's current research interests. Given the element of uncertainty involved in research and recognizing the continuous nature of research, a researcher may be tempted to submit a proposal for research that has already been totally or partially completed. Recognizing that it is difficult to delineate the degree of validity of a conclusion, the researcher may wish to continue the research to improve the validity of his conclusions. The merit of the proposal will be partially dependent on the value of increased validity that is assessed by the funding agency. If the researcher were to knowingly withhold information on the current status of the research, then the researcher would be acting fraudulently. He would be misrepresenting the facts in an effort to induce the funding agency to dispense public monies. It would also be a violation of professional codes of ethics, such as Canon 4 of the ASCE Code; the researcher would be accepting "... compensation from more than one party for services on the same project" (8).

It would be difficult to police such behavior. Funding agencies can request details on all current research funding from the researcher. By corresponding with other agencies that are funding similar research by the researcher, they may identify the potential of the proposal in extending the state of the art. However, if the researcher is intent on seeking funds in a fraudulent manner, action by the funding agency would have limited potential in identifying such fraudulent activity.

Professional societies could play a role by participating in the review process. Specifically, technical divisions of a professional society could serve to identify those individuals who would be most capable of assessing the value of the work. In interdisciplinary research, such professional society coordination would be especially valuable.

Fraud in the Submission of a Proposal

The quality of the personnel is a primary factor in assessing the merits of a proposal. Knowing this, those requesting funds attempt to strengthen their proposal packages by including resumes of the most qualified personnel possible. In some cases, the intended effort of each person is not clearly identified in the proposal. If this information is withheld in an attempt to deceive the funding agency, it is clearly a fraudulent activity.

In cases where a research organization does not have qualified in-house personnel they often attempt to strengthen their list of research associates by cooperating with others, such as faculty members at a local university. They request resumes be included with the proposal package, along with the

agreement that the outside person will be used as a consultant if the proposal is funded. If the research organization intends not to use the non "in-house" personnel, then they are acting unethically. Specifically, for example, they would be violating the second Fundamental Principle of the ASCE Code and possibly the fifth Fundamental Canon (8). With respect to the latter violation, they would also be negotiating a contract unfairly. In a legal sense, it would be fraudulent if one placed a value on the credentials of an individual. Funding agencies could minimize this practice by making it known that they expect the final time allocations to be a reasonable approximation to the budgeted values given in the proposal.

A problem similar to the preceding one occurs when the research organization obtains resumes for outside personnel, and then uses the resumes for additional proposals without informing the person that his or her resume is being used. This has the same ethical and legal implications of the previous practice and could easily be prevented if funding agencies would send a postcard to each person whose resume is in the proposal. Then, if the person cited is not a full-time employee of the research organization he could be notified that his resume had been used with a proposal.

Falsification of Research Data

It would be easy to provide examples in which engineering research has been quickly incorporated into engineering practice, and even easier to demonstrate the effect of engineering practice on human welfare; thus, there is a logical connection between engineering research and human welfare. The time frame of this connection is potentially critical. In the past, the time span between research and its use in practice was relatively long. However, in recent years, the time span has become much shorter. Because a relatively long time span would provide an opportunity to identify inaccurate research results, including those that are the result of fraudulent work, the decrease in the time span between research activity and its application should be of concern to the engineering profession. The decrease in the time span increases the likelihood that research based on falsified data will be incorporated into engineering practice.

Whether the research is theoretical or experimental data are likely to be involved, and this provides an opportunity for fraud. Through past experience, and possibly theoretical considerations, a researcher may develop certain biases about the research problem. This may lead to false hypotheses or misinterpretation of anomalous measurements. Anomalous data may then be falsified or omitted because the researcher cannot explain the results. In a sense, the researcher loses his objectivity. The researcher may sense that results containing anomalous data may not be accepted either when submitted to the grantor of the project funds or when included in a paper submitted for publication. This serves as motivation for data falsification. The researcher's value system, which is a function of many factors, is important.

Because of the potential consequences of fraudulent behavior in engineering research, especially with respect to human welfare, every effort should be made to eliminate this source of fraud. No deterrent, whether active or passive, can be totally effective in eliminating the potential for falsifying data. It would be impractical to require that an independent observer be present when the data are being collected. Given the length of time required for engineering research, it would not be cost effective. Funding agencies could require the researcher to maintain detailed logs of the data collection; however, funds would then be required to support the effort required to examine the database. It is questionable whether or not this would be cost effective. However, it may act as a passive deterrent to anyone who might be considering the falsification of data. If detailed logs are required, the researcher should be required to submit copies of the logs immediately following the data collection. This would minimize the time frame and, therefore, the potential for fraud.

An extreme solution might be to make it known that no future research funds will be given to a university or research institution that has a staff member who has previously engaged in fraudulent research activities. However, this would also punish all the other researchers at that institution. While this may appear to be a harsh punishment, this would force the other researchers to apply pressure on the administration to discharge the unethical researcher. Administrators cannot use tenure as an excuse for not firing any individual who has engaged in fraudulent research because fraudulent professional conduct is grounds for revocation of the tenure of the guilty individual. A more workable solution might be to withhold all future funding for anyone who engages in such activity, regardless of the individual's place of employment. While the former would place a greater need for the research institution to provide internal scrutiny of research activity, the latter deterrent is more in line with the principles of democratic law. It would also force an individual who has engaged in fraudulent research activities to seek employment outside of the engineering research.

Fraudulent Cost Overruns of Research Funding

Engineering research differs from engineering design in that the researcher is being asked to cross a new "frontier"; that is, there is an element of the unknown in research that is not usually present in design. This factor makes it somewhat more difficult to develop a budget to include along with the proposal for funding. Because of this measure of uncertainty, it is not unreasonable to expect a number of research proposals to be underbid, which may make it necessary for the researcher to submit a request for additional funding. Recognizing that funding agencies and clients understand this uncertainty, it is possible that researchers could use this as a mechanism for fraudulently obtaining an unfair advantage over competitors. Thus, by intentionally submitting a budget that is inadequate, the researcher could underbid other researchers; it would be fraudulent then to seek additional funds after the initial grant funds were used. It is important to note there is a value conflict only when the researcher intentionally underbids with the intention of seeking additional funds at a later time.

Fraudulent cost overruns could be avoided if the funding agency were to examine the funding record of researchers prior to awarding a contract. After all when a new employee is hired, character references are sought. Therefore, why shouldn't references be sought to verify that the researcher doesn't have a history of underbidding? This is not an unreasonable practice when one considers the funding for a single contract is most often many times greater than the salary commitment to a new employee. The funding agency could contact other funding agencies from which the researcher has obtained funds in the past.

Fraud in Multiple Source Funding

It is common practice to submit the same or a similar proposal to more than one funding agency. This is certainly a prudent practice and perfectly acceptable from both a moral and legal viewpoint. However, if a research organization receives funds from one agency, they cannot in good faith accept funds from another funding agency without notifying them that they have received funds from another source. This would certainly violate Fundamental Canon No. 6 of the ASCE Code of Ethics (8) because the researcher would knowingly be engaged in a business practice of a fraudulent, dishonest, and unethical nature. It could damage the credibility of the engineering profession if public finances were involved.

Unethical Practices in Publishing Research Results

Publishing of research results is a universal practice because the quantity and quality of publications serves both as an input to promotion and salary decisions, and as a consideration in awarding contracts for future research. The author may also find it personally gratifying and believe that it will benefit human welfare in the long run. Whatever the motivation, the process offers the opportunity for unethical and possibly fraudulent behavior. Editors of professional journals are concerned about both multiple submissions of one paper and the submission of two or more quite similar papers. Recognizing that leading journals have a rejection rate of 50% or more, and that the time between submission and publication may be a year or more, some authors may submit the same paper to more than one professional journal. In some cases the author may intend to withdraw the paper from one journal only after the paper has been accepted for publication in another journal. Even if the paper is withdrawn prior to publication, the individual acts unethically. Such a practice of multiple submission requires the time of editors and reviewers and the costs associated with the review process. Since it requires time by the professionals in the field, it is taking their time away from their research as well as time that could be spent reviewing other papers.

Submitting extremely similar papers to two different journals also tends to increase the difficulty of professionals in keeping up with the professional literature. Concerning the practice of submitting similar papers to different journals, some try to justify the practice by saying that: (1) It is common practice; (2) it is an attempt to reach different audiences; (3) they are required to submit brief papers for publication in conference proceedings if they are to present a paper at the conference, but they do not want to jeopardize the potential gain in the form of professional prestige from publishing in a refereed journal; and (4) there is not published criteria for the author of a manuscript to use to judge whether or not his paper is too similar to other papers. While there is some merit to each of these arguments, they do not justify the practice. These arguments do demonstrate there is a need for professional societies that publish research journals to take action before a significant problem develops. The following are possible courses of action. First, editors could develop and publish policy statements that set clear guidelines related to the practice. A copy of the policy should be sent to each individual who submits a paper to the editor. Second, punishments could be levied. For example, the editors of *Science* informed one author involved in multiple submission that papers with his name on it would not be considered for publication for a period of three years. Such policies based on punishment may serve as a greater deterrent if editors of different journals would have some measure of reciprocity built into the policy. Thus, an individual who was found guilty would not be able to publish in several journals. Third, authors should be encouraged to submit a list of their other papers on the same subject, including papers that have been submitted or those they were planning to submit to other journals. The editor could then request copies if they believed such was warranted. Failure to list a publication on this list would serve as prima-facie evidence of the intent to fraud. Finally, authors should only be required to submit an abstract for publication in conference proceedings if the author intended to submit a complete paper to a referred journal.

Myths and Truths

The previous fraudulent practices were not actual case studies. Thus, it would be easy to believe that it couldn't happen in engineering research; this is a myth. The truth is that unethical conduct has been reported in engineering research. Two of ASCE's professional conduct case studies deal with plagiarism and breach of copyright (14). In both cases, the charges were investigated to determine whether or not Article 9 of ASCE's Code of Ethics had been violated. In one case, ASCE's Board of Direction voted to suspend the accused, an author of a paper in one of ASCE's journals, for a period of two years. In the

second case, the Board recommended a suspension of membership for a period of five years; however, the individual allowed his membership to lapse before a Board hearing could be set. While these two actual cases may appear minor, at least with respect to costs and the effect on human welfare, they indicate the potential for fraud exists.

There is a myth that engineering research is self policing; that is, important engineering research is independently investigated by several researchers and if one would attempt to falsify data and publish the results, then other researchers would expose the fraudulent work. While this is possible, it is not a certainty. A significant portion of engineering research is supported by state and local governments. The results of such work may not receive the national or regional exposure that may be necessary to identify fraudulent work. Also, the results of the research may be incorporated into design manuals and used in design before additional research is performed. By then, it may be too late. Fraudulent research results that are used in the formulation of policy and design criteria could lead to inadequate designs. The potential impact on public safety is significant, and obvious.

Why would an engineer engage in fraudulent research activities? Many believe the myth that the "publish or perish" pressure is the cause of fraudulent acts. First, there is no documentation that fraud is increasing. It has been a part of research since the beginning of scientific inquiry. Even Leibniz was accused of plagiarizing some of Newton's work on differential calculus (6). Second, a strong case can be made that it is the change in value input sources. Bremer (2) hypothesized that business was the primary source of societal values rather than the traditional value input sources of religion, town and community, family, the agricultural society, and education. Others believe that television and the recent ethical failures of our elected officials contributed to fraudulent activities in many areas. There is no doubt that there is pressure to publish. However, professional pressure has existed in the past and it is a myth that the "publish or perish" pressure is the only cause of fraudulent research. This is not to say that it is not a factor but just that it is not the single primary cause. After all, there are tens of thousands of researchers who are under pressure to publish but do not choose the unethical path.

Conclusions

In recent years there has been a surge in interest in engineering ethics. This is evident from the significant increase in the number of publications addressing the subject, the number of conferences devoted to ethics in the professions, the increased expenditures for research on ethical issues, and the number of cases of professional misconduct. The interest in engineering ethics is the result of many factors, including a concern for the decline in societal values, cases of misconduct in other professions including the political arena, and increased concern for the potential loss of professional credibility that would result from cases involving professional engineers. Most of the attention has been directed towards the practicing engineer (1, 7, 13). This results because of the unique relationship between the engineer and his client.

Engineering research is well funded and highly competitive. Therefore, there exists a potential for fraud. It is important to consider this potential because of the significant impact of engineering research on society. The potential for fraud exists in all phases of the research process from the proposal-writing phase to the reporting of research results. Examples of potentially fraudulent activity in engineering research have been analyzed. A purpose of this has been to create a dialogue on the subject and hopefully identify and institute measures that will at least minimize the potential for such fraud. Hopefully, any measures that are adopted will not increase the amount of red tape. As Gutowsky (12) points out, the red tape is already retarding the productivity of basic research.

Professional societies must recognize their role in acting as a deterrent to fraudulent research. Professional codes of ethics certainly are just as applicable to those involved in research as they are to those in private practice. Therefore, the mechanism exists for disciplining members who act fraudulently, even though codes of ethics are not meant to be judicial instruments. Certainly, fraudulent research activity is grounds for loss of membership in engineering societies. While some professional journals have the mechanism for retracting papers that are based on fraudulent research, some do not have a well-established policy on this. Obviously, such a policy should be formulated.

REFERENCES

Benko, W.G., "Ethical Aspects of Engineer Recruitment," *Journal of Professional Practice*, Vol. 85, No. PP1, May, 1959, 1-4.

Bremer, D.A., "Is Business the Source of New Social Values?" *Harvard Business Review*, Nov.-Dec., 1971, 121-26.

Broad, W.J., "Imbroglio at Yale (I): Emergence of a Fraud," *Science*, Vol. 210, Oct. 3, 1980, 38-41.

Broad, W.J., "Imbroglio at Yale (II): A Top Job Lost," *Science*, Vol. 210, Oct. 10, 1980, 171-73.

Broad, W.J., "Fraud and the Structure of Science," *Science*, Vol. 212, Apr. 10, 1981, 137-441.

Broad, W.J., "Priority War: Discord in Pursuit of Glory," *Science*, Vol. 211, Jan. 30, 1981, 465-67.

Clayton, L.A., "Professional Ethics in Private Practice," *Engineering Issues—Journal of Professional Activities*, ASCE, Vol. 107. No. 212, Apr., 1981, 105-10.

Code of Ethics, American Society of Civil Engineers, ASCE, New York, NY, adopted Sept. 25, 1976, effective Jan. 1, 1977.

Cooke, J., "Jimmy's World: 8-year Old Heroin Addict Lives for a Fix," *The Washington Post*, Washington, DC, Sept. 28, 1980.

Engineering Education, American Society of Engineering Education, Vol. 71, No. 6, Mar., 1981. 1-128.

Grossberger, L., "The Pulitzer Prize Hoax," *Newsweek*, Apr. 27, 1981, 62-63.

Gutowsky, H.S., "Federal Funding of Basic Research: The Red Tape Mill," *Science*, Vol. 212, May 8, 1981.

McMinn, J., "Ethics in Inter-Firm Cooperation," *Engineering Issues—Journal of Professional Activities*, ASCE, Vol. 104, No. E14, Oct., 1978, 231-36.

Professional Conduct Case Studies, American Society of Civil Engineers, ASCE, New York, NY.

Wade, N., "A Diversion of the Quest for Truth," *Science*, Vol. 211, Mar. 6, 1981, 1022-25.

◆ ◆ ◆ ◆ ◆

TERRY L. TURNICK

Public Versus Client Interests—An Ethical Dilemma for the Engineer

The most obvious and inescapable effect of scientific technique is that it makes society more organic in the sense of increasing the interdependence of its various parts. (5, p. 11)

This observation by Bertrand Russell over 20 years ago well describes our present industrial-technological society. Our general knowledge has ascended to such vast proportions in so many areas that an individual is hardpressed to maintain a mastery of any specific field of endeavor. Society is therefore faced with groups of specialized people in a dynamic system. Each exerts an influence on society and likewise each is influenced by the remainder known as the public.

With the understanding gained through specialization usually comes a type of "tunnel vision" which somewhat limits perception of other areas. This breeds an acceptance of the remainder of society's functions without understanding the how and the why that produced them. Thus, the interdependence outlined by Bertrand Russell.

If society is to remain cohesive and to move forward by aim and not by accident, then each specialized group must apply its skills and knowledge to the benefit of the public. Today, it is generally agreed that greater knowledge brings greater responsibility (2). The educated professionals, in light of their specialized skills, carry a large burden of responsibility. Yet, in their specialization, they also carry the consequences of limited comprehension of the other facets of society and other fields of knowledge. Perhaps in the forefront of these nearsighted professionals are the people greatly responsible for today's technical society, the engineers.

With his technical expertise, the engineer has used the forces of nature and the properties of materials to produce some remarkable accomplishments. A list of these would encompass much of what is accepted as modern life. From the largest civil structures to the minute electronic circuitry of pocket calculators, almost all segments of society are touched in some way by the work of the engineer. Yet, for all his achievements, a change in public attitude toward the engineer has taken place.

As recently as the late 1950s the United States considered its engineering skills among the foremost reasons for national pride—as witness the great public disappointment that US engineers were not allowed to build the Aswan Dam. Today, engineering faces increasing disdain, mistrust, and fear (6, p. 19). Ill-conceived projects that damage the environment and far outweigh the benefits to society are darkening the engineer's reputation. Products which endanger life and health have been discovered long after their exposure to the public. But is the engineering profession to blame for its transgressions against society? The answer to this question requires an examination of the procedures of conception and design.

The Engineer-Client Relationship

As previously stated, the engineer is a specialist and in specialization has somewhat limited his view of society and its needs. He therefore has come to rely on the dictates of others who, by virtue of their broader spectrum of knowledge, supposedly know the desires and needs of the public whom the engineer is ultimately to serve. These would include private entrepreneurs, corporations, governmental bodies and agencies, and anyone who would engage the engineer and his services. The client and engineer form a symbiotic relationship with the client providing direction and the engineer the means.

The strength of this relationship and the responsibilities that accompany it are not taken lightly by the engineering profession. An examination of the American Society of Civil Engineers Code of Ethics reveals that two-thirds of the articles guiding professional conduct outline the engineer-client relationship, principally the engineer's duty to his client. This is understandable, for, along with providing direction, the client assumes many risks and must be insured of the engineer's faithful service.

In the past, the engineer was able to concern himself narrowly with the technical aspects of meeting his clients stated needs. His criteria included economy, functional efficiency, quite often style, if not esthetics. The engineer defined the limits of technical feasibility and strove to find the best solutions to problems within these bounds. Unless no solution presented itself, despite his most exhaustive and imaginative efforts, he seldom found a reason for questioning the wisdom of what the client wanted (1, p. 164).

Then the criticism began. Ralph Nader focused attention on every man's engineering marvel, the automobile, and made the public aware that the manufacturers were not giving all the safety that technology could provide and that common sense demanded.

The Sierra Club and other environmental protection groups began questioning the real benefits of the massive civil projects which had previously been such sources of pride. Ecology became a common word in the vocabulary as an anti-technology backlash swept the country. Advanced technology was no longer synonymous with progress and the engineer no longer a hero, for, in his devotion to serve the client, the engineer had failed the public who placed in his trust the power of technology. The engineer knows the full requirements and results of his technology better than any other segment of society. And yet, the profession is in no way fully competent to predict the full effect of its work on the environment and the remainder of society. Because of technology's ponderous effects, the engineer must seek the guidance of others in its administration.

Relying solely on his client for this responsibility must become a thing of the past. Lacking any system of public scrutiny, the client has a record of disregard or misunderstanding of public welfare. Where profit and economy are chief measures of success, public well-being is not always served.

The client-engineer bond also tends to promote economy over conscience. As "partners" in a venture which realistically should prove profitable to both, financial and personal pressures can be created which cloud issues of public welfare. By limiting discussion of these issues to the engineer and his client, society on the whole can suffer. However, too much public scrutiny can cause equal harm.

An undertaking of any magnitude will be met by some dissent. With public opinion being so diverse and public processes being so slow, a total referendum on any issue could cause unaffordable delays and cancellation of a beneficial proposition. Thus, the general public is not necessarily a good referral system for the engineer's work. The seeming contradiction of allegiance without respect is one of practicality and only adds to the engineer's dilemma.

Problems and Alternatives

The dilemma for the engineer is principally this—he must serve two masters whose wishes do not always coincide and whose opinions are not always in the best interest of all. Like most dilemmas, this has no suitable single solution. However, steps can be taken to help with resolution of the problem and to avoid future conflicts of this nature.

For the benefit of all, the engineer must gain a greater social consciousness. As man begins to develop a more enlightened view of his world as a unified system, the engineer's preview also seeks broader dimensions. His works are far too numerous, too massive, too powerful, and too pervading to continue to be viewed individually as mere technical services. Collectively, they form a major part of the framework of our environment (1, p. 165).

By establishing a more meaningful dialogue with other groups such as professional, private, and governmental agencies who speak authoritatively in representing the social and environmental interests that now interface so closely with the work of the engineer (1, p. 166), he can choose with greater discretion the solution to the conflict.

However, this does not resolve or redefine the conflict between client and public interest. Education only allows the engineer to see the questions more clearly and hopefully to select a proper course of action. By taking steps to align public and client interests, future conflict could be avoided.

One means of doing this would be more engineering counseling at the upper management levels where the initial directions of a project are determined. To provide such advice would take the concerted efforts of many groups, among which the engineering profession must be prominently represented (1, p. 165). This team of professionals could be tailored to the specific problems of each project, and lead by the discipline of who understands the total problem most completely and who can communicate most clearly the many aspects of the problems to technologists and laymen (4, p. 222).

Another direction would be greater public review of an undertaking. During conception, public sentiments could be expressed in the form of codes and laws that guide the client and engineer's design. Zoning laws, safety codes, and environmental impact studies are existing samples of this type of legislation. As the effects of technology become increasingly evident, it is conceivable that the future may require social impact studies covering a broad range of doctrines affected by a project. Boards of review could follow a project through execution and completion, settling any disputes that arise and insuring that all commitments be met. If these processes are to be workable programs that are truly beneficial and equitable, the engineer must play a major role in their conception and administration.

Finally, a procedure of due process should be established so that engineers can voice dissent without undue consequence. Faced with possible reprisal from employers, the engineer is pressured into silence. At the other extreme, the engineer faces unnecessary project delays if his questions, made public, prove unfounded. A "disinterested party" could hear grievances, review them, and make recommendations, without causing project delays, and still be responsible to the public interest. Whatever action was recommended, the engineer could be protected against unwarranted actions from his superiors by legislation and his colleagues in the professional societies. To require an act of courage for stating perceived truth is to foster a system of self-censorship and the demise of individual conscience against the organized (3).

The Periclean dictum, "In Athens, we think that silent men are useless," still applies in a twentieth-century democracy based on science and technology (2). The engineer has been silent for too long. It is time he realized the magnitude of his work while remembering its place in the framework of society.

The strength of the client-engineer relationship must remain, but also must be modified if it is truly to serve society's best interest. It must become more flexible and sensitive to issues other than dollar value and present technology.

For, while there are many guardians of "what might have been" or "what should be done," the engineer must bear a unique responsibility for "what was done" and "what can be done" (1, p. 167).

REFERENCES

Clarke, F.J., "The Engineer's Role," *Engineering Issues—Journal of Professional Activities*, ASCE, Vol. 98, No. PP2, Proc. Paper 8825. Apr., 1972, 163-67.

Mayer, J., "Science Without Conscience," *American Scholar*, Vol. XXXXI, Spring, 1972, 266.

Nader, R., "A Code for Professional Integrity," *The New York Times*, January 15, 1971, 43.

Novick, D., "The Civil Engineer in the Multidisciplinary Design Team," *Engineering Issues—Journal of Professional Activities*, ASCE, Vol. 98. No. PP2, Proc. paper 8826, Apr., 1972, 221-26.

Novick, D., and Schumacher, S., "The Civil Engineer of the Future—A Renaissance Man?" *Engineering Issues—Journal of Professional Activities*, ASCE, Vol. 99, No. PP1, Proc. Paper 9489, Jan., 1973, 9-18.

Roberts, K., "The Public Role of Engineering: The California State Water Project," *Engineering Issues—Journal of Professional* Activities, ASCE, Vol. 99. No. PP1, Proc. Paper 9492, Jan., 1973, 19-38.

◆ ◆ ◆ ◆ ◆

VIVIAN WEIL

Is Engineering Ethics Just Business Ethics? What Can Empirical Findings Tell Us?*

Introduction

How should we interpret the main question in the title? A plausible, and, I believe, illuminating way is to understand it as a question about professional ethics, more precisely, occupational ethics. I will not concentrate on how we use the terms, but will focus rather on two occupational groups to see whether they are the same or different. In this way, I give substance to the term "business ethics," suggesting that it has to do with the ethics of business managers, who form an occupational group.[1]

The distinction between professions and other occupations will be pivotal to my response to our question. I identify characteristic marks of professions on the basis of historical and empirical observation. Looking then at the recent history of engineers and business managers, I argue that engineers comprise a profession and business managers do not. I consider the claim that because engineers and managers operate in the same context, engineering decisions are not distinct from business decisions. I explain how they are distinct in light of the historical observations and recent empirical findings.

Further Interpretation of the Question

What does it mean to suggest that engineering ethics might be just business ethics? A popular understanding of the terms business ethics and engineering ethics is that they refer to the character or the behavior of business people or engineers. You can hear this sense of the term when someone asks, "Do business people or do engineers have any ethics?" In this sense, the question is largely empirical but very difficult to answer regarding engineers and managers in the aggregate, even assuming we could get agreement on the traits or behavior that would be indicative.

But perhaps we should take this question to suggest that the ethical guidelines for business managers are identical with those for engineers. According to one way of understanding that claim, it is correct. What we call the moral minimums, as captured, for example, in Bernard Gert's moral rules, hold for everyone, and so, of course, for engineers and managers.[2] But this is to deprive the question of any robustness.

Another reading of what this question suggests is that engineering ethics is somehow included in business ethics, perhaps a species of business ethics. Since most engineers and managers have positions in business organizations, if there are any ethical obligations specific to their callings and not just part of ordinary morality, these are obligations that derive from the character and operations of business organizations. Engineers' norms are all subsumed under the norms of business. The idea seems to be that the engineer's role is just one role in business and so it should be encompassed within business ethics. This suggestion that engineering ethics is just a specialization within business ethics seems likely to be the assumption which motivated this symposium, and it is the one to which I shall respond first.

Remarks on Professions

To lay the groundwork, we need to consider what differentiates professions from other occupational groups. The first point of interest is that certain occupational groups organize themselves in certain ways and present themselves as professions. They form professional societies and announce that they serve a social purpose. They adopt standards of education and performance that help them serve their social purpose. They do, of course, serve their own interests, obviously the interest of their members in earning a living. However, they also claim not to engage in the ordinary rough and tumble of the marketplace, but to have a special relation to the marketplace.

The understanding in any given profession about its special relation to the marketplace changes over time. In the past, professions claimed certain exemptions from the workings of the marketplace. Some changes in recent decades resulted from legal rulings that denied professions some of their former exemptions. For a case in point, recall that the American Bar Association had formerly held that the special relation of lawyers to the marketplace excluded advertising. A legal ruling ended that prohibition of advertising. Engineers' codes of ethics formerly contained provisions that barred them from competing on the basis of price. A legal ruling required engineers to give up these provisions. At one time professionals considered unionization to be incompatible with professional status. Some decades back, occupational groups such as university professors and government lawyers incorporated unionization in their stance toward the marketplace. Defining relations to the world of commerce is an ongoing process in all the professions.

Other characteristics by which professions are distinguished from other occupational groups also evolve over time. These include the nature and extent of the education needed to practice the profession and the definition of the primary responsibility of service to society. The changes need not result directly from external rulings. They also respond to conditions of practice and to less direct, more informal pressures from outside. In 1974, when the Engineers Council for Professional Development revised its Code of Ethics, it was very likely prompted to do so by strains in professional practice, as well as by external social pressures. Departing from traditional stress on gentlemanly conduct, the revised Code put emphasis on public welfare, offering as its First Canon:

> Engineers shall hold paramount the safety, health, and welfare of the public in the performance of their professional duties.

Originally the Code had enjoined engineers to show "due regard" for the public welfare. In the process of revision, the Engineers Council considered and rejected "proper regard" as too weak a statement. Here we get a glimpse of the deliberations that go into defining ethical standards. Of course, it is characteristic of professions to produce and revise codes of ethics and other formulated standards.

One other distinctive feature of professions deserves mention. It derives from the occupational group's organizing through professional societies and announcing the group's claim to be a profession. (As noted above, that claim itself is important to an occupational group's constituting itself as a profession.) In the process, a community of peers is created that reaches across and transcends individual clients, companies, agencies, and other employers. Collegiality is a distinctive relationship among peers. Publications such as the Institute of Electrical and Electronic Engineers' (IEEE) *Spectrum*, which circulates to a large, international membership, help to create and maintain a sense of a peer community among engineers. It is reasonable to regard codes of ethics as both reflecting and shaping the evolution of peer communities.

My approach so far has been to point out characteristic marks of professions rather than to propose a definition of necessary and sufficient conditions. This approach is closely allied to the historical, empirical way of proceeding I have adopted in the sections that follow. Since the relation to the marketplace is essential to the understanding of contemporary professions, historical comments need not reach back beyond the origins of modern market economies.

Distinctive History of Engineering

Because we are dealing with organizations and occupational groups that have histories, it would be a mistake to ignore those histories and simply fasten on the point that both roles of interest are roles in business organizations. We risk misunderstanding the character of the organizations and the roles that interest us if we abstract and focus on a static time-slice. It is also a mistake to fail to appreciate that these organizations and the roles within them continue to evolve. Some historical comments now, as well as subsequent comments dealing with current features and changes in business organizations, will therefore help to answer the question in the title.

The surge in growth in the engineering profession in the last quarter of the nineteenth century coincided with the rise of modern large-scale business organizations. It is not a mere coincidence that 75% of engineers in the United States are employed in large business organizations. The modern engineering profession was born in large industrial organizations. Engineers are needed to take some of the guesswork out of operations on a large scale. Large organizations have the resources to afford the knowledge and skills of professionally trained engineers. To emphasize this point is to concede that there is an intimate connection between engineers and business. At the same time it points to the distinctive feature of engineering that on a spectrum which has business at one end and science at the other, engineering falls somewhere between.

My comments earlier indicated that formal education or training is important to professional roles. In this respect, engineering has a long, relatively clear history, longer than managing. We can trace engineers' education to its origins in the late eighteenth century in the Ecole Polytechnique in France. This was the model for the first engineering school in the United States, West Point, which was established in 1802, before the clear emergence of civilian or civil engineering from its military parent. The eighteenth century French model is still discernible in the technical core of engineering education in this country today.

Recent writers, such as Walter Vincenti and Taft Broome, who have studied the nature of engineering knowledge, have pointed to another body of knowledge in addition to the technical core of formal education.[3] This is knowledge accumulated from engineers' experience and passed on in the course of practice. Though we can speak of engineering knowledge in this connection as if it were held by all engineers, it is knowledge closely tied to practice in the various fields of engineering—civil, mechanical, chemical, electrical, aerospace, materials, and so on. That is how it comes about that the knowledge is captured in tables, manuals, or standards of practice that are often industry-specific. Nevertheless, this shared knowledge of practitioners helps to constitute engineers as a professional community.

Moreover, since the middle of the last century engineers have been developing formal technical standards. Early in the nineteenth century, Oliver Evans, who had introduced the relatively high-pressure, non-condensing steam engine in the United States, published the first formula for computing the thickness of wrought iron to be used in boilers of various diameters carrying different working pressures. However, manufacturers did not heed this voluntary standard, and many disastrous steamboat boiler explosions occurred. Starting in the 1830s, efforts to formulate specifications for steamboat boilers and procedures for their operation contributed to the work of those trying to gain passage of federal legislation to impose and enforce safety standards. A federal law passed in 1852 incorporated recommendations made by an influential Illinois engineer on the basis of his own research, recommendations which corresponded to those made almost twenty years earlier by the Franklin Institute of Philadelphia.[4]

In the decades following passage of the law, the use of steam boilers spread to the railroads; insurance companies were organized to insure steam equipment that was manufactured and operated with proper regard for safety; and eventually, through the auspices of the American Society of Mechanical Engineers (ASME), uniform boiler codes were promulgated and adopted by states and municipalities.[5] The pattern to notice in this history is that engineers derived standards from engineering experience as well as formal research and eventually saw them adopted as legal codes through the agency of their professional societies. This is a pattern that has been repeated in other areas.

Engineers speak of the "state of the art," referring to standards, which might or might not have been formally adopted but nevertheless represent for a particular area the most advanced methods on which there is wide agreement. A student of mine this past fall, an older student who holds a responsible position as a chemical engineer, neatly invoked this standard to analyze an engineering ethics problem. When studying the Ford Pinto history, this student observed that there were no government regulations covering the gas tank placement on compact cars and therefore the engineers violated no legal standards. He pointed out, however, that the Pinto engineers submitted or acceded to a design for gas tank placement that was not up to the state of the art. Ford had in fact used a gas tank configuration that he identified as "state of the art" on an earlier small car in Europe. His suggestion was that the state of the art defined a standard of reasonable care.

The promulgation of codes of ethics by engineering professional societies began in this country in 1912. At various junctures in the intervening years, societies undertook to revise their codes, becoming most energetic about updating the codes in the mid-seventies. The point to be stressed is that the development of standards and codes, including codes of ethics, was internal to this occupational group. The professional societies and their members were, as we have noted, responding to various signals from outside and within the profession, but they themselves formulated and adopted codes which addressed the needs of all engineers. As early as 1975, the IEEE entered an *amicus curiae* brief in the law suit of whistleblowing engineers fired by the Bay Area Rapid Transit System. The IEEE's brief argued that the engineer's code of ethics should be regarded as an implied element of any employment contract.

When outsiders working on professional ethics focused on the engineering profession, they found these codes and standards already at hand, and they found activists within the profession who took the codes very seriously.

In this respect, even scholarly work on engineering ethics rests on what is internal to the profession.[6] Identifying safety as a distinctive and key concern of engineers, specialists on ethics could point to the paramount provision of the first canon for confirmation. Watching my colleagues in business ethics, I have been struck that theirs has been more an effort of figuring out how to bring standards in from outside. Unless I have misread the history, it was these ethics specialists who articulated the concept of stakeholders and showed how to put it to work. Although the notion of a code of ethics for managers that reaches across employer organizations is beginning to catch on, it is still the case that the codes of ethics of individual companies are far more visible. From these observations I conclude that the occupation of business managing has not yet organized itself as a profession, and business ethics is not yet professional ethics.

Decision Making: Recent Findings

But perhaps there remains a question about the extent to which engineering decisions and business decisions coincide or overlap; indeed it may be the question that generated this symposium. Before I respond, we should notice that we will have shifted from talking about the histories of two distinct occupational groups to concern with the nature of the decisions that members of these groups make. It may appear to some that both engineers and managers make business decisions, and that is the reason to say that engineering ethics is just business ethics.

To respond, I will comment on some empirical findings from a recent project on communication between engineers and managers in decision making.[7] Conducted by our Center under a grant from the Hitachi Foundation, the project was designed to get a better understanding of communication that supports responsible decision making. The interviewing, using prepared questionnaires, canvassed 29 engineers and 31 managers. The engineers represented all major fields of engineering. The ten companies in which we interviewed ranged from one employing four engineers to several employing thousands. Most of the companies were American, but they included one German and one Japanese transplant.

We had expected to find technical communication occurring within a relatively rigid command structure with strong barriers to communication across departments and along the chain of command. We expected engineers to advise and managers to decide. The interviews revealed a much less rigid process. In most companies, communication between departments was not only relatively easy but something managers actively encouraged. Even communication up the chain of command was easier than expected, although it was easier for personnel than for technical matters.

In general, managers did not make technical decisions; they sought agreement with their engineers. There was general agreement that engineers should have the last word on questions of safety or quality. Only when business considerations intervened—cost, schedule, or customer need—might engineers be overruled. And even then, the managers would try to reach consensus with their engineers rather than actually decide. Everyone seemed to think that deciding over the objections of an engineer was a sign of a bad decision.

This research underlines how intimately engineers are involved in business decisions and how thin the manager's role can be. Furthermore, there is other evidence showing that engineers are more valuable when they have a sense of the manager's concern with cost, time, resources, and customers' needs. Yet these findings should not be read as supporting the conclusion that engineering decisions are just business decisions, and, therefore, engineering ethics is just business ethics. There are good reasons to hold that it is a mistaken conclusion, for there is an underlying difference in the perspectives of engineers and managers and a different weighing of reasons.

The history of professionalization in engineering, the existence of standards and codes, and the centrality of the values of safety and quality shape the distinctive perspective of engineers in decision making. Engineers provide an overall technically-based judgment. That is what they are needed for; it is what their training, knowledge, and experience equip them to provide. Engineers are looked to for technically informed recommendations, and they are expected to act as advocates for their recommendations. Theirs is the authoritative word on safety and quality. The standard of care reasonably expected of engineers turns to a considerable extent on their ability to foresee consequences on the basis of their technical understanding. This engineering perspective has its place in newer, flatter structures and in the team approach, as well as in more traditional structures.

To summarize, I have taken our topic to be concerned with professional or occupational ethics, the two occupations in question being those of business managers and engineers. The two occupational groups have different histories; only one lays claim to being a profession, according to common criteria. It may nevertheless seem that both engineers and managers make business decisions and therefore the distinction between business ethics and engineering ethics that I have drawn cannot be maintained. In light of historical observations and recent empirical findings, I argue that there remains an underlying difference in decision making, and that difference survives reconstruction or deconstruction of business organizations.

NOTES

* For helpful comments on an earlier version of this paper thanks are due to Deborah Johnson and Fay Horton Sawyier. Comments by members of the audience at the Society for Business Ethics meeting at the APA contributed clarification. They seemed to take my question of whether business managers constitute a profession as addressing one component of business ethics, the ethics of managers.

1 The label "manager" in this connection does not refer to any kind of manager; public management, for example, is treated as a different occupation.

2 Bernard Gert. 1988. *Morality: A New Justification of the Moral Rules.* New York: Oxford University Press.

3 Walter G. Vincenti. 1990. *What Engineers Know and How They Know It.* Baltimore: Johns Hopkins University Press; Taft H. Broome, Jr. 1985. "Engineering the Philosophy of Science," *Metaphilosophy* Vol. 16, No. 1:47-57.

4 This story is well told by John G. Burke, 1966, "Bursting Boilers and the Federal Power," *Technology and Culture,* Vol. 17, No. 1:1-23.

5 Ibid.

6 For examples of the scholarly work, see Michael Davis's 1991 "Thinking Like an Engineer: The Place of a Code of Ethics in the Practice of a Profession," *Philosophy and Public Affairs,* Vol. 20, No. 2:150-67; Stephen H. Unger. 1987. "Would Helping Ethical Professionals Get Professional Societies Into Trouble?" *IEEE Technology and Society Magazine,* Vol. 6, No. 3:17-21; and Deborah Johnson (ed). 1991. *Ethical Issues in Engineering.* Englewood Cliffs, New Jersey: Prentice Hall.

7 For a more thorough report on this project, see Michael Davis's 1992 "Technical Communications Between Engineers and Managers: Preventing Engineering Disasters," a publication of IIT's Center for the Study of Ethics in the Professions.

THE WEST GATE BRIDGE: WHO WAS RESPONSIBLE?

JOANNE LAU

Case Description

Built between 1968 and 1978, the West Gate Bridge in Melbourne, Australia was to be a "masterpiece among bridges." Original in design, it is a vital link between Melbourne's city district and the industrial suburbs in the west. The length of the bridge is over 2.5 kilometers (1.6 miles), with the height above the Yarra River being 58 meters (190 feet). It is the world's largest cable-stayed girder bridge. At the time of its construction, it was the longest bridge in Australia and carries eight lanes of traffic. The West Gate Bridge is also the site of Australia's single worst workplace catastrophe.

Over 1,000 people were involved in the construction of the West Gate Bridge, including a host of notable designers, prime contractors, suppliers, and engineers. Two engineering firms, Maunsell and Freeman Fox Partners (FFP) were appointed as joint consultants for the design and preparation of tender documents. FFP was responsible for the structural design of the bridge. Two construction companies were awarded contracts, for building the foundations and concrete construction and steelwork construction respectively.

Unfortunately, relations between various groups soon began to deteriorate. The construction company responsible for steelwork claimed no responsibility for the joining of the bridge sections, and this role was transferred to FFP. Several work-delaying union strikes and poor on-site supervision meant that, in its first two years of construction, the building schedule fell seven months behind.

In June 1970, a counterpart of the West Gate Bridge in Wales—also designed by FFP—collapsed during construction, killing several workmen. This news created more problems for the West Gate Bridge project. Unions demanded greater safety measures for workers, and a mass stop-work meeting was held until assurances were given by project management that what had happened in Wales would not happen on the West Gate Bridge. A senior engineer from FFP present at the meeting unhesitatingly gave the assurance and work resumed.

It was common practice for the different sections of the bridge to be assembled on the ground, hoisted into place with cranes and bolted together. However, in August 1970, when two particular sections were brought together, it was discovered that the north section was 114 millimeters (4.5 inches) higher than the south section. Rather than take the sections down for correction, engineers decided to put several 8-ton weights on the high section to bring it level with the lower.

In September 1970, there was a major buckle.[1] Work came to a halt, followed by a month of deliberation. In October, the engineers decided to unbolt the two sections on each side of the buckle, theorizing that the weight of the higher section would cause it to lower and match the level of the lower section, and then it could be rebolted. However, before the process could be completed, the buckle became greater and the 2000-ton span collapsed, killing 35 of the 68 workers and causing AUD $10 million in damage. Several other workers were severely injured. The rebuilding cost AUD $31 million and the total cost of the bridge was three hundred million dollars, more than ten times the original estimated cost.

Ethical Analysis

A Royal Commission was established to investigate the cause of the collapse. It found that one of the main causes of the collapse was FFP's structural design. Other causes were "mistakes, miscalculations, errors of judgment, failure of communication and sheer inefficiency. In greater or less degree, the Authority itself, the designers, the contractors, even the labor engaged in the work, must all take some part of the blame."[2]

It is quite clear from the judgment that the Commission found various parties liable for the collapse. However, perhaps it is not the case that FFP should have been the *main* cause. One morally relevant issue in this case is the fact that the different parties all contributed to the end result. For example, the designers of the bridge were particularly proud of their original "box-girder" design and insisted that the engineers adhere to it, despite the fact that such a design had not been tested before. Perhaps if they had gone with a more conventional design, the risk of collapse would have been reduced, but at the cost of originality.

Another related issue is how directly related to the collapse a party's action has to be for liability to attach. For example, the unions held up construction with protests and stop-work meetings. Being already seven months behind, such delays in the construction probably contributed to the decision by the engineers to weigh down the section of the bridge that was too high, instead of having to demolish it and rebuild it, to try and make up time. Doing this would also be an extremely costly process for the client. How much weight should *this* be given?

Perhaps each party's actions were bound together in such a way that blame should not be attributed specifically to one group (such as FFP). It seems that, but for the actions of each of the parties involved, a collapse could have been avoided. If only one party acted irresponsibly, it seems that blame would have been much easier to attribute. However, in this case, where all the parties were connected in such a way that an action by one would irrevocably affect all the others, it may simply be the case that accountability could not be separated so simply.

It could also be a question of regulation. Engineers and builders, for instance, have different codes which govern the extent of their liability. However, the code for one industry is often written in isolation from another industry. If the level of liability varies between different industries, perhaps this should be made uniform for all industries involved in a project. However, the different roles that each party has initially may change as the project proceeds (as it did in this case) making it difficult to predetermine the extent of each party's liability.

The Royal Commission found that almost all the parties involved were liable. Only the suppliers were deemed to be blameless. The surviving designers, contractors, and engineers were dismissed. In 2004, on the thirty-fourth anniversary of the disaster, a memorial park was opened at the site of the collapse. 35 pillars were constructed, one for each worker who died.

Study Questions

1. The Royal Commission summed up its investigation of the collapse as follows:

    > "Error begat error ... and the events which led to the disaster moved with the inevitability of a Greek Tragedy."[3]

    Is this a fair description of the events? Consider the role of the engineers, the construction team, the unions and the designers. How much blame should be attributed to each party?

2. Suppose that the bridge had been completed without incident and opened to the public. Two years later, the bridge collapses, killing 35 people on their way to work. Who do you think would be to blame in this case? Would your answer be different if the bridge had collapsed five years later? Ten years later? Fifty years later?

3. Should there be different rules and regulations for the different groups involved in a large project like building a bridge? Why or why not?

4. Imagine that you are a builder at the stop-work meeting following the collapse of the FFP-designed bridge in Wales. Would you have believed the engineer who made assurances that the West Gate Bridge was safe? Why or why not?

5. In the engineering industry, originality and visual appeal in design is important, but having a structurally sound bridge is also crucial. How should the interests of originality and design be weighed against safety and social responsibility?

6. Sometimes experts can do everything right, and something can still go wrong. In this case, engineers deliberated for at least a month to decide how to deal with the buckle, and yet disaster still ensued. Presumably they had all the best knowledge of engineering principles at the time. To what extent is the expert responsible when things go wrong?

NOTES

1 Buckling is a sign of structural failure where a column is loaded too heavily for its capacity and bends or twists sharply and noticeably.

2 Report of Royal Commission into the failure of West Gate Bridge, VPRS 2591/P0, unit 14.

3 Ibid.

UNIT 3

Journalistic Ethics

AARON QUINN

Journalistic Ethics

Ironically, the very institution that aims to call upon government and big business to account for its ethical shortcomings is itself suffering from its moral missteps. Ethical issues in journalism arise at all levels: intrapersonally, interpersonally, organizationally and institutionally. Recently, numerous journalists have faced inquiry regarding questionable or in some cases clearly corrupt behavior.

Jayson Blair, a former *New York Times* reporter, resigned from the *Times* after he was found to have plagiarized or fabricated dozens of stories over several years. Blair's blatant disregard for journalistic professionalism led not only to his but other resignations at the *Times*, most notably Executive Editor Howell Raines, who was assumed partially responsible for failing to hold Blair accountable. Blair later wrote of his antics in a book, *Burning Down My Masters' House*, that not only offered Blair's somewhat unapologetic account of his actions, but gave a less-than-glamorous review of the contemporary institutional culture at the Grey Lady.

Just barely into the Post-Blair era at the *Times*, America's newspaper of record was again rife with scandal when reporter Judith Miller was accused of being so close with the Bush Administration that she failed to report accurately on claims of weapons of mass destruction in Iraq—Bush's initial rationale for the multi-year, multi-billion dollar military operation. Not long after pressure subsided from Miller's WMD fiasco, she was again in the limelight when she refused to divulge the identity of a confidential source to a grand jury investigating acts of political revenge suspected to have come from members of Vice-President Dick Cheney's staff. Miller later served more than 80 days in jail for protecting her source and subsequently resigned from the *Times* under pressure.

It is of course not only the *Times* that has suffered of late. Jack Kelly of *USA Today* came under fire for Blair-like fabrications, as have numerous other notable and less-public journalists. Ultimately, these ethical shortcomings have only fortified the belief among many in the public that journalists are less trustworthy than used-car salesmen. Thus, the pressing questions for journalists, media critics and academics involve not only the behavior of individual journalists, but of the organizations that employ them and the institutional governance that guides the industry.

Because fewer than a dozen media conglomerates own more than three-quarters of the US news media, news diversity—and the benefits that the public derives from it—are as scarce as ever. In effect, media owners such as *Fox*'s Rupert Murdoch can determine what topics make the news and how they are presented to a vast proportion of the public. And with the apparently increasing political alignment of news organizations, the potential effects on our democracy should be alarming.

Further concerns exist regarding the US media regulator, the Federal Communications Commission, which has recently promoted further concentration of media ownership. Though Congress blocked a recent FCC proposition that would have allowed the expansion of nation-wide audience reach for a single company from 35 per cent to 45 per cent, FCC panel members continue to push for expanding the compromised 39.5 per cent audience reach.

Let us not forget either the increasing role visual journalism has on media messages. Not only with the Web, but also in traditional print media, pictures and illustrations occupy more editorial space now than ever. This raises the stakes for news organizations to create firm standards for how to create, edit and present visual news in a truthful manner. Within the realm of visual journalism one of the chief concerns for ethics is setting firm standards for the editing of digital pictures, as now more than ever digital chicanery is both easy and creates believable results because of the powerful new tools at our disposal.

Of course, these issues are merely a drop in the proverbial bucket for journalism ethics. As the media landscape continues to shift to the Web, it would be naïve to think that currently unknown opportunities for unethical, self-serving behavior will not arrive along with the continued growth of this new public forum. Thus, we can only hope to keep addressing the issues, as the following authors have managed to do across many of the aforementioned topics, as well as other crucial issues in journalism ethics.

JOURNALISTS' OBLIGATIONS AND VIRTUES

DAVID DETMER

The Ethical Responsibilities of Journalists

Introduction

Democracies cannot function without an effective system of political communication. For if citizens are not aware of the policies that are carried out in their name, they are powerless to oppose them. Consequently, one of the chief responsibilities of journalists in a democracy is to provide their readers (or viewers or listeners) with news accounts that are accurate, reasonably comprehensive, and free from subordination to governmental or corporate power (or to that of other "special interests").

Certainly, most mass media journalists in the United States accept such a characterization of their responsibility, which they interpret as entailing an obligation on their part to present news in an "objective," "nonpartisan," "unbiased," "balanced," "nonideological," and "neutral" manner. Other journalists, however, interpret this same responsibility as justifying their adoption of a highly specific bias—that of acting as a "counterweight" to, or "watchdog" of, governmental power.[1] Despite this disagreement, there is a consensus among journalists holding it to be a serious breach of their professional ethics to tilt their news coverage heavily in *favor* of official US government perspectives, thus depriving their audience of the information needed to evaluate governmental policies critically. And yet these earnest professionals often do, though usually unwittingly, end up behaving in precisely this unethical fashion, and do so virtually without exception in the sphere of coverage of international affairs. In this essay I wish to (a) document that this is indeed the case, (b) offer an explanation as to why it is the case, and (c) suggest ways in which journalists might change their behavior so as to do a better job of meeting their ethical obligations.

Documenting the Problem

Let us begin by considering how the mainstream media cover censorship of the press when it is practiced in foreign countries. Since freedom of the press is obviously a value of great importance to journalists and to news organizations, and since press censorship presumably is "newsworthy," and of interest to readers and viewers of journalism, one would expect the press to be ever ready to focus on it. Obviously, this is not to say that it would be reasonable to expect the press to cover all, or even most, instances of censorship—there are too many such instances, and there is a finite amount of space in newspapers and time in news broadcasts available for such coverage. Thus, we might well expect even the most responsible of news media to ignore instances of censorship which are small in scale, minor in effect, or which occur in places that are otherwise of little current interest to their readers or viewers. But we would not expect a *responsible* press to highlight censorship activities of our "enemies," as defined by those who wield political power in our country, while ignoring much more serious instances of censorship perpetrated by those officially designated our "friends."

One good test of the responsibility of mainstream US journalism in its coverage of freedom of the press, then, would be to compare its coverage of censorship as practiced in the 1980s by the governments of Nicaragua and El Salvador. These two countries are geographically proximate to each other and to the US, and were in the 1980s of interest to the US news audience. (Or at least, there was at that time a great deal of news coverage of these two countries, in comparison to most foreign nations.) Thus, to the extent that the US press is unbiased and non-partisan, we should expect its relative coverage of censorship in the two countries to vary in accordance with such factors as the relative scale and severity of effects of the censorship in the two nations. On the other hand, since El Salvador was officially our "friend" and a "fledgling democracy," while Nicaragua under the Sandinistas was officially our "enemy" and a "totalitarian dungeon," we should expect a more partisan press, a less responsible one, to play up censorship in Nicaragua while ignoring it as much as possible in El Salvador. What, then, do we find?

Censorship in Nicaragua did indeed receive extensive coverage during the period in question. For example, one study of 104 articles from the *Boston Globe, New York Times*, and *Washington Post* dealing with the 1984 Nicaraguan elections, found that 65 mentioned press censorship.[2] Another study, con-ducted in 1988, found 263 references in the *New York Times* to the difficulties of the Nicaraguan newspaper *La Prensa* over a period of four years.[3]

Coverage of censorship in El Salvador, on the other hand, was so scanty that I cannot assume my readers to know of the existence of such censorship, let alone be familiar with its details. Thus, I quote the following from the September 1985 Americas Watch Report on El Salvador:

> Any discussion of press freedom in El Salvador must begin by pointing out the elimination of the country's two main opposition newspapers. *La Crónica del Pueblo* was closed in 1980 when members of the security forces raided a San Salvador coffee shop where the paper's editor and one of its photographers were meeting. Editor Jaime Suarez, a 31-year-old prize-winning poet, and Cesar Najarro, were disemboweled by machete and then shot. In 1981 *El Independiente* was closed when army tanks surrounded its offices. This was the culmination of a long series of attacks, which included the machinegunning of a 14-year-old newsboy, bombing and assassination attempts against editor Jorge Pinto. The Archdiocese's radio station, WMAX, spent several years out of commission after its offices were repeatedly bombed. Since 1981 the Salvadoran press has either supported the government or criticized it from a right-wing perspective. Daily newspapers do not publish criticism ... from a leftist perspective, nor do they print stories critical of government forces from a human rights standpoint.[4]

In contrast to the extensive coverage in the *New York Times* of censorship in Nicaragua, these far more serious abuses of press freedoms in El Salvador have gone unmentioned in that publication. The newspaper which claims to publish "all the news that's fit to print" has not seen fit to report the use of terrorism by the government of El Salvador against the press of that nation.[5] The story (or lack thereof) is very much the same when we turn to abuses of press freedoms in other "pro-US" nations. Thus, when security forces of the Guatemalan government in June 1988 succeeded in "persuading" the editor of *La Epoca* to shut down that weekly newspaper by firebombing its offices, stealing its valuable equipment, kidnapping its night watchman, and threatening to murder its "traitor journalists"—not a threat to be taken lightly in view of the fact that dozens of journalists in Guatemala already had been murdered in recent years—no report of these events was to be found in the *New York Times* or *Washington Post*.[6] Two months prior to these events, and one month following them, there were many articles in those two newspapers about lesser abuses of the press in Nicaragua.

In September 1988 Israeli security forces raided the offices of *Al-Fajr*, a leading daily newspaper in Jerusalem, arrested its managing editor, Hatem Abdel-Qader, and jailed him for six months without trial on unspecified grounds. This story was not covered in the *New York Times* or *Washington Post*.[7] In this non-coverage the two papers followed the precedent which they had set in 1986 when, during the height of their coverage of the suspension of publication of *La Prensa* in Nicaragua, they failed to inform their readers that the government of Israel had closed two newspapers, *Al-Mithaq* and *Al-Ahd*, on the grounds that their publication was "harmful to the state of Israel."[8]

An appropriately skeptical reader might object at this point that perhaps my examples are unfair. Of course it is easy, such a reader might argue, to find examples in which the US mass media irresponsibly ignores press censorship and other human rights abuses perpetrated by nations regarded as "friendly" by US political elites, while simultaneously, and hypocritically, trumpeting comparable or much lesser abuses carried out by "our enemies." The problem,

to conclude my imaginary reader's argument, is that there may be other cases in which the media exhibit the opposite bias, or even no bias at all, in which case I would be guilty of making my case by means of a highly selective presentation of evidence.

My response to this objection is that there is no need to be selective in marshalling the evidence for the simple reason that there is *no* counterevidence. To be sure, one can find a different "slant" in non-mainstream journals of opinion, such as *The Nation*, *Z Magazine*, or *The Progressive*, and an occasional isolated article of this sort occasionally finds its way into mass media publications as well. But one can never find a case in which, on balance, the *New York Times*, the *Washington Post*, *Time Magazine*, *Newsweek*, or ABC, CBS, or NBC news deals evenhandedly with the transgressions of "our friends" and "our enemies." Rather, these media always adopt the perspective of the US government, and never—literally never—develop an alternative, independent framework of their own.

Readers with a little time, energy, access to a good library, and eagerness to understand the world in which they live can easily verify this for themselves. Let me suggest one way of doing so. Many highly respected organizations are devoted to the task of investigating and documenting human rights abuses around the world. Their diversity is suggested by the following partial list: Amnesty International, Americas Watch, the International Association of Democratic Lawyers, the International Federation of Human Rights, the International League for the Rights of Man, the International Commission of Jurists, Writers and Scholars International, and the International Red Cross. I suggest that you pick any human rights issue that interests you—the use of torture, the imprisonment of political dissidents, press censorship, the staging of fraudulent elections, you name it. Now go through the reports of these organizations and find examples of comparable abuses carried out by two nations, one of which establishes policies and practices conducive to the financial interests of large US-based corporations (and which receives lots of US aid, both in terms of cash and weapons), and the other of which is readily condemned by US governmental officials as an enemy (or "communist" or "terrorist") state. Obviously, it is in the US corporate and governmental interest to play down the abuses in the former nation and to play up the ones occurring in the latter nation. And, in every case, that is how the US mass media, on balance, plays it.[9] You, dear reader, can refute me by finding a single counterexample. Good luck![10]

Explaining the Problem

Why do the mass media behave so irresponsibly? Must we conclude that they, together with the US government, are engaged in a gigantic conspiracy to keep information that would cast US foreign policy in an unflattering light from being published or broadcast?

As no evidence of such a conspiracy exists, to my knowledge, it is fortunate that one need not be invoked in order to explain the media's disastrous performance. While an adequate analysis would have to include many factors and deal with numerous subtleties and complexities, we can go a long way toward understanding the phenomena in question on the basis of three fairly simple and straightforward principles of news gathering and presentation, one economic and the other two ideological.

Beats and Handouts vs. Investigative Reporting

The economic principle is simply that almost all mass media news is generated either through established "beats"—places, such as the White House, Congress, city hall, the police station, the local football stadium, and so on, where news is regularly produced—or else is simply handed to reporters through press conferences and press releases. The reason is obvious. These two ways of gathering news require

little time, effort, or, most importantly, expense, and yet are guaranteed to yield usable news. Investigative reporting, in quite radical contrast, is expensive, time-consuming, labor-intensive, and speculative— it may or may not result in a good story. Thus, since all of these defects of investigative reporting are only exacerbated when it is conducted overseas, it is understandable that media outlets concerned with maximizing their profits should tend not to rely on this method of news gathering in their coverage of foreign affairs.

This economic factor alone goes a long way toward explaining why the news is tilted so heavily in one direction. For notice that only two sectors of society have the resources to provide the media with canned news regularly: the government and corporations, with their big public relations budgets. Thus, when a foreign nation acts against US governmental and corporate interests, these two powerful sectors of society have a strong motive to mobilize public opinion against that nation, and to lay the groundwork for intervention against it. One way to do so is to publicize its faults, both real and alleged, by bringing these to the attention of journalists. But when a foreign nation behaves in a manner that is favorable to US governmental and corporate interests, there is no motive to publicize its transgressions (quite the contrary), leaving journalists with the task of discovering these themselves. It is not advisable to hold one's breath, however, while waiting for this to happen.

Objectivity

Most mass media journalists subscribe to a theory of "objectivity," according to which reporters should present only "the facts" (which are said to be objective), while scrupulously omitting from their stories their opinions, interpretations, conclusions, theories, and value judgments (all of which are said to be "personal" and "subjective").

Such a conception of objectivity, in addition to its many other defects,[11] fosters journalistic irresponsibility of the sort described above in at least two ways. First, it discourages investigative journalism, since reporters who do their own investigations are pretty much obliged to draw their own conclusions, and this, according to the principle in question, is to inject their own "bias" and "personal opinions" into the news. Moreover, if a journalist were to investigate a foreign leader, favored by US governmental and corporate interests, and find that he is a brutal dictator, such a journalist would be constrained from saying so by "objectivity's" ban on value judgments. Thus, it is infinitely safer to present only those conclusions and value judgments that can be attributed to others—and we have already seen who these others will be, and why.

Secondly, since the journalistic theory of objectivity demands the impossible (that judgments and conclusions be rigorously separated from facts, when in fact these things are inextricably connected to one another in all thinking and writing), it encourages journalists to finesse the issue by presenting only those judgments and conclusions that neither they themselves nor the bulk of their audience will recognize as such. For, with regard to facts, typically one has to *reason*, on the basis of evidence of some kind, to the *conclusion* that something is a fact. Facts are often not self-evident. It requires theorizing, selective (intelligently guided) looking, and (sometimes) special knowledge to discover them. Thus, since concluding, theorizing, and the like are banned as supposedly inconsistent with "objectivity," what we tend to get in mainstream journalism are "obvious" facts—meaning those emerging from the consensus of mainstream political opinion, where no evidence is needed.

And as for value judgments, people think they are being neutral and objective when their value commitments, like the air they breathe, are invisible to them—and that only happens when they are of the assumed consensus mainstream variety. Radical, non-establishment, or otherwise non-consensus values, by contrast, stand out, are noticed as values,

and are thus excluded from mainstream journalism as non-objective.[12]

"Both Sides"

The other ideological principle of mass media journalism that tends to result in the journalistic irresponsibility discussed above is the idea that journalists, who, it must be recalled, are not to present their own opinions at all, can nonetheless achieve "objectivity," "balance," and "evenhandedness" in presenting the opinions of others simply by always being careful, when doing so, to give equal attention to "both sides" of every issue.

This supposed principle of fairness is open to a number of powerful objections,[13] the most important of which for our purposes is that the two sides to be heard from are rarely selected on the basis of their being most worthy of consideration in the light of the relevant evidence. Rather, they are selected on the basis of the economic and ideological principles discussed above, with the result that mass media "debates" in the United States almost always stick well within the narrow range of opinion to be found within the mainstreams of the two major political parties.

With regard to international affairs, this leads to a paltry debate indeed, since the two parties, despite their differences in connection with priorities, tactics, symbolism, and rhetoric, rarely disagree on fundamentals. They do not disagree, for example, on the identities of the "good guys" and "bad guys" around the world. Thus, when both the Democrats and the Republicans trumpet the human rights abuses of country A, while neither ever mentions the equal or greater abuses of country B, the idea that A is a totalitarian dungeon and B a land of freedom, democracy, and human rights begins to look not like a highly suspect conclusion or value judgment, but rather like an objective fact no matter how vehemently Amnesty International, the International Red Cross, the United Nations, the foreign press, world opinion, and the judgment of scholars might disagree.

Suggestions for Improvement

If the analysis presented above is cogent, there are at least five steps that journalists might take that would immediately enable them to do a much better job of meeting their fundamental ethical responsibilities.

First, journalists should engage in much more investigative reporting and rely much less on handouts from authority figures, since, in addition to the defects of such reliance noted above, "in the nature of public relations most authority figures issue a high quotient of imprecise and self-serving declarations."[14] To be sure, such a change might harm the media outfit's bottom line, but if journalism is correct in viewing itself as a genuinely honorable profession, it cannot allow its concern for profit to overwhelm its ethical responsibilities.

Secondly, insofar as it is necessary for journalists to rely on others to gather evidence for them, they should dramatically enlarge the pool of authorities from which they draw their information. Thus, with regard to international affairs, journalists would do well to engage in some library research, consulting the reports of the major human rights organizations mentioned above, as well as taking advantage of the findings of academics and foreign journalists. Similarly they might take advantage of the information that is readily available at such "beats" as the United Nations and the World Court. Finally, in consulting all of these alternative sources, there should be a concerted effort to find and to present to news audiences perspectives other than those of US corporate and governmental elites, so that these audiences might be better equipped to evaluate critically both mainstream perspectives and their competitors.

Thirdly, journalists should not allow US corporate and governmental spokespersons to "set the agenda" for media coverage of international affairs. Rather, the media should assert their own independence in this regard, as part of their professional responsibility. Thus, rather than remaining content to report the mainstream elite consensus, handed to reporters, that country A's elections are fraudulent because of factor X, while country B's are legitimate because of factor Y, the media would better serve us by drawing up a comprehensive list of the factors that tend to push an election in the direction of legitimacy or illegitimacy, and then check, preferably by direct investigation, but alternatively by a scrupulous assessment of a variety of independent sources, how different countries fare with regard to these factors.

Fourthly, journalists should abandon the confused and irresponsible doctrine of objectivity that currently guides the profession, and replace it with a more scientific or scholarly conception of objectivity. The difference between the two is this. While the former requires the (impossible) avoidance of opinions, conclusions, and theories, the latter allows, indeed insists upon, these, while demanding that they be well grounded in evidence, logic, and reasoning, and that they hold up under the pressure of counterargument and counterevidence. Objectivity in this scholarly sense is not undermined by taking a strong position, displaying emotion, or anything of that sort. To the contrary, a strong position might be warranted, or even required, by a scrupulous examination of the relevant facts and arguments, and strong feelings might be utterly fitting and appropriate. Moreover, to think that objectivity requires a "balanced," "play it down the middle" result is just a confusion. To be committed to drawing conclusions based solely on the evidence is to be committed to letting the conclusions fall where they may. Thus, the fact that a person arrives at a "one-sided" conclusion is no more evidence of a lack of objectivity on his or her part than would the fact that a referee in a basketball game called thirty fouls on one team and only twelve on another. Perhaps the one team simply committed way more fouls. Indeed, for all we know, the referee might have been biased the other way, so that a more appropriate job of officiating would have resulted in a margin of forty fouls to two.

Fifthly, journalists should also abandon the "both sides" approach to the presentation of opinion. To be sure, there is something to be said for airing more than one view when considering difficult or controversial issues, but no special magic should be accorded to the number two. On many issues, several different perspectives, as opposed to merely two, are worthy of consideration. Moreover, when multiple perspectives are aired, there is less chance that fundamental convictions held in common by the two sides usually heard from will go unchallenged. On the other hand, some issues, such as the question of whether or not cigarette smoking is harmful to health, are sufficiently well established as to make it a waste of time to consider "the other side." Such an insistence on always presenting "both sides" even when the currently available evidence is adequate to show that one is correct has the unfortunate consequence of suggesting that no issues ever are decidable on the basis of evidence, and that all issues are ultimately "subjective." Thus, journalists would be well advised to be guided by evidence in determining which views to include, as opposed to insisting on precisely two views (and two mainstream ones sharing most of the important contestable principles in common, at that).

In conclusion, it should be noted that these reforms, necessary though they may be if journalism is to meet its responsibilities in a democracy, are extremely unlikely to be undertaken. It is to be hoped that some journalists will attempt them, but this will require considerable courage on their part, since it is quite likely that any editor or reporter who behaved in the manner here recommended would quite quickly lose his or her job. Until these reforms are enacted, however, those US citizens who would like to understand the world in which they live would be well advised to turn to other sources—the foreign press, scholarly books and articles, and the "alternative" or non-mass media—to supplement their careful and critical use of mainstream journalism.

NOTES

1 Often this is put in more general terms, and it is not explicitly spelled out that the "power" which journalism is to confront in its zeal to unearth the truth is that of the government. Still, if power itself is what needs watching, one wonders why journalists do not see it as their duty to provide a counterweight to corporate power, given its enormous, and steadily increasing, dominance in American culture. I trust my readers will not regard me as overly cynical if I suggest that the answer lies in the fact that American mass media outlets, without exception, either are owned by giant corporations or else are such entities themselves.

2 Jack Spence, "The US Media: Covering (Over) Nicaragua," in Thomas W. Walker, ed., *Reagan versus the Sandinistas* (Boulder: Westview Press, 1987), 192.

3 Francisco Goldman, "Sad Tales of La Libertad de Prensa," *Harper's Magazine* (August 1988), cited in Noam Chomsky, *Necessary Illusions* (Boston: South End Press, 1989), 42.

4 Americas Watch, *The Continuing Terror: Seventh Supplement to the Report on Human Rights in El Salvador* (September 1985), cited in Spence, "The US Media," 192.

5 Spence, "The US Media," 192; Chomsky, *Necessary Illusions*, 41.

6 Chomsky, *Necessary Illusions*, 125, and sources cited in that work, 378, note 46.

7 Chomsky, *Necessary Illusions*, 125; *Boston Globe*, Sept. 5 1988.

8 Chomsky, *Necessary Illusions*, 127-28; Al-Hamishmar, July 25 1986 and August 13 1986; *Jerusalem Post*, Aug. 12 and Aug. 24 1986.

9 I should note one other protocol for this experiment. To make the comparison between the two nations fair, some care should be taken

to note the overall amount of coverage, as well as the favorable coverage, they each receive. Otherwise, one might claim to refute me by, for example, noting that the US pays more attention to political corruption in Canada than in some tiny "hostile" African nation of little interest to US political elites. Such a claim would be absurd, since US audiences are obviously much more interested in Canadian affairs than in those of this African nation, so that the greater attention to corruption in the former nation is clearly to be attributed to this rather than an anti-Canadian bias, a point that is also indicated by the comparatively vastly greater favorable coverage Canada receives.

10 Edward S. Herman and Noam Chomsky have made extensive and excellent use of this "matched pair" method, and it is a pleasure to acknowledge my great debt to their works. See especially their *Manufacturing Consent* (New York: Pantheon, 1988), Herman's *The Real Terror Network* (Boston: South End Press, 1982); and Chomsky's *Necessary Illusions*.

11 For more on these defects, see my "Covering up Iran," in Yahya R. Kamalipour, *The US Media and the Middle East* (Westport, CT: Greenwood Press, 1995), 98-100.

12 It is also worth noting that while journalists might indeed, with practice, become skilled at bracketing their "personal opinions" and "biases" when it comes to controversial domestic issues—ones about which there is disagreement within the mainstream spectrum of US political opinion—they obviously do not do so when it comes to international issues, where there is usually an elite consensus. When the US government declares another nation to be "our" friend or enemy, the media never—that is literally never—provide the slightest dissent or critical perspective. Biases shared by all respectable members of one's own society are not so easily bracketed.

13 See Alexander Cockburn, "The Tedium Twins," and Trudy Govier, "Are There Two Sides to Every Question?" both in Govier, ed., *Selected Issues in Logic and Communication* (Belmont, CA: Wadsworth, 1988); and my "Covering up Iran."

14 Ben H. Bagdikian, *The Media Monopoly*, 4th ed. (Boston: Beacon, 1992), 180.

◆ ◆ ◆ ◆ ◆

LORI ROBERTSON

Ethically Challenged

Dennis Love didn't need to do it. He wasn't manufacturing unheard-of stories, amazing tales that astounded editors and readers alike. He was a good reporter.

His editor still says so. But, perhaps, Love wasn't satisfied with "good," and besides, with the wealth of information on the Internet, "it was very easy," he says. It was also easy to get caught. On November 21, the *Sacramento Bee* fired Love for plagiarizing and fabricating material in his stories on the presidential campaign.

At first, he told editors he didn't know why he did what he did. But he's had some time to think about it. "I think several things contributed to it in my situation," says Love, 47. "No. 1, it's just a simple human fallibility of taking a shortcut where one was available, concerning some stories that maybe I didn't care as much about as some other stories. I know that sounds maybe sort of cavalier. But I really do think that it was a character weakness." There's still an element of mystery, however. "This is not something that I have historically done."

Love had been a political writer with the *Bee* for 20 months. His previous employer, the *Orange County Register*, investigated his work there and found no signs of misappropriation. Love says this is the first time he's done such a thing, and the weird aspect is that some of the stuff he took—from *US News & World Report*, *USA Today*, the *Boston Globe* and the *Dallas Morning News*—didn't seem to be absolutely necessary for the story he already had—"filler quotes," he calls them. In at least one instance, he says, he had interviewed a source but used somebody else's quotes from the same source anyway. Why would he do that?

Love's firing came at the outset of the most recent spate of plagiarism and fabrication episodes in the news industry. Northwestern University's Medill News Service said November 17 it could not verify information in two of its stories. (It did not name the author, Eric R. Drudis, a Northwestern journalism student.) Papers at which Drudis had previously interned—the *San Jose Mercury News*, the *Philadelphia Daily News* and the *San Francisco Examiner*—subsequently could not find proof that sources from 17 of Drudis' stories had existed. In late December, the *Detroit News* admitted to lifting a paragraph from a suburban weekly. Publisher and Editor Mark Silverman says a reporter and an editor were disciplined, though he would not provide details. About a week later, a *Mercury News* intern, David Cragin, was suspended—and shortly thereafter fired for plagiarizing material, including the words of the *Washington Post* and the *San Francisco Chronicle*. In its January 15 issue, *Business Week* apologized for using "information and wording without attribution" from the *Washington Post*. The column in question, by Marcia Stepanek, a journalist with about 20 years of experience, borrowed heavily from the *Post* article. After a two-month investigation, *Business Week* fired her. At Myrtle Beach, South Carolina's *Sun News*, Features Editor Mona Prufer stepped down January 15 after evidence of copying appeared in her weekly books column and a cooking column. And, on February 7, the Bloomsburg, Pennsylvania, *Press Enterprise* fired reporter Steven Helmer after he admitted to fabricating at least one person in a story about a local shopping mall.

Journalism has witnessed three or four of these flurries in the last few years, and every time it touches off columns and stories decrying the poor state of the industry. The clamor brings with it a sense that this is the worst thing that has ever happened, and it just goes to show that journalism ethics are on the decline. But wait—could the opposite be true? Has there actually been an increase in plagiarism and fabrication? Or is all the catching and firing indicative of a business that's just not going to take it anymore? Journalists scramble for a reason why, hoping to pin this on something, as if there couldn't be a way for this to happen again. But then, it does. Is there a why? Does the praised-and-blamed Internet play a role? And, most important, is there anything news organizations can do to prevent this wrongdoing from occurring in the first place?

"If imitation is the highest form of flattery, we seem to be entering an age not rivaled since royal courts teemed with bowing courtiers in plumed hats. Everywhere you look somebody is getting busted for plagiarism, which is imitation carried to its highest form, the exact copy."

That lead was written in 1991 by Jerry Carroll of the *San Francisco Chronicle*. It just as easily could have been written last month.

But each time a slew of people get caught, it's not necessarily indicative of a slip in journalistic standards, or even a trend. In fact, say many, ethical standards are higher today. And while it's important to talk of the seriousness of these sins, perhaps the actual number of cases is decreasing. After all, most organizations are quick to dismiss the purloiners—two plagiarists down, X more to go. Are the media actually cleaning up their act?

"We in the media have become more sensitive to ethical problems than we were perhaps 10 or 20 years ago," says Fred Brown, chairman of the Society of Professional Journalists' ethics committee and the *Denver Post*'s Capitol bureau chief. "We understand that in an environment where people are bombarded by all kinds of media ... it's important that serious media have credibility and are serious about maintaining it."

Philip Meyer, a journalism professor at the University of North Carolina at Chapel Hill, says "plagiarism that used to be acceptable is not anymore." In a May 1999 *USA Today* column, he cited a 1938 journalism textbook by C.D. MacDougall, which "advised concealing the source of rewritten material in order to make it seem original," Meyer wrote.

News organizations seem almost desperate to rebuild credibility in the public's eyes. It's the age of admit and reveal and explain. And, so, the media are admitting and revealing and explaining not only in their own outlets, but over the Internet. Now, everyone hears about almost every gaffe, whether it involves the *New York Times* or the Owensboro, Kentucky, *Messenger-Inquirer*.

Washington Post Supreme Court reporter Charles Lane was the editor of *The New Republic* in May 1998 when the magazine fired Stephen Glass for fabricating a story. What turned out to be Glass' chronic fictionalizing marked the start of a rash of plagiarism and fabrication cases that have come to light since. Lane says he sees the cluster as a sign of health of the industry, "in the same way that a fever is a good sign that your body is fighting an infection." News organizations "seem to be comfortable with coming forward and saying, 'We have a bad apple,'" he says.

A few months after Glass was exiled from journalism, Patricia Smith and then Mike Barnicle, *Boston Globe* star columnists, resigned because of fabrication charges. Smith admitted she had made people up; Barnicle maintained that a questioned column from 1995 was true. National media coverage of the episodes mushroomed for weeks. That attention, says *Globe* Editor Matthew V. Storin, has sprouted more detailed examinations of possible wrongdoing at other news organizations. "Now, between the Internet, which allows the transmittal of this information much quicker, and the effect of the Barnicle/Smith stories, there seems to be more attention paid to these instances," Storin says.

Some journalists and media critics do say plagiarism is on the rise, and an increase or decrease is almost impossible to measure. But most agree on one thing: The media are on high alert. One case causes a ripple through the industry, launching a plagiarist's past employers into a frenzy to restore their now-tainted credibility. Go ahead, journalism seems to be saying. Plagiarize. We'll catch you. And then we'll examine every story you've ever written.

The *New Republic* found evidence of fabrication in 27 of the 41 articles Glass wrote for the magazine. Lane says many saw that episode as a cautionary tale. "People broadly now are more aware that there's this fine line between trusting someone you work with and being a chump," he says. "And you definitely don't want to be a chump."

The first step in fixing a problem is to find out why it occurred. However, with plagiarism and fabrication, as with much human behavior, reasons aren't always clear. In a soul-searching way, Dennis Love runs through most of them: ambition, self-induced pressure, sheer opportunity. He says it may be "a reluctance to turn in a mediocre story.... You don't want to be ordinary, and there's nothing really wrong with being ordinary from time to time."

Most journalists want to gain approval. The difference is, most journalists don't plagiarize. Most journalists don't make it up.

Frank Ahrens, a staff writer for the *Washington Post*'s Style section, says everyone has been in the situation: You're on deadline; you didn't have time to do the research someone else had already done; your quotes are "banal or flat"; you think, "Wouldn't it be better if he said this instead?" "But you stop," Ahrens says. "You don't do that."

Whether from ambition, compulsion or laziness, fabricators often invent the unusual: Eric Drudis' 9-year-old boy who had been arrested more than 70 times; Stephen Glass' Wall Street investment company that housed a shrine to Alan Greenspan, complete with two Bic pens used by the Federal

Reserve chairman in 1993; Janet Cooke's 8-year-old heroin addict in her infamous 1981 *Washington Post* piece.

But Love's Warren Deering, a gun issues expert, doesn't budge an eyebrow. Of then Vice President Al Gore's tie-breaking vote on gun control legislation, the fictitious Deering said: "With that vote, Gore solidified his standing forever with gun-control advocates, and forever earned the enmity of the pro-gun lobby."

Surely, there must be no shortage of firearms pundits ready and willing to serve up such a quote. Love is one of many who have used quotes they could have easily obtained on their own or who have stolen rather innocuous material. He admits some character flaw "allowed me to hit the button to file my story. I mean, I knew what I was doing."

In such instances and in blatant plagiarism cases, the act may be one of compulsion, like shoplifting. It's a theory to which Philip Meyer is beginning to subscribe. "Some plagiarists act like they want to be caught," he says. Like some shoplifters, they don't even need the stuff they're taking.

All of these reasons, however, have been given for years. The one thing that's changed for Love and Cragin and others: the Internet.

It used to be to plagiarize from another publication, you'd have to type the information in letter by letter, staring at your source. It took a little more effort than what you can do now: cut and paste some words from a Web page you can call up in seconds. Love admits the availability tapped his weakness. The new medium changes the dynamics once again.

Almost everyone interviewed for this article mentioned the Net as a greater lure and a greater police officer in the game of plagiarism. "There are more eyes looking at more publications across the country," says *Sacramento Bee* Executive Editor Rick Rodriguez. "There's a potential for increased plagiarism, but I also think the potential to get caught is greater." Just as a writer can highlight and copy, an editor can hit the search button.

Rodriguez goes on to caution that the standards for print and online need to be the same. He says the *Bee*'s director of new media recently did a copyright violation search of the Web for a *Bee* review of a Shania Twain concert. The review popped up on about 100 Web sites, mostly fan sites and music pages, he says, without the paper's permission. Similarly, the Associated Press is running into more copyright violations as Web sites that aren't members post AP material. We all think the Web is free. And that idea, says the *Post*'s Ahrens, may cheapen the words on the screens, making plagiarism seem less of a crime.

"I'm always surprised when all my journalism friends say, 'I don't have cable ... I don't have a TV,'" says Ahrens. As if they're too good for it. "But TV is a cheap medium." That characteristic "tends to devalue the content on it.... Unlike a movie or a book," which costs money. "The Internet may cheapen the content on it, because it's right in front of you." It's easy. It's free for the taking.

And it's voluminous. Karen Dewitt, a Washington, DC-based writer and former senior editor at ABC News, says offenses are harder to catch because an editor can't read everything that's on the Web. "There's huge amounts of information that's easily accessible," she says.

But while the Internet may spell a frontier of freedom for some, it's fostered an age of the hyperlink for others. Says Meyer: "One thing that the Internet is encouraging us all to do is to cite sources with much greater care than in the past.... I try to drop the name of a book or the name of a Web site" into a column, to point readers to sources of more information.

The understanding of what constitutes plagiarism is not universally held. When Dewitt taught a freshman journalism class at Kansas State University during the 1989-90 school year, one of her students lifted whole paragraphs from a *Newsweek* article. Dewitt told the student she would receive an automatic F; the student protested that she had mentioned the *Newsweek* article in her piece. The fact that she still couldn't swipe chunks of another person's story "seemed a very difficult concept for her to grasp," Dewitt says, adding that it's a problem she's heard of at other universities as well.

The *San Jose Mercury News'* David Cragin didn't get it either. When he admitted to using passages from a story by the *Post's* Ahrens, he told the *Merc*, "I know it's pretty similar obviously, but that's just a small piece of the story." He didn't think what he'd done was unethical, but said, "evidently, I guess I'm wrong." (*Mercury News* Executive Editor David Yarnold, however, disagrees with that statement. "My guess is he knew that it was wrong at the time," Yarnold says.)

In a December 26 story on San Francisco families living in hotels, Cragin wrote: "Most of these hotels in the city are more than half a century old; they were built for the solitary working men who streamed into the city to toil at the wharves and the railway lines. They were never meant for families." Ahrens had written November 27: "Most of these hotels are more than a half-century old; they were built as hives for the working men who streamed to this city to toil at the wharves and the railway lines. They were never meant for families."

Ahrens, who was out of town when the plagiarism news broke, received a hearty, "'Way to go, congratulations,'" from *Post* colleagues, he says. His own reaction was that "it was odd," to see his words under someone else's name. "Writers tend to remember what they wrote.... I remember where I was when I was writing things." He recalls sweating over a "short, powerful" line that would pull readers into a long story: "They were never meant for families."

"I could see," Ahrens says, "in his story, it was like boilerplate."

Writers do remember their turns of phrase, the right word that finally came to them in the shower, their rhythm, the decision to go back and put in periods to make short, choppy sentences.

All of which makes the "accidental" plagiarism, the "it got mixed up in my notes" excuse, a little harder to believe. Ahrens, for one, isn't buying it. "That's baloney," he says. "That's a big pile of sliced baloney.... If you're not a halfwit or a felon ... you know what's going on."

Meyer also brings up the carelessness excuse, but then adds, "it doesn't sound viable for me."

Others can see it happening, however, and news organizations have accepted that plea. Ruth Shalit, for one, admitted to being "a klutz" when charged with plagiarism in two stories in *The New Republic* in 1994 and 1995. She continued working at the magazine, faced another incident in 1996—after which she took a leave of absence—and eventually left in January 1999.

Whether the cut-and-paste ease and the mass of electronic information will lead to more cases of plagiarism—or more firings—is unclear. Some editors, such as Rosemary Armao, wouldn't accept the "mistaken ownership" excuse. "I just don't think we have any room for it," says the *Sarasota Herald-Tribune* managing editor. "There is something that has to be absolute, and that's that it's an original work product."

She continues, "The Internet has certainly increased the number of resources and sources you can use." That doesn't mean you can't name those sources.

Editors seem to be most forgiving when copying involves news briefs or items based on wire and other news accounts. That's when a bungled attribution becomes more understandable. In July, *San Antonio Express-News* Sports Editor Mitchell Krugel apologized to readers, as did Editor Robert Rivard, for not crediting four paragraphs in Krugel's piece on Tiger Woods to *Fort Worth Star-Telegram* columnist Gil LeBreton. The story carried Krugel's byline and the tag line: "Express-News wire services contributed to this report." The LeBreton piece ran on the Knight Ridder/Tribune News Service wire. Krugel wrote in his apology that he was not trying to use LeBreton's words as his own, but he should have better attributed his material.

As a result, an *Express-News* committee took a look at the paper's policy. "Given the landscape," one of information saturation, says Krugel, "we should examine and reexamine attribution consistently, and this is a situation that helped raise the consciousness on doing better journalism."

After Charles Lane found himself duped by Stephen Glass, he adopted a more meticulous approach to checking out potential new hires. Say you got your bachelor's from Brown, for instance? He'd call and find out. Lane says that may be the only way to prevent fabricators from gaining a voice in journalism.

"I really think the most important thing you can do, which *The New Republic* really didn't do when it hired Stephen Glass, is screen people very carefully when they come in for integrity," he says. "Make sure you have sort of an honest person coming in the door."

The *Washington Post* could have benefited from such vetting. Janet Cooke had lied about graduating from Vassar College and speaking Portuguese.

To make sure staffers already on staff don't start fibbing in the future is more difficult, Lane says. "There's a small percentage of people who just aren't honest ... and don't care that they aren't honest." Shut the door before they make it in.

Editors who have dealt with plagiarism or fabrication often try to institute a reform or ethical reinforcement in the aftermath:

Before Patricia Smith and Mike Barnicle resigned in the summer of 1998, the *Boston Globe* had a policy under which editors were to ask for verification of unnamed or unknown sources in columns and news stories. "These policies were not being followed" as stringently as they should have been, Editor Storin says. "Suffice to say, they are being followed now, scrupulously." Phone numbers may be requested, but editors normally don't call sources. Also, Louisa Williams, managing editor for administration, talks with each hire about the paper's plagiarism and fabrication policies.

After Julie Amparano was fired by the *Arizona Republic* for fabrication in August 1999, the paper reworked its corrections policy, says Reader Advocate Richard de Uriarte. Corrections are seen by the entire newsroom; the paper creates "an electronic paper trail of each call, each concern, its resolution ... by editor, by the section, that kind of thing," he says. The message behind these correction chronicles is, "Look what has gone wrong; look what can be done better."

The *Sacramento Bee* had halted its usual brown-bag ethics lunches for about a year while it altered its pagination process. In the wake of the Love incident, Editor Rodriguez says the paper reinstituted the sessions in January. The episode fostered many discussions at the paper on what constitutes plagiarism. A "high-profile, unfortunate incident reinforces to people that we take the issue very seriously, and we'll deal with it very seriously," Rodriguez says.

Detroit News Publisher and Editor Mark Silverman talked to editors about gathering suburban news after the paper plagiarized a local weekly in December. They determined that the instance was isolated, but he sent a note out to remind staff of the paper's ethics policy. The paper also will hold "at least yearly" brown-bag ethics talks.

The *San Jose Mercury News* pledged to host a one-day seminar for new interns after Cragin's and Drudis' deeds were revealed. Executive Editor Yarnold says the paper will go over its news policies at the training sessions—"not just plagiarism or attribution, but to go through everything from when we name sources to when we name victims ... and make some things clear that we thought were obvious" and the journalism schools thought were obvious. The *Merc* will clarify its existing plagiarism and attribution policies as well.

After Love was fired by the *Bee*, his former employer, the *Orange County Register*, held a series of internal training sessions in its bureaus. Ombudsman Dennis Foley and Training Editor Larry Welbom led discussions on plagiarism and ethics, aimed mostly at younger reporters. Foley saw it as a "good opportunity to remind everybody that our craft and our ethics and our credibility ... is tied up in this," he says.

Other papers use high-profile cases to encourage discussion and awareness, as does Northwestern University. Ken Bode, the journalism school's dean, says the school would "stop the presses when anything like this happens in the real world of journalism," hosting ethics panels on the actual cases. "You hope that people don't have to learn the ethics and regulations of our profession on the run and on the road." (Bode was barred from talking about the Drudis case because of federal student privacy laws.)

But the idea that a news organization would implement plagiarism safeguards seems almost silly to some editors. "You're talking about one of the most basic sins in journalism, and we have a very detailed code of ethics," says *Business Week* Editor in Chief Stephen B. Shepard, "and it does not say, 'Do not steal,' on the assumption that anyone who works at *Business Week* bloody well knows that."

Some journalists may need a little reminding. "Maybe [news organizations] need to quit assuming that the basics are that well understood by people they hire," says SPJ's Fred Brown. "The other thing is to communicate with journalism schools to make sure they're teaching that lesson."

Business Week does fact-check stories, but only to verify the names of people, companies and institutions, says Shepard. The rest is the responsibility of the writer. Most newspapers, with daily deadlines, don't see fact-checking as a viable reform. And given Glass' ability to fool TNR's fact-checkers—he built a fake Web site, gave fake phone numbers—it's uncertain whether that would catch a determined fabricator or plagiarist before a story made it into print.

Since at least 1987, the *Orange County Register* has carried out accuracy checks. At first, the ombudsman would send out short surveys to news sources, asking how they had been treated by the paper, and then circulate the responses. Now, Foley sends letters

inviting sources to call him or have him come talk to them. While it may help the paper's credibility and news practices, the policy is not designed to catch stolen words or made-up people. "It's not intended to be the internal affairs investigation accusing the reporters of doing wrong," Foley says.

Besides, Storin and Lane aren't too sure a specific policy is the answer. "I think as much as it's important that we follow that procedure, I would like to think," says the *Globe*'s Storin, "that after the agony of what we went through and the effect that it had on the careers ... that this is the least likely paper where fabrication would occur."

Says Lane: "There's sort of a tendency to look for procedural fixes for this stuff.... If we only had more fact-checkers," or a better flow of copy. The *New Republic* bolstered its fact-checking roster and developed a written fact-checking policy. "It helped," Lane says, "but it didn't create any kind of guarantee."

Perhaps, Lane says, he should've been more doubtful of Glass. "If someone could never, ever show you the place he went to talk to this particular source," because it was too dangerous or secret; or if your reporter "always has the perfect quote ... that might be a bit of a warning," he says. Then again, some journalists are just that good. "Steve was so bent on doing what he was doing and then covering it up that there really, I think, in hindsight, was very little that could have been done prophylactically. It was just luck" that a writer with Forbes Digital Tool caught a lie.

But don't journalists corner the market on skepticism? Maybe not when it comes to one of their own. Geneva Overholser, a syndicated columnist with the Washington Post Writers Group and a journalism professor at the University of Missouri, says more skepticism may be what's needed. "At the very first suspicion you have to ask," she says, comparing editors to the spouses of alcoholics. They begin to suspect something. But they don't want to believe it.

When San Antonio's Krugel didn't give a columnist his proper credit, the paper gushed with apology to its readers. When the *Arizona Republic* fired Julie Amparano, it told readers on its front page and followed with a 2,800-word treatise on her ouster. When Rodriguez fired Love, he published a letter from the editor on the incident the next day. Most of the 30 to 40 calls and e-mails he then received from readers were supportive. "I think they were surprised that we dealt with it that directly and that publicly," he says. "Some of them thought we were being sanctimonious."

While there are still cases in which writers are barely disciplined or where they are not singled out by their news organizations, other media are more than happy to name names. In July, the *New York Times* acknowledged that material had been copied in an obituary of British spy-trainer Vera Atkins. An editors' note, which stressed the article had been "based substantially" on *Times* research, said "five brief passages in the [June 27] obituary closely reflected the phrasing of an obituary in *The Times* of London." The paper did not name the writer, Douglas Martin, though other outlets did. *Times* Managing Editor Bill Keller says only that the incident was "resolved as an internal disciplinary" matter, and the paper does not usually name writers in its corrections. Martin still writes obits for the paper; however, the issue led Obituaries Editor Charles Strum to initiate talks with writers on how to appropriately attribute material in obits, which are often based on other accounts.

Public embarrassment coupled with swift punishment may be the best deterrent to crimes of copying or out-and-out lying. It may also change the public's views: In an October 1998 survey by the Media Studies Center, 76 per cent of respondents believed that journalists often or sometimes plagiarize, and 66 per cent said they make stuff up.

To some observers, punishments dished out today tend to be more harsh than in the past. "I think there are more serious consequences than there used

to be," says SPJ's Brown. He feels the Smith/Barnicle cases "raised the bar."

Meyer says some penalties in the last few years were "way too heavy." Many journalists thought *Globe* editorial page columnist Jeff Jacoby's four-month suspension in July wasn't warranted. Jacoby's July 3 column on the signers of the Declaration of Independence was hardly an original idea—the gist of it was zipping around the Internet. His version resembled several other accounts, including one in a 1975 book by Paul Harvey.

Imagine if today a writer included factual errors in a review of an Elton John concert, and it turned out that writer had never picked up her press ticket. When Patricia Smith did so in 1986 at the *Chicago Sun-Times*, she received a lecture—ironically from then *Sun-Times* Editor Storin—and wasn't allowed to write for several months. In 2001, most papers would launch a full-scale investigation into the matter as well as the writer's past works.

News organizations' commitment to deal with plagiarists and fabricators firmly and immediately and the subsequent revelations to the public can only raise credibility and instill a greater fear in would-be thieves. But—and this is a big but—the industry is more than willing to grant second chances. The list of past offenders who made a comeback is long: National Public Radio's Nina Totenberg; the *New York Times*' Fox Butterfield; Salon.com columnist Ruth Shalit; Mike Barnicle, who joined the *New York Daily News* in March 1999; and Patricia Smith, who was hired by *Ms. Magazine* to write a column in January 2000, among many others. Of course—as evidenced by this story—those charges will haunt those writers, quite possibly for the rest of their careers.

"It will probably never go away," says Barnicle, who adds that the *Globe* rescinded its accusation of plagiarism. (Storin says that's a fair statement. The columnist ultimately left amid fabrication charges.) "It's always out there lurking in some people's minds, not the readers', I don't think ... but in the business." It is a heavy scarlet letter to bear. It's indicative of not only the gravity of the offenses, but the very small percentage of journalists who commit them. The surprising thing is that only one person interviewed for this article said that under no circumstances would she offer a job to someone who had made up material or stolen words.

Says Rosemary Annao: "If I knew about it, I wouldn't hire them. There are so many good people in the market, why take somebody with that mark against them?" She says she can hardly even read *Ms.* since it hired Smith.

Even Storin and Lane hedge. Each case is different, they say. "Is it a second or a third or a fourth chance?" Storin asks.

Lane's answer: "If anybody ever hired Steve Glass in journalism again, it would be a very sad day.... If on the other hand, there was somebody who really was going through a tough time personally and broke down and once or twice, but not much more than that, swiped some quotes from somebody else, should they be banished forever? I think no." If he was in the

position of hiring, he says, he would go over that person's background "with a fine-tooth comb."

Dennis Love says he's "trying to just accept responsibility for what I did with as much dignity as I can and move on." He is freelancing for some trade magazines and working on a biography of Stevie Wonder. Asked if he will pursue a newspaper career again, he says he's not sure if it's up to him. "I don't know if somebody in my situation gets a second chance or not," Love says. "I could see it happening, I guess.... But I don't know the answer.... In the future, I think that I would like to."

His old boss, Rodriguez, says it would probably be difficult for Love to find a job in journalism in the near future. But he's a believer in second chances as well. "He's such a good writer that you would hope at some point he would use that craft again."

Judging from history, Love could find a second journalistic life. But, in five, maybe 10 years, when AJR inevitably does another piece on plagiarism, his name, along with many of the rest, doubtless will appear again.

OBJECTIVITY

THEODORE L. GLASSER

Objectivity Precludes Responsibility

By objectivity I mean a particular view of journalism and the press, a frame of reference used by journalists to orient themselves in the newsroom and in the community. By objectivity I mean, to a degree, ideology; where ideology is defined as a set of beliefs that function as the journalist's "claim to action." As a set of beliefs, objectivity appears to be rooted in a positivist view of the world, an enduring commitment to the supremacy of observable and retrievable facts. This commitment in turn, impinges on news organizations' principal commodity—the day's news. Thus my argument, in part, is this: Today's news is indeed biased—as it must inevitably be—and this bias can be best understood by understanding the concept, the conventions, and the ethic of objectivity.

Specifically, objectivity in Journalism accounts for—or at least helps us understand—three principal developments in American journalism; each of these developments contributes to the bias or ideology of news. First, objective reporting is biased against what the press typically defines as its role in a democracy—that of a Fourth Estate, the watchdog role, an adversary press.

Indeed, objectivity in journalism is biased in favor of the status quo; it is inherently conservative to the extent that it encourages reporters to rely on what sociologist Alvin Gouldner so appropriately describes as the "managers of the status quo"—the prominent and the elite. Second, objective reporting is biased against independent thinking; it emasculates the intellect by treating it as a disinterested spectator. Finally, objective reporting is biased against the very idea of responsibility; the day's news is viewed as something journalists are compelled to report, not something they are responsible for creating.

This last point, I think, is most important. Despite a renewed interest in professional ethics, the discussion continues to evade questions of morality and responsibility. Of course, this doesn't mean that journalists are immoral.

Rather, it means that journalists today are largely amoral. Objectivity in journalism effectively erodes the very foundation on which rests a responsible press.

By most any of the many accounts of the history of objectivity in journalism, objective reporting began more as a commercial imperative than as a standard of responsible reporting. With the emergence of a truly popular press in the mid-1800s—the penny press—a press tied neither to the political parties nor the business elite, objectivity provided a presumably disinterested view of the world.

But the penny press was only one of many social, economic, political, and technological forces that converged in the mid- and late-1800s to bring about fundamental and lasting changes in American journalism. There was the advent of the telegraph, which for the first time separated communication from transportation. There were radical changes in printing technology, including the steam-powered press and later the rotary press. There was the formation of the Associated Press, an early effort by publishers to monopolize a new technology—in this case

the telegraph. There was, finally, the demise of community and the rise of society; there were now cities, "human settlements" where "strangers are likely to meet."

These are some of the many conditions that created the climate for objective reporting, a climate best understood in terms of the emergence of a new mass medium and the need for that medium to operate efficiently in the marketplace.

Efficiency is the key term here, for efficiency is the central meaning of objective reporting. It was efficient for the Associated Press to distribute only the "bare facts," and leave the opportunity for interpretation to individual members of the cooperative. It was efficient for newspapers not to offend readers and advertisers with partisan prose. It was efficient—perhaps expedient—for reporters to distance themselves from the sense and substance of what they reported.

To survive in the marketplace, and to enhance their status as a new and more democratic press, journalists principally publishers, who were becoming more and more removed from the editing and writing process—began to transform efficiency into a standard of professional competence, a standard later—several decades later—described as objectivity. This transformation was aided by two important developments in the early twentieth century: first, Oliver Wendell Holmes's effort to employ a marketplace metaphor to define the meaning of the First Amendment; and second, the growing popularity of the scientific method as the proper tool with which to discover and understand an increasingly alien reality.

In a dissenting opinion in 1919, Holmes popularized "the marketplace of ideas," a metaphor introduced by John Milton several centuries earlier. Metaphor or not, publishers took it quite literally. They argued—and continue with essentially the same argument today—that their opportunity to compete and ultimately survive in the marketplace is their First Amendment right, a Constitutional privilege. The American Newspaper Publishers Association, organized in 1887, led the cause of a free press. In the name of freedom of the press, the ANPA fought the Pure Food and Drug Act of 1906 on behalf of its advertisers; it fought the Post Office Act of 1912, which compelled sworn statements of ownership and circulation and thus threatened to reveal too much to advertisers; it fought efforts to regulate child labor, which would interfere with the control and exploitation of paper boys; it fought the collective bargaining provisions of the National Recovery Act in the mid-1930s; for similar reasons, it stood opposed to the American Newspaper Guild, the reporters' union; it tried—unsuccessfully—to prevent wire services from selling news to radio stations until after publication in the nearby newspaper.

Beyond using the First Amendment to shield and protect their economic interests in the marketplace, publishers were also able to use the canons of science to justify—indeed, legitimize—the canons of objective reporting. Here publishers were comforted by Walter Lippmann's writings in the early 1920s, particularly his plea for a new scientific journalism, a new realism; a call for journalists to remain "clear and free" of their irrational, their unexamined, their unacknowledged prejudgments.

By the early 1900s objectivity had become the acceptable way of doing reporting—or at least the respectable way. It was respectable because it was reliable, and it was reliable because it was standardized. In practice, this meant a preoccupation with how the news was presented, whether its form was reliable. And this concern for reliability quickly overshadowed any concern for the validity of the realities the journalists presented.

Thus emerged the conventions of objective reporting, a set of routine procedures journalists use to objectify their news stories. These are the conventions sociologist Gaye Tuchman describes as a kind of strategy journalists use to deflect criticism, the same kind of strategy social scientists use to defend the quality of their work. For the journalist,

this means interviews with sources; and it ordinarily means official sources with impeccable credentials. It means juxtaposing conflicting truth-claims, where truth-claims are reported as "fact" regardless of their validity. It means making a judgment about the news value of a truth-claim even if that judgment serves only to lend authority to what is known to be false or misleading.

As early as 1924 objectivity appeared as an ethic, an ideal subordinate only to truth itself. In his study of the Ethics of Journalism, Nelson Crawford devoted three full chapters to the principles of objectivity. Thirty years later, in 1954, Louis Lyons, then curator for the Nieman Fellowship program at Harvard, was describing objectivity as a "rock-bottom" imperative. Apparently unfazed by Wisconsin's Senator Joseph McCarthy, Lyons portrayed objectivity as the ultimate discipline of journalism. "It is at the bottom of all sound reporting indispensable as the core of the writer's capacity." More recently, in 1973, the Society of Professional Journalists, Sigma Delta Chi formally enshrined the idea of objectivity when it adopted as part of its Code of Ethics a paragraph characterizing objective reporting as an attainable goal and a standard of performance toward which journalists should strive. "We honor those who achieve it," the Society proclaimed.

So well ingrained are the principles of objective reporting that the judiciary is beginning to acknowledge them. In a 1977 federal appellate decision, *Edwards v. National Audubon Society*, a case described by media attorney Floyd Abrams as a landmark decision in that it may prove to be the next evolutionary stage in the development of the public law of libel, a new and novel privilege emerged. It was the first time the courts explicitly recognized objective reporting as a standard of journalism worthy of First Amendment protection.

In what appeared to be an inconsequential story published in *The New York Times* in 1972—on page 33—five scientists were accused of being paid liars, men paid by the pesticide industry to lie about the use of DOT and its effect on bird life. True to the form of objective reporting, the accusation was fully attributed—to a fully identified official of the National Audubon Society. The scientists, of course, were given an opportunity to deny the accusation. Only one of the scientists, however, was quoted by name and he described the accusation as "almost libelous." What was newsworthy about the story, obviously, was the accusation; and with the exception of one short paragraph, the reporter more or less provided a forum for the National Audubon Society.

Three of the five scientists filed suit. While denying punitive damages, a jury awarded compensatory damages against the *Times* and one of the Society's officials. The *Times*, in turn, asked a federal District Court to overturn the verdict. The *Times* argued that the "actual malice" standard had not been met; since the scientists were "public figures," they were required to show that the *Times* knowingly published a falsehood or there was, on the part of the *Times*, a reckless disregard for whether the accusation was true or false. The evidence before the court clearly indicated the latter—there was indeed a reckless disregard for whether the accusation was true or false. The reporter made virtually no effort to confirm the validity of the National Audubon Society's accusations. Also the story wasn't the kind, of "hot news" (a technical term used by the courts) that required immediate dissemination; in fact ten days before the story was published the *Times* learned that two of the five scientists were not employed by the pesticide industry and thus could not have been "paid liars."

The *Times* appealed to the Second Circuit Court of Appeals, where the lower court's decision was overturned. In reversing the District Court, the Court of Appeals created a new First Amendment right, a new Constitutional defense in libel law—the privilege of "neutral reportage." "We do not believe," the Court of Appeals ruled, "that the press may be required to suppress newsworthy statements merely because it has serious doubts regarding their truth." The First Amendment, the Court said, "protects the accurate and disinterested reporting" of newsworthy accusations "regardless of the reporter's private views regarding their validity."

I mention the details of the *Edwards* case only because it illustrates so well the consequences of the ethic of objectivity. First, it illustrates a very basic tension between objectivity and responsibility. Objective reporting virtually precludes responsible reporting, if by responsible reporting we mean a willingness on the part of the reporter to be accountable for what is reported. Objectivity requires only that reporters be accountable for how they report, not what they report. The *Edwards* Court made this very clear: "The public interest in being fully informed," the Court said, demands that the press be afforded the freedom to report newsworthy accusations "without assuming responsibility for them."

Second, the *Edwards* case illustrates the unfortunate bias of objective reporting—a bias in favor of leaders and officials, the prominent and the elite. It is an unfortunate bias because it runs counter to the important democratic assumption that statements made by ordinary citizens are as valuable as statements made by the prominent and the elite. In a democracy, public debate depends on separating individuals from their powers and privileges in the larger society; otherwise debate itself becomes a source of domination. But *Edwards* reinforces prominence as a news value; it reinforces the use of official sources, official records, official channels. Tom Wicker underscored the bias of the *Edwards* case when he observed recently that "objective journalism almost always favors Establishment positions and exists not least to avoid offense to them."

Objectivity also has unfortunate consequences for the reporter, the individual journalist. Objective reporting has stripped reporters of their creativity and their imagination; it has robbed journalists of their passion and their perspective. Objective reporting has transformed journalism into something more technical than intellectual; it has turned the art of story-telling into the technique of report writing. And most unfortunate of all, objective reporting has denied journalists their citizenship; as disinterested observers, as impartial reporters, journalists are expected to be morally disengaged and politically inactive.

Journalists have become—to borrow James Carey's terminology—"professional communicators," a relatively passive link between sources and audiences. With neither the need nor the opportunity to develop a critical perspective from which to assess the events, the issues, and the personalities he or she is assigned to cover, the objective reporter tends to function as a translator—translating the specialized language of sources into a language intelligible to a lay audience.

In his frequently cited study of Washington correspondents—a study published nearly fifty years ago—Leo Rosten found that a "pronounced majority" of the journalists he interviewed considered themselves inadequate to cope with the bewildering complexities of our nation's policies and politics. As Rosten described it, the Washington press corps was a frustrated and exasperated group of prominent journalists more or less resigned to their role as mediators, translators. "To do the job," one reporter told Rosten, "what you know or understand isn't important. You've got to know whom to ask." Even if you don't understand what's being said, Rosten was told, you just take careful notes and write it up verbatim: "Let my readers figure it out. I'm their reporter, not their teacher."

That was fifty years ago. Today, the story is pretty much the same. Two years ago another study of Washington correspondents was published, a book by Stephen Hess called *The Washington Reporters*. For the most part, Hess found, stories coming out of Washington were little more than a "mosaic of facts and quotations from sources" who were participants in an event or who had knowledge of the event. Incredibly, Hess found that for nearly three-quarters of the stories he studied, reporters relied on no documents—only interviews. And when re-

porters did use documents, those documents were typically press clippings—stories they had written or stories written by their colleagues.

And so what does objectivity mean? It means that sources supply the sense and substance of the day's news. Sources provide the arguments, the rebuttals, the explanations, the criticism. Sources put forth the ideas while other sources challenge those ideas. Journalists, in their role as professional communicators, merely provide a vehicle for these exchanges.

But if objectivity means that reporters must maintain a healthy distance from the world they report, the same standard does not apply to publishers. According to the SPJ.SDX Code of Ethics, "Journalists and their employers should conduct their personal lives in a manner which protects them from conflict of interest, real or apparent." Many journalists do just that—they avoid even an appearance of a conflict of interest. But certainly not their employers.

If it would be a conflict of interest for a reporter to accept, say, an expensive piano from a source at the Steinway Piano Company, it apparently wasn't a conflict of interest when CBS purchased the Steinway Piano Company.

Publishers and broadcasters today are a part of a large and growing and increasingly diversified industry. Not only are many newspapers owned by corporations that own a variety of non-media properties, but their boards of directors read like a Who's Who of the powerful and the elite. A recent study of the twenty-five largest newspaper companies found that the directors of these companies tend to be linked with "powerful business organizations, not with public interest groups; with management, not with labor; with well established think tanks and charities, not their grassroots counterparts."

But publishers and broadcasters contend that these connections have no bearing on how the day's news is reported—as though the ownership of a newspaper had no bearing on the newspaper's content; as though business decisions have no effect on editorial decisions; as though it wasn't economic considerations in the first place that brought about the incentives for many of the conventions of contemporary journalism.

No doubt the press has responded to many of the more serious consequences of objective reporting. But what is significant is that the response has been to amend the conventions of objectivity, not to abandon them. The press has merely relined the canons of objective reporting; it has not dislodged them.

What remains fundamentally unchanged is the journalist's naively empirical view of the world, a belief in the separation of facts and values, a belief in the existence of a reality—the reality of empirical facts. Nowhere is this belief more evident than when news is defined as something external to—and independent of—the journalist. The very vocabulary used by journalists when they talk about news underscores their belief that news is "out there," presumably waiting to be exposed or *uncovered* or at least *gathered*.

This is the essence of objectivity, and this is precisely why it is so very difficult for journalism to consider questions of ethics and morality. Since news exists "out there"—apparently independent of the reporter—journalists can't be held responsible for it. And since they are not responsible for the news being there, how can we expect journalists to be accountable for the consequences of merely reporting it?

What objectivity has brought about, in short, is a disregard for the consequences of newsmaking. A few years ago Walter Cronkite offered this interpretation of journalism: "I don't think it is any of our business what the moral, political, social, or economic effect of our reporting is. I say let's go with the job of reporting and let the chips fall where they may."

Contrast that to John Dewey's advice: that "our chief moral business is to become acquainted with consequences."

I am inclined to side with Dewey. Only to the extent that journalists are held accountable for the consequences of their actions can there be said to be a responsible press. But we are not going to be able to hold journalists accountable for the consequences of their actions until they acknowledge that news is their creation, a creation for which they are fully responsible. And we are not going to have much success convincing journalists that news is created, not reported, until we can successfully challenge the conventions of objectivity.

The task, then, is to liberate journalism from the burden of objectivity by demonstrating—as convincingly as we can—that objective reporting is more of a custom than a principle, more a habit of mind than a standard of performance. And by showing that objectivity is largely a matter of efficiency—efficiency that serves, as far as I can tell, only the needs and interest of the owners of the press, not the needs and interests of talented writers and certainly not the needs and interests of the larger society.

◆ ◆ ◆ ◆ ◆

MICHAEL RYAN

Journalistic Ethics, Objectivity, Existential Journalism, Standpoint Epistemology, and Public Journalism

Critics have hammered journalists for years for their alleged devotion to what Friedman (1998) called the "ideology" or "fantasy" of objective journalism. Indeed, "contemporary analyses of the news media have turned the once-transparent notion of objectivity into a hotly contested area of inquiry," Durham (1998) wrote. "Under scrutiny, its philosophical underpinnings have been challenged, revalued, and ultimately rejected" (117).[1]

Few observers base their critiques on precise definitions of objectivity—a critical failure, according to Gauthier (1993)—and most simply assume that (a) traditional objectivity is nothing more than uncritically reporting facts and opinions representing only two sides and (b) all journalists subscribe to this view. Both assumptions are false, and so the critiques, although not without some merit, are deeply flawed. This defense of objectivity begins with a definition.

A Definition of Objectivity

It is no accident that the evolution of journalistic objectivity parallels that of scientific objectivity, for objective journalism shares the core values of the scientific method. The overarching value for the objective journalist (or scientist) is the collection and dissemination of information that describes reality as accurately as possible.[2]

Philosophical constructs that underpin both science and objective journalism include (a) accuracy, completeness, precision, and clarity in information collection and dissemination; (b) receptivity to new evidence and alternative explanations; (c) skepticism, typically toward authority figures, the powerful, and the self-righteous; (d) initiative in finding ways, for example, to research difficult topics; (e) fairness, impartiality, and disinterestedness, in that no social-political agenda is served and the tenets of objectivity are observed; (f) imagination, creativity, and logical consistency in making strategic decisions (e.g., in selecting stories) and in presenting narratives in interesting and compelling ways; (g) honesty about personal idiosyncrasies and preferences; (h) communality and verification, in that results are freely shared; and (i) universalism, in that outcomes are not evaluated on the basis of the practitioner's personal characteristics (Koertge, 1996a; Merton, 1973; Nanda, 1998; Parsons, 1951).

The success of objective journalism or science depends on the integrity of practitioners and the norms to which they are committed. The process for the journalist—from story selection, to information collection, to news dissemination—is independent of acknowledged personal idiosyncrasies or preferences (Koertge, 1996a). Objective journalists refuse to serve or to support any political, social, economic, or cultural interests, even those that appear to some observers as laudatory (e.g., those that oppose gun control, abortion, or the status quo; that give voice to marginalized groups; that support gun control, abortion, or the status quo; or that ignore marginalized groups).

This does not mean that journalism is completely value-free, for as Dennis (1984) suggested, "Objectivity in journalism or science does not mean that all decisions do not have underlying values, only that within the 'rules of the game' a systematic attempt is made to achieve an impartial report" (118). Strategic decisions (e.g., selection of sources) are not based on a reporter's personal preference (e.g., for a source who cannot adequately clarify or defend an "unapproved" position), but on professional norms; that is, the reporter consistently seeks the most informed, qualified, forthcoming source available to address each side.

It also does not mean objective journalists cannot use analytical and interpretive skills in collecting and disseminating information. On the contrary, objective journalists cannot avoid applying these skills; they cannot, for example, fulfill the mandate for completeness if they cannot interpret and analyze information during information collection. They remain true to the norms of objectivity, however.

Objective journalists make every effort to ensure that all relevant information is obtained and disseminated—even that which they or powerful interests would prefer to see suppressed—for reports must be complete if they are (a) to describe (as they must) both the event or issue and the context within which persons act and events occur and (b) to help audiences decide which of several truth claims are, in fact, most compelling.

This means, among other things, that objective journalists gather facts and opinions that conflict, verify information carefully, seek to determine why accounts conflict and which most accurately reflect reality, and evaluate and fully identify sources. Objective journalists "realize that people and events are multifaceted and extremely complex. Simple descriptive 'tags' will not do; a person is far more than a 'liberal' or a 'conservative,' than a 'professor' or a 'legislator'" (Merrill and Lowenstein, 1979, 208).

Objective journalists gather facts and opinions that conflict, verify information carefully, [and] seek to determine why accounts conflict.

Objective journalists are accountable to their audiences, to the highest ethical and professional standards of objective journalism, and, finally, to their employers. They never assume that their employers, and not themselves, bear the ultimate responsibility for their behavior.

This definition assumes, of course, the existence of a "real" world about which human beings can be right or wrong. Objective journalists believe a real world exists and that one can produce a reasonably accurate description of that world. They do not guarantee their descriptions are accurate in every respect, only that they have followed a process that allows them to produce a description that is more accurate than any other process allows, and that allows society to move closer to an understanding of the real world.

It is difficult to overstate the importance to a free society, and to all the groups that comprise that society, of information that has been collected and disseminated by individuals who are committed to the ideals of objectivity, for objective reports are "the

necessary elements of a self-critical, authority-defying free society" (Nanda, 1998, 303). This is particularly true at a time when the number of information sources, many of which are unreliable, is expanding at an almost incomprehensible rate.

When the ideas of diverse political, social, economic, and cultural groups are not objectively reported, good decisions are unlikely, for, as Rachlin (1988) wrote,

> a press free from legal constraints imposed by an oppressive government can still undermine the possibility of pluralism and the requirements of democracy, if it is constrained instead by a narrow vision of the world that reproduces existing social relationships by inhibiting the possibility of realizing or even imagining alternative realities. (4)

Objective journalists are not constrained by this narrow vision.

A commitment to objective journalism is important to the news media as well. If the media enforce objectivity as a standard, they will flourish; if not, they will not, and Merrill and Lowenstein (1979) will be right:

> The "credibility gap" that we hear so much about today will probably not exist much longer. Why? Because nobody can believe *anything* in tomorrow's new world of subjective journalism; there will be no "gap"— only a credibility *vacuum*, a fuzzy kind of opinion world of journalistic dialectic with no solid foundation stones of verifiable fact. (213)

Not surprisingly, as increasing numbers of journalists have abandoned the quest for objectivity, audience confidence in the news media has dipped dramatically (Merritt, 1995, xv).[3]

Critiques of Objectivity

Critics have attacked objectivity for a wide range of sins, which seem to fall into eight broad, sometimes overlapping categories. I do not claim to demolish the critics' arguments here as that would require far too much space, but I do try to indicate the general nature of an objective journalist's rebuttal to each criticism.

Objectivity Is a Myth

Journalism has not escaped the influence of the relativists (e.g., Altheide, 1976; Harding, 1991; Longino, 1990; Shoemaker and Reese, 1991), who argue that absolutes do not exist in knowledge, morals, or values; that objectivity is not achievable; and that objectivity is not a useful goal. A foundation for the relativist critique is the social constructivist view, which holds as its "first principle that the standards of evaluation of truth, rationality, success, and progressiveness are relative to a culture's assumptions and that the ways of seeing further vary with gender, class, race, and caste in any given culture" (Nanda, 1998, 287).[4]

Reporters and editors are conditioned by many factors (e.g., gender, circumstance, education), which, when coupled with the need to be selective in choosing stories and details for stories, make it impossible for reporters and editors to be objective, Merrill (1984) argued. In short,

> objectivity is little more in substance than rhetoric, since the reporter is bound to accept the basic institutions of his society (the family, private enterprise, the corporations, the political system, etc.), and therefore sees society only in terms of them. (Smith, 1980, 65)

Comment. On need only read James Weldon Johnson's (1927) *The Autobiography of an Ex-Coloured Man* to understand that reality can be and is socially constructed. However, critics who argue that objectivity is a myth miss two important points: (a) An observer who tries to be objective, who recognizes personal and environmental influences and limitations and tries to transcend them, can describe reality with reasonable accuracy, and (b) an observer who tries to be objective will reconstruct reality more accurately than one who allows a personal agenda to influence strategic decisions. Indeed, the latter might well construct a "perceived reality" that has little or nothing to do with real life.

Objective Journalists Are Moral Spectators

Objective journalism means presenting only two sides of an issue or event without assessing the veracity of each side, according to some critics (e.g., Altschull, 1984; Hackett, 1984; Rosen, 1993). Stoker (1995) charged that this kind of objectivity "relegates journalists to subservient, spectator roles in serving the public interest" (11). In addition, Glasser (1984) argued that "objective reporting has denied journalists their citizenship; as disinterested observers, as impartial reporters, journalists are expected to be morally disengaged and politically inactive" (15).

The problem seems exacerbated by the organizational context within which journalists work. The Commission on Freedom of the Press (1947) said mass communication provides an essential service, but it noted that

> the element of personal responsibility, which is of the essence of the organization of such professions as law and medicine, is missing in communications. Here the writer works for an employer, and the employer, not the writer, takes the responsibility. (77)

Comment. Objective journalists are not moral spectators, unless one defines *objective* only as uncritically presenting two sides of a story. In fact, it is the moral duty of objective journalists to collect and to disseminate the information a community needs to make sound decisions. Objective journalists evaluate the veracity of all information, and they do reveal the superior sides of issues (when one side is, in fact, superior) by disseminating objective reports. It is a cliché, but the facts do speak for themselves. If one side is more compelling, that is apparent from the objective journalist's report. It is not necessary or desirable for the journalist to become an advocate for that position.

Objective journalists do not permit their employers to assume responsibility for their news reports or actions, as the Commission on Freedom of the Press (1947) asserted. They feel an ethical obligation to disseminate stories that describe reality as accurately as possible, and they are true to the highest standards of objective journalism—regardless of their employers' views.

Objectivity Stifles Progressive Politics

One consequence of an objective journalism that merely presents two sides uncritically is a stifling of critical thinking. As Durham (1998) noted, "The reportorial canon of presenting all perspectives without any engagement with the political valences of such perspectives effectively prevents any progressive or emancipatory politics from developing out of journalism" (125-26).

Comment. It is simply not true that the tenets of objectivity prohibit engagement with the political valences of differing perspectives. Although it is true that some journalists have tried to stifle progressive movements (e.g., Southern newspapers hindered efforts to expand voter registration lists early in the civil rights movement), these are failures of poor and irresponsible journalism, not of objectivity. Indeed, the discrimination in voter registration would have been adequately reported had the irresponsible Southern journalists subscribed to the tenets of objectivity.

Objectivity Obscures Truth

Objective journalists help the powerful maintain order and establish behavioral standards because objectivity, Altschull (1984) wrote, "hallows bias, for it safeguards the system against the explosive pressures for change. So long as 'both sides' are presented, neither side is glorified above the other, and the status quo remains unchallenged" (128).

Truth can be obscured also by source selection. Hackett (1984) asserted that objectivity ensures that information flows from bureaucracies, through the media, and to the public by introducing a bias toward sources who supply information most steadily. Koch (1990) seconded Hackett's assertion: "Reporters do not seek independent confirmation or use a critical method to test the statements issued by officials.... There is no real attempt to balance the official version against the contextual evidence" (174-75).

Comment. The powerful fear objective journalists, for they cannot be manipulated. They present all sides of a story, and if information suggests one side is superior, that is clear from their stories. Objective journalists do not shout, "This side is superior," as some critics seem to suggest they should, but the superiority is apparent. It is simply not accurate to argue that the status quo is not challenged by objective journalists.

Objectivity is less responsible for poor source selection than are deadline pressures, source or document unavailability, laziness, and confusion (Brown, Bybee, Wearden, and Straughan, 1987). Even objective journalists who recognize the need to obtain information from dissenting sources encounter difficulties. Dissenting sources may not be available; they may refuse to talk; or there may be too little time to contact them.

The powerful fear objective journalists, for they cannot be manipulated.

It also is difficult at times to know to whom one should talk. Who is, in fact, the leader of a marginalized group? Some Black individuals (e.g., Pearson, 2000) argue that the media should not give the Reverend Al Sharpton space or air time because he does not speak for the Black community; others (e.g., White, 2000) argue that he is a legitimate, though flawed, Black leader. Anyone, objective or not, would find such a situation confusing.

Journalists Deceive Themselves and Their Audiences

Journalists occasionally conclude during their investigations that official findings (e.g., about the guilt or innocence of a murder suspect) are "wrong" and that they, the journalists, have found the "right" answers. Those who respect the tenets of objectivity, critics argue, then try to find sources to state the journalists' opinions. Stoker (1995) concluded that such a journalist has

> deceived herself into believing that finding a willing source to state her opinion would eliminate the fact that she was writing her opinion based on the evidence. Second, she would deceive the audience into believing she had obtained her story by remaining objective. (11)

Comment. This criticism is a bit, well, odd. A journalist who suspects that official findings or actions are "wrong" (e.g., police have arrested the wrong person) has no business rushing into print or onto the air with his or her opinion. The journalist must seek evidence. This is not deceptive—this is how good journalists work, as journalism students at Northwestern University demonstrated when their research helped free a death row inmate (Belluck, 1999). The students, appropriately, contacted sources whom they knew or suspected had information about the inmate's case; it would have made

little sense for them to contact individuals who were ignorant about the case.

Objectivity Is Invoked for Protection

Objectivity is simply a ruse that journalists have devised to protect themselves from legal actions and criticism. Tuchman (1972) suggested that the journalist "can claim objectivity by citing procedures he has followed that exemplify the formal attributes of a news story or a newspaper. For instance, the newsman can suggest that he quoted other people instead of offering his own opinions" (660). Thus, objectivity is a strategic ritual that protects journalists from the risks of their trade.

Comment. This charge is beside the point. Objective journalists, when asked, tell how their information was obtained. Yes, the journalists are on solid legal, professional, and ethical ground if they have tried to be objective, but this seems analogous to airline mechanics who follow proper procedures and do excellent work; does it really matter whether they do good work to protect passengers or to protect themselves? The result either way is a safer aircraft. Certainly, though, objective journalists try to be objective because that is the right thing to do.

Objectivity Is Used to Build Audiences

Objectivity demands that journalists, to build their audiences, seek information from sources who are close to the political, economic, social, and cultural center and ignore sources who populate the more extreme positions, according to Ognianova and Endersby (1996):

> The journalistic convention of objectivity, we argue, resembles a strategy on the part of the media to present a centrist position in the ideological spectrum in order to appeal to the middle of the road audience and increase their market share. (1)

Comment. Objective reporting may build audiences, although that assertion is questionable in light of the anecdotal evidence. Huge audiences are attracted daily to sensational, biased, or clearly untrue "news" reports and programs and to radio and television talk shows that reflect definite biases.

If objectivity does build audiences, this is an incidental outcome. It is unlikely that critics could produce a single objective journalist who could say he or she ever heard an editor, publisher, or station manager say it is important to be objective because objectivity increases audience share or to ignore the views of marginalized groups because reporting their opinions might mean a loss of audience. It is likely that dedicated news consumers lose confidence in media that abandon objectivity, but that loss of confidence does not necessarily translate into a loss of audience.

Objectivity Is Used to Render Media Power Invisible

Friedman (1998) suggested that the "ideology of objectivity" is designed to make invisible the media's power to direct and to reinforce cultural standards and public opinion. "Objectivity asks us to think of the media not as an independent influence on American life, but only the transparent transmitter of already-existing information" (326).

Comment. It may be true that objective journalism obscures the media's power to influence culture and public opinion, although that assertion clearly is questionable, and it assumes mass audiences are composed of exceptionally dim bulbs. If the statement is true, however, this is another incidental result of objective journalism. It is unlikely that any objective journalist uses objectivity as a ruse to obscure the media's power. Further, one must assume that journalists are not particularly bright if their goal is to obscure media power; otherwise, why would they air and publish editorials or commentaries—or "Doonesbury," for that matter?

Alternatives to Objectivity

Critics have tried for decades to redefine journalism to resolve one or more of the problems that they attribute to the objective approach. Three current and widely discussed alternatives are existential journalism, standpoint epistemology, and public journalism, which have weaknesses of their own, but which contain philosophical constructs one can use to clarify and to improve the objective approach.

Existential Journalism

Existential journalism is difficult to define because existentialism is so complex and can manifest itself in so many ways (e.g., it can be moderate or extreme), as Merrill (1996) noted. In general, moderate existential journalism is extremely personal, requiring its practitioner to be independent, creative, passionate, committed, responsible, and subjective. It permits, or even requires, its practitioner to promote the freedom and welfare of others, and to define what *freedom* and *welfare* mean in various social, political, cultural, and economic contexts. According to Merrill, existential journalism "makes no *a priori* assumptions as to the direction the journalism should take.... It is mainly an orientation of being 'true to one's self,' however trite this may sound" (28) rather than to corporate or organizational interests. Stoker (1995) argued that "existential journalism focuses on the journalist as an autonomous moral agent" (12) who must accept moral responsibility and take the "right" or "responsible" actions, as he or she defines them, not the easy, safe, or most profitable actions. In addition, Merrill (1989) suggested that existential journalists "thrust themselves into the social maelstrom, seeking to harmonize their own self-interest with the wider public interest of society" (149). They do not worry about the commercial impact of their work, but about whether they have behaved ethically, have tried to become better journalists, and have promoted freedom and the general welfare.

Practitioners of existential journalism must examine their own subjective reactions to events and issues. "This means that ethical decision making begins with a recognition of one's biases, weaknesses, and background" (Stoker, 1995, 16).

Existential journalism, Merrill (1989) conceded, is subjective, but it does not ignore the objective world: "It is just that the *perception* of this objective world is emphasized, with substantial attention given to the journalist as the creator of the verbal or symbolic world that reflects the real world" (147).

Standpoint Epistemology

Standpoint epistemology originated with the feminist critique of objective scientific inquiry (e.g., Harding, 1991; Hekman, 1997).[5] Feminist standpoint epistemology is viewed as a counterhegemonic discourse that destabilizes hegemonic discourse (Hekman, 1997). "In science, this would mean that the scientists, the scientific communities that generate standards of knowledge, the methods of inquiry, and so on, would be put under the microscope, so to speak, as part of the research. This scrutiny would be as rigorous as that to which the 'objects' of research are subjected" (Durham, 1998, 128).

Standpoint epistemology also can destabilize hegemonic discourse in journalism, a desirable outcome because "journalism, like anthropology, is at best a second- or third-order reconstruction of an event that happened to other people, which brings the validity of the account—its objectivity, or realism, if you will—into question" (Durham, 1998, 130). Reporting should proceed from the perspective of the marginalized groups that are affected by events and issues so that

> the unrecognized weight of the socially dominant "insider" positions would be counterbalanced.... If this starting point is acknowledged and foregrounded, the resulting knowledge becomes less partial

and relativistic than the kind of knowledge that is presented by the journalist/insider as value free. (Durham, 1998, 132)

Journalists must view themselves as outsiders if they are to understand the consequences of their stories for marginalized groups, Durham (1998) suggested, but they must avoid privileging the views of the marginalized as that would produce a different sort of bias. "The trick for the standpoint reporter is to be able to decide on the validity of a knowledge claim regardless of who speaks it, while understanding that who speaks does have a bearing on what is made known" (134).

Public or Civic Journalism

Public journalism allows, or even requires, journalists to participate in social processes.[6] Rosen (1993) suggested that journalism is an appropriate institution to help Americans reconnect to the public life from which they have become disengaged; and Merritt (1995) argued that journalists are inextricably bound up with public life, whether they like it or not or acknowledge it or not, and that "journalism should be—and can be—a primary force in the revitalization of public life" (5).[7]

If journalists are to be vehicles for reconnection, Merritt (1995) said, they must cast aside some of the characteristics of modern journalism, one of which is the assumption that objectivity leads to increased media credibility. This does not mean journalists must start taking sides or privileging particular issues or groups, according to Friedland (1996). Public journalism "begins with a consideration of what will improve the public life, rather than what will make a good story, and it implies a commitment to solving community problems beyond the publication of one story or series" (Voakes, 1999, 759).

Public journalism can accomplish the goals set for it by its advocates in several ways. Public journalists must uncover problems and motivate citizens to seek solutions, but without being led by official policy makers. This "requires journalists not only to listen to and synthesize public commentary but to present independent research on alternative public views, so that citizens can be informed in their public judgment" (Voakes, 1999, 759). Journalists also must monitor closely official responses to various alternatives.

Journalists must help begin and sustain public discussions about community problems, even if that means convening participants. Journalists are in a good position to convene town meetings, for instance, because journalism is one of the few institutions that regularly addresses a wide range of issues across economic, cultural, political, social, and racial lines.

Conclusions

Alternatives to Objectivity

Durham (1998) asserted that objectivity's philosophical underpinnings have been analyzed carefully and rejected. She is wrong. Objectivity has been critiqued, certainly, but rarely with intellectual rigor; indeed, some critiques are intellectually dishonest in that they distort what objective journalism is. Furthermore, the critiques have had little effect. Just as the seasons come and go, so do objections and alternatives to objectivity. Advocacy journalism and the New Journalism of the 1960s and 1970s were relatively recent fads, but they ultimately had little impact on the practice of journalism.

The latest alternatives to objectivity share the fatal weakness that afflicted advocacy journalism and the New Journalism: Critics attempt to redefine journalistic practice to reflect their views of what is "good," and that, for them, means requiring that journalists start with personal agendas (e.g., to improve democracy, to adopt perspectives of marginalized groups, to expand freedom). All favor a "progres-

sive" journalism that requires deliberate ideological intervention.

Although it is difficult to disagree with the advocates of existential and public journalism that improving the community is an admirable goal, the argument becomes problematic as one considers specific cases: For example, whose view about what constitutes "improvement" should prevail? The *Houston Chronicle* embarrassed itself a few years ago with its relentless campaign to ensure that voters would approve funding for a new professional baseball stadium, a project that many in the community claimed would solve a number of urban problems. However, many citizens disagreed that the stadium represented civic improvement, and some suggested the *Chronicle* had not behaved responsibly.

Some proponents of public and existential journalism would argue that the *Chronicle's* unseemly support for the new stadium is not an example of public or existential journalism, but other advocates would argue that the *Chronicle's* campaign is a perfect example of identifying community problems and helping to solve them. The theoretical constructs underlying public and existential journalism cannot be used to resolve the discrepancy, for each proponent can hold a different view and cite the same philosophical constructs for support.

Advocates of standpoint epistemology have the same problem. Who decides when the views of dominant insiders must be counterbalanced by the views of the marginalized? Also, who decides which views of which marginalized groups should be considered first? Some might argue it is appropriate to approach a story about family values from the perspective of gays, for example, but others might argue it is better to approach the story from the perspective of Christian fundamentalists. Ethical standards are meaningless when the primary philosophical constructs can be debated virtually forever and when no clear guidance is available.

Who decides when the views of dominant insiders must be counterbalanced by the views of the marginalized?

Practitioners of these approaches can encounter unanticipated consequences. It is conceivable, for example, that one result of implementing any of the three alternatives is increased hegemony by a society's dominant elites (Switzer, McNamara, and Ryan, 1999). Everything depends on whose definition of *freedom* or *public good* or *approved marginalized group* holds sway.

Another result may be that audiences will have difficulty believing information from journalists who are personally involved. Most Americans recognize that some groups have been marginalized unfairly and that grievances must be addressed. It does not follow, however, that they want to see journalists approach stories from the perspectives of marginalized groups, as advocates of standpoint epistemology argue. They want to know what individuals on important sides of issues are thinking, but balance is not achieved by a journalist who approaches a story from a particular standpoint (whether that of a marginalized group or of a dominant power elite).

Objective journalists do not fret about where their limits are as advocates; how they can help "approved" groups achieve their goals; who decides what is beneficial for society and what is not; or how they can be activists and still retain their credibility, as do advocates of standpoint epistemology and of public and existential journalism. They do not worry because their job is not to persuade or to privilege but to report objectively.

It is ironic that, having trashed the tenets of objectivity, many supporters of standpoint epistemology and of public and existential journalism argue that objectivity is important. Merrill (1989) wrote that the will to be objective is important; objectivity seems to be the foundation for the public journalism described by Charity (1995); and Durham (1998) argued that standpoint epistemology produces "strong" objectivity.

Critics who attack and then embrace objectivity are on slippery intellectual and ethical turf. First, it is illogical on its face to attack and then to embrace a concept, particularly one that the critic has not precisely defined. Second, data reported by Starck and Soloski (1977) contradicted assertions by critics (e.g., Simpson, 1971) that "committed" journalists are able to come closer to truth than are those who try to be objective. In addition, the furor that erupted when many important inaccuracies were reported in Rigoberta Menchu's (1984) book about the lives of Guatemalan Indians suggested that objectivity that is practiced by "interested" or "committed" observers is not terribly successful. Indeed, they are open to the charge that they feign objectivity simply to give credibility to their work.

Implementation Is the Problem

Critics who argue that objectivity is responsible for journalism's failures, documented earlier, are not paying attention. As Pyle (2000) noted, the standards for responsible journalism have declined, and the demand for profit "seems increasingly to overrule the ethical and professional standards of reporters and their editors" (B10).

Fisher (2000) recounted the sordid story of the *Idaho Statesman* in Boise, which allowed Micron Technology officials to review stories about the company before publication. Paul Beebe was a business editor at the Gannett newspaper when he changed a lead about "a complaint by Taiwanese computer chip companies that Micron was dumping chips in Taiwan. That's the same charge Micron lodged earlier against Japanese competitors, one repeated by a number of Idaho politicians" (3F). He was fired after Micron complained.

Such failures cannot be attributed to the search for objectivity. The real problem is that too many journalists refuse to practice objectivity—and for many reasons. First, as Lippmann (1922) noted, many journalists view the sort of science-based objectivity he advocated as rigorous and difficult. It is far easier to argue that objectivity is a myth and then to simply slap one's opinions together to produce a story or to claim that objectivity is nothing more than uncritically reporting what sources on two sides have to say. It is easy to avoid the hard work of objective journalism when the climate of opinion is against objectivity and journalists do not feel obligated to adopt its norms.

Second, too many journalists are ill-prepared, as Kaniss (1991) found in her study of local news in Philadelphia. "As one reporter noted tellingly, journalists choose their profession because of the strength of their verbal skills—writing and interviewing—not because of any quantitative expertise" (5).

Third, many journalists evidently agree with Merrill and Lowenstein (1979), who suggested that objectivity "has become too staid, dull, pallid, and noncommitted for the new generations of audience members being raised in a climate of instant confrontation, dissent, and permissiveness" (214). In short, objectivity does not sell, and so it is not practiced.

Build on Common Ground

Journalists and their critics must abandon the idea that the best journalists are guided by personal agendas, as the proponents of standpoint epistemology and public and existential journalism seem to argue, and endorse a definition of objectivity that reflects the best of all four approaches. By combining the best elements of the four and insisting that professionals use them and professors teach them, some of the valid criticisms outlined earlier can be addressed. Fallows (1997) saw some hope for convergence, at least for public journalism and objectivity: "Beneath the apparent gulf that separates the public-journalism advocates from their elite critics is a broader ground of hopeful consensus" (265).

Proponents of public and existential journalism and of standpoint epistemology should be able to accept the definition of objectivity that is presented here, for it substantially reflects the critiques of and the alternatives to objectivity. For example, journalists who want to be objective must be willing to acknowledge their own biases and to accept that absolute objectivity seldom is achieved, as proponents of all three approaches argue. Further, they should agree to recognize and to give weight to the views of the marginalized and oppressed groups that are affected by their reports, as proponents of standpoint epistemology argue.

Advocates of existential journalism should approve the insistence on the moral responsibility of the individual journalist. It is simply not ethical for the journalist who wishes to be objective to become an amoral observer who refuses to wrestle with difficult ethical and strategic decisions or to shift responsibility for ethical lapses to, say, an employer.

Boosters of public journalism should approve the emphasis on reporting effectively about social, political, cultural, and economic issues, for the best service a news medium can render to its community is to supply fair, balanced, useful, accurate, compelling, impartial, and complete information about substantive problems and issues. Such reporting helps readers, listeners, and viewers understand the context within which news occurs; connects marginalized or alienated individuals to the system; and is the basis for informed decision making.

If proponents of different views can adopt a definition of objectivity that reflects most of their concerns, they may be able to turn their attention to a more important matter: trying to identify and to reform lazy or ideological journalists who have (a) essentially abandoned objectivity and (b) resorted to reporting opinionated, boring, useless, easily obtainable information. Such unethical journalism needs to be eliminated.

Critics would be more helpful if they would pressure journalists and teach potential journalists to adopt the highest standards of objectivity and to ensure that stories are reported in accord with these standards. One useful technique is to monitor the news media to find and publicize instances in which journalists have not performed well. Taking action to force journalists to "behave" could go far toward improving a journalism that has lost its way, that too often privileges dominant groups, that is unfair and lazy, that is too reliant on official sources, and that just does not command much respect.

NOTES

1 For additional critiques see Bennett (1983), Rhodes (1993), Rosen (1993), Schudson (1995), Stoker (1995), Streckfuss (1990), and Tuchman (1972).

2 The definition of *objectivity* is based on the work of several writers, including Dennis (1984); Gauthier (1993); Koertge (1996a); Merrill and Lowenstein (1979); Merton (1973); Nanda (1998); Parsons (1951); Switzer, McNamara, and Ryan (1999); and Tuchman (1972).

3 Declining media credibility has been documented also by the American Society of Newspaper Editors (1985, 1999), the Times Mirror Center (1995), and the Freedom Forum (1998). Furthermore, Izard (1985) found evidence that public confidence in the news media is diminished by journalists who are not objective (i.e., who make up information, present their own opinions in reports, and gather information improperly).

4 The attacks against journalism mirror the attacks against objective, scientific inquiry, attacks that ultimately had an impact on public school, college, and university curricula. When the critics could no longer be ignored, many scientists produced sometimes-devastating counterattacks. See, for example, Bunge (1996), Gross (1998), Koertge (1996b), Nanda (1998), and Sokal and Bricmont (1998).

5 Standpoint epistemology has been discredited in the sciences by, among others, Koertge (1996b), who argued that "*Social construction* or *constructivist* epistemology are trendy terms that, while they signal a certain sympathy towards nouveau ideas, have no precise referent" (266). See also Pinnick (1994) and Koertge (1996a).

6 *Public journalism* also is called *civic journalism* or *public-civic communication*. Although critics and journalists seem to use the terms interchangeably, Parisi (1997) said civic journalism seeks to increase citizen participation in public life by asking local citizens to define news agendas and to use local resources to solve problems. Public journalism also seeks solutions to local problems, "but it gives central narratorial responsibility to journalists themselves as a way of moving beyond community social resources to larger-scale public solutions" (683). See also; Lambeth, Meyer, and Thorson (1998) and Corrigan (1999).

7 For critiques of public journalism, see Barney (1997) and Hardt (1997), who wrote:

> Discussions of public or civic journalism ... appear as a rhetoric of change that claims neither theoretical depth nor historical consciousness, but insists on the need for a new understanding of journalism.... Missing is a critical examination of the underlying assumptions of journalism, professionalism, and freedom of expression, particularly in light of historical, social, political, and economic developments. (103-04)

REFERENCES

Altheide, D.L. (1976). *Creating Reality: How TV News Distorts Events*. Beverly Hills, CA: Sage.

Altschull, J.H. (1984). *Agents of Power: The Role of the News Media in Human Affairs*. New York: Longman.

American Society of Newspaper Editors. (1985). *Newspaper Credibility: Building Reader Trust.* Washington, DC: Author.

American Society of Newspaper Editors. (1999). *Examining our Credibility.* Washington, DC: Author.

Barney, R.D. (1997). "A Dangerous Drift? The Sirens' Call to Collectivism," in J. Black (Ed.), *Mixed News: The Public/Civic/Communitarian Journalism Debate* (72-90). Mahwah, NJ: Lawrence Erlbaum Associates, Inc.

Belluck, P. (1999, February 6). "Death Row Inmate Freed after 16 years: Investigation by Professor, Five Journalism Students Key to Release," *Houston Chronicle*, A3.

Bennett, W.L. (1983). *News: The Politics of Illusion.* New York: Longman.

Brown, J.D., Bybee, C.R, Wearden, S.T., and Straughan, D.M. (1987). "Invisible Power: Newspaper News Sources and the Limits of Diversity," *Journalism Quarterly* Vol. 64: 45-54.

Bunge, M. (1996). "In Praise of Intolerance to Charlatanism in Academia," in P.R Gross, N. Levitt, and M.W. Lewis (Eds.), *The Flight from Science and Reason* (97-115). New York: New York Academy of Sciences.

Charity, A. (1995). *Doing Public Journalism.* New York: Guilford.

Commission on Freedom of the Press. (1947). *A Free and Responsible Press: A General Report on Mass Communication: Newspapers, Radio, Motion Pictures, Magazines, and Books.* Chicago: University of Chicago Press.

Corrigan, D.H. (1999). *The Public Journalism Movement in America: Evangelists in the Newsroom.* Westport, CT: Praeger.

Dennis, E.E. (1984). "Journalistic Objectivity *is* Possible," in E.E. Dennis and J.C. Merrill, *Basic Issues in Mass Communication: A Debate* (111-18). New York: Macmillan.

Durham, M.G. (1998). "On the Relevance of Standpoint Epistemology to the Practice of Journalism: The Case for 'Strong Objectivity,'" *Communication Theory*, Vol. 8: 117-40.

Fallows, J. (1997). *Breaking the News: How the Media Undermine American Democracy.* New York: Vintage.

Fisher, J. (2000, February 13). "A Once-Proud Newspaper Becomes The Micron Statesman," *Lewiston Morning Tribune*, 3F.

Freedom Forum's Media Studies Center. (1998, October 16). "Recent Journalistic Lapses Little Noted by Most Americans, but Skepticism about Media Ethics Runs High." Retrieved December 27, 2000 from the World Wide Web: <http://www.freedomforum.org>.

Friedland, L.A. (1996). "Bringing the News Back Home: Public Journalism and Rebuilding Local Communities," *National Civic Review*, Vol. 85(3): 45-48.

Friedman, T. (1998). "From Heroic Objectivity to the News Stream: The Newseum's Strategies for Relegitimizing Journalism in the Information Age," *Critical Studies in Mass Communication*, Vol. 15: 325-35.

Gauthier, G. (1993). "In Defence of a Supposedly Outdated Notion: The Range of Application of Journalistic Objectivity," *Canadian Journal of Communication*, Vol. 18: 497-505.

Glasser, T. (1984, February). "The Puzzle of Objectivity I: Objectivity Precludes Responsibility," *Quill*, 12-16.

Gross, P.R. (1998). "Evidence-Free Forensics and Enemies of Objectivity," in N. Koertge (Ed.), *A House Built on Sand: Exposing Postmodernist Myths about Science* (99-118). New York: Oxford University Press.

Hackett, R. (1984). "Decline of a Paradigm? Bias and Objectivity in New Media Studies," *Critical Studies in Mass Communication*, Vol. 1: 229-59.

Harding, S. (1991). *Whose Science? Whose Knowledge? Thinking from Women's Lives.* Ithaca, NY: Cornell University Press.

Hardt, H. (1997). "The Quest for Public Journalism: A Review Essay," *Journal of Communication*, Vol. 47(3): 102-09.

Hekman, S. (1997). "Truth and Method: Feminist Standpoint Theory Revisited," *Signs: Journal of Women in Culture and Society*, Vol. 22: 341-65.

Izard, R.S. (1985). "Public Confidence in the News Media," *Journalism Quarterly*, Vol. 62: 247-55.

Johnson, J.W. (1927). *The Autobiography of an Ex-Coloured Man*. New York: Vintage.

Kaniss, P. (1991). *Making Local News*. Chicago: University of Chicago Press.

Koch, T. (1990). *The News as Myth: Fad and Context in Journalism*. New York: Greenwood.

Koertge, N. (1996a). "Feminist Epistemology: Stalking an Un-Dead Horse," in P.R. Gross, N. Levitt, and M.W. Lewis (Eds.), *The Flight from Science and Reason* (413-19). New York: New York Academy of Sciences.

Koertge, N. (1996b). "Wrestling with the Social Constructor," in P.R. Gross, N. Levitt, and M.W. Lewis (Eds.), *The Flight from Science and Reason* (266-73). New York: New York Academy of Sciences.

Lambeth, E.B., Meyer, P.E., and Thorson, E. (1998). *Assessing Public Journalism*. Columbia: University of Missouri Press.

Lippmann, W. (1922). *Public Opinion*. New York: Macmillan.

Longino, H. (1990). *Science as Social Knowledge: Values and Objectivity in Scientific Inquiry*. Princeton, NJ: Princeton University Press.

Menchu, R. (1984). *I, Rigoberta Menchu: An Indian Woman in Guatemala* (E. Burgos Debray, Ed.; A. Wright, Trans.). London: Verso.

Merrill, J.C. (1984). "Journalistic Objectivity is *not* Possible," in E.E. Dennis and J.C. Merrill, *Basic Issues in Mass Communication: A Debate* (104-10). New York: Macmillan.

Merrill, J.C. (1989). *The Dialectic in Journalism: Toward a Responsible Use of Press Freedom*. Baton Rouge: Louisiana State University Press.

Merrill, J.C. (1996). *Existential Journalism*. Ames: Iowa State University Press.

Merrill, J.C., and Lowenstein, R.L. (1979). *Media, Messages, and Men: New Perspectives in Communication* (2nd ed.). New York: Longman.

Merritt, D. (1995). *Public Journalism and Public Life: Why Telling the News is not Enough*. Hillsdale, NJ: Lawrence Erlbaum Associates, Inc.

Merton, R.K. (1973). *The Sociology of Science: Theoretical and Empirical Investigations*. Chicago: University of Chicago Press.

Nanda, M. (1998). "The Epistemic Charity of the Social Constructivist Critics of Science and Why the Third World Should Refuse the Offer," in N. Koertge (Ed.), *A House Built on Sand: Exposing Postmodernist Myths about Science* (286-311). New York: Oxford University Press.

Ognianova, E., and Endersby, J.W. (1996). "Objectivity Revisited: A Spatial Model of Political Ideology and Mass Communication," *Journalism & Mass Communication Monographs*, 159.

Parisi, P. (1997). "Toward a 'Philosophy of Framing': News Narratives for Public Journalism," *Journalism & Mass Communication Quarterly*, Vol. 74: 673-86.

Parsons, T. (1951). *The Social System*. New York: Free Press.

Pearson, H. (2000, February 29). "Enough of Al Sharpton's Masquerading as Leader," *Houston Chronicle*, A21.

Pinnick, C.L. (1994). "Feminist Epistemology: Implications for Philosophy of Science," *Philosophy of Science*, Vol. 61: 646-57.

Pyle, C.H. (2000, January 7). "Irresponsible Journalists are Jeopardizing Serious Investigations by the Press," *Chronicle of Higher Education*, B9-10.

Rachlin, A. (1988). *News as Hegemonic Reality: American Political Culture and the Framing of News Accounts*. New York: Praeger.

Rhodes, J. (1993). "The Visibility of Race and Media History," *Critical Studies in Mass Communication*, Vol. 10: 184-90.

Rosen, J. (1993). "Beyond Objectivity: It is a Myth, an Important One, but Often Crippling and it Needs to be Replaced with a More Inspiring Concept," *Nieman Reports*, Vol. 47(4): 48-53.

Schudson, M. (1995). *The Power of News*. Cambridge, MA: Harvard University Press.

Shoemaker, P.J., and Reese, S.D. (1991). *Mediating the Message: Theories of Influences on Mass Media Content*. New York: Longman.

Simpson, L. (1971, May-June). "Advocacy Reporting: Young Journalist Challenges System," *Grassroots Editor*, 12, 15.

Smith, A. (1980, May-June). "Is Objectivity Obsolete? Journalists Lost their Innocence in the Seventies—and Gained New Voices for the Eighties," *Columbia Journalism Review*, 61-65.

Sokal, A., and Bricmont, J. (1998). *Fashionable Nonsense: Postmodern Intellectuals' Abuse of Science*. New York: Picador USA.

Starck, K., and Soloski, J. (1977). "Effect of Reporter Predisposition in Covering Controversial Story," *Journalism Quarterly*, Vol. 55: 120-25.

Stoker, K. (1995). "Existential Objectivity: Freeing Journalists to be Ethical," *Journal of Mass Media Ethics*, Vol. 10: 5-22.

Streckfuss, R. (1990). "Objectivity in Journalism: A Search and a Reassessment," *Journalism Quarterly*, Vol. 67: 973-83.

Switzer, L., McNamara, J., and Ryan, M. (1999). "Critical-Cultural Studies in Research and Instruction," *Journalism & Mass Communication Educator*, Vol. 54(3): 23-42.

Times Mirror Center for the People and the Press. (1995). *The People, the Press, and their Leaders*. Washington, DC.

Tuchman, G. (1972). "Objectivity as Strategic Ritual: An Examination of Newsmen's Notions of Objectivity," *American Journal of Sociology*, Vol. 77: 660-79.

Voakes, P.S. (1999). "Civic Duties: Newspaper Journalists' Views on Public Journalism," *Journalism & Mass Communication Quarterly*, Vol. 76: 756-74.

White, J.E. (2000, March 6). "Big Al's Finest Hour: Sharpton Emerges as the Voice of Black Outrage," *Time*, 28.

◆ ◆ ◆ ◆ ◆

AARON QUINN

Accepting Manipulation or Manipulating What's Acceptable?

1. Introduction

Public trust in journalism is waning with each day that passes, but the press' role as watchdog is ever more necessary for a thriving democracy. One contribution to this decline in public trust is confusion about photographic integrity. Often for good reason, many people don't believe the images they see in print news are accurate and honest reflections of news events. The *New York Times'* photography critic, Andy Grundberg, predicted a tenuous prospect for documentary photography: "In the future, readers of newspapers and magazines will probably view news pictures more as illustrations than as reportage, since they can no longer distinguish between a genuine image and one that has been manipulated."[1] By determining proper ethical actions in photo manipulation, part of which is determining if journalists ought to rely on high-tech manipulations, we will establish guidelines that, if adopted, should rejuvenate some public trust in digital images and hence improve journalism's public standing in general.

There are two broad questions to be answered in this paper in regard to photographs and computers: (1) What are the proper ethical guidelines for post-shoot photo manipulations (manipulations made after the photo has been taken)? (2) How much should we rely on intra-camera exposure calculations instead of post-shoot manipulations? First, the initial question is essential because through analysis it illustrates ethical problems related to post-shoot manipulation, such as loss of integrity (in the form of losing the trust of readers/viewers), lack of consistency (which leads to diminished accuracy), and forsaking the photojournalistic duty of truthtelling, if for no other reason than that truthtelling is a theoretical principle of journalism that should not be sidestepped. Second, the final question asks us to consider ethical issues arising from giving the power of judgment to a machine (inside the camera) instead of the human mind in certain circumstances. That carries with it similar concerns with integrity, consistency, and truthtelling.

2. Making Choices

Before a news photographer lifts the camera to her eye she has the obligation to make choices—what lens to use, what settings best match the available light, and how close or far to stand from a subject to determine where the borders of the photo will be in terms of composition, among other considerations. Each of these choices, when put into action, is a form of manipulation (Elliot, Lester, 2003). Manipulation includes a neutral form that involves skilful use of the hands or a device. However, a second form of manipulation involves a deceptive element for the sake of personal or institutional gain. The former type of manipulation can be a matter of routine colour correction—changing colour in an image to correct unintended technical flaws—but the second type—the pejorative form—changes reality for the sake of news sensationalism or aesthetics.

2.1 Threading Ethical Theory

Journalists exist, in theory, to enhance the public good by providing accurate information that people can use to make decisions about public life. And all three of the main ethical doctrines—consequentialism, deontology, and virtue theory—can help photojournalists and news audiences better understand issues surrounding image manipulation and the way it affects people's ability to make those decisions. For example, utilitarianism—a form of consequentialism—can effectively help guide the practise of ethically acceptable photo manipulation in some cases, as maximising news value to the greatest number is often an ethically desirable end. One way of maximising news value, for example, is to maximise journalistic truth[2] and accuracy in dealing with photo manipulation. For without truth and accuracy, journalism is without moral grounding and credibility, therefore damaging one's ability to trust the information he or she receives from a news source.

Journalism professionals and the public also benefit from implementing carefully chosen virtues—such as integrity, accuracy, and truthtelling—because virtues help guide reporters and editors through the many less-than-obvious decision processes they confront. Virtues often complement or tactfully replace utilitarianism's agent-neutral status (considers all people equal) in decision making, primarily in dealing with important individual roles and actions, which often needs agent-relative (specific characteristics relevant to an individual) attention, left aside by consequentialism and deontology (Oakley, Cocking, 2001).

Finally, the third major ethical doctrine—deontology—is also worth inculcating into the photojournalistic psyche. By instilling Kant's Categorical Imperative, the journalistic duties of being accurate and telling the truth are grounded in what Kant refers to as a moral law—the action that a fully rational person would choose without question, regardless of its possible or actual consequences.

2.2 Categories of Image Manipulation

As mentioned earlier, we must consider what manipulations occur during the shoot at a news event, but also what happens to images in post-shoot manipulations. Manipulations that occur during the shoot include the manipulation of various camera settings that control the way the camera measures light, measures exposure, and frames an image. Post-shoot conduct, on the other hand, is the most commonly explored aspect of photo manipulation because it is the stage that presents the most technical challenges and therefore the most moral problems. Post-shoot manipulation involves digital "touch-ups" that can be ethical or unethical depending on whether the manipulations are deceptive, untruthful, or misleading.

Although unethical manipulations started with darkroom photography, and is more than a century old, the need for further exploration is evident because of the continuing decline in public trust in media, which is in part related to poor photojournalistic practise (Tompkins, 2002). Many scholars and journalists believe digital manipulation practises, both positive and negative, increased with new technology, because high-tech tools make manipulation faster (Lowrey, 1998).

3. Journalism Values and Virtues

However, to make determinations on good and bad professional practise, one must first refer to sound moral reasoning. Within journalism, professional ethics codes and rules of conduct have long been available but in some cases, poorly conveyed and unenforced. Therefore, developing professional standards and enforcing them is an important start in creating an ideal environment in news photography. Because the newsgathering processes of photojournalists and text reporters are so similar, they share the same general set of values, which are essentially journalistic virtues,[3] as they all have qualities that closely correspond to traditional epistemological virtues—virtues related to knowledge—and can be treated as such for guiding morally defensible behaviour. In a succinct summary of journalism values, Fred Mann (1998) offers photojournalism a handful of what can be considered journalistic virtues to guide morally good actions. To the right of Mann's suggested values are traditional virtues (both Cardinal and epistemic) to which these values correspond, showing journalism's natural theoretical identification with virtue theory:

- Balance/Fairness—Justice
- Credibility—Integrity
- Accuracy/Authenticity—Honesty/truthtelling
- News Judgment—Prudence

There are a number of interrelationships among these well-chosen values that we will now refer to as journalistic virtues. In fact, it is traditional in philosophy to consider an agent (in this case the agent is a journalist) a virtuous person only if he inculcates all of the virtues, not just one or a few where it is convenient. Each virtue does hold great importance, however, and single virtues can dominate specific considerations, and even compete with one another for prominence. The key factor in avoiding virtue abuse is to abstain from using a virtue out of convenience. For example, it would not be virtuous in most situations to claim that lying (violating the virtue of truthfulness) to obtain information or documents is acceptable because it is prudent in that it yields a desirable and instrumental end (using the virtue of prudence). Although lying may be instrumentally prudent in many situations, it should not dominate the virtues of honesty, integrity, and ultimately, credibility, when it is more morally damaging than progressive. A major presupposition to virtue theory is that humans possess the ability to reason, and it is reason that allows one to be virtuous by balancing virtues in difficult circumstances.

Now that we have established a description for using virtues, we must further explore Mann's journalism virtues for a better understanding of how they relate to philosophy and how they will be used in photojournalism. The balance/fairness journalism virtues relate closely to the traditional virtue of justice. Although justice has wide meaning and has received countless hours of conceptual analysis, we will consider justice a standard by which one makes decisions that are based on equity and equality. Therefore, balance and fairness are seamlessly analogous to justice. When photojournalists consider how to approach a story, capture images and manipulate images after a news event, they are required to consider the balance of the images that are used based on fair and equal representation of information, opinions, and demographics, among other factors.

The journalistic value of credibility is the most direct relative to the epistemological virtue of integrity, and is closely related to the sacred journalistic notion of objectivity.[4] Without an attempt by the photojournalist to be impartial to the news as an ideal objective journalist would, the visual newsgathering process becomes tainted with unknown bias and prejudice, which are symptoms of journalistic vice and renders the information passed onto the public either useless, tainted, or ambiguous.

Accuracy and authenticity are also seminal journalism values in regard to photo manipulation; they correspond closely to the traditional virtue of truthtelling. Since the goal of the photojournalist is, with obvious technical and philosophical limitations, to re-create reality, being accurate in terms of all of the technical (composition, light, shadows) and idealistic components (no posing subjects; reducing imposition on news event) is essential. But whenever one mentions accuracy as it relates to photo-

journalism, one ought not to mean exact reality, but an effort toward precision, conceding only to insurmountable technical limitations that photography and visual perception present.

Finally, news judgment is one of the most sensitive and worrisome areas in photojournalism because it is subject to the interpretation of the individual and is usually inconsistent in the way it is applied. However, this is an opportunity for well-trained photojournalists to use professional judgment to make the best of an imperfect process, which is a natural complement to the traditional virtue of prudence. News judgment in photojournalism involves making choices of content and context as to what appears in an image. Among nearly countless content and context considerations is: storytelling, maximising visual information, balancing representation of viewpoints, avoiding unfair juxtapositions, etc. Therefore, prudence, when it relates to photojournalism, is about making tough choices when there may be more than one good choice, or making a good choice when there are few good choices available. Nevertheless, photographers have a myriad of decisions to consider as they approach news assignments, and their prudent judgment affects the veracity and dynamics of the news content, which then affects the audience's ability to make good choices about public life. And so the dominoes fall.

This list of ethical essentials is not meant to be exhaustive, but certainly includes some of the most prominent and necessary virtues about which journalists should be aware. Additionally, these pairings of virtues and values are not as limited to those that were shown before. Essentially, the journalistic virtues listed by Mann can be paired with many or all traditional virtues in some cases, as each of the journalistic virtues are wide-ranging in their complement to traditional virtues. The pairings were made merely to illustrate the close relationships between journalistic values and traditional philosophical virtues.

4. Common Practises and Ethical Challenges

The aforementioned virtues are more than just theoretical tokens for academics and pretentious news managers to spout for posterity. They are meant to walk side by side with professionals on the streets and sit beside them in the digital laboratory. Therefore, we must explore the real areas of photojournalism that have the most ethical eggshells upon which we must walk. The photojournalistic practises that cause most ethical problems in terms of digital manipulation include: colour balancing, cropping, and the dodge-and-burn techniques. Colour balancing requires rendering a match (or the closest thing to a match) in colours in an image to that of the scene that was photographed. Colour balance commonly involves consistently correcting technical flaws (acceptable) and making aesthetic improvements (theoretically unacceptable). Cropping involves reducing an image from its outer edges inward to increase the impact of a prominent item or subject close to the centre of the image. Finally, the dodge-and-burn technique involves using digital computing tools, such as Adobe Photoshop software, to brighten or darken selected parts of a photograph.

Each of the three aforementioned practises has ethical implications when the process damages an image's truthtelling faculty, when it reduces integrity, when it causes or facilitates injustice, and/or when it damages the photojournalist's, publication's, or profession's credibility. As we will see, each practise can be considered unethical under some circumstances, sometimes under most circumstances.

4.1 Colour Correction

Colour balancing—making the colours in an image the most realistic colour quality—is often thought an innocuous task that has little or no ethical difficulty. However, in times that require the strictest ethical behaviour from news professionals because of their reputation for impropriety, they must abide carefully by honest and accurate practises. Therefore, we'll explore how the aforementioned virtues are best for the task of creating acceptable guidelines for colour balancing both during and after the photo shoot.

In the camera: The most widely used digital camera in the photojournalism industry as of the commencement of this paper, the Nikon D1, is well known for a few technical flaws, one of which is an ugly yellow haze that covers every image it records. No matter what camera lighting settings are adjusted for the various basic lighting scenarios (daylight, outdoor-cloudy, fluorescent, incandescent, tungsten, etc), the images always appear with this yellow scum—this scum, according to the naked eye, does not exist in reality and therefore must be removed. This is one situation in which Adobe Photoshop digital imaging software—the industry standard—is a saviour. It allows for colour corrections that bring an image to its fullest realisation of realism.

Outside of the camera: On the flip side, this function can be easily abused. For example, it is not uncommon for photographers to "warm" or "cool" photographs in the process of making a legitimate colour correction. Warming involves artificially infusing reds, yellows, or a combination thereof for aesthetics, which is analogous to someone wearing make-up—possibly pretty, but unnatural. Cooling involves artificially infusing shades of blue, and is popular for cold weather photos or for enhancing already existing blue and green colours. The mere act of legitimate colour correction often tempts photographers to make aesthetic enhancements that go beyond acceptable adjustments used to re-create reality, thus violating accuracy and integrity, which leads to a loss of credibility.

One possible—although imperfect—solution to this problem is to leave the colour balance and exposure work to the camera, except in the rare circumstances where cameras are known to fail—photographers are well aware of these situations through basic photography training. Although cameras have some small weaknesses in judging colour, the advantage they have is consistency in their errors, whereas photographers are inconsistent. Cameras use internal computers to judge colour, brightness, contrast, and a host of other things. Although these computers are not perfect in their colour rendering, they create a consistent and reliable measuring tool, whereas people do not have that consistency, and produce results ranging from near perfect to off base. Since every photojournalist uses a camera and most photojournalists are using the same camera model, it is feasible to let the camera make the judgment and avoid further colour manipulation at the office—especially since modern intra-camera computers are so accurate.

But there are exceptions. One exception is the aforementioned technical flaw in the Nikon D1 camera. It is acceptable to eliminate the yellow scum it records to its images, because it is a measurable inaccuracy that can be systematically and consistently eliminated from an image. Any mathematically measurable flaws (flaws in accuracy, not aesthetics) that can be repeatedly identified and eliminated with near-exactness, qualify as acceptable manipulations.

Another possible exception, for example, is if a head of state dies shortly after a flawed photo is captured. In this case, one must consider manipulating the colour balance to properly convey the subject's illness (in the case that camera flaw obscures the illness) because the news value outweighs other ethical considerations. This is an area, in philosophical terms, where virtues can help, for example, they help to sort through a utilitarian-deontological conundrum. On the one hand, one might say it is wrong to colour correct in an inconsistent way, as this situation would demand, because it would violate the Kantian-like maxim that might altogether decry manipulation or at least severely limit it to when it is necessary for the sake of truthtelling. On the other hand, utilitarians would ask whether it would create more pleasure for more people if news value (in the form of allowing imperfect manipulation) were given prominence over more consistent manipulation (as Kant demands). Historically, the utilitarians would win, because the news value overrides the conventional standard; the news is just too important to risk a bad image. Too much information—truth—could be lost, and in such an extreme circumstance as a presidential death, this would be too damaging.

4.2 Cropping

Cropping—reducing the size of an image by reducing its borders—can be an effective tool for creating visual impact. However, it can also cause a loss of vital visual information if it isn't executed carefully. The best advice: Crop only when you can increase the news value of an image. If there were no risk in shooting pictures with the intention of cropping, then photographers would shoot all of their images "loose," and set their cameras to record large, high-resolution files and then crop to their heart's delight. Modern technology allows for this because one can shoot massive image files, from which small fractions can be cropped, and the cropped image can then be enlarged while maintaining remarkable resolution. But by maximising news value—a utilitarianism goal—we can assure the most news value in an image with few ethical risks.

Because of problems that can develop from cropping, photographers are trusted to use their judgment on how to compose a newsworthy photograph rather than worry about subsequent alterations. But there is often relevant visual data in the secondary regions of an image that a photographer might overlook and eliminate in the cropping process if he isn't careful. So great care must be taken before a crop—and a loss of important information—is made. Careful cropping, then, will maximise the amount of visual information and impact an image can provide.

4.3 Dodge and Burn

One could go as far as to call a dodge or burn—artificially lightening or darkening regions in an image—a lie in almost all situations, so there is little question over what place this process ought to have in photojournalism: none. A lie is a violation of truth, and truth is a seminal journalistic virtue. But for the sake of choosing an ethical doctrine within which to analyse the dodge and burn, deontology's Categorical Imperative will be ideal: Many academics and professionals believe journalists should always tell the truth. Kant would likely say the same as truth would seemingly always be the dominant maxim for a journalist. So to break down how the dodge and burn is in violation of truth—and Kant's imperative—we'll use Sissela Bok's (1989) definition of a lie: "... any intentionally deceptive message which is stated" (Bok, 1989, 14).

Bok indicates that speaking or writing usually executes "stating." Since digital technology has its own form of statement, which is initiated by keystrokes and mouse-clicks, it requires a separate semantic representation. Essentially, the act of manipulating a dodge and burn—running a mouse cursor over a region of a photo—can be likened to a speaker who would manipulate a phrase in her mind before speaking. Therefore, the published word can be analogous to speech in regard to "stating."

Essentially, the photographer knows this manipulation technique is used to give artificial prominence to a subject, or a particular section of the photograph. Therefore, we have established a form of deception—the photojournalist knows the image is tainted either by the intention of making an aesthetic improvement, by attempting to assist understanding by highlighting central visual details, or simply in the doomed but well-intended attempt to correct perceived imperfections. All but the latter are obvious forms of deception and even the latter is indirectly deceiving, regardless if it is intended for good purposes.

Having established deception, now we must establish intent in order to satisfy Bok's definition of lying. As mentioned before, photojournalists know their altered photographs are intended for an audience. They also know their altered photographs are inaccurate because (1) they are altered for impact/understanding (2) aesthetics and/or (3) re-creating reality. Now, to prove that photojournalists often intend to deceive, one only needs to acknowledge the methods of manipulation with the fact that photojournalists know readers expect to have truth, accuracy, and reality—and are receiving something from a photojournalist that a photojournalist knows to be otherwise, despite other possible outcomes. This conscious knowledge of potential inaccuracy, therefore, arguably qualifies as intent in the form of a calculated risk.

Although this is a secondary notion of intent—meaning that photographers' primary intentions are not necessarily to deceive—there are few, if any, photojournalists or photo editors who don't know that their actions are likely to deceive at least some of the time (Irby, 2003). Therefore, although it may not be a robust intention to deceive readers, it is, for them, a calculated risk, which qualifies as intent, because of their knowledge that false information will reach the audience and it could have been prevented. As Kant's Categorical Imperative clearly implies, being truthful is a universal journalistic law, and this is undoubtedly an untruth.

5. Conclusions

Photojournalism is a profession that, as we have seen, invites pluralistic ethics. That is, we have shown that photojournalism can make effective use of multiple doctrines of ethical theory—deontology, consequentialism, and teleology (virtue theory)—to determine right ethical actions. Moreover, this pluralistic approach helps us cope with the multifaceted issues that arise from ever-increasing use of technology in media.

Although technology has not brought wholesale change to photojournalism manipulation, as similar manipulation existed 100 years ago, it has made manipulation easier and more pervasive, perhaps leading to a normalisation of questionable manipulation practises. This paper has questioned the ethical meaning of this ever-increasing normalisation. It has shown that no matter what advances come from technology, virtue, consequentialism, and deontology help weed out ethical problems. In virtue theory, truth, integrity, justice, and prudence have remained the standard for good professional decisions. In deontology, we know that whether one uses computers or dark rooms to make publishable images, telling the truth is still the journalistic imperative for imaging decisions. Finally, in a consequentialistic framework, we know that no matter what tools are used to bring an image to press or broadcast, photojournalists ought to cater to the public and serve its best interests. That interest is often, by default, the interest of the majority—the greatest happiness for the greatest number—as Jeremy Bentham, the famous utilitarian, said.

But no matter what ethical theories one uses to justify actions, because circumstances may dictate choice, it is crucial to consider all of the ethical options one has at one's disposal. Photojournalism, like and unlike other professions, affects the thoughts of millions of people every day. Without taking great care in the way photojournalists practise, they can knowingly or unwittingly contribute to growing social ailments—and technology is not solely to blame.

NOTES

1 Andy Grundberg, "Ask It No Questions: The Camera Can Lie," *The New York Times*, August 12, 1990, Sec. 2, 1.

2 Truth in journalism is often known as "journalistic truth" because information journalists provide is intended to be bits of truth about something, although it is usually impossible to get the "whole truth." Merrill, John (1997): *Journalism Ethics*. New York, St. Martin's Press, 105-08.

3 Virtue ethics enhance what Aristotle called the "good life" by adhering to sets of intrinsically good values (virtues) guided by "regulative ideals" that promote excellence in the way the virtues are interpreted. Oakley, J., Cocking, D. (2001): *Virtue Ethics and Professional Roles*. Cambridge, UK, Cambridge University Press, 25-38.

4 Objectivity in journalism is part truly objective in that journalists gather objective facts, but also more broadly theoretical in that the journalists themselves make an effort to eliminate personal bias and prejudice in newsgathering and in context, although those vices are impossible to eliminate altogether.

REFERENCES

Bok, S. (1989). *Lying: Moral Choice in Public and Private Life*. New York: Random House, 13.

Elliot, D., Lester, P. (2003). "Manipulation: A Word We Love to Hate," *News Photographer*, August 2003.

Grundberg, A. (1990). "Ask It No Questions: The Camera Can Lie," *The New York Times*, 12 August, 1990, Sec. 2, 1.

Irby, K. (2003). "A Photojournalistic Confession," *Poynter Institute for Media Studies Online*. [Found in the archives of the Poynter Institute for Media Studies' Web site on 8 August, 2003].

Mann, F. (1998). "Online Ethics," *Poynter Institute for Media Studies Online*. Posted 29 March, 1998. [Found 10 September, 2003].

Merrill, J. (1997). *Journalism Ethics*. New York, St. Martin's Press, 105-08.

Lowrey, W. (1998). "Photo Manipulation in the 1920s and 1990s," Paper presented to AEJMC conference and published in AEJMC online journal in October 1998.

Oakley, J., Cocking, D. (2001). *Virtue Ethics and Professional Roles*. Cambridge, UK, Cambridge University Press, 33-38.

Tompkins, A. (2002). "Sliding Sounds, Altered Images," *Poynter Institute for Media Ethics Online*. Posted 28 June, 2002. [Found: 19 November, 2003, <http://www.poynter.org/content/content_view.asp?id=3380>].

PRIVACY

SAMUEL P. WINCH[1]

Moral Justifications for Privacy and Intimacy

Privacy is a basic moral and social right in a democratic society, yet it has always been a troublesome concept for journalists. This is a tension that comes naturally, because while journalists actively seek out information about newsworthy individuals, Americans as a whole become alarmed when information about them—such as mothers' maiden names and social security numbers—is made public.

Perhaps the best way to frame the issue is to attempt to answer the question, "What is the right way for journalists to deal with concern for privacy?" This is a big question, related to the even bigger question posed by Socrates: "What is the right way to live?" (Plato, 340 BC/1941, 37). Such big questions have even bigger answers. Rather than thinking of the right to privacy as a roadblock (or "red-light ethic") to journalism, I hope that journalists will—after examining the roots of the concept—think of concern for privacy as an opportunity to be responsible and ethical.

We need to consider the basic moral principles regarding privacy and why it is important. From these foundational principles we can begin to understand how journalists should deal with concerns about privacy.

This article has two parts. In the first, I examine the basic moral arguments used to justify a right to privacy, tracing the history of the concept of privacy to the present day. I show how our commonsense conceptions of privacy do not flow seamlessly from historical conceptions of privacy. It turns out that some of our notions of privacy are rather new. In the second part, I critique some of the current thinking about privacy and public officials and argue for protection of intimate privacy for all.

Part I. Moral Justifications of Privacy

This effort to discover and examine the philosophical roots of privacy is intended to help journalists and others involved in mass communication understand why and how the conception of privacy has evolved from several different interrelated concepts, such as natural rights, liberty, property, individuality, intimacy, secrecy, autonomy, human dignity, and the concept of distinct public and private "spheres" of life. I try to show why certain philosophical justifications for privacy are stronger and more persuasive than others.

Schoeman (1984) said the arguments to morally justify the right to privacy have generally followed two strategies: (a) Respect for privacy is related to the more general theme of respect for human dignity, appealing to conditions such as moral integrity, individuality, consciousness of oneself with a distinct point of view and moral character; and (b) respect for privacy is related to "our understanding of ourselves as social beings with varying kinds of relationships," each important to a meaningful life

(8). Both arguments use the word *respect*, suggesting that privacy is conceived as a duty to others—it is not something you can give yourself.

All attempts to justify the existence of a right to privacy revolve around the "fact" that the desire for privacy is an innate aspect of human nature. For that reason, many have found that the most productive and credible way of justifying privacy is as a natural right aspect of human dignity.

Natural Rights and Property

Natural rights theories stress the importance of the concept that people are individual autonomous beings. Some philosophers argue that because we all have souls, or inviolable private sides that only we can control, we should have an express right to privacy. In other words, the argument goes, we are autonomous agents by nature so we should have a right to stay that way. Autonomy is usually understood as the right to be "self-legislating."

Francis Eterovich (1972) said "the theory of natural law was intended to lay the foundations of moral and socio-political thinking. It meant that the standard of moral and political conduct was to be discovered in man's very nature" (11). Thus, natural rights theories were developed to morally justify human behavior by looking at the nature of human beings.

Debates about natural rights from the fourteenth to the seventeenth centuries centered on questions of whether people had the right to liberty, which was equated with self-ownership, and whether they had the right to own property. Before the 1320s, church philosophers said that people should follow the example of the poverty of the Apostles and not own property. This was a particularly important question for the Franciscan monks, because they had considerable wealth in their holdings. In 1329, Pope John XXII enumerated a full natural rights theory when he wrote that "God's dominium over the earth was conceptually the same as man's dominium over his possessions" (Tuck, 1979, 22). So, in other words, humans should consider it a natural right to hold property in their possessions just as God holds property in the earth.

Ironically, the argument that people had the right to self-ownership was used as a moral defense by the Portuguese for the institution of slavery (Tuck, 1979). The argument went like this; If you own yourself, then you are entitled to sell yourself into slavery. Luis de Molina (as cited in Tuck, 1979), a Jesuit scholar, argued that no one can know if the Black slaves taken from Africa voluntarily sold themselves into slavery. He said that they may have voluntarily chosen slavery in return for a string of beads or perhaps for their life.

All rights theories are based on the idea of ownership; in particular, a person owns the liberty of his or her self. John Locke (1690/1924) argued that humans own the food they subsist on and the labor they produce, and no one can have a claim on them, because "[E]very man has a 'property' in his own 'person.' This nobody has any right to but himself" (129). Locke said that all the person becomes, and all he produces, become part of the person's property. A person's life, liberty, and estate are his own private property, according to Locke, whose entire conception of a just government rested on the idea that people must be allowed to own property, and that government exists in order to protect this ownership (Altschull, 1990).

Human nature and the earth provided natural rights advocates with sociological and historical evidence that helped legitimate their principles, but not the sort of philosophical "evidence" desired. For that reason, natural rights theories have come under heavy criticism. MacIntyre (1984), for instance, said natural rights—as well as all other theories of rights—are contemporary moral fictions that are not mentioned in any texts written in "Hebrew, Greek, Latin, or Arabic, classical or medieval, before about 1400, let alone in Old English, or in Japanese even as late as the mid-nineteenth century." And "every attempt to give good reasons for believing that there are such rights has failed" (69). MacIntyre said rights advocates like Locke (1690/1924) argued that natural rights are self-evident truths, but nothing can be self-evident in a comprehensive moral theory. Appeals to self-evidence are the sign of flimsy evidence.

Dworkin (1977), a modern proponent of rights, said that just because rights cannot be proven does not mean they do not exist. For Dworkin and many others, rights are a good idea in search of a justification. Natural rights theory has all but vanished from modern philosophical discussion simply because philosophers have been unable to prove that people have a right to anything. The exception is modern Roman Catholic ethics premised on the idea of human rights, which are, in essence, natural rights.

Public/Private Spheres of Life

Beginning in the Middle Ages and continuing into modern times, political philosophers have tried to delineate between public and private spheres of life primarily as a way to limit state power and to legitimate the concept of private property.

The different motivations for a justification of privacy have produced many different ways of arguing the case for privacy—or arguing against it.

According to Schoeman (1984), those arguing against the existence of a specific right to privacy have generally focused on two arguments: (a) The interests that privacy protects are not morally distinctive rights—they are enumerated in other rights; and (b) the protection of privacy may be harmful to both the individual and to society, because it makes people psychologically vulnerable and encourages an asocial or antisocial attitude.

Horwitz (1982), however, said the original purpose of natural rights theories was to set limits on state power over property and religious preferences. These types of concerns relate directly to the right to privacy, especially toward providing limitations on state intervention into the private sphere. In other words, rights theories were devised in order to delin-

eate between the public and private spheres of life (Tuck, 1979).

Saxonhouse's (1983) study of the classical Greek conceptions of public and private shows that citizens were motivated to public service because of a reward called *kleos*, which was a type of fame reserved for civic heroes. "Private life could offer no greatness for a Greek, no *kleos*" (363), said Saxonhouse. Most Greeks believed in the idea that service to the *polis*, or city-state, was the highest calling. Saxonhouse said that a common theme in Greek tragedies was that undue concern for individualism or for the family—above that for the *polis*—could spell ruin for society. "Private" is translated as *idion* in Greek. Saxonhouse said, "Within the political context, the use of the word *idion* was largely derogatory, for it referred to that which separates one out from the unity of the community, the humanity of the polis. The modern derivative 'idiot' gives some sense of this" (365). However, Swanson (1992) argued this interpretation of *idion* (which she traces to Hannah Arendt's [1959] classic *The Human Condition*) is faulty. Swanson also contended that Greeks such as Aristotle valued privacy as "essential to the self-sufficiency and happiness of the individual and of the body politic" (7).

Hanson (1970) said two forces pushed for distinctions between public and private. The first was the emergence of city-states and theories of sovereignty in the sixteenth and seventeenth centuries, which led to the idea of a distinctly public realm. Second, as a reaction to the claims of monarchs and, later on, parliaments, of their unrestrained power to make laws, the citizenry were seen to possess some powers. In effect, the emergences of democratic theories—the idea that individuals should have a say in government—helped form the concept of the public sphere of life, which caused people to think of the opposite sphere, the private.

Perhaps as a result of the emergence of democratic theories and the idea that people were not merely subjects of a ruler but should have a say in government, laws developed in England in the late medieval period that provided certain lands could not be claimed by the crown. These became public lands called "commons." Their establishment marked the beginning of a legally recognized public realm and probably contributed to the idea that the subjects of a particular ruler were entitled to certain benefits as citizens (Horwitz, 1982). A bit later in England, the concept of private property also developed, particularly in regard to farming and the ownership of land. For instance, prior to the seventeenth century, most farms in England were operated as community ventures, and were characteristically inefficient. During the seventeenth century, ownership of farmland by individual families proved to be a powerful incentive for more efficient and more profitable production—yet debate in England over the validity and morality of individually held property raged for decades (Appleby, 1978).

In America, the political dimension of the public/private distinction became more delineated with the advent of a market-dominated society. Laissez-faire capitalistic principles stipulated that government should allow transactions to remain unregulated. In other words, business transactions remain private, outside the sphere of publicly regulated activities. The influence of rights advocates in early America is evident in the language of the Bill of Rights and the Declaration of Independence. At the outset, the United States dedicated itself to the proposition that people had certain innate rights: to equality, liberty, and the pursuit of happiness.

Utilitarian Conceptions of Privacy

When people are allowed to do as they please, as long as they do not interfere with others, then they are thought to be free and to enjoy a certain level of autonomy over their lives. John Stuart Mill (1859/1956) wrote about the importance of autonomy and freedom in his book, *On Liberty*. Individuality and personal autonomy were what Mill considered to be the essential ingredients of liberty

and freedom, important to his utilitarian argument for autonomy. It is easy to see how this concern for individuality and autonomy relates to privacy, yet a concrete meaning for privacy is not easily extrapolated from Mill's writings.

The result of the 350-year debate over natural rights was a belief that people have a right to liberty and to own property, and that this right is derived from circumstances in which we find ourselves on this earth. It is a somewhat circular argument, but not much more circular than consequentialist (such as utilitarian) justifications of rights.

T.M. Scanlon (1978) noted that "rights themselves need to be justified somehow" (93), and he said it was utilitarians who saw that the best way to justify rights was to appeal to the good consequences that can result from them. Basically, utilitarianism requires moral agents to choose actions based on the calculated outcomes, always objectively choosing those that will result in the most good for the most people. One of the criticisms of this moral philosophy is that it contains a strong doctrine of "negative responsibility": It requires people to stop negative outcomes caused by others. This, some argue, reduces integrity because it forces people to stop doing the positive, good projects most dear to them whenever something else appears which, if not stopped, will produce a bad consequence (Scheffler, 1982; Smart and Williams, 1973).

To many, it is desirable to find moral justification for human rights outside of the actual benefits that the rights bring. Hard and fast principles seem more legitimate because they seem less flexible and less likely to be twisted through appeals to calculated desired outcomes.

An application of the utilitarian approach to journalistic dilemmas regarding the realm of privacy for public officials shows that it can be a cruel way to deal with individuals, because of its focus on overall outcomes. For instance, a utilitarian conceivably could argue that the maximum good for society will result from exposing all wrongdoing by public officials, and the only way to do this is to investigate the intimate details of all public officials, even innocent ones. Most would consider this unjust because it sacrifices people's privacy for the greater good. The additional problem with the utilitarian approach to this issue is that the calculations of consequences resulting from different scenarios are unreliable because these kinds of goods are qualitatively different, and indirect effects can never be anticipated. Who can say that the overall good is significantly greater when some insignificant fraud or hypocrisy is exposed if privacy is also sacrificed?

Deontological Conceptions of Privacy

Mill and the other utilitarians were not the only ones to argue for the importance of individual autonomy. Immanuel Kant (1785/1990) argued that everyone should be treated as autonomous, rational-willed beings, for only independent rational agents can choose to be ethical. This is Merrill's (1974) argument in *The Imperative of Freedom*: Journalists cannot be moral agents unless they are given the freedom to choose to be that way. Merrill was an optimist, believing that given the freedom to choose, most journalists will choose to be ethical.

Deontologists like Kant (1785/1990) believe morality is evident in the motivations for people's actions and rules, not in the consequences of them. Kant, in his "Kingdom of Ends," also argued that people should be treated as ends in themselves, never as merely a means to an end. Fried (1984), a modern disciple of Kant, wrote that privacy is a "necessary context" for love, friendship, and trust.

For Fried (1984), the right to privacy is justified by being a feature of autonomous life equally available to all people, a principle also expressed by Rawls (1986) in his influential writings on distributive justice. Rawls said that "each person should be given the maximum liberty compatible with a like liberty for all" (189).

Another deontologist, W.D. Ross (1930/1988), offered firm guidance about the kinds of duties and obligations we have as rational moral agents. Ross said we have certain prima facie duties, things which, on their face, we should do. He lists seven: (a) keep promises; (b) seek reparations for wrongful acts; (c) show gratitude when it is due; (d) seek justice; (e) help others; (f) improve ourselves; and (g) avoid harming others. It is easy to see how respect for privacy might come under several of these duties. Unfortunately, however, later in his seminal work, *The Right and the Good*, Ross injected some confusion for those trying to understand his views on privacy, because he contended that knowledge is an intrinsic good. Because privacy is often conceived as the control of knowledge about certain intimate aspects of our lives, knowledge about those private aspects of our lives is not always good, but can actually be evil. Several sociological researchers have argued that ignorance of certain kinds of information is a productive way of thinking about privacy, and that such ignorance serves important social functions (e.g., Lilly and Ball, 1981; Moore and Tumin 1949; Simmel, 1956). In the public/private dimensions of the term, knowledge should be considered an instrumental good, not an intrinsic good.

Other Conceptions of Privacy

Bok (1983) noted that the right of selective disclosure is control over our own secrets—something she said we naturally cherish. Control over the information we consider private is a part of autonomy and dignity, and, according to Bok, is important not only for our sense of self, but for our sanity and survival. Violations of our privacy and autonomy affect us on the inside, in our souls.

Konvitz (1966) said that as soon as a society makes the distinction between the physical body and the soul of a person, it has implied the difference between public and private. The public self, the physical body, is seen by all. The soul is private, is revealed only to those to whom the person wishes to reveal it to. In other words, people have autonomy over their soul. He noted that Socrates felt this way: When Crito asked how he would like to be buried, Socrates said that it did not matter because it was only his body, not him. He did not worry about his death because he knew the sanctity of his inner soul could not be disturbed by the state; it was out of the state's jurisdiction. Reiman (1984) offered a convincing argument that the value of privacy and intimacy is in the context in which private information is shared—in a loving, caring relationship intended to last. He said intimacy and private relationships are not indicated simply by the "swapping of information," because we do this with psychoanalysts, with whom we should feel open, but with whom our relationships should not spread to other activities.

In Summary

I have tried to show how privacy has been argued to be an important part of life yet has been morally justified in a number of conflicting ways. Natural rights theories, full of common sense, rely on the circular argument that it is in our nature to be private, so we deserve privacy. They ultimately offer very little in terms of logical evidence that privacy or any other rights exist, or should exist.

Consequentialist defenses of privacy also seem less than ideal because of internal inconsistency: Although they specify that people should have liberty and autonomy, they allow other indignities to negate these freedoms, such as allowing "greatest good" calculations to justify people being treated only as means to an end.

The deontological argument that autonomy is necessary for moral agency perhaps shows the greatest merit, simply because it is logically sound. How can one be ethical unless one is given the freedom to choose to be ethical? When we accept that autonomy is necessary for a moral life, we, of course, open the door to privacy. Autonomy implies control over one's person, and therefore, one's privacy.

Part II. An Argument for Equal Privacy for All

Once we morally justify a right to privacy, the difficulty is, of course, applying this to real-life journalism situations—complicated situations where there are no clear-cut answers.

The *Journal of Mass Media Ethics* recently devoted two whole issues (Vol. 9, Nos. 3 and 4. 1994) to the subject of privacy, in which several media ethics scholars contributed thoughtful articles on how journalists should deal with privacy concerns. Lou Hodges (1994) and Lee Wilkins (1994), in separate articles, offered guidelines for weighing privacy interests in political journalism. Both of them offered good insights and answers for journalists trying to respect privacy. Unfortunately, they both also ignored how some aspects of privacy should be equal to all—including public officials.

Hodges (1994) proposed the rule: "It is just to violate the privacy of an individual only if information about that individual is of overriding public importance and the public need cannot be met by other means" (203). His rule implied a consequentialist approach—first we must make calculations about public importance. Unfortunately, when journalists start making calculations about public importance, we start getting stories like *USA Today*'s exposé on the late Arthur Ashe's medical condition. Thankfully, Hodges made the important distinction between public interest and public importance. Hodges's rule has other problems, however, because it implies that people do not have an equal claim to intimate privacy. He said people in public office must sacrifice their claim to privacy in order to prevent secret frauds and hypocrisy in public institutions. This is more of a political/functional defense of invasion of privacy than a moral argument. Realistically, we know that public officials and those placing themselves in the spotlight of public attention automatically relinquish some privacy. They do not, however, relinquish the right to be humans deserving dignity.

Lee Wilkins (1994) stated matter-of-factly that the "character" of public officials "is appropriately the subject of news reports" (157) even though she recited a great body of evidence that seems to show that the character flaws of some of our country's greatest leaders—such as George Washington, Thomas Jefferson, and Franklin D. Roosevelt—would in today's media climate exclude them from consideration as leaders. The link between "character" (whatever that means) and the ability to lead or govern has never been established. The term "character" today often seems to focus on interpersonal relationships of an intimate nature. Journalists who continue to argue that the way a person handles intimate relationships says a lot about how they would govern are ignoring historical evidence to the contrary. A recent PHS documentary about the Civil War reported that Abraham Lincoln suffered from clinical depression, that his wife was certifiably insane, and that she beat him. This is interesting, intimate stuff, but it does not tell us whether Lincoln would be a good president. Many feel that he was our greatest president, regardless of his intimate private life.

I believe the focus on the intimate private lives and interpersonal relationships of politicians is unjust. To achieve justice in privacy, we need to distinguish between intimate and nonintimate kinds of private information. When we discuss the "character" of politicians, we should be looking at nonintimate aspects of their private lives such as finances and taxes. Politicians' business connections, finances, and tax returns—that is, whether they are crooks—are things that can be justified as being within the area of privacy disclosure expected of public officials, but not for private citizens.

Does it matter whether they are sexually abnormal, or even whether they are adulterers? When journalists consider whether they are invading a person's privacy they need to realize that certain areas of life should always be kept private—such as family, home, bodily functions, and as Reiman (1984), and

Inness (1992) pointed out, aspects of relationships involving intimacy, love, and caring.

In the interest of justice and equality, everyone, including public officials, deserves a measure of intimate privacy, and therefore I propose a maxim of privacy based on Rawls's (1986) principle of justice in a well-ordered society: Each person has an equal right to the most extensive scheme of intimate privacy compatible with a similar scheme of privacy for all.

This is a Kantian conception of privacy, because it acknowledges the autonomy, dignity, and equality of humans in regard to privacy. This maxim would prevent unwarranted revelations of intimate private details about public figures where the information made public is clearly not publicly important, but merely the subject of curiosity. As our world becomes more urbanized, crowded, and impersonal, we need to consider how to make life more full of dignity for all human beings. The current political/media climate makes one wonder how a "normal" person—one who values a measure of intimate privacy—would ever want to enter politics. Clearly, it is in society's interest to insure that normal people—and not just people with inflated egos—will want to get involved in public service.

The 1987 Gary Hart/Donna Rice scandal awakened many in journalism to the problems of indistinct delineations between the public and private, intimate aspects of the lives of politicians. Many journalists offered convincing arguments that Hart's blatant lying made his private life into something about which the public needed to know. Would these journalists argue that George Washington's alleged and FDR's documented marriage infidelities should have disqualified them from public office—particularly if they had denied them to journalists?

The 1991 Bill Clinton/Gennifer Flowers scandal brought these questions to the forefront of journalism ethics discussion again. This story differed from the Hart situation because the evidence was much less convincing—bought by a supermarket tabloid from a single, uncorroborated source who seemed to have a history of lying—and the alleged affair happened years before. Most news outlets reported the Clinton/Flowers story because it seemed similar to the Hart/Rice story. They continued to cover it because it looked like the story itself (regardless of whether it was true or not) might have an effect on Clinton's election chances (Rosenstiel, 1992). Hodges's (1994) rule for coverage of public officials could leave the door open to all "media stories" about the coverage of controversial private aspects of officials' lives, simply because stories about media coverage itself can have an "effect on their official performance" (205).

Journalists should carefully consider the relevance of a story as well as its source before reporting it—even if it means being "scooped" by the competition. The best advice for journalists is to be considerate, and to seek justice. Remember that—as Blum (1980) argued—to be ethical means to consider the "weal and woe" of others. Injustice can come either from unwarranted disclosure or from unwarranted concealment. Wilkins (1994) said that when we consider the "character" of political figures, we need to calculate the "need to know" (161). Unfortunately, these kinds of calculations lead us down a slippery slope. Did voters need to know about Thomas Jefferson's alleged slave girl concubine to evaluate his ability to govern (Brodie, 1974)? By all measures, Jefferson was one of our greatest political leaders. Journalists need to remember that calls for examining a politician's "character" usually come from that politician's political opponents. In other words, intimate information affects politics only to the degree that it is considered newsworthy by journalists.

Justice requires that public figures be treated the same as everyone else: Intimate private aspects of peoples' lives must be kept private, unless there is very clear evidence of a significant public injustice being hidden under the guise of privacy. All credible moral philosophy theories—deontological and teleological—argue that people must be treated equally, "with justice for all," and that includes politicians and celebrities. Journalists have a prima facie duty to correct or prevent injustice, as well as a professional duty to tell the truth.

Clearly, many journalists agree with the idea that everyone—even the most famous people—deserve some privacy. For example, American journalists have allowed Chelsea Clinton to live an almost normal life, free of the kind of intense scrutiny driven by curiosity which seems to follow the young sons of Britain's fractured royal family. This case is surely evidence that American journalists show they believe in the justice of equal privacy.

NOTE

1 The author would like to thank David Boeyink and Jim Bissland for their comments on an early version of this article.

REFERENCES

Altschull, J. (1990). *From Milton to McLuhan: The Ideas Behind American Journalism*. New York: Longman.

Appleby, J. (1978). *Economic Thought and Ideology in Seventeenth-Century England*. Princeton, NJ: Princeton University Press.

Arendt, H. (1959). *The Human Condition*. Garden City, NY: Doubleday.

Blum, L. (1980). *Friendship, Altruism, and Mortality*. London: Routledge & Kegan Paul.

Bok, S. (1983). *Secrets: On the Ethics of Concealment and Revelation*. New York: Vintage.

Brodie, F. (1974). *Thomas Jefferson: An Intimate History*. New York: Norton.

Dworkin, R. (1977). *Taking Rights Seriously*. Cambridge, MA: Harvard University Press.

Eterovich, F. (1972). *Approaches to Natural Law: From Plato to Kant*. New York: Exposition.

Fried, C. (1984). "Privacy [A Moral Analysis]," in F. Schoeman (ed.), *Philosophical Dimensions of Privacy* (203-22). Cambridge, UK: Cambridge University Press.

Hanson, D. (1970). *From Kingdom to Common-wealth: The Development of Civic Consciousness in English Political Thought*. Cambridge, MA: Harvard University Press.

Hodges, L. (1994). "The Journalist and Privacy," *Journal of Mass Media Ethics*, Vol. 9: 197-212.

Horwitz, M. (1982). "The History of the Public/Private Distinction," *University of Pennsylvania Law Review*, Vol. 130: 1423-28.

Inness, J. (1992). *Privacy, Intimacy, and Isolation*. New York: Oxford University Press.

Kant, I. (1990). *Foundations of the Metaphysics of Morals* (L.W. Beck, trans.). (2nd ed.). New York: Macmillan. (Original work published 1785)

Konvitz, M. (1966, Spring). "Privacy and the Law: A Philosophical Prelude," *Law and Contemporary Problems*, Vol. 31: 272-80.

Lilly, J., and Ball, R. (1981, July). "No-Tell Motel: The Management of Social Invisibility," *Urban Life*, Vol. 10: 179-97.

Locke, J. (1924). *The Second Treatise of Civil Government*. New York: Everyman's Library. (Original work published 1690)

MacIntyre, A. (1984). *After Virtue* (2nd ed.). Notre Dame, IN: University of Notre Dame Press.

Merrill, J. (1974). *The Imperative of Freedom: A Philosophy of Journalistic Autonomy*. New York: Hastings.

Mill, J. (1956). *On Liberty* (C.V. Shields, ed.). Indianapolis, IN: Bobbs-Merrill. (Original work published 1859)

Moore, W., and Tumin, M. (1949, December). "Some Social Functions of Ignorance," *American Sociological Review*, Vol. 14: 787-95.

Plato. (1941). *The Republic* (F.M. Cornford, trans.). London: Oxford University Press. (Original work published about 340 BC)

Rawls, J. (1986). "A Kantian Conception of Equality," in R.M. Stewart (ed.), *Readings in Social and Political Philosophy* (187-95). New York: Oxford University Press.

Reiman, J. (1984). "Privacy, Intimacy, and Personhood," in F. Schoeman (ed.), *Philosophical Dimensions of Privacy* (300-16). Cambridge, UK: Cambridge University Press.

Rosenstiel, T. (1992, January 29). "Clinton Allegation Raises Questions on Media's Role," *Los Angeles Times*, A1.

Ross, W. (1988). *The Right and the Good*. Indianapolis, IN: Hackett. (Original work published 1930)

Saxonhouse, A. (1983). "Classical Greek Conceptions of Public and Private," in S.I. Benn and G.F. Gaus (eds.), *Public and Private in Social Life* (363-84). New York: St. Martin's.

Scanlon, T. (1978). "Rights, Goals, and Fairness," in S. Hampshire (ed.), *Public and Private Morality* (93-111). Cambridge, UK: Cambridge University Press.

Scheffler, S. (1982). *The Rejection of Consequentialism*. Oxford, MA: Oxford University Press.

Schoeman, F. (1984). "Privacy: Philosophical Dimensions of the Literature," in F. Schoeman (ed.), *Philosophical Dimensions of Privacy* (1-33). Cambridge, UK: Cambridge University Press.

Simmel, G. (1956). "Knowledge and Ignorance," in E.F. Borgatta and H.J. Meyer (eds.), *Sociological Theory* (205-26). New York: Knopf.

Smart, J., and Williams, B. (1973). *Utilitarianism For and Against*. Cambridge, UK: Cambridge University Press.

Swanson, J. (1992). *The Public and the Private in Aristotle's Political Philosophy*. Ithaca, NY: Cornell University Press.

Tuck, R. (1979). *Natural Rights Theories: Their Origin and Development*. Cambridge, UK: Cambridge University Press.

Wilkins, L. (1994). "Journalists and the Character of Public Officials/Figures," *Journal of Mass Media Ethics*, Vol. 9: 157-68.

◆ ◆ ◆ ◆ ◆

LEE WILKINS
Journalists and the Character of Public Officials/Figures

Discussion of character in American politics dates at least to George Washington who, most school children know, never told a lie. However, some revisionists now also believe Washington may have had at least one extramarital affair.

Historians and political scientists will continue to debate the relationship between character and politics. But, recent political history has nudged the issue from the academic library shelf into popular political discourse.

Journalists questioned Nixon's character as early as 1952 over his handling of campaign finances. John Kennedy's character, in the form of his relationship to a Catholic God and his father's ability to buy elections, was examined by columnists far before knowledge of his extramarital relationships became public. Lyndon B. Johnson's character, including his widely reported capacity for political duplicity and strong-arm legislative tactics, was at the core of the debate over his conduct of the Vietnam War. Jimmy Carter, a human being of unquestionably decent character, was unable to survive a domestic agenda and historic events that transformed a sincere peacemaker into a wimp.

The contemporary list is longer. Is Congresswoman Pat Schroeder fit to be President after she cries in public—something Edmund Muskie was not allowed to do? Allegations of sexual harassment failed to derail the Supreme Court confirmation of Clarence Thomas. Six months later the same set of charges, brought by sources who were allowed to remain anonymous, halted the reelection campaign of Washington Senator Brock Adams. During the same time period, Nebraska Senator Bob Kerry, a decorated Vietnam War veteran who during his term as

Nebraska's governor lived in the state house with actress Debra Winger without a marriage license, spent more time in his presidential campaign answering questions about health care than he did about his close personal relationships.

This very rough and ready overview of some of the consistencies and contradictions in public examination of official character does reveal an important starting point. Character has always been, and will continue to be, political news. At its most fundamental, an examination of character can reveal much about the relationship between leaders and followers on which democratic society by definition depends.

The Ethical Question

Conceptualizations of character have changed significantly since the founding of the republic, where character was defined in Aristotelian terms—a collection of habits, virtues, and vices. Freudian psychology has altered that definition and has given academicians, historians, and journalists some potent theoretical tools with which to analyze the individual psyche (see, e.g., Davies, 1963; A. Freud, 1966; Maslow, 1970; Rejai and Phillips, 1973). Often that analysis focuses on areas of life—childhood experiences or patterns of behavior—that for the average person remain private.

For example, historian Fawn Brodie (Brodie, 1974) received a great deal of criticism for her biography of Thomas Jefferson in which she asserted he had conducted a long-term affair, and had several children with, a woman who was not only not his wife but also was his slave and part African American. Much of this criticism focused not on Brodie's reading of the evidence, which had been part of the historical record for decades, but on her apparent willingness to make such an assertion about a revered political figure.

Brodie's (1974) scholarly justification for such revelations is important. Jefferson was a key figure in American history, and certain areas of his private life—for example, his troubled relationship with his mother or a deathbed promise to his wife—reveal something about Jefferson the man. Thomas Jefferson the man speaks to Thomas Jefferson the writer, the friend, the international diplomat, the political visionary, and the President. In some tangible sense, scholars know more about Jefferson the public man because they are able to deeply understand some parts of who he was in private. Similar scholarly work has been done on less praiseworthy historical political figures.

Robert G.L. Waite's (1977) psychobiography of Hitler detailed the most intimate of behaviors—all with the goal of trying to explain how one human being was fashioned biologically and psychologically. Waite's biography spares few: Hitler's mother, who was his father's second cousin, his abusive father, and Hitler himself. Waite describes his deviant sexual practices and even a probable anatomical defect, being born with one testicle, that the psychiatric literature links to a variety of abnormal behaviors in adult men who have been physically abused as children.

Waite's biography invaded the most private areas of Hitler's humanity. Again, his justification is crucial. Hitler is among history's most notorious political leaders. His ability to gain power, to sway a nation, and to direct it to some of the most heinous acts against humanity are worthy of serious study. Hitler the man represents one of the darkest linkages between human character and political act.

The scholars who make such choices about the questions and subjects they investigate do so for an ethical reason. Privacy, as it has become defined in Western culture, is regarded as "a prima facie right that can be negated by other more compelling rights" (Grcic, 1986, 141). Public figures are powerful people. Ethicist Sissela Bok (1978) noted that when an unequal power relationship is involved, it is possible to justify what would otherwise be considered an unethical act. To paraphrase Bok, at the core of any serious investigation of the private character of public people is the notion that if the person one wishes

to investigate is also in the position to do one harm, then invading privacy in an attempt to counter that threat is justified. However, that invasion also needs to meet some tests. Ethical theory, including the legal and ethical theory of privacy, suggest the following.

First, the invasion must be placed in a larger context of facts and history. Because one of the definitions of invasion of privacy is the subject's loss of control over the context of information (Westin, 1967), an effort to study character must include enough context to provide meaning. For example, there have been many news accounts in the past decade about John F. Kennedy's extramarital affairs. These news accounts have aired and been broadcast despite the fact that while JFK is dead, his children and a host of other family members are still alive to read and hear the reports. However journalists may evaluate the Kennedy legacy, such accounts seem on the surface designed to titillate and hype rather than provide real understanding of the man and the political system. Contrast these news accounts with Doris Kearns Goodwin's (1989) treatment of JFK's sexual exploits. Goodwin placed JFK's constant "chasing" within a generational pattern that began with Joe and Rose Kennedy's marital agreements and was augmented by JFK's unique childhood experiences and personal qualities. Both accounts made the same essential invasion, but to a far different end. The context present in Goodwin's work provides understanding; the news accounts seem to imply only judgment.

Second, the revelation of private facts about political figures should meet the traditional tests of journalistic publicity and evidence. Private facts should be linked to public, political behaviors before publication or broadcast becomes ethically justifiable. An invasion of privacy in the reporting of character may be justified only if the journalist can treat the evidence resulting from the invasion the same way that he or she would treat other evidence. Publicity allows readers and viewers to form their own conclusions.

Publicity also follows ethical standards outlined by philosophers such as Bok (1978, 1983) and Rawls (1971) and adheres to the high professional standards to which journalists should subscribe. The Brock Adams story, as it was reported by the *Seattle Times*, provides an illustration of how high journalistic standards and a willingness to reveal evidence can add credibility to a story that could have been dismissed and which involved questions of privacy invasion. By choosing to reveal enough facts and background to allow readers to assess the motives of the women who charged Adams with sexual harassment, and by having the tenacity to report a pattern of behavior rather than a single instance, the newspaper essentially allowed its readers to make a judgment about the charges themselves and the motives of those who leveled them. In addition, it protected the privacy of women involved and promoted an understanding among readers that Adams's private behavior raised important public policy questions. Within this detailed and historically and politically grounded context, allowing Adams's accusers to remain off the record did not substantially diminish the overall credibility of the report or the paper itself. It had the further advantage of allowing readers some insight into the difficult decisions journalists must make when reporting the private activities of public figures.

As the Adams story illustrates, private behaviors need to be linked to public, political acts in significant ways. Take for example the recent spate of 1992 campaign stories about then President-elect Bill Clinton and President George Bush. Both men may or may not have had extramarital affairs, but that fact, by itself, does not provide journalists or their audiences with much understanding about how either man views or treats women, an important public policy issue. Yet, both men have a public record regarding women that can be documented. In their political lives, they have made appointments to a variety of offices, and have staffs where women are or are not people of influence. They have auth-

ored, voted on, and/or vetoed legislation that affects women in specific ways. All these are elements of a public political record that provide a context in which private behaviors—if they are made public—may be better understood. This public record also provides journalists with a context to be able to decide whether the publication of private facts furthers public understanding of political acts.

Third, the invasion of privacy must further the larger political discourse. This notion springs from the ethical justification for invading privacy delineated by the concepts of want to know, right to know, and need to know (Hodges, 1983). In contemporary society, political figures have celebrity status. Human curiosity means that viewers and readers want to know a great deal about celebrities. But media ethicists have long held that want to know is not an ethically compelling justification for the invasion of privacy, even privacy of public figures.

Rather, investigation of the character of political figures must meet a more demanding test: the need to know (Schoeman, 1984). Do readers and viewers need to know this information in order to make sense out of public life and political acts? Does such information more equally balance the power equation between the rulers and the ruled? Can an informed political choice be rooted in an understanding of private acts made public?

Careful reporting on character can pass these tests. Whether it is done by scholars, whose work has the goal of building a historic understanding, or journalists, writing a draft of history for more immediate consumption, a careful understanding of character can aid larger political understandings.

However, journalists must also be willing to weigh the harm done to others, particularly those who have not sought the public limelight, in investigating character. Although public officials do have the capacity to do harm, that argument is much less compelling when applied to parents, spouses, children, friends, and other family members. Journalistic investigation of character may often involve others, but publication or broadcast of what is learned should be considered only if public awareness of such facts furthers the political discourse. On such issues, the ethical governor should be a mature sense of discretion.

> At its best, discretion is the intuitive ability to discern what is and is not intrusive and injurious, and to use this discernment in responding to the conflicts everyone experiences as insider and outsider. It is an acquired capacity to navigate in and between the worlds of personal and shared experience, coping with the moral questions about what is fair or unfair, truthful or deceptive, helpful or harmful. Inconceivable without an awareness of the boundaries surrounding people, discretion requires a sense for when to hold back in order not to bruise, and for when to reach out. The word "tact" conveys the physical sense of touching that these boundaries evoke. (Bok, 1983, 41)

Discretion is not a word normally applied to the Journalistic enterprise. However, by employing it as one ethical standard for coverage of character, journalists and scholars could justify publication or broadcast of sensational "private" facts involving others who would normally be considered private persons only when those facts can be linked to public performance and the linkage documented. Merely publishing private information without this tie to a more public role is a form of tabloid journalism that casts doubt on journalistic motives and credibility. Perhaps more serious yet, such publication denigrates politicians in such a way that every official becomes a "crook," "liar," or "philanderer" without some larger understanding of why those character traits may or may not be important in doing the public's business.

Finally, reporting on the character of politicians should not be confused with psychological counseling or psychoanalysis. Psychoanalysis has as its goal understanding, treatment, and the alleviation (or cure) of pain and suffering. It is a medical effort with individual—not societal—ends. By necessity, it demands private revelation, but in a circumstance and under conditions that give substantial control to both the patient and the therapist. Psychoanalysis is very private work, conducted under well understood (if not always well obeyed) medical and ethical guidelines.

Public analysis of character may not have to delve as deeply into the individual psyche as psychoanalysis to be effective in promoting political debate. But, although coverage of the character of public officials asks some of the same questions as psychoanalysis, it asks other questions that are not normally part of the psychoanalytic process. And, it ties both sets of questions to public acts.

What journalists cover is *political character*. As I use the term, political character is the intersection of personality—viewed as a collection of traits, tendencies, and attitudes that may have either or both a biological and psychological basis—and public performance within a cultural and a historical context. Character is dynamic; it represents a synergistic interaction of a person within an environment (Davies, 1963). It is to those central elements of political character that this article now turns.

Coming Home: The Formation of Character and Identity

Childhood is the reservoir of much that politicians become as adults. An analysis of political character needs to consider the following aspects of childhood influence that have an impact on adult behavior in general and adult political behavior in particular.

The first aspect is the development of trust, a psychological activity that begins in infancy as a child relates to parents. The development of trust is such a fundamental psychological necessity that few journalists have stopped to examine it. However, there is probably no concept that is more central to the growth of a healthy personality than this one, and developmental psychologists such as Erik Erikson (1950, 1969b) have asserted that the development of trust is the first component of a matrix that the child uses to develop a sense of autonomous will and a sense of initiative during the first five years of life. Political leaders as adults have expressed their childhood engendered notions: Herbert Hoover believed that life and the environment are hostile and untrustworthy places to be subdued or avoided (Hofstadter, 1948), whereas Jimmy Carter believed that others are generally trustworthy and capable of being relied on and supportive.

The second aspect is a politician's own sense of self-worth and self-esteem. Contrast Franklin Roosevelt and Richard Nixon. It did not require impossibly deep investigation to uncover that Nixon had an unloving childhood that left a permanent mark on his sense of self. Historian Bruce Mazlish (1972) unearthed this essential component of Nixon's character in 1971 well before Watergate. Roosevelt was wrapped in adoration from the time he was born. FDR's biographers (Barber, 1977; Burns, 1978; Hofstadter, 1948) linked his healthy self-esteem with his White House management style. A politician's sense of self-worth, even Nixon as an adult admitted, has great impact on how he or she deals with crisis. Psychological theory indicates that sense of self also has a profound influence on how politicians view others, particularly others who are unlike them. Journalists certainly can and should write about such issues.

The third aspect is the development of a politician's relationship to authority. Like trust, psychological theory indicates that the development of a relationship to authority begins in the home, although it may be reinforced or altered by the child's interaction with a variety of influences including church, school, and peers (Langton, 1969; Lasswell, 1948). In Freudian terminology, a child's relationship to authority begins when the id encounters the ego and later, the ego ideal (A. Freud,

1966; S. Freud, 1923/1959, 1923/1960). Expressed in less Freudian terms, how and why a child learns to control and channel impulses will explain a great deal about many adult behaviors. Relationships with (and need for) authority figures, how a child views the role of the authority figure, and / or cooperates with others at the same level of authority, all find their expression in politics and political activity.

Political scientist James David Barber (1977) focused the concept of childhood relationships to authority as one important dimension of presidential character. How comfortable a politician is with authority, and how he or she chooses to exercise that authority, can have significant impact on public policy. As Barber (1977) noted:

> The power emphasis [is] reflected in the active-negative's concern with controlling his aggression ... The active negative lives in a dangerous world not only threatening in definite ways but also highly uncertain, a world one can cope with only by maintaining a tense, wary readiness for danger.... From the outside, he seems at first extraordinarily capable and then extraordinarily rigid, becoming more and more closed to experience, including advice of his ardent allies. (96-97)

The active-positive president that Barber describes shows a much richer and more varied range of emotional orientations that is available to the politician whose character is firmly rooted in self-recognition and self-love. This particular political figure is comfortable with exercising authority and with the inner self that must make such decisions.

Most political leaders have spent some time in legislatures or the governor's mansion where there is a discoverable record that provides insights about how political officials view themselves and the authority they acquire through the electoral process and amass on a more personal level. Such basic inclinations (or disinclinations) to use power in specific ways almost always evidence themselves in a legislative career. Senators such as Wayne Morse, who began standing on principle to the exclusion of almost all compromise during his tenure as dean of the University of Oregon law school, establish an important record that can be examined in a reelection campaign or a run for higher office (Wilkins, 1985). Such a legislative record also has the virtue of being quite public or of becoming public with enough digging. (Of course, backroom deals and power brokering are more difficult to uncover, but they do leave traces.) LBJ's wielding of legislative power, even including backroom activity, was part of the public political record of his legislative career. What remains is for journalists to put that political style into a context that provides it with meaning.

Early influences on adult policy outlook is the fourth aspect. Psychologists have generally asserted that adult identity formation begins in adolescence and continues through the early twenties. The experiences that a young person who becomes a politician has during these times, at least if the evidence of biography is an indication, can suggest a range of public policy views that can be important to an emerging political figure. Biographies of Nikita Kruschev indicate that his family's deaths at the hands of Stalin during these formative adolescent years was a major factor in his unprecedented (to that point) willingness to condemn Stalin within the Soviet system (Wilson, 1940). Similarly, LBJ, Carter, and Clinton have credited childhood or adolescent influences with their personal outlook on political questions such as poverty, racism, and the need for human rights as a focal point of US foreign policy. Uncovering such experiences—and the meaning behind them—requires journalistic digging. But, such digging, because it is done in the context of historical investigation, does not always involve an invasion of privacy either of the political figure or of friends, family and acquaintances. Such journalistic commitment requires that journalists examine not only

the political outlook, but also political action with regard to such issues.

The fifth aspect is how a politician establishes contact with people. The core of a legislative democracy is the belief that leaders need to be in touch with, and understand followers. In fact, historian, political scientist, and Pulitzer prize-winning biographer James MacGregor Burns (1978) said that this symbiotic psychological relationship forms the essence of leadership. There is no better evidence of this need for a deep understanding of constituency than the defining moment of the 1992 Presidential debates when a citizen asked President Bush, "How have you been personally effected by the recession?" One way in which people remain in touch is through their most intimate relations, but it is not the only way. Journalistic examination of character needs to focus on this issue, but not framed exclusively through the bedroom window. How people form friendships, who they listen to, how they listen, and who they are willing to allow into that most inner circle all explain this essential contact that political leaders must have in order to lead. It is this area of public political life that is probably most difficult for journalists to discover and understand at the time it is happening.

The flexibility, adaptability, and purposefulness of mature adulthood is the sixth aspect. Developmental psychologists have taken up research on adult research development where Freudian theory has essentially left off. Two of the most important efforts, by Erik Erikson and a team of psychologists led by Levison, have described specific stages of adult development in healthy personalities. In both studies, the adult is expected to continue to learn and adapt to the situations of maturity. Founded on the understandings of childhood and the developing sense of selfhood that emerges in adolescence, healthy adult development takes on an increasingly other-directed quality in the forties and fifties, a characteristic Erikson called generativity. This ability to flexibly encounter and cope with new situations, to empathize with others, to act for the good of others as well as for the good of self, and to show evidence of a drive to leave something behind to other generations can express themselves politically in a variety of ways. But, journalists can examine a past public record for evidence of political learning, a maturation of judgment, and a flexibility in coping styles. The danger here, of course, is to confound maturity and expediency, qualities that may look alike in the public record but which spring from vastly different psychological roots and needs. Covering this aspect of character requires that the journalist ask why and be willing to report the resulting answer in both a personal and historic context. Covering this aspect of character also requires that the journalist accept that the average political official seldom does things for only one reason, and that a specific action may serve a variety of purposes. In covering character, journalists must eschew reductionistic explanations for a more in-depth approach that acknowledges complexity.

The final aspect is the historical moment. Political leaders function at a particular time in history, something psychoanalyst Erik Erikson (1958, 1969a) made clear in his works on Martin Luther and Gandhi; Historical context works with and through political character. Jimmy Carter's presidency, at least as an international leader, would be evaluated much differently had he assumed office in 1988, as a political contemporary of Gorbachev, in a world that wanted to make peace. His political character was much less suited to the time he did become president. History, of course, is something that journalists cannot anticipate. However, an examination of character can reveal political potential in certain sorts of general situations. For example, most twentieth-century presidents have faced contrarian legislative bodies and several forms of external threat. Examining a previous legislative career, or a personal crisis of some sort, may provide some important indicators of how a political actor will respond in certain situations, providing that journalists remember these are merely tendencies that will be expressed in a unique way in particular historic situations.

Conclusions

I realize that my thesis about covering political character simultaneously urges journalists to reaffirm a commitment to something I think the profession has minimized—covering the historic and public political record of candidates—and to take new risks using psychological insights to inform analysis that will never fit the criterion of objective news reporting. Furthermore, some of those insights clearly violate what most would consider the traditional journalistic understanding of privacy, even privacy in public life. However, I do believe that good reporting and good writing and producing can make both the evidence and the analysis available to readers and viewers in such a way that political decision making, at least as it is part of the electoral process, is still well served. But, I also believe that covering political character badly is a profound disservice to the body politic (Lynn, 1977). Freud himself made this mistake in his psychoanalysis of Bullitt. Journalists should consider the long-term possibility for harm before they embark on stories that will require a great many resources from news organizations and individuals. Covering political character cannot be left until shortly before deadline.

Finally, there are some additional challenges that covering political character raises. I outline them not because I have answers but because they raise important questions.

Most psychological theory is really psychological theory about men. The academy knows too little about women and how they develop. At the same time, there are more women politicians. Analysis of women's political characters runs the great risk of too little intellectual base confounded by contradictory cultural expectations. Journalists need to know that right now women present a special case, not in the sense that they need to be treated differently but in the sense that there appear to be fewer analytic tools that provide real insight into character development in women.

Political psychology is not perfect, and it certainly is not perfectly predictive (Lifton, 1974). Political character should only be one aspect of political reporting, an important one, but one that does not take the place of other kinds of coverage, specifically candidate's stands on the issues. Quality coverage of political character can, at best, provide deep insights into the potential of individual political leaders. But, those people will interact with a larger culture and a historical moment that cannot realistically be expected to become part of the journalistic process.

Despite these acknowledged problems, covering political character is important work. It is work that the democratic political system needs to have done, and it requires the best of individual journalists and the support of news organizations. If, as contemporary critics of the political process such as E.J. Dionne (1991) suggest, the quality of democratic discourse has decayed, then a facile and reductionistic exploration of character can only speed that decline. But, an in-depth and nonjudgmental explanation of character may also serve to spur and expand the political debate, particularly if journalists treat character as one political story among many and if they are willing to imbed character in a history and political context Americans share. A deep exploration of character may help Americans think deeply about what we as a political system mean by and need from leadership. In a democratic society, there are few topics more worthy of discussion.

REFERENCES

Barber, J. (1977). *The Presidential Character*. Englewood Cliffs, NJ: Prentice-Hall.

Bok, S. (1978). *Lying: Moral Choice in Public and Private Life*. New York: Random House.

Bok, S. (1983). *Secrets*. New York: Random House.

Brodie, F. (1974). *Thomas Jefferson: An Intimate History*. New York: Norton.

Burns, J. (1978). *Leadership*. New York: Harper & Row.

Davies, J. (1963). *Human Nature in Politics*. New York: Wiley.

Dionne, E. (1991). *Why Americans Hate Politics*. New York: Simon & Schuster.

Erikson, E. (1950). *Childhood and Society*. New York: Norton.

Erikson, E. (1958). *Young Man Luther*. New York: Norton.

Erikson, E. (1969a). *Gandhi's Truth*. New York: Norton.

Erikson, E. (1969b). "Growth and Crises of the Healthy Personality," in H. Chiang and A. Maslow (eds.), *The Healthy Personality* (30-34). New York: Van Nostrand Reinhold.

Freud, A. (1966). *The Ego and the Mechanisms of Defense*. New York: International Universities Press, Inc.

Freud, S. (1959). *Inhibitions, Symptoms and Anxiety*. (J. Strachey, ed. and trans.). New York: Norton. (Original work published 1923)

Freud, S. (1960). *The Ego and the Id*. (J. Strachey, ed. and trans.). New York: Norton. (Original work published 1923)

Goodwin, D. (1989). *The Fitzgeralds and the Kennedys*. New York: Basic Books.

Grcic, J. (1986). "The Right to Privacy: Behavior as Property," *Journal of Values Inquiry*, Vol. 20: 137-44.

Hixson, R. (1987). *Privacy in a Public Society*. New York: Oxford University Press.

Hodges, L. (1983). "The Journalist and Privacy," *Social Responsibility: Journalism, Law and Medicine*, Vol. 9: 5-19.

Hofstadter, R. (1948). *The American Political Tradition*. New York: Vintage Books.

Langton, K. (1969). *Political Socialization*. New York: Oxford University Press.

Lasswell, H. (1948). *Power and Personality*. New York: Norton.

Lifton, R. (1974). *Explorations in Psychohistory*. New York: Simon & Schuster.

Lynn, K. (1977, January 16). "History's Reckless Psychologizing," *The Chronicle of Higher Education*, 48.

Maslow, A. (1970). *Motivation and Personality.* New York: Harper & Row.

Mazlish, B. (1972). *In Search of Nixon: A Psycho-historical Portrait.* New York: Basic Books.

Rawls, J. (1971). *A Theory of Justice.* Cambridge, MA: Harvard University Press.

Rejai, M., and Phillips, K. (1973). *Leaders of Revolution.* Beverly Hills, CA: Sage.

Schoeman, F. (ed.). (1984). *Philosophical Dimensions of Privacy: An Anthology.* Cambridge, UK: Cambridge University Press.

Waite, R. (1977). *The Psychopathic God: Adolph Hitler.* New York: Basic Books.

Westin, A. (1967). *Privacy and Freedom.* New York: Atheneum.

Wilkins, L. (1985). *Wayne Morse.* Westport, CT: Greenwood.

Wilson, E. (1940). *To the Finland Station.* New York: Doubleday.

◆ ◆ ◆ ◆ ◆

DENNIS F. THOMPSON
Privacy, Politics, and the Press

What should the press report about the private lives of public officials? The most common answer is based on what may be called the relevance standard: Private conduct should be publicized only if it is relevant to the official's performance in public office. Although this standard is often invoked by journalists and politicians, its justification has often been misunderstood, and the interpretation of its scope has been incomplete and overly broad. If the standard were more firmly grounded in the requirements of the democratic process, it would better serve as a guide to making and criticizing decisions about what to publicize about the private lives of public officials.[1]

Justification: Why Should the Press Respect the Privacy of Public Officials?

Any adequate justification for respecting the privacy of public officials must be based in part on what the democratic process requires. In virtually all conceptions of democracy, officials should be accountable to citizens.[2] Citizens should be able to hold public officials accountable for their decisions and policies, and therefore citizens must have information that enables them to judge how well officials are doing, or are likely to do, their jobs.

This accountability requirement provides a reason to override or diminish the right of privacy that officials otherwise have. It is clear enough that the requirement justifies making some conduct public that is ordinarily private: the financial affairs of officials and their family members; health records; drug use; names of friends, relatives, and close associates; gifts received; outside employment; and sexual activity related to the job. Sexual harassment, as now defined in the law on the subject, is not a private matter.[3]

The accountability requirement has another implication that is less noticed but no less important. The requirement provides a reason to *limit* publicity about private lives. When such publicity undermines the practice of accountability, the publicity should be limited. How can publicity undermine accountability? The most important way is through the operation of a political version of Gresham's law: Cheap talk drives out quality talk. This is not because people hoard the quality talk in the hope that they might be able to enjoy it later, as Gresham thought people would hoard higher-value currency, but because the cheap talk attracts readers and viewers, even those who, in their more reflective hours, would prefer quality talk.

Talk about private lives is "cheap" in two ways. First, the information is usually more immediately engaging and more readily comprehensible than information about job performance. Second, the information itself is less reliable, simply because it is usually less accessible and less comprehensive. We usually know less about private life not only in a particular case, but also in past cases, about which we need to know in order to make generalizations about the effects of private conduct on public performance.

Given these characteristics, information about private life has the tendency to dominate other forms of information, lower the overall quality of public discourse, and thereby diminish democratic accountability. Informing citizens about some matters makes it harder for them to be informed about other matters. The coverage of the Clinton-Lewinsky affair dominated media discussion of not only important new policy proposals on Social Security, health insurance, and campaign finance reform, but also attempts to explain the US position on Iraq in preparation for military action. Even if the tilt of political attention from the public to the private affects only opinion leaders and the political classes, it can still have the effect of weakening the system of accountability.

To be sure, in the absence of scandal, citizens will not necessarily pay more attention to the more important issues of the day. Some citizens would no doubt simply ignore political reporting completely. And reporting scandals might even sometimes increase interest in politics: Some viewers might turn on the news to find out the latest about Clinton and Lewinsky, and then stay to see a report on Iraq that they would otherwise have missed.

What exactly are the effects of the coverage of scandalous private conduct? This is an empirical question and one that unfortunately has received little serious investigation by social scientists.[4] But the considered judgments of most citizens in this and similar cases is that they do not need to know about the sexual affairs of their leaders,[5] and that the press pays too much attention to leaders' private lives.[6]

Comparative studies suggest that the US press is overly preoccupied with private life. Compared to the press in most other advanced democracies, our press is much more inclined to report on the private lives of officials. A recent study of journalists' attitudes in four European democracies and the United States found that "US journalists are the least scrupulous group when it comes to the private lives of public officials." Nearly 90 per cent disagreed with the statement that "journalists should not delve into their personal lives" (Donsbach 1995: 22).

Scope: What Privacy of Public Officials Should the Press Respect?

If the relevance standard is based on accountability, the scope of conduct that it would publicize is less than is often assumed. Two general features of the standard favor less publicity.

First, because the effects on accountability are a matter of degree, the standard focuses attention on questions of proportion. The issue should not be simply *whether*, but *to what extent*, private conduct should be publicized. The standard thus still has force in cases in which private conduct is relevant. Even when the standard does not prohibit coverage, it may require adjusting the amount of airtime or space devoted to private conduct compared to other issues.

A second consequence of basing the relevance standard on accountability is a shift in focus from conduct that affects job performance to conduct that citizens need to assess job performance. This shift builds into the standard some limits on intrusion. Citizens do not need to know, for example, about the drinking habits of an official because the alleged effects can be discovered by observing his actions on the job. More generally, in this interpretation of the standard, the press should concentrate more on the effects of private behavior and less on the behavior itself.

Four main types of conditions or considerations determine whether and to what extent private conduct is relevant.[7] The conditions refer to the publicness of the conduct, the character of the official in question, the reactions of the audience, and the effects on the political process. The significance of these conditions can be brought out by examining a case that has some parallels to recent events but is less cluttered with political contention. (The case also has the advantage of offering some insight into how editors think about this issue, because many spoke candidly about how they arrived at their decision to publish the story.)

In the mid-1980s, John Fedders, the chief of the enforcement division of the Securities and Exchange Commission (SEC), resigned shortly after the *Wall Street Journal* reported on its front page that he had repeatedly beaten his wife. Although his wife's charges had appeared in the public record at the start of the divorce proceedings nearly a year and a half earlier, virtually no one had taken notice until the *Journal*'s story appeared.[8] (The *Journal* had been told about the problem a year before but decided then against reporting it.) White House officials decided that once this information became so public, Fedders could not remain in office and asked for his resignation.

Can this disclosure be justified? The first refuge of a harried editor in face of such a story is to try to find some connection, however remote, between the private conduct and the job performance. The trouble was that Fedders's penchant for wife-beating had no noticeable effects on his job performance. By all accounts, Fedders's performance on the job had been exemplary.

Nevertheless, some editors, intent on publishing the story but not wanting to offend against the relevance standard, claimed that they *had* found an effect on performance. Demonstrating how far an editor is willing to stretch the relevance standard, Ben Bradlee of the *Washington Post* insisted that Fedders's private conduct "intrudes on his performance of his duties" because "the fact is that he's not at work, he's in court."[9] This argument is an abuse of the relevance standard because its claims can be shown to be false and can be shown to be so with-

out publicizing anything about Fedders's private life. If the claim is that an official is distracted from his public duties, the press can simply report that he is not on the job. (They could give some general description of the reason, such as his appearance in court, if necessary to indicate how long the absence is likely to be and whether it is justifiable.)

The managing editor of the *Journal*, Norman Pearlstine, said the decision to run the story was "the toughest call I've had to make since I've been in the job."[10] He finally decided to override the paper's general rule respecting the privacy of public officials because of the whole set of facts surrounding the case:

> [Fedders had] admitted in public the charges of wife-beating.... He is one of the important law enforcement officials in the country.... [There were] questions raised about his indebtedness ... The White House was aware of the issue of family violence and seemed to be concerned about it.[11]

Pearlstine's justification captures better than the claims of other editors the complexity of decisions of this kind and provides a useful start for analyzing the conditions that should be taken into account in applying the relevance standard.

Publicness of the Conduct

The first factor that almost all editors mentioned about this case is that the conduct was already on the public record. Abe Rosenthal, the executive editor of the *New York Times*, took this as a sufficient justification: "When stories of repeated wife-beating by a public official ... become part of the public record, they must be printed."[12]

Pearlstine was more careful. For him, Fedders's public admission of guilt, not just the publicness of the proceedings, was essential. This may be too strong a condition in some cases, as we may sometimes want an allegation of wrongdoing to be disclosed even if the accused denies it. But we ought to require some independent test of the plausibility of the charges beyond the fact that the charges are made in public.

This case illustrates clearly that the press itself often determines what is on the public record that counts. For Fedders, the difference between a court record and the front page of the *Journal* was the difference between holding public office or resigning in disgrace. More generally, the fact that conduct comes to light whether as a result of court proceedings or (more commonly) through less reputable means does not automatically justify giving it still more exposure. Just because an activity is public (even legitimately so) does not mean that it should be more widely publicized. Failure to make this simple distinction leads to the common mistake that Rosenthal made.

Similarly, the fact that the story is likely to be published elsewhere ("If we don't run it, somebody else will.") is not itself a sufficient justification. If it were, almost any story could be considered legitimate, whether actually public already or only imminently so—if not in the *Wall Street Journal*, then in the *Daily News*, or if not in the *Daily News*, then in the *Drudge Report*. On the relevance standard, properly interpreted, it makes a difference *where* the story is published—a difference that is becoming more important in the era of cyber-publicity. Publication in the *Journal* (or its local counterpart) gives a story more credibility and has more effect on political discussion and accountability than does publication in the tabloids or on most of the Internet.

The respectable press often tries to avoid this dilemma by a technique that may be called "meta-reporting": writing about the fact that the less respectable press is writing about private scandals. Thus the *New York Times* publishes a story about the unsubstantiated rumors that the *Daily News* has published about Clinton and Lewinsky—complete with miniature reproductions of the front pages of the *News*.[13] This technique might be more justifiable if the respectable press were not so much more

inclined to engage in meta-reporting about stories that feature sex than about stories that reveal other failings of their fellow journalists.

Thus, although the judgment that the private conduct is legitimately publicly known is a necessary condition for reporting about it, it is not sufficient—and certainly not for determining how extensive that reporting should be.

Unity of Character

A second condition is that the private conduct must reveal important character flaws that are relevant to the official's job. That is presumably what Pearlstine had in mind when he connected Fedders's personal debts and spousal abuse with his role as a law enforcement official. Citizens may reasonably want to know about an official's tendency toward domestic violence and personal indebtedness when that person is responsible for enforcing the law and regulating the finances of others.

Pearlstine's claim here is more specific than the more common use of the character argument, which is undiscriminatingly general. The general claim that private conduct reveals character flaws that are bound eventually to show up on the job is a psychological version of the classical idea of the unity of the virtues: A person who mistreats his wife is likely to mistreat his colleagues; a person who does not control his violent temper is not likely to resist the temptation to lie.

We should be wary of this argument because many people, especially politicians, are quite capable of compartmentalizing their lives in a way that the idea of the unity of virtues denies. Indeed, for some people, the private misbehavior may be cathartic, enabling them to behave better in public. And private virtue is no sign of public virtue. We should remember that most of the leading conspirators in the Watergate scandal led impeccable private lives. So evidently did most of the nearly one hundred political appointees who were indicted or charged with ethics offenses during the early years of the Reagan administration.[14]

More generally, as far as character is concerned, we should be primarily interested in the political virtues—respect for the law and the Constitution, a sense of fairness, honesty in official dealings. These virtues may not be correlated at all with personal ones. And the vices that the press seems most interested in—the sins of sex—are those that are probably least closely connected with the political vices.

Character is sometimes thought to be relevant in a different, more symbolic way. Officials represent us by who they are as much as by what they do: We need to know if their character makes them fit for moral leadership—for serving as role models for our youth and virtuous spokespeople for our nation. But this conception of public office is too demanding, as most citizens seem to recognize. They seek leaders whose characters display the political virtues, but most do not believe that even the president should be held to higher moral standards in his private life than ordinary citizens are.[15] The question is not whether it would be desirable to have a leader who is as moral in his private life as in his public life, but whether it is worth the sacrifice of privacy and the distortions of public debate that would be required to make private probity a job qualification.

If the character trait is specifically related to the job, the case for considering it relevant is stronger, even if the connection is only symbolic. This is perhaps part of the reason that Pearlstine thought that Fedders's domestic violence was relevant to his role as a law enforcement official: It was not that Fedders might actually condone violence or other law-breaking on the job, but that his private conduct symbolically repudiated the specific values that an official in his position is sworn to uphold. Even smoking cigarettes in the privacy of one's home may be a legitimate target in the case of some public officials. Responding to stories in the press, William Bennett had to give up smoking when he was head of the Drug Enforcement Agency.

Reactions of the Public

Pearlstine's allusion to the Reagan administration's campaign against domestic violence introduces a third condition. It refers to reactive effects: The private conduct affects job performance not because of what the officials themselves do but because of the reaction of other people when they find out about the conduct. If the Reagan administration had allowed Fedders to stay on the job, his reputation might have made it more difficult to continue the campaign against domestic violence and, more generally, the effort to promote family values. Anticipating these effects, an editor might reasonably find the private conduct relevant.

But we should be careful about appealing to reactive effects. The anticipated reaction of other people should almost never count as a sufficient reason to publicize further what would otherwise be private. The missing step in the argument—the one factor that Pearlstine and none of the editors mention is the assumption that the private conduct itself is morally wrong and that the anticipated reactions of other people are therefore morally justified.

Why this step is essential can be seen more clearly if we consider the cases of the "outing" of homosexuals in public office. The fact that constituents will vote against their conservative congressman if they find out he is gay is surely not a reason for publicizing his sexual orientation. The mainstream press was right not to disclose the fact that the chief spokesman for the Pentagon during the Gulf War is gay, even though some opponents of the military's policy of excluding gays from the military sought to publicize the fact.

If the congressman had actively opposed gay rights, or if the Pentagon spokesman had prominently defended the military's policy, the press would have had a reason to expose his sexual orientation. But the reason is not simply that these officials should be punished for their hypocrisy, but that their hypocrisy is serving a morally objectionable cause.

There is an important qualification to the general rule that reactive effects should not count as a reason for exposure unless the reactions are morally justified. If the official flagrantly disregards such reactions—in effect inviting scrutiny of private conduct that offends many people—the press may be justified in exposing it, whether or not it is in itself wrong. Perhaps the press should not spy on a prominent senator who goes off on a yacht for a rendezvous with his mistress, but when he declares himself a family man and dares the press to prove otherwise, the press has a reason, though not necessarily a sufficient reason, to expose his activities.[16] The senator is guilty of failing to take into account the reasonable reactions of citizens.

Officials who behave in this way display a form of the traditional vice of "giving scandal." In Thomist ethics, "giving scandal" is defined as providing the "occasion for another's fall" (Thomas Aquinas 1972: 109-37). In secular terms, we could say that a public official who fails to take into account the reasonable reactions of citizens fails to fulfill an important public duty, and citizens deserve to know about that failure. If the reports of President Clinton's escapades with Monica Lewinsky are true, he is guilty of "giving scandal." Except for the issue of perjury, this may ultimately be the strongest justification for the press's treating his affair differently from the more discreet alleged relationships of Bob Dole and George Bush.

If journalists invoke reactive effects when applying the relevance standard, they cannot escape making substantive moral judgments. Even when they decide to disclose on the grounds that citizens themselves should decide whether the conduct is justifiable, they are in effect judging that the anticipated reactions are not bad enough to outweigh the value of informing citizens about the conduct. Once the story is out, the decision has been made. Without judging the extent to which the reactions they are anticipating are justifiable, editors will not be able to distinguish between outing a homosexual and exposing a wife beater.

Priority in the Process

The fourth condition relates private conduct to other public issues: To what extent does knowing about this conduct help or hinder citizens' knowing about *other* matters they need to know to hold officials accountable?

In the Fedders case, it would be hard to argue that publicity about his private life distracted citizens from attending to more important traits or activities—whether his or those of the SEC or other officials and institutions. The publicity probably brought more attention to the SEC. (The number of people who learned for the first time that the SEC *had* an enforcement division must have increased substantially.) And the publicity indirectly gave a boost to the administration's campaigns against domestic abuse and for family values.

But in most cases—especially when they involve traditional personal vices such as drink, drugs, and sex—the Gresham effects are likely to be more salient. Even when this kind of private conduct has some clear relevance for judging the qualifications of a public official, it tends to assume more prominence than it deserves. In the confirmation hearings of Clarence Thomas, the press, the public, and the Senate Judiciary Committee paid more attention to Clarence Thomas's relationship with Anita Hill than to his judicial qualifications. The Gresham effects are especially damaging when, as in this and similar cases, irreversible decisions are made under tight constraints of time, so that any distortions in the process of accountability cannot be corrected.

The Gresham effects go well beyond particular cases like those of Clarence Thomas and Bill Clinton. The cumulative consequences of many cases, as they increase in number and prominence, create a pattern of media coverage that distorts our common practices of deliberation. Our habits of discourse—the considerations we easily identify, the distinctions we readily make, the reasons we immediately accept—become better adapted to controversies about private life than to public life. The more citizens hone their skills of deliberation on the finer points of sexual encounters (would he have really put her hand there?), the less they are prepared to develop their capacities to deliberate about the nuances of public policy (should he support this revision of Social Security?). Democratic deliberation gets into a rut—the rut of smut, it might be called. That is not the best place to conduct the discourse of democratic accountability.

Conclusion

To return to Pearlstine's decision: Should he have run the story about Fedders? The decision was justified because Fedders's conduct satisfies the relevance standard: It is the kind of conduct about which citizens or their representatives need to know to hold an official in Fedders's position accountable, and the extent of the publicity was proportionate to the relevance. More specifically, Fedders's conduct was already public, and legitimately so. The character flaws that the conduct revealed were closely and specifically connected to his job. There was reason to believe that the negative public reaction was morally justified because the conduct is a serious moral wrong. And most important, there were no significant Gresham effects.

Just as important as noting the factors that justify the story is recognizing the factors that should not count at all. Just because the conduct was already public does not justify publicizing it more widely. Just because the conduct reveals a character defect does not make it relevant to public office. And just because the public or some part of it is likely to react negatively does not license disclosing it.

Our interest is not in the conclusion about this particular case, but in the reasons for it. Those reasons can help identify some general principles that should guide journalists in making—and just as importantly, citizens in judging—decisions about reporting on the private lives of public officials. Those decisions affect not only what we read and watch,

but also ultimately the quality of the discourse of the democratic politics we experience. That discourse is too important to be left to the vagaries of Gresham's law.

NOTES

An earlier version of this article was presented at the conference on Politics and the Media at the University of Nebraska in April 1998. I am grateful to Robert Audi and the conference participants for their comments.

1 For an earlier and more comprehensive discussion (written not only pre-Lewinsky, but even pre-Hart), see Thompson 1981: 221-47.

2 For a fuller discussion of accountability, see Gutmann and Thompson 1996: 128-64.

3 Even some conduct that does not, strictly speaking, violate the law may still be relevant if it reveals a pattern of unwanted sexual advances to subordinates. The press therefore should not be faulted for publicizing Senator Bob Packwood's sexual encounters, which the Senate Ethics Committee found constituted a "pattern of abuse of his position of power and authority" (Senate Ethics Counsel 1995: 125). Indeed, one might criticize the decision not to publish the allegations from the women until after the election in 1992.

4 A comparative content analysis of the press coverage of Gary Hart in the 1988 campaign and Bill Clinton in 1992 found that the stories of the affairs dominated the coverage of Hart's campaign but "did not fully eclipse" discussion of Clinton's issue positions because the press "cast more doubt on the accuser, Gennifer Flowers, and the medium, the *Star*" (Payne and Mercuri 1993: 295, 298).

5 Sixty-four per cent of respondents in a February 1998 survey said that it is not important for the public to know "what the relationship was" between Clinton and Lewinsky. Distinguishing the relationship from legal testimony

about it, 61 per cent said that it is important for the public to know whether Clinton encouraged Lewinsky to lie. (James Bennet with Janet Elder, "Despite Intern, President Stays in Good Graces," *New York Times*, Feb. 24, 1998: 1A, 14A.)

6   In February 1998, 80 per cent of the respondents in a national survey said that they thought the media coverage of the Clinton-Lewinsky story was "excessive." (Roper Center for Survey Research and Analysis [Roper Center], "Clinton Lewinsky News Coverage Survey" [conducted Jan. 30-Feb. 4], released Feb. 6, 1998, University of Connecticut: Public Opinion Online.) Sixty per cent agreed with the more general proposition that the media have "gone too far in disclosing the details of Clinton's private life," while only nine per cent thought the media had not gone "far enough." (Roper Center, "Clinton Lewinsky News Coverage Survey," Feb. 6, 1998.) Even before the recent scandals, 60 per cent of respondents said that the news media is paying too much attention to Clinton's private life. (Roper Center, "Princeton Survey Research Associates, Newsweek" [conducted May 6], released May 1994, University of Connecticut: Public Opinion Online.) Since the 1980s, there has been a steady and substantial increase in the number of people who say that the "increased attention being given to the private lives of public officials and candidates" is a "bad thing" (from 39 per cent in 1989 to 47 per cent in 1993). (Gallup Organization, "Gallup, Newsweek" [conducted June 1-2], released June 1989, University of Connecticut: Public Opinion Online; and Gallup Organization, "Gallup, Newsweek" [conducted Mar. 9-10], released Mar. 20, 1993, Roper Center, University of Connecticut: Public Opinion Online.)

7   For other institutional factors that should be considered, such as the level and type of office, see Thompson 1981: 129-32.

8   Brooks Jackson, "John Fedders of SEC Is Pummeled by Legal and Personal Problems," *Wall Street Journal*, Feb. 25, 1985.

9   Stuart Taylor, "Life in the Spotlight: Agony of Getting Burned," *New York Times*, Feb. 27, 1985.

10   Ibid.

11   Ibid. Pearlstine also mentioned two other factors: "that [Fedders] had indicated that he would resign his position at the S.E.C. if that would get his wife to take him back" and "the issues in the Southland case" (in which a former law client had been charged with a cover-up of a bribery scheme). Ibid.

12   Ibid.

13   Janny Scott, "Media Notebook: Focus Turns Elsewhere in Newspapers and on TV," *New York Times*, Feb. 4, 1998.

14   George Lardner Jr., "Conduct Unbecoming an Administration," *Washington Post National Weekly Edition*, Jan. 3, 1988.

15   About 53 per cent of the respondents in a national survey in 1998 in the aftermath of the Lewinsky publicity said that "when it comes to conduct in one's personal life the President should be held to the same standard you hold yourself," while 44 per cent said that he should be held to a higher standard. (Roper Center, "CBS News, New York Times" [conducted Feb. 19-21], released Feb. 23, 1998, University of Connecticut: Public Opinion Online.) An overwhelming majority, 84 per cent, agree that "someone can still be a good president even if they do things in their personal life that you disapprove of." (Ibid.)

16   Maureen Dowd, "Change of Hart," *New York Times*, Mar. 22, 1998.

REFERENCES

Donsbach, Wolfgang. 1995. "Lapdogs, Watchdogs, and Junkyard Dogs," *Media Studies Journal* Vol. 9(4): 17-31.

Gutmann, Amy, and Dennis Thompson. 1996. *Democracy and Disagreement*. Cambridge, MA: Harvard University Press.

Payne, J. Gregory, and Kevin Mercuri. 1993. "Private Lives, Public Officials: The Challenge to Mainstream Media," *American Behavioral Scientist* Vol. 37(2): 291-301.

Senate Ethics Counsel. 1995. *The Packwood Report*. New York: Times Books.

Thomas Aquinas, Saint. 1972. Question 43, "Scandal," *Summa Theologiae* Vol. 35. New York: Blackfriars with McGraw-Hill.

Thompson, Dennis F. 1981. "The Private Lives of Public Officials," in *Public Duties: The Moral Obligations of Government Officials*, ed. Joel L. Fleishman, Lance Liebman, and Mark H. Moore. Cambridge, MA: Harvard University Press. Reprinted in *Essentials of Government Ethics*, ed. Peter Madsen and Jay Shafritz. New York: Penguin, 1992.

◆ ◆ ◆ ◆ ◆

JUDITH LICHTENBERG

Truth, Neutrality, and Conflict of Interest

April 1989: Several reporters from the *New York Times* and the *Washington Post*, including the *Time*'s Supreme Court reporter Linda Greenhouse, participate in an abortion rights demonstration in Washington. They are later criticized by their editors, who claim that such actions violate their newspapers' conflict-of-interest policies.[1]

February 1999: Four members of the executive committee of the Periodical Press Gallery, one of four Congressional viewing galleries for journalists, are unseated after they support a rule that would require journalists to disclose sources of income—although not amounts—for admission to the gallery.[2]

Widely discussed among journalists and by media-watchers outside the profession as well, these incidents upset a fragile and uneasy balance of conflicting values and expectations. On the one hand, we may wonder how can we trust journalists to tell us the truth if they are not themselves disinterested. On the other, it seems unreasonable to expect journalists to hold no views about the issues they cover and to be wholly isolated from interested parties. Total agnosticism and isolation seem not only unnatural but also undesirable.

I discovered after extended reflection that my own responses to these cases were more complex than I had anticipated. And the attempt to reconcile my intuitions was accordingly more difficult.

The Novelty of Journalistic Conflicts of Interest

These questions have not always been with us. When we think of the circumstances in which the classical theory of freedom of the press was formulated, we think of revolutionaries, freethinkers, partisans, impassioned pamphleteers, believers in causes; we think of "a struggle between combatants fighting under hostile banners."[3]

Yet the contemporary journalist working for a major daily, a news magazine, or a television network is expected to be neutral, fair, balanced, objective, and altogether "value-free." These traits form part of the norm of objectivity, which is a cornerstone of the professional ideology of journalists in liberal democracies.

Clearly our demands and expectations vary depending on the kind of journalism involved. Peter Jennings has to satisfy conditions of neutrality that a documentary filmmaker does not. Similarly, the *New York Times* and the *Wall Street Journal* are subject to different expectations than the *Nation* and the *National Review*. Nevertheless, in every corner of journalism charges of bias and conflict of interest have become increasingly common.

What caused this shift to the values of objectivity and neutrality in journalism? The reasons have much to do with the nature of the contemporary mass media, which, unlike their ancestors, constitute not simply voices in the public forum but the forum itself. As a result, mass media organizations have in crucial respects become public institutions. Vested with enormous power, they must maintain at least the appearance of neutrality or impartiality.

We might elaborate this point in two related ways. First, evidence of nonneutrality, of a point of view, would be seen as an abuse of public responsibility and trust, and so would subject the journalist or media organization to censure. Second, the organization's economic drive to appeal to a vast audience compels it to upset the settled convictions of as few viewers or readers as possible.

That a news article or program secures widespread and ready agreement within a society does not prove, of course, that it is objective or neutral. It may simply mirror its audience's assumptions—held so strongly and deeply they go unrecognized as assumptions capable of challenge. It takes a certain degree of reflection and self-consciousness to see that "what goes without saying" may involve premises that those from a different culture might question, and that it is not simply irrational to challenge. Consensus does not entail neutrality. On the other hand, members of a diverse society may regard all but the most banal truths as highly charged and nonneutral.

Case I: The Journalist as Tabula Rasa

Should journalists participate in politically controversial activities? I want to consider four arguments for the view that they shouldn't.

1. *"Journalists shouldn't have opinions on controversial issues; they should be neutral."* This is a bad argument. An intelligent person will inevitably form opinions about some important moral and political issues. Even if opinionlessness were possible, it is not a trait we ought to cultivate. Engaged and informed people naturally form views about issues that confront them, and journalists may be expected to do likewise.

The question is whether the mere possession by journalists of opinions about the issues they cover—on moral, political, scientific, religious, or other subjects—envelops them in conflicts of interest. The argument for an affirmative answer goes something like this: The journalist's duty is to report, or at least to seek, the truth. But if the journalist holds an opinion on an issue she is covering, that will bias her, she will abuse her position to advance her own view or at least she will fail to seek the truth because she believes she already possesses it.

This argument focuses simply on the possession of an opinion, ignoring its genesis and the manner in which it is held. But this is a mistake, and one that predisposes the conclusion.

So, for example, we might say that insofar as a person's belief about an issue possesses the right kind of pedigree or lineage, holding the belief does not conflict with the journalist's duty to seek the truth. If I have arrived at a view through a fair and careful consideration of the evidence or of the arguments on all sides, I am involved in no conflict of interest. Why not? First, I have no hidden interest pushing me to one view or the other; my aim is to discover the most rational or defensible position. Second, insofar as I proceed fairly in considering the issues, I am unlikely, even having settled on a view, simply to dismiss the other side.

Is this an excessively rationalistic picture of belief formation? No doubt. We can, if we are so inclined, find causes to undermine even beliefs with impeccable pedigrees. But unless we are prepared to slide down the slope to the conclusion that everyone is biased and no one ever believes anything for good reasons—in which case we may as well give up altogether on the idea of good journalism—we need some way to distinguish holding a view in light of the arguments, the evidence, the facts, and other less worthy routes to belief.

We often put this difference in terms of whether a person has a "vested interest" in a position or not. The question is whether there is "something in it for him"—whether he has some motive for believing it apart from a desire to believe the truth. The most common understanding of a vested interest suggests a material or personal interest: my stocks will go up or my brother will get hired. But someone with strong ideological commitments can likewise have a vested interest in a position. His belief system depends upon things being one way or another. We judge this question—essentially whether a person has an "open mind"—largely in terms of the extent to which she can appreciate another's point of view.

Practically speaking, then, the manner in which a belief is held matters more than its genesis. In light of our typical ignorance of the origins of people's beliefs and the ease with which we may cast doubt on them, how you came to have the beliefs you do matters less than how you hold them: whether with a certain detachment or distance, whether with an appreciation of your own fallibility and the capacity to see other ways of looking at things.

In any case, the mere holding of a belief, even one relevant to a subject one is reporting, cannot involve one in a conflict of interest. Such a criterion is too stringent, because complete agnosticism is neither possible nor desirable. We may note in addition that a piece of reporting rarely threatens one's beliefs in the direct way that the assumption of conflict of interest supposes.

2. *"Any journalist who gets politically involved has beliefs too strong to allow for fair journalism."* Exactly what is the claim here? Is it that people who demonstrate or who join political organizations necessarily have stronger political beliefs than those who do not? Although some psychological experiments indicate that taking action can deepen commitment, it doesn't follow that joiners are always more committed than nonjoiners. And even if joining meant a stronger commitment or belief, that in itself would not justify prohibiting political involvements. For the crucial question is not how strong a journalist's beliefs are but whether they disable him from fair and accurate reporting. Without evidence of a connection between the two, the prohibition remains unsupported.

Some people, of course, are dogmatically committed to their beliefs. Immune to contrary evidence or arguments, they lack the virtues of skepticism and open-mindedness that make for good reporting. Perhaps there are journalists animated by a single-minded passion, who show us things we would not otherwise see while blinding them to other ways of looking. But such people are rare.

Presumably, part of an editor's job is to assess the extent to which reporters possess the virtues necessary to their role—not to eliminate those who hold opinions, but to purge those whose opinions prevent them from reporting fairly. But they should decide these questions by examining a reporter's work, rather than her extracurricular activities.

We must recognize, however, the limitations in this approach. First, editors, like everyone else, will have trouble recognizing biases that match their own. Second, examining a news story is rarely sufficient to expose its biases; for that we need to know not only what it contains but what it leaves out. The sins of bias are largely sins of omission. This is a deep problem for the critique of journalism.

The conclusion nonetheless remains: the prohibition on political action cannot rest on the argument that action in itself demonstrates attitudes inappropriate for journalists.

3. *"Journalists' political commitments will entangle them in relationships that compromise their ability to report news stories fairly and accurately."* This is a serious concern. It is not so much journalists' political beliefs themselves that create the danger of bias but rather the personal and institutional relationships that normally flow from political involvement. A reporter actively involved in a political organiza-

tion will probably find it difficult to write critically about it. Members of the group are his friends, his comrades.

This example points up one of the most fundamental sources of conflicts of interest: personal relationships, which can exert a powerful pull at odds with professional duty. Few people can distance themselves adequately from their ties to friends, family, colleagues, comrades. For many purposes we count that as a virtue, not a vice. But it does create a professional conflict of interest.

4. *"Journalists' political involvements create the appearance of bias and conflict of interest, and ought to be prohibited on that account."* According to this argument, public political commitments create the appearance of conflict of interest because the public is likely to infer that a reporter is biased and incapable of fair and accurate reporting from knowledge of her political involvements. In support of this view one might point to the common assumption that liberal reporters (reporters who happen to be liberals) inevitably or generally write liberal journalism (journalism with a liberal bias).

Furthermore, potential sources may draw the same conclusion. They may be reluctant to talk to reporters they perceive as holding political beliefs contrary to their own. Since this could prevent a reporter from doing his job well, it is understandable that news organizations would prefer that their journalists' political affiliations remain unknown.

But arguments that rest policy conclusions on the mere appearance of impropriety require special justification. They naturally arouse suspicion: where appearance and reality diverge, why should we rest policy on mere and misleading appearances? Where they coincide, why not argue directly from reality? If, as I have argued, one's political beliefs or involvements need not taint one's reporting, why should one be bound to keep them under wraps? Having asserted that neutrality is nearly impossible and in any case undesirable, isn't the noninvolvement policy hypocritical?

To answer these questions, we must distinguish two different appearance-of-impropriety arguments. According to the first, the appearance of impropriety serves as a basis for policy just because it provides good reason to suspect genuine impropriety. On this view, if noninvolvement policies are justified on grounds of the appearance of conflict of interest, that is because the belief that such involvements bias journalists is a reasonable one.

Is this belief reasonable? It depends partly on how we characterize it. Is it the belief that people in general tend to be biased by their beliefs, or that journalists are? Journalists' professional training might make them less biased by their political beliefs than the ordinary person—not for reasons of moral or intellectual superiority but because journalists possess incentives to be unbiased that the ordinary person does not.

At the same time, the belief that political commitments bias journalists seems reasonable to the extent that—as I argued in the previous section—such commitments entangle journalists in personal relationships that make detachment and fairness difficult.

This first appearance-of-impropriety argument, then, gives modest support to prohibiting journalists' political involvements. According to the second argument, although the appearance of impropriety may be misleading, it does not follow that we should ignore it. If people believe that journalists' political views distort their work, that will undermine journalism's credibility. And this is a legitimate reason for instituting policies to counteract such beliefs.

Yet sometimes it seems downright wrong to fashion policies to suit people's false or unjustified beliefs. Even though people's racist or sexist beliefs may be very powerful, we do not think policies should be shaped around them. What's the difference? At least this: racist or sexist beliefs seriously demean and degrade minorities and women. But the belief that journalists' political commitments bias them does not degrade them in the same way. There is,

I conclude, nothing wrong with designing policies around people's false beliefs, if the beliefs do not seriously degrade other people and if there is little hope of changing them.

To endorse the noninvolvement policy while denying that reporters can be or should be neutral is likely to invite condemnation from both sides. For the most natural defense of the policy relies on the premise of journalistic neutrality, while opponents tend to assert that neutrality is a fiction. Let me say a bit more, then, to defend my view.

First, I do not mean to deny that reporters (like everyone else) possess biases, and that these biases may influence their reporting. No one is perfectly detached and distanced from her opinions. But having opinions is not the same as being biased by them. The idea that bias is inescapable and poisonous leaves us no way to separate better reporting from worse. If we insist that every opinion is a bias we will simply have to invent a new distinction to separate good reporting from bad.

Second, I believe it is a common fallacy to overestimate the influence of journalists' personal beliefs on their reporting. The reason is mainly that we are likely to ignore structural and institutional forces and biases which, although often more subtle than personal political commitments, are also more powerful.

Among these forces are editors who act as critics and eliminate obvious slants and value judgments. There are also journalists' own professional values, which may conflict with their political beliefs: the desire for a good story, for professional recognition and success may provide incentives to fairness, and the assumption of moral virtue is not required. Extremely important are the institutional constraints of news organizations and the natural tendencies of particular media, which may also pull against the reporter's personal views. So, for example, a reporter's liberal political views may be insufficient to overcome the inherent conservatism of journalists' reliance on official sources, the ability of powerful political figures to use the media to their own advantage, and the effects of news organizations' formal and informal ties to large corporations.

My justification for the prohibition on political involvement rests, then, on the surprising view that audiences are more likely to be biased by knowing journalists' beliefs than journalists are by having them. We can, of course, imagine circumstances in which the prohibition ought to be over-ridden. In emergencies, pressing moral and political concerns—civil rights, the threat of totalitarianism—may leave the professional with no alternative.

The force of the foregoing arguments must be evaluated in light of several variables:

Public acts and private acts. My view that reporters should not engage in political action rests largely on the public nature of their activities. But political involvement can be more or less public. A journalist might donate money to a cause, march anonymously in a demonstration, or work behind the scenes for an organization. On the other hand, she might sign petitions published in newspapers, testify before Congress, or in some other way make her commitments known.

How visible a person's actions are depends not only on the actions but on the person. Acts that would call immediate attention to Diane Sawyer or Ted Koppel might go entirely unnoticed if done by a reporter for a small city newspaper.

The relation between a journalist's political activities and her beat. If a journalist's political activities are thought to undermine either her credibility or her ability to report fairly, it stands to reason that some connection must exist between her beat and her political interests. We might see why a reporter active in the abortion-rights movement shouldn't cover abortion, but why shouldn't a reporter involved in environmentalism cover abortion?

Two reasons might be offered. First, reporters often change beats, and so even if a reporter's political activities do not overlap with her coverage today, that does not mean they never will. Second, political issues do not divide into neat packages. It is easy to see how a reporter's involvement in abortion might have implications for her views about animal rights or population growth; it does not require a great leap to see how her views about environmental questions might also be affected.

The journalist's specific role and the nature of the organization for which she works. I have defended my view primarily with an eye to the news reporter for a mass media organization. By contrast, we don't expect writers for smaller-circulation periodicals whose audiences have a specifiable point of view to be neutral in the same way. And of course editorialists are permitted—even paid—to be opinionated.

Case II: The Sound of Money Talking

Should journalists accept income derived from sources other than the news organization for which they work? Ought they to disclose the sources, and even the amounts, of their income? These are the questions raised by the Periodical Press Gallery case.

We must consider three basic policy alternatives: (1) honoraria not accepted; (2) honoraria accepted; sources (and possibly amounts) disclosed; (3) honoraria accepted; sources not disclosed.

I believe that the first policy is best, but I do not regard it as a practical possibility, because journalists as a group would refuse to accept such a sweeping limitation on their earning power (or, as they are more likely to put it, on their freedom). Clearly this claim is arguable, but let us make it nevertheless. Which of the other alternatives is preferable?

To answer this question we must explain why ideally prohibiting honoraria altogether would be best. The rationale is hardly obscure: financial interests pose genuine threats to professional duty, because those who benefit materially from a source have a strong incentive to favor information supportive of it and to ignore information damaging to it.

In accepting such a view we mark a difference between the pull of material interests and the pull of prior beliefs and values. As I have acknowledged, beliefs and values no doubt bias those who hold them to some extent. But we do not count them prejudicial in the same way as material interests. Why not?

Here are several reasons. (a) Many of people's beliefs have some rational basis; i.e., they bear some connection to truth. The strength of the connection is a matter of dispute, but we can assert at least this much: that a person believes a given proposition provides some reason for thinking it true; that a person has a material interest in the truth of a given proposition provides no reason for thinking it true. (b) The investment most people have in particular political, social, economic, and other worldly beliefs—those beliefs reflected in the news—is rarely so great as to render them immune to change of view in light of contrary evidence or argument. The exceptions we call ideologues or fanatics or true believers. (c) When money talks, most people listen.

Yet none of these reasons alone supports the weight of the conclusion, because the truth of each is qualified. Even together, we may question how well they distinguish the biases of material interests from the biases of belief. Further doubt may be cast by those who, arguing in defense of journalists, find the imputation of greed and even bribery implausible and insulting.

For the motives of most journalists, including those who accept honoraria, are probably honorable. Journalists do not sell their souls when they give speeches for money. Indeed, the typical lecture-circuit journalist probably gives essentially the same talk (to go with lunch: light on substance and controversy so as not to cause indigestion) to whatever organization invites him, no matter what its political orientation. So what's the problem?

The conflict of interest arises, however, not because most journalists can be bought in the crude way. Most people do not simply abandon all their scruples for money. For them the force of material conflicts of interest derives primarily from the relationship created between donor and beneficiary. It will be difficult for the reporter to write an exposé of the lobbying group that has just paid him thousands of dollars to give a speech. He now knows some members of the group; a relationship has been established; the group has benefited him. Unless something has gone wrong—they treated him badly, didn't pay what they had promised, or in some other way fumbled—turning his investigative arsenal on them will probably feel like a betrayal.

Seen in this way, the underlying force of material conflicts of interest is of a piece with the other most common species: personal relationships, which can exert a powerful pull at odds with professional duty. In both cases, the primary source of the conflict resides in the existence of a relationship rather than in greed.

What has been forgotten in the current hand-wringing about "ethics in America" is that our vulnerability to conflicts of interest speaks as much of our virtues—our connectedness to other people—as of our vices. Of course some professionals are corrupted by garden-variety self-interest. And others can separate their professional duty from their feelings: they can take the money and run, writing a critical story that bites the hand that fed it. (Ironically, as we admire their "professionalism" we may suspect them as human beings.) Nevertheless, conflicts of interest often arise from personal traits that we value highly.

Returning to the practical question, if we cannot expect journalists to forego honoraria, should we at least expect them to disclose them? Yes, because, as I have been arguing, honoraria pose a genuine threat of conflict of interest. Disclosure can serve two valuable functions: first, to alert the public to the possibility of conflicts; and second, to deter journalists from undertaking relationships that breed conflicts.

Is there any inconsistency in journalists' keeping their beliefs to themselves to avoid creating an appearance of impropriety while disclosing their finances, which may create the same appearance? I don't think so. Because material interests are more biasing

than prior beliefs, the appearance of conflict of interest created by disclosure of honoraria is less misleading than the appearance of conflict created by public political involvement. And there are other asymmetries between the cases as well.

First, although each policy requires sacrifice, presumably journalists would prefer the option of political involvement, while they would rather not disclose sources of income—refraining from public political commitments, unlike refusing honoraria, is already deeply embedded in journalistic norms. It does not appear to demand more of journalists than can realistically be expected. In a different culture—fifth-century Athens or the founding fathers'—where public commitment was considered essential to a full life, this demand might be unreasonable.

Second, receiving honoraria reinforces the conservative institutional biases created by the corporate interests of news organizations and journalists' dependence on official sources, since large honoraria tend to come from powerful sources. By contrast, the biases, if any, created by journalists' political views spread out more evenly along the political spectrum.

Finally, journalists have long exerted pressure on politicians and public officials to disclose their financial involvements, on the assumption that these entangle them in conflicts of interest. Journalists' lack of embarrassment at failing to practice what they preach is remarkable. Their standard response, when they bother to make one at all, is that they are not public employees and so do not bear the same duties as politicians and public officials.

But in crucial respects the contemporary mass media are public institutions. As I argued earlier, they are not simply voices in the public debate; today they constitute the forum itself, where all significant debate takes place and to which anyone who hopes to make a difference must gain access. Just the concerns that justify financial disclosure by politicians and public officials apply to reporters for mass media organizations, who remind us of their public function whenever they invoke the First Amendment.

Journalists are neither more nor less susceptible to compromising conflicts than the politicians they cover. In both cases, the question is whether they have motives at odds with their professional duties.

But suppose that a journalist only gives speeches for free. Does she not, by my argument, still form some of the ties that create conflicts of interest—meeting people, developing relationships, and the like?

She does, but not, perhaps, with the same degree of indebtedness. Conflicts of interest cannot be entirely eliminated; the argument for financial disclosure is that such a measure can at least contain them. Other conflicts, however, will exist as long as journalists have relationships with other people. The long-term relationships between journalists and sources provide an ineradicable source of conflict. Journalists who depend extraordinarily on the cooperation of regular sources—i.e., many reporters with important beats—must be tempted to avoid critical stories if not to write flattering ones. Those who attend parties with the people they write about are at special risk.

Conflicts of interest, then, constitute an occupational hazard for journalists. Compared to the others, those involving money are easy to avoid.

NOTES

1 *New York Times*, April 16, 1989, 28.
2 See, e.g., Eleanor Randolph, "Query Makes Reporters Cringe," *Washington Post*, January 25, 1989, and Cass Peterson, "4 Press Gallery Incumbents Lose Seats in Disclosure Flap," *Washington Post*, February 5, 1989, A14.
3 *On Liberty* (Indianapolis: Robbs-Merrill, 1956), 58.

CASE STUDY

BREAKING A PROMISE TO PREVENT A LIE
AARON QUINN

Case Description

Journalism is replete with ethical controversy and never more than in the recent past. Special federal prosecutor Patrick J. Fitzgerald was assigned to investigate the senior Bush Administration source(s) who apparently leaked confidential information to journalists that potentially threatened national security and the safety of an undercover CIA agent. Subsequently, at least two journalists were ordered by a federal grand jury to reveal the confidential source (or sources) who leaked the identity of CIA agent Valerie Plame. Matthew Cooper of *Time* and Judith Miller of the *The New York Times* were ordered to reveal the identity of a source or sources who, apparently out of political revenge, leaked Plame's name to reporters because of her husband's role in publicly criticizing the Bush Administration's rationale for going to war in Iraq.

Plame's husband, Joseph C. Wilson, was commissioned to investigate whether it was likely the pre-invasion Iraqi government either succeeded in or attempted to acquire uranium for the purpose of making weapons of mass destruction. After his investigation, Wilson concluded that there was no evidence to indicate that uranium had been acquired or sought by Iraqi government or military officials. In an op-ed column he authored for *The New York Times*, Wilson criticized the Bush Administration for attempting to justify the invasion of Iraq on the grounds that it had, or was developing, weapons of mass destruction.

The matter first gained prominence after Plame's name was published in a column written by conservative columnist Robert Novak, as it sparked worry in the intelligence community that there was a threat of further dangerous intelligence leaks. When contacted by Fitzgerald, Novak agreed to give testimony about his source(s), but both Cooper and Miller initially refused, citing their interest in maintaining their confidential agreements. Though *Time* and its reporter Matthew Cooper relented to the judicial pressure and the threat of imprisonment, Miller was eventually jailed for 85 days for her refusal to comply with the grand jury's order, despite having never published a story mentioning Plame.

Fitzgerald, meanwhile, continues to seek information about what role Vice President Dick Cheney's Chief of Staff, I. Lewis Libby, and senior Bush advisor Karl Rove, might have played in the leak. Though Libby claims he has not participated in leaking information, he was indicted on charges of obstruction of justice, perjury and making false statements. Rove, on the other hand, has not been charged as of early December 2005, but remains involved in an ongoing investigation. Several reporters, including *Time*'s Viveca Novak (no relation to Robert Novak), told Fitzgerald that Rove was Cooper's source for information about Plame.

Ethical Analysis

There are a number of moral matters at issue in this case, and we will focus on those most crucial to journalists. First and foremost is the matter of whether journalists are always bound to keeping confidential agreements with sources. This of course raises matters both legal and moral. Legally, it has become increasingly common for journalists to make written agreements with confidential sources regarding the conditions of their confidentiality agreements. Miller claims to have been legally bound to maintain her confidentiality agreement based on one such contract, but later agreed to offer limited testimony once her source(s) relieved her of her contractual obligation. It is less clear with Cooper or either of the Novaks whether their agreements were written contracts or more traditional oral agreements.

Nevertheless, there is the additional matter of what a journalist's moral obligation ought to be when confidential agreements bring about conflicting duties. On the one hand, journalists are morally obligated to keep their promises, which includes maintaining confidentiality agreements to which they have agreed. On the other hand, there may be legitimate duties that conflict with keeping their confidentiality agreement, such as aiding law enforcement in bringing about justice when there are few or no alternative sources of information for authorities. In the Plame affair, many journalists and media critics alike have suggested that Miller's stronger duty might have been to reveal her confidential source(s) because maintaining the confidence would make her complicit in a moral and legal wrong—leaking intelligence information that may threaten both national security and the safety of an innocent, Valerie Plame.

Journalists, as many of their ethics codes and traditions reveal, rarely if ever are comfortable in breaking confidentiality agreements. Most journalists think breaking confidences undermines the very trust on which journalism's social value rests. Conversely, many in the judiciary believe journalists have the same legal and moral obligation as all citizens, which is to comply with grand jury and judicial subpoenas that aim to bring justice. Ultimately, this impasse boils down to a disagreement about what moral costs journalists ought to incur in such moral conflicts—does one risk losing public trust by breaking confidential agreements, or does one instead weaken the justice system by failing to contribute crucial information to it?

Journalists have long argued that complying with subpoenas in instances in which they are not protected by "shield laws"—state statutes that sometimes allow journalists to refuse testimony without legal penalty—makes them an unofficial branch of law enforcement to be used (or abused) at will. Moreover, journalists have never had an official professional status—other than scattered shield laws—that recognizes them as anything other than ordinary citizens who have a legal and moral obligation as citizens to promote justice. Conversely, medical doctors and lawyers have a legal obligation to maintain confidential information about their patients and clients.

Journalists' confusion about moral conflicts in confidential sourcing represents part of an interesting debate in professional ethics between what is commonly labeled role morality—following the moral mandates and guidelines specific to the goals and purposes of an occupation—and universalizable ethics—mandates and guidelines to be followed in any circumstance, occupational or otherwise. As mentioned above, journalists are typically inclined to follow a journalistic role morality that emphasizes maintaining confidential agreements and by extension their public trust. Nevertheless, critics decry this steadfast adherence to journalistic convention because of its occasional incompatibility with the more universal pursuit of justice.

Study Questions

1. Should journalists maintain confidential sources under all conditions, or are there circumstances that mitigate their promise-keeping obligations?

2. Should journalists make written contractual agreements with sources?

3. Are the contractual obligations of journalists (legal or moral) nullified when their sources lie to or mislead them?

4. What is a more important goal for journalists when their journalistic duties conflict with their duties as ordinary citizens: to achieve ends that best advance the profession or to achieve ends that a good citizen would promote?

5. Should journalists be afforded special legal and social privileges like absolute shield laws because of their special duties related to informing the public?

UNIT 4

Legal Ethics

FRITZ ALLHOFF

Legal Ethics

Why is it that lawyers are often derided as among the most unethical professionals? Certainly there is a perception that they will do whatever it takes to win their cases; but does that make them unethical? Or does ethics *require* that they zealously advocate on behalf of their clients, so long as their actions stay within the bounds of the law? Consider a famous example, which is offered by Monroe Freedman in his famous essay "Professional Responsibility of the Criminal Defense Lawyer: The Three Hardest Questions" (reprinted in this volume). In this hypothetical situation, we might imagine a defense lawyer to know the guilt of his client, though know that a conviction will only be possible with the incriminating testimony of an elderly witness. Further imagine that, while the lawyer knows the testimony to be true, she could levy any number of assaults against its integrity, challenging the vision, mental competence, etc. of the witness. *Ethically*, then, what should the lawyer do: leave the truthful testimony unchallenged (thus ensuring a conviction for her client) or else vociferously attack it, hoping to create reasonable doubt in the minds of the jurors and to secure an acquittal for her client?

This is a *very* tough question that quickly gets to the heart of many of the complicated issues in legal ethics. The lawyer, it seems, is party to competing interests: those of her client and those of justice. When such a conflict attains, as they undoubtedly do in criminal defense, what should the lawyer do? Follow the interests of the client and attempt to secure an acquittal? Or else follow the interests of justice and be complicit in the conviction (by not seeking to discredit the testimony)? Freedman takes a controversial stand on this question (as on the other two that he posits) by saying that the lawyer *must* serve the interests of the client, and that the demands of justice are irrelevant to the functional role that the

lawyer occupies. While this might sound like an extreme position, Freedman, of course, has reasons to defend it: he argues that zealous advocacy is *required* by the legal system that we have and that anything short thereof is inconsistent with its proper functioning and self-defeating.

What does this mean? Or, more specifically, what sort of legal system *do* we have? Ours is commonly referred to as an *adversarial* system, which might be contrasted with some European inquisitorial systems. The adversarial legal system is characterized by two legal teams (*viz*, the prosecution and the defense) who *compete* against each other in such a way that, absent mistrials, one team *wins* and the other team *loses*. There is no reason that legal systems have to work this way (and, as mentioned above, many do not). Rather, there could be inquests which are *led by* (rather than facilitated by) the judge and in which the legal teams, if they exist at all, have comparatively minor roles.

Why does any of this matter? Freedman, for example, argues that the *moral responsibilities* of lawyers depend upon the systems that they inhabit. In the adversarial system, both the prosecution and the defense are supposed to try to win; if the criminal defense attorneys give less than their all in defense of their clients, the balance would be tipped in favor of the more zealous prosecutors. This would, ultimately, be a disservice to all criminal defendants (both the guilty and the innocent), so Freedman, as well as the American Bar Association's Model Rules of Professional Conduct, thinks that lawyers owe their best efforts; such efforts are required to preserve the integrity of the system itself.

Whatever you think about such an argument, it is an extremely powerful one and shapes many of the current debates in legal ethics, as well as the chosen selections in this volume. One of the most powerful objections to Freedman's position comes from David Luban, who argues that, while Freedman might be right in arguing that the system justifies the actions of its constituents, we should only be swayed by such an argument if the *system* is morally justifiable in the first place. Luban then goes on to raise various objections to the adversarial legal system, and eventually concludes that the system does not have the sort of moral justification that it would need to license many of the behaviors by lawyers that Freedman aims to sanction.

After these foundational discussions, we offer selections on confidentiality and on duty to represent. Certainly the adversarial legal system places a high premium on confidentiality: without it, clients might not disclose information to their lawyers that might otherwise be useful in a defense. Nevertheless, it does not follow from this alone that there should be no *limits* to confidentiality; in fact, several are widely codified into law.

Finally, we offer two articles on the duty to represent. Imagine, for example, that a lawyer is approached for a legal defense by a client whom the lawyer finds morally detestable (e.g., imagine that the client is a Nazi sympathizer); does the lawyer have a *duty* to represent the client? Imagine further that no other lawyer is available (or is as equally qualified); does this change the situation at all? If we think that lawyers do *not* have a duty to represent certain clients, then we might be in a quandary such that those would-be clients are without legal representation altogether. No matter how morally repulsive someone is, should they nevertheless be afforded a quality legal defense? Relatedly, to what extent should lawyers have the *discretion* to choose what clients they will represent?

LAWYERS' OBLIGATIONS AND VIRTUES

MONROE H. FREEDMAN

Professional Responsibility of the Criminal Defense Lawyer: The Three Hardest Questions

In almost any area of legal counseling and advocacy, the lawyer may be faced with the dilemma of either betraying the confidential communications of his client or participating to some extent in the purposeful deception of the court. This problem is nowhere more acute than in the practice of criminal law, particularly in the representation of the indigent accused. The purpose of this article is to analyze and attempt to resolve three of the most difficult issues in this general area:

1. Is it proper to cross-examine for the purpose of discrediting the reliability or credibility of an adverse witness whom you know to be telling the truth?
2. Is it proper to put a witness on the stand when you know he will commit perjury?
3. Is it proper to give your client legal advice when you have reason to believe that the knowledge you give him will tempt him to commit perjury?

These questions present serious difficulties with respect to a lawyer's ethical responsibilities. Moreover, if one admits the possibility of an affirmative answer, it is difficult even to discuss them without appearing to some to be unethical.[1] It is not surprising, therefore, that reasonable, rational discussion of these issues has been uncommon and that the problems have for so long remained unresolved. In this regard it should be recognized that the Canons of Ethics, which were promulgated in 1900 "as a general guide,"[2] are both inadequate and self-contradictory.

1. The Adversary System and the Necessity for Confidentiality

At the outset, we should dispose of some common question-begging responses. The attorney is indeed an officer of the court, and he does participate in a search for truth. These two propositions, however, merely serve to state the problem in different words: As an officer of the court, participating in a search for truths, what is the attorney's special responsibility, and how does that responsibility affect his resolution of the questions posed above?

The attorney functions in an adversary system based upon the presupposition that the most effective means of determining truth is to present to a judge and jury a clash between proponents of conflicting views. It is essential to the effective function of this system that each adversary have, in the words of Canon 15, "entire devotion to the interest of the client, warm zeal in the maintenance and defense of his rights and the exertion of his utmost learning and ability." It is also essential to maintain the fullest uninhibited communication between the client and his attorney, so that the attorney can most effectively counsel his client and advocate the latter's cause. This policy is safeguarded by the requirement that the lawyer must, in the words of Canon 37, "preserve his client's confidences." Canon 15 does, of course, qualify these obligations by stating that "the office of attorney does not permit, much less does it demand of him for any client, violations of law or any manner of fraud or chicane." In addition, Canon 22 requires candor toward the court.

The problem presented by these salutary generalities of the Canons in the context of particular litigation is illustrated by the personal experience of Samuel Williston, which was related in his autobiography.[3] Because of his examination of a client's correspondence file, Williston learned of a fact extremely damaging to his client's case. When the judge announced his decision, it was apparent that a critical factor in the favorable judgment for Williston's client was the judge's ignorance of this fact. Williston remained silent and did not thereafter inform the judge of what he knew. He was convinced, and Charles Curtis[4] agrees with him, that it was his duty to remain silent.

In an opinion by the American Bar Association Committee on Professional Ethics and Grievances, an eminent panel headed by Henry Drinker held that a lawyer should remain silent when his client lies to the judge by saying that he has no prior record, despite the attorney's knowledge to the contrary.[5] The majority of the panel distinguished the situation in which the attorney has learned of the client's prior record from a source other than the client himself. William B. Jones, a distinguished trial lawyer and now a judge in the United States District Court for the District of Columbia, wrote a separate opinion in which he asserted that in neither event should the lawyer expose his client's lie. If these two cases do not constitute "fraud or chicane" or lack of candor within the meaning of the Canons (and I agree with the authorities cited that they do not), it is clear that the meaning of the Canons is ambiguous.

The adversary system has further ramifications in a criminal case. The defendant is presumed to be innocent. The burden is on the prosecution to prove beyond a reasonable doubt that the defendant is guilty. The plea of not guilty does not necessarily mean "not guilty in fact," for the defendant may mean "not legally guilty." Even the accused who knows that he committed the crime is entitled to put the government to its proof. Indeed, the accused who knows that he is guilty has an absolute constitutional right to remain silent.[6] The moralist might quite reasonably understand this to mean that, under these circumstances, the defendant and his lawyer are privileged to "lie" to the court in pleading not guilty. In my judgment the moralist is right. However, our adversary system and related notions of the proper administration of criminal justice sanction the lie.

Some derive solace from the sophistry of calling the lie a "legal fiction," but this is hardly an adequate answer to the moralist. Moreover, this answer has no particular appeal for the practicing attorney, who knows that the plea of not guilty commits him to the most effective advocacy of which he is capable. Criminal defense lawyers do not win their cases by arguing reasonable doubt. Effective trial advocacy requires that the attorney's every word, action, and attitude be consistent with the conclusion that his client is innocent. As every trial lawyer knows, the jury is certain that the defense attorney knows whether his client is guilty. The jury is therefore alert to, and will be enormously affected by, any indication by the attorney that he believes the defendant to be guilty. Thus, the plea of not guilty commits the advocate to a trial, including a closing argument, in which he must argue that "not guilty" means "not guilty in fact."[7]

There is, of course, a simple way to evade the dilemma raised by the not guilty plea. Some attorneys rationalize the problem by insisting that a lawyer never knows for sure whether his client is guilty. The client who insists upon his guilt may in fact be protecting his wife, or may know that he pulled the trigger and that the victim was killed, but not that his gun was loaded with blanks and that the fatal shot was fired from across the street. For anyone who finds this reasoning satisfactory, there is, of course, no need to think further about the issue.

It is also argued that a defense attorney can remain selectively ignorant. He can insist in his first interview with his client that, if his client is guilty, he simply does not want to know. It is inconceivable, however, that an attorney could give adequate counsel under such circumstances. How is the client to know, for example, precisely which relevant circumstances his lawyer does not want to be told? The lawyer might ask whether his client has a prior record. The client, assuming that this is the kind of

knowledge that might present ethical problems for his lawyer, might respond that he has no record. The lawyer would then put the defendant on the stand and, on cross-examination, be appalled to learn that his client has two prior convictions for offenses identical to that for which he is being tried.

Of course, an attorney can guard against this specific problem by telling his client that he must know about the client's past record. However, a lawyer can never anticipate all of the innumerable and potentially critical factors that his client, once cautioned, may decide not to reveal. In one instance, for example, the defendant assumed that his lawyer would prefer to be ignorant of the fact that the client had been having sexual relations with the chief defense witness. The client was innocent of the robbery with which he was charged, but was found guilty by the jury—probably because he was guilty of fornication, a far less serious offense for which he had not even been charged.

The problem is compounded by the practice of plea bargaining. It is considered improper for a defendant to plead guilty to a lesser offense unless he is in fact guilty. Nevertheless, it is common knowledge that plea bargaining frequently results in improper guilty pleas by innocent people. For example, a defendant falsely accused of robbery may plead guilty to simple assault, rather than risk a robbery conviction and a substantial prison term. If an attorney is to be scrupulous in bargaining pleas, however, he must know in advance that his client is guilty, since the guilty plea is improper if the defendant is innocent. Of course, if the attempt to bargain for a lesser offense should fail, the lawyer would know the truth and thereafter be unable to rationalize that he was uncertain of his client's guilt.

If one recognizes that professional responsibility requires that an advocate have full knowledge of every pertinent fact, it follows that he must seek the truth from his client, not shun it.[8] This means that he will have to dig and pry and cajole, and, even then, he will not be successful unless he can convince the client that full and confidential disclosure to his lawyer will never result in prejudice to the client by any word or action of the lawyer. This is, perhaps, particularly true in the case of the indigent defendant, who meets his lawyer for the first time in the cell block or the rotunda. He did not choose the lawyer, nor does he know him. The lawyer has been sent by the judge and is part of the system that is attempting to punish the defendant. It is no easy task to persuade this client that he can talk freely without fear of prejudice. However, the inclination to mislead one's lawyer is not restricted to the indigent or even to the criminal defendant. Randolph Paul has observed a similar phenomenon among a wealthier class in a far more congenial atmosphere:

> The tax adviser will sometimes have to dynamite the facts of his case out of the unwilling witnesses on his own side—witnesses who are nervous, witnesses who are confused about their own interest, witnesses who try to be too smart for their own good, and witnesses who subconsciously do not want to understand what has happened despite the fact that they must if they are to testify coherently.[9]

Paul goes on to explain that the truth can be obtained only by persuading the client that it would be a violation of a sacred obligation for the lawyer ever to reveal a client's confidence. Beyond any question, once a lawyer has persuaded his client of the obligation of confidentiality, he must respect that obligation scrupulously.

II. The Specific Questions

The first of the difficult problems posed above will now be considered: Is it proper to cross-examine for the purpose of discrediting the reliability or the credibility of a witness whom you know to be telling the truth? Assume the following situation. Your client has been falsely accused of a robbery committed at 16th and P Streets at 11:00 p.m. He tells you at first that at no time on the evening of the crime was he within six blocks of that location. However, you are able to persuade him that he must tell you the truth and that doing so will in no way prejudice him. He then reveals to you that he was at 15th and P Streets at 10:55 p.m. that evening, but that he was walking east, away from the scene of the crime, and that, by 11:00 p.m., he was six blocks away. At the trial, there are two prosecution witnesses. The first mistakenly, but with some degree of persuasion, identifies your client as the criminal. At that point, the prosecution's case depends on this single witness, who might or might not be believed. Since your client has a prior record, you do not want to put him on the stand, but you feel that there is at least a chance for acquittal. The second prosecution witness is an elderly woman who is somewhat nervous and who wears glasses. She testifies truthfully and accurately that she saw your client at 15th and P Streets at 10:55 p.m. She has corroborated the erroneous testimony of the first witness and made conviction virtually certain. However, if you destroy her reliability through cross-examination designed to show that she is easily confused and has poor eyesight, you may not only eliminate the corroboration, but also cast doubt in the jury's mind on the prosecution's entire case. On the other hand, if you should refuse to cross-examine her because she is telling the truth, your client may well feel betrayed, since you knew of the witness's veracity only because your client confided in you, under your assurance that his truthfulness would not prejudice him.

The client would be right. Viewed strictly, the attorney's failure to cross-examine would not be violative of the client's confidence because it would not constitute a disclosure. However, the same policy that supports the obligation of confidentiality precludes the attorney from prejudicing his client's interest in any other way because of knowledge gained in his professional capacity. When a lawyer fails to cross-examine only because his client, placing confidence in the lawyer, has been candid with him, the basis for such confidence and candor collapses. Our legal system cannot tolerate such a result.

> The purposes and necessities of the relation between a client and his attorney require, in many cases, on the part of the client, the fullest and freest disclosures to the attorney of the client's objects, motives and acts.... To permit the attorney to reveal to others what is so disclosed, would be not only a gross violation of a sacred trust upon his part, but it would utterly destroy and prevent the usefulness and benefits to be derived from professional assistance.[10]

The client's confidences must "upon all occasions be inviolable," to avoid the "greater mischiefs" that would probably result if a client could not feel free "to repose [confidence] in the attorney to whom he resorts for legal advice and assistance."[11] Destroy that confidence, and "a man would not venture to consult any skillful person, or would only dare to tell his counsellor half his case."[12]

Therefore, one must conclude that the attorney is obligated to attack, if he can, the reliability or credibility of an opposing witness whom he knows to be truthful. The contrary result would inevitably impair the "perfect freedom of consultation by client with attorney," which is "essential to the administration of justice."[13]

The second question is generally considered to be the hardest of all: is it proper to put a witness on the stand when you know he will commit perjury? Assume, for example, that the witness in question is the accused himself, and that he has admitted to you, in response to your assurances of confidentiality, that he is guilty. However, he insists upon taking the stand to protest his innocence. There is a clear consensus among prosecutors and defense attorneys that the likelihood of conviction is increased enormously when the defendant does not take the stand. Consequently, the attorney who prevents his client

from testifying only because the client has confided his guilt to him is violating that confidence by acting upon the information in a way that will seriously prejudice his client's interests.

Perhaps the most common method for avoiding the ethical problem just posed is for the lawyer to withdraw from the case, at least if there is sufficient time before trial for the client to retain another attorney.[14] The client will then go to the nearest law office, realizing that the obligation of confidentiality is not what it has been represented to be, and withhold incriminating information or the fact of his guilt from his new attorney. On ethical grounds, the practice of withdrawing from a case under such circumstances is indefensible, since the identical perjured testimony will ultimately be presented. More important, perhaps, is the practical consideration that the new attorney will be ignorant of the perjury and therefore will be in no position to attempt to discourage the client from presenting it. Only the original attorney, who knows the truth, has that opportunity, but he loses it in the very act of evading the ethical problem.

The problem is all the more difficult when the client is indigent. He cannot retain other counsel, and in many jurisdictions, including the District of Columbia, it is impossible for appointed counsel to withdraw from a case except for extraordinary reasons. Thus, appointed counsel, unless he lies to the judge, can successfully withdraw only by revealing to the judge that the attorney has received knowledge of his client's guilt. Such a revelation in itself should seem to be a sufficiently serious violation of the obligation of confidentiality to merit severe condemnation. In fact, however, the situation is far worse, since it is entirely possible that the same judge who permits the attorney to withdraw will subsequently hear the case and sentence the defendant. When he does so, of course, he will have had personal knowledge of the defendant's guilt before the trial began.[15] Moreover, this will be knowledge of which the newly appointed counsel for the defendant will probably be ignorant.

The difficulty is further aggravated when the client informs the lawyer for the first time during trial that he intends to take the stand and commit perjury. The perjury in question may not necessarily be a protestation of innocence by a guilty man. Referring to the earlier hypothetical of the defendant wrongly accused of a robbery at 16th and P. the only perjury may be his denial or the truthful, but highly damaging, testimony of the corroborating witness who placed him one block away from the intersection five minutes prior to the crime. Of course, if he tells the truth and thus verifies the corroborating witness, the jury will be far more inclined to accept the inaccurate testimony of the principal witness, who specifically identified him as the criminal.[16]

If a lawyer has discovered his client's intent to perjure himself, one possible solution to this problem is for the lawyer to approach the bench, explain his ethical difficulty to the judge, and ask to be relieved, thereby causing a mistrial. This request is certain to be denied, if only because it would empower the defendant to cause a series of mistrials in the same fashion. At this point, some feel that the lawyer has avoided the ethical problem and can put the defendant on the stand. However, one objection to this solution, apart from the violation of confidentiality, is that the lawyer's ethical problem has not been solved, but has only been transferred to the judge. Moreover, the client in such a case might well have grounds for appeal on the basis of deprivation of due process and denial of the right to counsel, since he will leave been tried before, and sentenced by, a judge who has been informed of the client's guilt by his own attorney.

A solution even less satisfactory that informing the judge of the defendant's guilt would be to let the client take the stand without the attorney's participation and to omit reference to the client's testimony in closing argument. The latter solution, of course, would be as damaging as to fail entirely to argue the case to the jury, and failing to argue the case is "as improper as though the attorney had told the jury

that his client had uttered a falsehood in making the statement."[17]

Therefore, the obligation of confidentiality, in the context of our adversary system, apparently allows the attorney no alternative to putting a perjurious witness on the stand without explicit or implicit disclosure of the attorney's knowledge to either the judge or the jury. Canon 37 does not proscribe this conclusion; the canon recognizes only two exceptions to the obligation of confidentiality. The first relates to the lawyer who is accused by his client and may disclose the truth to defend himself. The other exception relates to the "announced intention of a client to commit a crime." On the basis of the ethical and practical considerations discussed above, the Canon's exception to the obligation of confidentiality cannot logically be understood to include the crime of perjury committed during the specific case in which the lawyer is serving. Moreover, even when the intention is to commit a crime in the future, Canon 37 does not require disclosure, but only permits it. Furthermore, Canon 15, which does proscribe "violation of law" by the attorney for his client, does not apply to the lawyer who unwillingly puts a perjurious client on the stand after having made every effort to dissuade him from committing perjury. Such an act by the attorney cannot properly be found to be subornation—corrupt inducement—of perjury. Canon 29 requires counsel to inform the prosecuting authorities of perjury committed in a case in which he has been involved, but this can only refer to perjury by opposing witnesses. For an attorney to disclose his client's perjury "would involve a direct violation of Canon 37."[18] Despite Canon 29, therefore, the attorney should not reveal his client's perjury "to the court or to the authorities."[19]

Of course, before the client testifies perjuriously, the lawyer has a duty to attempt to dissuade him on grounds of both law and morality. In addition, the client should be impressed with the fact that his untruthful alibi is tactically dangerous. There is always a strong possibility that the prosecutor will expose the perjury on cross-examination. However, for the reasons already given, the final decision must necessarily be the client's. The lawyer's best course thereafter would be to avoid any further professional relationship with a client whom he knew to have perjured himself.

The third question is whether it is proper to give your client legal advice when you have reason to believe that the knowledge you give him will tempt him to commit perjury. This may indeed be the most difficult problem of all, because giving such advice creates the appearance that the attorney is encouraging and condoning perjury.

If the lawyer is not certain what the facts are when he gives the advice, the problem is substantially minimized, if not eliminated. It is not the lawyer's function to prejudge his client as a perjurer. He cannot presume that the client will make unlawful use of his advice. Apart from this, there is a natural predisposition in most people to recollect facts, entirely honestly, in a way most favorable to their own interest. As Randolph Paul has observed, some witnesses are nervous, some are confused about their own interests, some try to be too smart for their own good, and some subconsciously do not want to understand what has happened to them.[20] Before he begins to remember essential facts, the client is entitled to know what his own interests are.

The above argument does not apply merely to factual questions such as whether a particular event occurred at 10:15 or at 10:45.[21] One of the most critical problems in a criminal case, as in many others, is intention. A German writer, considering the question of intention as a test of legal consequences, suggests the following situation.[22] A young man and a young woman decide to get married. Each has a thousand dollars. They decide to begin a business with these funds, and the young lady gives her money to the young man for this purpose. Was the intention to form a joint venture or a partnership? Did they intend that the young man be an agent or a trustee? Was the transaction a gift or a loan? If the couple should subsequently visit a tax attorney and discover that it is in their interest that the transaction be viewed as a gift, it is submitted that they could, with complete honesty, so remember it. On the other hand, should their engagement be broken and the young woman consult an attorney for the purpose of recovering her money, she could with equal honesty remember that her intention was to make a loan.

Assume that your client, on trial for his life in a first-degree murder case, has killed another man with a penknife but insists that the killing was in self-defense. You ask him, "Do you customarily carry the penknife in your pocket, do you carry it frequently or infrequently, or did you take it with you only on this occasion?" He replies, "Why do you ask me a question like that?" It is entirely appropriate to inform him that his carrying the knife only on this occasion, or infrequently, supports an inference of premeditation, while if he carried the knife constantly, or frequently, the inference of premeditation would be negated. Thus, your client's life may depend upon his recollection as to whether he carried the knife frequently or infrequently. Despite the possibility that the client or a third party might infer that the lawyer was prompting the client to lie, the lawyer must apprise the defendant of the significance of his answer. There is no conceivable ethical requirement that the lawyer trap his client into a hasty and ill-considered answer before telling him the significance of the question.

A similar problem is created if the client has given the lawyer incriminating information before being fully aware of its significance. For example, assume that a man consults a tax lawyer and says, "I am fifty years old. Nobody in my immediate family has lived past fifty. Therefore, I would like to put my affairs in order. Specifically, I understand that I can avoid substantial estate taxes by setting up a trust. Can I do it?" The lawyer informs the client that he can successfully avoid the estate taxes only if he lives at least three years after establishing the trust or, should he die within three years, if the trust is found not to have been created in contemplation of death. The client then might ask who decides whether the trust is in contemplation of death. After learning that the determination is made by the court, the client might inquire about the factors on which such a decision would be based.

At this point, the lawyer can do one of two things. He can refuse to answer the question, or he can inform the client that the court will consider the wording of the trust instrument and will hear evidence about any conversations which he may have or any letters he may write expressing motives other than avoidance of estate taxes. It is likely that virtually every tax attorney in the country would answer the client's question, and that no one would consider the answer unethical. However, the lawyer might well appear to have prompted his client to deceive the Internal Revenue Service and the courts, and this appearance would remain regardless of the lawyer's explicit disclaimer to the client of any intent so to prompt him. Nevertheless, it should not be unethical for the lawyer to give the advice.

In a criminal case, a lawyer may be representing a client who protests his innocence, and whom the lawyer believes to be innocent. Assume, for example, that the charge is assault with intent to kill, that the prosecution has erroneous but credible eyewitness testimony against the defendant, and that the defendant's truthful alibi witness is impeachable on the basis of several felony convictions. The prosecutor, perhaps having doubts about the case, offers to permit the defendant to plead guilty to simple assault. If the defendant should go to trial and be convicted, he might well be sent to jail for fifteen years; on a plea of simple assault, the maximum penalty would be one year, and sentence might well be suspended.

The common practice of conveying the prosecutor's offer to the defendant should not be considered unethical, even if the defense lawyer is convinced of his client's innocence. Yet the lawyer is clearly in the position of prompting his client to lie, since the defendant cannot make the plea without saying to the judge that he is pleading guilty because he is guilty. Furthermore, if the client does decide to plead guilty, it would be improper for the lawyer to inform the court that his client is innocent, thereby compelling the defendant to stand trial and take the substantial risk of fifteen years' imprisonment.[23]

Essentially no different from the problem discussed above, but apparently more difficult, is the so-called *Anatomy of a Murder* situation.[24] The lawyer, who has received from his client an incriminating story of murder in the first degree, says, "If the facts are as you have stated them so far, you have no defense, and you will probably be electrocuted. On the other hand, if you acted in a blind rage, there is a possibility of saving your life. Think it over, and we will talk about it tomorrow." As in the tax case, and as in the case of the plea of guilty to a lesser offense, the lawyer has given his client a legal opinion that might induce the client to lie. This is information which the lawyer himself would have, without advice, were he in the client's position. It is submitted that the client is entitled to have this information about the law and to make his own decision as to whether to act upon it. To decide otherwise would not only penalize the less well-educated defendant, but would also prejudice the client because of his initial truthfulness in telling his story in confidence to the attorney.

III. Conclusion

The lawyer is an officer of the court, participating in a search for truth. Yet no lawyer would consider that he had acted unethically in pleading the statute of frauds or the statute of limitations as a bar to a just claim. Similarly, no lawyer would consider it unethical to prevent the introduction of evidence such as a murder weapon seized in violation of the fourth amendment or a truthful but involuntary confession, or to defend a guilty man on grounds of denial of a speedy trial.[25] Such actions are permissible because there are policy considerations that at times justify frustrating the search for truth and the prosecution of a just claim. Similarly, there are policies that justify an affirmative answer to the three questions that have been posed in this article. These policies include the maintenance of an adversary system, the presumption of innocence, the prosecution's burden to prove guilt beyond a reasonable doubt, the right to counsel, and the objection of confidentiality between lawyer and client.

Postscript[†]

At the beginning of this article, some common question-begging responses were suggested. Professor John Noonan has added yet another: the role of the advocate is to promote a wise and informed judgment by the finder of fact.[26] This is the position of the 1958 Joint Conference on Professional Responsibility of the Association at American Law Schools and of the American Bar Association, and it is, of course, the primary basis of Professor Noonan's argument.

Professor Noonan graciously compliments me on "[making the] principles vital by showing how they would govern particular cases."[27] He adds, "this scholarly explication of what is often taken for granted serves a very useful function."[28] At the risk of appearing ungrateful, I am compelled to observe that Professor Noonan's own position fails in precisely that respect. His general proposition simply does not decide specific cases, nor does he make the effort to demonstrate how it might do so. Indeed, Professor Noonan occasionally appears to be struggling against confronting the particular cases.

---

† Because Mr. Bress' article was not received in time for Professor Freedman to prepare a reply, his comments in this brief postscript are restricted to Professor Noonan's article—Ed.

For example, how would the Joint Conference principle resolve the situation where the prosecution witness testifies that the crime was committed at 10:15, and where the lawyer knows that his client has an honest alibi for 10:15, but that he actually committed the crime in question at 10:45?[29] Can the lawyer refuse to present the honest alibi? Is he contributing to wise and informed judgment when he does so? If he should decide that he cannot present the alibi, how should he proceed in withdrawing from the case? Does it matter whether he has forewarned his client that he would withdraw if he discovers that his client is in fact guilty? Will it contribute to wise and informed judgment if the client obtains another lawyer and withholds from him the fact of his guilt?[30] Similar questions might be asked regarding the problem of the guilty plea by the innocent defendant.[31] One might ask, in addition, whether such a plea is really a lie to the court, in the moral sense, or whether it is just a convention, which is Professor Noonan's view of the not-guilty plea by the guilty defendant.

In the situation involving avoidance of estate taxes,[32] the Joint Conference principle would probably require that the lawyer refuse to answer his client's question. Such a result would be required because, in the assumed circumstances, an answer could be justified as contributing to wise and informed judgment only by what Professor Noonan characterizes as "brute rationalization."[33] However, is it realistic to disregard as irrelevant the undoubted fact that virtually every tax lawyer in the country would answer the client?

Finally, Professor Noonan argues that it would be better to let the truthful (but misleading) witness remain unimpeached and to trust the trier of fact to draw the right conclusions. This is necessary, he contends, because "repeated acts of confidence in the rationality of the trial system are necessary if the decision-making process is to approach rationality."[34] This means that the fortunes, liberty, and lives of today's clients can properly be jeopardized for the sake of creating a more rational system for tomorrow's litigants. It is hard to believe that Professor Noonan either wants or expects members of the bar to act on this advice.

Thus, Professor Noonan does not realistically face up to the lawyer's practical problems in attempting to act ethically. Unfortunately, it is precisely when one tries to act on abstract ethical advice that the practicalities intrude, often rendering unethical the well-intended act.[35]

NOTES

1 The substance of this paper was recently presented to a Criminal Trial Institute attended by forty-five members of the District of Columbia Bar. As a consequence, several judges (none of whom had either heard the lecture or read it) complained to the Committee on Admissions and Grievances of the District Court for the District of Columbia, urging the author's disbarment or suspension. Only after four months of proceedings, including a hearing, two meetings and a *de novo* review by eleven federal district court judges, did the Committee announce its decision to "proceed no further in the matter."

2 American Bar Association, *Canons of Professional Ethics*, Preamble (1908).

3 Williston, *Life and Law* 271 (1940).

4 Curtis, *It's Your Law*, 17-21 (1954). See also Curtis, "The Ethics of Advocacy," *Stan. L. Rev.* Vol. 4: 3, 9-10 (1951); Drinker, "Some Remarks on Mr. Curtis' 'The Ethics of Advocacy,'" *Stan. L. Rev.* Vol. 4: 349, 350-51 (1952).

5 Opinion 287, Committee on Professional Ethics and Grievances of the American Bar Association (1953).

6 *Escobedo v. Illinois*, 378 U.S. 478, 485, 491 (1964).

7 "The failure to argue the case before the jury, while ordinarily only a trial tactic not subject to review, manifestly enters the field of incompe-tency when the reason assigned is the attorney's conscience. It is as improper as though the attorney had told the jury that his client had uttered a falsehood in making the statement. The right to an attorney embraces effective representation throughout all stages of the trial, and where the representation is of such low caliber as to amount to no representation, the guarantee of due process has been violated." *Johns v. Smyth*, 176 F. Supp. 949, 953 (E.D. Va. 1959): Schwartz, *Cases on Professional Responsibility and the Administration of Criminal Justice* 79 (1962).

8 "[C]ouncil cannot properly perform their duties without knowing the truth." Opinion 23, Committee on Professional Ethics and Grievances of the American Bar Association (1930).

9 Paul, "The Responsibilities of the Tax Adviser," *Harv. L. Rev.* Vol. 65: 377, 383 (1950).

10 *Mechem Agency* Vol. 2: § 2297 (2nd ed. 1914).

11 Opinion 150, Committee on Professional Ethics and Grievances of the American Bar Association (1956), quoting Thornton, *Attorneys at Law* § 94 (1914). See also Opinion 23, *supra* note 8.

12 *Greenough v. Gaskell, Myl, & K.* Vol. 1: 98, 103, *Eng. Rep* Vol. 39: 618, 621 (Ch. 1833) (Lord Chancellor Brougham).

13 Opinion 91, Committee on Professional Ethics and Grievances of the American Bar Association (1933).

14 See Orkin, "Defense of One Known To Be Guilty," *Grim L. W.* 170, 174 (1956). Unless the lawyer has told the client at the outset that he will withdraw if he learns that the client is guilty, "it is plain enough as a matter of good morals and professional ethics" that the lawyer should not withdraw on this ground. Opinion 90. Committee on Professional Ethics and Grievances of the American Bar Association (1932). As to the difficulties inherent in the

lawyer's telling the client that he wants to remain ignorant of crucial facts, see note 8 *supra* and accompanying text.

15 The judge may infer that the situation is worse than it is in fact. In the case related in note 25 *infra*, the attorney's actual difficulty was that he did not want to permit a plea of guilty by the client who was maintaining his innocence. However, as is commonly done, he told the judge only that he had to withdraw because of "an ethical problem." The judge reasonably inferred that the defendant had admitted his guilt and wanted to offer a perjured alibi.

16 One lawyer, who considers it clearly for the attorney to present the alibi in this hypothetical case, found no ethical difficulty himself in the following case. His client was prosecuted for robbery. The prosecution witness testified that the robbery had taken place at 10:15, and identified the defendant as the criminal. However, the defendant had a convincing alibi for 10:00 to 10:30. The attorney presented the alibi, and the client was acquitted. The alibi was truthful, but the attorney knew that the prosecution witness had been confused about the time, and that his client had in fact committed the crime at 10:45.

17 See note 7 *supra*.

18 Opinion 287, Committee on Professional Ethics and Grievances of the American Bar Association (1953).

19 Ibid.

20 See Paul, *supra* note 9.

21 Even this kind of "objective fact" is subject to honest error. See note 16 *supra*.

22 Wurzel, *Das Juristische Denken* 82 (1904), translated in Fuller, *Basic Contract Law* 67 (1964).

23 In a recent case, the defendant was accused of unauthorised use of an automobile, for which the maximum penalty is five years. He told his court-appointed attorney that he had borrowed the car from a man known to him only as "Junior," that he had not known the car was stolen, and that he had an alibi for the time of the theft. The defendant had three prior convictions for larceny, and the alibi was weak. The prosecutor offered to accept a guilty plea to two misdemeanours (taking property without right and petty larceny) carrying a combined maximum sentence of eighteen months. The defendant was willing to plead guilty to the lesser offenses, but the attorney felt that, because of his client's alibi, he could not permit him to do so. The lawyer therefore informed the judge that he had an ethical problem and asked to be relieved. The attorney who was appointed in his place permitted the client to plead guilty to the two lesser offenses, and the defendant was sentenced to nine months. The alternative would have been five or six months in jail while the defendant waited for his jury trial, and a very substantial risk of conviction and a much heavier sentence. Neither the client nor justice would have been well served by compelling the defendant to go to trial against his will under these circumstances.

24 See Traver, *Anatomy of a Murder* (1958).

25 Cf. Kamisar, "Equal Justice in the Gatehouses and Mansions of American Criminal Procedure," in *Criminal Justice in Our Time* 77-78 (Howard ed. 1965): Yes, the presence of counsel in the police station may result in the suppression of truth, just as the presence of counsel at the trial may, when a client is advised not to take the stand, or when an objection is made to the admissibility of trustworthy, but illegally seized "real" evidence.

If the subject of police interrogation not only cannot be "coerced" into making a statement, but need not volunteer one, why shouldn't he be so advised? And why shouldn't court-appointed counsel, as well as retained counsel, so advise him?

26 Noonan, "The Purposes of Advocacy and the Limits of Confidentiality," Mich. L. Rev Vol. 64: 1485 (1966). Professor Noonan adds a further *petitio principii* when he argues, in the language of Canon 15, that the lawyer "must obey his own conscience." It may be that the wisest course is to make each lawyer's conscience his ultimate guide. It should be recognised, however, that this view is wholly inconsistent with the notion of professional ethics which, by definition, supersede personal ethics. In addition, it should be noted that personal ethics, in the context of acting in a professional capacity for another, can require a conclusion different from that which one might reach when acting for himself. For example, the fact that a lawyer would not commit perjury on his own behalf does not in any way preclude a decision to put on the witness stand a client who intends to perjure himself in his behalf.

27 Noonan, *supra* note 26, at 1486.

28 Ibid.

29 See note 16 *supra*.

30 As has been noted earlier, the most significant practical difference between the lawyer who knows the truth and the one who does not is that only the former will have reason to attempt to dissuade the client from perjuring himself.

31 See note 23 *supra*.

32 See text accompanying note 23 *supra*.

33 Noonan, *supra* note 26, at 1488.

34 Ibid. at 1487-88.

35 See, e.g., note 15 *supra*.

◆ ◆ ◆ ◆ ◆

DAVID LUBAN

The Adversary System Excuse

Again, if we suggest that the agent should adopt as rule and incarnation of his conscience some extraneous interest, system or authority, serving henceforth that objectified Principle with punctual fidelity and unflinching zeal, we are no longer holding on to a morality of Conscience.... A conscience thus put out to lease is not conscience but the evasion of it, except for that specious semblance of conscience which may be discerned in one's blind obedience to the authority that happens to be in command.
—Aurel Kolnai, "Erroneous Conscience," in *Ethics, Value and Reality*, edited by Bernard Williams and David Wiggins (Indianapolis: Hackett, 1978), 7.

It is not the lawyer's responsibility to believe or not to believe—the lawyer is a technician.... Law is an adversarial profession. The other side is out to get your client. Your job is to protect your client and the nonsense they hand out in these ethics courses today—if the young people listen to this kind of nonsense, there isn't going to be such a thing as an intelligent defense in a civil or criminal case.
—Roy Cohn, interview, *National Law Journal*, December 1, 1980, 46.

I. Introduction

Holding forth at table in 1831, Samuel Taylor Coleridge turned to the behavior of lawyers. "There is undoubtedly a limit to the exertions of an advocate for his client," he said, for "the advocate has no right, nor is it his duty, to do that for his client which his client *in fo conscientiae* has no right to do for himself."[1] Thirteen years later, William Whewell elaborated the same point:

> [E]very man is, in an unofficial sense, by being a moral agent, a judge of right and wrong, and an Advocate of what is right.... This general character of a moral agent, he cannot put off, by putting on any professional character.... If he mixes up his character as an Advocate, with his character as a Moral Agent ... he acts immorally. He makes the Moral Rule subordinate to the Professional Rule. He sells to his Client, not only his skill and learning, but himself. He makes it the Supreme Object of his life to be, not a good man, but a successful Lawyer.[2]

Whewell's position is not commonly acknowledged to be valid. George Sharswood, whose 1854 *Legal Ethics* is the great-grandparent of the current ABA Code of Professional Responsibility, wrote: "The lawyer, who refuses his professional assistance because in his judgment the case is unjust and indefensible, usurps the functions of both judge and jury."[3] A lawyer is not to judge the morality of the client's cause; it is irrelevant to the morality of the representation. That, I think, is the official view of most lawyers: the lawyer's morality is distinct from, and not implicated in, the client's. Murray Schwartz calls this the "Principle of Nonaccountability":

> When acting as an advocate for a client ... a lawyer is neither legally, professionally, nor morally accountable for the means used or the ends achieved.[4]

Add to this the "Principle of Professionalism":

> When acting as an advocate, a lawyer must, within the established constraints upon professional behavior, maximize the likelihood that the client will prevail.[5]

and you get what is usually taken to be the professional morality of lawyers. Gerald Postema calls it the "standard conception of the lawyer's role,"[6] William Simon says that these principles (which he calls the "Principle of Neutrality" and the "Principle of Partisanship") define partisan advocacy.[7] Shortly after introducing these principles, Schwartz raises two points about them:

> It might be argued, that the law cannot convert an immoral act into a moral one, nor a moral act into an immoral one, by simple fiat. Or, more fundamentally, the lawyer's nonaccountability might be illusory if it depends upon the morality of the adversary system and if that system is immoral ... if either [of these challenges] were to prove persuasive, the justification for the application of the Principle of Nonaccountability to moral accountability would disappear.[8]

Schwartz raises these issues but does not address them. My purpose in this paper is to meet them head-on. I shall argue (1) that a lawyer's nonaccountability does depend on the adversary system; (2) that the adversary system is not a sufficient basis for it; and (3) thus, that while the Principle of Professionalism may be true, the Principle of Nonaccountability is not.

This, I believe, will defend the morality of conscience—the position of Coleridge and Whewell—against the claim that professional obligation can override it.

II. Institutional Excuses

On February 7, 1973, Richard Helms, the former director of the Central Intelligence Agency, lied to a Senate committee about American involvement in the overthrow of the Allende government in Chile. Santiago proved to be Helms's Waterloo: he was caught out in his perjury and prosecuted.[9] Helms claimed that requirements of national security led him to lie to Congress. We can only speculate, however, on how the court would have viewed this excuse, for in fact the case never came to trial; Helms's lawyer, the redoubtable Edward Bennett Williams, found an ingenious way to back the government down. He argued that national security information was relevant to Helms's defense and must be turned over to Helms, thereby confronting the government with the unpleasant choice of dropping the action or making public classified and presumably vital information. The government chose the first option and allowed Helms to plead guilty to a misdemeanor charge.[10]

I don't know if anyone ever asked Williams to justify his actions; had anyone attempted to do so, they would presumably have been told that Williams was simply doing his job as a criminal defense attorney. The parallel with Helms's own excuse is clear—he was doing his job, Williams was doing his—but it is hard to miss the irony. Helms tried to conceal national security information; therefore he lied. Williams, acting on Helms's behalf, threatened to reveal national security information as part of a tactic that has come to be called "graymailing." One man's ends are another man's means. Neither lying nor graymailing (to say nothing of destabilizing elected regimes) are morally pretty, but a job is a job and that was the job that was. So, at any rate, runs the excuse.

We may want to reject these "good soldier" excuses or we may find them valid and persuasive. That is the issue I shall address here. A second graymailing example will warm us to our topic:

> In instances [of merger cases involving firms in competition with each other] in which the [Federal Trade] commission's legal case looked particularly good and none of the usual defenses appeared likely to work, the staff was confronted several times with the argument that if they did not refrain from prosecution and allow the merger, one of the proposed merger partners would close

down its operations and dismiss its employees.... of course, the mere announcement of the threat to close the plant generates enormous political pressure on the prosecutor not to go forward. Ought lawyers to be engaged in such strategies for the purpose of consummating an otherwise anticompetitive and illegal transaction involving the joinder of two substantial competitors?[11]

On the lawyers' advice, the firms played a nice game of chicken: closing down by stages, they laid off a few workers each day until the FTC cried uncle.

What could justify the conduct of these lawyers? A famous answer is the following statement of Lord Henry Brougham:

> An advocate, in the discharge of his duty, knows but one person in all the world, and that person is his client. To save that client by all means and expedients, and at all hazards and costs to other persons, and, amongst them, to himself, is his first and only duty; and in performing this duty he must not regard the alarm, the torments, the destruction which he may bring upon others. Separating the duty of a patriot from that of an advocate, he must go on reckless of consequences, though it should be his unhappy fate to involve his country in confusion.[12]

This speech, made in his 1820 defense of Queen Caroline against King George IV's charge of adultery, was itself an act of graymail. Reminiscing years later, Brougham said that the king would recognize in it a tacit threat to reveal his secret marriage to a Catholic, a marriage that, were it to become public knowledge, would cost him his crown.[13] Knowing this background of Brougham's oft-quoted statement might make us take a dim view of it; it has, nevertheless, frequently been admired as the most eloquent encapsulation of the advocate's job.

Brougham's statement invites philosophical reflection for at first blush it is equally baffling to utilitarianism, and moral rights theory, and Kantianism. The client's utility matters more than that of the rest of the world put together. No one else's moral rights matter. Other people are merely means to the client's ends.[14] Moral theory seems simply to reject Brougham's imperatives.

They are, however, universalizable over lawyers, or so it is claimed. The idea seems to be that the role of lawyer, hence the social institutions that set up this role, reparse the Moral Law, relaxing some moral obligations and imposing new ones. In the words of an Australian appellate court, "Our system of administering justice necessarily imposes upon those who practice advocacy duties which have no analogies, and the system cannot dispense with their strict observance."[15]

The system of which the court speaks is the so-called "adversary system of justice." My main question is this: does the adversary system really justify Brougham's position? I hope that the example of Helms and his lawyers has convinced you that a more general issue is lurking here, the issue of what I shall call *institutional excuses*. We can state the main question in full generality in this way: can a person appeal to a social institution in which he or she occupies a role in order to excuse conduct that would be morally culpable were anyone else to do it? Plausibly, examples exist in which the answer is yes: we do not call it murder when a soldier kills a sleeping enemy, although it is surely immoral for you or me to do it. There are also cases where the answer is no, as in the job "concentration camp commandant" or "professional strikebreaker." Here, we feel, the immorality of the job is so great that it accuses, not excuses, the person who holds it.

This suggests that an important feature of a successful institutional excuse is that the institution is itself justified. I think that is partly right, but I do not think it is the whole story: I shall argue that the kind of justification that can be offered of the institution is germane to the success of the excuses it provides.

III. The Adversary System and the Two Principles

Sometimes a lawyer pursuing a case finds him or herself compelled to do something outrageous. Graymailing is one example. A second is the Lake Pleasant bodies case, in which lawyers Frank Beige and Frank Armani, having been told by their client Robert Garrow of two murders he committed, found and photographed the bodies but kept the information to themselves for half a year—this despite the fact that the father of one of the victims, knowing that Armani was representing an accused murderer, personally pleaded with him to tell him if he knew anything about his daughter.[16]

Such spectacular examples could be multiplied, but I think the point is made. A more important point is that it is not just the spectacular examples that are the problem—they only dramatize it. I dare say that all litigators have had cases where, in their heart of hearts, they wanted their client to lose or wished that a distasteful action did not need to be performed. The problem is that (recollecting Brougham's words) "to save that client ... [the lawyer] must not regard the alarm, the torments, the destruction which he may bring upon others."[17] On the face of it, this is as terse a characterization as one could hope to find of amorality; it is reminiscent of Nietzsche's description of the old Teutonic code: "To practice loyalty and, for the sake of loyalty, to risk honor and blood even for evil and dangerous things."[18]

The way it is currently phrased, in the ABA's Code of Professional Responsibility, is this:

> The duty of a lawyer, both to his client and to the legal system, is to represent his client zealously within the bounds of the law.... in our government of laws and not of men, each member of our society is entitled ...

to seek any lawful objective through legally permissible means; and to present for adjudication any lawful claim, issue, or defense.[19]

It sounds nicer than Zarathustra or Brougham, but in fact there is no difference: the zealous advocate is supposed to press the client's interests to the limit of the legal, regardless of the "torments or destruction" this wreaks on others.

Nor does the phrase "within the bounds of the law" mitigate this. For the law is inherently double-edged: any rule imposed to limit zealous advocacy (or any other form of conduct, for that matter) may be used by an adversary as an offensive weapon. In the words of former Judge Marvin E. Frankel "the object always is to beat every plowshare into a sword."[20] The rules of discovery, for example, initiated to enable one side to find out crucial facts from the other are used nowadays to delay trial or impose added expense on the other side; conversely, one might respond to an interrogatory by delivering to the discoverer several tons of miscellaneous documents, to run up their legal bills or conceal a needle in a haystack.

To take another example: rules barring lawyers from representations involving conflicts of interest are now regularly used by adversaries to drive up the other side's legal costs by having their counsel disqualified.[21] The general problem of double-edgedness is described by the novelist Yasunari Kawabata:

> When a law is made, the cunning that finds loopholes goes to work. We cannot deny that there is a certain slyness ..., a slyness which, when rules are written to prevent slyness, makes use of the rules themselves.[22]

It is not just the rules governing lawyer conduct that are double-edged—double-edgedness is an essential feature of any law because any restraint imposed on human behavior in the name of just social policy may be used to restrain behavior when circumstances make this an unjust outcome. This is the unbridgeable gap between formal and substantive justice. David Mellinkoff gives these examples:

> The law intended to stop sharpers from claiming money that is not owed (the Statute of Frauds) may sometimes defeat a just debt, because the claim was not in writing.
>
> The law intended to stop a man from holding off suit until defense becomes impossible—memories grown dim, witnesses dead or missing—(the Statute of Limitations) may sometimes defeat a just suit, because it was not filed fast enough.
>
> The law intended to prevent designing grown-ups from imposing on children (the defense of infancy) may defeat a just claim, because the man who signed the contract was 20 instead of 21.
>
> The law intended to give a man, for all his misfortunes, a new start in life (the bankruptcy laws) may defeat a widow's just claim for the money she needs to live on.[23]

The double-edgedness of law underlines the moral problem involved in representing a client "zealously within the bounds of the law." If on the one hand this means forwarding legal claims that are morally dubious, as in Mellinkoff's examples, on the other, it means pushing claims to the limit of the law and then a bit further, into the realm of what is "colorably" the limit of the law.[24] "Zeal" means zeal at the margin of the legal, and thus well past the margin of whatever moral and political insight constitutes the "spirit" of the law in question. The limits of the law inevitably lie beyond moral limits, and zealous advocacy always means zeal at the margin.

It is at this point that the adversary system looms large, for it provides the institutional excuse for the duty of zealous advocacy. Each side of an adversary proceeding is represented by a lawyer whose sole obligation is to present that side as forcefully as possible; anything less, it is claimed, would subvert the operation of the system. The ABA code states the matter quite clearly: "The duty of a lawyer to his client and his duty to the legal system are the same: to represent his client zealously within the bounds of the law."[25]

Everything rides on this argument. Lawyers have to assert legal interests unsupported by moral rights all the time; asserting legal interests is what they do, and everyone can't be in the right on all issues. Unless zealous advocacy could be justified by relating it to some larger social good, the lawyer's role would be morally impossible. That larger social good, we are told, is justice, and the adversary system is supposed to be the best way of attaining it.

Indeed, it is misleading to call this Justification by the Adversary System an *argument*. It is more like a presupposition accepted by all parties before the arguments begin. Even lawyers with nothing good to say about the legal system in general believe that their current actions are justified or excused by the nature of the adversary system.

The point deserves to be labored a bit, for the universal acceptance among lawyers of the Justification by the Adversary System is a startling thing, a marvelous thing, a thing to behold. It can go something like this: one talks with a pragmatic and hard-boiled attorney. At the mention of legal ethics, he smiles sardonically and informs one that it is a joke. One presses the subject and produces examples such as the buried bodies case. The smile fades, the forehead furrows, he retreats into a nearby phone booth and returns moments later clothed in the Adversary System, trailing clouds of glory. Distant angels sing. The discussion usually gets no further.

This portrait is drawn from life, but I do not tell the story just to be snide. It is meant to suggest that discussions of the adversary system usually stop where they ought to start, with a chorus of deeply felt but basically unexamined rhetoric.

What, then, is the adversary system? We may distinguish narrow and wide senses. In the narrow sense, it is a method of adjudication characterized by three things: an impartial tribunal of defined jurisdiction, formal procedural rules, and most importantly for the present discussion, assignment to the parties of the responsibility to present their own cases and challenge their opponents'.[26] The attorneys are their clients' agents in the latter task. The duty of a lawyer in an adversary proceeding is therefore one-sided partisan zeal in advocating his or her client's position. This in turn carries with it familiar collateral duties, the most important of which are *disinterestedness*[27] and *confidentiality*.[28] Each of these is best viewed as a prophylactic designed to enhance the quality of partisan advocacy: forbidding lawyers who have conflicts of interest from advocating a client's cause is meant to forestall the possibility of diluted zeal; and forbidding lawyers from divulging clients' confidences and secrets is meant to encourage clients to give their lawyers information necessary for effective advocacy. These duties of zeal, disinterestedness, and confidentiality—which I have elsewhere called the Three Pillars of Advocacy[29]—form the core of an attorney's professional obligations.

The structure of the adversary system, then—its fission of adjudication into a clash of one-sided representations—explains why Schwartz's Principle of Professionalism holds. But it explains the Principle of Moral Nonaccountability as well. If advocates restrain their zeal because of moral compunctions, they are not fulfilling their assigned role in the adversary proceeding. But, if lawyers must hold themselves morally accountable for what they do in the course of the representation, they will be morally obliged to restrain their zeal whenever they find that "the means used or the ends achieved" in the advocacy are morally wrong. Therefore, or so the syllogism goes, the structure of adversary adjudication must relieve them of moral accountability, and that is how the adversary system entails Schwartz's Principle of Nonaccountability—how, that is, the adversary system is supposed to provide an institutional excuse for moral ruthlessness.

All this holds (if hold it does) only within the context of adjudication. Lawyers, however, commonly act as though Schwartz's two principles characterized their relationship with clients even when the representations do not involve the courtroom.[30] Thus, there is a *wide* sense of the adversary system in which it is defined by the structure of the lawyer-client relationship rather than the structure of adjudication. When lawyers assume Schwartz's two principles in negotiations and counseling as well as courtroom advocacy, and attribute this to the adversary system, they are speaking of it in the wide sense.[31]

Lawyers often equivocate between the narrow and wide conceptions, appealing to the virtues of adversary adjudication in order to justify ruthless behavior on behalf of clients in nonlitigation contexts. Getting paid by the client, of course, makes it easier to ignore the difference between courtroom and other activities: $200 an hour has been known to buy a lot of Professionalism and will even stand in quite nicely for Moral Nonaccountability, especially around the first of the month—and an hour is an hour, in or out of court.[32] Rather than pursue this equivocation, however, I shall ask if an institutional excuse can be based on the adversary system conceived in the narrow sense. If problems crop up even there, certainly they will be worse outside of a legitimately adversarial institution.

IV. Criminal versus Noncriminal Contexts

I have suggested that the adversary system excuse may be only as good as the adversary system. The question of how good that is, however, is often ignored by discussions that stop where they ought to start. Indeed, there is a tendency among many people to treat reservations about the adversary system as assaults on the American Way. Monroe Freedman, for example, has written what is arguably the best modern book on lawyers' ethics.[33] He shows how the duty to put a perjurious client on the stand, or brutally cross-examine a witness known by the lawyer to be telling the truth, follows from the adversary system. But he defends the adversary system primarily by contrasting the nonadversarial systems in "totalitarian states" such as Cuba and Bulgaria, with American concern for the "dignity of the individual."[34] Left in their bare state, phrases like these can be only slogans.

Freedman's rhetorical point still contains an important argument. That argument is that zealous adversary advocacy of those accused of crimes is the greatest safeguard of individual liberty against the encroachment of the state. The good criminal defense lawyer puts the state to its proof in the most stringent and uncompromising way possible. Better, we say, that a hundred criminals go free than that one person be wrongly convicted.[35]

I think this is right as far as it goes, but as general defense of the adversary system, it is beside the point for two related reasons. The first is that it pertains only to criminal defense and thus is irrelevant to the enormous number of civil cases tried each year. The latter are in a way much more morally troubling. It inflicts no tangible harm on anyone when a criminal evades punishment. This is not to deny that people may be legitimately outraged (consider the Nixon pardon, the trial of Dan White in San Francisco, the acquittals of policemen that led to the 1980 riots in Miami). But no one's life is made materially worse off. However, when A wins an unjust personal injury claim against B, every dollar in A's pocket comes out of B's. A's lawyer, in my book, has a lot of explaining to do.

This point is worth emphasizing. Most people I have spoken with about lawyers' ethics assume that the paradigm of the morally dubious representation is the defense of the guilty criminal, the defense that gets a murderer back out on the street. This, I suspect, is a reflection of a perception of the justice system as primarily concerned with protecting the lives and property of Decent People (meaning us) from You Know Who (meaning you know who). It is You Know Who that needs watching, not the real estate speculator, the slumlord, the redliner, the discriminatory employer, the finance company, the welfare officials who won't give recipients their due, or the police.

It is this public preoccupation with crime and criminals, I think that leads writers like Freedman and David Mellinkoff to focus their justifications of Broughamesque advocacy on criminal defense.[36] They are reacting to an assault from the Right, an assault that sees the rights of the accused as a liberal invention leading to anarchy. Now, emphasizing the role of lawyers in safeguarding individual liberty may indeed be the best defense against the Law and Order attack on lawyers. Criminal defense is, so to speak, the "worst-case scenario," and it might be assumed that any defense of advocacy that works there works everywhere else as well.

In fact, and this is my second point, criminal defense is a very special case in which the zealous advocate serves atypical social goals. The point is one of political theory. The goal of zealous advocacy in criminal defense is to curtail the power of the state over its citizens. We want to handicap the state in its power even legitimately to punish us. And so the adversary system is justified, not because it is a good way of achieving justice, but because it is a good way of hobbling the government and we have political reasons for wanting this. The argument, in other words, does not claim that the adversary system is the best way of obtaining justice. It claims just the opposite, that it is the best way of impeding justice in the name of more fundamental political ends, namely keeping the government's hands off people. Nothing, of course, is wrong with that; indeed, I believe that Brougham's imperative may well hold in criminal defense. My point is merely that criminal defense is an exceptional part of the legal system, one that aims at protection rather than justice.

One might adopt Aristotelian language and say that the "final cause" of the adversary system is different in criminal and noncriminal contexts. In the latter, the primary end of adversary adjudication is

legal justice, the assignment of rewards and remedies on the basis of parties' behavior as prescribed by legal norms. The adversary method is supposed to yield accurate accounts of past behavior and legitimate interpretations of the law. In the criminal context, on the other hand, the primary end of the adversary system is not legal justice but the protection of accused individuals against the state or, more generally, the preservation of the proper relation between the state and its subjects. (This suggests one qualification to what I have just said: some noncriminal matters, such as administrative hearings, can raise the same issues of state versus subject and should be treated similarly. The reader should therefore read "criminal context" as an abbreviation for "criminal and quasi-criminal contexts.")

It seems, then, that focusing on the adversary system in the criminal context obscures the issue of how it works as a system of justice, and for this reason I shall talk only about arguments attempting to vindicate it as a system of justice. There are two sorts of arguments: those claiming that the adversary system is the best way of accomplishing various goals (consequentialist arguments), and those claiming that it is intrinsically good (nonconsequentialist arguments). To begin, we shall look at three versions of the former: (1) that the adversary system is the best way of ferreting out truth, (2) that it is the best way of defending people's legal rights, and (3) that by establishing checks and balances it is the best way of safeguarding against excesses.

V. Consequentialist Justifications of the Adversary System

A. Truth

The question whether the adversary system is, all in all, the best way of uncovering the facts of a case at bar sounds like an empirical question. I happen to think that it is—an empirical question, moreover, that has scarcely been investigated, and that is most likely impossible to answer. This last is because one does not, after a trial is over, find the parties coming forth to make a clean breast of it and enlighten the world as to what *really* happened. A trial is not a quiz show with the right answer waiting in a sealed envelope. We can't learn directly whether the facts are really as the trier determined them because we don't ever find out the facts.

The kind of empirical research that can be done, then, is laboratory simulations: social psychology experiments intended to model the adversary proceeding. Obviously, there are inherent limitations on how closely such experiments can correspond to actual trials, no matter how skillfully they are done. In fact, the only experiments of the sort I know of are those of Thibaut, Walker, and their associates,[37] and these are far from perfect modelings of the adversary and "inquisitorial"—meaning French- and German-style—systems that they are comparing.[38] Even so, the results are instructive: they show that in some situations the adversary system works better while in others the inquisitorial system does, and furthermore, that the participants cannot tell which situation they are in. This would hardly surprise us: it would be much more astounding to discover a greater difference in veracity between the Anglo-American and Continental systems, for surely such a difference would after so many centuries have become a commonplace in our folklore.

Given all this, it is unsurprising to discover that the arguments purporting to show the advantages of the adversary system as a factfinder have mostly been nonempirical, a mix of a priori theories of inquiry and armchair psychology.

Here is one, based on the idea, very similar to Sir Karl Popper's theory of scientific rationality, that the way to get at the truth is a wholehearted dialectic of assertion and refutation.[39] If each side attempts to prove its case, with the other trying as energetically as possible to assault the steps of the proof, it is more likely that all of the aspects of the situation will be presented to the factfinder than if

it attempts to investigate for itself with the help of the lawyers.

This theory is open to a number of objections. First of all, the analogy to Popperian scientific methodology is not a good one. Perhaps science proceeds by advancing conjectures and then trying to refute them,[40] but it does not proceed by advancing conjectures that the scientist knows to be false and then using procedural rules to exclude probative evidence.[41]

The two adversary attorneys, moreover, are each under an obligation to present the facts in the manner most consistent with their client's position—to prevent the introduction of unfavorable evidence, to undermine the credibility of opposing witnesses, to set unfavorable facts in a context in which their importance is minimized, to attempt to provoke inferences in their client's favor. The assumption is that two such accounts will cancel out, leaving the truth of the matter. But there is no earthly reason to think this is so; they may simply pile up the confusion.

This is particularly likely in those frequent cases when the facts in question concern someone's character or state of mind. Out comes the parade of psychiatrists, what Hannah Arendt once called "the comedy of the soul-experts."[42] Needless to say, they have been prepared by the lawyers, sometimes without knowing it. A clinical law teacher explained to a class that when you first contact a psychiatrist and sketch the facts of the case, you mention only the favorable ones. That way, he or she has an initial bias in your favor and tends to discount the unfavorable facts when you finally get around to mentioning them.

The other side, of course, can cross-examine such a witness to get the truth out. Irving Younger, perhaps the most popular lecturer on trial tactics in the country, tells how. Among his famous "Ten Commandments of Cross-Examination" are these:

- Never ask anything but a leading question.
- Never ask a question to which you don't already know the answer.

- Never permit the witness to explain his or her answers.
- Don't bring out your conclusions in the cross-examination. Save them for closing arguments when the witness is in no position to refute them.[43]

Of course, the opposition may be prepared for this; they may have seen Younger's three-hour, $425 videotape on how to examine expert witnesses. They may know, therefore, that the cross-examiner is saving his or her conclusions for the closing argument. Not to worry! Younger knows how to stop an attorney from distorting the truth in closing arguments. "If the opposing lawyer is holding the jury spellbound ... the spell must be broken at all cost [sic]. [Younger] suggests the attorney leap to his or her feet and make furious and spurious objections. They will be overruled, but they might at least break the opposing counsel's concentration."[44]

My guess is that this is not quite what Sir Karl Popper had in mind when he wrote, "The Western rationalist tradition ... is the tradition of critical discussion—of examining and testing propositions or theories by attempting to refute them."[45]

A skeptic, in fact, might try this scientific analogy: a beam of invisible electrically charged particles—charge and origin unknown—travels through a distorting magnetic field of unknown strength, then through an opposite field of unknown, but probably different, strength. The beam strikes a detector of undeterminable reliability, from which we are supposed to infer the nature and location of the beam's source. That is the adversary system at its worst.

Let us try another argument, this one taken from the ABA's official justification of the adversary system, the *Joint Conference Report* of the ABA-AALS. The heart of the argument is this:

> Any arbiter who attempts to decide a dispute without the aid of partisan advocacy ... must undertake not only the role of judge, but that of representative for both of the litigants. Each of these roles must be played to the full without being muted by qualifications derived from the others. When he is developing for each side the most effective statement of his case, the arbiter must put aside his neutrality and permit himself to be moved by a sympathetic identification sufficiently intense to draw from his mind all that it is capable of giving,—in analysis, patience and creative power. When he resumes his neutral position, he must be able to view with distrust the fruits of this identification and be ready to reject the products of his own best mental efforts. The difficulties of this undertaking are obvious. If it is true that a man in his time must play many parts, it is scarcely given to him to play them all at once.[46]

Psychologically, the argument says, a nonadversarial trial is like trying to play chess against yourself: neither white nor black pieces get played very well, and second-rate games result.

The argument, however, begs the question. True, if the facts are best discovered by a battle between two conflicting points of view, then one person won't do as well at it as two adversaries. But to suppose that that is how factual inquiry best proceeds is simply to take as a premise that the adversary system is best, when that was supposed to have been the conclusion.

It is not, moreover, as attractive a premise as it appears at first glance. It trades on an ambiguity in the idea that the judge in a nonadversary proceeding must be the "representative for both of the litigants." It is true that the judge must take the *interests* and *legal claims* of both litigants into account in order to grant them due process of law: in this sense he or she must "represent" both of them. But that is not to say that the judge will find the facts by somehow balancing the parties' factual claims against each other as if these were the parties' interests. Is the best way to find out about an event to ask only parties who have special interests at stake in it? The *Joint Conference Report*, assuming that truth is gotten at by making sure that both sides' versions of every aspect of the story are represented, comes close to the undergraduate fallacy of thinking that because everyone has a right to his or her opinion, everyone's opinion on any topic whatsoever is equally worthy of being taken into account. Although frequently there are versions of the truth, truth does not necessarily come in versions. Thus, there is no reason to suppose that a judge making factual inquiries must "represent" the points of view of both litigants to be fair.

No trial lawyer seriously believes that the best way to get at the truth is through the clash of opposing points of view. If a lawyer did believe this, the logical way to prepare a case for trial would be to hire two investigators, one taking one side of every issue and one taking the other. After all, the lawyer needs the facts, and if those are best discovered through an adversary process, the lawyer would be irresponsible not to set one up. That no lawyer would dream of such a crazy procedure should tip us off that the *Joint Conference Report* premise is flawed.[47]

The *Joint Conference Report* employs two subsidiary psychological arguments as well. The first is that the adversary system will "hold the case ... in suspension between two opposing interpretations of it,"[48] so the finder of fact will not jump to hasty conclusions. The second is that if the judge and not the lawyer had to "absorb" the disappointments of his or her theory of the case being refuted, he or she would be "under a strong temptation to keep the hearing moving within the boundaries originally set for it"; then it would not be a fair trial so much as a "public confirmation for what the tribunal considers it has already established in private."[49]

Let me reiterate that these arguments, however plausible they sound on paper, are untested speculations from the armchair. But let us suppose for the sake of argument that they are right. They still do not show why we must have an adversary system.

Consider three other possible systems: (1) a three-judge panel, two of whom investigate and present the case from the points of view of the respective litigants, making the strongest arguments they can but also pointing out weaknesses in their side's case and strengths in the other; (2) a system like our own, except that the advocates are under an affirmative duty to point out facts or arguments in the other side's favor if the adversary is unaware of them (or, perhaps, a system in which the court awards attorneys' fees on the basis of how helpful they are in the overall search for truth); (3) the French system in which one judge investigates the case beforehand and presents a dossier to the trial judge.

Now, I don't recommend any of these as a practical alternative to the existing adversary system; they have their drawbacks. But notice that (1) and (2) do just as good a job as the adversary system at holding the case in suspension, while all three do just as good a job at shifting the onus of being wrong away from the tribunal. All three, moreover, sever the search for truth from the attorney's need to win, which under the adversary system ties the attorney to the client's victory by bond of self-interest. All three, therefore, are likely to avoid the most extravagant tactics currently employed by lawyers. The *Joint Conference Report* does not even consider this as a possibility.

Indeed, it seems to take as a premise the idea that truth is served by self-interested rather than disinterested investigation. "The lawyer appearing as an advocate before a tribunal presents, as persuasively as he can, the facts and the law of the case *as seen from the standpoint of his client's interest*" [emphasis added].[50] The emphasized phrase is accurate, but it gives the game away. For there is all the difference in the world between "the facts seen from X's standpoint" and "the facts seen from the standpoint of X's interest." Of course it is important to hear the former—the more perspectives we have, the better informed our judgment. But to hear the latter is not helpful at all. It is in the murderer's *interest* not to have been at the scene of the crime, consequently the "facts of the case as seen from the standpoint of [the] client's interest" are that the client was elsewhere that weekend. From the standpoint of my *interest* the world is my cupcake with a cherry on top; from the standpoint of yours, its streets are paved with gold. Combining the two does not change folly to truth.

All this does not mean that the adversary system may not in fact get at the truth in many hard cases. (Trial lawyers' war stories are mixed.) I suppose that it is as good as its rivals. But, to repeat the point I began with, nobody knows how good that is.[51]

B. Legal Rights

It is sometimes said, however, that the point of the adversary system is *not* that it is the best way of getting at the truth, but rather the best way of defending individuals' legal rights. It is, in the words of the current attorney general of Maryland, "a celebration of other values" than truth.[52] Freedman points out that if the sole purpose of a trial were to get at the truth we would not have our Fourth, Fifth, and Sixth Amendment rights; that improperly obtained evidence cannot be used against us and that we cannot be required to testify against ourselves indicate that our society considers other values more central than truth.[53] And, according to the theory we shall now consider, these other values have to do with legal rights.[54]

The argument is that the best way to guarantee that an individual's legal rights are protected is to provide him or her with a zealous adversary advocate who will further the client's interest.

This argument, we should note, is slightly different from Freedman's, according to which counsel by a zealous advocate is not merely the best way of defending one's legal rights, but is itself one of those rights.[55] That, of course, would make the adversary system necessary for the defense of legal rights, but only in the trivial sense that taking away counsel infringes a person's right to counsel and you can't defend a right by infringing it. Freedman suggests that adversary advocacy is a constitutional value,[56] but

this is not obvious. The Constitution makes no explicit mention of the adversary system. Now, it may be, as Theodore Koskoff says, a "fact, so basic that the Constitution does not even mention it, that our system of justice is an adversary system."[57] Certainly the Supreme Court has asserted that we have an adversary system.[58] What is unclear is whether this means only that under an adversary system, due process of law requires adversary advocacy. It is not clear that the Court would find common-law tinkering with the adversary format a denial of due process, and it is not clear that a constitutional amendment would be required to change to a nonadversarial system. It is true that the Sixth Amendment gives persons accused of crimes the right to counsel, but this says nothing about the adversary system as such. If we used a nonadversarial system, the Sixth Amendment right could be fulfilled by giving the accused a nonadversary advocate.

The argument we are considering is rather that, right to counsel aside, adversary advocacy is the best defense of our *other* legal rights. The no-holds-barred zealous advocate tries to get everything the law can give (if that is the client's wish) and thereby does a better job of defending the client's legal rights than a less committed lawyer would do.

Put this way, however, it is clear that the argument trades on a confusion. My legal rights are *everything I am in fact legally entitled to*, not *everything the law can be made to give*. For obviously a good lawyer may be able to get me things to which I am not entitled, but this, to call a spade a spade, is an example of infringing my opponent's legal rights, not defending mine. Every lawyer knows tricks of the trade that can be used to do opponents out of their legal deserts—using delaying tactics, for example, to make it too costly for an opponent without much money to prosecute a lengthy suit even though the law is on his or her side.

To this it might be replied that looking at it this way leaves the opponent's lawyer out of the picture. Of course, the reply continues, no one is claiming that a zealous adversary advocate is attempting to *defend* legal rights: he or she is attempting to win. The claim is only that the clash of two such adversaries will in fact defend legal rights most effectively.

But what reason do we have to believe this, other than a question-begging analogy to eighteenth-century economic theories of the Invisible Hand, theories that are themselves myth rather than fact? Every skill an advocate is taught is bent to winning cases no matter where the legal right lies. If the opponent manages to counter a lawyer's move with a better one, this has precisely nothing to do with legal rights. In the Middle Ages lawsuits were frequently tried by combat between hired champions. Each was charged with defending the legal right of his employer, but surely the fact that one swordsman successfully fileted the other did not mean that a right was established. Now, of course judicial combat did not involve argument *about* rights. But neither does graymailing, "dollaring to death," driving up an opponent's costs by getting his or her law firm disqualified, peremptorily challenging a juror because he or she seems too smart, or even masking an invalid argument with what Titus Castricius called "the orator's privilege to make statements that are untrue, daring, crafty, deceptive and sophistical, provided they have some semblance of truth and can by any artifice be made to insinuate themselves into the minds of the persons who are to be influenced."[59]

It is obvious that litigators pride themselves on their won-lost record. The *National Law Journal* describes "the world's most successful criminal lawyer—229 murder acquittals without a loss!" and describes the Inner Circle, a lawyers' club whose membership requirement is winning a seven-figure verdict.[60] You never know, of course—maybe each of these cases really had legal right on its side. And when a coin comes up heads 229 times in a row it may be fair, but there *is* another explanation. Lawyers themselves do not see the point of what they do as defending their clients' legal rights, but as using the law to get their clients what they want.

It is true, of course, that one way for society to guarantee that lawyers do their best to defend their clients' rights is to commit them to defending every claim a client has to a right, whether valid or not. That kind of overkill is reassuring to each client, of course. But suppose we look at it from the point of view of the whole process, rather than of the individual clients. It is hard to see then why an adversary system is the best defender of legal rights. Why not, for example, a system in which both attorneys are committed to defending the legal rights of both parties, if they seem to be getting trampled? I am not recommending such a system: my point is only that we have no reason at all to believe that when two overkillers slug it out the better case, rather than the better lawyer, wins.

Let me be clear about what the objection is. It is not that the flaw in the adversary system as a defender of legal rights is overkill on the part of morally imperfect, victory-hungry lawyers. The objection is that under the adversary system an *exemplary* lawyer is required to indulge in overkill to obtain as legal rights benefits that in fact may not be legal rights.

At this point an objection can be raised to my argument. The argument depends on a distinction I have drawn between *what a person is in fact legally entitled to* and *what the lazy can be made to give*. But this is a suspect distinction because it is based on the notion that there are legal entitlements other than what the law in fact gives. American Realism, the dominant jurisprudential theory of this century, was primarily responsible for throwing cold water on the notion of entitlements-in-themselves floating around in some sort of noumenal never-never land. The law is nothing other than what the courts say it is.

The objection fails, however, for it cuts the ground out from under itself. If legal rights are strictly identical with what the courts decide they are, then it is simply false that the adversary system is the best defender of legal rights. *Any* system whatsoever would defend legal rights equally well, as long as on the basis of that system courts decided cases.

There is, however, a legitimate insight concealed in the Realist objection. Whether or not legal rights are anything beyond what the courts say they are, it is the courts that are charged with adjudicating them. And—the point continues—if lawyers were given discretion to back off from zealous advocacy, they would have to prejudge the case themselves by deciding what the legal rights actually are in order to exercise this discretion. Lawyers would be usurping the judicial function.

Now, it must be said that this insight cannot be used to defend the innumerable tactics lawyers use to force favorable settlements of cases outside of court; if anything, the argument should condemn such practices inasmuch as they preempt the adjudicatory process. Nor does it militate against requiring lawyers to disclose adverse information and arguments, since doing so does not usurp the judicial function. But I do not wish to focus on these points for I think that the insight contains an important argument for the adversary system that we have not yet considered.

C. Ethical Division of Labor

This argument is no longer that the excesses of zealous advocacy are excused by appealing to the promotion of truth or the defense of legal rights. Rather, it is that they are excused by what Thomas Nagel calls "ethical division of labor." He says, in a discussion of the peculiarly ruthless and result-oriented role morality of public officials,

> that the constraints of public morality are not imposed as a whole in the same way on all public actions or on all public offices. Because public agency is itself complex and divided, there is a corresponding ethical division of labor, or ethical specialization. Different aspects of public morality are in the hands of different officials. This can create the illusion that public morality is more

consequentialist or less restrictive than it is, because the general conditions may be wrongly identified with the boundaries of a particular role. But in fact those boundaries usually presuppose a larger institutional structure without which they would be illegitimate. (The most conspicuous example is the legitimacy conferred on legislative decisions by the limitation of constitutional protections enforced by the courts.)[61]

The idea is that behavior that looks wrong from the point of view of ordinary morality is justified by the fact that other social roles exist whose purpose is to counteract the excesses resulting from role-behavior. Zealous adversary advocacy is justified by the fact that the other side is also furnished with a zealous advocate; the impartial arbiter provides a further check.

This is in fact one of the most commonly heard defenses for pugnacious advocacy: "he had a lawyer, too"; "I'm not supposed to do his lawyer's job for him"; or quoting Sharswood once again, "The lawyer, who refuses his professional assistance because in his judgment the case is unjust and indefensible, usurps the functions of both judge and jury."[62]

The idea is really a checks-and-balances theory, in which social engineering or "wise legislation" is supposed to relieve some of the strain on individual conscience. A functionary in a well-designed checks-and-balances system can simply go ahead and perform his or her duties secure in the knowledge that injuries inflicted or wrongs committed in the course of those duties will be rectified by other parts of the system.

Will this do the trick? The answer, I am afraid, is no. Suppose that a lawyer is about to embark on a course of action that is unjustified from the point of view of ordinary morality, such as attempting to win an unfair, lopsided judgment for a client from a hapless and innocent party. Or think of our second graymailing example. A zealous adversary advocate will do whatever he or she can to avoid the opposing counsel's attempt to foil his or her designs. But such an advocate surely cannot claim that the existence of the opposing counsel morally justifies these actions. Certainly the fact that a man has a bodyguard in no way excuses you for trying to kill him, particularly if you bend all your ingenuity to avoiding the bodyguard.

The problem is this. The checks-and-balances notion is desirable because if other parts of the system exist to rectify one's excesses, one will be able to devote undivided attention to the job at hand and do it better. It is analogous to wearing protective clothing in a sport such as fencing: knowing that one's opponent is protected, one is justified in going all out in the match. But in the adversary system the situation is different, since the attorney is actively trying to get around the checks and balances: here the analogy is to a fencer who uses a special foil that can cut through the opponent's protective clothing. To put the point another way, the adversary advocate attempts to evade the system of checks and balances, not rely on it to save his or her opponents.

There is another problem with the notion of ethical division of labor. It attempts to justify a system of roles by the fact that the system is self-correcting, in other words that injuries perpetrated by one part of the system will be rectified by another. Rectification, however, carries with it high transaction costs in terms of money, time, worry, energy, and (generally) an arduous passage through the bureaucratic straits. These transaction costs are, so to speak, a general background "noise" in the system, a penalty imposed on one simply for becoming embroiled in it. This can be justified only if the system itself is justified, but then the checks-and-balances argument seems merely to gild the lily. Had we found a justification for the adversary system on other grounds, we would not have needed to turn to the ethical division-of-labor argument to begin with.

A somewhat different division-of-labor argument has been offered by Virginia Held.[63] She argues that different institutional systems utilize different forms of moral argument; specifically, "deontological justification is especially characteristic of and appropriate to legal systems, teleological justification especially characteristic of and appropriate to political systems."[64] By "legal justification," Held is referring primarily to the sort of justification we expect judges to offer for their decisions; they are supposed to appeal to legal rules, not moral consequences. Since lawyers are also officers of the legal system, the argument might be extended to include them. In that case, lawyers would be justified in following the institutionally prescribed rule and forgoing consideration of wider moral consequences.

That this is a division-of-labor argument may be seen from Held's reason for holding it:

> The justification for such a division of appropriate forms of justification ... seems to rest on a judgment that such a division, over time, is morally salutary. It provides an institutional balance, or system of checks within the social system which each system [legal and political] exerts upon the other, allowing both ... more nearly to approach moral justification than could either system alone using no distinct form of justification.[65]

Now, this is certainly a plausible theory; however, I do not think it extends to the moral behavior of lawyers. Whichever form of moral argument one uses, deontological or teleological, one is still constrained by what I take to be a requirement on moral arguments in general: that the argument take into consideration the interests of and obligations toward all the parties in the situation. It's just that the judge and the politician do this in different ways and perhaps arrive at different results.

The defender of the adversary advocate, however, is arguing something different, namely, that the division of moral labor assigns the lawyer to take only the client's interests into account. This is neither a deontological nor teleological moral argument: such one-sidedness is not moral thinking at all. It will not do to say that the lawyer has a deontological duty to bracket all but the client's interests, for that begs the very question at issue, the question of what the lawyer's duties are.

This is a very troubling and difficult topic. The structure of bureaucratic institutions such as the legal system lends itself to divided responsibility. Those who write the rules, those who give the orders, and those who carry them out each have some basis for claiming that they are not at fault for any wrong that results. But this is unacceptable. As Hannah Arendt observed,

> In a fully developed bureaucracy there is nobody left with whom one can argue.... Bureaucracy is the form of government in which everybody is deprived of ... the power to act; for the rule of Nobody is not no-rule, and where all are equally powerless we have a tyranny without a tyrant.[66]

If moral agency divides along lines of institutional authority, it seems to me that every agent in the institution will wind up abdicating moral responsibility. It is for this reason that division-of-labor arguments must walk a thin line between the legitimate notion that different patterns of moral thought are appropriate in different institutional contexts—what I take to be Held's point—and the unacceptable notion that moral responsibility is itself diminished or "divided down" by institutional structure.

A final division-of-labor argument exists different from those we have just been considering. This is the general line of argument of the *Joint Conference Report*. It is based on a point emphasized by the Realists, namely, that lawyers spend very little of their time or attention on actual litigation. Mostly they are involved in other activities: document-drafting, deal-making, negotiation, giving advice, and so forth. The *Joint Conference Report* seizes on this fact to argue for a separation of lawyerly func-

tions, with a corresponding separation of norms of professional behavior in accord with the nature of those functions. The report restricts no-holds-barred zeal to the role of advocate, a role that, to repeat, lawyers do not occupy very much of the time. The real key to the lawyer's function in society, according to the report, lies not in litigation but in wise counsel and airtight draftsmanship, which make litigation unnecessary. As to the morally troubling cases, the lawyer is permitted or even required to advise the client against "a course of conduct technically permissible under existing law, though inconsistent with its underlying spirit and purpose."[67] This the lawyer does by reminding the client of the "long-run costs" of such conduct.[68]

I do not think we need to take this argument very seriously, for it trades on a sleight-of-hand and a key omission. The sleight-of-hand lies in the tricky phrase "long-run costs." Costs to whom? Society at large? I suppose some clients engaged in morally shady projects may be dissuaded by being told how they are harming society, but surely these are just the people least likely to listen. Perhaps the long-run costs are to the client, costs in the form of loss of respect in the community, hard feelings, inability to do business with people in the future, etc. But why suppose that these inevitably accompany morally unworthy litigation? It is a commonplace that we live in a litigious society, and the fact that a person or corporation makes effective use of an arsenal of legal weapons is not often held against him. We have, for better or worse, learned to expect such behavior and ruthless, hard-driving entrepreneurship that eagerly goes to the legal mat is more likely to win respect than enmity if it is successful. You'd be surprised what a lot of money will do to make people like an amoral wheeler-dealer. The *Joint Conference Report's* ominous rumbling about long-run costs is mere Panglossian piety, which harmonizes society's loss with the client's, when in fact society's loss is often the client's gain.

The argument also omits the key point that, after lawyers have offered their "quiet counsel," they will still have to press forward with the representation if the client won't be dissuaded. Perhaps the lawyer can say that he or she gave morality the old college try, and his or her heart is pure. Our worry, however, was not about impure hearts, but about dirty hands. And those haven't become any cleaner.

The *Joint Conference Report*'s theory that most lawyerly functions are nonadversarial is, I might add, bad sociology. Lawyers, I have suggested, commonly act as though all their functions were governed by the Principles of Professionalism and Nonaccountability. It follows, then, that lawyers commonly act as though all their functions were adversarial. This is true even of the counseling and drafting functions, the report's prime examples of nonadversarial legal activities. As Judge Frankel puts it, "if not combat soldiers—if, indeed, their main mission is to avoid combat—most lawyers pattern their advice and their arrangements by imagining who might sue whom for what, and with what chances of success."[69] If lawyers' "advice and arrangements" forestall litigation, this is because they were shrewd enough that potential adversaries are sure to lose. The counseling and drafting functions, in other words, work in daily life the way nuclear deterrents work in international affairs: they keep the peace, but it would be odd to call them "non-adversarial." You needn't look hard to see the bottom line.

Thus, the division of functions within a lawyer's own professional life fares no better than the division of functions within the legal system as a whole: neither is sufficient to provide the moral timbering of adversary advocacy.

VI. Nonconsequentialist Justifications of the Adversary System

It may be thought, however, that assessing the adversary system in consequentialist terms of how it will get some job done misses the point. Some social institutions, such as participatory democracy, are justifiable despite the fact that—maybe even *be-cause*—they are inefficient. The moral standing of such institutions has a noninstrumental basis.

I wish to consider two nonconsequentialist justifications of the adversary system. The first and perhaps boldest is an attempt to justify the adversary system in the wide sense: it is the argument that the traditional lawyer-client relation is an intrinsic moral good. The second is a cluster of related arguments: that adversary adjudication is a valued and valuable tradition, that it enjoys the consent of the governed, and that it is thus an integral part of our social fabric.

A. Adversary Advocacy as Intrinsically Good

When we seek out the services of a professional, it seems to me that we generally see more to the relationship than a mere quid pro quo. Perhaps this is because the quo may be of vital importance to us; perhaps it is because a lot of quid may be required to hire those services. In any event, we have the sense of entrusting a large chunk of our life to this person, and the fact that he or she takes on so intimate a burden and handles it in a trustworthy and skillful manner when the stakes are high seems commendable in itself. Nor does the fact that the professional makes a living by providing this service seem to mitigate the praiseworthiness of it. The business aspect moves along a different moral dimension: it explains how the relationship came about, not what it involves.[70] Finally, our being able to bare our weaknesses and mistakes to the professional and receive assistance without condemnation enhances our sense that beneficence or moral graciousness is at work here. Our lawyer, *mirabile dictu*, forgives us our transgressions.

Feelings such as these are quite real; the question is whether they have merely subjective significance. If they do not, if they mean something more, that may show that Schwartz's two principles, and thus the adversary system and the behavior it countenances, are themselves positive moral goods. Such arguments are, in fact, frequently made: they are based on the idea that providing service is intrinsically good. No finer statement of this exists, in my opinion, than Mellinkoff's. He sees the paradigm client as the "man-in-trouble."

> Cruelty, oppression, deception, unhappiness, worry, strain, incomprehension, frustration, bewilderment—a sorcerer's bag of misery. These become the expected. Then the saddest of all human cries: "Who will help me?" Try God, and politics, and medicine, and a soft shoulder, sooner or later a lawyer. Too many do.
>
> The lawyer, as lawyer, is no sweet kind loving moralizer. He assumes he is needed, and that no one comes to see him to pass the time of day. He is a prober, an analyzer, a scrapper, a man with a strange devotion to his client. Beautifully strange, or so it seems to the man-in-trouble; ugly strange to the untroubled onlooker.[71]

Charles Fried thinks of the lawyer as a "special-purpose friend" whose activity—enhancing the client's autonomy and individuality—is an intrinsic moral good.[72] This is true even when the lawyer's "friendship" consists in assisting the profiteering slumlord to evict an indigent tenant or enabling the wealthy debtor to run the statute of limitations to avoid an honest debt to an old (and less well-off) friend.

I mention Mellinkoff's and Fried's arguments together because, it seems to me, they express similar ideas, while the unsavory conclusion of the latter exposes the limitations of the former. Both arguments are attempts to show that a lawyer serving a client is engaged in an intrinsic moral good. Mellinkoff's, however, really shows something much weaker, that a lawyer serving a man-in-trouble is (even more cautiously: can be) engaged in an intrinsic moral good. If the client is one of Daniel Schwartz's graymailing companies,[73] or Fried's friends-in-need, we are confronted with no man-in-trouble, and the intuitions to which Mellinkoff's argument appeals disappear.

Indeed, if these were the typical clients, the real men-in-trouble—the victims of these predators—might be better off taking their chances in the war of all against all than seeking to have their "autonomy" vindicated legally. The trouble with Mellinkoff's argument is that he makes clients look more pitiable than they are.

Fried, on the other hand, is willing to bite the bullet and argue that it is morally good to represent the man-in-no-trouble-in-particular, the man-who-troubles-others. Your friendly neighborhood anticompetitive multiglomerate is nobly served by a special-purpose friend who helps extract that pound of flesh. Fried constructs a "concentric-circles morality" in which, beginning with an absolute right to self-love based on our own moral standing, we work outward toward those closest to us, then to those whose connections are more remote. Fried's idea is that the abstract connection between a remote person (even a person-in-trouble) and the agent exercises too slight a claim on the agent to override this inclination toward concrete others. This justifies lavishing special care on our friends, even at the expense of "abstract others," and since lavishing care is morally praiseworthy, once we swallow the notion that a lawyer is a special-purpose friend we are home free with the intrinsic moral worth of the lawyer-client relation.

Several of Fried's critics focus on the fact that the friendship analogy is question-begging: Fried builds enough lawyerly qualities into his concept of friendship that the rest of the argument virtually writes itself.[74] It does seem to me, however, that the analogy captures, albeit in a distorted form, some of the legitimate notion of professionals as devoted by the nature of their calling to the service of their clients. Fried's analogy contains a grain of truth.

This does not, however, vindicate the adversary system. For the friendship analogy undercuts rather than establishes the Principle of Nonaccountability. We are *not*—except for Nietzsche's Teutons and G. Gordon Liddy—willing to do grossly immoral things to help our friends, nor should we be. Lord

Brougham's apology may be many things, but it is not a credo of human friendship in any of its forms. Fried realizes the danger, for he confesses that

> not only would I not lie or steal for ... my friends, I probably also would not pursue socially noxious schemes, foreclose the mortgages of widows or orphans, or assist in the avoidance of just punishment. So we must be careful lest the whole argument unravel on us at this point.[75]

The method for saving the argument, however, is disappointing. Fried distinguishes between *personal* wrongs committed by a lawyer, such as abusing a witness, and *institutional* wrongs occasioned by the lawyer, such as foreclosing on widows. The latter are precisely those done by the lawyer in his or her proper role of advancing the client's legal autonomy and—preestablished harmony?—they are precisely the ones that are morally O.K. That is because the lawyer isn't really doing them, the system is.

This last distinction has not been very popular since World War II, and Fried takes pains to restrict it to "generally just and decent" systems, not Nazi Germany. With this qualification, he can more comfortably assert: "We should absolve the lawyer of personal moral responsibility for the result he accomplishes because the wrong is wholly institutional."[76]

This last sentence, however, is nothing but the assertion that institutional excuses work for lawyers, and this should tip us off that Fried's argument will be useless for our purposes. For consider: our whole line of argument has been an attempt to justify the adversary system by showing that the traditional lawyer-client relation is an intrinsic moral good. Now it seems that this can be established by Fried's argument only if we are permitted to cancel the moral debit column by means of an institutional excuse; but that can work only if the institution is justified, and we are back where we started.

Part of the problem is that Fried considers the wrong institution: the context of the lawyer's behavior is not simply the system of laws in general, which he assumes to be just and decent, but the adversary system in particular with its peculiar requirement of one-sided zeal at the margin. It is the adversary system and not the system of laws that shapes the lawyer-client relationship.

The more fundamental problem, however, is that Fried takes the lawyer to be the mere occasion rather than the agent of morally-bad-but-legally-legitimate outcomes. The system did it; it "was just one of those things difficult to pre-visualize—like a cow, say, getting hit by lightning."[77]

This is false in three respects: first, because it discounts the extent to which the lawyer has had a creative hand in advocating the outcome, at times even reversing the law—a skilled lawyer, after all, argues, advocates, bargains, and persuades. Second, because the system is not an abstract structure of propositions but a social structure of interacting human beings, so that the actions of its agents *are* the system. Third, because the lawyer is indeed acting *in propria persona* by "pulling the levers of the legal machinery."[78] Fried's image seems to trade on a Rube Goldberg insight: if the apparatus is complex enough, then the lever-puller doesn't really look Mike the agent. But that cannot be right. *I* chop the broccoli, whether I do it with a knife or merely push the button on the blender. The legal levers are pulled by the lawyer: no one else can do it.

B. The Social Fabric Argument

The remaining arguments are distinct but closely related. They are two variants of the following idea, which may be called the "social fabric argument":

> Regardless of whether the adversary system is efficacious, it is an integral part of our culture, and that fact by itself justifies it.

The first variation is based on democratic theory: it claims that the adversary system is justified because it enjoys the consent of the governed. The second variation is based on conservative theory: it claims that the adversary system is justified because it is a deeply rooted part of our tradition.

According to the social fabric argument, the moral reason for staying with our institutions is precisely that they are ours. We live under them, adapt our lives and practices to them, assess our neighbors' behavior in their light, employ them as a standard against which to measure other ways of life. Traditional institutions bind us—morally and legitimately bind us—because we assimilate ourselves to our tradition (Variation 2). In the language of political theory, we *consent* to them (Variation 1). They express who we are and what we stand for.

This way of looking at the adversary system is quite different from the claim that it promotes the discovery of truth, or the protection of legal rights, or the rectification of wrongs. Those arguments are consequentialist in character: they are attempts to justify the adversary system on the basis of what *it* does. The social fabric argument justifies it on the basis of what *we* do, or who we are. Let us look at the variants.

The *consent argument* claims that the adversary system is part of the social contract. The adversary system is justified because it enjoys the consent of the governed, the highest moral compliment that can be paid to it in a democracy. An immediate problem with the argument, however, is that we obviously do not *explicitly* consent to the adversary system. Nobody asked us, and I don't suppose anyone intends to. If the argument is to work, the consent must be *tacit* consent, and then we are entitled to wonder how we can tell that it has been given. One test is simply that, over an extended period of time, we have incorporated the institution into our shared practices. Michael Walzer makes this suggestion: "Over a long period of time, shared experiences and cooperative activity of many different kinds shape a common life. 'Contract' is a metaphor for a process of association and mutuality."[79]

There is a problem with this account, however: just because people do not have the energy, inclination, or courage to replace their institutions we should not conclude that they want them or approve of them. But unless they want them or approve of them, people's endurance of institutions does not make the institutions morally good. The verb "consent" can mean either "put up with" or "actively approve." Only the latter has the moral force required to show that the institution is a positive moral good, but only the former is revealed by the mere existence of "our common life."

To see this, recall the original point of consent theory—classically, the theory that we incur political obligations and forfeit political rights only through our own consent. The intuition behind consent theory is that human beings are morally autonomous. For classic consent theorists such as Locke this autonomy was expressed in the concept of natural right, but other conceptual vocabularies may be used to capture the same idea. In each version, regardless of vocabulary, consent theory assumes that coercion is prima facie wrong and that this prima facie wrongness may normally be overridden only by the fact that we have consented to submit to coercive institutions. It is a theory of governmental legitimacy that assumes government is illegitimate until proven otherwise, and that specifies the standard form of such proof: demonstration of the consent of the governed.

Such a demonstration—and this is the important conclusion of the preceding paragraph—shows that a coercive institution is *not illegitimate*, that it is *acceptable*. It does not show that it is good and thus does not provide an argument in favor of it. Think of this analogy: you ask me for a two-week extension on repaying some money you owe me. I grant the extension—I consent to it. That shows that you *may* wait two more weeks before repaying me, but it does not show that you *should* wait two more weeks, or that it is good for you to wait two more weeks.

Thus, the most we get from tacit consent arguments, such as Walzer's appeal to our "common life," is a demonstration that we are not obliged to dismantle the adversary system. To get anything stronger we must appeal to a different concept in democratic theory from consent: we must show that people want the adversary system. In Rousseau's language, we must show that having an adversary system is our "general will."

Does the adversary system pass such a test? The answer, I think, is clearly no. Few of our institutions are trusted less than adversary adjudication, precisely because it seems to license lawyers to trample the truth, and legal rights, and common morality. David Mellinkoff begins *The Conscience of a Lawyer* with a history of lawyer-hating that is quite eloquent in this regard. At one point he notes:

> The full force of the complaint is not alone the denial of truth, even coupled with avarice, but that with a God given talent the lawyer stands in the way of every man's birthright, the right to justice. The lawyer, in John Stuart Mill's phrase, is ready to "frustrate justice with his tongue."[80]

Is this because of the adversary system? Indeed it is, for it is the adversary system that makes zealous advocacy of the client's interests the pillar of professional obligation. The *Joint Conference Report* puts it best:

> At the first meeting of the Conference the general problem discussed was that of bringing home to the law student, the lawyer and the public an understanding of the nature of the lawyer's professional responsibilities. All present considered that the chief obstacle to the success of this undertaking lay in "the adversary system." ... Those who had attempted to teach ethical principles to law students found that the students were uneasy about the adversary system, some thinking of it as an unwhole-

some compromise with the combativeness of human nature, others vaguely approving of it but disturbed by their inability to articulate its proper limits.... Confronted by the layman's charge that he is nothing but a hired brain and voice, the lawyer often finds it difficult to convey an insight into the value of the adversary system.[81]

Even law students, then, are suspicious of the adversary system (though not for long). There is irony here: the need to justify the adversary system lies, according to the *Joint Conference Report*, in the fact that no one seems to trust it or the conduct it countenances; our current argument purports to justify it by claiming that we all tacitly approve of it. The argument fails.

Seeing that it fails and why can motivate the second variation, which we may call the *tradition argument*. Consent theorists assume that we have no political obligations except those we consent to, but as Hume noted, "would these reasoners look abroad into the world, they would meet with nothing that, in the least, corresponds to their ideas, or can warrant so refined and philosophical a system."[82] On the contrary, as Hume argued, people commonly consent to institutions because they take themselves to be obligated to them, rather than the other way around. We feel that traditional institutions lay claim to us, even when they themselves originated through violence or usurpation.

The power of the past to move us and bind us is enormous; compared with such deep feelings, the ideas of consent theory seem shallow and alien to human experience. This criticism is most familiar in Burke (though it is implicit in Hume as well):

> Society is indeed a contract ... but the state ought not to be considered as nothing better than a partnership agreement in a trade of pepper and coffee, callico or tobacco, or some such low concern, to be taken up for a little temporary interest, and to be dis-

solved by the fancy of the parties.... it is ... a partnership not only between those who are living, but between those who are living, those who are dead, and those who are to be born. Each contract of each particular state is but a clause in the great primaeval contract of eternal society.... The municipal corporations of that universal kingdom are not morally at liberty at their pleasure, and on the speculations of a contingent improvement, wholly to separate and tear asunder the bonds of their subordinate community, and to dissolve it into an unsocial, uncivil, unconnected chaos of elementary principles.[83]

A Burkean argument for the adversary system would appeal to its place in our traditions and claim that we are under a moral obligation to spurn "speculations of a contingent improvement" that would tear this tradition apart. There is much to be said for Burkean argument, if for no other reason than its rejection of a shallow and Philistine conception of progress.[84] But it does not apply to the adversary system.

In the first place, it ignores the fact that there is no constant tradition: common law constantly modifies the adversary system. Indeed, the adversary advocate is a recent invention within that changing tradition. In Great Britain, criminal defense lawyers were not permitted to address the courts until 1836;[85] in America, criminal defendants were not guaranteed counsel until 1963.[86] Civil litigants are still not guaranteed counsel, even in quasi-criminal matters such as a state's attempt to take a child from its parent.[87] It is hard to see the adversary system as "a clause in the great primaeval contract."

In the second place, the adversary system is an ancillary institution compared with those with which Burke was concerned. In William Simon's words,

I think the argument will seem rather out of proportion to the subject. It's one thing to talk about the dangers of utopian change when you're talking about ripping the whole society apart to restructure it from top to bottom. But there are plenty of ways of abolishing adversary ethics which from a larger point of view are really just marginal social reforms which, whether good or bad, hardly suggest the likelihood of Burkean dangers. It's like making a Burkean argument against no-fault or social security.[88]

The Burkean argument is in effect a demurrer to the demand that we justify the adversary system: it suggests that the system is too central to the "great primaeval contract" to be put to the justificatory test. To this argument the reply is simply that the tradition does not clearly incorporate the adversary system, and that the system is too marginal for us to let Burkean considerations permit the demurrer.

VII. The Adversary System Excuse

A. Pragmatic Justification

So far the course of argument has been purely negative, a persecution and assassination of the adversary system. By this time you are entitled to ask what I propose putting in its place. The answer is: nothing, for I think the adversary system is justified.

I do not, let me quickly say, have an argumentative novelty to produce. It would be strange indeed for a social institution to be justified on the basis of virtues other than the tried and true ones, virtues that no one had noticed in it before. My justification is rather aversion of the tradition argument, but purged of its ideological overtones: I shall call it the "pragmatic justification" or "pragmatic argument" to suggest its affinity with the relaxed, problem-oriented, and historicist notion of justification associated with American pragmatism. The justification is this:

First, the adversary system, despite its imperfections, irrationalities, loopholes, and perversities, seems to do as good a job as any at finding truth and protecting legal rights. None of its existing rivals, in particular the inquisitorial system and the socialist system, are demonstrably better, and some, such as trial by ordeal, are demonstrably worse. Indeed, even if one of the other systems were slightly better, the human costs—in terms of effort, confusion, anxiety, disorientation, inadvertent miscarriages of justice due to improper understanding, retraining, resentment, loss of tradition, you name it—would outweigh reasons for replacing the existing system.

Second, *some* adjudicatory system is necessary.

Third, it's the way we have always done things.

These propositions constitute a pragmatic argument: if a social institution does a reasonable enough job of its sort that the costs of replacing it outweigh the benefits, and if we need that sort of job done, we should stay with what we have.

A cynic might say that the insight underlying a pragmatic justification is twofold: first, what has been called the Law of Conservation of Trouble, and second, the principle that the devil you know is better than the devil you don't. The suspicion is that even if the adversary system murders truth (and legal rights and morality) in its characteristic way, whatever we replace it with will do so in new and unexpected ways. Why, then, go through the trauma of change?

That this is a very relaxed sort of justification may be seen from the fact that it works equally well for the inquisitorial system in France and the socialist system in Bulgaria. A pragmatic justification is weak as well because it crumbles in the face of a demonstration that, contrary to what we believe, the institution is awful enough to replace. The argument, in other words, does not really endorse an institution—it only endures it.

Accepting a pragmatic justification of the adversary system, it should be added, does not commit one to a blanket conservatism. One can believe that our society should be drastically changed or that our legal system *in praxi* is hopelessly unjust and still accept that a changed society or overhauled legal system should utilize adversary adjudication. Thus, while the argument leads to a conservative conclusion, it does so in a nonideological way, and the conclusion extends no further than the institution for which the argument is offered.

In my opinion, many of our social institutions are like the adversary system in that they admit only of pragmatic justification, Some are not intended to serve any positive moral good; some serve it badly. That these institutions are not worth replacing may be a measure of nothing more than social lethargy and our inability to come up with a better idea; my point is that this is a real reason. A pragmatic argument is logically weak—it justifies institutions without showing that they are better than their rivals, or even that they are particularly good—but in practice it is overwhelmingly powerful. Institutions, like bodies, obey Newton's First Law.

B. Pragmatic Justification and Institutional Excuses

Because this is so typical of institutions it is worth asking about the effect of pragmatic argument on the moral obligations of institutional functionaries (such as lawyers). The position I want to press is roughly that a social institution that can receive only a pragmatic justification is not capable of providing institutional excuses for immoral acts. To do that, an institution must be justified in a much stronger way, by showing that it is a positive moral good. A pragmatic argument, by contrast, need show only that it is not much more mediocre than its rivals.

Let me spell this out by criticizing what I shall call the Transitivity Argument, which goes as follows:

1. The institution is justified.
2. The institution requires its functionary to do A.
3. Therefore, the functionary is justified in doing A.

This plausible-looking defense of institutional excuses can be criticized by denying the first premise; however, I am accepting the pragmatic justification of the adversary system and thus accepting the premise. Or it could be criticized by attacking the second premise: thus, William Simon and Richard Abel have argued that the role morality of lawyers is so riddled with contradictions that it is impossible to derive any coherent set of professional requirements from it.[89] My strategy, however, is to deny that the conclusion follows from the premises. The institutional obligation is only a prima facie obligation, and the weaker the justification of the institution, the weaker the force of this obligation in overriding other morally relevant factors.

To get the argument underway, let us look at the way an institutional excuse might work when the institution is strongly justified, when it is a positive moral good.

Consider, as an example, a charitable organization whose sole function is to distribute food to famine-stricken people in impoverished areas of the world. We will call this the *institution*. Division of labor within it creates different jobs or *institutional tasks* each of which has specified duties or *role-obligations*. These may be quite general: the logistics officer, for example, might have as his role-obligation procuring means of transporting food. To carry out the role-obligation, he must perform various actions, call them the *role-acts*.

Let us suppose that to get food to a remote village the logistics officer must obtain several trucks from a local, very powerful gangster, P. As it happens, P is involved in a number of unsavory activities, including a plan to murder a local man, because P wants to sleep with the man's wife. Imagine further that the logistics officer overhears P dispatching a murderer to kill the man that very night, that P discovers that the logistics officer has overheard him, and that P tells the officer that if the man is warned and escapes, P will not provide the trucks.

The officer is in a moral dilemma. Other things being equal, he is under a moral obligation to warn the man. Let us, at any rate, suppose that this is so. But here, if anywhere, we may wish to permit an institutional excuse. Suppose the officer complies with P's demand. Asked to justify this, he says, "My job is more important." This is an institutional excuse, the structure of which may be spelled out as follows: he points out that the role-act of complying with P is required by his role-obligation, which in turn is necessary to perform the institutional task, which (finally) is justified by the positive moral good of the institution—the saving of many innocent lives.

The general problem, which creates the dilemma, is that the propositions

> The institution is a morally good one

> and

> The institution imposes role-obligations on its officers some of which may mandate morally bad role-acts

can both be true.

In such a case, the institutional excuse, fully spelled out, will take the form I have indicated: the agent justifies the role-act by showing it is required by the role-obligation, justifies the obligation by showing it derives from the institutional task, justifies the institutional task by appealing to the structure of the institution, and justifies the institution by demonstrating its moral goodness.

Let us apply this form of argument to a legal example. Freedman uses it in his analysis of the Lake Pleasant bodies case.[90] The lawyer's role-act (preserving the defendant's confidence) was required by the general duty of confidentiality (the role-obligation). This is justified by arguing that the duty is required in order to guarantee adequate criminal defense (the institutional task). (That argument is somewhat detailed, and I will not go into it here. Let me note that this stage of the argument is where most policy disputes in legal ethics are located.) The next step is to show that such defense is required by the adversary system, and this in turn, or so it is claimed and so I have agreed, serves the positive moral good of preserving individual rights against the encroachment of the state.

I am *not* claiming that an institutional excuse is inevitably appropriate when the institution is strongly justified. You and I may differ in our assessment even of the examples. I am claiming only that in such cases a difficult moral dilemma exists, from which an institutional excuse is one possible way out.

If, on the other hand, an institution is justified only by pragmatic argument, the sides of the dilemma do not have equal weight and the institutional excuse collapses. For in that case it reads as follows:

> It is true that I am morally wronging you. But that is required by my role-obligations, which are essential to my institutional task, which is necessary to the structure of the institution, which is justified
>
> because it is there.
>
> because it's the way we do things around here.
>
> because it's not worth the trouble to replace it.

This, I think, will not do. The excuse rests on an elephant that stands on a tortoise that floats in the sky. But the sky is falling.

Compare this real-life example with the Lake Pleasant case: A youth, Spaulding, badly injured in an automobile wreck, sued for damages. The conscientious defense lawyer had his own doctor examine the youth; the doctor discovered a life-threatening aortic aneurism, apparently caused by the accident, that Spaulding's doctors had not found. Spaulding was willing to settle the case for $6500, but the defense lawyer realized that if the youth learned of the aneurism he would demand a much higher amount.[91]

The defense lawyer concealed the information and settled for $6500. How could this be justified? Presumably, the argument would have to track Freedman's defense in the Lake Pleasant case, but

the final step would be missing. In this case the adversary system is not strongly justified by the liberal argument about keeping the state's hands off people accused of a crime. No one is accused of a crime in this case. Uncharitably put, the basis of confidentiality here is the need to save money for a client or (more likely) an insurance company. Charitably put, it is that the adversary system is weakly justified—justified because it is there. That may be a reason to risk one's own life on a mountain, but it is not a reason to risk Spaulding's life in a law office.

It might be objected to this line of criticism that the pragmatic argument for the adversary system is a strong justification for it, even in noncriminal cases. After all, what better justification of the system can there be than saying that it performs a necessary function as well as any of its competitors? What absolute yardstick is used to measure it and find it wanting?

The answer to these questions has already been given in our discussion of the difference between the criminal and noncriminal context.[92] In the noncriminal context, the primary end of adversary adjudication is the assignment of rewards and remedies on the basis of parties' behavior as prescribed by legal norms: legal justice, rather than protection from the state, is the goal. The adversary method is supposed to yield accurate accounts of facts and legitimate interpretations of the law. That is the absolute yardstick: if the adversary system yields legal justice, it is a positive moral good. But, as I have argued, we have no reason to believe that it does yield legal justice in the hard cases.

An analogy may clarify this point. Scientists at times accept and use a theory because it is the best account going, even though they do not have much confidence in its truth. Such a theory is pragmatically justified in much the same way as the adversary system: it is as good as its competitors, some theory is necessary, and it is there. It's just that most scientists in the field think the theory will turn out to be false—and for that reason it is weakly, not strongly, justified.[93]

The general point is that some practices carry absolute criteria of success. The criterion of success for a scientific theory is truth; the criterion of success for mountain climbing is getting to the top and back. Other practices carry criteria that are merely relative (the fastest runner in the world is *ipso facto* a successful runner). A pragmatic argument strongly justifies only the latter sort of practices, but, if I am right, the adversary system is of the former sort.

Let us return to the two confidentiality examples. Their general point is that one can be excused from a moral obligation only by another moral consideration that outweighs it: an institution provides a moral excuse only if it has moral cachet. If the institution is justified only because it is there, it possesses only the minutest quantum of force to excuse an immoral act. The Transitivity Argument fails.

Another way to see this, derived from a point made by Gerald Postema and Bernard Williams,[94] can also be offered. Suppose that the Transitivity Argument were valid. Then it would not be immoral for lawyers to engage in ruthless, rights-violating activity. They would therefore have no occasion for moral regret at their actions. But, and this is Postema's and Williams's point, we want agents in "dirty hands" situations to feel regret at what they must do since otherwise they will not develop the sort of moral character that enables them to judge when they should refrain from ruthless action. It follows that we should accept the Transitivity Argument only if we are willing to accept lawyers who are incapable of turning off their own adversariality. But that is absurd, because such a lawyer would be unable to draw adequate lines in any sort of situation that requires normative judgment, and that is inconsistent with what it takes to practice law at all.

The basic problem with the Transitivity Argument is that it exempts officers of an institution from ordinary moral requirements that conflict with role-obligations, even though the institution itself is in place only because we have always done it that way. The result is to place conformity to existing institutions beyond the very possibility of moral criticism. This, however, is no longer justified conservatism: rather, it is fetishism of tradition.

Pragmatic arguments do not really praise institutions; they merely give reason for not burying them. Since their force is more inertial than moral, they create insufficient counterweight to resolve dilemmas in favor of the role-obligation. An excuse based on institutions justified in this way is simply a "good soldier" argument with little more to be said.

VIII. Conclusion and Peroration

By this point, I think, the argument has just about exhausted itself. It is time to summarize.

Perhaps the best way to see the import of the arguments I have been offering is not as an attack on the adversary system (for, after all, I have not suggested that it should be replaced) so much as an attack on an ideology consisting of these ideas:

1. The adversary system is the best system of justice ever devised.
2. It is a delicately poised instrument in which the generation of just outcomes depends on the regular functioning of each of its parts.
3. Hence the pursuit of justice morally obligates an attorney to assume a one-sided Broughamesque role.
4. The adversary system, in consequence, institutionally excuses lawyers from ordinary moral obligations conflicting with their professional obligations.
5. Broughamesque advocacy is, moreover, a cornerstone of our system of political liberties, for it is the last defense of the hapless criminal-accused against the awesome power of the state. To restrict the advocate is to invite totalitarianism.

I have argued, I hope convincingly, against the first four of these propositions. About the fifth a more cautious conclusion is in order. The argument it offered that the criminal defense lawyer "must not regard the alarm, the torments, the destruction which he may bring upon others" (Brougham, again) is rather persuasive, but only because of two special features of the criminal context: that we have political reasons for handicapping the government in its role as enforcer, and that the criminal defendant comes closest to the paradigm of the man-in-trouble. The argument, then, countenances adversarial ruthlessness as a blanket policy only in criminal and quasi-criminal defense, and thus only in these situations is the adversary system available as an institutional excuse. Criminal defense is the exception that proves the ordinary moral rule.

What does all this mean in noncriminal contexts, where this institutional excuse based on political theory is unavailable? The answer, very simply, is this. The adversary system possesses only the slightest moral force, and thus appealing to it can excuse only the slightest moral wrongs. Anything else that is morally wrong for a nonlawyer to do on behalf of another person is morally wrong for a lawyer to do as well. The lawyer's role carries no moral privileges and immunities.

This does not mean that zealous advocacy is immoral, not even when it frustrates the search for truth or violates legal rights. Sometimes frustrating the search for truth may be a morally worthy thing to do, and sometimes moral rights are ill served by legal rights. All I am insisting on is that the standards by which such judgments are made are the same for lawyers and nonlawyers. If a lawyer is permitted to puff, bluff, or threaten on certain occasions, this is not because of the adversary system and the Principle of Nonaccountability, but because, in such circumstances, anyone would be permitted to do these things. Nothing justifies doing them on behalf of a predator.

But, it will be objected, my argument leads to a paradox, for I have claimed to offer a vindication, albeit a weak one, of the adversary system, and therefore of the duties of partisan advocacy that it entails.

Am I not saying that a lawyer may be professionally obligated to do A and morally obligated not to do A?

That is indeed what I am saying, but there is no contradiction here. The adversary system and the system of professional obligation it mandates are justified only in that, lacking a clearly superior alternative, they should not be replaced. This implies, I have argued, that when professional and moral obligation conflict, moral obligation takes precedence. When they don't conflict, professional obligations rule the day. The Principle of Professionalism follows from the fact that we have an adversary system; the Principle of Nonaccountability does not. The point of elaborating the former is to tell the lawyer what, in this system, professionalism requires—to say that it requires zeal, for example, even when cutting corners might be more profitable or pleasant. Professionalism can tell a lawyer not to cut corners; my point is that it cannot mandate him or her to cut throats. When moral obligation conflicts with professional obligation, the lawyer must become a civil disobedient.

Not that this is likely to happen. Lawyers get paid for their services, not for their consciences. But so does everyone else. As we do not expect the world to strike a truce in the war of all against all, we should not expect lawyers to. Shen Te, the Good Woman of Setzuan, says:

> I'd like to be good, it's true, but there's the rent to pay. And that's not all: I sell myself for a living. Even so I can't make ends meet, there's too much competition.[95]

That, of course, is the way the world is, and criticizing an ideology won't change the world. The point of the exercise, I suppose, is merely to get our moral ideas straight. One less ideology is, after all, one less excuse.

NOTES

1 Samuel Taylor Coleridge, "Duties and Needs of an Advocate," in *The Table Talk and Omiana of Samuel Taylor Coleridge*, edited by T.

Ashe (London: George Bell and Sons, 1888), 140-41.

2 William Whewell, *The Elements of Morality, Including Polity* 2 vols (London: John W. Parker, 1845), Vol. 1, 258-59.

3 George Sharswood, *A Compend of Lectures on the Aims and Duties of the Profession of the Law* (Philadelphia: T. & J.W. Johnson, 1854), 84.

4 Murray Schwartz, "The Professionalism and Accountability of Lawyers," *California Law Review* Vol. 66 (1978): 673.

5 Ibid.

6 Gerald J. Postema, "Moral Responsibility in Professional Ethics," *New York University Law Review* Vol. 55 (1980): 73.

7 William Simon, "The Ideology of Advocacy: Procedural Justice and Professional Ethics," *Wisconsin Law Review* 1978 (1978): 36-37.

8 Schwartz, "Professionalism and Accountability," 674.

9 Mitchell Rogovin, "'Graymail': Shaded Variant of a Darker Hue," *Legal Times of Washington*, March 26, 1979; see Lawrence Meyer, "Justice Dept. is Examining Helms' Testimony on CIA," *The Washington Post*, February 12, 1975, A1, A12.

10 Joe Trenton "Inside the Helms File," *National Law Journal*, December 22, 1980, 1.

11 Daniel Schwartz, "The 'New' Legal Ethics and the Administrative Law Bar," Chapter 10, this volume, 247-48.

12 J. Nightingale, ed., *Trial of Queen Caroline*, 3 vols (London: J. Robins & Co., Albion Press, 1820-21), Vol. 2, 8.

13 David Mellinkoff, *The Conscience of a Lawyer* (St. Paul, MN: West, 1973), 188.

14 See Edward Dauer and Arthur Leff, "Correspondence: The Lawyer as Friend," *Yale Law Journal* Vol. 86 (1977): 581.

15 *Tukiar and the King*, 52 Commw. L.R. 335, 347 (Austin 1934), quoted in Mellinkoff, *The Conscience of a Lawyer*, 273.

16 A lengthy discussion of this well-known case, with documents and interviews, is found in Patrick A. Keenan, ed., *Teaching Professional Responsibility: Materials and Proceedings from the National Conference* (Detroit: University of Detroit Press, 1979), 233-324.

17 The damages to all concerned in the Lake Pleasant bodies case were considerable: the parents of the victims were anguished, the public aghast, the tourism business in Lake Pleasant harmed because of the unsolved disappearances, Garrow convicted and sentenced to 35-years-to-life, Belge and Armani nearly ruined.

18 Friedrich Nietzsche, *Thus Spoke Zarathustra*, in *The Portable Nietzsche*, edited and translated by Walter Kaufmann (New York: Viking Press, 1954), 171.

19 *ABA Model Code of Professional Responsibility* (1974 revision), EC 7-1.

20 Marvin Frankel, *Partisan Justice* (New York: Hill and Wang, 1980), 18.

21 See Martha Mills, "Motions to Disqualify: Caveat Advocatus," *Litigation* Vol. 6 (1979): 47-50 and, for a pioneering but not altogether satisfactory analysis, Lawrence Crocker, "Comment: The Ethics of Moving to Disqualify Opposing Counsel for Conflict of Interest," *Duke Law Journal* 1979 (1979): 1310-34. For general background, see "Developments in the Law—Conflicts of Interest in the Legal Profession," *Harvard Law Review* Vol. 94 (1981): 1244-1503.

22 Yasunari Kawabata, *The Master of Go*, translated by Edward Seidensticker (New York: Alfred A. Knopf, 1972), 54.

23 Mellinkoff, *The Conscience of a Lawyer*, 157.

24 *ABA Code*, EC 7-1 to 7-5 are clear on this point.

25 Ibid., EC 7-19.

26 See Murray Schwartz, "Professionalism and Accountability," 672; Lon Fuller, "The Adversary

System," in *Talks on American Law*, edited by Harold J. Berman (New York: Vintage Books, 1961), 30-32; Martin Golding, "On the Adversary System and Justice," in *Philosophical Law*, edited by Richard Bronaugh (Westport, CT: Greenwood Press, 1978), 105.

27 *ABA Code*, Canon 5.

28 Ibid., Canon 6.

29 David Luban, "Professional Ethics: A New Code for Lawyers?" *The Hastings Center Report* Vol. 10 (June 1980): 12.

30 A sophisticated attempt to characterize the principles of lawyers' ethics through the nature of the lawyer-client relationship rather than the adversary system is Charles Fried, "The Lawyer as Friend: The Moral Foundations of the Lawyer-Client Relation," *Yale Law Journal* Vol. 85 (1976): 1060-89. See also Charles Fried, *Right and Wrong* (Cambridge, MA: Harvard University Press, 1978), 167-94.

31 Indeed, one of Schwartz's reasons for writing the article (see note 4) was to propose a reform according to which the principles do not apply in the context of negotiation. Currently, negotiation is seen as a subject calling for as much "hardball" as courtroom advocacy.

32 An attempt to argue that the real purpose of lawyers' codes of conduct is market-control from the supply side is Richard L. Abel, "Why Does the ABA Promulgate Ethical Rules?" *Texas Law Review* Vol. 59 (1981): 639-88.

33 Monroe Freedman, *Lawyers' Ethics in an Adversary System* (Indianapolis: Bobbs-Merrill, 1975).

34 Ibid., 2, 4.

35 John Griffiths suggests that this way of thinking reflects "little more than the concerns of the middle class in connection with the rare occasions on which it has to fear prosecution." ("Ideology in Criminal Procedure or A Third 'Model' of the Criminal Process," *Yale Law Journal* Vol. 79 [1970]: 415.) It is clear, of course, that despite the official rhetoric of the bar indigent criminal defendants do not often get the zealous advocacy the rhetoric promises; it is hard to see, though, why it would not benefit them if they did get it, and thus why it is a strictly "middle class" concern. Griffiths's point seems to be that treating the exceptional case of genuine zeal as a paradigm simply reinforces a false liberal political philosophy "assuming the inevitability of a state of irreconcilable hostility between the individual and the state" (413)— a political philosophy that is "middle class." Now, I do not wish to defend liberalism as a general political philosophy, for I think that trafficking in abstractions such as "the individual" and "the state" is essentially misleading. (For the same reason, I think that Griffiths's own proposal of the "fundamental reconcilability" of individual and state is as misleading as the position he attacks.) Neither is it true that *every* criminal defendant is equally set-upon by the state—think, for example, of the Watergate defendants. Thus, there *are* significant class differences in the way criminal procedure actually proceeds. Nevertheless, the liberal abstraction is a rather good first approximation of the relationship between defendant and state. Maurice Nadjari, lecturing his fellow prosecutors, told them that their "true purpose is to convict the guilty man who sits at the defense table, and to go for the jugular as viciously and rapidly as possible.... You must never forget that your goal is total annihilation" (quoted in Frankel, *Partisan Justice*, 32). If that isn't "Irreconcilable hostility," what is? The criminal defense situation may, in fact, be the only one of which liberal political theory is true. The *real* objection to "Better a hundred criminals go free" is not that it is a middle-class bromide, but rather that the middle class is so willing to abandon it the moment that a suspected mugger or burglar enters the docket.

36 In *The Conscience of a Lawyer*.

37 John Thibaut and Laurens Walker, *Procedural Justice: A Psychological Analysis* (Hillsdale, NJ: Lawrence Erlbaum Associates, 1975).

38 See Mirjan Damaska, "Presentation of Evidence and Fact-finding Precision," *University of Pennsylvania Law Review* 123 (1975): 1083-106.

39 Karl Popper, *Conjectures and Refutations: The Growth of Scientific Knowledge* (New York: Harper & Row, 1963), iv, 33-65, 114-19, 352, 355-63. See Marvin Frankel, "The Search for Truth: An Umpireal View," *University of Pennsylvania Law Review* Vol. 123 (1975): 1036; and Monroe Freedman, "Judge Frankel's Search for Truth," *University of Pennsylvania Law Review* Vol. 123 (1975): 1060-61.

40 And then again, perhaps not. See Imre Lakatos, "Falsification and the Methodology of Scientific Research Programmes," in *Criticism and the Growth of Knowledge*, edited by Imre Lakatos and Alan Musgrave (Cambridge: Cambridge University Press, 1970); Paul Feyerabend, *Against Method* (London: New Left Books, 1975); and *Science in a Free Society* (London: New Left Books, 1978).

41 Feyerabend to the contrary (*Against Method, Science in a Free Society*). But his view is widely rejected, and anyway he does not claim that truth is the outcome of the process.

42 Hannah Arendt, *Eichmann in Jerusalem: A Report on the Banality of Evil* (New York: Viking Press, 1964), 2nd ed., 26.

43 Frank Moya, "The Teacher Takes the Final Exam," *National Law Journal*, November 17, 1981, 22.

44 Ibid.

45 Popper, *Conjectures and Refutations*, 352.

46 Lon Fuller and John D. Randall, "Professional Responsibility: Report of the Joint Conference," *ABA Journal* 44 (1958): 1160. Cited hereafter as *Joint Conference Report*.

47 A similar argument is used by William Simon, "The Ideology of Advocacy," 76.

48 *Joint Conference Report*, 1160.

49 Ibid., 1161.

50 Ibid., 1160.

51 For related arguments expressing skepticism about the truth-finding function of the adversary system, see Golding, "On the Adversary System and Justice," note 26 above, 106-12; and Alan H. Goldman, *The Moral Foundations of Professional Ethics* (Totowa, NJ: Rowman and Littlefield, 1980), 112-16. Geoffrey Hazard, the Reporter who drafted the current ABA Model Rules of Professional Conduct, acknowledges that "there is no proof that the adversary system of trial yields truth more often than other systems of trial; that ... is an article of faith, because there is no way to conduct a reliable experiment." "Rules of Legal Ethics: The Drafting Task," *The Record of the Association of the Bar of the City of New York* Vol. 36 (March 1981): 93.

52 Steven Sachs, untitled and unpublished speech, 1980.

53 Freedman, *Lawyers' Ethics*, 3-4.

54 It should be noted that other values than truth and legal rights are also implicated in trial procedure. For example, in a personal injury negligence case evidence that the defendant has repaired the site of an accident after it happened is not admissible, even though it would indirectly establish that the defendant really had been negligent. The reason for this policy is that to do otherwise would discourage the repair and so enhance a menace to the public. It is thus an oversimplification to suggest that the whole purpose of the trial process is to protect the interests of the court (by getting at the truth) or the parties. The public interest is also involved.

55 Freedman, *Lawyers' Ethics*, 3-4.

56 Ibid., 8. See also James L. Oakes, "Lawyer and Judge: The Ethical Duty of Competency," in

Ethics and Advocacy (Washington, DC: The Roscoe Pound-American Trial Lawyers Foundation, 1978), 60, who argues that the adversary system is required by Article III and Amendments V, VI, and VII of the Constitution.

57 Theodore Koskoff, "Introduction" to *The American Lawyer's Code of Conduct Public Discussion Draft* (Washington, DC: The Roscoe Pound-American Trial Lawyers Foundation, 1980), ii.

58 See, for example *Hickman v. Taylor*, 329 U.S. 495, 514 (1946); or *Herring v. New York*, 422 U.S. 853, 857-58 (1974).

59 *The Attic Nights of Aulus Gellius*, translated by John C. Rolfe (Cambridge, MA: Harvard University Press, 1954), l. vi. 4-5 (quoted in Golding, "On the Adversary System and Justice").

60 Advertisement, *National Law Journal*, June 2, 1980, 30.

61 Thomas Nagel, "Ruthlessness in Public Life," in *Public and Private Morality*, edited by Stuart Hampshire (Cambridge: Cambridge University Press, 1978), 85.

62 Sharswood, *A Compend of Lectures*, note 3 above, 84.

63 Virginia Held, "Justification: Legal and Political," *Ethics* Vol. 86 (October 1975): 1-16.

64 Ibid., 11.

65 Ibid. It is this argument, justifying an institutional division of labor by its "morally salutary" results, that leads me to classify Held's theory as consequentialist, though it has nothing to do with simple utilitarian arguments. See also Chapter 3, this volume.

66 Hannah Arendt, *On Violence* (New York: Harcourt, Brace & World, 1970), 81.

67 *Joint Conference Report*, 1161.

68 Ibid.

69 Frankel, *Partisan Justice*, 4.

70 Fried, "The Lawyer as Friend," 1075.

71 Mellinkoff, *The Conscience of a Lawyer*, 270.

72 Fried, "The Lawyer as Friend," 1068-73.

73 See text accompanying note 11 above.

74 See Dauer and Leff, "Correspondence: The Lawyer as Friend," note 14 above, 577-78; Simon, "The Ideology of Advocacy," note 7 above, 108-09.

75 Fried, *Right and Wrong*, 191.

76 Ibid., 192.

77 Galway Kinney, *The Book of Nightmares* (Boston: Houghton Mifflin, 1971), 43.

78 Slightly paraphrased from Fried, *Right and Wrong*, 192 and "The Lawyer as Friend," 1085.

79 Michael Walzer, *Just and Unjust Wars: A Moral Argument with Historical Illustrations* (New York: Basic Books, 1977), 54.

80 Mellinkoff, *The Conscience of a Lawyer*, 12.

81 *Joint Conference Report*, 1159.

82 David Hume, "Of the Original Contract," in *Essays, Literary, Moral and Political* (London: George Routledge and Sons, n.d.), 272.

83 Edmund Burke, *Reflections on the Revolution in France* (Garden City, NY: Anchor Books, 1973), 110.

84 My view here is heavily influenced by Walter Benjamin's brilliant but gnomic "Theses on the Philosophy of History," in *Illuminations*, edited by Hannah Arendt, translated by Harry Zohn (New York: Schocken books, 1969). See particularly Thesis XV, 261.

85 Mellinkoff, *The Conscience of a Lawyer*, 47.

86 *Gideon v. Wainwright*, 372 U.S. 335 (1963).

87 See, most recently, *Lassiter v. Department of Social Services of Durham, NC*, 452 U.S. 18 (1981).

88 Letter to the author, January 31, 1981.

89 Abel, "Why Does the ABA Promulgate Ethical Rules?" note 32 above; Simon, "The Ideology of Advocacy," note 7 above.

90 Freedman, *Lawyers' Ethics*, chap. 1.

91 *Spaulding v. Zimmerman*, 116 N, W. 2d 704 (1962).

92 See 91-93 above.

93 I am indebted to Victoria Choy for this point.

94 Gerald Postema, "Moral Responsibility in Professional Ethics," note 6 above, 79-80. Bernard Williams, "Politics and Moral Character," in *Public and Private Morality*, edited by Stuart Hampshire (Cambridge: Cambridge University Press, 1978), 61-65; Chapter 11, this volume.

95 Bertolt Brecht, *The Good Woman of Setzuan*, translated by Eric Bentley (New York: Grove Press, 1947), 24.

This much-traveled and often-revised paper has received the criticism and comments of too many people to acknowledge all by name. Portions were presented to the staff of the Center for Philosophy and Public Policy; the Center for Philosophy and Public Policy Working Group on Legal Ethics; the Ethics and Public Policy Workshop; and the Society for the Study of Professional Ethics 1981 meeting at the Western Division of the American Philosophical Association. I wish to thank the participants in these meetings for their helpful advice. Major repairs in the argument resulted from comments by Robert Fullinwider, Virginia Held, Douglas MacLean, George Sher, Henry Shue, and William Simon. Needless to say, the reader is safe in assuming that the inadequacies in what he or she now has in hand are entirely the fault of its author.

This research was funded in part by the Maryland Bar Foundation and NEH Grant No. EH-20045-81-0658. Neither sponsor should be held responsible for the views expressed in the paper.

◆ ◆ ◆ ◆ ◆

ELLIOT D. COHEN

Pure Legal Advocates and Moral Agents: Two Concepts of a Lawyer in an Adversary System

It is sometimes asked whether a good lawyer in an adversary system can also be a good person. We must first notice that there are two different senses of the term *good* employed in this question. In its first occurrence, *good* may be taken in its instrumental sense to mean, roughly, *effective*. In its second occurrence, *good* may be taken in its moral sense to mean *morally good*. Thus the question is whether an effective lawyer can also be a morally good person. And the latter question, it is clear, can be answered only if we have some idea of what we mean by a morally good person, and by an effective lawyer.

Accordingly, in this paper I shall first outline what we take to be salient marks of a morally good person. Second, I shall examine one sense of a lawyer, what we call the *pure legal advocate concept*, in which a good lawyer does *not* satisfy our criteria of a morally good person. Third, I shall examine a further concept of a lawyer, what might be called the *moral agent concept*, according to which a good lawyer is, *ipso facto*, a morally good person.

Morally Good Persons

Following one tradition, let us say that a morally good person is a person who, through exercise and training, has cultivated certain morally desirable traits of character; the latter traits being constituted by dispositions to act, think, and feel in certain ways, under certain conditions, which are *themselves* morally desirable.[1] What traits of character in particular are morally desirable and to what extent and in what combinations they must be cultivated in order for a person to be morally good are admittedly no settled matters. Still, there are some traits which at least most of us would countenance as being important, if not essential, ingredients of the morally good personality. It is such traits of character with which I shall be concerned, particularly those among them which seem to be the most relevant to legal practice.

What then are some such characteristic marks of a morally good person?

1. We would not ordinarily countenance a person as being morally good if we believed that he was not a *just* person, that is, if we thought that he was not disposed toward treating others justly. There are, however, two senses of *just* and *unjust* in which a person may be said to treat others justly or unjustly.

First, a person may be said to treat others justly when, in distributing some good or service among them, she observes the principle of treating relevantly similar cases in a similar fashion; and she may be said to treat others *unjustly*, in this sense, when she violates this principle. For example, a physician who consistently distributes medical service among the ill on the basis of medical need would, *ceteris paribas*, be acting justly in this sense; whereas one who distributes such service without regard to medical needs, but instead with regard to race or religion, would, in this sense, be acting unjustly. This is so because we typically regard medical need as the controlling factor in distributing health care; whereas race and religion appear to be quite irrelevant in such a context.

We may, however, be said to treat others justly when we are respectful of their legal and moral rights, or when we give to them what they rightfully deserve; and we may be said to treat others unjustly when we intrude upon their legal or moral rights, or when we treat them in ways in which they do not deserve to be treated. For example, one acts justly, in this sense, when he keeps an agreement with an individual who has the right to insist upon its being kept; or a judge acts justly, in this sense, when he hands down a well-deserved punishment to a legal offender; whereas a person perpetrates an injustice

upon another, in this sense, when he fails to uphold a binding agreement or when he inflicts injury upon an innocent party.

Let us say, then, that the just person is one who is disposed toward treating others justly in both of the above senses. That is, she tends to be consistent in her treatment of others—she does not normally make biased or arbitrary exceptions. But she is also the sort of person who respects individual rights and can usually be counted upon to make good on her obligations to others.

2. Being morally good would also appear to require being *truthful*. By truthful person is meant one who is in the habit of asserting things only if he *believes* them to be true. Thus he is in the habit of asserting things with the intention of *informing* his hearers, and not deceiving them, about the truth. An *untruthful* person, on the other hand, is in the habit of asserting things which she *disbelieves*; and this she does with the intention of deceiving her hearers about the truth. Moreover, the untruthful person may deceive not merely through her spoken word, but also by other means. She may, for example, leave false clues or simply remain silent where such measures are calculated to mislead as to the truth. This is not to suggest that such tactics are never justified; it is rather to say that, when they constitute the rule instead of the exception, the person in question has fallen below that level of truthfulness which we should normally require of a morally good person.

3. Being a morally good person would also seem to demand at least *some* measure of *moral courage*. Indeed, it would appear that a person could not be just or truthful if he did not have any such measure; for it often takes courage to be honest or to do what is just. By a *morally* courageous person we mean a person who is disposed toward doing what he thinks is morally right even when he believes that his doing so means, or is likely to mean, his suffering some substantial hardship. As Aristotle suggests, it is "the mark of a brave man to face things that are, and

seem, terrible for a man, because it is noble to do so and disgraceful not to do so."[2]

And, therefore, we can say, along with Aristotle, that a person who endures hardship just for the sake of some reward—such as fame or fortune—or for the sake of avoiding some punishment—such as public disfavor or legal sanctions—is not truly acting courageously in this sense, for he acts not because it is morally right to do so, but to gain a reward or avoid a punishment.

4. The moral quality of a person is no doubt often revealed through her monetary habits. Indeed, for some individuals, the making of money constitutes an end in itself for which they willfully transgress the bounds of morally permissible conduct—for example, the pimp, the drug dealer, the thief, and the hit man. And some—those whom we characterize as being stingy, miserly, tight—cling to their money with such tenacity that they would sooner allow great iniquities to occur than surrender a dollar.

The morally good person, on the other hand, would appear to be one who has developed *morally respectable* monetary habits. Such a person Aristotle calls a *liberal* person, one who, he states, "will both give and spend the right amounts and on the right objects, alike in small things and in great, and that with pleasure; he will also take the right amounts and from the right sources."[3] Following Aristotle, let us say then that a morally good person must also be, to some degree, a *liberal* person.

5. We should also expect a morally good person to be *benevolent*. By this we mean that she is disposed to do good for others when she is reasonably situated, and to do no harm. And the concern she has for the well-being of others does not arise out of some ulterior motive but rather *for its own sake*. Furthermore, she is disposed toward *feeling* certain ways under certain conditions—for example, feeling sorrow over another's misfortune or taking pleasure in another's good fortune or in helping another.

It is not supposed, however, that in order to be a morally good person one must be disposed toward benefiting others at great sacrifice to oneself; nor is it supposed that such a person must go very far to benefit or feel sympathetic toward those who do not stand in any concrete personal relation such as friendship or kinship. Still, a person who does not go an inch to benefit anyone—unless justice demands it—and who sympathizes with no one is perhaps at most a minimally good person. But one who intentionally harms others, as a matter of course, with pleasure or without regret, cannot normally be regarded as being benevolent. Indeed, such is a mark of a malevolent or morally base person.

6. So, too, would we expect to find *trustworthiness* in a morally good person. That is, we should expect such a person to be in a habit of keeping the confidences and agreements which he freely accepts or enters upon. Indeed, the person who breaks faith for no good reason is not just being dishonest; he is also being a "traitor" or a "double-crosser."

This, however, is not to suppose that an individual must *never* breach a trust if he is to be a morally good person. There are, undoubtedly, some extenuating circumstances in which breaking a trust would be the morally right thing to do—as when keeping it involves working some greater injustice upon someone than that involved in breaking it. Nor is it to be supposed that trustworthiness is a *sufficient* condition of being morally good. There may be loyalty among thieves, for instance, but we should not, for that reason alone, take their lot to be morally good.

7. A morally good person, I would suggest, is one who is regularly disposed to do her *own* moral thinking—that is, to come to her own decisions about moral issues on the basis of her own moral principles; and then, in turn, to act upon her considered judgment. Kant expressed this fact by saying that the will of a morally good person (that is, a morally good will) is one which is determined "autonomously." Following his usage, let us say then that a morally good person is a person who possesses *moral autonomy*.

Being such a person is undoubtedly no easy matter, for moral decisions are frequently difficult ones to make. For instance, in cases of conflict between one's moral principles, one must weigh one principle against another and then "strike a moral balance"—as, for instance, in a case where keeping a promise involves inflicting harm upon another; or when, in determining the value of the consequences of an act, one must balance the good consequences against the bad ones. And such determinations are clearly no mere matter of logical deduction. All that one can reasonably be expected to do in such cases is to try one's level best. But it is a mark of a morally autonomous person, and thus of a morally good person, that he actually makes such an earnest effort.

Keeping the foregoing criteria of a morally good person in mind, let us now turn to an analysis of lawyers.

The Pure Legal Advocate Concept

Following one traditional usage, we can say that the concept of a lawyer is a *functional* concept—that is, it may be defined in terms of the function or role which a lawyer *qua* lawyer is supposed to perform, in an analogous manner in which a watchdog may be defined in terms of its function of guarding property, or in which a carpenter's hammer may be defined in terms of its function of driving in nails. Hence, just as a good (effective) watchdog may be defined as a dog which performs well the function of guarding property so too may a good (effective) lawyer be defined as a person who performs well the function or role of a lawyer. What, then, we may ask, is the function or role of a lawyer?

One sense of *lawyer* is that in which the role of a lawyer is restricted to that of the client's legal advocate, and in which a good lawyer is thus conceived as being *simply* an effective legal advocate. This sense, which we shall hereafter call the *pure legal advocate concept*, is exemplified in the classic statement made by Lord Brougham when he was defending Queen

Caroline against George IV in their divorce case before the House of Lords. He states:

> An advocate, in discharge of his duty, knows but one person in all the world, and that person is his client. To save that client by all means and expedients, and at all hazards and costs to other persons, and, amongst them, to himself, is his first and only duty.[4]

The pure legal advocate concept is also more recently suggested by Canon 15 of the ABA *Canons of Professional Ethics*, which states that

> the lawyer owes "entire devotion to the interest of the client, warm zeal in the maintenance and defense of his rights and the exertion of his utmost learning and ability," to the end that nothing be taken or be withheld from him, save by the rules of law, legally applied.

Given the pure legal advocate concept, it is easy for one to conclude that the necessary and sufficient mark of a good lawyer is her tendency to win cases by all legal means. For, as was said, this concept supposes that a good lawyer is simply an effective legal advocate; and it is easy to suppose that the necessary and sufficient mark of an effective legal advocate is her tendency to legally win cases. A good lawyer hence emerges as a legal technician skillful in manipulating legal rules for the advancement of her clients' legal interests; in this sense, the good lawyer is no different than a skillful chess player able to manipulate the rules of chess to win *his* game.

Furthermore, given this concept, a lawyer may, and indeed is required, to do certain kinds of things on behalf of his client which would ordinarily be regarded as being morally objectionable. In such instances all that matters, so far as lawyering is concerned, is that such acts are legal means of advancing the client's legal interests. For instance, a defense attorney in a rape case may cross-examine the prosecutrix, whom he knows to be telling the truth, about her chastity for purposes of casting doubt upon her truthful testimony. Or, he may permit his client to take the stand knowing full well that the client will perjure himself. Or, a lawyer in a civil case may invoke a legal technicality (for example, the statute of limitations) on behalf of his client in order to defeat a just cause against him. Or, a corporate lawyer on a continuing retainer may represent a client who seeks to keep a factory in operation which creates a public health hazard by emitting harmful pollutants into the air.

However, some who countenance the pure legal advocate concept—namely, those sometimes referred to as rule utilitarians—hold that such immoralities as the above-mentioned ones are the necessary evils of maintaining an adversary system which itself does the greatest good. The working assumption here is that the adversarial form of legal administration, wherein two zealous advocates are pitted against each other before an impartial judge, constitutes the best-known way of maximizing truth and justice; and that, furthermore, this system works best when lawyers disregard their personal moral convictions and hereby restrict their professional activities to the zealous legal representation of their clients.

If the rule utilitarian is correct, then lawyering, so conceived, can be said to be a morally justified function, notwithstanding that, on that view, a lawyer may be required to engage in conduct which, by common standards, is morally objectionable. Thus, when seen in this light, the lawyer emerges as a promoter of the highly prized ends of justice and truth, and as an individual who, because of her service to society, is worthy of praise and admiration. Indeed, she begins to seem like a morally good person.

Nevertheless, I want to suggest that the appearance is deceiving, that, on the contrary, the lawyer, so conceived, will inevitably fall short of our marks of a morally good person. Moreover, I want to suggest that, as a result of such shortcomings, there is substantial disutility in the pure legal advocate con-

cept of lawyering which its utilitarian exponents rarely take into account in their utilitarian justification of it.

Let me emphasize that I am supposing, along with Aristotle, that it takes exercise and training to cultivate the character traits of a morally good person: one is not simply born with them. My claim is, accordingly, that the legal function as construed under the pure legal advocate concept, with its emphasis on suppression of the individual lawyer's personal moral convictions, does not allow for the cultivation of these traits and is, in fact, quite conducive to their corresponding vices.

Furthermore, I am supposing that a lawyer cannot easily detach his professional life from his private life and thereby cannot easily be one sort of person with one set of values in the one life, and a quite different sort with quite different values in the other life.

The latter supposition is justified by the substantial amount of empirical evidence that now exists correlating the personality traits of individuals with their specific vocations. One ambiguity, however, is whether individual vocations influence personality traits, or personality traits influence choice of vocation, or some combination of both; for any one of these hypotheses would explain the correlation.

Some studies have supported the hypothesis that personality traits influence choice of profession—that is, that people with certain personalities are attracted to certain professions in order to satisfy their individual needs. But even *if* this hypothesis is true, and the other above-mentioned hypotheses are false, it is clear that the kind of person found in a profession will remain a function of the way the profession itself is conceived. Specifically, on the hypothesis in question: we would expect the personalities of those choosing careers in law to depend upon their conception of a lawyer. But, if I am correct, then legal practice as construed on the pure legal advocate model could seem attractive only to those individuals contemplating a career in law who would feel comfortable in a professional climate which discourages, rather than promotes, the personality traits of a morally good person as here understood.

Moral Shortcomings of the Pure Legal Advocate

1. It appears that a lawyer, on the pure legal advocate concept, will inevitably fall short of being a *just* person. For although she does not violate the principle of treating relevantly similar cases similarly when she gives special preference to her client—inasmuch as being a client would appear to be a relevant dissimilarity for the purposes of an adversary system—she does, indeed, work injustices through the violation of the moral *rights* of individuals. For on this concept the lawyer's fundamental professional obligation is to do whatever she can, within legal limits, to advance the legal interests of her clients. But from this basic obligation there derives a more specific one which, contra Kant, may be expressed thus: "Whenever legally possible treat others not as ends but as means toward winning your case."

For example, the criminal defense lawyer is thereby authorized to knowingly destroy the testimony of an innocent rape victim in order to get an acquittal for his client; and a civil lawyer is authorized to knowingly deprive another of what he rightfully deserves by invoking the statute of limitations for the purpose of furthering his client's interests. But we shall concur with Kant in maintaining that lawyers, like anyone else, have a duty to treat others with the respect which they, as persons, have a right to insist upon.

2. Nor will the pure legal advocate meet the mark of *truthfulness*. For, from her cardinal obligation there derives the secondary obligation of being untruthful where doing so can legally contribute toward winning the case. An example of a lawyer who complies with this obligation is one who remains silent when she knows that her client has, under oath, lied to the court. The lawyer, by wittingly saying nothing,

engages in deceptive behavior—she contributes to the court's being deceived as to the truth—and is on that count *herself* guilty of being untruthful. Indeed, scrupulous adherence to *this* obligation could hardly support anything but an untruthful habit.

3. Nor does the concept in question support *moral courage*. For, according to it, personal moral convictions of a lawyer are irrelevant to his function and should not serve as reasons for zealous representation of clients, or for any sacrifices—of time, money, reputation, and the like—which he may make on their behalf. Indeed, if he is to do his job well, then he must get into the habit of *not* being influenced by his moral outlook. Rather, any sacrifice he may make should be for the sake of obtaining a legal victory, be it a moral one or not. It is plausible to suppose, however, that where morality takes a back seat, ulterior motives, such as the self-aggrandizement obtained through winning, will serve as the primary motivation.

4. Nor does the pure legal advocate concept support *liberality*; for the pure legal advocate, through her unconcern with the moral character of her clients and the purposes for which they hire her, gets into the habit of taking money from dishonorable individuals for unsavory purposes. She thus emerges as a professional who can be hired, for a good sum, to do the dirty work of a villain or a scoundrel. Indeed, she then begins to sound more like a hired assassin than like the liberal person whom Aristotle had in view. The high-priced corporate lawyer who wittingly helps her corporate client to market a dangerous product provides us with one example of such a lawyer; and the high-priced criminal lawyer who specializes in defending mass murderers is another.

5. Furthermore, the pure legal advocate concept does not appear to satisfy the minimum condition of *benevolence*—that is, the nonmalevolence expected of a morally good person. For, from his primary obligation, there derives the secondary obligation to employ even such means to forward a client's inter-

ests as are injurious to others, so long, of course, as they are legal. But this also means that a lawyer must learn to put off sympathetic feelings which a benevolent person would normally have. In particular, he must get used to working injury upon others without having any strong feelings of guilt, sorrow, or regret. For, to be sure, such feelings could only serve to interfere with the execution of his basic obligation to his client. The result is thus a callous attitude in his dealings with others.

6. Prima facie, it appears that the morally desirable character trait of *trustworthiness* receives strong support from the pure legal advocate concept. For, indeed, it appears that a lawyer cannot put on the most effective representation of her client's interests unless she is also prepared to hold in confidence the secrets entrusted to her by her client. A problem with this view, however, arises in the case in which there is a conflict between a lawyer's obligation to keep her client's confidence and some other moral obligation—for instance, that of not harming innocent persons. In such a case, the restricted lawyer is required to keep her client's confidence so long as it is legally possible and in her client's best interest to do so. Her considered judgment as to what is, under the circumstances, morally best is then quite irrelevant. But it is a mark of a morally good person to choose what she thinks is, all things considered, the morally right thing to do in such a situation. Hence, whereas a morally good person sees his obligation to keep confidences as one among several moral principles which may at times override one another, the pure legal advocate sees her professional obligation to keep her clients' confidences as binding upon her quite independently of the moral propriety of doing so in any particular case.

In any event, even *if* it is admitted that the pure legal advocate concept reinforces trustworthiness which, *in itself*, is a morally good trait, this still does not show that the good lawyer, on this conception, can be a morally good person. For, as we have seen, there are further requisites of a morally good life.

7. I have suggested that an important quality of a morally good person is that he has *moral autonomy*. However, the pure legal advocate concept offers no stimulus to the cultivation of this trait. For, as we have seen, the pure legal advocate inhabits a world in which his moral judgment is quite beside the point. If morality is relevant, it is so at the level of the judge or the legislator, but it is quite outside the purview of the lawyer's function. The lawyer must know the law and must know that he owes his undivided allegiance to his client. Given the latter he can easily accommodate himself to the requirements of the law. His decisions are, in effect, made *for him* by the system he serves. He is more like a cog in a machine and less like a person. But the moral world is inhabited by *persons*—that is, individuals who autonomously confront their moral responsibilities; so that, for a lawyer who has grown comfortable with passing the buck of moral responsibility, there is little hope of his aspiring to the morally good life.

The Moral Agent Concept

If I am correct, then it appears that the pure legal advocate who scrupulously adheres to her restricted role, far from being a morally good person, will be given ample opportunity for becoming—if she is not already—quite the opposite. For she will thereby be placed in a professional climate conducive to her being unjust instead of just; untruthful instead of truthful; unmotivated by a moral outlook instead of morally courageous; illiberal instead of liberal; callous instead of benevolent; morally irresponsible instead of morally autonomous. In short, she will fall well below the minimum standards of a morally good person.

But if all this is right, then there will, it seems, be a good deal of *disutility* in the pure legal advocate concept which, indeed, any utilitarian exponent of it ought to consider in computing its overall balance of utility. For it appears that such personality traits as those mentioned above, when associated with our concept of a lawyer, can serve only to bring disrespect upon the legal profession and, by association, upon the legal system as a whole. And this low regard may well lead to a commonplace view of the adversary system as a haven for the guilty and the wicked and as something of which the innocent and the morally good ought to steer clear. It can very well serve to discourage persons of strong moral character from entering the legal profession. It is also quite plausible that pure legal advocates who, by virtue of their knowledge of, and relation to, the law, are uniquely situated to contribute to needed changes in unjust laws, will not concern themselves with such moral reformation. Moreover, add to these the disutility involved in the unsavory acts performed by pure legal advocates on behalf of their clients in the normal course of discharging their professional obligations—the injuries thereby done to individual litigants as well as to others—and there is at least a strong prima facie case for abandoning the adversary system entirely in favor of a different model (an inquisitorial model for instance) or for adopting a concept of a lawyer in an adversary system which avoids these disutilities.

Fortunately, there is a further concept of a lawyer which, while not abandoning the adversarial approach, serves to avoid much of the disutility mentioned above.

This farther sense, hereafter called the *moral agent concept*, is exemplified, for example, in the remarks on advocacy made by Lord Chief Justice Cockburn, in the presence of Lord Brougham, at a dinner given in honor of M. Berryer on November 8, 1864. He stated:

> My noble and learned friend, Lord Brougham, whose words are the words of wisdom, said that an advocate should be fearless in carrying out the interests of his client: but I couple that with this qualification and this restriction—that the arms which he wields are to be the arms of the warrior and not of the assassin. It is his duty to strive to accomplish the interest of his clients per fas, but not per nefas; it is his duty, to the utmost of his power, to seek to reconcile the interests he is bound to maintain, and the duty it is incumbent upon him to discharge, with the eternal and immutable interests of truth and justice.[5]

The moral agent concept was also expressed, more recently, by John Noonan when he remarked that

> a lawyer should not impose his conscience on his client; neither can he accept his client's decision and remain entirely free from all moral responsibility, subject only to the restraints of the criminal law. The framework of the adversary system provides only the first set of guidelines for a lawyer's conduct. He is also a human being and cannot submerge his humanity by playing a technician's role.[6]

And this concept is suggested elsewhere by Richard Wasserstrom, Jeremy Bentham, and *The Report of the Joint Conference on Professional Responsibility.*[7]

Given the moral agent concept, we may no longer say that the good lawyer is simply the effective legal advocate; he is, rather, one who is effective in morally as well as legally advocating his client's cause. Hence, one cannot infer from this concept that the good lawyer is one who tends to win his cases. For, on this concept, he is not merely a good legal technician; he is also one who conducts himself in the manner of a morally good person—that is, as a person with morally desirable character traits.

It is evident, however, that a lawyer cannot so conduct herself unless she also subscribes to the moral principles to which a morally good person would subscribe were she to participate in an adversarial process. If our analysis of a morally good person is supposed, then such principles would need to be ones supportive of the personality traits set forth in that analysis. To wit, from these character traits we may derive a corresponding set of moral principles which are adjusted to an adversarial context. I suggest the following formulations, although other similar formulations are possible:

- Treat others as ends in themselves and not as mere means to winning cases. (Principle of Individual Justice)
- Treat clients and other professional relations who are relevantly similar in a similar fashion. (Principle of Distributive Justice)
- Do not deliberately engage in behavior apt to deceive the court as to the truth. (Principle of Truthfulness)
- Be willing, if necessary, to make reasonable personal sacrifices—of time, money, popularity, and so on—for what you justifiably believe to be a morally good cause. (Principle of Moral Courage)
- Do not give money to, or accept money from, clients for wrongful purposes or in wrongful amounts. (Principle of Liberality)
- Avoid harming others in the process of representing your client. (Principle of Nonmalevolence)
- Be loyal to your client, and do not betray his confidences. (Principle of Trustworthiness)
- Make your *own* moral decisions to the best of your ability and act consistently upon them. (Principle of Moral Autonomy)

We can say that the above principles, or ones like them, at least in part *constitute or define* the moral agent concept of a lawyer; for they are principles to which a lawyer's conduct must to some extent conform if he is to function not simply as a legal advocate but also as a morally good person.

I am *not* suggesting that these principles are unconditional ones. Indeed, to say so would be unrealistic since they will inevitably come into conflict with each other when applied to specific contexts, thereby making it impossible for the lawyer to satisfy all principles at once. (That is, in order to be truthful, a lawyer may need to betray a client's trust, and conversely.) Rather, what I am suggesting is that such principles impose upon a lawyer *conditional—* or prima facie—obligations which, in cases of conflict, must be weighed, one against the other, by the lawyer in question in the context in question.

Let me offer an example which will illustrate the difference between applying, in conflict situations, the above multi-principle model and the pure legal advocate model. In *Lawyers' Ethics in an Adversary System* Monroe Freedman cites the following:

> In a recent case in Lake Pleasant, New York, a defendant in a murder case told his lawyers about two other people he had killed and where their bodies had been hidden. The lawyers went there, observed the bodies, and took photographs of them. They did not, however, inform the authorities about the bodies until several months later, when their client had confessed to those crimes. In addition to withholding the information from police and prosecutors, one of the attorneys denied information to one of the victims' parents, who came to him in the course of seeking his missing daughter.[8]

According to Freedman, the lawyers in the above cited case were simply discharging their *unconditional* professional obligation to represent their clients' legal interests. However, if the moral agent concept is supposed, then it is clear that the above lawyers could have revealed where the bodies were buried. Admittedly, according to the Principle of Trustworthiness, a lawyer has a (prima facie) obligation to keep his client's confidences. But he also has further (prima facie) obligations such as those of Truthfulness, Individual Justice, and Non-malevolence. I think that a plausible case can be made that the latter principles were sacrificed to some extent by the lawyers in the Lake Pleasant case at least insofar as their treatment of the relatives of the deceased was concerned. And it is plausible, I believe, to argue that the moral weight of the latter principles, taken collectively, out-weighed that of the Principle of Trustworthiness taken by itself in the situation in question. This need not have been what the lawyers in the cited case should have finally decided to be the correct balancing of principles. The point I want to make is rather that the lawyers *did have* in the first place, on the conception in question, the *moral autonomy* (as legitimized by our Principle of Moral Autonomy) to make such a judgment on the matter. It is just such moral autonomy—with its weighing of competing moral principles, one against the other—that the pure legal advocate concept disallows.

Of course, if lawyers are allowed such autonomy, there arises the difficulty of providing *criteria* for arbitrating between conflicting principles. This difficulty, we have seen, does not arise on the pure legal advocate model since the pure legal advocate is, in effect, insulated from making moral tradeoffs by her unconditional allegiance to her client's legal interests.

One normative view regarding how a lawyer, in accordance with the moral agent concept, might go about solving moral dilemmas takes the form of a "pure" utilitarianism. According to such an ethic, all eight of our principles are to be understood as receiving their ultimate justification from the principle of utility. Hence, in case of conflict the final court of appeal will be the principle of utility itself.

I do not think, however, that such a basis for solving lawyers' moral dilemmas would be adequate. My objection is that which has traditionally been made against utilitarian ethics which are not tempered by justice considerations. Suppose, for example, a criminal lawyer is defending an influential politician accused of rape. Suppose also that the politician admits his guilt to his attorney but nevertheless informs her of his intention to testify under oath (to that which is false) that the defendant first made sexual advances toward him. Now suppose that the politician in question is in the process of bringing

about a change in taxation which would mean substantial tax reductions for millions of Americans, and that, furthermore, these efforts would most likely be defeated if the politician in question were convicted of rape. On the pure utilitarian criterion, it would appear that the attorney in question would be committed to allowing the politician to perjure himself notwithstanding the defeat of the true rape claim; for the greatest good would (*ex hypothesi*) be served by allowing the politician to escape the charge of rape through his perjured testimony. But in such a case it would seem unjust (by the Principle of Individual Justice) to sacrifice the well-being of the truthful rape victim for the tax reduction. Indeed, in doing so, the lawyer would arguably be committing a grossly immoral act. But, if so, the principle of utility untempered by some principle(s) of justice—such as the Principle of Individual Justice or the Principle of Distributive Justice—would be an inadequate criterion for settling lawyers' moral dilemmas.

How then is a lawyer, on the moral agent conception, to resolve antinomies arising between those principles? Although I do not see any formula for doing so, this is not to suggest that one resolution is just as respectable as any other. For one thing, there is a difference between the ethical judgment of a lawyer that is *factually enlightened* and one that is not. For example, the judgment of a lawyer who allows trustworthiness to override harm in a particular case without adequate knowledge of the nature and extent of the harm is less respectable than the judgment of a lawyer who takes account of such facts.

Still, once the facts are known a decision must be made in their light; and I think it would be intellectually dishonest to suggest that there is some principle(s) from which we may logically deduce our decision. Principles take us just so far, leaving the final verdict in our hands.

It is the lack of clear noncontroversial criteria or resolving moral dilemmas, and the ensuing feeling that ethics is, in the end, a matter of "fiat" or "personal preference," that may make some feel uncomfortable about giving lawyers moral autonomy. However, it should be kept in mind by those who worry about the "gray" areas of ethics that the making of ethical decisions is already an accepted and unavoidable part of the role of *some* officials in our legal system. For example, given the "open-textured" quality of legal rules and precedents themselves, judges often need to rely upon their own *moral* evaluations in deciding whether a given set of facts falls under a given legal rule or precedent. But if judges can handle their moral problems—and I believe that, in general, they do handle them—then there appears to be less reason to fear that lawyers cannot or will not handle their moral problems.

NOTES

1 See Aristotle, *Nicomachean Ethics*, Book II.

2 Ibid., 1117a16.

3 Ibid., 1120b29-31.

4 M.H. Freedman, *Lawyers' Ethics in an Adversary System* (Indianapolis: Bobbs-Merrill, 1975), 9.

5 Costigan, "The Full Remarks on Advocacy of Lord Brougham and Lord Chief Justice Cockburn at the Dinner to M. Berryer on November 8, 1864," *California Law Review* Vol. 19: 523 (1931).

6 Noonan, "The Purposes of Advocacy and the Limits of Confidentiality," *Michigan Law Review* Vol. 64: 1492 (1966).

7 See, respectively, Wasserstrom, "Lawyers as Professionals: Some Moral Issues," *Human Rights* Vol. 5: 8 (1975); Bentham, "Rationale of Judicial Evidence," book 9, chapter 5, in *The Works of Jeremy Bentham* (J. Bowring, ed), 1843; American Bar Association and the Association of American Law Schools, "Professional Responsibility: Report of the Joint Conference," *American Bar Association Journal* Vol. 44: 1161 (1958).

8 M. Freedman, *supra* note 4 at 1.

♦ ♦ ♦ ♦ ♦

AMY GUTMANN

Can Virtue Be Taught to Lawyers?

"Can virtue be taught?" Plato rightly thought this a most challenging question. But our question—Can virtue be taught to lawyers?—presents a still greater challenge. We can begin to meet the challenge, as Socrates might suggest, by addressing the prior question: What is virtue for lawyers? For without figuring out what legal virtue is, we can only pretend to know whether lawyers can be taught virtue, or learn it.

What virtues are fitting for lawyers in their most common activities as advocates and counselors in a constitutional democracy? My aim in this essay is not to offer anything close to a comprehensive answer, but to contribute to a more adequate understanding of legal virtue by briefly assessing three answers commonly offered by contemporary legal theorists. Each reflects an important conception of legal virtue: the "standard conception" recommends zealous advocacy of clients' interests; the "justice conception" that lawyers be above all dedicated to the pursuit of social justice; and the "character conception" that they live a good life in the law, a life characterized by the exercise of practical judgment.

I argue that despite their different relative merits, these conceptions are similarly incomplete. Each neglects a virtue that is increasingly relevant to lawyering because we live in a society where legally-relevant decision making is increasingly complex. The missing virtue is the disposition and capacity of lawyers to deliberate with nonlawyers (call us ordinary people) about the practical implications of legal action and its alternatives. By deliberation I mean a mutual interchange of information and understanding oriented toward decision making about both ends and means. I suggest some reasons why the obligation of lawyers to deliberate with their clients about legal means and ends is endemic to legal ethics in a constitutional democracy. And I suggest why each conception of legal ethics should explicitly defend the deliberative obligations of lawyers. I conclude that the question, What is legal virtue?, true to its Socratic inspiration, points to a more deliberative conception of lawyering and legal education. Lawyers should deliberate with clients, and legal education should prepare them to do so.

Consider the view of legal virtue offered by the standard conception of lawyering. "When acting as an advocate, a lawyer must, within the established constraints upon professional behavior, maximize the likelihood that the client will prevail."[1] To maximize the likelihood that your client prevails, you must be not just an advocate of your client's preferences or interest, but a zealous advocate.

The obligation of zealous advocacy has been amply criticized by David Luban, among others, for losing sight of the larger aim of the law in furthering social justice.[2] The standard conception makes most sense in the context of the adversary process of criminal law, which does not of course comprehend most of what lawyers do. Even zealous advocates of their clients' preferences or interests may be held responsible—legally, professionally, and morally—for their actions. Authorization by clients does not immunize lawyers from responsibility for doing wrong any more than authorization by military officers exonerates soldiers from wrongdoing. What constitutes legal wrongdoing is often a tricky question, but the principle of responsibility does not stand or fall on hard cases.

A partial truth of the standard conception remains, and I want to pursue its implications here. Far worse than being a zealous lawyer is being a lazy or incompetent one, unwilling or unable to take on someone else's cause as your own. Lawyers who represent their clients simply for the sake of making a living, and therefore do not represent them well as long as they can get away with it, use their clients merely as means to their own self-interested ends. In criticizing the standard conception, we should not lose sight of the virtue of ardent (and perhaps at times zealous) advocacy. This is a virtue entailed in the legal obligation to argue other people's causes, not one's own. The advocacy virtues are necessary to safeguarding the basic interests of citizens in the face of threats to their civil and political rights.

But they are not sufficient, and for a reason that even proponents of the standard conception should acknowledge. The standard critique of zealous advocacy focuses on the need for lawyers to temper their defense of clients' causes with an appreciation of the larger purpose of their legal actions: social justice. Before we consider tempering advocacy for the sake of social justice, we should look carefully at the requirements of advocacy itself. What constitutes adequate representation? Ardent legal advocates, like good doctors, need to know not just the preferences of their clients, but their informed preferences. Like good friends, good lawyers do not take every and any preference of their clients as dispositive of what they should do in their clients' defense.[3] Unlike good friends, good lawyers know, or should know a lot more than their clients about the probable consequences for their clients' lives of various legal strategies. Proponents of the standard conception and critics alike can grant that ardent advocacy is sometimes a great virtue of lawyers. But we also should recognize that lawyers are not in a position to know what their obligation of ardent advocacy entails unless they understand their clients' informed preferences. Such an understanding cannot be taken for granted, or assumed to be apparent from simply asking clients about their preferences for legal services.

An internal critique of the standard conception follows from its central premise. The case of an ardent advocate should reflect her clients' informed preferences. In general, if lawyers do not make special efforts to understand the informed preferences of their clients, then the standard conception becomes indistinguishable from the indefensible claim that lawyers cannot be held accountable for anything to which their clients consent, whether or not they are well informed.

Clients are typically not experts in the law, or at least not in the part of the law for which they seek legal counsel. We need to rely upon legal counsel to develop informed preferences regarding legal services. Whether we know it or not, we are dependent on lawyers for becoming informed about the nature of legal processes and outcomes, and their likely impact on our lives. But the process of legal understanding is not one-way. Lawyers also depend, or should depend, upon their clients for understanding whether and what legal strategies would best serve their clients' interests. And clients depend on lawyers for advising us on whether and how to proceed with our cases. The decision in the end is ours, not theirs. But lawyers have a responsibility for helping us make an informed decision by engaging with us in a deliberative process which entails the give-and-take of information, understanding, and even argument about our alternatives. Whenever ardent advocacy is a legal virtue, so is the willingness and ability of lawyers to deliberate with clients, explaining the aims and likely consequences of alternate strategies, listening to the clients' concerns, reacting to them, and arriving at an understanding of their clients' informed preferences after mutual evaluation of the possibilities. The deliberative virtues include the disposition to discuss various legal strategies with clients, and to understand clients' goals and their informed reaction to relevant legal strategies to the extent feasible. These deliberative virtues are a precondition of good advocacy.

A mundane example illustrates this internal criticism of the standard conception. Suppose a group of divorce lawyers are excellent at arguing court cases for their clients but spend little or no time trying to understand their clients' informed preferences with regard to marriage and divorce. The vast majority of their clients do not start out with anything close to an expert knowledge of legal possibilities, let alone of the probable consequences and experiences

attached to arguing their cases in court or settling them out of court. The lawyers take their clients' preferences at face value. When a client comes into their office saying that he does not want to pay his spouse a penny if he can get away with it, they tell him they will do whatever they can within the limits of the law to help him. They can threaten his spouse with litigation over custody and scare her into settling for a minimum amount of child support.[4] And the lawyers often succeed in this strategy or in others that are also well-designed to satisfy their clients' expressed preferences. Their clients, on the other hand, typically fail miserably. They are never encouraged to consider the bad consequences of their desire to punish their spouses, and by extension, their children, who may never forgive them for the excessive misery wrought on their family for the sake of selfishness or revenge.

This group of successful divorce lawyers could practice their profession differently and still be successful as zealous advocates, far more successful in one important sense. They could help their clients examine the broader implications of their initial preferences, and explore with them the pros and cons of alternative strategies. The initial preferences of clients are sometimes, perhaps often, contrary to what their informed preferences would be. It is not reasonable to expect clients to inform themselves, even to know the questions they need to ask, independently of the guidance of legal counsel. These divorce lawyers, therefore, may seem like ardent advocates but in one critical sense they fail to fulfill the responsibilities of ardent advocates. They have not tried to understand, and to help their clients understand, their informed preferences. These lawyers bear some responsibility (not necessarily "full" responsibility) for their clients' uninformed preferences, because clients typically have no reasonable alternative but to depend on lawyers for informing them about the pitfalls and possibilities of the legal strategies available to them. (These lawyers do not bear full responsibility because clients also have some responsibility for informing themselves, and public officials are also responsible for instituting legal reforms that make it easier for ordinary people to inform themselves about the law.) On its own terms, the standard conception is incomplete if it does not ally the virtues of deliberation with clients with those of ardent advocacy.

But this defense of deliberative virtues is incomplete, and we can expose its incompleteness by considering a more compelling conception of law: the justice conception. Ardent advocacy may be a necessary virtue for lawyers in their roles as advocates, but lawyers cannot know if and when they should be advocates without thinking about the larger social purposes of law, in particular about the central place of law in serving social justice in a constitutional democracy. (Of course, this is not to say that legal practices as we know them consistently serve the cause of social justice, but rather that the social justification of some legal services rests critically on their doing so.) The core of the justice conception is captured by the Model Rule's characterization of a lawyer as a "public citizen having special responsibility for the quality of justice."[5]

The justice conception, as one might infer from its label, shifts the primary virtue of lawyering from advocacy to justice. Advocacy, even zealous advocacy, may still be an important virtue for (some) lawyers, but only insofar as justice demands. It would be surprising, moreover, especially in a society where some people are economically disadvantaged and socially stigmatized, to find that justice always, or even generally, demands zealous advocacy of lawyers regardless of the nature of their clients' cause. The justice conception does not demand that lawyers aim directly at what they deem just, even if that means arguing against their clients' cause. Where the adversary system is justified, so are lawyers justified in ardently arguing their clients' cases. But the adversary system is not justified in all legal contexts, and even where it is, it may not justify zealous advocacy, meaning maximizing the likelihood that one's cli-

ent cause will prevail (which is what the standard conception requires). The virtue of justice, to follow David Luban's "fourfold root of sufficient reasoning," requires that lawyers be able to justify (1) the legal institution within which they act (e.g., the adversary system of criminal justice), (2) their legal role (e.g., advocate for clients) as necessary to that institution, (3) their role obligation (e.g., zealousness in advocacy) as necessary to the role, and (4) their role acts (e.g., cross-examining an alleged victim of rape about her irrelevant sexual history) as necessary to the role obligation.[6] If the justification fails at any stage, as it does in stages three and four of the parenthetical example, then lawyers are not justified in acting as zealous advocates.

Whereas the standard conception defends zealous advocacy as the primary legal virtue, the justice conception views as virtuous only those dispositions and acts required by the legal pursuit of social justice. The justice conception highlights an important legal virtue that the standard conception neglects, or even denies: the willingness and capacity of lawyers to act according to the demands of justice, rather than the preferences (even the informed preferences) of their clients when the two conflict. Partisan advocacy is not justified for all legal roles. Even when advocacy is justified, zealous advocacy may not be. And zealous advocacy does not justify certain tactics on behalf of one's clients (such as discrediting a plaintiff by raising irrelevant facts about her sexual history).

Louis Brandeis is sometimes cited as the paradigm of a virtuous lawyer on the justice conception—someone who put justice first in the practice of law. When he was acting as legal counsel to William McElwain, the owner of a large shoe factory embroiled in a labor dispute, Brandeis told McElwain in front of John Tobin, who was representing the striking workers, that Tobin was "absolutely right."[7] Brandeis proceeded to convince McElwain to end the seasonality of employment that was troubling his labor force. McElwain's company flourished. What should we make of the Brandeis example? I think that it demonstrates that the demands of justice on lawyers are both greater and less than what proponents of the justice conception commonly convey.

What more could the justice conception demand than that lawyers follow Luban's fourfold root of sufficient legal reasoning? We need not question whether the fourfold root is sufficient to reasoning to wonder whether legal reasoning of this sort is sufficient to acting justly as a lawyer. In focusing on the steps of legal reasoning that must be satisfied by justified legal action, proponents of the justice conception take something critical for granted concerning the lawyer-client relation that some questioning of the Brandeis example may reveal. Suppose Brandeis told McElwain in front of Tobin that Tobin was "absolutely right" and left it at that. Brandeis still would have represented the right position to his client, but McElwain would have been far less likely to abide by it. He might well have fired Brandeis and gotten himself a lawyer more sympathetic to his cause. Or he might have gone along with Brandeis out of deference to Brandeis's legal expertise even though Brandeis's moral position on this matter was largely, if not entirely, independent of his legal expertise. Or suppose Brandeis had deceived McElwain into doing the right thing, thereby pursuing the cause of justice with morally suspect means. For lawyers to work effectively in bringing both the means and ends of law into conformity with social justice, they must be disposed not to deceive their clients into doing the right thing, but rather aid their clients in deliberating about the demands of social justice.

Proponents of the justice conception conflate the idea that lawyers have a greater responsibility to pursue justice (by virtue of their role and/or their having more power to do so) with the idea that they are more likely to subscribe to the correct conception of justice (by virtue of their practical judgment). The practical judgment of lawyers, their capacity for "logical thinking, a nose for facts, good judgment of people, toleration"[8] does not translate into a comparative advantage over other thoughtful people in discerning what constitutes just social policy or the most justifiable of competing principles of social justice. Deception of clients in the service of social justice is therefore suspect for both deontological and consequentialist reasons. Justice is not well-served by authorizing lawyers to pursue just ends independently of their clients' authorization, because the unauthorized means are morally suspect, and the ends lawyers choose to pursue may be worse than those that would be chosen by well-informed clients.

Had Brandeis deceived McElwain or simply quit as his legal counsel because he deemed McElwain's cause unjust, the story would illustrate a weakness of the justice conception as commonly articulated, rather than its potential strength. The commitment of lawyers to pursuing (what they believe are) just causes is only half the conception, the most commonly articulated half. The neglected half is a disposition to deliberate with their clients with the aim of arriving at a mutual understanding of what justice in a constitutional democracy permits or demands. By its very nature, deliberation is subverted by deceptive means.

If their cause is just, why be so concerned with the means that lawyers use to pursue justice? Why recommend deliberation between lawyers and clients, a sharing of information and understanding on relevant matters, rather than that lawyers use their legal expertise and authority simply to convince clients to do what they, the expert lawyers, believe is just? Luban uses the Brandeis model to illustrate the noblesse oblige tradition of law, where lawyers use their authority and expertise to pursue that understanding of social justice they think best.[9] This is not the deliberative model even if it eschews deception. Deliberation demands far more. It requires an active engagement with clients that aims at a better understanding of the value of legal action and its alternatives than either party to the deliberation probably had at the outset. The value of the best legal action on behalf of a client may often be its contribution to the pursuit of social justice, but social justice cannot routinely be pursued by a legal counsel independently of the client's informed consent.

The demand for deliberative virtues has two distinct sources internal to the justice conception of law, and one external to it (to which I will return in discussing the character conception of legal virtue). The first internal source has to do with the distribution of the virtue of justice, the second with its content. Regarding the distribution of justice as a virtue, it is not in practice reasonable to rely upon lawyers as a group for a firmer commitment to social justice (beyond the rule of law) or just social policies than their clients. Lawyers are more expert in navigating the law than their clients, but they are also, by virtue of their expertise and professional autonomy, politically more powerful and therefore potentially more likely to subvert social justice in pursuit of their own professional or personal interests. Legal expertise does not make lawyers more committed to the cause of social justice than their clients, and it is hard to see why it would. The justice conception therefore cannot credibly claim that the disposition to pursue just ends is a virtue more distinctive to lawyers than their clients. Nor can it authorize lawyers to act upon their substantive conception of justice independently of deliberating with their clients about its content. Were the justice conception to recommend such independent action beyond upholding the rule of law, it would be justifying a form of tyranny.

It does not follow that lawyers must defer to their clients' preferences as required by the standard conception, but rather that deliberation with clients places an important internal constraint on (and opportunity for) the legal pursuit of justice. This constraint is important both because it respects the principle of informed consent, and because it increases the chances that justice will actually be pursued and the virtue of justice will be as widely distributed among citizens as constitutional democracies require. An analogous (although relevantly different) set of internal constraints applies to judg-

es, where judicial deliberation issues in one or more opinions that are informed by, and addressed to, competing legal and moral perspectives on the case.

The recommendation that lawyers deliberate with their clients follows also from an understanding of the content of social justice in a constitutional democracy. Constitutional democracies are created to cope with reasonable disagreements, including disagreements over the content of social justice and just social policy. At the same time, constitutional democracies must be constituted by, and authorize public officials to act upon, a public conception of social justice which itself is not universally accepted. Ongoing deliberation over its contents is one requirement of a conception of social justice suitable to constitutional democracy. Saying that lawyers should deliberate with their clients about justice is another way of saying that they should act justly, where the conception of justice now includes consideration of the social process of reasoning, not just its content. Reasoning by lawyers themselves is not enough, however logical, cognizant of the facts, tolerant and understanding of human nature legal reasoning is. Neither is deliberation a sufficient condition of legal justice, although it is both necessary and neglected.

I have outlined two reasons internal to the justice conception for lawyers to deliberate with their clients. There is a third reason that becomes apparent only after considering the limited scope of the justice conception in motivating what many lawyers do for a living. The justice conception would of course claim too much were it to require lawyers always to manifest the virtue of justice in their actions. In some situations of adversary justice, we rely upon legal institutions rather than lawyers for pursuing justice. This is the insight the standard conception carries too far. But there is yet another limit of the justice conception that rests on the distinction between furthering social justice and helping people live good lives according to their best lights, where social justice does not demand such help but simply permits it. Social justice need not be the primary aim of legal counsel and action on behalf of clients. Helping people live good lives is an aim of legal counsel consistent with social justice but not dictated by it or directly aimed at it. Some legal services simply help people live good lives according to their best lights.

Whereas the standard conception needs to be revised at the level of justification, the justice conception needs modification at the level of motivation. The commitment to deliberating about the law from the perspective of social justice seems to be inadequately motivated by a great deal of legitimate legal practice, which is aimed not at social justice but at helping people live good lives consistent with, but not dictated by, social justice. Many people need lawyers on occasion to help them deliberate not about social justice, but about their own well-being. Helping people deliberate about their own well-being is surely a reasonable, indeed admirable use of the law, as long as the means and ends of such legal aid are not unjust. It also adds another motivating reason for good people to enter the legal profession. The legal profession is, or at least can be, a "helping profession" in this regard.

We often need help in thinking about our own well-being, and lawyers can help us in situations where legal services are a potential means of furthering individual well-being. Many nonadversarial legal services are only indirectly relevant to social justice, but directly relevant to a client's well-being. Lawyers who further the well-being of their clients without injuring others do good in the world, even if they do not contribute to the cause of justice. The differential ability of citizens to afford legal counsel is of course a matter of social justice, but income maldistribution does not obliterate the good of this common form of legal counsel. Wherever legal services have the potential for enhancing human well-being, they also have the potential for harm, which is yet another reason why the disposition of lawyers to deliberate with their clients is a legal virtue. Delibera-

tion is a necessary condition for informed consent, and informed consent is a safeguard against the potential tyranny of legal counsel.

What can motivate good people to enter a profession where advocacy is more often better rewarded than the pursuit of social justice and where the pursuit of social justice is often not a realistic aim of legal counsel? Law can be an attractive career not only because people make good money in it or pursue social justice by its means, but also because lawyers can live a good life in the law by helping other people live good lives. The character conception of legal virtue builds upon this understanding of legal purposes, which is potentially more inclusive than advocacy in an adversary process or the pursuit of social justice.

The character conception, as articulated by Anthony Kronman, runs roughly as follows. Law is a habit-forming profession. The good habit that it can cultivate is practical judgment, *phronesis*. Living a good life in the law means living a life characterized primarily by practical judgment, not by client advocacy or the pursuit of social justice by means of the law. Both client advocacy and the pursuit of social justice are too instrumental to serve as adequate motivations for good people to become lawyers. Kronman worries that "the lawyer who chooses his career for public-spirited reasons alone, may see himself merely as the instrument by which some communal good is to be achieved. He may even hate his work, find it dull and unrewarding in itself, but still consider it the most economical route to whatever political arrangements he values for their own sake."[10]

This particular worry is not warranted for two reasons. One relates to Kronman's overly restrictive understanding of the public-spirited reasons for becoming a lawyer, and the other relates to a narrow notion of the nature of practical judgment in law. The insight of the character conception is that law at its best requires the virtue of practical judgment. But the conception, as Kronman proposes it, unnecessarily separates public-spirited reasons for becoming a lawyer from the exercise of practical judgment. Suppose you have public-spirited reasons for becoming a lawyer. You want to contribute in some small way to defending people's legal rights and obligations. Another element of your public-spiritedness is that you believe that the equal defense of every citizen's legal rights and obligations constitutes an essential element of the public good in a constitutional democracy. You correctly believe that by the very process of competently defending people's rights and obligations, you are contributing to social justice. In being motivated by social justice, you therefore need not have anything resembling a purely instrumental relation to your work.

Even if your attitude toward legal work is not purely instrumental, could it be, as Kronman also suggests, that the legal practice of defending citizens' rights and obligations is dull and unrewarding, especially by contrast to the practice of practical judgment? Even this more qualified claim rests on a misunderstanding of how lawyers can best defend citizens' rights and obligations. Lawyers should not simply enlist what they consider the best legal means to pursue what they consider the most justified ends for their clients. In the service of social justice, law at its best enlists the practical judgment of lawyers, and (as we have seen) the exercise of practical judgment by lawyers requires deliberation with clients, the mutual interchange of relevant information, and understanding. If a life dedicated to the exercise of practical judgment is rewarding in itself, as the character conception rightly suggests it can be, then legal practice in defense of social justice may also be rewarding in itself, because it too enlists the virtue of practical judgment.

Kronman describes a person of practical judgment as combining "a compassionate survey of alternatives viewed simultaneously from a distance,"[11] and as someone who "knows more than others do because he feels what they do not."[12] Practical judgment is "marked as much by affective dispositions as

by intellectual powers."[13] There is much to be said for this understanding of practical judgment insofar as it includes the disposition of lawyers to sympathize with, and thereby better understand, the situation of their clients. But practical judgment in legal practice cannot simply be assimilated to practical judgment more generally. According to Kronman, practical judgment requires more than knowledge of the law and cleverness; it requires

> the same combination of sympathy and detachment that a person must possess in order to deliberate wisely about his own ends. The wise counselor is one who is able to see his client's situation from within and yet, at the same time, from a distance, and thus give advice that is at once compassionate and objective.[14]

What is missing from this description of practical judgment in the law? The lawyer of practical judgment gives advice, but he never (according to Kronman's many descriptions) needs to consider the judgments of clients, their understanding of what is good or just. By now, it will come as no surprise that the element that I think is missing from this understanding of practical judgment is the disposition of lawyers to deliberate, to engage with their clients in the mutual interchange of information and understanding, rather than the one-way flow that Kronman's description recommends, his Aristotelian sympathies notwithstanding. The addition of deliberation to our understanding of practical judgment in the law would only strengthen the character conception's claim that people can live a good life in the law, a life that, unlike the nondeliberative exercise of practical judgment by lawyers, would be free of problematic paternalism. The exercise of practical judgment in the law can be all the more rewarding when it issues in deliberation by both lawyers and clients.

Practical judgment is a generally valuable virtue. The character conception is therefore correct in recommending practical judgment as a constitutive part of a good life. But the demands of practical judgment differ importantly from one realm of life to another. In private life, practical judgment often does not require the disposition and skills of deliberation. In many matters of private life, we need not engage in the mutual exchange of reasons, empirical and moral understandings with other people in order to divide neatly between private and public realms. In some matters of law, for example, clients may know precisely what they want, and know enough about the law to be confident that their preferences are informed and therefore in need of nothing but technical input from legal counsel. This is that attractively unsanctimonious view of lawyers that Anthony Trollope attributes to John Bold, the political reformer:

> Bold was not very fond of his attorney but, as he said, merely wanted a man who knew the forms of law, and who would do what he was told for his money. He had no idea of putting himself in the hands of a lawyer. He wanted law from a lawyer as he did a coat from a tailor, because he could not make it so well himself.[15]

Because our options for legally pursuing even mundane matters these days are so complex in their implications for our own and other people's lives, this view of lawyers as hired hands is unrealistic at best and dangerous at worst.

Complex professional decisions typically require deliberation between professional and client, if only (but not only) to figure out what a client wants, and how a professional can best help the client without making things worse (by using means, for example, that are incompatible with some other valued end that only deliberation brings to light). Deliberation is a constitutive part of practical judgment with regard to complex professional decisions that affect the interests of other people, and practical judgment is, as the character conception correctly suggests, an indispensable virtue of good lawyering. If lawyers do not deliberate with their clients, if they pursue their own independently-arrived-at conception of their clients' interests or social justice, then they act paternalistically, treating their clients as children, and even unjustly, using them as mere means rather than ends in themselves, as constitutional democracy demands. If lawyers deliberate with their clients not only, or even primarily, about social justice, but about the ways in which the law can contribute to their well-being, then many kinds of legal practices can be motivated for public-spirited reasons and because they are conducive to living a good life as a lawyer. Living a good life in the law is dependent upon doing good with the law, but lawyers can do good even when they are not self-consciously serving the cause of social justice. This is an important insight of the character conception of law. Another public-spirited reason for being a lawyer is to help people by deliberating with them about how the law can (and cannot) help them live a good life. Helping people in this way requires lawyers to have the virtue of practical judgment, and a necessary element of practical judgment in the legal realm is the disposition to deliberate with clients.

To summarize: The standard conception of law, the justice conception, and the character conception, as commonly articulated, neglect the virtue of deliberation in legal practice. Yet consistently pursued, all three point to the moral importance for lawyers of the disposition to deliberate. Whether the law aims at ardent advocacy of clients' informed preferences, the pursuit of social justice, or the ability of lawyers to live a good life in the law, deliberation becomes a necessary (but not sufficient) virtue for lawyers. Each of these three conceptions of the law is incomplete. The law actually and ideally aims at elements of all three conceptions which have yet to be synthesized into a more comprehensive view.

We need not choose among the three conceptions, or arrive at a more comprehensive conception to acknowledge the importance of legal deliberation. Can lawyers be taught the disposition to deliberate with clients, and the skills of deliberation? Yes, if legal education is self-consciously aimed at teaching the deliberative virtues, and if legal practices are better designed to encourage lawyers to deliberate. These are of course two big "ifs," which I now must leave largely in the hypothetical.

In conclusion, I can only mention, briefly and tentatively, two ways of moving legal education further in the direction of teaching the deliberative virtues. The first is a change in law school education that would parallel what has been happening in many medical schools and for related reasons: the expansion of clinical practice for the purpose of teaching future lawyers how better to communicate with their clients. Clinical practice is perhaps more often viewed as a means of encouraging law students to pursue public interest law, but clinical work need not be motivated only or even primarily by this purpose. Clinical practice can also be designed and directed to cultivate the skills and dispositions of deliberation, which should characterize good lawyers, whether they enter the world of corporate, private, prosecutorial, or public defense law.

A second way of moving legal education further in the direction of teaching deliberation is for regular law school courses to teach more of the knowledge and understanding that is necessary to make informed judgments about alternative legal strategies. This entails teaching students to think in philosophically and empirically rigorous ways about the value and consequences of pursuing alternate legal strategies and defending different legal doctrines. Learning to think like a lawyer would mean learning to think rigorously not only about legal doctrine but also about the consequences and moral values of alternate legal (and nonlegal) decisions. And also to understand the different evaluations people may place on various legal alternatives in light of their own distinctive conceptions of the good life. The Socratic method employed for the sake of delibera-

tion would have students engaging in the give-and-take of argument about the value of various legal strategies in light of considerations of social justice and conceptions of the good life in a constitutional democracy.

There is obviously a lot more to be said about whether and how the deliberative virtues can be taught to lawyers. I have offered some reasons why the disposition to deliberate and the skills of deliberation should be considered an important part of legal virtue, whether one subscribes to the standard conception, the justice conception, the character conception, or a more (yet to be articulated) comprehensive conception of law. Deliberation, I have argued elsewhere, is also a disposition that public education should try to teach all democratic citizens.[16] It is not the unique responsibility of law schools or legal institutions to teach deliberation. But deliberation is not easy to teach, and a constitutional democracy can use all the help it can get, not only but especially from lawyers and professors of law.

NOTES

1 Murray L. Schwartz, "The Professionalism and Accountability of Lawyers," *Cal. L. Rev.* Vol. 66: 673 (1978).

2 David Luban, *Lawyers and Justice: An Ethical Study* 3-147, 393-403 (1988).

3 See Charles Fried, "The Lawyer as Friend: The Moral Foundations of the Lawyer-Client Relation," *Yale L.J.* Vol. 85: 1060, 1060-69 (1975).

4 I am grateful to Andrew Koppelman for this example.

5 *Model Rules of Professional Conduct*, Preamble (1989).

6 For a detailed description and defense of this conception of legal ethics, see Luban, *supra* note 2.

7 Philippa Strum, *Louis D. Brandeis: Justice for the People* 96-97 (1984).

8 David Luban, "The *Noblesse Oblige* Tradition in the Practice of Law," *Vand. L. Rev.* Vol. 41: 717, 725 (1988).

9 Ibid. at 720-27.

10 Anthony T. Kronman, "Living in the Law," *U. Chi. L. Rev.* Vol. 54: 835, 843-44 (1987).

11 Ibid. at 853.

12 Ibid. at 858.

13 Ibid.

14 Ibid. at 866.

15 Anthony Trollope, *The Warden* 25 (David Skilton ed., Oxford University Press, 1980) (1855).

16 Amy Gutmann, *Democratic Education* 50-52 (1987).

CONFIDENTIALITY BETWEEN LAWYER AND CLIENT

BRUCE M. LANDESMAN

Confidentiality and the Lawyer-Client Relationship

I. Introduction

Lawyers are expected to keep information learned from their clients confidential. This obligation has two parts: the narrower attorney-client privilege that bars lawyers from testifying in court, and a broader obligation not to reveal information in other contexts.[1] The grounds for this obligation are succinctly stated in *McCormick's Handbook on the Law of Evidence*:

> ... claims and disputes which may lead to litigation can most justly and expeditiously be handled by practised experts, namely lawyers, and ... such experts can act effectively only if they are fully advised of the facts by the parties whom they represent. Such full disclosure will be promoted only if the client knows that what he tells his lawyer cannot, over his objection, be extorted in court from the lawyer's lips.[2]

The same concern supports lawyer nondisclosure out of court as well. According to the American Bar Association's Code of Professional Responsibility, however, lawyers may sometimes reveal information learned in the course of the lawyer-client relationship. Thus lawyers may make known a client's intention to commit a crime and the information necessary to prevent the crime;[3] and lawyers may reveal information when necessary to collect their fee or to defend themselves against charges of wrongful conduct.[4] The code may also allow lawyers to reveal perjury, although this is a matter of dispute.[5] In any event, the obligation of confidentiality is not taken to be absolute. There is therefore a serious question about the *extent* and *limits* of the obligation. How much and what sorts of information should it cover? What sorts of information, if any, should be left unprotected? Where the confidentiality obligation exists, when, if ever, may it be overridden? I attempt to address these questions in this essay. I do not challenge the basic obligation of lawyer-client confidentiality. Rather, I am concerned primarily with developing a reasonable view of its scope.

The appropriate extent of confidentiality is a subject of serious current dispute in a number of areas, and I shall briefly mention four of them:

1. *Future wrongdoing.* The code, as we have seen, permits an attorney to disclose a client's intention to commit a crime. But some crimes are trivial, and some seriously injurious acts may not be crimes. And it is not always easy to draw a clear distinction

between past and future crimes.[6] Further, it is not obvious why the lawyer should have the discretion to disclose rather than being required to disclose, at least in the case of acts that are likely to cause death or serious injury. Thus the obligation to prevent harm, implicit in these exceptions, could be specified in several alternative ways.

2. *Perjury and misapprehensions.* The code tells lawyers that if the client has perpetrated a fraud upon a person or the court, they must get the client to rectify the fraud and, if they fail, they must disclose it. But this may be done only when the information revealed is not "protected as a privileged communication."[7] In reality, this means that lawyers will be required to disclose only in those rare cases in which their knowledge of the fraud does not come from the client. On the other hand, a recent (January 1980) version of the newly proposed Model Rules of Professional Conduct put forward by an ABA committee unambiguously requires the disclosure of perjury and misapprehensions in both civil proceedings and in almost all criminal proceedings.[8] For yet a third view, a new code presented by the American Trial Lawyers Foundation—reflecting the well-known views of its reporter Monroe Freedman—prohibits completely the disclosure of perjury and misapprehensions.[9] What is at issue here is the relative weights of the obligation to promote justice and the interests of the client.

3. *Corporate misconduct.* We have seen that the code permits lawyers to disclose the intention to commit a crime; presumably this covers corporate crimes as well as other crimes. But the rule does not give much guidance. The January 1980 version of the Model Rules, however, requires a corporate lawyer to take steps within an organization to prevent acts that are both illegal and substantially harmful to the corporation. It then permits, but does not require, disclosure to outside sources if the highest authority in the corporation refuses to act because of its own personal or financial interests.[10] But it is not obvious why such disclosure should be discretionary rather than mandatory. Nor is it clear why the financial interests of the highest authority are relevant or why mandatory internal efforts are required only when the act is both illegal *and* harmful to the corporation. Why not require efforts if the act is simply illegal? Why not require efforts if the harm is not to the corporation but to consumers or employees? To answer these and similar questions, we need a plausible account of the appropriate relationship between the lawyer and the corporation, given that most corporations are not relatively powerless individuals, but social institutions capable of doing great good or evil. How much should the lawyer identify with the corporation or with its group of officers? How much should the lawyer represent an independent public interest? Here we must balance loyalties to a very special client against obligations to the public.

4. *Lawyer self-defense.* The code allows lawyers to reveal confidences in order to collect their fee or to defend themselves against charges of misconduct.[11] But if confidentiality is so important, why may it be breached in this case and not where third-party interests are involved? What makes this disclosure more important than disclosure for the good of the public or to promote justice? This exception seems self-serving. Of course, one appropriate response is that lawyers may be deterred from taking cases and rendered excessively cautious in legal proceedings when they fear nonpayment or malpractice charges.[12] Other plausible responses are that it is unfair and expects too much to require lawyers not to defend themselves from clients who are swindling or accusing them, or that by refusing to pay or accusing the lawyer the client is violating an implicit contract so that the lawyer's duty of confidentiality is voided. There is a good deal to these responses. But protecting confidentiality usually means sacrificing some other aims, and the special significance of this exception needs further justification, especially if the lawyer's interests are to be protected while the interests of innocent third parties are left in jeopardy.

In these disputed areas what is at issue is the lawyer's duty to his or her client as opposed to his or her duties to prevent harm or promote justice or as opposed to his or her right to protect his or her own interests. Thus an adequate view of the scope and limits of lawyer-client confidentiality requires an account that will enable us to weigh these competing values and interests. To make progress toward such an account, I think it best not to tackle the issues directly, but to look at confidentiality at a more fundamental level. Thus in Sections II and III, I make some suggestions about the moral basis, complexity, and limits of confidentiality. I focus in these sections on ordinary, nonprofessional contexts, leaving aside the attorney-client situation. I also consider the more general question of passing on information about other people, whether or not it has been given in confidence. In Section IV, I return to the question of confidentiality in the legal context. I argue for the appropriateness of more liberalized disclosure provisions than are involved in the code or in current practice, although I am not able to say enough to claim that the conclusion is fully justified. My tentativeness and the exploratory nature of my remarks are calculated. The discussions of lawyer-client confidentiality of which I am aware do not seem to me to go very deep.[13] In the disputed cases, as we have seen, valid competing interests are at stake: those of the client, the court, the public, the truth, etc. Those who discuss the issue tend to weigh these interests differently, backing their weightings with arguments that do not meet each other. I intend to avoid this pattern and suggest some ways to move beyond it.

II. The Use and Misuse of Personal Information

When one person conveys information about himself or herself to a second person, let's call the first person the *speaker*, the second person the *hearer*, and the sort of information conveyed *personal information*.[14] If the hearer discloses the information to a third person, let's call that person a *listener*. Such information might or might not be given with an understanding that it be kept confidential, and such an understanding might be explicit or implicit. It is explicit when the hearer has made a promise (in many but not all cases requested by the speaker) not to pass on the information, implicit when there is no expressed promise but, because of the relationship between the parties or the nature of the information, there is an unspoken understanding that the information is not to be transferred. I want to suggest that confidentiality grows out of the ordinary communication of personal information, and that the line between the nonconfidential and confidential expression of information is not sharp.

To see this, let's note first that even when information is given without confidentiality, there will often be good moral reasons for not passing it on. Information conveyed by a speaker could be used by a hearer to harm or embarrass the speaker, interfere with his or her interests, thwart his or her plans, invade his or her privacy, or upset, disturb, or harm third parties. I take it that there is a more or less stringent obligation not to affect other people "negatively," i.e., not to harm or injure them or thwart their interests, at least not without good reasons.[15] Thus there will often be good moral reasons for not disclosing nonconfidential information, and we are certainly not morally free to do whatever we want with such information. In fact, I suggest we accept and are more or less governed by a fairly subtle, complex, and imprecise set of principles concerning what we may and may not do in disclosing personal information conveyed to us by others. How we should use such information will be a function of a variety of factors such as the nature of the information revealed, the consequences of disclosure, the hearer's relationship to the speaker and the potential listener, the speaker's relationship to the listener, and the uses the listener is likely to make of the information.

As an illustration of this, consider a case in which a speaker imparts to a hearer some embarrassing personal information without explicitly asking that the information be kept secret. To whom might the hearer reveal the information? A sweeping answer that it might be revealed to anyone or to no one would surely be incorrect. Much will depend on the factors just listed. Very likely, it would be wrong for the hearer to disclose the information to a listener who would use it to embarrass or harm the speaker. Even if the information is not used detrimentally or put to any use at all, conveying it to certain listeners might constitute an unjustified invasion of the speaker's privacy simply because others are made aware of the embarrassing fact. Consider now the imparting of the information to a listener who is a caring friend of the speaker, and who could use the information to help the speaker. The appropriateness of such disclosure will depend on whether the friend really can help, whether the speaker would welcome the help, whether the speaker would mind the information's being disclosed, whether the information is really as embarrassing as the speaker perceives it to be, whether the listener can be trusted to use the information appropriately, etc. The speaker's decision will raise difficult questions about when and how to help others, when to respect their autonomy and privacy, and when to intervene paternalistically—that is, for another's good, independent of or against his wishes. All these issues will arise even when the information is not given in confidence. And even if the information has been given in confidence, there still may be a case for revealing it.

Consider now two more variations on our case. Suppose the embarrassing information is not really as embarrassing as the speaker supposes: friends are not surprised to hear of it and perhaps cherish it as an interesting, even lovable, idiosyncrasy of the speaker. Would it be wrong for the hearer to reveal it, even gossip about it, to one of the speaker's friends? to a gathering of such friends? Such revelation may be at least a minor indiscretion, perhaps a sort of betrayal. But it might be said that there is a natural human tendency to be interested in other people, especially one's friends, to talk and gossip about them—and

people sometimes are too easily embarrassed, no "real" harm is done, etc. So there may be nothing seriously wrong about such gossip. And what about the propriety of the hearer revealing genuinely embarrassing information, even information given in confidence, to a spouse or to the person with whom the hearer shares his or her life? I think people are not generally expected to keep a good deal of detrimental and confidential information from their mates, although this will be affected by the particulars of the context, and in particular by whether one's mate can in turn be trusted to keep a secret!

My aim in presenting these examples has been to suggest that the transfer of personal information is a morally complex matter, even without confidentiality, and to suggest that confidentiality is neither necessary nor sufficient for the appropriateness of nondisclosure. I now turn to another related point, that the line between confidential and nonconfidential contexts is not sharp. Confidentiality, I noted earlier, may be either explicit or implicit. I want to suggest that the revelation of damaging personal information frequently carries with it an *implicit* understanding that the hearer keep the information confidential, or is often ambiguous as to whether there is such an understanding.[16] I shall argue below that confidentiality is based on a complex need of the speaker, a need to express information while at the same time retaining control of it, keeping "title" to it. When information is given in confidence our obligation not to disclose it is based on (at least) three factors: our respect for the speaker's need, the bad consequences for the speaker of disclosure, and our duty to keep our promises. When a speaker expresses negative information, we can often assume that the complex need for expression—to express but retain—exists and that disclosure would be damaging; in many cases willingly hearing such information carries with it an implicit understanding that it not be further disclosed and therefore amounts to a tacit promise. (The same may be true of other information that could be used to harm the speaker, such as the whereabouts of his or her children who are the likely victims of a kidnapper.) Or, to put the point more weakly, whether there is an implicit understanding may be uncertain; one may have reason to think there is but not be entirely sure. In many cases the request for a promise of confidentiality is simply a way for the speaker to make sure that the tacit understanding really exists or to produce it with certainty when the situation is ambiguous. And when the hearer really does assume that the information is to be kept confidential, to be asked to keep it secret can be irritating, taken as expressing an unwarranted lack of trust. Yet it may be very important to the speaker to make sure that the understanding is really there, despite this consequence.

In sum, expressing personal information, especially of the negative sort, can be dangerous. But we often need to do this. The consequence is that we recognize an obligation to others to treat such information with care, and this gives rise to a complex moral practice. Confidentiality arises in a natural and inevitable way out of the expression of negative information and is not something "tacked on" as an extra and extraneous element. As I said earlier, it "grows out" of the ordinary communication of information in an easily understandable way. Confidentiality, in effect, provides an *additional* reason for respecting the speaker's need to express information without adverse consequences. Setting confidentiality against this broader background will give us a better chance of understanding the special obligation of confidentiality, a task to which I now turn.

III. *The Case for Confidentiality*

Confidentiality—the speaker's revelation of information with the explicit or implicit understanding that it will not be disclosed further—can be "attached" to many different sorts of information. I have restricted the discussion to personal information, that is, information about one's self. Other sorts of information might be kept confidential, but I am not

dealing here with the questions these raise. I would now like to distinguish five different categories of confidential information and then turn to the basic reasons for confidentiality.

The first sort of information is *embarrassing* information, information that simply embarrasses or shames the speaker, but need not involve wrongful or illegal acts. From this, we can distinguish *guilty* information, information that the speaker has done something wrong that, if imparted to the appropriate listener, would cause the speaker to be sanctioned by formal punishment or by informal blame, disapproval, chastisement, etc. Information about a speaker's crime, a speaker's betrayal, or a child's mischievousness would all count as guilty information. Third, there is *dangerous* information, information that the speaker intends to commit some harm, injury, or other damage to the interests of a third party. A fourth category of information is *planning* information, information about a speaker's plans, intentions, projects, or purposes. The key reason for confidentiality here would be that revealing such information might cause the speaker's plans to be thwarted by others. The fifth and final category of information I call simply *positive* information, information involving good or indifferent facts about a person. Such information, though not intrinsically damaging, could be used by others to harm the speaker or his or her interests, as when the whereabouts of a diplomat are conveyed to an enemy terrorist.

These categories are not meant to be exhaustive or exclusive, but only a good rough classification for the purposes of understanding the limits of confidentiality. After making clear a conflict that I take to be inherent in confidentiality, I shall argue that the moral force of the obligation of confidentiality will differ with respect to these different types of information.

People may reveal embarrassing, guilty, or dangerous information for a number of reasons. They may wish advice, seek sympathy, desire the human response of another person, need to express what is on their mind, to confess or admit or just share their knowledge and feelings. Or they may want to boast or enlist hearers as confederates in some plan of action. The main point is that the speaker wishes both to retain the privacy of the information and at the same time to express it to someone else. Confidentiality is the device for doing this.

This dual nature of confidentiality can be understood in a somewhat metaphorical way: when a speaker delivers information in confidence, the speaker attempts to make the hearer a part of his or her own self, or "extended self," with respect to the information revealed. It is true that the speaker needs the hearer to be another person, another "ear" and mind who can register the information and respond to it; "revealing" a confidence to a wall or a dog is no substitute for telling a person. But at the same time, the speaker needs the hearer not to be another person, but to be a part of his or her own self so that the information will not be used except as he or she chooses. Dropping the metaphorical notion of an extended self, the idea is that the hearer is not an autonomous moral agent with regard to the piece of information revealed. This is not a merely arbitrary restriction on the hearer because the need to confide information in another person is a normal human need that the hearer may also be expected to experience on occasion. The information, in effect, still "belongs" to the speaker who would not have "lent" it without being sure of retaining control of it. I suggest that both the speaker and hearer in a situation in which information is imparted in confidence perceive the situation this way or at least realize that this is how it is supposed to be perceived.

The situation of the hearer just presented is characterized by inevitable moral conflict. On the one hand, the hearer has given up moral autonomy with respect to a certain piece of information. On the other hand, the hearer still remains an autonomous moral agent with the capacity for moral deliberation and choice. Morally speaking, his or her autonomy with respect to the information received cannot be

given up. He or she remains a moral being and thus free to deliberate about what to do with the information once it has been received. That it has been revealed in confidence is a powerful reason for keeping it secret, but cannot settle the issue. The hearer cannot remain a moral agent without retaining the right to consider the information in light of other factors that may, all things considered, provide even stronger reasons for revealing it.

We all implicitly realize this about confidentiality. On the one hand, we need the confidential transfer of information and the consequent inclusion of the hearer into the speaker's wider self. Yet, on the other hand, the presuppositions of this relationship cannot be realized simultaneously; the hearer cannot be expected to give up moral autonomy. Revealing information to others is a dangerous act, involving both trust that they will keep the information secret and fear not only that they will not but that they justifiably will not, that they will perceive the situation as one in which other moral demands rightly overcome the demand to keep the information secret.[17] Of course, we fear also the hearer's moral weakness, temptations to reveal gossip to others for frivolous or self-serving reasons, and betrayal out of neglect or malevolence. Yet these are not the only concerns involved when we reveal information.

It might be argued that my claim that people cannot give up autonomy proves too much. It might be taken to mean that a moral agent cannot make any commitments—no promises, contracts, or undertakings of any sort—because to do so is to give up moral autonomy. Since making commitments is a fundamental and pervasive feature of moral life, this would be a conclusive objection. But moral autonomy does not mean that one may not undertake commitments. It means that one always remains free to act against a commitment if the balance of reasons requires that one do so, and this always remains a moral possibility. Commitments constitute strong moral reasons for action, which need to be taken very seriously. But they do not constitute, all by themselves, conclusive reasons, and other moral features of the situation will often be relevant. Moral deliberation concerning the details of the particular case is always in order; the moral life involves both deliberation and attention to circumstances.

Some will reject this account of the moral life, especially those who think there are certain absolute or exceptionless commands or prohibitions, e.g., certain things that must never or always be done regardless of the circumstances or consequences. My view thus amounts to a rejection of this form of absolutism. It may be thought, then, that it is simply a version of utilitarianism or some kind of "pragmatic" or situational version of morality. But it is clearly compatible with a deontological view that recognizes a plurality of moral obligations and moral reasons for action and a need to assess their weight when they conflict. Moral autonomy means that such assessment is always appropriate.[18]

But what about people who either surrender their moral judgment to some external agency, e.g., a religious authority or a political doctrine, or who take some principle as absolute, never to be violated? Such people fall into two groups. The first group are willing to deliberate about particular moral questions and concede that competing moral considerations might override the requirements of the authority or the absolute principle; nevertheless, in each case, they conclude that, all things considered, the commands of the authority or the principle are to be followed. Such persons do exercise moral autonomy, if their deliberations are genuine, for they do deliberate and attend to circumstances; they therefore present no problem for my view. The second group do not deliberate about particular moral questions, but just automatically act and consider themselves bound to act on all occasions as the authority or principle dictates. They do not even consider it possible that the commands of the authority or principle could be overridden. Are these people no longer moral agents? Certainly they will see themselves as doing what they morally ought to do and they will often be described

by others as people who do what they at least believe they ought to do. To say that such people, nevertheless, are not genuinely moral agents, I need to make clear whether my claim is intended as a conceptual or normative one. While I think a case can be made on conceptual grounds,[19] this will be inconclusive and I believe that ultimately this claim must be a normative one: a claim about how one ought to act and deliberate to be a genuine moral agent. I shall not, however, try to defend this normative claim here, and I thus concede that my thesis must take a conditional form for now—that if autonomy can be analyzed as I have suggested, confidentiality involves a kind of "contradiction," the surrender of something that (morally) cannot be surrendered.[20]

Let me summarize. I take it that there is a prima facie obligation not to reveal personal information given in confidence that is based on three things: respect for the need of the person to express but retain control of the information; the possible bad consequences for the speaker of disclosure; and, finally, the duty to keep one's word based on the explicit or implicit promise of confidentiality one has made. My remarks about the tensions involved in confidentiality have been meant to emphasize that, as strong as these reasons may be—and in many cases they are very strong—they cannot be strong enough to remove the hearer's own moral autonomy, his or her right and duty to act on stronger countervailing considerations.

Just how strong are the reasons on both sides? I have claimed that two of the reasons for an obligation of confidentiality are the needs that motivate the expression of information and the consequences, good and bad, of disclosure. I want to suggest that these also affect the strength of the obligation. To illustrate this, I want to compare some of the types of information mentioned above.

The speaker's need to reveal *guilty* information—information that the speaker has done some wrong for which he or she could be sanctioned—will often be deep and serious, deserving of respect. The speaker's need to reveal *dangerous* information—information that the speaker intends to harm another—will often be less compelling. On what facts are these generalizations based? Quite often, the motive to reveal guilty information is the speaker's need to confess, to share the knowledge and burden of guilt, to express thoughts and feelings, and to receive advice about what to do. These are important needs, and much can be gained by permitting wrongdoers this opportunity to express themselves with impunity. On the other hand, a speaker might reveal dangerous information from boastfulness, as an expression of revenge (against the potential victim), or from the desire to enlist the hearer as a confederate or keep the hearer quiet. Such disclosure may surely come from better motives, such as seeking advice or hoping to be talked out of the wrongful act; conversely, guilty information could be confided from boastfulness, revenge, or other less admirable motives. I am inclined, nevertheless, to think there is a typical difference between motives of the sort mentioned.

Furthermore, there is a difference with respect to consequences. Revealing dangerous information can often, with near certainty, have very good consequences: the prevention of injury and harm. The consequence of disclosing guilty information—usually the sanctioning of the offender—in many cases is less important to society than preventing impending harm. One reason for this is that the punishment of any particular offender may not matter so much if the general system of punishment is maintained. Also, the punishment may do no good if the offender is not inclined to commit other wrongs. And the offender, if allowed the opportunity to confess, may sooner or later reveal the wrongdoing publicly and thus undergo sanctions without disclosure by the hearer. I admit that these claims are controversial and hold at best in a general way, but if correct they underlie the intuition that there are often stronger reasons for not disclosing guilty information than for not disclosing dangerous information. This intuition may very well be at the basis of the fact that

the ABA code and the Model Rules treat differently the disclosure of future and of past crimes or wrongful acts.

If we focus just on the consequences of revealing embarrassing information, it may seem that the obligation of confidentiality is weakened by the fact that the consequences of disclosure will often not be very bad. On the other hand, disclosure is unlikely to attain good consequences or prevent bad consequences, so there is little compelling reason for revelation. Consequences do not play a very important role here. What are important are the needs for self-expression and understanding that move people to reveal embarrassing information. These needs deserve respect and thus may strengthen the obligation to keep such information confidential. Here we might also recall our earlier discussion of cases in which disclosure may help the speaker. In such cases, there will be reasons for disclosure, although these raise the complex issue of paternalism. *Planning* and *positive* information are difficult to generalize about since no typical needs or consequences seem to characterize imparting them.

The point implicit in this rough survey is that it does matter what wants or needs give rise to expressing information and what consequences will follow disclosure. These features affect the strength of the obligation of confidentiality. But a third feature is relevant: the fact of having made, explicitly or implicitly, a promise. Some people will concede that in a particular case the consequences of disclosure will be very good, of nondisclosure very bad, and the needs that motivated expression nonworthy ones—but still they will judge it wrong to disclose because the hearer has given his or her word not to do so. For them a promise carries great weight, perhaps absolute weight. Others, however, will find the promise less weighty and will be more apt to find exceptions to the duty to keep promises. It sounds like we have a knotty dispute here that opposes familiar consequentialist and deontological considerations. Can anything be said to shed light on this?

It is helpful to distinguish two different grounds for the obligation to keep promises. The *purely deontological* ground is the mere fact that one has given a promise. This ground involves the claim that the principle that promises ought to be kept is a fundamental one, needing no defense in terms of other sorts of considerations. That an act is the keeping of a promise is a basic or *intrinsic* moral reason for doing it. The *systemic ground* considers certain of the effects of promise-breaking. One effect is the *interpersonal effect*: if I break my promise to *Y*, *Y* will be less likely to accept my promises in the future and various beneficial consequences will be lost. A second effect is the *personal effect*: if I break my promise to *Y* and "get away" with it, I may be more inclined to break other promises in the future with damage to my integrity and loss of other beneficial consequences. A third effect is the *contagion effect*: my promise-breaking may motivate others to break promises so that a beneficial practice of making certain sorts of promises among some group of people is damaged or destroyed. A final effect is the *hypothetical effect*: bad consequences might result if everyone broke promises, or the particular sort of promise I am contemplating breaking. Effects such as these underlie widely different types of theories that attempt to justify a very strong rule against promise-breaking that either forbids or looks with great caution at judging and acting in terms of the consequences of a particular act. Whatever their differences, each theory appeals to the systemic consequences mentioned to justify following rules even in situations in which there seem to be very persuasive grounds for violating the rules.

The obligation to keep information confidential is stronger, I think, the more a systemic case can be made; it is weaker when nothing more than the purely deontological ground can be cited. Given this, I want to suggest that in most ordinary contexts a strong case on systemic grounds can *not* be made. It is usually unlikely that one instance of breaking a confidence will be damagingly contagious; the personal effect may seem negligible and any negative

interpersonal effects worth the price; and the appeal to what I called the hypothetical effect is notoriously controversial. I think the systemic ground is most important in specialized contexts, such as the law, where the practice of confidentiality is taken to be necessary to achieve some definite aim and where the contagious effects of violations are thought to be likely and serious. The greater relevance of the systemic ground seems to me to be the crucial difference between ordinary and legal contexts with regard to confidentiality.

Before turning to the legal context directly, let me make one qualification. I have said that the obligation to keep promises is stronger when systemic grounds are added to the purely deontological ground. But to say it is stronger is not to assert or justify the claim that the obligation is weak when it rests on the purely deontological ground alone. Some may accept the claim about comparative strength and weakness, but still argue that the purely deontological obligation is very strong. So we are left with the controversial question of the strength of such obligations; I have tried only to point out a comparative difference that sheds some light on the special significance of confidentiality in the law.

IV. Confidentiality in Legal Contexts

To tackle the question of lawyer-client confidentiality, we need to note first that there are three possible categories of permissible disclosure of information. First, some information that is permissible to disclose might be considered to be entirely outside the domain of confidentiality—completely unprotected. As I noted earlier, the ABA code permits a lawyer to disclose a client's intention to commit a crime; such information might therefore be thought of as falling outside the protected domain of confidentiality or consider that the code requires a lawyer to hold confidential the confidences and secrets of clients, where a confidence is information protected by the attorney-client privilege and a secret is other information that would be embarrassing or otherwise detrimental to the client or that the client has requested be held inviolate.[21] It seems, then, that positive information—neither embarrassing nor otherwise detrimental—for which confidence has not been requested is not protected.[22] This suggests, then, that there is no indiscretion when such information is revealed at, say, a cocktail party. Perhaps this is unintended, but—and this is my only point—it seems that we have here another case of information falling outside the domain of confidentiality.

The second category is this: some information might be considered confidential in most situations or for most purposes, but there might be understood to be certain instances in which disclosure is permitted or required. Such information is prima facie confidential, or confidential other things being equal—it falls within the domain of confidentiality, but in certain situations the requirement of confidentiality is overcome. The overriding conditions might be spelled out in codes of conduct. Consider the information a lawyer would have to disclose in order to reveal perjury or correct misapprehensions; this will be quite ordinary information about the case learned from the client or through the lawyer's research and that needs to be held confidential except in such circumstances. The information revealed by lawyers to collect their fee or protect themselves from misconduct charges will also tend to fall into this category.

A third category is also possible, absolutely protected information that may be revealed under no circumstances. I do not think that the ABA code has such a category, since no restriction is made on what, for example, lawyers might reveal to collect their fee or defend themselves. But such a category is possible. We have, then, three categories in which to classify information: (1) outside the domain of confidentiality, *totally unprotected*; (2) within the domain of confidentiality but permissible to reveal in certain circumstances, *prima facie protected*; and (3) within the domain of confidentiality and never to be revealed, *absolutely protected*. In elucidating a view

on the scope of confidentiality, we need to be able to say into which of these categories various types of information should be put.

Let us distinguish three views concerning the scope of confidentiality, each of which has a strong and weak version. A very simple and natural view is that the information to be protected is *all* and *only* the information relevant to the particular case for which the client has sought the lawyer's aid. Let's call this the *particular case* theory. In a strong version, the information would be absolutely protected, under no conditions to be revealed. On a weaker version such information would be prima facie protected and might be revealed, for example, to prevent perjury. On either version many sorts of information would go unprotected, including information about past crimes, information about the intention to commit future crimes, and positive and negative information totally unrelated to the case. Examples of this might be the client's finances, occupational record, or prior mental or physical health history.

Because so much information is unprotected, many will find the particular case theory inadequate. A natural and opposed alternative is that *anything* the client tells the lawyer, whether or not it is relevant to the case, should be confidential. Let's call this the *holistic* theory. This, too, will have two versions: on the strong version the information will be absolutely protected, never to be revealed; on the weaker version it will be prima facie protected, with confidentiality overridden in certain instances. A third view, which falls between these two, brings all negative or detrimental information within the domain of confidentiality, whether or not it concerns the particular case, but leaves positive information unprotected. We can call this the *negative information* theory. And, in the obvious ways, it will also have strong and weak versions.

I am going to concentrate for now on the extent of the domain of confidentiality, with how much and what kinds of information should fall into it, and leave for later the question of whether information within the domain is absolutely or only prima facie protected. Let's look at the particular case theory, which allows in the domain only information about the particular case. This theory seems implausible, for several psychological or social reasons. When a client receives the services of a professional, they will have occasion to discuss many things that are not relevant to the professional matter. They may chat about family affairs or the client's work simply as a means of warming up to each other or because they have developed a friendship or taken an interest in each other. (They are people after all, not just lawyers and clients in the abstract.) Or their chat may just be typical small talk. The client may disclose information that should not be revealed to others by the lawyer, whether or not it is explicitly given in confidence. But this obligation of confidentiality results not so much from the inherent requirements of the lawyer-client relationship as from the mutual understanding presupposed in the ordinary communication of personal information, as discussed above. This added dimension of ordinary confidentiality is part of the reason why the scope of confidentiality is wider than the particular case view allows. Further, in a relationship characterized by confidentiality in some areas, the habit of confidentiality is likely to be extended to other areas. This extension may be sought by the client who, having found an advisor on one issue, seeks his or her advice on other issues. It may be acquiesced in by the lawyer because it enhances the smooth functioning of the relationship, because the lawyer enjoys the role, or for other reasons. Most likely the extension is unconscious and undeliberate for either party. Again, the domain of confidentiality is extended for reasons that stem from the professional relationship only insofar as the attorney-client relationship is embedded in ordinary communication between persons.

Although these "psychological" reasons for a broader domain of confidentiality do not invoke the inherent demands of the lawyer-client relationship, it is possible to give an argument that does invoke such demands and leads away from the particular case view to the holistic view. I will call the argument the "spread" argument because those who give it want to spread the veil of confidentiality from information about the particular case to all information imparted to the lawyer. The argument begins with the plausible assumption that for lawyers to present the best possible case for their client, they need to know everything of relevance to the case. From this premise it infers, also plausibly, that clients must be able to tell their lawyers, in confidence, anything they know that is relevant to the facts. The next, crucial premise lays down certain conditions for clients to be able to disclose such information. There are several possible versions of this premise. One version, as put by Monroe Freedman, is that the "client is not ordinarily competent to evaluate the relevance or significance of particular facts. What may seem incriminating to the client may actually be exculpatory."[23] Alternatively, it might be held not that clients lack competence to evaluate the facts, but that the relevance of any particular fact cannot be determined in isolation: all the facts the client has in mind need to be brought out before the lawyer can determine which are genuinely relevant.

A third possibility is that the relevant information is often "intertwined" in the client's mind with other information that is not, logically, relevant to the case, and the client will be able to express the relevant information only if he or she also has the "space" to express a lot of nonrelevant information as well. The point is not that clients are not competent to assess relevance but that people need to express themselves in their own special ways and this requires freedom to go beyond the particular case. Whichever additional premise is used, it follows that clients must be free to say in confidence anything that is on their mind, leaving the assessment of relevance to the lawyer after all the facts have been brought out. If certain areas were exempted from the scope of confidentiality, clients would want to ensure that they did not reveal damaging information that falls into those areas. But since such information is, in one of the ways mentioned, connected with relevant information, clients are likely to omit relevant information as well. So any restrictions on the domain of confidentiality will make clients cautious and thus will have an unacceptable "chilling effect"; if lawyers are to represent clients effectively, confidentiality must therefore apply to all information.

The first two versions of the crucial premise of the spread argument are implausible, as can be seen by rather obvious counterexamples. *A* is charged with robbing *B*. *A* can know with certainty that at least regarding this particular robbery his sister-in-law's maiden name or his favorite baseball team are irrelevant. *A* is not likely to be mistaken on this nor must he know everything in order to know this. On the other hand, whether *A* was or was not at the scene of the robbery when it occurred can be known with certainty by him to be relevant. So the claim that people cannot assess relevance at all or cannot assess it piecemeal is an implausible exaggeration.

The third version of the premise—the claim that relevant and irrelevant information is mentally "intertwined" for most people—is more satisfactory. It says, in effect, that people are not well-programmed computers who can communicate "the facts and nothing but the facts"; rather, in the course of giving out the facts, they need the freedom to express themselves in their own peculiar ways and this means bringing in more than the facts. Lawyers must therefore set up a situation in which clients feel free to talk about all sorts of things and the obvious condition of this freedom is that clients know they won't be betrayed. Thus it seems reasonable to think that, in the course of interviewing, lawyers are likely to learn not only the facts relevant to the case but other information that is embarrassing or otherwise detrimental or that is, though not negative, the sort of information that people usually keep private.

These psychological facts about the intertwining of information, if plausible, show that the particular case view is too restricted. Do they support the holistic theory? While people intertwine information and require freedom to talk about more than the particular case, they are not totally unable to discern differences, distinguish contexts, and categorize information. To say that they must be able to say *anything*, if they are to reveal relevant facts, is surely to overstate the case.[24] Most clients are unlikely to make fine distinctions among categories of information, however, and so may lose confidence in a lawyer who reveals information too freely, even information that has nothing to do with the present case. But likewise we are likely to lose confidence in friends who reveal even our trivial confidences too casually, though this certainly does not mean that a holistic duty of confidentiality holds among friends. Where information is clearly irrelevant to the case in hand and is in no way intertwined with information that is relevant to it, it would seem that the lawyer's duty of confidentiality to a client begins to approximate our ordinary assumptions discussed earlier regarding communications of personal information.

What emerges from this, I think, is that the domain of confidentiality must be wider than the particular case theory allows, but its scope is not captured adequately by the holistic theory. Nor does the negative information theory do the job here. The trouble with the negative information view is that some nonnegative information should be included in the domain (the sort usually held private) and much negative information need not be included (the sort that is clearly not intertwined with the pertinent facts). So we have a vague domain of confidential information about the particular case plus other intertwined information "radiating out" from there. This additional information does not include everything known to the client, but it is difficult to give a precise demarcation of it that would fit every client's needs. This is probably why the extent of the domain of confidentiality is generally left quite vague in the various codes and systems of rules.

It might now be said that it is fine to speak of the domain of confidentiality as lacking clear boundaries, but this is not of much help to practitioners who need a rule to give them guidance. What then, for practical purposes, should the rule be? To answer this we need to stop talking about information in general and consider some of the controversial types of information mentioned in the introduction. I will focus, then, on the following two questions:

1. Should information about future crimes and/or acts that injure others fall within the domain of confidentiality?
2. Should the disclosure of information about the particular case be permitted or required in order to prevent or rectify perjury?

Discussing these issues will help us give a partial outline of the most plausible practical rule.

With respect to the client's intention to commit a crime, the major reason for disclosure is to prevent the harm and injury the crime involves. This is a compelling ground. Also relevant is a concern for the lawyer's own moral status: if such information may be disclosed the lawyer is not put in the morally difficult position of having to stand by while something dreadful happens to others. We should also note that the information to be disclosed is not about the particular case nor is it likely that the lawyer would need to know that information in order to present the best possible case. What is clearly relevant to presenting, for example, the best defense in a criminal trial is what the client did, what his or her motives were, what the circumstances were, and so forth. It is unlikely that future intentions will, logically, bear on these matters. And, as I argued earlier, the needs that prompt a client to express such information are in many cases not worthy ones. Thus there are persuasive grounds for omitting such information from the domain of confidentiality.

In response, the case against revealing such information must, I think, appeal to three considerations. The first is the possibility that information about the

intention to commit a crime may be intertwined with information directly relevant to the case. But while it is possible that some clients may be unable to discuss the particular case without revealing future criminal plans, I doubt this is very common. It is certainly not common enough to outweigh the considerations that favor disclosure.

Second, it may be held that the client's knowledge that the lawyer may report intentions to commit a crime will have a significant chilling effect, interfering with the confidence the client must have in the lawyer in order to reveal all pertinent information. I have already suggested that this sort of remark is an overstatement, most clients will not need this sort of immunity in order to have enough "space" to talk freely on the matter at issue. Nevertheless, this objection does suggest a general problem. It may be that allowing each one of a number of categories of information separately to be disclosed would have no significant chilling effect. But allowing all of them would have such an effect. So there may be a case for allowing disclosure of information of type A, of type B, of type C, etc., but not of A *and* B *and* C, etc. If all were disposable a threshold would be reached in which the client's "space" would be diminished enough so that confidence in the lawyer would disappear. This means we must take into account the combined results of various disclosure provisions, which may involve ranking the importance of various provisions and accepting only the most crucial. Since preventing imminent harm is a fundamental moral aim, this provision should survive this "combined effect" objection.

The third response to the argument is very interesting. If lawyers "blow the whistle" on clients' crimes, some harm will be prevented. But if clients come to know that lawyers will do this, most of them will cease informing lawyers of their criminal intentions. So the harm this disclosure is designed to prevent will not be prevented. Further, if disclosure is protected a lawyer will sometimes succeed in persuading a client not to follow through with criminal intentions. But if such disclosure is not protected, the information will not be revealed and the crime will be committed. So, it is argued, the long-term result of allowing disclosure of information about likely criminal acts, in terms of harm to others, is either no different or worse than the policy protecting such information.[25]

This is a powerful argument, though I think the facts may be challenged to some extent. Even if information about future crimes is not considered confidential, some clients are likely to reveal such information anyway and some harm will be prevented either through persuasion or revelation. So some crucial benefits may still be gained by permitting disclosure. Still, the net gain may be minimal, and a case for disclosure based solely on consequentialist considerations would not be very strong. But something else is involved: the lawyer's own moral status and worth. If disclosure is not allowed, the lawyer will sometimes be forced to permit something quite evil to happen. The policy of disclosure avoids or minimizes this. I think that no one should be forced or required by social rules to stand by while genuine evil occurs; the damage to one's moral personality is unacceptable (and possibly habit-forming). I conclude that this weighty concern for the lawyer's own moral status tips the scales in favor of disclosure.

I have spoken so far about the intention to commit a crime. But there are crimes and crimes; some are awful, some trivial. And it may sometimes be right to break the law. Also the lawyer's belief that the client will commit a crime will differ in reliability from case to case and time to time. I am inclined to think that the most important thing is the prevention of serious harm that is nearly certain to occur. Given this, I find most acceptable a rule that would make mandatory the revelation of information when necessary to prevent death or serious bodily harm to another person, but leaves the reporting of other wrongful activity to the lawyer's discretion.[26] Such a rule seems to me most likely to preserve the lawyer's moral autonomy and worth and to prevent evils, while minimizing any potential chilling effects.

I now turn to the disclosure of perjury. Here we are concerned with information about the particular case that must be considered prima facie confidential. The question is whether confidentiality is overridden when the client commits perjury. The issue of perjury poses the question of what a lawyer may do for a client. Clearly, the lawyer may and should present the strongest and best case. But what is the strongest and best case? Although a case involving perjured testimony and manufactured evidence may be very strong, neither the client nor lawyer is entitled to present *this* case, despite its strength. On the other hand, they need not be confined to what they really believe, based on the evidence, is the strongest case. Uncounterfeit evidence may be treated with flexibility, welcome facts may be stressed, unwelcome facts played down, and the whole interpreted in the most favorable light.[27] The distinction between perjured or manufactured evidence and evidence that is given greater emphasis than the client or lawyer believes it deserves may or may not be arbitrary. Both cases involve a kind of deception. But perjury seems to be a reasonable place to draw the line, since permitting perjury may place impossible burdens on judges and juries, while forbidding any stretching of evidence would negate a person's day in court, also the adversary process arguably has the resources to correct such stretching. So the prohibition of perjury makes sense in terms of the nature of the adversary system and its aim of achieving justice while permitting people to present their case as they best see fit.

For these reasons there is a prima facie case for requiring lawyers not to allow perjury and for having a rule that requires them to attempt to dissuade clients from lying and to reveal the lie to the judge if a client goes through with it. What, then, are the arguments against this? The most typical is the familiar appeal to the "chilling effect": clients will not feel free to speak openly about the particular case if they know the lawyer can reveal perjury. To examine this, consider that we have two kinds of clients. The first have no intentions of committing perjury. These persons will not be chilled by the attorney's duty of disclosure. (And surely these clients are in the majority!) The second might want to commit perjury. They will be chilled. If they know in advance that they intend to lie, they will have to be very careful what they tell the lawyer and they may well omit relevant facts. And if they decide they want to commit perjury after they have revealed the damning facts, they won't be able to get away with it. So such people will suffer bad consequences if perjury may be disclosed. But why should this trouble any one else? They have, after all, no right to commit perjury, and if their attempt to do what they have no right to do gets them into difficulties, the responsibility is theirs. They can simply avoid the difficulties by giving up the intention to lie.[28]

It is true that if a client believes that all client conversations must be held in confidence so that the lawyer cannot reveal perjury, he or she will feel betrayed if the lawyer then does so. Monroe Freedman says that revealing perjury "would be a betrayal of the assurances of confidentiality given by the attorney in order to induce the client to reveal everything, however damaging it might appear." And so it would be if the client had been given to believe that perjury may not be revealed. But there is no such betrayal if the client knows in advance that confidentiality may be overridden when the client lies. Freedman's argument in his well-known discussion of "the perjury trilemma"—the conflict between a lawyer's duty to know all the facts, keep information in confidence, and be frank with the court[29]—plays on the ambiguity of revealing information when a promise has been made that it won't be revealed (which is betrayal) and when no such promise has been made. Of course Freedman would say that a client who knows in advance that perjury may be revealed will not speak freely. But we have already seen that this is not so with clients who do not wish to lie, and, for those who wish to lie, it is a consequence they cannot complain about. I conclude then that there are good reasons for disclosing

perjury to the court and the reasons that can be cited against this are unpersuasive.

V. Conclusion

I have argued that rules permitting or requiring the disclosure of information to prevent crimes and serious injuries and to reveal perjury are reasonable and will not damage the basic functions of confidentiality. Thus a social rule to guide practitioners should allow the disclosure of such information. Information about intended crimes should probably fall outside the domain of confidentiality, while information concerning perjury, being information about the particular case, will be prima facie confidential: it is in the domain, but it may be revealed when the client lies. For a complete discussion of attorney-client confidentiality and for the formulation of a social rule to govern all cases, we would need to discuss some of the other types of information mentioned in the introduction: facts concerning past crimes and crimes in the corporate context, facts needed to correct misapprehensions, and information lawyers may need to reveal to protect themselves against charges or to win a suit to collect their fee. We shall also need to pay more attention to the differences between criminal and civil cases and among different legal contexts, e.g., litigation, negotiation, counseling, etc. We also need to pay attention to a point mentioned earlier—the cumulative effect of a number of different disclosure provisions, each of which may be reasonable in itself. But I believe that the types of considerations I have mentioned and the framework I have set out will help us deal with these issues.

I said at the beginning that I would not present a complete and detailed argument for my conclusions and I have not. Much more needs to be said, but I believe progress has been made. Exclusive stress on confidentiality and on the obligation to the client leads to an unjustifiable surrender of moral autonomy and gives rise to the amorality and impersonality of the lawyer's role that has often been noticed.[30] By emphasizing moral autonomy and the moral status and worth of the lawyer, and by expressing some skepticism toward the systemic arguments for a wide and near-absolute domain of confidentiality (i.e., the "spread" argument, the chilling effect, etc.) I hope to have made plausible the idea that confidentiality must be restrained out of respect for autonomy and the lawyer's moral status, and that this can be done in a manner that achieves the important functions of confidentiality. In any case, I trust that enough has been said to show that "ideological" appeals either to zealous advocacy of the client's cause, on the one hand, or to the truth, on the other, are likely only to simplify the moral complexity of these issues.

NOTES

This paper is an extensively revised and expanded version of my "Confidentiality and the Lawyer-Client Relationship," *Utah Law Review* 1980 (1980): 765-86.

1 *ABA Code of Professional Responsibility* (1976 revision), DR 4-101.

2 Edward W. Cleary et al., *McCormick's Handbook on the Law of Evidence*, 2nd ed. (St. Paul, MN: West Publishing Co., 1972), 175.

3 *ABA Code*, DR 4-101 (C) (3).

4 Ibid., DR 4-101 (C) (4).

5 Ibid., DR 7-102 (A) (4), DR 7-102 (B) (1). An illuminating discussion of the ambiguities of the perjury rules can be found in "Note: Client Fraud and the Lawyer—An Ethical Analysis," *Minnesota Law Review* Vol. 62 (1977): 89-118.

6 See the discussion of this in Geoffrey Hazard, *Ethics in the Practice of Law* (New Haven, CT: Yale University Press, 1918), 30.

7 *ABA Code*, DR 7-102 (B) (1).

8 ABA Commission on Evaluation of Professional Standards, *Model Rules of Professional Conduct* (discussion draft, January 1980), Rule 3.1 (b).

9 The Roscoe Pound-American Trial Lawyers Foundation Commission on Professional Responsibility, *The American Trial Lawyers Code of Conduct* (public discussion draft, June 1980), Rule 1. For Monroe Freedman's views, see his *Lawyers' Ethics in an Adversary System* (Indianapolis: Bobbs-Merrill, 1975).

10 *ABA Model Rules*, Rule 1.13(b), (c).

11 *ABA Code*, DR 4-101(c)(4).

12 For a statement of this sort, see Cleary et al., *McCormick on Evidence*, 191.

13 Among the standard essays on the subject are Monroe Freedman, *Lawyers' Ethics*; Charles Curtis, "The Ethics of Advocacy," *Stanford Law Review* Vol. 3 (1951); Henry Drinker, "Some Remarks on Mr. Curtis' 'The Ethics of Advocacy,'" *Stanford Law Review* Vol. 4 (1952); Marvin Frankel, "The Search for Truth: An Umpireal View," *University of Pennsylvania Law Review* Vol. 123 (1975); Monroe Freedman, "Professional Responsibility and the Criminal Defense Lawyer: The Three Hardest Questions," *Michigan Law Review* Vol. 64 (1966). See also David Luban, "Professional Ethics: A New Code for Lawyers?" *Hastings Center Report* Vol. 10 (1980): Thomas D. Morgan, "The Evolving Concept of Professional Responsibility," *Harvard Law Review* Vol. 90 (1977); and Murray Schwartz, "The Professionalism and Accountability of Lawyers," *California Law Review* Vol. 66 (1978).

14 There are of course other sorts of information that might be conveyed, e.g., about third parties, about the facts. I am simply not considering the disclosure of such information in this paper.

15 I use the term "obligation" in a loose way such that whenever it is appropriate to say of someone that they morally ought to do something, they can be said to have an obligation to do it. Philosophers who wish to restrict the term "obligation" to contexts in which there are

social rules and institutions will not like my usage, but I don't think it begs any substantive questions.

16 By contrast, positive, nondamaging information is typically nonconfidential unless confidentiality is requested.

17 These other demands, incidentally, may involve not only obligations to third parties but to the speaker himself, when revealing the information would be for the speaker's own good.

18 I think that ethical theories (e.g., utilitarianism) that contain only one basic principle or theories (e.g., Rawls's) that contain a number of principles but rank them in accord with strict priority rules do not show enough sensitivity to moral autonomy, which requires leaving open the possibility of judgment opposed to the principle or the priority rules if the balance of reasons seems to go that way.

19 See the two notions of a moral position that Ronald Dworkin discusses in his treatment of the enforcement of community morality, *Taking Rights Seriously* (Cambridge, MA: Harvard University Press, 1978), 248-53.

20 The general obligation of loyalty and the obligation to fill the demands of a role one plays can perhaps also be understood along these lines. To have obligations based on loyalty to someone or some entity, or to have an obligation because one fills a role, is to consider oneself unfree to act in certain respects as an autonomous moral agent, because one is under the moral control of the person or role and must act according to their wishes or requirements. I cannot pursue this more general issue here. For a provocative discussion of how this may characterize the lawyer's role, see Richard Wasserstrom, "Lawyers as Professionals: Some Moral Issues," *Human Rights* Vol. 5 (1975): 1-24.

21 *ABA Code*, DR 4-101 (A).

22 At least one court has ruled that all client communications, even of positive information, are protected by Canon 4: *Doe v. A Corp.*, 330 E Supp. 1352, 1355-56 (S.D.N.Y. 1971), *aff'd. sub nom Hall v. A Corp.*, 453 F. 2d 1375 (1972).

23 Freedman, *Lawyers' Ethics*, 4.

24 The claim that everything the client may feel inclined to say must be kept confidential has a great deal of cogency if applied to a psychotherapist; in such a context any information may have a symbolic meaning for the problem at hand. But the lawyer does not have the same job as a therapist. (In *Tarasoff v. Regents of University of California*, 551 P. 2d 334 [1976], however, it was ruled that psychotherapists are liable at tort if they don't reveal dangerous information that results in someone's death.)

25 An interesting version of this argument, applied to medical contexts, is given by Kenneth Kipnis, "Review Article: Alan Goldman's The Moral Foundations of Professional Ethics," *Westminster Institute Review* Vol. 1, No. 3 (October 1981): 8-10.

26 The 1980 version of the Model Rules contained a rule of this form (*ABA Model Rules*, Rule 1.7(b), (c). But they have now been changed to make discretionary the disclosure of information needed to protect someone from death or serious injury.

27 Criminal cases, civil cases, and negotiations will obviously need relatively different treatment in these respects.

28 Freedman, *Lawyers' Ethics*, 31.

29 Ibid., chap. 3.

30 See Wasserstrom, "Lawyers as Professionals." For another discussion that also emphasizes the lawyer's own autonomy, see John J. Flynn, "Professional Ethics and the Lawyer's Duty to Self," *Washington University Law Quarterly* 1976 (1976): 429-44.

◆ ◆ ◆ ◆ ◆

LEE A. PIZZIMENTI

Informing Clients About Limits to Confidentiality

The legal ethics rules concerning the maintenance of client confidences are varied and confusing, and many exceptions exist allowing or mandating the lawyer to disclose confidences. For example, lawyers must disclose client perjury in many states, and they often have discretion to report future crimes, or to disclose information necessary to protect themselves or collect a fee.[1] Yet, clients expect lawyers to keep their secrets. Lawyers encourage that belief, either by misstating the scope of protections or by saying nothing to clients and allowing television or friends to serve as the source of information.[2] In a recent survey of attorneys, Professor Zacharias found that 22.6% "almost never" informed clients abut confidentiality, and 59.7% stated that they informed clients in less than 50% of their cases.[3] In fact, 72.1% of the lawyers surveyed admitted they told clients "only generally that all communications are confidential."[4] As a result, many clients believe that anything they tell their lawyers will never be disclosed to anyone.[5]

Suppose, then, that a lawyer discloses client information. The client may feel that the lawyer has misled him, or, at a minimum, has not provided him with an adequate opportunity to consider whether he should share information with the lawyer. That is, his decision to confide in the lawyer was not an informed one. The question then becomes whether the client should be the one to make that choice, and, if so, whether other considerations outweigh that right.

Rule 1.4 of the Model Rules of Professional Conduct recognizes that lawyers must provide information to the extent "reasonably necessary to permit the client to make informed decisions regarding the representation." However, not all decisions are to be made by the client. The traditional approach is that "procedural," or tactical, decisions are to be made by the lawyer, while the client makes "substantive" decisions.[6] The notion supporting this dichotomy is that a lawyer is in a better position to evaluate those tactical decisions requiring professional discretion.

A lawyer may argue that whether a client should be told about confidentiality exceptions demands an examination of personal and professional ethics that transcends the attorney-client relationship. She may support that position by recognizing that client consent is but one of many exceptions to the rule requiring confidentiality. Thus, one could view the decision as akin to a professional, tactical one rather than a substantive client decision.

While it may be concluded after consideration that lawyers should refrain from informing clients about confidentiality exceptions, it is improper to conflate the questions of making disclosures to third parties and giving clients information about that possibility. Just as a lawyer should not decide to disclose client information until after she undertakes a careful balancing of rights at stake, the lawyer should not withhold information from the client until she has made that analysis. I will undertake to consider that question now.

Using the substance/procedure analysis to determine what rights are at stake is not useful, because issues that are ostensibly procedural can have a profound impact upon clients. Professor David Luban provides the example of an innocent client being prosecuted for murder who forbade counsel from calling an alibi witness. While one might claim that choice of witnesses is a tactical matter, the client refused for what he viewed to be a "substantive" reason: the witness was his best friend's wife, who would testify that he had been with her during the time the crime had been committed.[7] A less provocative example might be that a client negotiating a long term contract would prefer that a lawyer be accommodating to the other party to assure a comfortable working relationship with him, while the lawyer might wish to allow no compromise in order to effect the best possible agreement.

Recognizing the artificial distinction between substance and procedure, commentators agree that the appropriate focus should be on client expectations rather than upon whether the lawyer historically has made decisions of the type contemplated.[8] Instead, the lawyer should consider whether the client would view the information as material to his decisionmaking. This focus is consistent with the doctrine of informed consent in the medical profession and with Model Rule 1.4.[9] More important, it helps assure that the lawyer will treat her client as an individual rather than merely as a means to illustrate her professional skill and standards.[10] Thus, to determine whether it is appropriate to withhold information, one must balance the rights implicated by the failure to allow informed consent against countervailing rights affected if clients are apprised of confidentiality's limits.[11]

A requirement of informed consent is necessary to protect the right of autonomy, which is derived from the Kantian notion of respect for persons as ends in themselves rather than as simply means to another goal.[12] As Gerald Dworkin explains, the ability to make decisions reaffirms our sense that we are individuals able to control our own destiny.[13] Thus, the ability to make autonomous choices reaffirms our status as persons.

To assure that autonomy, lawyers must recognize their duty of veracity toward clients, which includes not only the duty to refrain from misstatements, but also the affirmative responsibility of candor.[14] Veracity is critical to the maintenance of autonomy, because a lack of it creates two obstacles to autonomous decisionmaking: limiting information limits choices, and, almost inevitably, the client may be manipulated if an attorney withholds or misstates information.[15] Thus, failure to share the material fact that secrets may be disclosed has an immediate and substantial impact on client autonomy.

In most cases, failure to disclose limits to confidentiality should be deemed an intentional act as a lawyer is bound to know the requirements of the code of ethics in her state.[16] Intentional deception creates additional strains upon the attorney-client relationship, even if the client is unaware of the deception. First, the lawyer may feel compelled to make additional false statements to avoid discovery of the original deception.[17] Moreover, the attorney may become less sensitive to the morality of her actions: "lies seem more necessary, less reprehensible; the ability to make moral distinctions can coarsen; the liar's perception of his chances of being caught may warp."[18] Finally, the lawyer who successfully deceives may view her client as being easily duped. Consequently, the attorney's respect for the client as an autonomous moral agent may be reduced.[19] Perhaps she may develop a general unwillingness to respect the client's rights, or those of other clients.[20] A lack of informed consent about limits on confidentiality also presents an interesting irony: the lawyer makes a misrepresentation regarding secrecy to clients to create an atmosphere encouraging candor. Such lawyers "would prefer, in other words, a 'free-rider' status, giving them the benefit of lying without the risks of being lied to."[21]

It is clear, then, that deception concerning confidentiality can immediately destroy the foundation of the attorney-client relationship and the client's right to autonomy. Of course, the right to autonomy is not absolute. Although increasing autonomy is good in the abstract, it may not be justified in cases where autonomous decisionmaking leads to immoral results.[22] Thus, one must also consider the rights of the lawyer or third parties at stake if the lawyer informs the client of exceptions to confidentiality and the client chooses to refrain from confiding in the lawyer.[23] However, autonomy is a "prima-facie" right entitled to great deference,[24] and the lawyer attempting to justify deception must overcome a strong presumption that the client is entitled to information.[25]

Deception is most justified when it prevents imminent bodily harm to a third party.[26] Such deception is justified for three reasons: there is a limited time available to evaluate alternatives; the right to bodily integrity is a strong countervailing one; and deception typically occurs in such isolated instances that it probably will not encourage others to lie.[27] Such a rationale might, for example, serve as a justification for failure to inform the parent of a child who is admitted to an emergency room with injuries clearly stemming from abuse that the incident must be reported. Otherwise, the parent may remove the child, who then would not receive care. In the attorney-client context, deception may be appropriate where the client has a history of violent behavior, making it more likely that third parties might be harmed.[28]

The difficulty with this analysis is that it assumes that clients will not inform of their intention to commit a harmful act absent a promise of confidentiality, and lawyers will therefore be unable to prevent harm. In fact, clients may tell lawyers anyway, either because they feel compelled to confess or because they recognize they will receive better representation if they talk to their lawyers.[29]

There is, in addition, an analytical problem with using the paradigm of avoidance of bodily harm as a blanket justification for deception. Deception about possible disclosure occurs from the commencement of the relationship, when it is unclear whether anyone's interests are implicated, let alone an innocent third party's interest in bodily integrity. Thus, the lawyer cannot evaluate the alternatives, nor can she determine the likelihood or severity of an infringement of a third party's rights at the time of the deception. Thus, the lawyer cannot evaluate the strength of the justification for the deception at the time it occurs. Moreover, a policy of not disclosing limits on confidences, if intentional, goes beyond the isolated incident that will not encourage others to lie. Rather, it reflects an ongoing practice of deception.

If the possibility of averting bodily injury does not serve to justify a policy of deception, it follows that deception is not justified by the possibility of perjury, or that a lawyer may avoid harm to herself if

her competence is challenged or if she must collect a fee.[30] In fact, if situations invoking those exceptions arise more often than threats of bodily harm, the greater likelihood of occurrence makes the information more material to the client.

Lawyers may fear that informing clients of the limits to confidentiality will chill attorney-client communications. Other than the possibility of harm to the lawyer or third parties, which is too speculative to serve as support for deception, the only danger of a chilling effect is that the client may not confide information the attorney finds necessary for competent representation. One can analogize this argument to the discredited and paternalistic notion that patients should not be told of risks because they might not submit to procedures that are "good" for them.[31] So long as a client is made aware that the lawyer may be hampered in her representation if the client does not confide in her, the choice of whether to confide belongs to the client.

One exception to the notion that lawyers may not consider the chilling effect that informing the client might have is where the client appears extraordinarily nervous and mistrustful, and the lawyer feels immediate warnings will destroy the relationship before it is established. Commentators have recognized that short term paternalism may be necessary to enhance autonomy in the long run.[32] However, as David Luban indicates, there are strict limits to when deception is justified, even for a brief period: the decisionmaker's capacity must be impaired; the constraint must be as limited and temporary as possible, and the threatened damage must be severe and irreversible.[33] I would add that if the attorney believes that confidences potentially damaging to the client are imminent, deception even in the short term is unjustified as the impact on autonomy would be irreversible. Absent these special circumstances, however, a presumption arises that informing clients about limits to confidentiality is necessary.

One obvious question that arises is how much information the lawyer should share. Providing the client with an equivalent of a law school education by explaining all of the nuances of confidentiality rules seems unnecessary and, in fact, would be counterproductive, as studies have shown that providing too much information reduces the recipient's ability to understand. However, the attorney should give a general explanation of the duty of confidentiality and its major exceptions. In that way, the client will have enough information to enable him to ask intelligent questions as specific confidentiality issues arise. If it becomes clear to the attorney as the representation progresses that the client needs more specific information because an exception may apply, she should raise the issue again.

Of course, not all information is material to every client. Three variables might be considered in determining when to inform the client. First, the lawyer might evaluate the relative sophistication of her client. A lawyer dealing with in-house corporate counsel may assume the client is aware of confidentiality sections. Although some cases have shown corporate officials are unaware of the nuances of legal representation,[34] one may assume they are generally more sophisticated than some other clients. Arguably, knowledgeable clients do not require warnings to make informed decisions.

Next, the lawyer could evaluate the likelihood that information might be confided. For example, Model Rule 2.2 requires that a lawyer serving as intermediary between clients inform them that no attorney-client privilege exists regarding communications between any of them and the lawyer. Similarly, Model Rule 1.13 requires that a lawyer inform a corporate officer that she is not his attorney. Both rules are based on the notion that it is foreseeable that problems could arise. For example, this factor would support a rule that lawyers should warn criminal clients about the potential for disclosure of future crimes or of fraud on a tribunal. If fee disputes are common, that exception should be disclosed.

Finally, the nature of the confidences to be shared is relevant. A client will be more concerned about disclosures involving highly private or harmful information than about more innocuous information. Perhaps, then, exceptions concerning crimes or frauds should be raised, but the fee exception need not be as only general information is disclosed. The client might also be interested in learning that a lawyer may exculpate herself by inculpating the client.

While use of these factors would be better than giving no consideration to client concerns, there are two grave problems with relying on them. First, selective information may be more misleading than no information at all. Recitation of some exceptions may lead the client to believe there are no others.

Second, use of the factors tends to treat clients as groups rather than as individuals, which is contrary to the central notion of the informed consent requirement. Rather than enhancing autonomy of the individual client in an individual case, the lawyer relying on the factors above runs the risk of creating "a standardized person to whom he attributes standardized ends,"[35] and "acting for the hypothetical client rather than the one before him."[36] This approach depersonalizes the client and treats him as an object. To assure true autonomy, the lawyer must not decide what she thinks the client wants or needs, but must explore the client's actual goals with him.

As a result, while the above factors might be useful, they cannot be dispositive. The lawyer must engage the client in an ongoing, personal discussion to enable her to determine what matters to the client. Perhaps that discussion could begin with a statement such as the following one, which is drafted to apply to a criminal client:

> You should know that I work for you and that I consider it very important to keep your confidences. The attorney-client privilege essentially means that I cannot be forced to disclose information about discussions we have. For example, judges sometimes can order lawyers to disclose information, but they can't make me tell them

about whether you committed the crime.[37] You should know about some limits to the privilege, however. I am an officer of the court, and I cannot help you commit any frauds upon the court. Therefore, if I learn that you will lie or have lied on the witness stand, I must report that.[38] I am also allowed to report if you tell me you are going to commit a crime. I may also report limited information to defend against claims made against me or to collect my fee, but I am allowed to report only that information necessary to meet those goals. For example, if we fight about my fee, I might be able to show my billing records, but I couldn't just reveal all the things I know about you. Although there are times I may feel it is necessary to report information, I want to remind you that I take the privilege very seriously and would never lightly decide to share information.

Those reading this suggested statement might believe all of this sounds terrible and the client would view the lawyer as greedy and self-protective.[39] This response is like shooting the messenger rather than wishing the message were different. The ethics rules provide for these exceptions, and if they sound as if ethical priorities are misplaced, the rules should be changed. So long as they exist, however, the client should be aware of them. Of course, absent modification of the rules, one alternative to revealing the more self-serving of those exceptions is that an individual attorney may decide as a matter of personal ethics not to warn regarding those exceptions, because she intends never to invoke them. In this way, no deception occurs.[40]

Assuming no explanation of exceptions occurs, and the client confides evidence he would not have absent a belief it would remain confidential, the client has lost the right to make autonomous decisions with adequate information. The lawyer should be held responsible for that loss. First, a lawyer may be disciplined for violation of Model Rule 1.4. Moreover, the client could bring an action for lack of informed consent. If there are no actual damages from the lack of informed consent, at least nominal damages and possibly attorney fees should be assessed.[41] Because an action for breach of the fiduciary duty of candor is a tort claim,[42] emotional distress damages, if proved, should be allowed. Punitive damages may be appropriate where reckless disregard is shown.[43]

Although informing clients of limitations on confidentiality might inhibit the rights of the lawyer or third parties, those rights are varied and speculative. Conversely, deception regarding limitations has an immediate impact of reducing autonomy and impairing the attorney-client relationship. Thus, an attorney is morally required, and should be legally required, to be forthright with a client and to allow the client to choose whether the risks of disclosure outweigh its benefits.

NOTES

This paper is adapted from *The Lawyer's Duty to Warn Clients About Limits on Confidentiality*, 39 Catholic U. L. Rev. 801 (1990), copyright 1990 Catholic University of America. It is printed with their permission.

1 See, e.g., *Model Code of Professional Responsibility* DR 4-101(c) (1980); *Model Rules of Professional Conduct* 1.6(b), 3.3 (1983) (hereinafter *Model Rules*). Confidentiality rules vary greatly among states. See Pizzimenti, "The Lawyer's Duty to Warn Clients About Limits on Confidentiality," *Cath. U.L. Rev.* Vol. 39: 801, 810 n.34; 829 n.126 (1990).

2 Zacharias, "Rethinking Confidentiality," *Iowa L. Rev.* Vol. 74: 351, 382-83 (1989).

3 Ibid.

4 Ibid. at 386.

5 Ibid. at 383. Of those clients surveyed regarding confidentiality, 42.4% believed that confidentiality requirements were absolute.

6   See *Model Rules, supra* note 1, at 1.2(a).

7   Luban, "Paternalism and the Legal Profession," *Wis. L. Rev.* 454, 456 (1981). For other example of procedural issues with substantive impact, see Ibid. at 454-59.

8   See, e.g., Maute, "Allocation of Decision-making Authority Under the Model Rules of Professional Conduct," *U.C. Davis L. Rev.* Vol. 17: 1049, 1080-1105 (1984) (tactics/substance dichotomy not dispositive); Spiegel, "Lawyering and Client Decisionmaking: Informed Consent and the Legal Profession," *U. Pa. L. Rev.* Vol. 128: 41, 72-133 (1979) (same); Strauss, "Toward a Revised Model of Attorney-Client Relationship: The Argument for Autonomy," *N.C. L. Rev.* Vol. 65: 315, 336-49 (1987) (same).

9   Such a shift in emphasis would track developments in informed consent in the medical profession. See Martyn, "Informed Consent in the Practice of Law," *Geo. Wash. L. Rev.* Vol. 48: 307, 333-40 (1980). Prior to the decision in Canterbury v. Spence, 464 F.2d 772, 787 (D.C. Cir.), *cert. denied*, 409 U.S. 1060 (1972), reasonableness of disclosures was examined in light of medical custom; that is, from the perspective of doctors rather than patients. See Martyn, *supra*, at 336. In *Canterbury*, recognizing the fiduciary nature of the doctor-patient relationship and the primacy of patient expectations, the court held that "the patient's right of self-decision [is] the factor that determines the scope of the duty to reveal." Ibid. at 337. See also *Canterbury*, 464 F.2d at 786. Under the *Canterbury* approach, the scope of the requirement of informed consent in medical practice is now determined not by the custom of medical professionals but by the patient's right to information necessary for making an intelligent choice. Martyn, *supra*, at 338. *Canterbury* did not go far enough, however, because it used an objective standard of materiality rather than a subjective inquiry into the client's needs. See, *infra* notes 35-36 and accompanying text.

10 This is not to say that a lawyer should always do the bidding of her client. See *infra* notes 22-23 and accompanying text. It simply means that the lawyer must take into account the impact on client autonomy when evaluating the morality of an action.

11 I do not by suggesting the need for balancing rights implicated by an action mean to advocate adoption of a utilitarian standard. See *infra* note 23. However, justifications using a utilitarian theory can be raised. See, e.g., note 13 *infra*.

12 Kant provided a deontological approach to determining morality. A deontological theory is one based on the notion that the "right, the obligatory and the morally good" are not determined by reviewing the consequences of an action, but by reviewing the intrinsic morality of the act itself. W. Frankena, *Ethics* 14 (1963).

Kant is perhaps the best known rule-deontologist. Rule deontologists recognize that standards of right and wrong may be expressed through general rules. Kant articulated a basic principle, the categorical imperative, as the standard by which to determine which acts are moral: "*Act as if the maxim of your action were to become through your will a* Universal Law of Nature." I. Kant, *Groundwork of the Metaphysics of Morals*, 89, 96 (H. Paton, trans. 1964) Further, Kant adds to the imperative that one should "[a]ct in such a way that you always treat humanity ... never simply as means, but always at the same time as an end." Ibid. at 96 (footnotes omitted). Kant posits that human beings have a *duty* to act in a manner consistent with the categorical imperative. See ibid. at 19.

The formula, simply put, asks whether the proposed rule may be equally applied to everyone, without exception, and whether the proposed rule treats persons as ends in themselves and not only as means to some end which is not their own. That is, we must ask whether the proposed act uses people ... and whether the rule applies to everyone....

R. Wright, *Human Values in Health Care: The Practice of Ethics* 32 (1987). It should be noted that to pass this test, the actor must will the rule to be applied recognizing that he may be on the "receiving end" of such a rule on some occasion. W. Frankena, *supra* at 25. For an excellent explanation of the categorical imperative, see T. Mappes and J. Zembaty, *Biomedical Ethics* 17-22 (2nd ed. 1986).

Other deontological theorists have articulated somewhat more specific duties consistent with the requirement of universal generalization and respect for persons. For example, W.D. Ross finds duties of fidelity (based on implicit promises to tell the truth); reparation (based on a previous wrongful act); gratitude (based on previous services on actor's behalf); justice (distribution of happiness according to merit); non-maleficence (duty to refrain from harming others); beneficence (duty to promote good, based on possibility we can improve the lives of others); and self-improvement (based on ability to improve our own lives). W.D. Ross, *The Right and the Good* 21-23 (London: Oxford Press, 1930).

The notion that human beings must be treated with respect and as ends in themselves leads naturally to the idea that we have some inherent rights because of our status as human beings. R. Wright, *supra* at 37. See also, R. Faden and T. Beauchamp, *A History and Theory of Informed Consent* (New York: Oxford Press, 1986); W. Frankena, *supra* at 45 (moral rights and duties are correlative). Medical scholars

first articulated rights-based theories as resting on the notion that inherent rights are given by God and cannot be taken away by man. R. Wright, *supra* at 37. The primary non-theological basis of inherent rights is found in the notion of autonomy: since human beings have the inherent right to self determination, it is improper to interfere with that process. Ibid.; see R. Faden and T. Beauchamp *supra* at 7-9.

13 Dworkin, "Autonomy and Informed Consent," in President's Comm. for the Study of Ethical Problems in Medicine & Biomedical & Behavior Research, *Making Health Care Decisions: The Ethical and Legal Implications of Informed Consent in the Patient-Practitioner Relationship* Vol: 3: 74 (1982) (quoted in Strauss, *supra* note 8, at 337.) Thus, autonomy is justifiable as a good in itself. Dworkin, *supra*, at 73-74. Moreover, principles of utility justify informed consent: they assure that individual choice is maximized, resulting in client satisfaction; attorney and client are protected from the dangers of poor communication; the public may be less skeptical of the legal profession; and they encourage self-scrutiny. Strauss, *supra* note 8, at 338. See Martyn, *supra* note 9, at 318-21 (informed consent increases self-scrutiny and public involvement in affairs of profession).

14 This right is drawn from the fiduciary nature of the attorney-client relationship. M. Bayles, *Professional Ethics* 72 (2nd ed. 1989).

15 R. Wright, *supra* note 12, at 94 (1987).

16 Nondisclosure may not be intentional, however, when an attorney mistakenly believes the information withheld is not relevant to a client. While such failure is not as morally culpable as deliberate nondisclosure, it still violates client autonomy, which is the value underlying an attorney's duty to inquire in order to determine what the client thinks is material. See Martyn, *supra* note 9 at 323 (citing J. Story, *Commentaries on Equity Jurisprudence* § 208 [fiduciary

has affirmative duty to disclose facts and circumstances principal would find important]).

17 S. Bok, *Lying: Moral Choice in Public and Private Life* 15 (1978).

18 Ibid.

19 The lawyer may reach this conclusion to reduce his or her own feelings of guilt. The attorney may conclude it is the client's "fault" that deception was necessary, or the client's "fault" that he is too dense to recognize the deception.

20 Disdain for the client's right or ability to make intelligent decisions may result even when the lawyer lies for the client's "own good." The lawyer may come to view the client as unable or unworthy to decide for himself. S. Bok, *supra* note 17, at 76.

21 S. Bok, *supra* note 17 at 23. The fact that the client trusted the lawyer will exacerbate the inevitable feelings of betrayal that will result if the client learns the lawyer has disclosed private information, regardless of whether the lawyer intended to mislead.

22 See Luban, "The Lysistratian Prerogative: A Response to Stephen Pepper," *Am. B. Found. Res. J.* 637, 639 (1986).

23 Because apprising clients of confidentiality enhances the right of autonomy but may implicate other rights, one must determine which performance would result in the greatest balance of right over wrong. W.D. Ross, *supra* note 12, at 41 (1930). Recognizing that one should consider immoral results, as well as the intrinsic features of an act, does not result in the adoption of a utilitarian theory. Ross explained the difference:

> If I have promised to meet a friend at a particular time for some trivial purpose, I should certainly think myself justified in breaking my engagement if by doing so I could prevent a serious accident or bring relief to the victims of one. And the

supporters of the view we are examining hold that my thinking so is due to my thinking that I shall bring more good into existence by the one action than by the other. A different account may, however, be given of the matter, an account which will, I believe, show itself to be the true one. It may be said that besides the duty of fulfilling promises I have and recognize a duty of relieving distress, and that *when I think it right to do the latter at the cost of not doing the former, it is not because I think I shall produce more good thereby but because I think it the duty which is in the circumstances more of a duty.*

W.D. Ross, *supra* note 12 at 18 (emphasis added). See also, ibid. at 33 (act is right only with reference to its "whole nature"). One can see the distinction if he keeps in mind the idea that the failure of utilitarianism is its inability to recognize a just result in a particular case.

> The essential defect of the "ideal utilitarian" theory is that it ignores, or at least does not do full justice to, the highly personal character of duty. If the only duty is to produce the maximum of good, the question who is to have the good—whether it is myself, or my benefactor, or a person to whom I have made a promise to confer that good on him, or a mere fellow man to whom I stand in no such special relation—should make no difference to my having a duty to produce that good. But we are all in fact sure that it makes a vast difference.

W.D. Ross, *supra* note 12, at 22.

24 Rule deontological theories such as Kant's were problematic because theorists viewed both formulating a universalized rule with no exceptions and developing rules which do not

conflict with one another as impossible. W. Frankena, *supra* note 12, at 23. W.D. Ross attempted to deal with this problem through a theory of "prima-facie" duties. W. D. Ross, *supra* note 12, at 20. Ross posits that there may be exceptions to rules regarding "actual duties," which prescribe what should be done in a particular situation. Ibid. Prima facie duties, however, are essentially presumptions that certain duties are morally required to be performed absent some countervailing interest. Ibid. Ross also explains that "prima-facie" terminology is not intended to connote an illusory or easily ignored right. Ibid. The prima facie rules are universal and do not have exceptions; however, they might conflict with other prima facie duties. W. Frankena, *supra* note 12, at 24. As Ross explains, a "prima-facie duty ... [is] a brief way of referring to the characteristic ... which an act has ... of being [one] which would be [an actual duty] if it were not at the same time [another act] which is morally significant." W.D. Ross, *supra* note 12, at 19. For example, keeping a confidence regarding a client's intent to murder a third party contemplates two acts with moral significance: maintaining client autonomy (a fiduciary's prima facie duty), and arguably giving aid to a person causing death (which violates the prima facie duty of non-maleficence). Both duties are compelling; the question becomes how to balance those duties. See *supra* note 23. The notion of prima facie rules can also be applied to rights. Deontological moral philosophers have generally accepted the notion that certain duties and rights are prima facie moral demands which can be overridden only in the most compelling of circumstances. See T. Beauchamp and J. Childress, *Principles of Biomedical Ethics* 345-47 (1979); R. Faden and T. Beauchamp, *supra* note 12, at 16-17; R. Wright, *supra* note 12, at 36-38; Landesman, "Confidentiality and the Lawyer Client Relationship," in D. Luban, *The Good Lawyer: Lawyers' Roles and Lawyers' Ethics* 191, 200 (1985); Moore, "Limits to Attorney-client Confidentiality: A 'Philosophically Informed' and Comparative Approach to Legal and Medical Ethics," *Case W. Res. L. Rev.* Vol. 36: 177, 192 n. 68 (1985). See also W. Frankena, *supra* note 12 at 35 (moral rights and duties are correlative). In fact, the example provided above could be phrased in terms of prima facie rights: The prima facie right of client autonomy conflicts with the prima facie right of the third party to life.

25 Bok adds that because liars tend to provide a "more benevolent" interpretation of their actions than would others, S. Bok, *supra* note 17, at 86-7, any justification must withstand the test of publicity and appeal to a common view of propriety. Ibid. at 91. Kant would allow no justification for deception, finding the duty of truthfulness "a sacred and absolutely commanding degree of reason, limited by no expediency." Truth is required regardless of the harm to the liar or innocent third parties. Kant, "On a Supposed Right to Lie from Altruistic Motives," reprinted in S. Bok, *supra* note 17, at 267-269. Most commentators recognize that deception is excused in certain circumstances. *See* S. Bok, *supra* note 17 at 39-42, R. Wright, *supra* note 12, at 95.

26 S. Bok, *supra* note 17, at 105-09.

27 Ibid.

28 Although the rights of third parties are most clearly at issue in such a case, the information is also more material to the client, and of a more private nature than some confidences. Perhaps as a result, most commentators believe that patients who are tested for AIDS should be informed of the doctor's responsibility to report results, and of the economic and social consequences that may follow disclosure. See, e.g., McDonald, "Ethical Problems for Physicians

Raised by AIDS and HIV Infection: Conflicting Legal Obligations of Confidentiality and Disclosure," *U.C. Davis L. Rev.* Vol. 22: 557, 588 (1989) (duty to advise clients in high risk categories); Swartz, "AIDS Testing and Informed Consent," *J. Health Pol., Pol'y & Law* Vol. 13: 607, 613-15 (1988) (doctors should explain implications to health and lifestyle); Weldon-Linne, Weldon-Linne, and Murphy, "AIDS-Virus Antibody Testing: Issues of Informed Consent and Patient Confidentiality," *Ill. B.J.* Vol: 75: 206, 210 (1986) (duty to warn of ramifications of testing, including possibility of disclosure). See *People v. Younghanz*, 156 Cal. App. 3d 811, 202 Cal. Rptr. 907 (1984) (psychologist must inform patient of duty to report child abuse in order to protect patient privacy).

29 Subin, "The Lawyer as Superego: Disclosure of Client Confidences to Prevent Harm," *Iowa L. Rev.* Vol. 70: 1091, 1163-64 (1985); Zacharias, *supra* note 2, at 369.

30 For a discussion of the moral justifications for the various exceptions to confidentiality rules, see Pizzimenti, *supra* note 1, at 827-31, and sources cited therein.

31 The desire to do what is best for the client is a laudable one, based on the principle of beneficence, or providing benefits (which includes both prevention of harm and promotion of welfare). See T. Beauchamp and J. Childress, *supra* note 24, at 194-95. However, failure to provide informed consent for the client's "own good" creates a conflict between the principles of beneficence and autonomy. Ibid. at 210. In medical ethics, it is generally recognized that beneficence must give way to promotion of autonomy, at least where the patient is competent.

> The primary goal of health care in general is to maximize each patient's well-being. However, merely acting in a patient's best interests without recognizing the individual as the pivotal decisionmaker would fail to respect each person's interest in self-determination ... When the conflicts that arise between a competent patient's self-determination and his or her apparent well-being remain unresolved after adequate deliberation, a competent patient's self-determination is and usually should be given greater weight than other people's views on that individual's well-being ...
>
> Respect for the self-determination of competent patients is of special importance ... The patient [should have] the final authority to decide.

Ibid. at 210, (quoting President's Commission, *supra* note 13, at 26-27, 44 [1983]).

32 See T. Mappes and J. Zembaty, *Biomedical Ethics* 55 (2nd ed. 1986).

33 Luban, *supra* note 7, at 465.

34 See, e.g., *Brown v. E.F. Hutton*, 305 F. Supp. 371 (S.D. Tex. 1969) (corporate officer unaware attorney did not represent him as well as corporation).

35 Lehman, "The Pursuit of a Client's Interest," *Mich. L. Rev.* Vol. 77: 1078, 1087 (1977). See Anderson, "Informed Decisionmaking in an Office Practice," *B.C.L. Rev.* Vol. 28: 225, 233 (1987) (using the "reasonable client" approach to materiality assumes that clients fit into categories and that it is permissible to treat them alike).

36 Lehman, *supra* note 35, at 1087.

37 In another setting, the lawyer might say the court cannot force her to disclose her client's negligence, breach of contract, or other past act which is the subject of the representation.

38 This statement assumes the lawyer lives in a jurisdiction where such disclosures are mandated. Professor Judith Andre suggested in response to my talk that lawyers should re-

mind clients that lawyers will not aid clients in wrongdoing. She reasoned that absent a clear message that perjury is unacceptable, the information that lawyers must disclose serves as an aid in violating the law, as a "fuzzbuster" would. Articulating a concern for the law would, she added, render the speech instead analogous to providing information about traffic laws. I recognize that the problem of an intelligent client getting the message that it is fine to lie so long as the lawyer is unaware of the lie is unavoidable. However, because it is impossible to evaluate the likelihood or seriousness of perjury at the time the lawyer deceives the client, the lawyer must inform the client of the perjury exception. Professor Andre's formulation might deter some clients from lying, so I am grateful for the suggestion.

39 It may also be argued that the client may be deterred from making disclosures. To the extent this is an exercise in client autonomy, this response is appropriate. To the extent it may frighten an individual so much he is unable to make a decision, it may be morally justifiable to delay disclosures about limits, but only if several requirements are met. See *supra* notes 32-33 and accompanying text.

40 An attorney may also decide as a matter of personal ethics to refrain from disclosing perjury, but she thereby runs the risk of violating an ethics rule and subjecting herself to discipline.

41 Anderson, *supra* note 35, at 250.

42 Cf. *Olfe v. Gordon* (breach of the fiduciary duty of following client instructions is malpractice).

43 Anderson, *supra* note 35, at 249-50.

IS THERE A DUTY TO REPRESENT?

CHARLES W. WOLFRAM

A Lawyer's Duty to Represent Clients, Repugnant and Otherwise

In the course of a conversation about some differences between legal and moral obligations, my colleague Steven Munzer once offered the example of an executioner in a state that had established the legality of capital punishment. His brief analysis was that the executioner's work could well be regarded as legally appropriate—or at least legally neutral (subject to no legal sanction of disapproval)—but morally objectionable. In some senses it is not overly drastic to substitute the figure of the lawyer for that of the executioner. Indeed, the executioner in a capital pun-

ishment jurisdiction can do no grisly work until a prosecutor has employed considerable lawyerly skills and persuasively urged a judge or jury to impose the death penalty. If, then, one supposes that the executioner's act is morally objectionable, although legally permissible, is not the prosecuting lawyer's the same? Or can it be said, as many lawyers would say, that a lawyer enjoys a special moral immunity from judgments about acts taken in behalf of a client?

A lawyer's decision whether or not to represent a prospective client whose objectives are morally objectionable raises two separate issues, the second of which I will pursue here. The first, and extensively debated, issue is whether, once a decision to represent the client has been made, the lawyer may be tarred with the same brush as the client. Many of the essays in this collection skillfully elucidate various facets of this problem. A time-honored focus of this debate is the conduct of the criminal defense lawyer in defending a person known by the lawyer to be guilty of the crime charged. There are probably disparities between the professional and the lay resolutions of this problem. The professional view is that defense of the known guilty person is appropriate in order that the established governmental system, and not private lawyer perceptions, determine guilt and innocence. This professional stance is supported by a principle of professional detachment under which a lawyer is not to be regarded as endorsing the client's political, economic, social, or moral views.[1] The nonprofessional view probably does not so readily or so often put distance between the lawyerly agent and the client principal. Despite the familiarity and attractiveness of the professional view, to my way of thinking the problem remains a troublesome one.

The principle of professional detachment does not claim that in fact all lawyers are innocent of moral views about a client's objectives. It seems instead to assume that a lawyer will typically be willing to sublimate moral repulsion to the requirements of the service function of providing legal assistance, or of the economic function of making a living or living well. But suppose a perhaps unusual case. Suppose that a lawyer in fact feels unwilling, at least at the outset, to set aside personal moral values to further the immoral ends of a prospective client. Is the lawyer nonetheless required to represent the client? A variety of settings suggest themselves. One of the most prominent in recent years was raised by the decision of ACLU lawyers to accept as clients members of the American Nazi party who had been refused permission by local authorities to hold an anti-Jewish parade in Skokie, a predominantly Jewish community near Chicago.[2] Or consider a case in which the operator of a "dirty bookstore" wishes representation to resist efforts of governmental officials or private citizens to limit or altogether ban distribution of pornography. Or consider a lawyer asked by an embattled president of the United States to represent him personally in resisting attempts to force

disclosure of potentially damaging materials in the course of an investigation into widespread corruption of the political process.[3] Or consider a lawyer asked to represent a chemical company in resisting the efforts of a governmental agency to restrict its operations pending investigations concerning serious public health risks posed by them.

Many lawyers would find it repugnant to support or further in a personal way the cause of the "deserving guilty," Nazis, pornographers, a president who has corrupted the political system, or environmental polluters. The untutored instinct is that the representation of any such client should, at most, be left to the discretion of the lawyer asked to undertake it. On closer examination, however, both the moral and to some extent the legal dimensions of these, I hope, representative and interesting settings give rise to a substantial doubt that a lawyer never is obliged to accept a case of a repugnant client.

But starting with the repugnant client is starting backwards. It must first be established whether or not there is a duty to represent in any case, including the much more usual situation in which no strong moral objection to the client's objectives is present. It is clear that if no general duty exists, a duty to represent morally objectionable clients becomes impossible to support.

I will first review briefly the "professional" regulations that lawyers have drafted for themselves. The view apparently reflected there is that no duty exists to represent any client except in a very specialized case: where a court or bar association appoints the lawyer. Beyond the professional obligation, however, it appears that in many other situations lawyers of normal moral sensitivity personally would feel compelled to represent a client whose case they would not otherwise handle. In these situations the necessitous client has a compelling need for legal services that can be satisfied only by the lawyer who is requested by the client to take the case. After this review, I will return to the specialized problem of the repugnant client.

Professional Regulations

At present, under the American Bar Association Code of Professional Responsibility, there is no firm basis for stating that any obligation to represent a client exists that will be enforced by professional discipline, some suggestion that an ethical (non-enforceable) obligation to represent a client exists only if the lawyer is appointed by a court or bar association to defend a person accused of a crime, and some basis for concluding that a lawyer is ethically permitted (but not obliged) to represent any person in any other case. The special problem of the lawyer's moral objections to a client's objectives is mentioned only tangentially.

The ABA's code, as is well known to lawyers, is divided into "Disciplinary Rules," which are enforceable by formal disciplinary procedures, and "Ethical Considerations," which are said to be merely unenforceable ethical aspirations.4 No Disciplinary Rule bears upon our question, but a number of Ethical Considerations (ECs) mention it. EC 2-26 states that the objective of making legal services fully available means that "a lawyer should not lightly decline proffered employment" and "requires acceptance by a lawyer of his share of tendered employment which may be unattractive both to him and the bar generally." Yet, earlier in EC 2-26 it is stated that "a lawyer is under no obligation to act as advisor or advocate for every person who may wish to become his client...." On the subject of "unpopular clients and causes," EC 2-27 invokes a history "replete with instances of distinguished and sacrificial services by lawyers who have represented unpopular clients and causes." It continues, "regardless of his personal feelings, a lawyer should not decline representation because a client or cause is unpopular or community reaction is adverse." But EC 2-30 states that a lawyer should not "accept" employment "if the intensity of his personal feeling, as distinguished from a community attitude, may impair his effective representation of a prospective client." Unpopular clients are

specifically mentioned in EC 2-28, which states that a lawyer's desire not to antagonize judges, other lawyers, public officials, or influential members of the community "does not justify his rejection of proffered employment." The implicit notion is that employment can be rejected, but only for good reasons, and that fear of antagonizing powerful adversaries or others is not a good reason.

Ethical Consideration 2-29 states a general ethical obligation of lawyers to accept appointments by a court or bar association to represent a person who is unable, "whether for financial or other reasons," to obtain other counsel. A lawyer should "seek to be excused from such appointments only for 'compelling reasons,'" and these "do not include such factors as the repugnance of the subject matter of the proceeding, the identity or position of a person involved in the case, the belief of the lawyer that the defendant in a criminal proceeding is guilty, or the belief of the lawyer regarding the merits of the civil case." Appointments of the kind alluded to occur very commonly in criminal defense representations, but relatively rarely in civil cases in the United States. And, while EC 2-29 is open to the implication that a lawyer who is not under the special obligations of an appointment may reject a prospective client for uncompelling reasons, such a reading would conflict with the explicit statements in EC 2-27 and EC 2-28 of an obligation not to decline representation of an unpopular client or cause because of popular feelings alone.

In distilled form, under the ABA code a lawyer has professional discretion to accept or reject any proposed representation. Even the obligation to accept a court or bar association appointment is stated only in an Ethical Consideration and thus, at least as far as the code is concerned, is an ethical and not a disciplinary obligation. In exercising that discretion, the lawyer is told by the code not to decline representation lightly and not to reject a client because of the unpopularity of the client or cause unless the lawyer's personal feelings on the matter would prevent effective representation. The code is silent, however, on whether a lawyer whose feelings would not prevent able advocacy may nonetheless decline a representation because of moral qualms about the client's objectives or methods.[5]

The American Bar Association recently replaced the code with a redrafted Model Rules of Professional Conduct.[6] This contains a rule that makes mandatory, and thus a ground for professional discipline, the ethical prescription of the present code that a lawyer accept appointed cases. Rule 6.2 states that "a lawyer shall not seek to avoid appointment" but allows that "good cause" provides an excuse. And Rule 6.2(c) states that good cause includes the fact that "the client or the cause is so repugnant to the lawyer as to be likely to impair the client-lawyer relationship or the lawyer's ability to represent the client." The official commentary to Rule 6.2 states flatly that "a lawyer ordinarily is not obliged to accept a client whose character or cause the lawyer regards as repugnant."[7]

Thus, under the new Model Rules as under the existing code, it appears that a lawyer has professional discretion to accept or reject any case, except for an appointed case. In fact, unlike the code in EC 2-26, the Model Rules and commentary do not suggest that a lawyer in a nonappointment situation must have a reason at all, good or bad, to decline a representation. And there is no requirement that a lawyer represent a repugnant client, in a nonappointment setting, even if the lawyer's feelings would not prevent an adequate relationship and representation.

Dimensions of a Moral Duty to Accept a Client

Given the present professional regulations, it seems quite unlikely that professional discipline would be visited upon a lawyer for declining to represent a client for any reason aside from court appointments. But that observation does not, of course, end the inquiry, for a lawyer of normal moral instincts will not lead a

professional life impelled only by the direct and sanctionable commands of professional regulations. The important question remains: is there a moral duty to represent? Parenthetically, I might add that if one did conclude that a professional regulation with the force of law required a lawyer to accept a representation— for example, as the new Model Rules clearly do in the instance of a court appointment—then, unless the legal duty were morally objectionable, it would create a moral obligation to obey.

The problem of defining and elaborating the moral obligations and prerogatives of a lawyer confronted with a request to represent someone whom he or she is not disposed or legally required to represent calls forth the image, known both to law and to philosophy, of the rescuer. In law, courts in the United States and in other common-law countries generally have rejected a duty to rescue a person in peril unless there exists one of a relatively narrowly defined kind of special pre-existing relationships.[8] But the reasons given for rejecting a general legal duty to rescue have nothing to do with morality. Instead, they are based on a tradition in the common law to find liability only where affirmative acts have caused injury and, more important perhaps, on apprehensions about difficulties in administering a legal duty to rescue.[9] But while denying that the potential rescuer who fails to act may be held liable in damages, judges have left little doubt that they regard the unmoved spectator as a moral derelict.[10] Thus, an adult on a bridge who fails to throw an available rope to a drowning child may escape legal liability but will incur the moral condemnation of almost every lawyer and judge.

The philosophical basis for a duty to rescue is explicable whether one's starting point is a theory based on utilities or one based on rights and obligations that are posited for reasons not related necessarily to consequences. On a utilitarian calculus, at least where the cost to the rescuer is nonexistent or slight and the benefit to the victim is great, a duty clearly stands out.[11] Indeed, because of the importance of protecting the victim and the assumed small cost to the rescuer, the possibly more substantial intellectual task for the utilitarian is to put meaningful limits on a duty to act benevolently.[12] Philosophical theories based on rights and nonutility-based obligations also recognize a duty to rescue. Concern for the rights of the victim calls forth an obligation on the part of available rescuers to supply aid. Even within individualistic ethical systems that give great attention to the right of the potential rescuer to act on the basis of self-interest, where the inconvenience of rescue to the rescuer is slight or nonexistent, little can be said to resist the intuitive appeal of a duty to rescue.[13]

The generally recognized moral duty of an adult, for example, to save the life of a drowning child by throwing a readily available rope does not immediately translate, of course, into a general duty on the part of every lawyer to lend assistance to every client in need of legal services. Several additional factors remain to be considered: the capacities of the lawyer, the risk that may be incurred by the lawyer or caused to others, and the nature of the client's legal needs.

Capacity to Rescue

No one would suppose that a duty to rescue should be visited upon one who was incapable of discharging it. So a lawyer will not be bound to accept a case in which he or she is not competent to render the kind of legal service that other available lawyers could provide. Indeed, in an era in which specialized knowledge and skills are required for capable performance in many areas of practice, the lawyer's lack of competence strongly operates as a reason not to accept the client. As will be seen, a special problem of competence is presented when the lawyer's personal repugnance to the client is so strong as to preclude effective representation. Yet it is important to note that the "rescue" contemplated need not be a perfect one. That the lawyer may be less competent than other lawyers, none of whom will accept the case, does not mean that the lawyer's assistance

will be entirely ineffectual. If the lawyer's assistance would materially aid the client, even if not perfectly, then there might be a duty to give such assistance as is possible. For example, the lawyer may render assistance by helping the potential client to find another lawyer who could handle the case quite competently. Or the lawyer may assist the client by preparing legal documents even though the lawyer would not be permitted to appear in court in the client's behalf because, for example, the lawyer is not admitted to practice before that court.

Risk to the Rescuer and Others

A duty to rescue is modulated by the extent to which the potential rescuer is exposed to risk. To toss a drowning child a rope that lies nearby is one thing; to plunge into a raging torrent is another. A potential rescuer may properly take into account the extent of personal risk. Similarly, no moral fault can be found if the would-be rescuer makes a decision for morally acceptable reasons to save one drowning child rather than another, where only one can be saved. This is true as well where the decision is personalized, or arguably "selfish," as where the child chosen to be saved is the rescuer's own or even is saved from a significant but lesser danger, for example, from the risk of a serious crippling injury but not death. The duty to rescue can be overridden by other compelling duties, loyalties, or interests.

Yet there are limits on the risks that negate a duty to rescue. Minor inconvenience, it seems, should not suffice. A casual distaste for young children or a desire not to soil a fine new pair of gloves on a dirty rope would not excuse a failure to rescue a drowning child. In the middle range will be difficult questions of degree in which the morally appropriate decision will require a careful balancing of the risk that the rescuer would incur against the certainty and magnitude of the danger confronting the victim.

Among these difficult, middle-ground problems are issues of economics. To what extent, if any, should a claimed duty to rescue give way where effecting a rescue would be uneconomical for the potential rescuer? For example, while morality would not require a sea captain to subject his or her own ship and crew to certain danger to rescue the crew of another ship, what if the time required to effect the rescue would merely spoil a perishable cargo? Or what if the sea captain would become personally liable for additional days' wages for the crew or would lose additional cargoes waiting in port that would go to other ships because of the delay? Most moral systems would conclude that, while rescue under these circumstances is morally correct, even morally heroic, it is not required due to the sacrifice of the rescuer's own substantial interests that would be involved. This idea is captured in some of the literature by the concept of the "easy rescue."[14]

As applied to a lawyer, these ideas imply a duty to accept a case only where a similar lack of risk to the lawyer or to others would be present. If there is time in the working day, the task is within the normal competence of the lawyer, no great financial sacrifice would be required, and no competing professional, family, or personal need would be seriously compromised, then acceptance of the client would seem required—at least in "necessitous" instances.

Danger to the "Necessitous" Victim

A duty to rescue will also depend on a high likelihood of a significant danger to the victim whose rescue uniquely requires the rescuer's labors. At the outset, of course, the victim's plight would have to be known. Beyond that, the perceived probability of danger must be high. A probabilistically remote danger might strike the potential rescuer as so unlikely as not to require intervention. In part this idea turns on the probability that the danger will be able to be averted in some other way, perhaps by the victim personally. To the extent that this is not true, even a remote danger may, depending on its magnitude, require some kind of intervention.

The danger must also be substantial. A risk that a child tottering on the edge of a shallow puddle will get wet without apparent risk to life or health would raise no duty. A prospect of certain drowning clearly would.

A final element of necessitousness is that the rescuer's efforts are uniquely required by the victim. Buster Crabb can help himself in deep water, and even if the victim is knocked unconscious an onlooker might be entitled to assume that a lifeguard who has gone to the rescue can do the job without further aid. But if a potential rescuer knows that all members of a crowd of spineless spectators are unwilling to render assistance, then the simple presence of a crowd should not justify inaction.

For the lawyer, determining a potential client's "necessitousness" will require an inquiry into the client's circumstances. Trivial or minor client matters, such as enforcement of parking tickets, would give rise to no duty, Among these would be cases in which only small monetary values, relative to the client's needs, are at stake—return of a property deposit from a landlord, and the like. In other situations the client can do without a lawyer's aid, either through self-help or through the assistance of others. There is also no duty to represent clients seeking something which a just law does not allow. And, as we will see, in the case of a repugnant client, other distinctions along these lines may be required. For the moment, the basic proposition is that in the absence of particularly serious harm to the client no duty to represent exists.

The client must also be in danger of losing a significant legal interest specifically because of the absence of *this* lawyer's legal assistance. If many other lawyers are available and willing to handle the client's case, our lawyer is not required to lend assistance. Thus, in the normal case a lawyer need have no moral qualms about concentrating in a narrow legal specialty even if that means sending away potential clients with real legal needs, so long as other lawyers are available to service those needs. Not surprisingly, therefore, there can be no moral objection—although some have imagined one[15]—to a "public interest" practice confined to a set of clients (and not to their adversaries) who are identified by political, economic, or social criteria. Alleged polluters, for example, are not deprived of needed representation because an environmental public interest lawyer group represents only the victims of pollution.

But what if the potential client is in dire need of this lawyer's assistance because, although other competent lawyers are available, they refuse to assist, perhaps systematically, and perhaps for morally objectionable reasons? Suppose, for example, that our lawyer feels, rightly, that more than a "fair share" of necessitous clients have already come to him or her because other lawyers have failed to perform their moral duty to assist needful clients? Can our lawyer now act similarly, on the ground that the client's necessitousness is caused by the dereliction of moral duty on the part of the other lawyers?

No: a duty to supply available food to a starving person is not excused if the victim's starvation is someone else's fault. Indeed, the moral duty to rescue a starving person exists even when the starvation is the result of a deliberate state policy; the duty to represent a necessitous client exists even when a professional regulation or custom states that there is no duty of representation. It is the client's need, and not the third-party cause of it, that generates a duty to act.

A related question arises when the number of potential necessitous clients is large. Does a lawyer's duty to act lessen as the number of victims requiring aid increases? Does the duty exhaust itself once one potential victim is assisted? Again, my answer is negative. Unless one loses sight of the fact that each victim is a separate person with a separate need, one victim's claim is not lessened because many others have similar claims. Of course, the plight of many may be relevant to a rescuer's decision about strategies for helping.[16] The good person with an abundance of food will feel a compulsion to share this

surplus with those who are hungry. But one would not condemn this person for refusing to share part of the abundance with *X* because the abundance has been depleted by sharing it with *Y, Z*, and others. So a lawyer may defensibly decide to represent only necessitous welfare claimants and not to accept as clients criminal defendants. Relatedly, once one's abundance of food has already been depleted by sharing, one's moral duty has been quitted. There is no moral duty to impose significantly upon oneself or one's own family in order to assist others, even others who are in greater need. To this extent, then, once a lawyer has committed significant resources to the representation of necessitous clients, the lawyer's moral obligations are satisfied even though the legal needs of other unrepresented persons are still unmet.

A final matter concerning necessitousness—windfalls—requires attention. Does the duty to rescue extend only to preventing dangers or also to assisting a "victim" who would be able to achieve a fortuitous advantage? Suppose a rich aunt is writing a will and, because she mistakenly thinks the law requires it, she intends reluctantly to give her estate to a ne'er-do-well niece instead of to a valued friend who is not a relative. Or suppose that, because of her mistaken notion, she intends to give the estate to charity or, more radically, to convert it to cash, which she will burn. Does a person in the unique position of knowing the aunt's intentions have a duty to the aunt's friend to intervene to ensure that she receives the bequest or does the fact, which we will assume, that the friend has no need for these funds preclude a duty to rescue? My tentative notion is that any duty to assist that might exist here is one of considerably lesser force. The question will be pursued further in connection with the repugnant client problem.

The duty to represent that this "rescue" analysis posits is, I assert, a not inconsiderable one. The American system currently relies very heavily upon private-practitioner representation in most areas of legal rights other than criminal defense, an area in which public defender and similar, governmentally supported systems have recently been established in most locations. In other areas of legal right, the American system has placed lawyers in a position like that of a public-utility monopoly. No one but a certified lawyer may render legal services. And, because of the legal system's complexity and inaccessibility, legal services are virtually indispensable in many contexts if persons are to be assured of their legal rights. To the extent that lawyers are not available to render needed legal assistance, then, in fact, prospective clients will not obtain what the law otherwise would have allowed. Given the collective resources of the private bar, it is probable (although anything approaching firm statistics are lacking) that American lawyers as a group are not fulfilling a moral duty to provide legal services to those who are badly in need of them. Presumably it is to fulfill more adequately such a responsibility that proposals are being urged to make pro bono practice by lawyers mandatory.[17]

A Duty to Represent a Repugnant Client

Does a Nazi, whose views are repugnant to the lawyer, stand in the lawyer's office in the same posture as any other necessitous client? Or is a lawyer ethically entitled to reject this representation on the ground that Nazi tenets are repugnant? If so in some cases, is this true in all? I believe that the necessitous but repugnant prospective client should be represented in some cases, but only if (1) the client's claim is legally just, (2) the client's claim is a morally important and compelling one, and (3) the client's need for this particular lawyer's services is truly pressing. Overall, my view is that necessitousness should here be considered in a special sense that permits the moral lawyer to take fully into account the precise moral nature of the legal claim that the repugnant client wishes to assert.

Capacity to Represent Effectively

Some lawyers would probably claim that their emotional and philosophical revulsion against Nazism and, to some extent, against one who espoused it was so strong that they could not competently represent such a client. The claim must be taken seriously. The lawyer's role in the United States is typically one in which some significant—at least vicarious, but perhaps more personal—identification occurs between lawyer and client. One need not embrace the ultimate prescription of William Kunstler that he would only represent a client whom he loved. Somewhat less dramatically, many lawyers believe that they function best if they are able to share and agree with the values, beliefs, and goals of the client. This lawyer-client identification is doubtless sometimes feigned. But often it must be real. There is no reason to think that American lawyers as a group—who, as a group, seem so comfortable with their clients' objectives—are particularly good actors or possess in unusual measure the psychological hardihood (or, possibly, even defects of character) that would permit daily work in behalf of persons whose goals and beliefs were sharply divergent from their own.[18]

Much of this follows from the American style—perhaps found nowhere else in such vigor—of intense lawyer loyalty to the client in adversarial representations. Now, as a century ago, a client typically is represented by a lawyer who is expected to, and most often does, throw himself or herself into the representation with little emotional or personal reserve. The "exertions" of an American lawyer in behalf of a client are not merely physical—time spent, energy expended—although these may be substantial. More than this, American lawyers and their models (F. Lee Bailey, Percy Foreman, Melvin Belli) often perform with great investments of emotional resources.

Personal repugnance, then, may create a situation in which some lawyers cannot make the customary emotional commitment. As a result, those lawyers' representations might be defective in the normal emotional commitment that those lawyers would make in other representations and that other lawyers—including the lawyer on the other side—would make in the present case. Competence here is not merely a flat-voiced recitation of the leading cases and statutes that support the client's position. It is, if called for, an impassioned plea, and all the rhetorical rest. If it is lacking, then adversaries, judges, jurors, peers, and one's own client might well notice and act upon the difference, and the lawyer's work will not be of the same value to the client as another's would have been.

Nevertheless, if the choice is between this kind of flawed representation and no representation at all, and so long as the client chooses knowingly, it seems that even a representation that may be hobbled by the lawyer's personal rejection may be better that none and, if other criteria are fulfilled, may even be required.

Risk to Rescuer and Others

Would a lawyer be morally justified in refusing legal assistance to a repugnant client because of the harm that might be inflicted upon the lawyer and the lawyer's other clients and family as a result of the representation? Take the decision of the American Civil Liberties Union and its lawyers to represent the American Nazi party in its effort to stage an anti-Jewish march through Skokie. Setting aside any strategic decisions about defending civil liberties, would a duty to represent have existed if one could have foreseen the quite considerable harm that the ACLU suffered as a result of its decision to provide representation?

One with a sensible set of moral values would hesitate a long time before foisting extreme heroism upon ordinary moral agents. A desire not to ruin one's private practice or one's organization, not to impair seriously the extent to which one can make credible arguments in behalf of other clients, not to bring public scorn upon one's family and friends—these and similar concerns are legitimately compelling. And, depending upon the extent of the hypothetical Nazi client's need, they might prevent any duty to represent from arising.

An additional element is that a representation that is forced upon a lawyer necessarily requires the lawyer to compromise or to surrender a considerable measure of personal autonomy. Those who hold, as I do, that individualism, at least in the realm of ideas and beliefs, is an important moral value must take into account the fact that a duty to represent a repugnant client will require the lawyer to suspend, if not to sacrifice, an important part of his or her intellectual and moral freedom. In striking a balance here, some measure of the strength of the prospective client's claim to representation must also be taken into account.

What Counts as Repugnance?

In order to strike a balance between the intellectual and moral freedom of a lawyer and the legal needs of a repugnant client, the concept of "repugnance" requires more elaboration that it has thus far received. This is true both with respect to the reasons that legitimately count in generating a characterization of repugnance and with respect to the possible reach of such a characterization.

First, what makes a client "repugnant" and thus serves as a reason for refusing legal assistance to one in need of it? Repugnance may be virtually self-defining for many in the case of representing a Nazi to further the morally objectionable propaganda projects of Nazism. What of a prospective client who is repugnant, not because of an ideology, but because of a different defect of character—for example, a remorseless murderer? Or a grasping entrepreneur who, quite profitably, is engaged in the business of manufacturing "Saturday Night Specials"—small firearms that are used by purchasers chiefly for illegal and often deadly purposes?[19] Or a greedy manipulator who uses legal technicalities to seize the property of the poor?[20] Are all deficient characters to be treated the same? Are remorseless jaywalkers the same as murderers? What of persons of different political parties from the lawyer's? Persons who enjoy popular music or otherwise display unsound aesthetic values?

Second, does a lawyer's moral repugnance legitimately reach only the particular legal matter—the particular morally repugnant project or incident in which the client is involved? Or are some persons—such as a Nazi, a remorseless murderer, a cold-hearted land speculator, and the like—so pervaded by a repugnant characteristic or character that any legal matter brought to a lawyer by such a client would be properly rejectable, regardless of whether or not it was directly related to the source of the lawyer's abhorrence?

Certainly not all possible reasons for differing from another person can count as grounds for "repugnance." Some reasons would have to be rejected as trifling or as the overly judgmental reactions of a senselessly severe moral, political, or aesthetic prudery. To refuse to represent a prospective client, who otherwise would be forced to proceed without a lawyer, on the ground that he or she is a member of another major political party is to demonstrate a failure of ethical judgment, not an abundance of it. Of course, in unusual situations an attorney may have a reasonable conscientious objection to the project that the prospective client has undertaken and for which legal assistance is needed. A lawyer, for example, may conscientiously object to filing suit to block certification of the election of a prospective client's political adversary if the lawyer reasonably believes that the law unwisely gives some support to the prospective client's position.[21] On the other hand, if a newspaper illegally refuses to print a political advertisement of a Republican, even a lawyer who disagrees with Republicanism and with the specific message sought to be published would probably feel that this ideological difference is not a sufficient reason to reject a representation that seeks to uphold the values of free expression. The difference from

the election suit is that here, presumably, the lawyer has no conscientious scruple with the law protecting free expression and, while differing with it, no strong moral objection to the advertisement.

Repugnance might stem not from ideology but from character defects of the prospective client— such as the remorseless murderer. It is readily imaginable that a lawyer would find that too heavy a sacrifice of his or her reasonably held beliefs about goodness would be entailed by accepting such a representation. Suppose, for example, that a remorseless person has been convicted on overwhelming evidence of a horrible murder. The convicted person wishes the lawyer to handle a discretionary appeal (for which there is no right to a court-appointed lawyer). A lawyer who feels that the conviction was morally justified may reasonably feel strong moral scruples against obtaining release of the deservedly convicted person on possible technical grounds unrelated to the fact of guilt or innocence. Such a lawyer should not be considered to be under a moral obligation to deny those scruples and to accept the representation to file the appeal.

Professor Murray Schwartz argues in Chapter 6 that a moral duty to afford representation in civil cases may exist regardless of the immorality of the client's ends. This is said to be true when the client could not function effectively in the legal system without counsel and the client has a legal entitlement to claim a morally objectionable "good." But the moral duty is not borne by individual lawyers. Each remains free in most instances to reject morally repugnant representations. The concept is one of social justice rather than one of individual morality: the moral duty is borne by "the legal system" and not by individual lawyers. But it is not clear to me that a legal system that leaves immoral claimants of legal rights unrepresented (although not preventing them from obtaining counsel if individual lawyers are willing to represent them) is necessarily unjust.

Professor Schwartz is concerned chiefly with a situation in which the manufacturer of "Saturday

Night Specials" is threatened with an unlawful attempt by a town council to close his business.[22] Professor Schwartz's formulation attempts to take account of the prospective client's immorality and the gravity of the harm to the prospective client, but apparently he is prepared to find these criteria satisfied for this prospective client.

I do not agree that a legal system should be accounted unjust if it leaves unrepresented this particular litigant whom no lawyer will represent because of moral objections. The gun manufacturer, to be sure, will probably lose future profits and might even be unable to shift operations to a morally unobjectionable product and so perhaps will lose the value of the business itself. The injustice of leaving this and similar shady operators to the collective moral judgment of lawyers apparently springs from a perceived defect in a legal system that accords legal rights that are unenforceable because of the seriatim refusal of lawyers to lend their skilled and necessary assistance to enforce them. But why is this society unjust?

The answer does not lie in some assumed categorical supremacy of legal rights over moral claims, for Professor Schwartz is willing to give dominance to some moral claims over some legal entitlements. Nor does his position seem to depend upon some calculus of utilities; we are given no reason to think that the entrepreneur's loss through nonrepresentation would be nonutilitarian. Professor Schwartz's position incorporates a formula from, but is not compelled by, two dicta in decisions of the United States Supreme Court. The first decision rejected a claimed constitutional right to a hearing prior to agency termination of disability benefits; the second rejected a claim of constitutional right to appointed counsel in the case of an impoverished parent whose children were taken away in an uncounseled proceeding.[23] In the course of each decision, the Court majority conceded arguendo that a right to counsel might exist in some civil cases. But the concession, as lawyers know, was quite unnecessary to the decision in the particular cases, and the Court would

probably feel free in a future decision to deny that any such right existed in any case.

Instead, the justification for Professor Schwartz's position seems based upon a notion that a right to legal representation is both superior (at times) to moral claims and instincts and is separable from the immorality of the ends to which prospective clients seek to put the imperfect machinery of the law. Representation in this view becomes an end in itself. But legal representation seems without significance apart from the uses to which it is put. It is merely process and is not detachable from the outcomes it produces. If we were to change the hypothetical situation and assume that the morality of the acts of the gun manufacturer is unclear, then the process value of legal representation becomes more compelling. At least then one can say that the resolution of doubtful moral positions should be shouldered by a just society in order to ensure that erroneous moral judgments do not prevent morally deserving claimants of legal rights from obtaining their legal and moral due.[24] But that is a different situation from the one portrayed by Professor Schwartz in which we are to stipulate the moral wrongness of the prospective client's alms.

In any event, for present purposes I assume that the decision on representation confronts an individual lawyer and does not involve a decision about the justness of an entire legal system. I also assume that the lawyer acts reasonably and on adequate information in determining that the prospective client's goals are morally objectionable. Such a lawyer, in my view, is always entitled to take this into account in deciding whether to represent.

Ethical "Shunning"?

What about a legal matter brought to the lawyer in which the client does not seek directly to further goals that the lawyer regards as repugnant? May a lawyer refuse to assist a Nazi, or a remorseless murderer, or a handgun manufacturer, or a grasping land speculator, to buy a personal home? To adopt a child? To defend against an attempt to terminate welfare? Or to defend against the state's attempt to take away parental rights?

Is "ethical shunning" of this kind legitimate? The lawyer could argue that there is no moral obligation to give legal support and comfort to an ethically worthless person. Ethical instincts of this kind seem to inform many people's attitudes and actions in everyday life. Persons with ongoing immoral projects and with prominent immoral acts in their past frequently find themselves avoided by others with whom they might wish to deal.

But one may properly be concerned that such a position might give insufficient regard to the human dignity even of moral reprobates. Ethical shunning is an extreme stance that intuitively seems legitimate only with respect to extreme instances of unrepentant moral agents. It strikes me that it would be inappropriate if carried to the extent of attempting to legitimize rejection of representation on all unrelated legal matters brought by any person whose representation the lawyer properly may have rejected on another matter. For example, the unrepentant political activist who wishes to take advantage of an unwise law to unseat an elected opponent does not seem to have acted in a way that forfeits his or her claim for legal services on totally unrelated matters. To take a more difficult case, it seems to me that under present social and political conditions in the United States, it goes too far to reject the case of the unrepentant Nazi with unrelated welfare or parental rights problems.

Who Is a "Necessitous" Client?

Recall that even in the instance of an unrepugnant prospective client, a duty to represent does not arise for minor legal matters. A duty lies only where the hurt to the client because of the lack of representation threatens to become severe. A fortiori, the loss to a prospective repugnant client normally must be even greater. The problem that remains is to supply more precisely articulated measures of the "weight" to be accorded to different client needs.

At one extreme, consider an innocent Nazi erroneously accused of a serious crime who comes to a competent defense lawyer after being rejected by many other lawyers. Assume that the situation had arisen at a time when there was no right to a court-appointed lawyer in criminal cases. May this lawyer decline the representation on the ground of a strong revulsion against Nazism and its adherents? Even if the prospective client's Nazi beliefs have something to do with the charged offense, still I believe that a duty to represent may exist. For example, if the offense charged was murder and the Nazi had killed the decedent in self-defense against an attack that was caused by the decedent's strong anti-Nazi sentiments, the threatened imprisonment of an innocent would be critical. Even if the Nazi refused to regret the death, even delighted that it was necessary and that a skilled lawyer might obtain an acquittal, still the unwarranted threat to the Nazi's freedom from the impending criminal proceeding would create a duty to rescue.

Suppose, in contrast, that the Nazi seeks the vindication of a right of free speech in order to be able in the future to spread, legally but viciously, Nazi gospel about Jews and blacks. If a lawsuit could protect that right, is a lawyer entitled to refuse the representation, even if this means that the Nazi's legal right to speak will not be vindicated? My conclusion is that no lawyer has any duty to assist such a representation. This situation and that of the innocent Nazi accused of murder are different in several ways. Unlike the murder situation, here the abhorrent ideology of Nazism is central to the proposed course of conduct. With the lawyer's assistance the ideology can be broadcast; without it, it will be suppressed, even if against the legal right of the Nazi to free expression. Critically different from the unjust murder charge, here the Nazi proposes to engage in future elective behavior. Moreover, it is behavior that will impose harm upon the targets of the speech, Jews and blacks, whereas an acquittal of an unjust murder charge will have no "victims." Note that there still is a reason why a lawyer of normal moral instincts might decide to accept the representation: unlawful governmental interference with free speech may encourage more governmental lawlessness. But that threat does not seem so great as to override by itself a lawyer's conscientious scruple against the representation.

Nor do I think that "necessitousness" is present in the following situation. Suppose now that the Nazi wishes to purchase a house, a transaction that, we will assume, requires legal assistance that no other lawyer will provide. As in the criminal defense situation, one could view this as an instance in which the Nazi is sanctioned by the practical need for legal representation and by the refusal of lawyers to provide it. As in the criminal defense situation, moreover, the Nazi is innocent of any wrong that would legally deprive him or her of the entitlement to housing; Nazis are not for that reason barred by law from purchasing houses. And, finally, unlike the free speech situation, here the lawyer's assistance would not have the direct effect of facilitating an act that the lawyer finds reprehensible (publication of Nazi racial views). How, then, can it be that the lawyer is freer in this instance to decline the representation than in the innocent defense situation?

The answer, to my mind, depends less on the nature of the legal rights that might be asserted by the client than upon the sort of human need that vindication of the legal right will fulfill in the particular case. In short, "necessitousness" for our purposes should not take its meaning primarily from legal concepts, but from the needs of human beings. The needs for freedom and dignity are implicated strongly, for example, when an innocent is accused of crime. But basic needs are much less strongly implicated when someone wishes to hold a parade or give a speech (unless all or most other avenues of expression are also closed). Similarly, these needs would typically not be implicated in a Nazi's desire to buy a house, unless, as would be highly unlikely, the purchase were necessary in order to provide essential shelter not available through other common means, such as rental.

Also excluded from the category of necessitousness would be "windfall" situations and certainly those in which vindication of the repugnant client's legal rights would be at another person's expense. Consider a case in which a person convicted of murder on overwhelming evidence is released following an appeal. The appellate court, we will imagine, concludes that the trial was fair and that a guilty verdict was inescapable under the evidence presented. Nonetheless, the court reverses for a reason that has nothing to do with fairness of the proceeding or accuracy of the determination—for example, because the legislature had mistakenly repealed the statute upon which the prosecution was based. The accused, released from all further obligation to stand trial as a defendant in a criminal trial by a legal technicality, comes to a lawyer for assistance in securing an inheritance from the murdered decedent. On the assumption that it would be legally possible for a civil trial to result in granting the murderer the inheritance, the objectionability of such a result, the outrageousness of the murder, and the lack of any compelling need for the inheritance would plainly permit any lawyer to decline the representation, even if this would mean that the murderer was unrepresented in efforts to obtain the inheritance.

In general then, the "rescue" obligation arises only when the prospective client seeks to vindicate a legal right to an essential human need. For anything else, I believe that the lawyer with moral objection to the prospective repugnant client may decline a representation. A fortiori, this means that a lawyer would never be required to undertake a representation in which the client's objective or the client's chosen means were clearly morally objectionable. This follows because the concept of essential human needs includes no right to act immorally or for immoral ends. Thus, a Nazi seeking to protect a legal right to circulate hate literature seeks no basic human right of his or her own. The grasping land speculator seeking to dispossess an impoverished householder seeks through law no basic human need; indeed, the speculator may be seeking to deprive the victim of satisfaction of such a need.

This overall view entails discrimination among various legal rights. For the limited purpose of determining whether a moral obligation to represent a client exists, most legal rights are thus viewed as nonabsolutes whose value and claim for recognition will wax and wane with the circumstances of their expression and with the extent to which they are important in vindicating underlying human needs. Rights of free expression, as I have developed in the example of the Nazi client, thus are not of unitary value. Racial hate (and pornography and other immoral, even if legal, expression) does not stand on the same footing as other forms of expression. Even a right to freedom, if based upon legal technicalities of the kind I have described, is not absolute, but can be ignored by a lawyer who on strong conscientious grounds determines not to represent the "deserving guilty."

The Problem of the "Lawyers' Trump"

Yet the image of an unrepresented client losing a valuable and legally defensible right because all lawyers refuse to lend their aid does not rest entirely comfortably on the mind. The refusal of any lawyer to provide assistance to a morally repugnant client takes on the appearance of an exceptional social policy forced upon a person because of rejection of his or her otherwise lawful or at least legally immune (if immoral) actions. It might be objected that the persistent refusal of lawyers to represent such persons places the seriatim, uniform judgment of lawyers in a position of veto over the considered judgment of public officials—those who promulgated the legal right to free speech regardless of its vicious content or to inherit from one's murdered victim in some circumstances. The resulting "lawyers' trump" replaces official judgments and policies with private

moral ones. Unless some mechanism were invented for testing lawyers' opinions by a court of review, we would have to defend the imposition of consequences through a process that is both informal and, arguably, illegitimate in a representational democracy. Nonetheless, I believe that limiting a duty to represent in the way proposed is justifiable.

Perhaps the most telling response to the "lawyers' trump" objection is that it is addressed more to reasons why a society might decide to enact laws requiring lawyers to represent even repugnant clients, or some of them in some situations. It is not an argument that uniformly held moral refusals to provide legal services are necessarily unjust. Political institutions sometimes do enact prophylactic laws because of a legislative suspicion about the process or the product of private judgments. Certain laws dealing with racial discrimination, for example, may be written broadly so as to sanction both morally inappropriate and morally appropriate behavior. A business, for example, will be precluded by law from participating in government contracts unless an announced percentage of the contractor's workforce are members of minority races. That the employer, in good faith and with great effort, has been unable to hire a sufficient number of minority workers may be legally irrelevant. Automobiles are legally constrained to operate at a speed of no higher than 55 miles per hour regardless of the safety of a higher speed at a particular time and regardless of the demonstrably greater gasoline economy of a higher speed for a particular automobile. In law, individuation may be either administratively infeasible or impossible to monitor because intent, motive, or similar internal sentiments may be a significant or the only relevant determinant.

But there should be no moral imperative to act in a particular way solely for the reason that other moral agents might act immorally in the same circumstances. Moral philosophy is all about individual states of mind, about subjective knowledge, intentions, and wishes. And on the level of just social arrangements, many kinds of commonly held moral judgments are not subjected to legal control although, similar to the "lawyers' trump," they can achieve a kind of uniform application that suggests extralegal legislation. Employers might uniformly refuse employment to a Nazi, legally in most jurisdictions as far as I know. Persons who know of a Nazi's beliefs might refuse them their friendship, refuse to greet them on the street, refuse to contract with them, move away from them in public places. We have assumed from the beginning that certain deeply held feelings of repugnance—toward Nazis, murderers, grasping entrepreneurs and others—are entirely defensible on moral grounds. If uniformity in moral judgments produces a de facto kind of extralegal social control, so long as the shunning is not itself unlawful, then it would seem that it is morally justified.

Yet a political system well might conclude that universal provision of legal services is still plainly warranted even if not compelled by individual morality. A legal system might determine for example that in fact many lawyers are failing in their moral responsibility to provide legal services to clients in need of them. It might be concluded that regardless of actual immoral practices of lawyers a legal system should always provide a method of last resort for reasons of appearances—some type of mandatory lawyer appointment—to assure even skeptics that no one has been deprived of a legal right because of a morally indefensible decision by individual lawyers not to provide representation.

Most importantly the analysis pursued here leaves two very numerous classes of potential clients without representation. The first class is composed of those whose representation would impose too great a burden on the lawyer, most obviously an economic one. The second class is composed of prospective clients asserting legal rights to what I have denominated nonessential human needs. A great many members of both sets will be persons whose lack of lawyer assistance is attributable to poverty. Recent severe restrictions of federal funding for legal services have exacerbated their plight. On my analysis individual lawyers are not required by good morals to make extraordinary efforts in the first case or any effort in the second. But a system that in effect permits access to its justice system to be allocated according to the ability of holders of legal rights to pay might truly be counted unjust. Both justice and sound policy may place demands for income redistribution upon a legal system that are radically different from the demands that morality places upon individuals for voluntary contributions to others who are in need.

NOTES

1 The Principle is implicit in Ethical Considerations 7-8 and 7-9 of the *American Bar Association Model Code of Professional Responsibility* and is stated explicitly in the code proposed to replace it—Rule 1.2(b) of *ABA Model Rules of Professional Conduct* (approved August 1983). See e.g., Murray Schwartz, "The Professionalism and Accountability of Lawyers," *California Law Review* Vol. 66 (1978): 609, where the principle of professional detachment is described. The principle of course is the subject of telling criticism in other chapters of this volume.

2 The legal position of the Nazis was ultimately vindicated by the United States Supreme Court. In *National Socialist Party v. Village of Skokie*, 432 U.S. 43 (1977) (per curiam), the Court held that the Illinois Supreme Court had erred when it refused to grant a stay of an Illinois trial court's broad injunction against the petitioners' marching, parading, and distributing pamphlets to incite or promote hatred against Jews. At later points in this paper, I take various liberties with hypothetical variants on the facts of this case.

3 Transparently, the reference is to *United States v. Nixon*, 418 U.S. 683 (1974).

4 *ABA Model Code of Professional Responsibility*, "Preliminary Statement."

5 Occasional statements can be found of a "duty" to accept unpopular clients or causes on the part of individual lawyers (see, e.g., Justice Marshall, concurring, in *re Primus*, 436 U.S. 412 470 [1978]) or on the part of the organized bar as an entity (see, e.g., Proceedings of the House of Delegates, *American Bar Association Report* 78 [1953]: 118, 133; Special Committee on Individual Rights as Affected by National Security, "Report," *American Bar Association Report* Vol. 78 [1953]: 304). The references seem always to be invoking an ethical, rather than a legal, imperative.

6 See *ABA Model Rules of Professional Conduct* (approved August 1983).

7 *ABA Model Rules of Professional Conduct* Rule 6.2, comment.

8 See, e.g., William Prosser, *Handbook of the Law of Torts*, 4th ed. (St. Paul, MN: West Publishing Company, 1971), 340-43; Fowler Harper and Fleming James, *Law of Torts* (Boston: Little, Brown, 1956), 1044-53. The rule of tort law has long been criticized on grounds as diverse as those of morality and of economics. See James Barr Ames, "Law and Morals," *Harvard Law Review* Vol. 22 (1908): 97, 110; William M. Landes and Richard A. Posner, "Salvors, Finders, Rescuers, and Other Good Samaritans: An Economic Study of Law and Altruism," *Journal of Legal Studies* Vol. 7 (1978): 83, 119-27.

9 See the critique in Ernest J. Weinrib, "The Case for a Duty to Rescue," *Yale Law Journal* Vol. 90 (1980): 247. Henderson, "Process Constraints in Torts," *Cornell Law Review* Vol. 67 (1982): 901, 925-43, criticizes Weinrib's failure to account for the "process" difficulties in defining and enforcing a duty to rescue. Henderson concludes that problems with comprehensibility, verifiability, conformability, and manageability of a legally enforceable duty to rescue

fully support the refusal of courts to create a general legal duty to rescue.

10 See, e.g., *Buch v. Amory Mfg. Co.*, 69 N.H. 257, 260, 44 A. 809, 810 (1897) (the nonrescuer "may, perhaps, justly be styled a ruthless savage and moral monster but he is not liable in damages ..."). Prosser, himself given at times to strong statement, recounted that common-law decisions refusing to end liability "are revolting to any moral sense" and noted that "they have been denounced with vigor by legal writers." Prosser, *Handbook*, 341.

11 Weinrib, "The Case for a Duty to Rescue," 280, 283, cites both Bentham and Mill.

12 Such an attempt is made by Weinrib, ibid., 281-86. Weinrib finds the necessary limitations upon what otherwise would threaten to become a senselessly broad duty of altruism in a need to avoid reliance upon assistance. This concern generates a postulate that requires that the victim face an emergency. This, in turn, has the effect both of reducing the incidence of the duty and of preventing victim self-generation of a duty to rescue.

13 Weinrib, ibid., 286-92, relies mainly upon Kant for a deontologically based duty to rescue. Even individualist thinkers are prepared to accept that wrongs can be committed under some circumstances by depriving a victim of assistance. See Charles Fried, *Right and Wrong* (Cambridge, MA: Harvard University Press, 1978), 114. Truly radical libertarian philosophers may not.

14 See Weinrib, "The Case for a Duty to Rescue," 279 ff.

15 In ABA Formal Opinion 334 (1974), the ABA Ethics Committee opined that there were only a limited number of criteria on which a legal services ("public interest") organization could decline to represent prospective clients. The source of the obligations, and the persons who bore them, were not identified. The opinion is

criticized in Gary Bellow and Jeanne Kettleson, "From Ethics to Politics: Confronting Scarcity and Fairness in Public Interest Practice," *Boston University Law Review* Vol. 58 (1978): 337.

16 The point seems to be missed in Robert Nozick, *Philosophical Explanations* (Cambridge, MA: Harvard University Press, 1981), 467 and 732 n. 63, where he attempts to refute the "stringent view" that a person is responsible for every evil that he or she could have prevented. Nozick argues that this would mean that such a person would be responsible for failing to prevent the sum total of all evil that could have been prevented. One may agree with Nozick that there is something counterintuitive about the claim that the nonactor is responsible for each evil not prevented, but disagree with the claim that the nonactor is responsible for none.

17 There has been little in the recent controversy over mandatory pro bono service by lawyers that throws much light on the philosophical question whether a moral obligation to represent may exist in certain circumstances. For example, David L. Shapiro has surveyed history, judicial decisions, the United States Constitution, economics, and the practices of other countries, and concludes that individual lawyers should not be under a formal professional mandate to serve clients without compensation. "The Enigma of the Lawyer's Duty to Serve," *New York University Law Review* Vol. 55 (1980): 735. With respect to matters of ethics, Shapiro leaves "the whole matter mired in difficult moral issues." Ibid., 792. His colleague Charles Fried, for one, has rejected the notion that there is ever a moral duty to serve without compensation. "The Lawyer as Friend: The Moral Foundations of the Lawyer-Client Relation," *Yale Law Journal* Vol. 85 (1976): 1060, 1079.

18 The point is made powerfully in Chapter 12 of *The Good Lawyer: Lawyers' Roles and Law-*

yers' Ethics, ed. D. Luban (Totowa, NJ: Rowman and Allanheld, 1983) by Andreas Eshete, "Does a Lawyer's Character Matter?" part ii. In Chapter 13, Gerald Postema also deals persuasively with the problem of professional character and moral character in his "Self-Image, Integrity, and Professional Responsibility." See also the excellent examination of this problem in his "Moral Responsibility in Professional Ethics," *New York University Law Review* Vol. 55 (1980): 60.

19 I take the example from Professor Murray Schwartz's "The Zeal of the Civil Advocate," Chapter 6, D. Luban, ed., *The Good Lawyer*.

20 Some earlier discussions in the symposia that gave rise to these essays involve the example of a real estate operator in a large city who assiduously scouted the tax rolls of the city for tax-delinquent property to buy. The law was assumed to be such that the speculator could quite legally buy up irrevocably the property of a poor person for a small fraction of its real value.

21 So, under the circumstances in *Brown v. Hartlage*, 456 U.S. 45, 102 S. Ct. 1532, 71 L. Ed. 2d 732 (1982), a lawyer might feel that denial of an otherwise fair election result to a candidate who made a campaign promise to reduce his or her government salary if elected, because of a dubious law that might treat such a promise as a "bribe," would be quite unwise and unfair. Indeed, a unanimous Supreme Court held that application of the law on such facts was unconstitutional. My point is that a lawyer may legitimately reject the representation on the ground that the law, whether constitutional or not, would in this instance reach a morally and politically objectionable end.

22 Schwartz, "The Zeal of the Civil Advocate," 165.

23 See *Mathews v. Eldridge*, 424 U.S. 319 (1976); and *Lassiter v. Department of Social Services*, 452 U.S. 18 (1981).

24 Perhaps this is the basis for Alan Donagan's dictum, upon which Professor Schwartz relies (Schwartz, 165), to the effect that a society would be unjust if it "denied" claimants of legal rights a fair opportunity to obtain representation. See Alan Donagan, "Justifying Legal Practice in the Adversary System," Chapter 5, D. Luban, ed., *The Good Lawyer*.

◆ ◆ ◆ ◆ ◆

KENNETH KIPNIS

Responsibility for the Distribution of Legal Services

Distributive Justice and Legal Services

When goods of any type—including services—are distributed in society, a choice can be made whether these will enter the market to be bought and sold there, or whether they will be distributed or rationed wholly or in part in accordance with some principle other than the ability and willingness to pay the market price. Few would question that with respect to some goods—aftershave lotion, for example—market mechanisms are a reasonable and appropriate means of distribution. In efforts to maximize their profits, designers, manufacturers, and distributors compete with one another to make available the highest-quality goods at the lowest cost. Purchasers in turn make independent judgments about whether the goods offered for sale are worth the price. However for some other goods—childhood vaccinations, elementary education, firefighting services—distributions are not nearly so dependent upon transactions made between the end-users of the goods and their suppliers. Accordingly, we can distinguish

broadly between market systems of distribution and rationing systems, understanding by the latter all systems in which ability and willingness to pay the market price for the goods are not the sole preconditions for receipt.

In some cases, the justification for a rationing system involves an appeal to goals that are shared, more or less, by the community as a whole. We may all be more secure if conflagrations are contained as quickly as possible. The community's interests in speed and efficiency are not served if those who need to have fires put out have to negotiate with vendors while their homes, businesses, and factories go up in flames. In a second category, the justification of rationing systems involves an appeal to some right. It is arguable that police protection services, legal services in serious criminal proceedings and elementary education must be provided where needed, not merely because it is in the public interest that this be done, but, rather, because the beneficiary of the good has an entitlement to it. The victim who is being beaten up has a right to the assistance of a law enforcement officer. Those accused of criminal wrongs have a right to legal assistance in proceedings that would be unfairly imposed in the absence of such help. And children have a right to be taught skills that are essential to a decent life in the complex society we will leave them.

In a third category of case—and it will be one of these that will interest us here—nonmarket mechanisms may be justified, not by an appeal to a right enjoyed by the beneficiary of the good, but, rather, by appeal to a duty or special responsibility assumed by those designated to provide the good. We may wish to say, for example, that where it is vital to their well-being, children should receive medical care, not because they have a basic right to health care—we may believe that no one does—but, rather, because in becoming parents, mothers and fathers have assumed a social responsibility to provide that care. The child is what lawyers would call a "third-party beneficiary."

Unlike criminal law, in a civil case there is characteristically a dispute between two private parties over some matter of legal right. Familiar examples include unintended personal injuries and breaches of contract. In the United States, legal services in civil proceedings are for the most part made available through market distribution systems. To be sure, many attorneys and firms provide services for free or at reduced fees to those who might otherwise have to go without legal advice or representation. Additionally, private organizations (the American Civil Liberties Union or the National Association for the Advancement of Colored People) and government-funded organizations (the Legal Services Corporation) also make available legal services without reliance upon market pricing systems. In its state and national bar associations, the organized legal profession has often played a role in the provision of legal services to those who cannot obtain them because of an inability to pay. While it is clear that legal services in civil matters have been made available outside of market distribution systems, it is less clear that these services have been adequate to meet the general need. But it will not be our purpose here to explore the dimensions of any such shortcomings. Rather, the concern will be to identify who it is that has central responsibility for the provision of such services, the form that such responsibility takes, and the grounds for that obligation.

Let us accept that our community has committed itself to an adversary system of adjudication. For the sake of the discussion that follows, we assume here that a public commitment to adjudication secures for each member of the community the following four rights: (1) the right to submit certain types of complaint to a judge or tribunal, (2) the right to have the other party to the dispute summoned to court to answer the complaint, (3) the right to have the judge make a decision in the case, and, if it is favorable, (4) the right to have the judge's decision enforced. Let us further assume that in an adversary system of adjudication responsibility for gathering evidence and marshaling legal arguments rests with the parties to the dispute. It is the judge's job (1) to create a forum in which the parties can argue their cases, (2) to issue a decision in the case, (3) to declare a rule applicable in all relevantly similar cases, and (4) to disclose the reasoning behind the decision. Finally, we assume that the overriding purpose of such a system is to make it as likely as possible that (1) the judge's decision will be just, and (2) that it will be accepted by the parties to the dispute and by the community as a whole.[1]

The Conditions of Information and Exercise

It would seem that for any legal system worthy of respect, the protection and support that the community provides for some should be made available to all whose claims are similar. To the extent that the community fails to make this protection so available, it fails to provide equal protection: It fails to be just. Two conditions must be met if the protection afforded by legal rights is to be available to all with sound claims to it. First, it should be possible for citizens to obtain, at least generally, *information* about what the law requires or permits. There may be some cases, as when the law is unsettled, when only educated guesses are possible: Adequate authoritative information is not available because it does not exist. To be sure, even when rights are problematic, a commitment to adjudication as a means of resolving disputes, secures for members of the community a right to an authoritative clarifying judgment in the event of a dispute. But when information does exist, it should be possible for a member of the community to find out what the legal standards are. Legal rights have little value (and legal obligations can be unfairly perilous) to those who cannot find out which ones they have.

Second, when members of the community have a legal right to something that has been denied to them, it should be possible for them to obtain what-ever protection and support the community guar-antees to them as a matter of law. In other words, it should be possible for them to *exercise* what rights they have. Thus if Potter has the legal right that Watson not build the towering orange fence on the boundary separating their two lots, it should be possible for her to commence some commun-ity-constituted process that will have as its effect the rectification of Watson's wrong. Potter might be able to invoke some legal requirement that Watson re-move, relocate, reconfigure or repaint the fence or that he compensate her for a continuing encroach-ment upon her interests.

If the community is serious in its commitment to adjudication as a means of clarifying and securing legal rights for its citizenry, it must begin by secur-ing generally for all citizens a right to information about what the law permits and requires, and a right as well to appeal to the law to secure that which the law guarantees to them.

Adversarial systems seem to have the serious disadvantage that complaints may not be made and cases may be wrongly decided if the party in the right doesn't bring the case or loses it because of an inability to present intelligibly and persuasively what is, in fact, a solid case. Some citizens—let us call them nonparticipants—may be effectively ex-cluded from the courts because of inadequate re-sources of one kind or another. Since the judge in an adversarial proceeding depends upon the par-ties to do the investigative work and to present the results to the court in a useful way, serious injus-tices may be tolerated when they shouldn't be or cases may be wrongly decided if one of the parties is unable to meet the requirements of adversarial adjudication. Where this happens, the judicial sys-tem may serve generally to protect some perpetra-tors of injustice. It may become an instrument of injustice. Certain sectors of the community may be forced to put up with wrongs that the rest of us would not tolerate. Being unable to participate in

the adjudicatory procedures that the community provides for the settling of disputes, these persons will be exposed to wrongs without the prospect of legal recourse.

If such infractions are ever to be rectified, those who are wronged may have to take measures that are outside the law. However, if in taking "direct ac-tion," further wrongs are committed against those who are not similarly excluded from participation in the system, then the legal system will protect the victims of the nonparticipants in a way that it won't protect the nonparticipants when they are victim-ized. One thinks of the looting and destruction in America's periodic ghetto riots.

In contrast with adversarial systems, inquisitor-ial systems of adjudication seem not to have these same problems, since a judge and an investigating magistrate together have the responsibility for doing the work of both sides: investigating the facts and interpreting the law. Independent attorneys are less critical to its operation. Injustices stemming from inequality in the resources of the parties are there-fore less likely to occur in these nonadversarial sys-tems that are also used throughout the world. So if the community opts for an adversarial model—and there are some reasons for doing so[2]—it will have to address this problem.

Convivial and Sophisticated Legal Systems

At the broadest level, adversarial legal systems can meet the conditions of information and exercise in a variety of ways. Because each approach ameliorates some difficulties while, at the same time, exacerbat-ing others, each may be thought of as representing different agendas: With what kinds of problem do we choose to be occupied?

The easiest solution is that of the "convivial" legal system.[3] In such a system care is taken so that people can generally be expected to understand their legal positions with respect to most matters and to be able to function within the legal system without assistance. This is brought about by (1) employing programs of mass legal education to ensure that virtually everyone has the knowledge and skill that are needed, and (2) opting for a simple legal system so that only minimal instruction is required.

The system can be kept simple using a number of methods. Judges can be limited in the degree to which they are able to become specialists. They might receive only a small amount of specialized training, perhaps only after they are selected. And they could be rotated in and out of short single terms in office. Because in terms of training and experience judges would not be very different from the litigants, courtroom discourse would not differ strikingly from the language of everyday life. Indeed, experience in the courtroom, as litigant and as judge, might be fairly commonplace among members of such a community. A convivial arrangement has the advantage that each person would know just about everything anyone would need to know about the legal system: both what the law was on most matters and how to function in the courts. It would have the disadvantage—perhaps this is a disadvantage—that legal relationships and their derivative social institutions could never be so complicated as to require a specialist to understand what is involved in them.[4] Difficult-to-discern injustices might persist because the expertise required to identify and deal with them might not be developed. In essence, a convivial system meets the conditions of information and exercise by means of mass legal education and simplicity.

On the other hand, the community could choose to make no effort whatever to educate the general public to the point at which it has an adequate understanding of the provisions of the law and the niceties of legal procedure. The legal system itself could be permitted to become as complicated as it may, with only highly educated and experienced specialists sitting on the bench. In such a "sophisticated" system, the ordinary person cannot be expected to understand his or her legal position

with respect to many matters, and neither can the layman be expected to secure, all alone, what the law guarantees. In a legal system like this, justice requires that there exist some mechanism for making available both information about the requirements of the law and skilled legal assistance. Without such a mechanism, a sophisticated legal system cannot be justified. Justice can thus require that a sophisticated adversarial system of adjudication be a "professionalized" system.[5]

Unlike the convivial arrangement, sophisticated legal systems do not provide for mass legal education, nor do they incorporate structural features that serve to limit the complexity of the system. Accordingly, in order to meet the conditions of information and exercise, they must provide for some sort of intermediary between laypersons and what will generally be a mysterious and intimidating legal system. There are three main approaches to the provision of such an intermediary: the free market, the liberal profession, and the public agency. Each of these will be considered in turn.

The Free Market

In the absence of mass legal education, judicial specialists create the need for lawyers. Just as—historically—shoemakers and repairers of appliances can materialize without invitation, so pettifoggers will appear about the courts to make specialized services available to those who have business there. In exchange for a fee, these self-designated attorneys will give legal advice, draft legal documents, and, with the judge's permission, represent clients before the court. It is important to appreciate how these "proto-professionals" differ from what we now know as attorneys. They will not have standardized educational experiences, nor will they be certified in familiar ways. Though some may have been to "law school," completion of such a course of study will not be a prerequisite to the practice of law. Just as anyone can hold himself out as a gardener or as an automobile front-end specialist—and let the buyer beware!—so pettifoggers will fall all along the spectra of competence and integrity. There will be virtually no formal restrictions on entry into the field. Of course, some may not be able to earn a living in the legal services business and will be forced to take up other livelihoods. Consumer evaluation services may alleviate some of the problems created by variations in quality; they can sell information to potential customers about the relative merits of attorneys. Still, the consumer of legal services may have no assurance (except for the word of the attorney) that the goods received are of their putative quality.

Should pettifoggers decide to organize, their distinctive form of society will be the "trade association," set up to further the economic interests of the membership. The trade as a whole may have problems that are best addressed by means of some kind of collective action. Perhaps there are too many people entering the business, causing excessive competition and driving down the average income of the membership. Perhaps a few "rotten apples" have given pettifoggery a bad name and there is therefore a public-relations problem that needs attention. Perhaps programs can be set up that will help to keep lawyers current on legal developments.

A legal-services trade has the advantage that it may require little attention by the larger community. If disparities in financial resources are not too large among the citizenry, if the costs of litigation are unduly burdensome, and if reliable information is available concerning the quality of practicing lawyers, the conditions of information and exercise can be met.

Sectors of the community that are without adequate legal services will almost naturally generate their own specialists as legal tradesmen seek out untapped markets. On the other hand, where poverty is significant in sectors of the community or where legal services are for other reasons not made available by market forces, the problems may be more difficult. Still, the proto-professional lawyer may nobly offer legal services "pro bono publico" (for the good of the public). A sufficient level of such charity may serve adequately to address the community's concern to meet the conditions of information and exercise. It is important to note that pettifoggers would seem not to be under an obligation to do work for anyone other than their paying customers. Appliance-repair services need not fix the vacuum cleaners of those too poor to pay for the work. If the gratuitous charity of the legal trade will not suffice, the community can always choose to subsidize the purchase of legal services for those too poor to pay.

The Liberal Profession

The development of a trade into a profession is a lengthy process, and occupations can be located at virtually any point along the continuum. In American legal history, the process of professionalization can perhaps be said to have begun in 1870 with the organization of the Association of the Bar of the City of New York.[6] Samuel J. Tilden, addressing the first meeting of the first modern legal professional association, warned:

> Sir, [I] should not be unwilling that the Bar should combine to restore any power or influence which it has lost, except such power and influence as it may have deservedly lost. As a class, as a portion of a community, I do not desire to see the Bar combined, except for two objects. The one is to elevate itself—to elevate its own standards; the other object is for the common and public good. For itself, nothing; for that noble and generous and elevated profession of which it is the representative, everything.
>
> Sir, it cannot be doubted—we can none of us shut our eyes to the fact—that there has been, in the last quarter of a century, a serious decline in the character, in the training, in the education, and in the mor-

ality of our Bar; and the first work for this Association to do is to elevate the profession to a higher and a better standard. If the Bar is to become merely a method of making money, making it in the most convenient way possible; but making it at all hazards, then the Bar is degraded. If the Bar is to be merely an institution that seeks to win causes and to win them by backdoor access to the judiciary, then it is not only degraded, but it is corrupt.[7]

Tilden's language signals a new role for the bar, a new conception of the responsibility of lawyers, a striking departure from the idea of lawyering as a trade, and a commitment to the development of the modern legal profession, much as we now understand it. The transition from something close to what we have described as a "free market" to the modern legal profession took many decades, but the three critical steps in the process are roughly as follows.[8]

First, practitioners within the trade begin to make a *claim to maximal competence*. Some lawyers, in virtue of superior training, education, and experience, exceed all others in knowledge and skill. There must be an organization of practitioners within the favored class; not necessarily all, but enough to warrant a claim to speak for the whole class. And there must be a criterion for deciding who belongs to the class and who does not. Because of the special knowledge and skill possessed by these practitioners, those outside the favored class appear to lack the standing to judge the competence of these specialists. As the public comes to accept the profession's claim to maximal competence, it becomes reasonable to let the select class of practitioners certify and evaluate itself, excluding from practice those of dubious expertise. The favored practitioners, in association, stand ready to assume this responsibility.

Second, since in a society that is committed to a sophisticated adversarial system, special legal knowledge and skill are vital to the achievement of justice,

the process of professionalization requires that the profession make a *public commitment to use its distinctive abilities in the realization of that significant social value*. The profession publicly pledges to give due attention to the special responsibilities it assumes in ensuring that the system of adversarial adjudication succeeds in the task of addressing disputes emerging within the community. The American Bar Association's Code of Professional Responsibility includes the words:

> Lawyers, as guardians of the law, play a vital role in the preservation of society. The fulfillment of this role requires an understanding by lawyers of their relationship with and functions in our legal system. A consequent obligation of lawyers is to maintain the highest standards of ethical conduct.

In characterizing itself as a guardian of the law, a guardian of the foundation of justice, the legal profession represents itself as dedicated to an ideal of social service.

Third and most important, the process of professionalization culminates in the community's recognition of the members of the profession as *the sole means* by which legal skill and knowledge are to be applied. This *exclusive social reliance* upon licensed attorneys is grounded on the preceding two stages. For if there is confidence that the favored members of the class of practitioners possess maximal competence in matters legal, and if there is trust that these same lawyers are reliably committed to the responsible application of their distinctive skills, then there will seem to be neither the ability nor the need to designate nonprofessionals as overseers of professional practice. As the profession secures trust and confidence, it takes control over the selection and training of candidates, the accreditation of professional schools and programs, the certification of new members, and the promulgation and enforcement of standards of professional conduct. It becomes, in essence, an unregulated legal monopoly with respect to legal services, unauthorized practice being a criminal offense.[9] In the end, of course, it is the citizenry who, through representatives, have the power to delegate responsibility to professions or to relieve them of it. Though permission to practice in the courts—admission to the bar—is initially granted by the judiciary, the privileges that lawyers enjoy can, within perhaps some limits, be ratified, extended, and revoked by legislatures.

The Model Rules of Professional Conduct evidence a sensitive appreciation for the essential connection between the professional responsibilities of lawyers and the responsibilities of the legal profession. Its preamble contains the following:

> To the extent that lawyers meet the obligations of their professional calling, the occasion for government regulation is obviated. Self-regulation also helps maintain the legal profession's independence from government domination. An independent legal profession is an important force in preserving government under law, for abuse of legal authority is more readily challenged by a profession whose members are not dependent on government for the right to practice.
>
> The legal profession's relative autonomy carries with it special responsibilities of self-government. The profession has a responsibility to assure that its regulations are conceived in the public interest and not in furtherance of parochial or self-interested concerns of the bar. Every lawyer is responsible for observance of the Rules of Professional Conduct. A lawyer should also aid in securing their observance by other lawyers. Neglect of these responsibilities compromises the independence of the profession and the public interest which it serves.

It is helpful to compare the monopoly status of public utilities with the standing of the professional-ized bar.[10] Corporations that operate as public utilities receive from the community an exclusive legal right to distribute some good or service within a defined geographical area. It is a great advantage to the corporation to have the assurance that it will not face competition and, because of this, it may be able to keep its costs low and achieve economies of scale. From the point of view of the citizenry however, the deal makes sense only if the corporation assumes the responsibility of providing reasonable service to all those within its area. As the United States Supreme Court put it in 1918:

> Corporations which devote their property to a public use may not pick and choose, serving only the portions of the territory covered by their franchises which it is presently profitable for them to serve, and restricting the development of the remaining portions by leaving their inhabitants in discomfort without the service which they alone can render.[11]

Without the commitment to provide service, the granting of the exclusive right to the corporation—the barring of all others from entering the market—does not make sense.

Likewise, in the absence of a commitment from the legal profession to provide service to all who need it, the granting of an exclusive right to the bar becomes a decision to exclude some sectors of the community from participation in the system of adjudication. Where only attorneys are permitted to advise and represent members of the community, but where no attorneys will agree to serve some community members with need for legal assistance, the community does not meet the conditions of information and exercise and is to that extent unjust. One mechanism for meeting the two conditions is a responsible legal profession. Those in it would possess the knowledge and skill that the ordinary members of the community would lack. They would have an exclusive right to counsel and represent clients in legal matters. And finally, the profession as a whole would acknowledge its obligation to serve adequately as the necessary intermediary between the public and an otherwise inaccessible judiciary. Understood in this way, the liberal legal profession serves as an integral part of the legal system: Though they retain their autonomy, lawyers are *officers* of the court. Thus a serious failure of the legal profession is a serious failure of the legal system. The standards of practice that the profession as a whole imposes upon its members must ensure that the counseling and representational services that must be made available if the legal system is to make sense are made available to the public in an adequate way.

Speaking through professional associations in codes of ethics, lawyers have acknowledged the bar's duty to serve all members of the community. Thus the first Ethical Consideration of the American Bar Association's Code of Professional Responsibility begins:

> A basic tenet of the professional responsibility of lawyers is that *every person* in our society should have ready access to the independent professional services of a lawyer of integrity and competence.

The legal profession, the collectivity of licensed attorneys, thus does provide a guarantee to the community as a whole that competent and responsible attorneys will be available to those with need for it. Were it the case that large numbers of attorneys publicly disavow these representations made by organizations undertaking to speak on behalf of the profession, then one would have reason to believe that the public commitment expressed by the codes does not represent a public responsibility undertaken by the profession. But in the absence of widespread and visible disassociation, one can only suppose that the codes express a commitment that is generally acknowledged. To be sure, the possibility exists, as Tilden foresaw, that the bar associations of today are merely yesterday's trade associations with

improved public-relations programs. And it may be that the codes are not intended—perhaps were never intended—to bind lawyers to responsible levels of public service. Perhaps they were enunciated merely to convey the illusion of concerned attention. To the extent that this is so, the liberal profession will have failed, professional responsibility will have failed. Some other mechanism must be instituted to meet the conditions of information and exercise.

Students of contract law may have detected here the equitable doctrine of promissory estoppel. Ordinarily, a gratuitous promise does not create a legal obligation. Not owing the money in any sense, W promises to B that he will give B twenty dollars tomorrow. Other things being equal, no legal obligation is created. But if B has made it clear to W that he will be acting to his detriment in reliance upon W's promise, that he will be giving up something of value if W doesn't come through, then a legally binding obligation may be created. Suppose B were to say to W: "Because you will be giving me twenty dollars tomorrow, today I will put down a nonrefundable twenty dollar deposit on a coat I have wanted, and I will promise the merchant to pay the balance tomorrow when I receive the money from you." At that point the law may well acknowledge a contract. When the maker of a promise ought reasonably to expect that the promise will induce a particular kind of action or forbearance on the part of the promisee, and where the promise does induce the action or forbearance, the obligation is no longer merely "moral": the promise may be held to be legally binding.[12]

In granting the legal profession monopoly status, the community relies to its detriment upon the profession's collective representation that it will meet the conditions of information and exercise. The community loses something universally acknowledged to be of inestimable value if the legal profession fails to meet the responsibilities it has assumed in the process of professionalization. Of course, if we assume that the granting of monopoly status to the bar is the "consideration" that the bar receives in return for having agreed to meet the conditions of information and exercise, then the contract is a much more ordinary one. In either event, unlike the free-market pettifogger, professional attorneys have a clear duty to address the legal needs of nonparticipants; indeed, a duty to see to it that there are no nonparticipants. It is not a matter of gratuitous charity "pro bono publico." It is a "basic tenet" of the bar's professional responsibility.

The Public Agency

The community takes the third approach to providing the intermediary between the lay public and the sophisticated adversarial system when it decides to employ attorneys directly, much as it does with fire fighters, judges, and police officers. If the interest that citizens have is important enough (it is difficult to think of a more important interest than civil justice), if neither the free market nor the liberal profession can be relied upon to do the job, and if the inquisitorial and convivial approaches are ruled out, the principal remaining option is directly to employ attorneys in public agencies set up to provide legal services to the general public. Though lawyers will *work for* their clients (just as teachers work for their students), they will be *paid by* and will have some of their working conditions set by their employers—in this case, civil government. Where gratuitous charity and professional responsibility have failed, "conditions of employment" that are set by the community can perhaps succeed.

The most serious problem that can emerge within the public agency approach is, as the Preamble to the Model Rules observes, the compromising of professional autonomy, the damaging erosion of the bar's independence. Even though agency attorneys are nominally employed to provide legal services to the public, government officials may try to discourage these lawyers from bringing certain types of complaint—especially complaints against the government and its officials—even when the cases are

legitimate. Government, the employer of attorneys, may be able to limit the degree to which citizens can challenge the state for having exceeded its proper authority. As the legal profession's "boss," it will do this by setting conditions of employment, both formal and informal, that restrict the types of case that can be brought to court. In controlling the legal profession—and thus access to the judiciary—the state can circumvent legal limits to its authority. Though in some sense or other citizens may still "enjoy" legal rights against the government, they will not be able to appeal to the courts to obtain that which the law guarantees to them. Their rights will not have been secured.

Autonomy problems within legal-services agencies can be addressed by carefully attending to the structure of the organization. In universities, for example, the problem of unwarranted encroachment upon professional autonomy has been extensively addressed under the general heading of "academic freedom." In practice, this entails a separation of administrative and professional functions within the institution so as to guarantee that academicians have the latitude that is required if they are to do their work. It *is a secured limitation on the employer's right to determine the conditions and content of the professional's job.* At most American colleges and universities, neither the administration nor the governing board can fire a professor for publishing ideas to which they object. Substantial control is in the hands of the faculty. By far the most important factor in securing professional autonomy within an employing organization is the type of association created by the professionals themselves.

We have seen how trade associations and professional associations are the characteristic forms of occupational organization with respect to the free market and the liberal profession. The social organization that can be expected to emerge among publicly employed attorneys is the public sector labor union. Labor unions exist primarily to negotiate with the employer (in this case, the community) the terms and conditions of employment. The distinction drawn earlier between trade associations and professional associations parallels the two distinct sets of interests that can be furthered by a public-sector legal-services labor union. Employed attorneys may identify themselves as employees. They may feel that the work they are doing is not really their work but, rather, the agency's work. If the quality of service provided is low, that is not the employee's responsibility. Think of an assembly-line worker, building a badly engineered product. "I am just doing my job, earning a living. It is the company's car." To the extent that attorneys think of themselves in this way, the collective bargaining process will focus upon "bread and butter" issues: wages, hours, and general working conditions. The employee's posture will in essence be "more money for less work," mirroring the employer's posture of "more work for less money."

On the other hand, attorneys may identify themselves as professionals; not being paid for their work but, *in order that they may do their work.*[13] Employed professionals have the option to focus, not upon their interests as employees, but upon their interests as professionals, with final responsibility for the quality of their work. Decent salaries and appropriate working conditions may be important, not because it is nice to earn more in better circumstances, but because adequate attention must be given to these matters if the agency and its professional staff are to serve their public purpose. Likewise, if professional autonomy is under attack by administrators (or even by fellow professionals), the membership of a public sector labor union has the option of placing those values high upon its agenda in negotiations. Of course, where the community as a whole adequately appreciates the argument for an independent bar, it is unlikely that employer and employee will be at odds on this issue. Still, provided that lawyers have not lost their sense of responsibility in their roles as employees, labor unions can serve to further professionalism and buttress autonomy should the need arise to protect these critical values.

Some Final Thoughts

A system of law sets out powers, obligations and prohibitions that citizens will do well to understand. For such a system to be more than an elaborate pretense, citizens must be able to understand their legal situations and secure that to which they are entitled. They need access to the system. But while it may be essential for society to adopt some process for resolving civil disputes—if only to ensure the blessings of peace—there are a variety of approaches that can serve the purpose. And the responsibilities of government, judges, lawyers (if the system requires them) and citizens will vary depending on which procedure is implemented. The basic structures are "in play": not carved into historical granite.

In the United States and some other parts of the world, the liberal profession has been favored by history. For the reasons set out above, the burden of ensuring fair access to legal services in civil cases falls largely on the shoulders of the legal profession. Though I have not explored them here, the profession itself may have a variety of options that it can implement in discharging this important social obligation. But if the argument above is correct, it does not have the option of ignoring this aspect of its professional responsibility.[14]

NOTES

1 The issues referenced in this paragraph are elaborated in Kenneth Kipnis, *Legal Ethics* (Englewood Cliffs: Prentice-Hall, 1986), Chapter Two, 15-39.

2 The contrasts between adversarial and inquisitorial systems is addressed in Kenneth Kipnis, *op. cit.*, 29-30.

3 I have taken the term "convivial" from the chapter entitled "Institutional Spectrum" in Ivan Illich's *Deschooling Society* (New York: Harper & Row, 1972).

4 For an illuminating description of a legal system that approaches conviviality, see Victor

Li's account of the Chinese legal system in *Law Without Lawyers* (Boulder: Westview Press, 1978).

5 It is somewhat misleading to say that specialists are required because the system is complex. While this has no doubt become true, a more discerning account would disclose that a system can become complicated just because it has been, over time, given over to a relatively closed community of specialists. This is not to say that complexity and sophistication are bad things; only that they create problems that need to be solved.

6 R. Pound, *The Lawyer from Antiquity to Modern Times* 5 (1953), note 7 at 249. Pound describes the period between 1836 and 1870 as the "Era of Decadence," 223-49.

7 Quoted in R.F. Marks, K. Leswing, and B. Fortinsky, *The Lawyer, the Public, and Professional Responsibility* (Chicago: The American Bar Foundation, 1972), 13.

8 The process by which an occupation becomes a profession is more fully described in Kenneth Kipnis, *op. cit.*, Chapter One, 1-14.

9 The New Mexico Supreme Court, in *Norvell v. Credit Bur. of Albuquerque, Inc.*, 85, N.M. 521, 514 P.2d 40 (1973), recognized the following "indicia" of the "practice of law":

> (1) representation of parties before judicial or administrative bodies, (2) preparation of pleadings and other papers incident to actions and special proceedings, (3) management of such action and proceeding; and non-court-related activities such as (4) giving legal advice and counsel, (5) rendering a service that requires the use of legal knowledge or skill, (6) preparing instruments and contracts by which legal rights are secured.

These issues are to be considered by the courts in determining whether an individual is guilty of the unauthorized practice of law.

10 The characterization of the legal profession as a public utility has been developed by Marks, et al. in *The Lawyer, the Public, and Professional Responsibility*, 288-93. Some of the key elements of their general view were developed decades earlier by Karl Llewellyn in "The Bar Specializes—With What Results?" *Annals of the American Academy of Political and Social Science* Vol. 167 (May 1933): 177-92; and "The Bar's Troubles and Poultices—and Cures?" *Law and Contemporary Problems* Vol. 5 (1938): 104.

11 *New York and Queens Gas Co. v. McCall*, 245 U.S. 345, 351. On the ethical responsibility of public utilities, see Kenneth Sayre, ed., *Values in the Electric Power Industry* (Notre Dame: Notre Dame University Press, 1977). See especially Chapter 3, Charles Murdock, "Legal and Economic Aspects of the Electric Utility's 'Mandate to Serve.'"

12 *Fried* v. *Fisher*, 328 Pa 497, 196 A 39 (1938).

13 Lawrence Haworth, *Decadence and Objectivity* (Toronto: University of Toronto Press, 1978), 112.

14 This article is descended from "Distributive Justice and Civil Justice: Professional Responsibility and the Allocation of Legal Services" published in *Economic Justice: Private Rights and Public Responsibilities*, an AMINTAPHIL volume edited by Kenneth Kipnis and Diana T. Meyers (Rowman and Allanheld, 1985). That article later appeared as "Professional Responsibility and the Distribution of Legal Services," Chapter Six of Kenneth Kipnis, *Legal Ethics* (Englewood Cliffs: Prentice-Hall, 1986). This third instantiation incorporates two decades of supplementary reflection.

WILLFUL IGNORANCE AND THE LIMITS OF ADVOCACY

HANS ALLHOFF

Case Description

Daniel Kellington was a lawyer in private practice in Medford, Oregon, specializing in personal injury law and trusts and estates.

One Saturday afternoon, a United States Marshal phoned Kellington to tell him a former client of his, "Richard Parker," was really Peter MacFarlane, a fugitive wanted in Vermont on drug trafficking charges. MacFarlane had been arrested in Appelgate, Oregon, was in jail, and wished to speak with Kellington. Kellington took his call. He had represented MacFarlane about a year previously in a few matters connected with MacFarlane's business, Metalhead Boat Works.

Kellington told MacFarlane he was not a criminal lawyer, but agreed to visit MacFarlane anyway regarding, in MacFarlane's words, "some matters related to a boat business." Their meeting lasted for about ten minutes. MacFarlane admitted to Kellington he was in fact Peter MacFarlane and not Richard Parker. He also told him he owed time for a prior drug conviction and intended to serve it. MacFarlane then asked Kellington to contact an employee named Norm Young, and to have Young remove some things from MacFarlane's home. Those things included: stereo equipment, files, a black attaché case, money stuffed underneath a mattress, a laptop computer, electronic organizers, and a boat. In addition, MacFarlane wrote out some instructions for Young, which read, "Chair in bedroom, right side of arm, envelope. Please destroy as soon as possible."

Kellington returned to his office, immediately called Young, and began to pass on instructions from his conversation with MacFarlane. Young asked him how he should destroy the envelope; Kellington said he could burn it. Young also asked Kellington why he was calling him and not Mr. "Parker"; Kellington told him Mr. "Parker" was in jail, but said nothing more. When Young asked Kellington if he could get into any kind of trouble for doing what MacFarlane was asking of him, Kellington told him he could not—but also to stop if he ran into police or "somebody bigger than you."

Young, more or less, did as he was instructed. But, after discovering a driver's license with MacFarlane's picture and another name (not Parker *or* MacFarlane) in the envelope he was told to burn, as well as $20,000 in cash in a bag he removed, Young panicked and drove home. When he later drove back to MacFarlane's house to put things back in their place, he was confronted by federal officials who were there to execute a search warrant. Young told them what, through Kellington, MacFarlane had instructed him to do.

The federal officials then arranged for Young to initiate a tape-recorded phone call to Kellington. During this call, Young told Kellington about the fake I.D. and the large amount of money. When Kellington asked Young if he had "heard from anybody" Young said he had not. Kellington then suggested they take an inventory of everything, and he would then take possession. When Young asked Kellington whether they should report this to authorities, Kellington said, "Well, I don't think you have to do that." Kellington said, "I have a duty to my client to protect his assets that, that they can't get and when they.... If they, if somebody uh, come and, comes and says hey we're attaching that money because it's ill gotten gains or something.... Well then

I have to turn it over to them, but in the meantime it's his money, and it's his money and he may need to defend uh, you know pay a lawyer." When Kellington left Young's house with MacFarlane's belongings, federal agents detained him.

Ethical Analysis

These facts, names included, are taken almost verbatim from a real case, *United States v. Kellington*, in which Kellington was arrested and, along with MacFarlane, charged with obstructing justice by "knowingly ... engaging in misleading conduct toward another person, with intent to alter, destroy, mutilate, or conceal an object with intent to impair the object's integrity or availability for use in an official proceeding."

At trial, Kellington played dumb. For all he knew, the envelope he was directing Young to destroy contained a love letter. In hindsight, he admitted, he should have been more inquisitive of MacFarlane's demands, but when he and MacFarlane met he assumed MacFarlane merely wanted to make sure his things were in good hands. Why did he tell Young so little? Because, Kellington maintained, it is his policy not to disclose to third parties information he learns in confidence from clients.

The real issue at trial, and on appeal, was whether Kellington, unlike MacFarlane, could avail himself of a defense grounded in legal ethics norms. Specifically, the trial judge, in his instruction to the jury, said, "[T]his is not a case on legal lawyer ethics. A crime has been charged and I'm not going to permit ethics type of arguments here." On appeal, the Ninth Circuit Court of Appeals rejected this framing. An expert on legal ethics had testified on Kellington's behalf, and the Ninth Circuit thought his testimony was quite relevant: "When you have a lawyer who has been in private practice on the civil side—and Mr. Kellington has been for the better part of 30 years—it does not come as a surprise to me that in this context he did not immediately flash upon what

I think would be known to you or to maybe others, that, by God, this is a—you know, I'm being asked to destroy evidence here." On this analysis, Kellington's ignorance, naïveté—call it what you will—coupled with his sense of client loyalty, would seem to rebut an obstruction of justice charge.

Study Questions

1. During his taped phone conversation with Young, Young asked Kellington whether they should alert authorities, against what MacFarlane's wishes obviously would have been. Kellington replied, "I have a duty to my client to protect his assets that, that they can't get and when they ... If they, if somebody uh, come and, comes and says hey we're attaching that money because it's ill gotten gains or something ... Well then I have to turn it over to them, but in the meantime it's his money, and it's his money and he may need to defend uh, you know pay a lawyer." What do you make of Kellington's response? Can Kellington's claim of naïveté be accepted?

2. It certainly would not have been a crime for Kellington to have gone straight to the police after his initial phone conversation with MacFarlane. Should he have? Or are you satisfied with a rule saying, "If you're a lawyer and you don't know what your client is asking you to do is illegal, you can go ahead and do it"?

3. Kellington said MacFarlane was a client of his. But was he? Once a lawyer for MacFarlane, always a lawyer for MacFarlane? Doesn't this amount to conscripting Kellington into an ethical dilemma?

4. In connection with this case and the readings in this section, ask yourself whether lawyering requires an ethics of its own. Is common-sense moral philosophy just not enough? Do we want lawyers to have certain moral duties and exemptions beyond those we have as ordinary people?

UNIT 5

Medical Ethics

FRITZ ALLHOFF

Medical Ethics

Of all the professions, medicine has the longest tradition of recognizing its ethical dimensions. The patriarch of medical ethics is usually recognized as Hippocrates (460 BC-370 BC), who was from the Greek island of Kos and was a physician as well as a teacher. Hippocrates' most enduring legacy is the Hippocratic Oath (reprinted in this volume), though there is a debate about whether he wrote it himself or one of his disciples did so after his death. The Hippocratic Oath established the basis of medical ethics, and it has shaped the profession for nearly 2500 years.

The Hippocratic Oath lays out four core values for the medical profession: beneficence, nonmaleficence, confidentiality, and honor. Beneficence is the idea that physicians are supposed to *help* patients: physicians, through their specialized training, are in a unique position to bring benefits to their charges. Nonmaleficence holds that physicians should *not harm* their patients; while nonmaleficence might sound straightforward enough, it gives rise to some of the more controversial elements of the Oath, specifically its proscriptions on euthanasia and abortion. Confidentiality requires that physicians not share information gained through the treatment of patients. Again, this might seem an obvious requirement for doctors, though the moral status of confidentiality extends beyond mere respect for persons: the existence of confidentiality will engender *better* medical care insofar as patients will disclose medical information that they might otherwise hold back were these protections not there.[1] Finally, physicians, in nearly all societies and at all times, have been afforded a special and esteemed status: the Hippocratic Oath recognizes this and requires physicians to carry themselves honorably in order to preserve the integrity of the profession. For example, the Oath cautions physicians about inappropriate relationships with their patients, and it concludes by promising physicians eternal honor should they follow its requirements.

As mentioned above, the Hippocratic Oath has had a profound impact upon the development of medical ethics; many of the contemporary debates in the field stem from challenges to or refinements of this classical doctrine. In this unit, we will survey some of these contemporary debates, never losing sight of their origins. Following the Hippocratic Oath, we will look at an article by Edmund Pellegrino who, in 2005, became the chairman of the President's Council of Bioethics. Pellegrino argues for a special moral status of medicine, which primarily derives from the fact that patients are, by definition, in a vulnerable position; this vulnerability requires us to recognize certain moral norms for the profession.

Many of the discussions in medical ethics speak to duties of the physician or else to rights of the patient, but the *relationship* between the physician and the patient could also be explored. For example, we might think that such a relationship should be *paternalistic*: physicians stand to their patients as parents stand to their children; the former order or advise and the latter follow. Alternatively, we might think that such a model does not respect a patient's *autonomy*, and that a better model might be one that treats the patient more as an equal than as a subordinate; such concerns might motivate a *partnership* or *friend* model for the relationship.

In the second section, we look at trust and confidentiality in more detail; this is one of the most fecund areas of contemporary debate. While it might seem obvious that trust and confidentiality are important medical values, it is less clear whether there should be *limits* to such trust and confidentiality. Regarding trust, is it ever justifiable for a physician to lie to a patient or else to withhold the truth? The Hippocratic Oath would suggest not, though some of the cases can get tricky. Imagine, for example, that there could be *benefits* to the patient through dishonesty; these might be manifest through psychosomatic effects, which is to say that the truth might *depress* the patient to the extent that his medical prognosis worsens. In these cases, should the physician lie or withhold the truth? Does the principle of beneficence *require* such actions? Confidentiality can also lead to tough cases. Imagine that a physician is treating both a husband and wife and that one of the two has a contagious health condition that could affect the other. Further imagine that the afflicted does not want to share the information (perhaps because it would reveal marital transgressions), despite the health risks to the spouse. Now imagine that the spouse comes in for treatment: can the physician disclose the health risk? Beneficence towards the current patient would seem to require such a disclosure, yet the confidentiality owed to the former patient would seem to prohibit it: what should physicians do in such conflicts?

Finally, in the third section, we will look at informed consent, competence, and surrogate decision making. Informed consent, often taken to be the most important concept in modern medical ethics, was conspicuously absent from Hippocrates' original suggestions. The idea is straightforward enough: many of us would think that physicians should not trick patients into accepting treatments; rather, patients should be able to make decisions about their own treatments. But is informed consent really an important medical value? Or else, given other values, such as beneficence, is it *superfluous*? An emphasis on consent presupposes that patients are *able* to give

it, which is not always the case. At the boundaries of consent, physicians might have to make determinations about *competence*, by which we mean the circumstances under which patients can or should be able to make decisions on their own behalf. Imagine, for example, that a patient is in a tremendous amount of pain and requests passive euthanasia (e.g., removal from some life-sustaining device). Should such a request be honored, or does the debilitating pain somehow serve to invalidate it? And, other than the cases of borderline competence, there are at least some cases where patient consent is clearly inappropriate, such as when a patient might be unconscious. Obviously medical decisions will still have to be made, but how? In these cases, we would usually recognize some procedure for *surrogate decision making* by some third party on behalf of the patient.

NOTE

1   Note that these protections are not necessarily absolute or uncontroversial. In times of public health crises, for example, it might be the case that individual protections (including those of confidentiality) might be justifiably suspended.

THE VIRTUOUS PHYSICIAN AND THE DOCTOR-PATIENT RELATIONSHIP

The Hippocratic Oath

Little is known about the life of Hippocrates, a Greek physician born about 460 BC. A collection of documents known as the *Hippocratic Writings* (largely written from the fifth to the fourth century BC) is believed to represent the remains of the Hippocratic school of medicine. Some of the works in this collection are credited to Hippocrates. The oath reprinted here, however, is believed to have been written by a

philosophical sect known as the Pythagoreans in the latter part of the fourth century BC. For the Middle Ages and later centuries, the Hippocratic Oath embodied the highest aspirations of the physician. It sets forth two sets of duties: (1) duties to the patient and (2) duties to the other members of the guild (profession) of medicine. In regard to the patient, it includes a set of absolute prohibitions (e.g., against abortion and euthanasia) as well as a statement of the physician's obligation to help and not to harm the patient.

I swear by Apollo Physician and Asclepius and Hygieia and Panaceia and all the gods and goddesses, making them my witnesses, that I will fulfill according to my ability and judgment this oath and this covenant:

To hold him who has taught me this art as equal to my parents and to live my life in partnership with him, and if he is in need of money to give him a share of mine, and to regard his offspring as equal to my brothers in male lineage and to teach them this art—if they desire to learn it—without fee and covenant; to give a share of precepts and oral instruction and all the other learning to my sons and to the sons of him who has instructed me and to pupils who have signed the covenant and have taken an oath according to the medical law, but to no one else.

I will apply dietetic measures for the benefit of the sick according to my ability and judgment; I will keep them from harm and injustice.

I will neither give a deadly drug to anybody if asked for it, nor will I make a suggestion to this effect. Similarly I will not give to a woman an abortive remedy. In purity and holiness I will guard my life and my art.

I will not use the knife, not even on sufferers from stone, but will withdraw in favor of such men as are engaged in this work.

Whatever houses I may visit, I will come for the benefit of the sick, remaining free of all intentional injustice, of all mischief and in particular of sexual relations with both female and male persons, be they free or slaves.

What I may see or hear in the course of the treatment or even outside of the treatment in regard to the life of men, which on no account one must spread abroad, I will keep to myself holding such things shameful to be spoken about.

If I fulfill this oath and do not violate it, may it be granted to me to enjoy life and art, being honored with fame among all men for all time to come; if I transgress it and swear falsely, may the opposite of all this be my lot.

◆ ◆ ◆ ◆ ◆

EDMUND D. PELLEGRINO

The Virtuous Physician and the Ethics of Medicine

... In most professional ethical codes, virtue and duty-based ethics are intermingled. The Hippocratic Oath, for example, imposes certain duties like protection of confidentiality, avoiding abortion, not harming the patient. But the Hippocratic physician also pledges: "... in purity and holiness I will guard my life and my art." This is an exhortation to be a good person and a virtuous physician, in order to serve patients in an ethically responsible way.

Likewise, in one of the most humanistic statements in medical literature, the first century AD writer, Scribonius Largus, made *humanitas* (compassion) an essential virtue. It is thus really a role-specific duty. In doing so he was applying the Stoic doctrine of virtue to medicine [1, 5].

The latest version (1980) of the AMA "Principles of Medical Ethics" similarly intermingles duties, rights, and exhortations to virtue. It speaks of "standards of behaviour," "essentials of honorable behavior," dealing "honestly" with patients and colleagues and exposing colleagues "deficient in character." The *Declaration of Geneva*, which must meet the challenge of the widest array of value systems, nonetheless calls for practice "with conscience and dignity" in keeping with "the honor and noble traditions of the profession." Though their first allegiance must be to the Communist ethos, even the Soviet physician is urged to preserve "the high title of physician," "to keep and develop the beneficial traditions of medicine" and to "dedicate" all his "knowledge and strength to the care of the sick."

Those who are cynical of any protestation of virtue on the part of physicians will interpret these excerpts as the last remnants of a dying tradition of altruistic benevolence. But at the very least, they attest to the recognition that the good of the patient cannot be fully protected by rights and duties alone. Some degree of supererogation is built into the nature of the relationship of those who are ill and those who profess to help them.

This too may be why many graduating classes, still idealistic about their calling, choose the Prayer of Maimonides (not by Maimonides at all) over the more deontological Oath of Hippocrates. In that "prayer" the physician asks: "... may neither avarice nor miserliness, nor thirst for glory or for a great reputation engage my mind; for the enemies of truth and philanthropy may easily deceive me and make me forgetful of my lofty aim of doing good to thy children." This is an unequivocal call to virtue and it is hard to imagine even the most cynical graduate failing to comprehend its message.

All professional medical codes, then, are built of a three-tiered system of obligations related to the special roles of physicians in society. In the ascending order of ethical sensitivity they are: observance of the laws of the land, then observance of rights and fulfillment of duties, and finally the practice of virtue.

A legally based ethic concentrates on the minimum requirements—the duties imposed by human laws which protect against the grosser aberrations of personal rights. Licensure, the laws of torts and contracts, prohibitions against discrimination, good Samaritan laws, definitions of death, and the protection of human subjects of experimentation are elements of a legalistic ethic.

At the next level is the ethics of rights and duties which spells out obligations beyond what law defines. Here, benevolence and beneficence take on more than their legal meaning. The ideal of service, of responsiveness to the special needs of those who are ill, some degree of compassion, kindliness, promise-keeping, truth-telling, and non-maleficence and specific obligations like confidentiality and autonomy, are included. How these principles are applied, and conflicts among them resolved in the patient's best interests, are subjects of widely varying interpretation. How sensitively these issues are confronted depends more on the physician's character than his capability at ethical discourse or moral casuistry.

Virtue-based ethics goes beyond these first two levels. We expect the virtuous person to do the right and the good even at the expense of personal sacrifice and legitimate self-interest. Virtue ethics expands the notions of benevolence, beneficence, conscientiousness, compassion, and fidelity well beyond what strict duty might require. It makes some degree of supererogation mandatory because it calls for standards of ethical performance that exceed those prevalent in the rest of society [6].

At each of these three levels there are certain dangers from over-zealous or misguided observance. Legalistic ethical systems tend toward a justification for minimalistic ethics, a narrow definition of benevolence or beneficence, and a contract-minded physician-patient relationship. Duty- and rights-based ethics may be distorted by too strict adherence to the letter of ethical principles without the modulations and nuances the spirit of those principles implies. Virtue-based ethics, being the least specific, can more easily lapse into self-righteous paternalism or an unwelcome over-involvement in the personal life of the patient. Misapplication of any moral system even with good intent converts benevolence into maleficence. The virtuous person might be expected to be more sensitive to these aberrations than someone whose ethics is more deontologically or legally flavored.

The more we yearn for ethical sensitivity the less we lean on rights, duties, rules, and principles and the more we lean on the character traits of the moral agent. Paradoxically, without rules, rights, and duties specifically spelled out, we cannot predict what form a particular person's expression of virtue will take. In a pluralistic society, we need laws, rules and principles to assure a dependable minimum level of moral conduct. But that minimal level is insufficient in the complex and often unpredictable circumstances of decision-making, where technical and value desiderata intersect so inextricably.

The virtuous physician does not act from unreasoned, uncritical intuitions about what feels good. His dispositions are ordered in accord with that "right reason" which both Aristotle and Aquinas considered essential to virtue. Medicine is itself ultimately an exercise of practical wisdom—a right way of acting in difficult and uncertain circumstances for a specific end, i.e., the good of a particular person who is ill. It is when the choice of a right and good action becomes more difficult, when the temptations to self-interest are most insistent, when unexpected nuances of good and evil arise and no one is looking, that the differences between an ethics based in virtue and an ethics based in law and/or duty can most clearly be distinguished.

Virtue-based professional ethics distinguishes itself, therefore, less in the avoidance of overtly immoral practices than in avoidance of those at the margin of moral responsibility. Physicians are confronted, in today's morally relaxed climate, with an increasing number of new practices that pit altruism against self-interest. Most are not illegal, or, strictly speaking, immoral in a rights- or duty-based ethic. But they are not consistent with the higher levels of moral sensitivity that a virtue-ethics demands. These practices usually involve opportunities for profit from the illness of others, narrowing the concept of service for personal convenience, taking a proprietary attitude with respect to medical knowledge, and placing loyalty to the profession above loyalty to patients.

Under the first heading, we might include such things as investment in and ownership of for-profit hospitals, hospital chains, nursing homes, dialysis units, tie-in arrangements with radiological or laboratory services, escalation of fees for repetitive, high-volume procedures, and lax indications for their use, especially when third party payers "allow" such charges.

The second heading might include the ever decreasing availability and accessibility of physicians, the diffusion of individual patient responsibility in group practice so that the patient never knows whom he will see or who is on call, the itinerant emergency room physician who works two days and skips three with little commitment to hospital or community, and the growing overindulgence of physicians in vacations, recreation, and "self-development."

The third category might include such things as "selling one's services" for whatever the market will bear, providing what the market demands and not necessarily what the community needs, patenting new procedures or keeping them secret from potential competitor-colleagues, looking at the investment of time, effort, and capital in a medical education as justification of "making it back," or forgetting that medical knowledge is drawn from the cumulative experience of a multitude of patients, clinicians, and investigators.

Under the last category might be included referrals on the basis of friendship and reciprocity rather than skill, resisting consultations and second opinions as affronts to one's competence, placing the interest of the referring physician above those of the patients, looking the other way in the face of incompetence or even dishonesty in one's professional colleagues.

These and many other practices are defended today by sincere physicians and even encouraged in this era of competition, legalism, and self-indulgence. Some can be rationalized even in a deontological ethic. But it would be impossible to envision the physician committed to the virtues assenting to these practices. A virtue-based ethics simply does not fluctuate with what the dominant social mores will tolerate. It must interpret benevolence, beneficence, and responsibility in a way that reduces self-interest and enhances altruism. It is the only convincing answer the profession can give to the growing perception clearly manifest in the legal commentaries in the FTC ruling that medicine is nothing more than business and should be regulated as such.

A virtue-based ethic is inherently elitist, in the best sense, because its adherents demand more of themselves than the prevailing morality. It calls forth that extra measure of dedication that has made the best physicians in every era exemplars of what the human spirit can achieve. No matter to what depths a society may fall, virtuous persons will always be the beacons that light the way back to moral sensitivity; virtuous physicians are the beacons that show the way back to moral credibility for the whole profession.

Albert Jonsen, rightly I believe, diagnoses the central paradox in medicine as the tension between self-interest and altruism [4]. No amount of deft juggling of rights, duties, or principles will suffice to resolve that tension. We are all too good at rationalizing what we want to do so that personal gain can be converted from vice to virtue. Only a character formed by the virtues can feel the nausea of such intellectual hypocrisy.

To be sure, the twin themes of self-interest and altruism have been inextricably joined in the history of medicine. There have always been physicians who reject the virtues or, more often, claim them falsely. But, in addition, there have been physicians, more often than the critics of medicine would allow, who have been truly virtuous both in intent and act. They have been, and remain, the leaven of the profession and the hope of all who are ill. They form the seawall that will not be eroded even by the powerful forces of commercialization, bureaucratization, and mechanization inevitable in modern medicine.

We cannot, need not, and indeed must not, wait for a medical analogue of MacIntyre's "new St. Benedict" to show us the way. There is no new concept of virtue waiting to be discovered that is peculiarly suited to the dilemmas of our own dark age. We must recapture the courage to speak of character, virtue, and perfection in living a good life. We must encourage those who are willing to dedicate themselves to a "higher standard of self effacement" [2]. We need

the courage, too, to accept the obvious split in the profession between those who see and feel the altruistic imperatives in medicine, and those who do not. Those who at heart believe that the pursuit of private self-interest serves the public good are very different from those who believe in the restraint of self-interest. We forget that physicians since the beginnings of the profession have subscribed to different values and virtues. We need only recall that the Hippocratic Oath was the Oath of physicians of the Pythagorean school at a time when most Greek physicians followed essentially a craft ethic [3]. A perusal of the Hippocratic Corpus itself, which intersperses ethics and etiquette, will show how differently its treatises deal with fees, the care of incurable patients, and the business aspects of the craft.

The illusion that all physicians share a common devotion to a high-flown set of ethical principles has done damage to medicine by raising expectations some members of the profession could not, or will not, fulfill. Today, we must be more forthright about the differences in value commitment among physicians. Professional codes must be more explicit about the relationships between duties, rights, and virtues. Such explicitness encourages a more honest relationship between physicians and patients and removes the hypocrisy of verbal assent to a general code, to which an individual physician may not really subscribe. Explicitness enables patients to choose among physicians on the basis of their ethical commitments as well as their reputations for technical expertise.

Conceptual clarity will not assure virtuous behavior. Indeed, virtues are usually distorted if they are the subject of too conscious a design. But conceptual clarity will distinguish between motives and provide criteria for judging the moral commitment one can expect from the profession and from its individual members. It can also inspire those whose virtuous inclinations need reinforcement in the current climate of commercialization of the healing relationship.

To this end the current resurgence of interest in virtue-based ethics is altogether salubrious. Linked to a theory of patient good and a theory of rights and duties, it could provide the needed groundwork for a reconstruction of professional medical ethics as that work matures. Perhaps even more progress can be made if we take Shakespeare's advice in *Hamlet*: "Assume the virtue if you have it not.... For use almost can change the stamp of nature."

BIBLIOGRAPHY

[1] Cicero: 1967, *Moral Obligations*, J. Higginbotham (trans.), University of California Press, Berkeley and Los Angeles.

[2] Cushing, H.: 1929, *Consecratio Medici and Other Papers*, Little, Brown and Co., Boston.

[3] Edelstein, L.: 1967, "The Professional Ethics of the Greek Physician," in O. Temkin (ed.), *Ancient Medicine: Selected Papers of Ludwig Edelstein*, Johns Hopkins University Press, Baltimore.

[4] Jonsen, A.: 1983, "Watching the Doctor," *New England Journal of Medicine* Vol. 308: 25, 1531-35.

[5] Pellegrino, E.: 1983, "*Scribonius Largus* and the Origins of Medical Humanism," address to the American Osler Society.

[6] Reader, J.: 1982, "Beneficence, Supererogation, and Role Duty," in E. Shelp (ed.), *Beneficence and Health Care*, D. Reidel, Dordrecht, Holland, 83-108.

◆ ◆ ◆ ◆ ◆

EZEKIEL J. EMANUEL and LINDA L. EMANUEL
Four Models of the Physician-Patient Relationship

During the last two decades or so, there has been a struggle over the patient's role in medical decision making that is often characterized as a conflict between autonomy and health, between the values of the patient and the values of the physician. Seeking to curtail physician dominance, many have advocated an ideal of greater patient control. Others question this ideal because it fails to acknowledge the potentially imbalanced nature of this interaction when one party is sick and searching for security, and when judgments entail the interpretation of technical information. Still others are trying to delineate a more mutual relationship. This struggle shapes the expectations of physicians and patients as well as the ethical and legal standards for the physician's duties, informed consent, and medical malpractice. This struggle forces us to ask, What should be the ideal physician-patient relationship?

We shall outline four models of the physician-patient interaction, emphasizing the different understandings of (1) the goals of the physician-patient interaction, (2) the physician's obligations, (3) the role of patient values, and (4) the conception of patient autonomy. To elaborate the abstract description of these four models, we shall indicate the types of response the models might suggest in a clinical situation. Third, we shall also indicate how these models inform the current debate about the ideal physician-patient relationship. Finally, we shall evaluate these models and recommend one as the preferred model.

As outlined, the models are Weberian ideal types. They may not describe any particular physician-patient interactions but they highlight, free from complicating details, different visions of the essential characteristics of the physician-patient interaction. Consequently, they do not embody minimum ethical or legal standards, but rather constitute regulative ideals that are "higher than the law" but not "above the law."

The Paternalistic Model

First is the *paternalistic* model, sometimes called the parental or priestly model. In this model, the physician-patient interaction ensures that patients receive the interventions that best promote their health and well-being. To this end, physicians use their skills to determine the patient's medical condition and his or her stage in the disease process and to identify the medical tests and treatments most likely to restore the patient's health or ameliorate pain. Then the physician presents the patient with selected information that will encourage the patient to consent to the intervention the physician considers best. At the extreme, the physician authoritatively informs the patient when the intervention will be initiated.

The paternalistic model assumes that there are shared objective criteria for determining what is best. Hence the physician can discern what is in the patient's best interest with limited patient participation. Ultimately it is assumed that the patient will be thankful for decisions made by the physician even if he or she would not agree to them at the time. In the tension between the patient's autonomy and well-being, between choice and health, the paternalistic physician's main emphasis is toward the latter.

In the paternalistic model, the physician acts as the patient's guardian, articulating and implementing what is best for the patient. As such, the physician has obligations, including that of placing the patient's interest above his or her own and soliciting the views of others when lacking adequate knowledge. The conception of patient autonomy is patient assent, either at the time or later, to the physician's determinations of what is best.

The Informative Model

Second is the *informative* model, sometimes called the scientific, engineering, or consumer model. In this model, the objective of the physician-patient interaction is for the physician to provide the patient with all relevant information, for the patient to select the medical interventions he or she wants, and for the physician to execute the selected interventions. To this end, the physician informs the patient of his or her disease state, the nature of possible diagnostic and therapeutic interventions, the nature and probability of risks and benefits associated with the interventions, and any uncertainties of knowledge. At the extreme, patients could come to know all medical information relevant to their disease and available interventions and select the interventions that best realize their values.

The informative model assumes a fairly clear distinction between facts and values. The patient's values are well defined and known; what the patient lacks is facts. It is the physician's obligation to provide all the available facts, and the patient's values then determine what treatments are to be given. There is no role for the physician's values, the physician's understanding of the patient's values, or his or her judgment of the worth of the patient's values. In the informative model, the physician is a purveyor of technical expertise, providing the patient with the means to exercise control. As technical experts, physicians have important obligations to provide truthful information, to maintain competence in their area of expertise, and to consult others when their knowledge or skills are lacking. The conception of patient autonomy is patient control over medical decision making.

The Interpretive Model

The third model is the *interpretive* model. The aim of the physician-patient interaction is to elucidate the patient's values and what he or she actually wants, and to help the patient select the available medical interventions that realize these values. Like the informative physician, the interpretive physician provides the patient with information on the nature of the condition and the risks and benefits of possible interventions. Beyond this, however, the interpretive physician assists the patient in elucidating and articulating his or her values and in determining what medical interventions best realize the specified values, thus helping to interpret the patient's values for the patient.

According to the interpretive model, the patient's values are not necessarily fixed and known to the patient. They are often inchoate, and the patient may only partially understand them, they may conflict when applied to specific situations. Consequently, the physician working with the patient must elucidate and make coherent these values. To do this, the physician works with the patient to reconstruct the patient's goals and aspirations, commitments and character. At the extreme, the physician must conceive of the patient's life as a narrative whole, and from this specify the patient's values and their priorities. Then the physician determines which tests and treatments best realize these values. Importantly, the physician does not dictate to the patient; it is the patient who ultimately decides which values and course of action best fit who he or she is. Neither is the physician judging the patient's values; he or she helps the patient to understand and use them in the medical situation.

In the interpretive model, the physician is a counselor, analogous to a cabinet minister's advisory role to a head of state, supplying relevant information, helping to elucidate values, and suggesting what medical interventions realize these values. Thus the physician's obligations include those enumerated in the informative model but also require engaging the patient in a joint process of understanding. Accordingly, the conception of patient autonomy is self-understanding; the patient comes to know more clearly who he or she is and how the various medical options bear on his or her identity.

The Deliberative Model

Fourth is the *deliberative* model. The aim of the physician-patient interaction is to help the patient determine and choose the best health-related values that can be realized in the clinical situation. To this end, the physician must delineate information on the patient's clinical situation and then help elucidate the types of values embodied in the available options. The physician's objectives include suggesting why certain health-related values are more worthy and should be aspired to. At the extreme, the physician and patient engage in deliberation about what kind of health related values the patient could and ultimately should pursue. The physician discusses only health-related values, that is, values that affect or are affected by the patient's disease and treatments; he or she recognizes that many elements of morality are unrelated to the patient's disease or treatment and beyond the scope of their professional relationship. Further, the physician aims at no more than moral persuasion; ultimately, coercion is avoided, and the patient must define his or her life and select the ordering of values to be espoused. By engaging in moral deliberation, the physician and patient judge the worthiness and importance of the health-related values.

In the deliberative model, the physician acts as a teacher or friend, engaging the patient in dialogue on what course of action would be best. Not only does the physician indicate what the patient could do, but, knowing the patient and wishing what is best, the physician indicates what the patient should do—what decision regarding medical therapy would be admirable. The conception of patient autonomy is moral self-development; the patient is empowered not simply to follow unexamined preferences or examined values, but to consider, through dialogue, alternative health-related values, their worthiness, and their implications for treatment.

Comparing the Four Models

Importantly, all models have a role for patient autonomy; a main factor that differentiates the models is their particular conceptions of patient autonomy. Therefore, no single model can be endorsed because it alone promotes patient autonomy. Instead the models must be compared and evaluated, at least in part, by evaluating the adequacy of their particular conceptions of patient autonomy.

The four models are not exhaustive. At a minimum, there might be added a fifth: the instrumental model. In this model, the patient's values are irrelevant; the physician aims for some goal independent of the patient, such as the good of society or the furtherance of scientific knowledge. The Tuskegee syphilis experiment and the Willowbrook hepatitis study are examples of this model. As the moral condemnation of these cases reveals, this model is not an ideal, but an aberration. Thus we have not elaborated on it herein.

A Clinical Case

To make tangible these abstract descriptions and to crystallize essential differences among the models, we will illustrate the responses they suggest in a clinical situation, that of a 43-year-old pre-menopausal woman who has recently discovered a breast mass. Surgery reveals a 3.5-cm ductal carcinoma with no lymph node involvement that is estrogen receptor positive. Chest roentgenogram, bone scan, and liver function tests reveal no evidence of metastatic disease. The patient was recently divorced and has gone back to work as a legal aide to support herself. What should the physician say to this patient?

In the paternalistic model a physician might say, "There are two alternative therapies to protect against recurrence of cancer in your breast: mastectomy or radiation. We now know that the survival with lumpectomy combined with radiation therapy is equal to that with mastectomy. Because lumpectomy and radiation offers the best survival and the best cosmetic result, it is to be preferred. I have asked the radiation therapist to come and discuss radiation treatment with you. We also need to protect you against the spread of the cancer to other parts of your body. Even though the chance of recurrence is low, you are young, and we should not leave any therapeutic possibilities untried. Recent studies involving chemotherapy suggest improvements in survival without recurrence of breast cancer. Indeed, the National Cancer Institute (NCI) recommends chemotherapy for women with your type of breast cancer. Chemotherapy has side effects. Nevertheless, a few months of hardship now are worth the potential added years of life without cancer."

In the informative model, a physician might say, "With node-negative breast cancer there are two issues before you: local control and systemic control. For local control, the options are mastectomy or lumpectomy with or without radiation. From many studies we know that mastectomy and lumpectomy with radiation result in identical overall survival, about 80 per cent 10-year survival. Lumpectomy without radiation results in a 30 per cent to 40 per cent chance of tumor recurrence in the breast. The second issue relates to systemic control. We know that chemotherapy prolongs survival for premenopausal women who have axillary nodes involved with tumor. The role for women with node-negative breast cancer is less clear. Individual studies suggest that chemotherapy is of no benefit in terms of improving overall survival, but a comprehensive review of all studies suggests that there is a survival benefit. Several years ago, the NCI suggested that for women like yourself, chemotherapy can have a positive therapeutic impact. Finally, let me inform you that there are clinical trials, for which you are eligible, to evaluate the benefits of chemotherapy for patients with node-negative breast cancer. I can enroll you in a study if you want. I will be happy to give you any further information you feel you need."

The interpretive physician might outline much of the same information as the informative physician, then engage in discussion to elucidate the patient's wishes, and conclude, "It sounds to me as if you have conflicting wishes. Understandably, you seem uncertain how to balance the demands required for receiving additional treatment, rejuvenating your personal affairs, and maintaining your psychological equilibrium. Let me try to express a perspective that fits your position. Fighting your cancer is important, but it must leave you with a healthy self-image and quality time outside the hospital. This view seems compatible with undergoing radiation therapy but not chemotherapy. A lumpectomy with radiation maximizes your chance of surviving while preserving your breast. Radiotherapy fights your breast cancer without disfigurement. Conversely, chemotherapy would prolong the duration of therapy by many months. Further, the benefits of chemotherapy in terms of survival are smaller and more controversial. Given the recent changes in your life, you have too many new preoccupations to undergo months of chemotherapy for a questionable benefit. Do I understand you? We can talk again in a few days."

The deliberative physician might begin by outlining the same factual information, then engage in a conversation to elucidate the patient's values, but continue, "It seems clear that you should undergo radiation therapy. It offers maximal survival with minimal risk, disfigurement, and disruption of your life. The issue of chemotherapy is different, fraught with conflicting data. Balancing all the options, I think the best one for you is to enter a trial that is investigating the potential benefit of chemotherapy for women with node-negative breast cancer. First, it ensures that you receive excellent medical care. At this point, we do not know which therapy maximizes survival. In a clinical study the schedule of follow-up visits, tests, and decisions is specified by leading breast cancer experts to ensure that all the women receive care that is the best available anywhere. A second reason to participate in a trial is altruistic; it allows you to contribute something to women with breast cancer in the future who will face difficult choices. Over decades, thousands of women have participated in studies that inform our current treatment practices. Without those women, and the knowledge they made possible, we would probably still be giving you and all other women with breast cancer mastectomies. By enrolling in a trial you participate in a tradition in which women of one generation receive the highest standard of care available but also enhance the care of women in future generations because medicine has learned something about which interventions are better. I must tell you that I am not involved in the study; if you elect to enroll in this trial, you will initially see another breast cancer expert to plan your therapy. I have sought to explain our current knowledge and offer my recommendation so you can make the best possible decision."

Lacking the normal interchange with patients, these statements may seem contrived, even caricatures. Nevertheless, they highlight the essence of each model and suggest how the objectives and assumptions of each inform a physician's approach to his or her patients. Similar statements can be imagined for other clinical situations such as an obstetrician discussing prenatal testing or a cardiologist discussing cholesterol-reducing interventions.

The Current Debate and the Four Models

In recent decades there has been a call for greater patient autonomy or, as some have called it, "patient sovereignty" conceived as patient *choice* and *control* over medical decisions. This shift toward the informative model is embodied in the adoption of business terms for medicine, as when physicians are described as health care providers and patients as consumers. It can also be found in the propagation of patient rights statements, in the promotion of living-will laws, and in rules regarding human experimentation. For instance, the opening sentences of one law state: "The

Rights of the Terminally Ill Act authorizes an adult person to *control* decisions regarding administration of life-sustaining treatment. The Act merely provides one way by which a terminally ill patient's *desires* regarding the use of life-sustaining procedures can be legally implemented" (emphasis added).[1] Indeed, living-will laws do not require or encourage patients to discuss the issue of terminating care with their physicians before signing such documents. Similarly, decisions in "right-to-die" cases emphasize patient control over medical decisions. As one court put it:

> The right to refuse medical treatment is basic and fundamental.... Its exercise requires no one's approval.... *[T]he controlling decision belongs to a competent informed patient.... It is not a medical decision for her physicians to make ... It is a moral and philosophical decision that, being a competent adult, is [the patient's] alone.*[2] (emphasis added)

Probably the most forceful endorsement of the informative model as the ideal inheres in informed consent standards. Prior to the 1970s, the standard for informed consent was "physician based." Since 1972 and the *Canterbury* case, however, the emphasis has been on a "patient-oriented" standard of informed consent in which the physician has a "duty" to provide appropriate medical facts to empower the patient to use his or her values to determine what interventions should be implemented.

> True consent to what happens to one's self is the informed exercise of a choice, and that entails an opportunity to evaluate knowledgeably the options available and the risks attendant upon each.... *[I]t is the prerogative of the patient, not the physician, to determine for himself the direction in which his interests seem to lie.* To enable the patient to chart his course understandably, some familiarity with the therapeutic alternatives and their hazards becomes essential.[3] (emphasis added)

Shared Decision Making

Despite its dominance, many have found the informative model somewhat "arid."[4] The President's Commission and others contend that the ideal relationship does not vest moral authority and medical decision-making power exclusively in the patient but must be a process of shared decision making constructed around "mutual participation and respect."[5] The President's Commission argues that the physician's role is "to help the patient understand the medical situation and available courses of action, and the patient conveys his or her concerns and wishes."[6] Brock and Wartman[7] stress this fact-value "division of labor"—having the physician provide information while the patient makes value decisions—by describing "shared decision making" as a collaborative process

> in which both physicians and patients make active and essential contributions. Physicians bring their medical training, knowledge, and expertise—including an understanding of the available treatment alternatives—to the diagnosis and management of patients' conditions. Patients bring knowledge of their own subjective aims and values, through which risks and benefits of various treatment options can be evaluated. With this approach, selecting the best treatment for a particular patient requires the contribution of both parties.

Similarly, in discussing ideal medical decision making, Eddy[8] argues for this fact-value division of labor between the physician and patient as the ideal:

> It is important to separate the decision process into these two steps.... The first step is a question of facts. The anchor is empirical evidence.... [T]he second step is a question not of facts but of personal values or preferences. The thought process is not analytic but personal and subjective.... [I]t is the

patient's preferences that should determine the decision.... Ideally, you and I [the physicians] are not in the picture. What matters is what Mrs. Smith thinks.

This view of shared decision making seems to vest the medical decision-making authority with the patient while relegating physicians to technicians "transmitting medical information and using their technical skills as the patient directs."9 Thus, while the advocates of "shared decision making" may aspire toward a mutual dialogue between physician and patient, the substantive view informing their ideal reembodies the informative model under a different label.

Other commentators have articulated more mutual models of the physician-patient interaction. Prominent among these efforts is Katz's10 *The Silent World of Doctor and Patient*. Relying on a Freudian view in which self-knowledge and self-determination are inherently limited because of unconscious influences, Katz views dialogue as a mechanism for greater self-understanding of one's values and objectives. According to Katz, this view places a duty on physicians and patients to reflect and communicate so that patients can gain a greater self-understanding and self-determination. Katz's insight is also available on grounds other than Freudian psychological theory and is consistent with the interpretive model.

Objections to the Paternalistic Model

It is widely recognized that the paternalistic model is justified during emergencies when the time taken to obtain patient consent might irreversibly harm the patient. Beyond such limited circumstances, however, it is no longer tenable to assume that the physician and patient espouse similar values and views of what constitutes a benefit. Consequently, even physicians rarely advocate the paternalistic model as an ideal for routine physician-patient interactions.

Objections to the Informative Model

The informative model seems both descriptively and prescriptively inaccurate. First, this model seems to have no place for essential qualities of the ideal physician-patient relationship. The informative physician cares for the patient in the sense of competently implementing the patient's selected interventions. However, the informative physician lacks a caring approach that requires understanding what the patient values or should value and how his or her illness impinges on these values. Patients seem to expect their physician to have a caring approach; they deem a technically proficient but detached physician as deficient, and properly condemned. Further, the informative physician is proscribed from giving a recommendation for fear of imposing his or her will on the patient and thereby competing for the decision-making control that has been given to the patient. Yet, if one of the essential qualities of the ideal physician is the ability to assimilate medical facts, prior experience of similar situations, and intimate knowledge of the patient's view into a recommendation designed for the patient's specific medical and personal condition, then the informative physician cannot be ideal.

Second, in the informative model, the ideal physician is a highly trained subspecialist who provides detailed factual information and competently implements the patient's preferred medical intervention. Hence, the informative model perpetuates and accentuates the trend toward specialization and impersonalization within the medical profession.

Most importantly, the informative model's conception of patient autonomy seems philosophically untenable. The informative model presupposes that persons possess known and fixed values, but this is inaccurate. People are often uncertain about what they actually want. Further, unlike animals, people have what philosophers call "second-order desires,"11 that is, the capacity to reflect on their wishes and to revise their own desires and preferences. In fact, freedom of the will and autonomy inhere in having "second-order desires" and being able to change our preferences and modify our identities. Self-reflection and the capacity to change what we want often require a "process" of moral deliberation in which we assess the value of what we want. And this is a process that occurs with other people who know us well and can articulate a vision of who we ought to be that we can assent to. Even though changes in health or implementation of alternative interventions can have profound effects on what we desire and how we realize our desires, self-reflection and deliberation play no essential role in the informative physician-patient interaction. The informative model's conception of autonomy is incompatible with a vision of autonomy that incorporates second-order desires.

Objections to the Interpretive Model

The interpretive model rectifies this deficiency by recognizing that persons have second-order desires and dynamic value structures and placing the elucidation of values in the context of the patient's medical condition at the center of the physician-patient interaction. Nevertheless, there are objections to the interpretive model. Technical specialization militates against physicians cultivating the skills necessary to the interpretive model. With limited interpretive talents and limited time, physicians may unwittingly impose their own values under the guise of articulating the patient's values. And patients, overwhelmed by their medical condition and uncertain of their own views, may too easily accept this imposition. Such circumstances may push the interpretive model toward the paternalistic model in actual practice.

Further, autonomy viewed as self-understanding excludes evaluative judgment of the patient's values or attempts to persuade the patient to adopt her values. This constrains the guidance and recommendations the physician can offer. Yet in practice, especially in preventive medicine and risk-reduction interventions, physicians often attempt to persuade patients to adopt particular health-related values.

Physicians frequently urge patients with high cholesterol levels who smoke to change their dietary habits, quit smoking, and begin exercise programs before initiating drug therapy. The justification given for these changes is that patients should value their health more than they do. Similarly, physicians are encouraged to persuade their human immunodeficiency virus (HIV)-infected patients who might be engaging in unsafe sexual practices either to abstain or, realistically, to adopt "safer sex" practices. Such appeals are not made to promote the HIV-infected patient's own health, but are grounded on an appeal for the patient to assume responsibility for the good of others. Consequently, by excluding valuative judgments, the interpretive model seems to characterize inaccurately ideal physician-patient interactions.

Objections to the Deliberative Model

The fundamental objections to the deliberative model focus on whether it is proper for physicians to judge patients' values and promote particular health-related values. First, physicians do not possess privileged knowledge of the priority of health-related values relative to other values. Indeed, since ours is a pluralistic society in which people espouse incommensurable values, it is likely that a physician's values and view of which values are higher will conflict with those of other physicians and those of his or her patients.

Second, the nature of the moral deliberation between physician and patient, the physician's recommended interventions, and the actual treatments used will depend on the values of the particular physician treating the patient. However, recommendations and care provided to patients should not depend on the physician's judgment of the worthiness of the patient's values or on the physician's particular values. As one bioethicist put it:

> The hand is broken; the physician can repair the hand; therefore the physician must

repair the hand—as well as possible—without regard to personal values that might lead the physician to think ill of the patient or of the patient's values.... [A]t the level of clinical practice, medicine should be value-free in the sense that the personal values of the physician should not distort the making of medical decisions.[12]

Third, it may be argued that the deliberative model misconstrues the purpose of the physician-patient interaction. Patients see their physicians to receive health care, not to engage in moral deliberation or to revise their values. Finally, like the interpretive model, the deliberative model may easily metamorphose into unintended paternalism, the very practice that generated the public debate over proper physician-patient interaction.

The Preferred Model and the Practical Implications

Clearly, under different clinical circumstances, different models may be appropriate. Indeed, at different times, all four models may justifiably guide physicians and patients. Nevertheless, it is important to specify one model as the shared, paradigmatic reference; exceptions to use other models would not be automatically condemned, but would require justification based on the circumstances of a particular situation. Thus, it is widely agreed that in an emergency where delays in treatment to obtain informed consent might irreversibly harm the patient, the paternalistic model correctly guides physician-patient interactions. Conversely, for patients who have clear but conflicting values, the interpretive model is probable justified. For instance, a 65-year-old woman who has been treated for acute leukemia may have clearly decided against reinduction chemotherapy if she relapses. Several months before the anticipated birth of her first grandchild, the patient relapses. The patient becomes torn about whether to endure the risks of reinduction chemotherapy in order to live to see her first grandchild or whether to refuse therapy, resigning herself to not seeing her grandchild. In such cases, the physician may justifiably adopt the interpretive approach. In other circumstances, where there is only a one-time physician-patient interaction without an ongoing relationship in which the patient's values can be elucidated and compared with ideals, such as in a walk-in center, the informative model may be justified.

Descriptively and prescriptively, we claim that the ideal physician-patient relationship is the deliberative model. We will adduce six points to justify this claim. First, the deliberative model more nearly embodies our ideal of autonomy. It is an oversimplification and distortion of the Western tradition to view respecting autonomy as simply permitting a person to select, unrestricted by coercion, ignorance, physical interference, and the like, his or her preferred course of action from a comprehensive list of available options. Freedom and control over medical decisions alone do not constitute patient autonomy. Autonomy requires that individuals critically assess their own values and preferences; determine whether they are desirable; affirm, upon reflection, these values as ones that should justify their actions; and then be free to initiate action to realize the values. The process of deliberation integral to the deliberative model is essential for realizing patient autonomy understood in this way.

Second, our society's image of an ideal physician is not limited to one who knows and communicates to the patient relevant factual information and competently implements medical interventions. The ideal physician—often embodied in literature, art, and popular culture—is a caring physician who integrates the information and relevant values to make a recommendation and through discussion, attempts to persuade the patient to accept this recommendation as the intervention that best promotes his or her overall well-being. Thus, we expect the best physicians to engage their patients in evaluative discussions of health issues and related values. The physician's discussion does not invoke values that are unrelated or tangentially related to the patient's illness and potential therapies. Importantly, these efforts are not restricted to situations in which patients might make "irrational and harmful" choices[13] but extend to all health care decisions.

Third, the deliberative model is not a disguised form of paternalism. Previously there may have been category mistakes in which instances of the deliberative model have been erroneously identified as physician paternalism. And no doubt, in practice, the deliberative physician may occasionally lapse into paternalism. However, like the ideal teacher, the deliberative physician attempts to persuade the patient of the worthiness of certain values, not to impose those values paternalistically; the physician's aim is not to subject the patient to his or her will, but to persuade the patient of a course of action as desirable. In the *Laws*, Plato[14] characterizes this fundamental distinction between persuasion and imposition for medical practice that distinguishes the deliberative from the paternalistic model:

> A physician to slaves never gives his patient any account of his illness.... [T]he physician offers some orders gleaned from experience with an air of infallible knowledge, in the brusque fashion of a dictator.... The free physician, who usually cares for free men, treats their disease first by thoroughly discussing with the patient and his friends his ailment. This way he learns something from the sufferer and simultaneously instructs him. Then the physician does not give his medications until he has persuaded the patient; the physician aims at complete restoration of health by persuading the patient to comply with his therapy.

Fourth, physician values are relevant to patients and do inform their choice of a physician. When a pregnant woman chooses an obstetrician who does not routinely perform a battery of prenatal tests or, alternatively, one who strongly favors them; and when patients seek an aggressive cardiologist who favors procedural interventions or one who concentrates therapy on dietary changes, stress reduction, and life-style modifications, they are, consciously or not, selecting a physician based on the values that guide their medical decisions. And, when disagreements between physicians and patients arise, there are discussions over which values are more important and should be realized in medical care. Occasionally, when such disagreements undermine the physician-patient relationship and a caring attitude, a patient's care is transferred to another physician. Indeed, in the informative model the grounds for transferring care to a new physician is either the physician's ignorance or incompetence. But patients seem to switch physicians because they do not "like" a particular physician or that physician's attitude or approach.

Fifth, we seem to believe that physicians should not only help fit therapies to the patients' elucidated values, but should also promote health-related values. As noted, we expect physicians to promote certain values, such as "safer sex" for patients with HIV or abstaining from or limiting alcohol use. Similarly, patients are willing to adjust their values and actions to be more compatible with health-promoting values. This is in the nature of seeking a caring medical recommendation.

Finally, it may well be that many physicians currently lack the training and capacity to articulate the values underlying their recommendations and persuade patients that these values are worthy. But, in part, this deficiency is a consequence of the tendencies toward specialization and the avoidance of discussions of values by physicians that are perpetuated and justified by the dominant informative model. Therefore, if the deliberative model seems most appropriate, then we need to implement changes in medical care and education to encourage a more caring approach. We must stress understanding rather than mere provisions of factual information in keeping with the legal standards of informed consent and medical malpractice; we must educate physicians not just to spend more time in physician-patient communication but to elucidate and articulate the values underlying their medical care decisions, including routine ones; we must shift the publicly assumed conception of patient autonomy that shapes both the physician's and the patient's expectations from patient control to moral development. Most important, we must recognize that developing a deliberative physician-patient relationship requires a considerable amount of time. We must develop a health care financing system that properly reimburses—rather than penalizes—physicians for taking the time to discuss values with their patients.

Conclusion

Over the last few decades, the discourse regarding the physician-patient relationship has focused on two extremes: autonomy and paternalism. Many have attacked physicians as paternalistic, urging the empowerment of patients to control their own care. This view, the informative model, has become dominant in bioethics and legal standards. This model embodies a defective conception of patient autonomy, and it reduces the physician's role to that of a technologist. The essence of doctoring is a fabric of knowledge, understanding, teaching, and action, in which the caring physician integrates the patient's medical condition and health-related values, makes a recommendation on the appropriate course of action, and tries to persuade the patient of the worthiness of this approach and the values it realizes. The physician with a caring attitude is the ideal embodied in the deliberative model, the ideal that should inform laws and policies that regulate the physician-patient interaction.

Finally, it may be worth noting that the four models outlined herein are not limited to the medical realm; they may inform the public conception of other professional interactions as well. We suggest that the ideal relationship between lawyer and client, religious mentor and laity, and educator and student are well described by the deliberative model, at least in some of their essential aspects.

NOTES

1   "Uniform Rights of the Terminally Ill Act," in *Handbook of Living Will Laws* (New York, NY: Society for the Right to Die, 1987), 135-47.

2   *Bouvia v. Superior Court*, 225 Cal Rptr 297 (1986).

3   *Canterbury v. Spence*, 464 F2d 772 (D.C. Cir 1572).

4   President's Commission for the Study of Ethical Problems in Medicine and Biomedical and Behavioral Research. *Making Health Care Decisions* (Washington, DC: US Government Printing Office, 1982).

5   Ibid; Crock D. "The Ideal of Shared Decision-Making between Physicians and Patients," *Kennedy Institute J Ethics* (1991) Vol. 1: 28-47.

6   President's Commission, op. cit.

7   Brock D.W., Wartman S.A. "When Competent Patients Make Irrational Choices," *N Engl J Med.* (1990) Vol. 322: 1595-99.

8   Eddy D.M. "Anatomy of a Decision," *JAMA* (1990) Vol. 263: 441-43.

9   President's Commission, op. cit.

10 Katz J. *The Silent World of Doctor and Patient* (New York, NY: Free Press, 1984).

11 Frankfurt H. "Freedom of the Will and the Concept of a Person," *J. Philosophy* (1971) Vol. 68: 5-20.

12 Gorovitz S. *Doctors' Dilemmas: Moral Conflict and Medical Care* (New York, NY: Oxford University Press Inc, 1982), chap 6.

13 Brock, D.W., Wartman S.A., op. cit.

14 Plato; Hamilton E., Cairns H. eds; Emanuel E.J., trans. *Plato: The Collected Dialogues* (Princeton, NJ: Princeton University Press, 1961), 720 c-e.

TRUST AND CONFIDENTIALITY

DAVID C. THOMASMA

Telling the Truth to Patients: A Clinical Ethics Exploration

Of all tyrannies a tyranny sincerely exercised for the good of its victims may be the most oppressive.

—C.S. Lewis (1970)

Introduction

In this essay I will examine why the truth is so important to human communication in general, the types of truth, and why truth is only a relative value. After those introductory points, I will sketch the ways in which the truth is overridden or trumped by other concerns in the clinical setting. I will then discuss cases that fall into five distinct categories. The conclusion emphasizes the importance of truth telling and its primacy among secondary goods in the healthcare professional-patient relationship.

Reasons for Telling the Truth

Is there ever a circumstance in human affairs when it might be better not to know the truth to protect our values? This question occurs now and then in our lives, and it is a traumatic one. For the most part, we assume that knowledge is power. It is important, we might reason, at all times to know the truth so that we can act on it by making informed choices. Perhaps the most significant form of this priority doctrine (the truth comes first) in healthcare is found in the principle of informed consent. Through it, all persons are guaranteed sufficient information to make intelligent decisions about their care based on their values. On the face of it, we would be hard pressed to consider any time or circumstance when the truth would not take precedence over other considerations. Not to receive the truth would be a form of unacceptable paternalism. Persons would be "protecting" us from harm by destroying our autonomy. This would hardly be a way of truly protecting us.[1]

The matter is more complex than that, however. In all human relationships, the truth is told for a myriad of reasons. A summary of the prominent reasons are that it is a right, a utility, and a kindness.

It is a right to be told the truth because respect for the person demands it. As Kant argued, human society would soon collapse without truth telling, because it is the basis of interpersonal trust, covenants, contracts, and promises.

The truth is a utility as well, because persons need to make informed judgments about their actions. It is a mark of maturity that individuals advance and grow morally by becoming more and more self-aware of their needs, their motives, and their limitations. All these steps toward maturity require honest and forthright communication, first from parents and later also from siblings, friends, lovers, spouses, children, colleagues, co-workers, and caregivers.[2]

Finally, it is a kindness to be told the truth, a kindness rooted in virtue precisely because persons to whom lies are told will of necessity withdraw from important, sometimes life-sustaining and life-saving relationships. Similarly, those who tell lies poison not only their relationships but themselves, rendering themselves incapable of virtue and moral growth.[3] Recently, a question was raised about the link of virtue and imagination with regard to the life and bitter wit of Dorothy Parker:

> People are always telling us how there is
> no connection between moral strength

and artistic strength; how Picasso preyed on women, how Wagner hated Jews, how you can be a terrible person and still be a great artist. But the case of Parker reminds us that, while the relation between morality and imagination may be a complicated one, it does exist. Hope, forgiveness—these are not just moral actions. They are enlargements of the mind. Without them you remain in the tunnel of the self. Parker was morally a child all her life. She had a clear vision of the bad, but it never taught her anything about the good.[4]

Both as a necessity for the person and as a condition for relations, then, the truth is required.

Kinds of Truth

There are at least four broad categories of truth in human relationships. The first we might call direct truth. This is a response to an interrogatory question for which an answer is rather straightforward. A "yes" or "no" will suffice in most instances. "Are we going to the concert tonight?" might be a good example of such a question. A second, related type of truth might be called factual truth. This truth references objective reality. The fact that it is raining out is a truth to be told, should someone inquire. This would allow the inquirer to prepare to get an umbrella to go out to the car. Sometimes we might wish to withhold the truth or even lie about objective reality to tease a person. In any case, it is easily checked by the recipient of our joke, and little harm is done.

More important for our consideration are the next two types of truth, personal truth and interpretive truth.

Personal truth requires the speaker to inform the listener, and vice versa, about interior reality. It requires self-disclosure. Often self-disclosure is developmental; it is revealed over time as a relationship solidifies. Personal feelings are a good example of these truths. To tell another how one is truly feel-ing is important, so that lingering problems about feelings do not fester. If a husband says he does not mind if his beloved wants to dance with an old boyfriend but actually does mind a whole lot, that lack of truthfulness will spoil the evening for him and later, I am sure, for her, when his resentment comes out. If a patient does not truthfully reveal how she is feeling to her doctor, then the first step in diagnosis or therapy will be misled, to the detriment both of the patient and the relationship itself.

Interpretative or hermeneutical truth is the most complex of all truths, closely mirroring the complexity of human relationships and communication. In it, the responder tries to interpret the real reasons an individual makes an inquiry. This truth is important for how the other person, most often the caregiver in healthcare, thinks of us or how we respond to that other person. A good example might be those occasions during which values seem more important than the truth: a married couple might not be able sometimes to tell each other the truth about how they appear to one another for fear that that information needlessly might "crush" the other person. "Tell me how I look, honey" might become an open invitation to destroy the husband or wife who has gained 50 pounds over the years. The spouse may look positively porcine by now. Diplomacy on the part of the inquisitive spouse here cements the bonds of love. It seems to take precedence over the bald truth. In fact, the truth is interpreted in the sense that the responder looks for the reasons behind the question, and instead of responding factually to the question responds to those presumed or interpreted reasons. In this instance the reasons are a request for assurance that one is still loved and appreciated.

Overriding the Truth

When we stop and think of it, there are times when, at least for the moment, protecting us from the truth can save our egos, our self-respect, and even our most cherished values. Not all of us act rationally and autonomously at all times. Sometimes we are under sufficient stress that others must act to protect us from harm. This is called necessary paternalism. Should we become seriously ill, others must step in and rescue us if we are incapable of doing it ourselves. Consider how the comedian and actor John Belushi's family and friends watched him deteriorate on drugs but continued to say, "John's an adult; he can take care of himself."[5] But Belushi was not capable of making that move. He subsequently died without the intervention he needed.

In General Relationships

In each of the three main reasons why the truth must be told, as a right, a utility, and a kindness, lurk values that may from time to time become more important than the truth. When this occurs, the rule of truth telling is trumped, that is, overridden by a temporarily more important principle. The ultimate value in all instances is the survival of the community and/or the well-being of the individual. Does this mean for paternalistic reasons, without the person's consent, the right to the truth, the utility, and the kindness, can be shunted aside? The answer is "yes." The truth in a relationship responds to a multivariate complexity of values, the context for which helps determine which values in that relationship should predominate.

Nothing I have said thus far suggests that the truth may be treated in a cavalier fashion or that it can be withheld from those who deserve it for frivolous reasons. The only values that can trump the truth are recipient survival, community survival, and the ability to absorb the full impact of the truth at a particular time. All these are only temporary trump cards in any event. They only can be played under certain limited conditions because respect for persons is a foundational value in all relationships.

In Healthcare Relationships

It is time to look more carefully at one particular form of human relationship, the relationship between the doctor and the patient or sometimes between other healthcare providers and the patient.

Early in the 1960s, studies were done that revealed the majority of physicians would not disclose a diagnosis of cancer to a patient. Reasons cited were mostly those that derived from nonmaleficence. Physicians were concerned that such a diagnosis might disturb the equanimity of a patient and might lead to desperate acts. Primarily physicians did not want to destroy their patients' hope. By the middle 1970s, however, repeat studies brought to light a radical shift in physician attitudes. Unlike earlier views, physicians now emphasized patient autonomy and informed consent over paternalism. In the doctor-patient relation, this meant the majority of physicians stressed the patient's right to full disclosure of diagnosis and prognosis.

One might be tempted to ascribe this shift of attitudes to the growing patients' rights and autonomy movements in the philosophy of medicine and in public affairs. No doubt some of the change can be attributed to this movement. But also treatment interventions for cancer led to greater optimism about modalities that could offer some hope to patients. Thus, to offer them full disclosure of their diagnosis no longer was equivalent to a death sentence. Former powerlessness of the healer was supplanted with technological and pharmaceutical potentialities.

A more philosophical analysis of the reasons for a shift comes from a consideration of the goal of medicine. The goal of all healthcare relations is to receive/provide help for an illness such that no further harm is done to the patient, especially in that patient's vulnerable state.[6] The vulnerability arises because of increased dependency. Presumably, the doctor will not take advantage of this vulnerable condition by adding to it through inappropriate use of power or the lack of compassion. Instead, the vulnerable person should be assisted back to a state of human equality, if possible, free from the prior dependency.[7]

First, the goal of the healthcare giver-patient relation is essentially to restore the patient's autonomy. Thus, respect for the right of the patient to the truth is measured against the goal. If nothing toward that goal can be gained by telling the truth at a particular time, still it must be told for other reasons. Yet, if the truth would impair the restoration of autonomy, then it may be withheld on grounds of potential harm. Thus the goal of the healing relationship enters into the calculus of values that are to be protected.

Second, most healthcare relationships of an interventionist character are temporary, whereas relationships involving primary care, prevention, and chronic or dying care are more permanent. These differences also have a bearing on truth telling. During a short encounter with healthcare strangers, patients and healthcare providers will of necessity require the truth more readily than during a long-term relation among near friends. In the short term, decisions, often dramatically important ones, need to be made in a compressed period. There is less opportunity to maneuver or delay for other reasons, even if there are concerns about the truth's impact on the person.

Over a longer period, the truth may be withheld for compassionate reasons more readily. Here, the patient and physician or nurse know one another. They are more likely to have shared some of their values. In this context, it is more justifiable to withhold the truth temporarily in favor of more important long-term values, which are known in the relationship.

Finally, the goal of healthcare relations is treatment of an illness. An illness is far broader than its subset, disease. Illness can be viewed as a disturbance in the life of an individual, perhaps due to many nonmedical factors. A disease, by contrast, is a medically caused event that may respond to more interventionist strategies.[8]

Helping one through an illness is a far greater personal task than doing so for a disease. A greater, more enduring bond is formed. The strength of this bond may justify withholding the truth as well, although in the end "the truth will always out."

Clinical Case Categories

The general principles about truth telling have been reviewed, as well as possible modifications formed from the particularities of the healthcare professional-patient relationship. Now I turn to some contemporary examples of how clinical ethics might analyze the hierarchy of values surrounding truth telling.

There are at least five clinical case categories in which truth telling becomes problematic: intervention cases, long-term care cases, cases of dying patients, prevention cases, and nonintervention cases.

Intervention Cases

Of all clinically different times to tell the truth, two typical cases stand out. The first usually involves a mother of advanced age with cancer. The family might beg the surgeon not to tell her what has been discovered for fear that "Mom might just go off the deep end." The movie *Dad*, starring Jack Lemmon, had as its centerpiece the notion that Dad could not tolerate the idea of cancer. Once told, he went into a psychotic shock that ruptured standard relationships with the doctors, the hospital, and the family. However, because this diagnosis requires patient participation for chemotherapeutic interventions and the time is short, the truth must be faced directly. Only if there is not to be intervention might one withhold the truth from the patient for a while, at the family's request, until the patient is able to cope with the reality. A contract about the time allowed before telling the truth might be a good idea.

The second case is that of ambiguous genitalia. A woman, 19 years old, comes for a checkup because she plans to get married and has not yet had a period. She is very mildly retarded. It turns out that she has no vagina, uterus, or ovaries but does have an undescended testicle in her abdomen. She is actually a he. Should she be told this fundamental truth about herself? Those who argue for the truth do so on grounds that she will eventually find out, and more of her subsequent life will have been ruined by the lies and disingenuousness of others. Those who argue against the truth usually prevail. National standards exist in this regard. The young woman is told that she has something like a "gonadal mass" in her abdomen that might turn into cancer if not removed, and an operation is performed. She is assisted to remain a female.

More complicated still is a case of a young Hispanic woman, a trauma accident victim, who is gradually coming out of a coma. She responds only to commands such as "move your toes." Because she is now incompetent, her mother and father are making all care decisions in her case. Her boyfriend is a welcome addition to the large, extended family. However, the physicians discover that she is pregnant. The fetus is about 5 weeks old. Eventually, if she does not recover, her surrogate decision makers will have to be told about the pregnancy, because they will be involved in the terrible decisions about continuing the life of the fetus even if it is a risk to the mother's recovery from the coma. This revelation will almost certainly disrupt current family relationships and the role of the boyfriend. Further, if the mother is incompetent to decide, should not the boyfriend, as presumed father, have a say in the decision about his own child?

In this case, revelation of the truth must be carefully managed. The pregnancy should be revealed only on a "need to know" basis, that is, only when the survival of the young woman becomes critical. She is still progressing moderately towards a stable state.

Long-term Cases

Rehabilitation medicine provides one problem of truth telling in this category. If a young man has been paralyzed by a football accident, his recovery to some level of function will depend upon holding out hope. As he struggles to strengthen himself, the motivation might be a hope that caregivers know to be false, that he may someday be able to walk again. Yet, this falsehood is not corrected, lest he slip into despair. Hence, because this is a long-term relationship, the truth will be gradually discovered by the patient under the aegis of encouragement by his physical therapists, nurses, and physicians, who enter his life as near friends.

Cases of Dying Patients

Sometimes, during the dying process, the patient asks directly, "Doctor, am I dying?" Physicians are frequently reluctant to "play God" and tell the patient how many days or months or years they have left. This reluctance sometimes bleeds over into a less-than-forthright answer to the question just asked. A surgeon with whom I make rounds once answered this question posed by a terminally ill cancer patient by telling her that she did not have to worry about her insurance running out!

Yet in every case of dying patients, the truth can be gradually revealed such that the patient learns about dying even before the family or others who are resisting telling the truth. Sometimes, without directly saying "you are dying," we are able to use interpretive truth and comfort the patient. If a car driver who has been in an accident and is dying asks about other family members in the car who ware already dead, there is no necessity to tell him the truth. Instead, he can be told that "they are being cared for" and that the important thing right now is that he be comfortable and not in pain. One avoids the awful truth because he may feel responsible and guilt ridden during his own dying hours if he knew that the rest of his family were already dead.

Prevention Cases

A good example of problems associated with truth telling in preventive medicine might come from screening. The high prevalence of prostate cancer among men over 50 years old may suggest the utility of cancer screening. An annual checkup for men over 40 years old is recommended. Latent and asymptomatic prostate cancer is often clinically unsuspected and is present in approximately 30% of men over 50 years of age. If screening were to take place, about 16.5 million men in the United States alone would be diagnosed with prostate cancer, or about 2.4 million men each year. As of now, only 120,000 cases are newly diagnosed each year. Thus, as Timothy Moon noted in a recent sketch of the disease, "a majority of patients with prostate cancer that is not clinically diagnosed will experience a benign course throughout their lifetime."9

The high incidence of prostate cancer coupled with a very low malignant potential would entail a whole host of problems if subjected to screening. Detection would force patients and physicians to make very difficult and life-altering treatment decisions. Among them are removal of the gland (with impotence a possible outcome), radiation treatment, and most effective of all, surgical removal of the gonads (orchiectomy). But why consider these rather violent interventions if the probable outcome of neglect will overwhelmingly be benign? For this reason the US Preventive Services Task Force does not recommend either for or against screening for prostate cancer.10 Quality-of-life issues would take precedence over the need to know.

Nonintervention Cases

This last example more closely approximates the kind of information one might receive as a result of genes mapping. This information could tell you of the likelihood or probability of encountering a number of diseases through genetic heritage, for example, adult onset or type II diabetes, but could not offer major interventions for most of them (unlike a probability for diabetes).

Some evidence exists from recent studies that the principle of truth telling now predominates in the doctor-patient relationship. Doctors were asked about revealing diagnosis for Huntington's disease and multiple sclerosis, neither of which is subject to a cure at present. An overwhelming majority would consider full disclosure. This means that, even in the face of diseases for which we have no cure, truth telling seems to take precedence over protecting the patient from imagined harms.

The question of full disclosure acquires greater poignancy in today's medicine, especially with respect to Alzheimer's disease and genetic disorders that may be diagnosed in utero. There are times when our own scientific endeavors lack a sufficient conceptual and cultural framework around which to assemble facts. The facts can overwhelm us without such conceptual frameworks.11 The future of genetics poses just such a problem. In consideration of the new genetics, this might be the time to stress values over the truth.

Conclusion

Truth in the clinical relationship is factored in with knowledge and values.

First, truth is contextual. Its revelation depends upon the nature of the relationship between the doctor and patient and the duration of that relationship.

Second, truth is a secondary good. Although important, other primary values take precedence over the truth. The most important of these values is survival of the individual and the community. A close second would be preservation of the relationship itself.

Third, truth is essential for healing an illness. It may not be as important for curing a disease. That is why, for example, we might withhold the truth from the woman with ambiguous genitalia, curing her disease (having a gonad) in favor of maintaining her health (being a woman).

Fourth, withholding the truth is only a temporary measure. *In vino, veritas* it is said. The truth will eventually come out, even if in a slip of the tongue. Its revelation, if it is to be controlled, must always aim at the good of the patient for the moment.

At all times, the default mode should be that the truth is told. If, for some important reason, it is not to be immediately revealed in a particular case, a truth-management protocol should be instituted so that all caregivers on the team understand how the truth will eventually be revealed.

NOTES

1 Pellegrino, E.D., Thomasma, D.C., *For the Patient's Good: The Restoration of Beneficence in Health Care* (New York: Oxford University Press, 1988).

2 Bok, S., *Lying: Moral Choice in Public and Personal Life* (New York: Vintage Books, 1989).

3 Pellegrino, E.D., Thomasma, D.C., *The Virtues in Medical Practice* (New York: Oxford University Press, 1993).

4 Acocella, J., "After the Laughs [on Dorothy Parker]," *The New Yorker* 1993 Aug. 26, 64(26): 76-81 (quote from 80).

5 Woodward, B., *Wired: The Short Life and Fast Times of John Belushi.* Book Club Ed (New York: Simon & Schuster, 1984).

6 See note 1, Pellegrino, Thomasma, 1988.

7 Cassell, E., "The Nature of Suffering and the Goals of Medicine," *New England Journal of Medicine* (1982) Vol. 306(11): 639-45.

8 See Nordenfelt, L., issue editor, "Concepts of Health and their Consequences for Health Care," *Theoretical Medicine* (1993) Vol. 14(4).

9 Moon, T.D., "Prostate Cancer," *Journal of the American Geriatrics Society* (1992) Vol. 40: 622-27 (quote from 626).

10 Ibid.

11 This was the driving assumption of Robert Maynard Hutchins during his tenure as President of the University of Chicago. During that time he and a circle of scholars tried to

implement an innovative humanities-oriented curriculum at the University of Chicago that stressed ideas over facts, thinking over researching, the historical probity of Western civilization over the fractious scientific meandering of the present day. Ashmore, H.S., *Unseasonable Truths: The Life of Robert Maynard Hutchins* (New York: Little, Brown, 1989).

◆ ◆ ◆ ◆ ◆

MARK SIEGLER

Confidentiality in Medicine —A Decrepit Concept

Medical confidentiality, as it has traditionally been understood by patients and doctors, no longer exists. This ancient medical principle, which has been included in every physician's oath and code of ethics since Hippocratic times, has become old, worn-out, and useless; it is a decrepit concept. Efforts to preserve it appear doomed to failure and often give rise to more problems than solutions. Psychiatrists have tacitly acknowledged the impossibility of ensuring the confidentiality of medical records by choosing to establish a separate, more secret record. The following case illustrates how the confidentiality principle is compromised systematically in the course of routine medical care.

A patient of mine with mild chronic obstructive pulmonary disease was transferred from the surgical intensive-care unit to a surgical nursing floor two days after an elective cholecystectomy. On the day of transfer, the patient saw a respiratory therapist writing in his medical chart (the therapist was recording the results of an arterial blood gas analysis) and became concerned about the confidentiality of his hospital records. The patient threatened to leave the hospital prematurely unless I could guarantee that the confidentiality of his hospital record would be respected.

This patient's complaint prompted me to enumerate the number of persons who had both access to his hospital record and a reason to examine it. I was amazed to learn that at least 25 and possibly as many as 100 health professionals and administrative personnel at our university hospital had access to the patient's record and that all of them had a legitimate need, indeed a professional responsibility, to open and use that chart. These persons included six attending physicians (the primary physician, the surgeon, the pulmonary consultant, and others); 12 house officers (medical, surgical, intensive-care unit, and "covering" house staff); 20 nursing personnel (on three shifts); six respiratory therapists; three nutritionists; two clinical pharmacists; 15 students (from medicine, nursing, respiratory therapy, and clinical pharmacy); four unit secretaries; four hospital financial officers; and four chart reviewers (utilization review, quality assurance review, tissue review, and insurance auditor). It is of interest that this patient's problem was straightforward, and he therefore did not require many other technical and support services that the modern hospital provides. For example, he did not need multiple consultants and fellows, such specialized procedures as dialysis, or social workers, chaplains, physical therapists, occupational therapists, and the like.

Upon completing my survey I reported to the patient that I estimated that at least 75 health professionals and hospital personnel had access to his medical record. I suggested to the patient that these people were all involved in providing or supporting his health-care services. They were, I assured him, working for him. Despite my reassurances the patient was obviously distressed and retorted, "I always believed that medical confidentiality was a part of a doctor's code of ethics. Perhaps you should tell me just what you people mean by 'confidentiality'!"

Two Aspects of Medical Confidentiality

Confidentiality and Third-Party Interests

Previous discussions of medical confidentiality usually have focused on the tension between a physician's responsibility to keep information divulged by patients secret and a physician's legal and moral duty, on occasion, to reveal such confidences to third parties, such as families, employers, public-health authorities, or police authorities. In all these instances, the central question relates to the stringency of the physician's obligation to maintain patient confidentiality when the health, well-being, and safety of identifiable others or of society in general would be threatened by a failure to reveal information about the patient. The tension in such cases is between the good of the patient and the good of others.

Confidentiality and the Patient's Interest

As the example above illustrates, further challenges to confidentiality arise because the patient's personal interest in maintaining confidentiality comes into conflict with his personal interest in receiving the best possible health care. Modern high-technology health care is available principally in hospitals (often, teaching hospitals), requires many trained and specialized workers (a "health-care team"), and is very costly. The existence of such teams means that information that previously had been held in confidence by an individual physician will now necessarily be disseminated to many members of the team. Furthermore, since health-care teams are expensive and few patients can afford to pay such costs directly, it becomes essential to grant access to the patient's medical record to persons who are responsible for obtaining third-party payment. These persons include chart reviewers, financial officers, insurance auditors, and quality-of-care assessors. Finally, as medicine expands from a narrow, disease-based model to a model that encompasses psychological, social, and economic problems, not only will the size of the health-care team and medical costs increase, but more sensitive information (such as one's personal habits and financial condition) will now be included in the medical record and will no longer be confidential.

The point I wish to establish is that hospital medicine, the rise of health-care teams, the existence of third-party insurance programs, and the expanding limits of medicine all appear to be responses to the wishes of people for better and more comprehensive medical care. But each of these developments necessarily modifies our traditional understanding of medical confidentiality.

The Role of Confidentiality in Medicine

Confidentiality serves a dual purpose in medicine. In the first place, it acknowledges respect for the patient's sense of individuality and privacy. The patient's most personal physical and psychological secrets are kept confidential in order to decrease a sense of shame and vulnerability. Secondly, confidentiality is important in improving the patient's health care—a basic goal of medicine. The promise of confidentiality permits people to trust (i.e., have confidence) that information revealed to a physician in the course of a medical encounter will not be disseminated further. In this way patients are encouraged to communicate honestly and forthrightly with their doctors. This bond of trust between patient and doctor is vitally important both in the diagnostic process (which relies on an accurate history) and subsequently in the treatment phase, which often depends as much on the patient's trust in the physician as it does on medications and surgery. These two important functions of confidentiality are as important now as they were in the past. They will not be supplanted entirely either by improvements in medical technology or by recent changes in relations between some patients and doctors toward a rights-based, consumerist model.

Possible Solutions to the Confidentiality Problem

First of all, in all nonbureaucratic, noninstitutional medical encounters—that is, in the millions of doctor-patient encounters that take place in physicians' offices, where more privacy can be preserved—meticulous care should be taken to guarantee that patients' medical and personal information will be kept confidential.

Secondly, in such settings as hospitals or large-scale group practices, where many persons have opportunities to examine the medical record, we should aim to provide access only to those who have "a need to know." This could be accomplished through such administrative changes as dividing the entire record into several sections—for example, a medical and financial section—and permitting only health professionals access to the medical information.

The approach favored by many psychiatrists—that of keeping a psychiatric record separate from the general medical record—is an understandable strategy but one that is not entirely satisfactory and that should not be generalized. The keeping of separate psychiatric records implies that psychiatry and medicine are different undertakings and thus drives deeper the wedge between them and between physical and psychological illness. Furthermore, it is often vitally important for internists or surgeons to know that a patient is being seen by a psychiatrist or is taking a particular medication. When separate records are kept, this information may not be available. Finally, if generalized, the practice of keeping a separate psychiatric record could lead to the unacceptable consequence of having a separate record for each type of medical problem.

Patients should be informed about what is meant by "medical confidentiality." We should establish the distinction between information about the patient that generally will be kept confidential regardless of the interest of third parties and information that will be exchanged among members of the healthcare team in order to provide care for the patient. Patients should be made aware of the large number of persons in the modern hospital who require access to the medical record in order to serve the patient's medical and financial interests.

Finally, at some point most patients should have an opportunity to review their medical record and to make informed choices about whether their entire record is to be available to everyone or whether certain portions of the record are privileged and should be accessible only to their principal physician or to others designated explicitly by the patient. This approach would rely on traditional informed-consent procedural standards and might permit the patient to balance the personal value of medical confidentiality against the personal value of high-technology, team health care. There is no reason that the same procedure should not be used with psychiatric records instead of the arbitrary system now employed, in which everything related to psychiatry is kept secret.

Afterthought: Confidentiality and Indiscretion

There is one additional aspect of confidentiality that is rarely included in discussions of the subject. I am referring here to the wanton, often inadvertent, but avoidable exchanges of confidential information that occur frequently in hospital rooms, elevators, cafeterias, doctors' offices, and at cocktail parties. Of course, as more people have access to medical information about the patient the potential for this irresponsible abuse of confidentiality increases geometrically.

Such mundane breaches of confidentiality are probably of greater concern to most patients than the broader issue of whether their medical records may be entered into a computerized data bank or whether a respiratory therapist is reviewing the results of an arterial blood gas determination. Somehow, privacy is violated and a sense of shame is heightened when intimate secrets are revealed to people one knows or is close to—friends, neighbors, acquaintances, or hospital roommates—rather than when they are disclosed to an anonymous bureaucrat sitting at a computer terminal in a distant city or to a health professional who is acting in an official capacity.

I suspect that the principles of medical confidentiality, particularly those reflected in most medical codes of ethics, were designed principally to prevent just this sort of embarrassing personal indiscretion rather than to maintain (for social, political, or economic reasons) the absolute secrecy of doctor-patient communications. In this regard, it is worth noting that Percival's Code of Medical Ethics (1803) includes the following admonition: "Patients should be interrogated concerning their complaint in a tone of voice which cannot be overheard."[1] We in the medical profession frequently neglect these simple courtesies.

Conclusion

The principle of medical confidentiality described in medical codes of ethics and still believed in by patients no longer exists. In this respect, it is a decrepit concept. Rather than perpetuate the myth of confidentiality and invest energy vainly to preserve it, the public and the profession would be better served if they devoted their attention to determining which aspects of the original principle of confidentiality are worth retaining. Efforts could then be directed to salvaging those.[2]

NOTES

1 Leake, C.D., ed., *Percival's Medical Ethics* (Baltimore: Williams & Wilkins, 1927).

2 Supported by a grant (OSS-8018097) from the National Science Foundation and by the National Endowment for the Humanities. The views expressed are those of the author and do not necessarily reflect those of the National Science Foundation or the National Endowment for the Humanities.

ANNOTATED BIBLIOGRAPHY

Annas, George J.: "The Emerging Stowaway: Patients' Rights in the 1980s," *Law, Medicine, and Health Care* Vol. 10 (February 1982), 32-46. Annas characterizes and criticizes the values and factual assumptions underlying the paternalistic attitudes that lead physicians to downplay patients' rights. He asserts five rights intended to humanize the hospital environment.

——: *The Rights of Patients.* 2nd ed. (Carbondale, IL: Southern Illinois University Press. 1989). This American Civil Liberties Union handbook on the rights of hospital patients is a guide for those directly affected by the problems discussed. Using a question-and-answer approach, the book provides a statement of the rights patients had under the law when the guidebook was written.

Bayer, Ronald, and Kathleen E. Toomey: "HIV Prevention and the Two Faces of Partner Notification," *American Journal of Public Health* Vol. 82 (August 1992), 1158-64. Bayer and Toomey begin by contrasting the respective histories and rationales of two approaches to notifying sexual or needle-sharing partners at risk—the moral "duty to warn" ethic and the contact-tracing approach. They then argue that confusing these approaches in the context of the AIDS epidemic can lead us to "mischaracterize processes that are fundamentally voluntary as mandatory, and processes that respect confidentiality as invasive of privacy."

Benjamin, Martin, and Joy Curtis: *Ethics in Nursing.* 3rd ed. (New York: Oxford University Press, 1992). The intent of this book is to give nursing students and nurses an introduction to the identification and analysis of ethical issues in nursing. The book includes a large number of actual cases, many of which are explored in detail.

Blustein, Jeffrey: "The Family in Medical Decisionmaking," *Hastings Center Report* Vol. 23 (May-June 1993), 6-13. Blustein argues that the ethos of patient autonomy survives two important challenges that would shift some of the decision-making authority currently granted to patients to families instead: John Hardwig's fairness-based argument and a challenge stemming from communitarian theory. Nevertheless, he contends, medical practice and medical ethics are at fault for not giving the family a more prominent role in medical decision making for competent patients.

Cohen, Elliot D.: "Confidentiality, Counseling, and Clients Who Have AIDS," *Journal of Counseling & Development* Vol. 68 (January/February 1990), 282-86. Cohen uses ethical theory in exploring the limits of confidentiality that mental health professionals should observe in dealing with sexually active clients who have AIDS. He proposes a model rule to guide such decisions.

Corcoran, Sheila: "Toward Operationalizing an Advocacy Role," *Journal of Professional Nursing* Vol. 4 (July-August 1988), 242-48. Corcoran begins by contrasting two models of nursing advocacy—the legal rights model and the existential advocacy model. Accepting the second model, Corcoran describes an approach that nurses might take when they attempt to perform the advocacy function of helping patients to make decisions.

Daley, Dennis W.: "*Tarasoff v. Regents of the University of California* (Cal. 528 P2nd 553) and the Psychotherapist's Duty to Warn," *San Diego Law Review* Vol. 12 (July 1975), 932-51. Daley analyzes the practical problems and potential consequences for psychiatry stemming from the *Tarasoff* decision. He discusses in more detail the same types of issues set forth in Justice Clark's dissenting opinion in the case, such as the difficulty of predicting violence and the importance of confidentiality in the therapist-patient relationship.

Kuhse, Helga: "Clinical Ethics and Nursing: 'Yes' to Caring, but 'No' to a Female Ethics of Care,"

Bioethics Vol. 9 (July 1995), 207-19. Kuhse argues that, while care—a sensitivity and responsiveness to the particularities of a situation and to people's needs—is necessary for nursing ethics, the "ethics of care" is seriously inadequate for nursing ethics and as a general moral theory.

Macklin, Ruth: "HIV-Infected Psychiatric Patients: Beyond Confidentiality," *Ethics & Behavior* Vol. 1 (1991), 3-20. Macklin examines ethical issues concerning HIV-infected psychiatric patients. Devoting most of her analysis to professionals' conflicting obligations of confidentiality and protecting persons at risk, she defends some limits to the first obligation before turning to other kinds of ethical dilemmas.

Nelson, Hilde Lindemann, and James Lindemann Nelson: *The Patient in the Family* (New York: Routledge, 1995). This book explores the moral relationship between two major institutions of modern life: health care and family. Using a wide variety of examples based on actual encounters between families and medicine, the authors attempt to develop a robust ethics of the family and demonstrate how the latter can reframe and illuminate various issues in biomedical ethics.

Nelson, James Lindemann: "Taking Families Seriously," *Hastings Center Report* Vol. 22 (July-August 1992), 6-12. Nelson defends a presumption that a competent patient's informed consent is necessary and sufficient to authorize treatment but argues that consideration of the interests of family members and others intimately involved with the patient can justify overriding this presumption in some cases.

Pence, Terry: "Nursing's Most Pressing Moral Issue," *Bioethics Forum* Vol. 10 (Winter 1994), 3-9. In defending the thesis that nurses' appropriate role is one of advocacy for patients, Pence offers an account of the concept of advocacy, argues that advocacy's ascendance as a moral metaphor was a major turning point in nursing history, and responds to leading criticisms of the advocacy model.

Salsberry, Pamela J.: "Caring, Virtue Theory, and a Foundation for Nursing Ethics," *Scholarly Inquiry for Nursing Practice* Vol. 6 (Summer 1992), 155-67. Salsberry critically examines virtue ethics as a foundation for a nursing ethics based on the ideal of caring. She argues that, while virtue ethics can meet some of the conditions of an adequate foundation, it ultimately fails to provide a viable alternative to a duty-based approach as a foundation for nursing ethics.

Winslow, Betty J., and Gerald R. Winslow: "Integrity and Compromise in Nursing Ethics," *Journal of Medicine and Philosophy* Vol. 16 (June 1991), 307-23. The authors grapple with ethical issues that arise for nurses when they consider compromise as a means of resolving conflicts in which they are entangled. They argue that compromise is compatible with moral integrity if certain conditions are met.

◆ ◆ ◆ ◆ ◆

KENNETH KIPNIS

A Defense of Unqualified Medical Confidentiality[1]

The Infected Spouse

The following fictionalized case is based on an actual incident.

1982: After moving to Honolulu, Wilma and Andrew Long visit your office and ask you to be their family physician. They have been your patients ever since.

1988: Six years later the two decide to separate. Wilma leaves for the Mainland, occasionally sending you a postcard. Though you do not see her professionally, you still think of yourself as her doctor.

1990: Andrew comes in and says that he has embarked upon a more sophisticated social life. He has been hearing about some new sexually transmitted diseases and wants to be tested. He is positive for the AIDS virus and receives appropriate counseling.

1991: Visiting your office for a checkup, Andrew tells you Wilma is returning to Hawaii for reconciliation with him. She arrives this afternoon and will be staying at the Moana Hotel. Despite your best efforts to persuade him, he leaves without giving you assurance that he will tell Wilma about his infection or protect her against becoming infected.

Do you take steps to see that Wilma is warned?

If you decide to warn Wilma, what do you say to Andrew when, two days later, he shows up at your office asking how you could reveal his confidential test results?

If you decide not to warn Wilma, what do you say to her when, two years later in 1993, she shows up at your office asking how you, her doctor, could possibly stand idly by as her husband infected her with a deadly virus. She now knows she is positive for the virus, that she was infected by her husband, and that you—her doctor—knew, before they reconciled, that her husband would probably infect her.

The ethical challenges here emerge from an apparent head-on collision between medical confidentiality and the duty to protect imperiled third parties. Notwithstanding Andrew's expectation of privacy and the professional duty to remain silent, it can seem unforgivable for anyone to withhold vital assistance in such a crisis, let alone a doctor. The case for breaching confidentiality is supported by at least five considerations. First, the doctor knows, to a medical certainty, that Andrew is both infected with HIV and infectious. Second, knowing Wilma as a patient, the doctor reasonably believes (let us suppose) that she is not infected. (Wilma cannot be at risk of contracting the disease if she is infected already.)

Third, Wilma's vulnerability is both serious and real. HIV infection is both debilitating and, during those years, invariably fatal. The couple's sexuality makes eventual infection highly likely. Fourth, assuming that preventing Wilma's death is the goal, it is probable that, were Wilma to be told of Andrew's infection, she would avoid exposing herself to the risk. This is not a trivial condition: many people knowingly risk illness and injury out of love and other honorable motivations. Molokai's Father Damien contracted and died from Hansen's disease while caring for patients he knew might infect him. Soldiers, police and firefighters commonly expose themselves to grave risk. It is not enough that a warning would discharge a duty to Wilma, merely so she could make an informed choice. Plainly, the paramount concern has to be to save Wilma's life. Finally, Wilma is not a mere stranger. Instead she has an important relationship with her doctor—you—that serves as a basis for special obligations: You have a special duty to look out for her health.

In the light of these five considerations, it should not be a surprise that the conventional wisdom in medical ethics overwhelmingly supports either an ethical obligation to breach confidentiality in cases like this one or, occasionally and less stringently, the ethical permissibility of doing so (Lo 1995). Notwithstanding this consensus, it is my intention to challenge the received view. I will argue in what follows that confidentiality in clinical medicine is far closer to an absolute obligation than it has generally been taken to be; doctors should honor confidentiality even in cases like this one. Although the focus here is on *The Infected Spouse*, the background idea is that, if it can be demonstrated that confidentiality should be scrupulously honored in this one case where so many considerations support breaching it, the duty of confidentiality should be taken as unqualified in virtually all other cases as well (Kottow, 1986). I shall not, however, defend that broader conclusion here.

Although this essay specifically addresses the obligations of doctors, its approach applies more broadly to all professions that take seriously the responsibility to provide distressed practitioners with authoritative guidance (Wicclair 1985; Kipnis 1986, 63-79). With its focus narrowly on "professional obligations," the methodology used below also represents something of a challenge to much of the conventional thinking in medical ethics.

Clearing the Ground: What Professional Obligations are Not

Among philosophers, it is commonplace that if people are not asking the same questions, they are unlikely to arrive at the same answers. It may be that the main reason doctors have difficulty reaching consensus in ethics is that, in general, systematic discussion about professional responsibility is commonly confused with at least three other types of conversation. When one asks whether one should call the hotel to warn Wilma, one can be asking what the law requires, what one's personal morality requires (as an Orthodox Jew, a Roman Catholic, etc.), or what is required by one's most deeply held personal values (preventing deaths or scrupulously honoring other obligations). Discussions can meander mindlessly over all three areas without attending to boundary crossings. More to the point, effective deliberation about professional obligations, as I will try to show, differs importantly from all three of these discussions. Accordingly, it is necessary to identify and bracket these other perspectives in order to mark off the intellectual space within which practitioners can productively reflect on questions of professional responsibility. Let us examine these different conversations.

Law

The conventional wisdom on the ethics of medical confidentiality has been largely shaped by a single legal case: *Tarasoff v. Regents of the University of California* (Tarasoff 1974). In 1969, Prosenjit Poddar, a student at Berkeley, told a university psychologist

he intended to kill a Ms. Tatiana Tarasoff, a young woman who had spurned his affections. The psychologist dutifully reported him to the campus police who held him briefly and then set him free. Shortly afterwards, Poddar did as he said he would, stabbing the young woman to death. The Tarasoff family sued the University of California for their daughter's death, finally prevailing in their contention that the psychologist (and, by implication, the University) had failed in their duty to protect. The University was found liable and had to compensate the family for its loss. Today it is hard to find discussions of the ethics of confidentiality that do not appeal to this legal parable and, occasionally, to its California Supreme Court moral: "The protective privilege ends where the public peril begins."

Taking its cue from *Tarasoff*, the prevailing standard in medical ethics now holds that the obligation of confidentiality will give way when a doctor is aware that a patient will seriously injure some identified other person. (One might ask why disclosure is not required when a patient will seriously injure many unidentified persons. Under the narrower standard, there is no duty to alert others about an HIV-infected prostitute who neither informs nor protects a large number of anonymous at-risk clients.) We assume that the physician knows Andrew is seropositive, that Wilma is likely seronegative, that the two will likely engage in activities that transmit the virus, that breaching confidentiality will probably result in those activities not occurring and Wilma's not becoming infected. Thus, a physician's warning in *The Infected Spouse* will mean that Wilma is very likely to remain infection-free and a failure to warn her is very likely to result in her eventual death from AIDS.

Focusing on the legal standard, it is useful to distinguish between "special" and "general" legal duties. Special duties can apply to individuals occupying certain roles. A parent, but not a bystander, has a (special) duty to rescue a drowning daughter; firefighters and police officers have (special) duties to take certain occupational risks, and doctors have many (special) duties toward their patients: confidentiality is a good example. In contrast, virtually everyone has a (general) duty to be scrupulously careful when handling explosives, to pay taxes on income, to respect others' property, and so on. It is notable that the duty to warn in *Tarasoff* is a special duty, applicable only to those occupying special roles. So if my neighbor casually assures me he is going to kill his girlfriend tomorrow, the *Tarasoff* ruling does not require me to warn her.

It is surprising to many that the default standard in Anglo-American jurisprudence is that there is no general duty to improve the prospects of the precariously placed, no legal obligation to undertake even an easy rescue. As first-year law students discover, one can stand on a pier with a lifeline in hand and, with complete impunity, allow a stranger to drown nearby. Although we will pass over it, it is notable that, in general, the parties who are legally obligated to warn are those who are otherwise ethically obligated not to disclose. One should reflect on the absence of a general duty to warn.

The easy transition from law to ethics reflects a common error. The mistake is to move from the premise that some action is legally required (what the *Tarasoff* opinion establishes in the jurisdictions that have followed it) to the conclusion that the same action is ethically required. But ethical obligations can conflict with legal ones. Journalists, for example, are sometimes ordered by the courts to reveal the identities of their confidential sources. Although law demands disclosure, professional ethics requires silence. Reporters famously go to jail rather than betray sources. Journalists can find themselves in a quandary: while good citizens obey the law and good professionals honor their professional codes, laws requiring journalists to violate their duties to confidential sources force a tragic choice between acting illegally and acting unethically. Conscientious persons should not have to face such decisions.

Similarly in pediatrics, statutes may require doctors to report suspicions of child abuse. But where

protective agencies are inept and overworked and foster care is dangerous or unavailable, a doctor's report is more likely to result in termination of therapy and further injury to the child instead of protection and care. To obey the law under these appalling, but too common, circumstances is most likely to abandon and even cause harm to the minor patient, both of which are ethically prohibited in medicine. To assume that legal obligations always trump or settle ethical ones is to blind oneself to the possibility of conflict. Professions have to face these dilemmas head-on instead of masking them with language that conflates legal standards and ethical ones. They must conceive professional ethics as separate from the law's mandate. When law requires what professional responsibility prohibits (or prohibits what professional responsibility requires), professional organizations must press the public, legislatures, and the courts to cease demanding that conscientious practitioners dishonor the duties of their craft. This is an important responsibility of professional organizations. It is a mistake to configure professional obligations merely to mirror the law's requirements. Rather the law's requirements must be configured so that they do not conflict with well-considered professional obligations. Law is a human artifact that can be crafted well or badly. In a well-ordered society no one will have to choose between illegality and immorality. Since the law can require conduct that violates ethical standards (and ethical standards can require conduct that violates the law), it cannot be the case that legal obligations automatically create ethical obligations. As the tradition of civil disobedience shows, it can be ethically permissible or obligatory (though not legal) to violate an unjust law.

Even though laws cannot create ethical obligations by fiat, professions need to distinguish between the state's reasonable interests in the work of doctors—e.g., preventing serious harm to children—and the specific legal mandates a state imposes—e.g., requiring doctors to report suspicion of child abuse to an incompetent state agency. Just as patients can make ill-considered demands that should not be satisfied, so too can the state and its courts.

Accordingly, it is assumed that the state has a legitimate interest in preventing harm to people, and that doctors have an ethical obligation to further that important public objective. The focus in this essay is on the shape of the resulting ethical obligation as it applies narrowly to cases like those involving Wilma Long and Tatiana Tarasoff. Because they introduce complexities that will carry us far afield, we set aside cases involving (1) children brought in by parents (Kipnis, 2004); (2) patients referred for independent medical evaluation; (3) mentally ill or retarded patients in the custody of health care institutions; (4) health care that is the subject of litigation; (5) gunshot, knife wounds, and the like; (6) workers' compensation cases; and a few others. While a much longer discussion could cover these areas, many readers can extend the analysis offered here to discern much of what I would want to say about those other cases.

Though I will not discuss them, institutional policies (hospital rules, for example) function very much like laws. Both involve standards that can be imposed externally upon practitioners. Both can be formulated knowledgeably and wisely or with a disregard for essential professional responsibilities.

Personal Morality

We will understand a "morality" as a set of beliefs about obligations. There are plainly many such sets of beliefs: the morality of Confucius has little in common with the moralities of George W. Bush and Thomas Aquinas. For most of us, morality is uncritically absorbed in childhood, coming to consciousness when we encounter others whose moral beliefs differ.

There are still parts of the world in which virtually all members of a community are participants in a common morality. But moral pluralism now seems a permanent part of the social order. Con-

sider a Jehovah's Witness physician who is opposed, on religious grounds, to administering blood transfusions. If this doctor were the only physician on duty when his patient needed an immediate transfusion, a choice would have to be made between being a good Jehovah's Witness and being a good doctor. The doctor's personal moral convictions are here inconsistent with professional obligations. It follows that clarity about personal morality is not the same as clarity about medical ethics. Professionalism can require that one set aside one's personal morality or carefully limit one's exposure to certain professional responsibilities. Here the rule has to be that doctors will not take on responsibilities that might conflict with their personal morality. Problems could be sidestepped if the Jehovah's Witness doctor specialized in a field that didn't involve transfusion (e.g., dermatology) or always worked with colleagues who could administer them. If I am morally against the death penalty, I shouldn't take on work as an executioner. If I am deeply opposed to the morning-after pill, I shouldn't counsel patients at a rape treatment center. To teach medical ethics in a pluralistic professional community is to try to create an intellectual space within which persons from varied backgrounds can agree upon responsible standards for professional conduct. Participants in such a conversation may have to leave personal morality at the door. For some, it may be a mistake to choose a career in medicine.

If ethics is critical reflection on our moralities, then the hope implicit in the field of medical ethics is that we might some day reach a responsible consensus on doctors' obligations. While medicine has dozens of codes, it is not hard to observe commonalities: the standards for informed consent, for example. At a deeper level, there can also be consensus on the justifications for those standards. One role for the philosopher is, as in this essay, to assess carefully the soundness of those arguments. A major task for professions is to move beyond the various personal moralities embraced by practitioners and to reach a responsible consensus on common professional standards.

Personal Values

Values are commonly a part of an explanation of personal conduct. It is always reasonable to ask of any rational action: what good was it intended to promote? While some wear shoes to avoid hurting their feet (embracing the value of comfort) others think they look better in shoes (embracing aesthetic values). Where we have to make personal decisions, often we consider how each option can further and frustrate our values and try to decide among the good and bad consequences.

This strategy can serve when the question is "What should I do?" But the question "What should a good doctor do?" calls for a different type of inquiry. For while I have many personal values, the "good doctor" is an abstraction. She is neither Protestant nor Buddhist, doesn't prefer chocolate to vanilla, and doesn't care about money more than leisure time. Questions about professional ethics cannot be answered in terms of personal values.

A second difficulty appears when we consider that one can give perfect expression to one's most deeply held personal values and still act unethically. Hannibal Lecter in *Silence of the Lambs* and Mozart's Don Giovanni are despicable villains who give vigorous effect to deeply held if contemptible personal values. While personal values can determine action, they do not guarantee that the favored actions are ethical.

Accordingly, we cannot appeal to our personal values to inquire about what physicians in general ought to do. Medicine has no personal values, only individual physicians do. When a physician must decide whether or not to resuscitate a patient, personal values should have nothing to do with the issue. Whether you like the patient or detest him, whether you are an atheist or a fundamentalist believer in a joyous hereafter, should not weigh in the balance. A key part of professionalism involves being able to set personal values aside. While medical students have much to gain by becoming clear about their personal values, that clarity is not the same as responsible certainty about professional obligations.

To summarize the argument so far, discussion about professional obligations in medicine is not the same as discussion about legal and institutional obligations, personal morality or personal values. If a responsible ethical consensus is to be achieved by a profession, it is necessary for physicians to learn to bracket their personal moral and value commitments and to set aside, at least temporarily, their consideration of legal or institutional rules and policies. The practical task is to create an intellectual space within which responsible consensus can be achieved on how physicians, as professionals, ought to act. I will now describe one way in which this might be done.

The Concept of a Professional Obligation

Professional ethics involves disciplined discussion about the obligations of professionals. One place to begin is with a distinction between personal values, already discussed, and what can be called "core professional values." A physician can prefer (1) pistachios to Brazil nuts and (2) confidentiality to universal candor. While the preference for pistachios is merely personal, the preference for confidentiality is a value all doctors ought to possess. The distinction between personal values and "core professional values" is critical here. There is what this flesh-and-blood doctor happens to care about personally, and what the good doctor ought to care about. This idea of a "good doctor" is a social construction, an aspect of a determinate social role, an integral element of medical professionalism. Our idea of a good doctor includes a certain technical/intellectual mastery coupled with a certain commitment to specific professional values. As with the Jehovah's Witness doctor, personal and professional values may be in conflict. As part of an appreciation of the ethical claims of professionalism, physicians must be prepared to set aside their personal values and morality, to set aside what the legal system and their employers want them to care about, and to take up instead the question of what the responsible physician ought to care about. The profession's core values inform those purposes that each medical professional should have in common with colleagues. In discussing the professionally favored resolution of ethically problematic cases (*The Infected Spouse*, for example) physicians can ask—together—how medicine's core professional values ought to be respected in those circumstances.

We have alluded to some of these core professional values. Trustworthiness needs to be on the list. Beneficence toward the patient's health needs is essential. Respect for patient autonomy is a third. Others might be collegiality (duties to colleagues), and perhaps a few others: nondiscrimination and a certain deference to families are among the most commonly mentioned candidates. If we were to leave out that doctors should care about the well-being of the public, the argument for confidentiality would be easy. But it too properly goes on the list. Anyone seeing no point in furthering and securing these values would be ill-suited for the practice of medicine.

Each of these professional values has two dimensions. Along one vector, they define the shared aspiration of a profession. At any time, medicine's ability to benefit patients will be limited. But it is a part of the profession's commitment to push its envelope, to enlarge its collective competency and draw upon its knowledge and skill. Those who master and extend the profession's broadest capabilities are exemplary contributors, but practitioners do not discredit themselves by failing to serve in this estimable way.

Along the second vector, values define a bottom line beneath which practitioners shall not sink. Paraphrasing Hippocrates, although you may not always be able to benefit your patients, it is far more important that you take care not to harm them. Knowingly to harm a patient (on balance) is not merely a failure to realize the value of beneficence. It is a culpable betrayal of that value, a far more serious matter.

All the values above can be understood in this second way. Trustworthiness entails that I not lie to patients, or deliberately withhold information they have an interest in knowing. Respect for patient autonomy can require that I not use force or fraud upon them. And the concern for the well-being of the public requires that that interest somehow appear prominently upon every practitioner's radar screen, that doctors not stand idly by in the face of perils the profession can help to avert and, as a lower limit, that they not do anything to increase public peril. Consider that the overutilization of antibiotics, resulting in drug-resistant infectious agents, is professional misconduct that increases public peril.

Ethical problems can arise, first, when core values appear to be in conflict, as with *The Infected Spouse*. At issue are trustworthiness toward Andrew on one side and beneficence toward Wilma and a concern for the well-being of the public on the other. If the conflict is real, what is required is a priority rule. For example, the concept of decisional capacity is part of a priority rule resolving the well-studied conflict between beneficence and autonomy: when do physicians have to respect a patient's refusal of life-saving treatment? There is what the patient wants and what the patient needs. But when a patient is decisionally capacitated and informed, his or her refusal trumps the doctor's recommendation.

Second, ethical problems can also arise when it is unclear what some core professional value requires one to do. Though we can all agree that doctors should avoid harming their patients, there is no professional consensus on whether deliberately causing the deaths of certain unfortunate patients, those experiencing irremediable and intense suffering, is always a betrayal of beneficence. Likewise, although doctors may be in a position to prevent harm to third parties, it is not well understood what they must do out of respect for that value. When core values conflict, what is required is a priority rule. When they are unclear, what is required is removal of ambiguity: what philosophers call "disambiguation." These two tasks—prioritizing and disambiguating core professional values—need to be carried out with a high degree of intellectual responsibility.

The above list of medicine's core values is not controversial. Propose a toast to them at an assemblage of physicians and all can likely drink with enthusiasm. What is less clear is why such a consensus should obligate professionals. A criminal organization can celebrate its shared commitment to the oath of silence. But it doesn't follow that those who cooperate with the police are unethical. In addition to organizational "celebratability," three additional elements are required to establish a professional obligation.

The first element is that attention to core values has to be a part of professional education. Most medical education is aimed at beneficence. The procedures used in informed consent express a commitment to respect for patient autonomy and trustworthiness. If the profession wholly fails to equip its novices to further its core values, it can be argued that it is not serious about those professed values. Its public commitments will begin to look like they are intended to convey an illusion of concerned attention. In replicating itself, a profession must replicate its commitment. Students of medicine must come to care about the goods that doctors ought to care about. Because justice is rarely explored as a topic in medical education, I do not think it can be counted as a core professional value. However some parts of justice—nondiscrimination for example—are routinely covered.

The second element is critical. The core values are not just goods that doctors care about and that doctors want other doctors to care about. They are also goods that the rest of us want our doctors to care about. I want my doctor to be trustworthy, to be intent on benefiting my health, to take my informed refusals seriously, and so on. And we want our doctors to look out for the well-being of the public. The core professional values are also social values. (Consider that it is not reasonable to want our mobsters to respect their oaths of silence.)

The third element flows from the second: an exclusive social reliance upon the profession as the means by which certain matters are to receive due attention. We mostly respect medical competence. But it is precisely because, as a community, we have also come to accept that doctors are reliably committed to their values (our values), that we have, through state legislatures, granted the medical profession an exclusive monopoly on the delivery of medical services. The unauthorized practice of medicine is a punishable crime. If, like the medical profession, one were to make a public claim that, because of unique skills and dedication, some important social concern ought to be exclusively entrusted to you, and the public believes you and entrusts those important matters to you, incidentally prohibiting all others from encroachment upon what is now your privilege, you would have thereby assumed an ethical obligation to give those important matters due attention. Collectively, the medical profession has done exactly this in securing its monopoly on the delivery of certain types of health care. Accordingly the profession has a collective obligation to organize itself so that the shared responsibilities it has assumed in the political process of professionalization are properly discharged by its membership.

A sound code of ethics consists of a set of standards that, if adhered to broadly by the profession's membership, will result in the profession as a whole discharging its responsibilities. Where physician behavior brings it about that a public loses that essential trust, society may have to withdraw the monopolistic privilege and seek a better way of organizing health care. Professionalization is but one way of organizing an essential service. There are others.

Summarizing: the medical profession has ethical obligations toward patients, families and the community because of its public commitment to secure and further certain critical social values and because of society's exclusive reliance on the profession as its means of delivering certain forms of health care. With the professional privilege comes a reciprocal collective responsibility (Kipnis 1986, 1-14). We can now turn our attention to medicine's responsibility to diminish public perils.

The Duty to Diminish Risks to Third Parties

There is an implication for the way in which we must now understand the problem in *The Infected Spouse*. The opening question "Do you take steps to warn Wilma?" has to be understood as a question about medical ethics and not about "you." We want to know what the "good doctor" should do under those circumstances. Each doctor is ethically required to do what a responsible doctor ought to do: in order to properly respect the core values of the profession. To become a doctor without a proper commitment to respect the profession's values is to be unfit for the practice of medicine. So how are trustworthiness and confidentiality to be understood in relationship to medicine's commitment to diminish risks to third parties?

The Infected Spouse poses its question in 1991, after the doctor-family relationship has been in place for a decade. The dilemma arises during and immediately after a single office visit, forcing a choice between calling Wilma or not, and having to explain to Andrew, in two days, why you disclosed his infection to his wife, or having to explain to Wilma, in two years, why you did not disclose his infection to her. Each option has a bad outcome: the betrayal of Andrew's trust or the fatal infection of Wilma. Either way, you will need to account for yourself.

Infection seems a far worse consequence for Wilma than betrayal is for Andrew. Much of the literature on confidentiality has been shaped by this fact, and perhaps the standard strategy for resolving the problem calls attention to the magnitude and

probability of the bad outcomes associated with each option. While predictions of harm can sometimes be wrong, it can be evident that Tatiana Tarasoff and Wilma Long are at grave risk and, accordingly, it can seem honorable to diminish the danger to vulnerable parties like them. Justice Tobriner appeals to a version of this consequentialist argument in *Tarasoff*:

> Weighing the uncertain and conjectural character of the alleged damage done the patient by such a warning against the peril to the victim's life, we conclude that professional inaccuracy in predicting violence [or deadly infection] cannot negate the therapist's duty to protect the threatened victim.

Beauchamp and Childress, in their widely read *Principles of Biomedical Ethics* (Beauchamp and Childress 2001), urge clinicians to take into account "the probability that a harm will materialize and the magnitude of that harm" in any decision to breach confidentiality. (While they also urge that clinicians take into account the potential impact of disclosure on policies and laws regarding confidentiality, they are not very clear about how this assessment is to be carried out.) In brief, the very bad consequences to Wilma—disease and death and the betrayal of her trust—outweigh the not-all-that-bad consequence to Andrew. Your explanation to Andrew could cover those points.

The preferred argument would go something like this: The state's interest in preventing harm is weighty. Medicine has an obligation to protect the well-being of the community. Because the seriousness of threatened grave injury to another outweighs the damage done to a patient by breaching confidentiality, the obligation of confidentiality must give way to a duty to prevent serious harm to others. Accordingly, despite confidentiality, warning or reporting is obligatory when it will likely avert very bad outcomes in this way. Of course clinicians should try to obtain waivers of confidentiality before disclosure, thereby avoiding the need to breach a duty. But the failure to obtain a waiver does not, on this argument, affect the overriding obligation to report.

A Defense of Unqualified Confidentiality

As powerful as this justification is, there are problems with it. Go back to 1990, when Andrew comes in to be tested for sexually transmitted diseases. Suppose he asks: "If I am infected, can I trust you not to disclose this to others?" If, following the arguments set out in the previous paragraphs, we are clear that confidentiality must be breached to protect third parties like Wilma, then the only truthful answer to Andrew's question is "No. You can't trust me." If the profession accepts that its broad promise of confidentiality must sometimes be broken, then any unqualified assurances are fraudulent and the profession should stop making them. If there are exceptions, clinicians have a duty to be forthcoming about what they are and how they work. Patients should know up front when they can trust doctors, and when they can't. To withhold this important information is to betray the value of trustworthiness.

Accordingly, the argument for breaching confidentiality has to be modified to support a qualified confidentiality rule, one that carves out an exception from the very beginning, acknowledging an overriding duty to report under defined circumstances. (In contrast, an unqualified confidentiality rule contemplates no exceptions.) Instead of undertaking duties of confidentiality and then violating them, doctors must qualify their expressed obligations so they will be able to honor them. Commentators who have walked through the issues surrounding confidentiality have long understood the ethical necessity of "Miranda warnings" (Bok 1983, Goldman 1980): A clinician would have to say early on: "Certain things that I learn from you may have to be disclosed to ... under the following circumstances: ..., and the following things might occur to you as a result of

my disclosure...." If doctors are ethically obligated to report, they need to say in advance what will be passed along, when, to whom, and what could happen then. They should never encourage or accept trust only to betray their patients afterwards. To do so is to betray the value of trustworthiness.

But now a second problem emerges. If prospective patients must understand in advance that a doctor will report evidence of a threat to others, they will only be willing to disclose such evidence to the doctor if they are willing to accept that those others will come to know. If it is important to them that the evidence not be reported, they will have a weighty reason not to disclose it to those who are obligated to report it.

Some have questioned this proposition, arguing that there is no empirical evidence that prospective patients will avoid or delay seeking medical attention or conceal medically relevant information if confidentiality is qualified in this way. Despite widespread reporting practices, waiting rooms have not emptied and no one really knows if people stop talking openly to their doctors when confidentiality is breached.

Three responses are possible regarding this claim. First, there is a serious difficulty doing empirical research in this area. How, for example, do we determine the number of child-abusing parents who have not brought their injured children to doctors out of a fear that they will get into trouble with the authorities? How many HIV+ patients avoid telling their doctors all about their unsafe sexual practices? How many of us would volunteer unflattering truthful answers to direct questions on these and other shameful matters? It is notoriously difficult to gather reliable data on the embarrassing, criminal, irresponsible things people do, and the steps they take to avoid exposure, especially if those are wrongful too. I don't want to suggest that these problems are insurmountable (Reddy 2002), but they are decidedly there and they often make it hard to study the effects of these betrayals.

Second, despite the problems, certain types of indirect evidence can occasionally emerge. Here are two anecdotal examples from Honolulu. There was a time, not long ago, when military enlistees who were troubled by their sexual orientation knew that military doctors and psychologists would report these problems to their officers. Many of these troubled soldiers therefore obtained the services of private psychologists and psychiatrists in Honolulu, despite the fact that free services were available in military clinics. The second example emerged from the failure of the Japanese medical system to keep diagnoses of HIV infection confidential. Many Japanese who could afford it traveled to Honolulu for diagnosis and treatment, avoiding clinics in Japan. At the same time Japanese data on the prevalence of HIV infection were unrealistically low, especially considering the popularity of Japanese sex tours to the HIV-infected brothels of Thailand. Evidence of this sort can confirm that the failure to respect confidentiality can impair the ability of doctors to do their job.

And third, there is an argument based on the motivational principle that if one strongly desires that event E does not occur, and one knows that doing act A will bring about event E, then one has a weighty reason not to do act A. The criminal justice system is based on this idea. We attach artificial and broadly unwelcome consequences (imprisonment and other forms of punishment) to wrongful, harmful conduct with the expectation that, even if inclined, most people will decide against the conduct in order to avoid the unwelcome consequence. If I don't want to go to prison, and a career in burglary will likely result in my going to prison, then I have a weighty reason to choose a different career. Likewise, if I don't want my marriage to be destroyed by my wife's discovery that I am HIV+, and I know that telling my doctor about reconciliation will result in her discovering just that, then I have a weighty reason not to tell my doctor. The presumption must be in favor of the truth of this seemingly self-evident principle. If critics allege that it is false or otherwise

unworthy of endorsement, it seems the burden of disproof belongs to them. It is their responsibility to come up with disconfirming evidence. It can be argued, in rebuttal, that people still commit burglary and, despite reporting laws, people still go to doctors for HIV testing, even knowing that confidentiality has its limits. But no one would maintain that punishing convicted criminals totally prevents crime and that breaching confidentiality results in all people avoiding or delaying medical treatment, or concealing aspects of their lives. The situation is more complicated.

Consider that Andrew belongs to one of two groups of prospective patients. Members of the first group are willing enough to have reports made to others. Members of the second are deterred from disclosure by the fear of a report. Of course we can't know in advance which type of patient Andrew is, but if both groups are treated alike, uncertainty will not be a problem. (While this division into two groups may be oversimplified, working through the qualifications would take us too far afield.)

Consider the first group: patients who would be willing to have a report made. Recall that the physician in *The Infected Spouse* tried to obtain assurance that Wilma would be protected. Under an unqualified confidentiality rule—no exceptions—if the patient were willing to have reports made to others, the doctor should be able to obtain a waiver of confidentiality and Wilma could then be informed. Once permission to report is given, the ethical dilemma disappears. Notice that for this group of patients an exceptionless confidentiality rule works just as well as a rule requiring doctors to override confidentiality when necessary to protect endangered third parties. At-risk parties will be warned just the same, but with appropriate permission from patients. In these cases there is no need to trim back the obligation of confidentiality since patients in this first group are, by definition, willing to have a report made.

Difficulties arise with the second type of patient: those who will not want credible threats reported.

Notice that these prospective patients are in control of the evidence doctors need to secure protection for parties at risk. If a patient cannot be drawn into a therapeutic alliance—a relationship of trust and confidence—then doctors will not receive the information they need to protect imperiled third parties (at least so long as patients have options). As a result, doctors will not be able to mobilize protection. When one traces out the implications of a reporting rule on what needs to be said in 1990 (when Andrew asked to be tested and the doctor disclosed the limits to confidentiality), it becomes evident that Wilma will not be protected if Andrew (1) does not want her to know and (2) understands that disclosure to his doctor will result in her knowing. Depending on his options and the strength of his preferences, he will be careful about what he discloses to his doctor, or will go without medical advice and care, or will find another physician who can be kept in ignorance about his personal life.

We began by characterizing *The Infected Spouse* as an apparent head-on collision between the doctor's duty of confidentiality and the duty to protect imperiled third parties. But if the argument above is sound, there is no collision. The obligation to warn third parties does not provide added protection to those at-risk. In particular, a no-exceptions confidentiality rule has a better chance of getting the facts on the table, at least to the extent that honest promises of confidentiality can make it so. To be sure, clinicians would have to set aside the vexing "Should I report?" conundrum and search for creative solutions instead. These strategies will not always prevent harm, but they will sometimes. The nub of the matter is that these strategies can never work if they can't be implemented. And they can't be implemented if the fear of reporting deters patients from disclosure. Accordingly there is no justification for trimming back the obligation of confidentiality since doing so actually reduces protection to endangered third parties, increasing public peril.

The argument advanced here is that—paradoxically—ethical and legal duties to report make it less likely that endangered parties will be protected. Depending on the prospective patient, these duties are either unnecessary (when waivers can be obtained) or counterproductive (when disclosure to the doctor is deterred and interventions other than disclosure are prevented).

In part, the conventional wisdom on confidentiality errs in focusing on the decision of the individual clinician at the point when the choice has to be made to disclose or not. The decision to violate confidentiality reaches backwards to the HIV test administered years earlier and, as we shall see, even before. Perhaps little will be lost if one doctor betrays a single patient one time, or if betrayals are extremely rare. But medical ethics is not about a single decision by an individual clinician. The consequences and implications of a rule governing professional practice may be quite different from those of a single act. Better to ask, what if every doctor did that?

While it is accepted here that doctors have an overriding obligation to prevent public peril, it has been argued that they do not honor that obligation by breaching or chipping away at confidentiality. This is because the protective purpose to be furthered by reporting is defeated by the practice of reporting. The best public protection is achieved where doctors do their best work and, there, trustworthiness is probably the most important prerequisite. Physicians damage both their professional capabilities and their communities when they compromise their trustworthiness.

If the argument above is sound and confidentiality must be respected in this case, we must now return to the question of what the doctor must say to Wilma when, now infected, she returns to the office two years after the reconciliation. Though this question has finally to be faced in 1993, it is on the table before her return to Honolulu. It is there even before Andrew asks to be tested in 1990, and you then have to decide whether to live out the trust he has placed in you or disabuse him of it. In fact, the problem is on the table in 1982, when the couple first enters your office and asks you to be their physician. As a doctor, you have obligations of beneficence and confidentiality and you owe both to each. But now—having read this far—you are aware that something can happen that you cannot control; and, if it does, you will face those apparently conflicting obligations. You can only provide what you owe to one if you betray your obligation to the other. That is the choice you will have to make in 1993, unless you (and the medical profession) contour professional responsibilities now.

If, in choosing a governing ethical principle, the end-in-view is to protect vulnerable third parties; and if this can be done best, as I have tried to show, by honoring confidentiality and doing one's best to protect imperiled third parties within that framework; then what you must say to both Wilma and Andrew, when they enter your office in 1982, should be something like this:

> There is an ethical problem physicians sometimes face in taking on a married couple as patients. It can happen that one partner becomes infected with a transmissible disease, potentially endangering the other. If the infected partner won't share information with me because he or she fears I will warn the other, there will be no protection at all for the partner at risk. There may, however, be things I can do if I can talk with the infected partner. What I promise both of you is, if that were to happen, I will do everything I possibly can to protect the endangered partner, except for violating confidentiality, which I will not do. You both need to remember that you should not count on me to guarantee the wholesomeness of your spouse, if doing this means betrayal.

It is in these words that the final explanation to Wilma can be found. If Wilma understands from the beginning that medical confidentiality will not be breached; if she (and the public generally) understand that the precariously placed are safer under unqualified confidentiality, she will understand she has final responsibility for her choices. If you are clear enough about it, she will grasp that she can't depend on you to protect her at the cost of betrayal, and that she is better off because of that. Both the doctor and the medical profession collectively need to work through these issues and fully disclose the favored standard to prospective patients before the occasion arises when a doctor must appeal to it. The view defended here is that the profession should continue to make an unqualified pledge of confidentiality, and mean it.

It is also appropriate to consider what should be said to Andrew as he is about to leave your office in 1991 to prepare for a romantic dinner with Wilma. I once spent part of an afternoon with a health care professional who had served in Vietnam. He had counseled married enlistees who had returned from visits with their wives and had been diagnosed with a venereal disease that was probably contracted before they left. These men may have infected their wives. This clinician had learned how to persuade these men to agree to disclosure. He stressed that their wives would likely find out eventually and that the emotional and medical consequences would be far more severe because of the delay. More importantly—given the soldiers' tentative decisions not to let their at-risk spouses know—he would ask whether this was a marriage they really wanted to preserve? I recall that he claimed a near perfect record in obtaining permission to notify the at-risk spouses. It would be useful if there were skilled allied caregivers, bound by confidentiality, who could routinely conduct these specialized counseling sessions. While this is not the place to set out the full range of options for a profession reliably committed to trustworthiness, it will suffice to point out a direction for professional and institutional development.

Concluding Remarks

Even if the foregoing is accepted, what may trouble doctors still is a painful fear that they will learn about an endangered person and be barred by this no-exceptions confidentiality rule from doing anything. (Actually there is only one thing they cannot do: disclose. All other paths remain open.) Even if a reporting rule keeps many prospective patients out of the office, or silences them while they are there, the rule protects doctors from the moral risk of having to allow injury to third parties when a simple disclosure would prevent it. This distress is significant and has to be faced.

Here we must return to an error discussed earlier: the conflation of personal morality and professional ethics. Like law, personal morality can also conflict with professional responsibility. We considered a Jehovah's Witness surgeon, morally prohibited from administering blood transfusions to patients needing them. Likewise a Catholic doctor may be unable to discuss certain reproduction-related options. And despite understandable moral misgivings, doctors everywhere must be prepared to administer high-risk treatments they know will cause the deaths of some of their patients. Paradoxically, a personal inability to risk killing patients can disqualify one for the practice of medicine. While personal morality can play a decisive role in career choice, it shouldn't play a decisive role within medical ethics.

Many enter medicine believing that good citizens must prevent serious injury to others, even if that means violating other obligations. But the task of professional ethics in medicine is to set out principles that, if broadly followed, will allow the profession to discharge its collective responsibilities to patients and society. Confidentiality, I have argued, is effective at getting more patients into therapeutic alliances more quickly, it is more effective in bringing about better outcomes for more of them and—counter-intuitively—it is most likely to prevent serious harm to the largest number of at-risk third parties. Now it is ethically praiseworthy for honorable people to belong to a profession that, on balance, diminishes the amount of harm to others, even though these same professionals must sometimes knowingly allow (and sometimes even cause) harm to occur. Although doctors may feel guilty about these foreseeable consequences of their actions and inactions, they are not guilty of anything. They are acting exactly as it is reasonable to want doctors to act.

It is hard enough to create therapeutic alliances that meet patients' needs. But if doctors take on the added duty to mobilize protective responses without waivers of confidentiality, their work may become impossible in too many important cases. And all of us will be the worse for that. The thinking that places the moral comfort of clinicians above the well-being of patients and their victims is in conflict with the requirements of professional responsibility, properly understood. While it will be a challenge for many honorable physicians to measure up to this standard, no one ever said it was easy to be a good doctor.

NOTE

1 A longer version of this article will appear as "Medical Confidentiality" in *The Blackwell Guide to Bioethics*, edited by Rosamond Rhodes, Anita Silvers, and Leslie Francis (Oxford: Blackwell Publishers Ltd., 2006).

REFERENCES

Beauchamp, T.L., and J.F. Childress. 2001. *Principles of Biomedical Ethics* (New York: Oxford University Press).

Bok, S. 1983. *Secrets* (New York: Pantheon Books).

Goldman, A. 1980. *The Philosophical Foundations of Professional Ethics* (Totowa: Rowman & Littlefield).

Kipnis, K. 2004. "Gender, Sex, and Professional Ethics in Child and Adolescent Psychiatry," in *Child and Adolescent Psychiatry: Clinics of North America*. July Vol. 13(3): 695-708.

Kipnis, K. 1986. *Legal Ethics* (Englewood Cliffs: Prentice-Hall).

Kottow, M. 1986. "Medical Confidentiality: An Intransigent and Absolute Obligation," *Journal of Medical Ethics* Vol. 12: 117-22.

Lo, B. 1995. *Resolving Ethical Dilemmas: A Guide for Clinicians* (Baltimore: Williams and Wilkins).

Reddy, D.M., R. Fleming, C. Swain. 2002. "Effect of Mandatory Parental Notification on Adolescent Girls' Use of Sexual Health Care Services," in *Journal of the American Medical Association* Vol. 288: 710-14.

Tarasoff v. Regents of the University of California, Supreme Court of California: 529 P.2d 553 (Cal. 1974).

Wicclair, Mark. 1985. "A Shield Right for Reporters vs. the Administration of Justice and the Right to a Fair Trial: Is there a Conflict?" in *Business & Professional Ethics Journal* Vol. 4(2).

INFORMED CONSENT, COMPETENCE, AND SURROGATE DECISION MAKING

JAY KATZ[*]

Informed Consent—Must It Remain a Fairy Tale?[**]

When the editors of the *Journal of Contemporary Health Law and Policy* asked me to contribute an article to their issue in honor of my friend, colleague and dean, Guido Calabresi, I accepted their invitation with pleasure. Since I had reflected about informed consent for two decades, I welcomed this opportunity to set forth my final thoughts and conclusions, however briefly and summarily, on this doctrine and its impact on physician-patient decisionmaking. This essay gives a good account of what I shall ever be able to say about informed consent.

It is appropriate that I choose this topic for this occasion because Guido has had a long standing interest in law and medicine. Twenty-five years ago, he published his remarkable paper, *Reflections on Medical Experimentation in Humans*,[1] and since then he has periodically written on issues in law and medicine. He has not, however, ever explored in depth the problematics of the legal doctrine of informed consent and, to the extent he has, only in the contexts of human experimentation and organ transplantation. If this essay will stimulate this great torts law scholar and teacher to give us his analysis and insights, we can only benefit from his wisdom.

In his article on human experimentation, Guido was mainly concerned with one crucial tension inherent in medical research: "our fundamental need constantly to reaffirm our belief in the sanctity of life and our practical placing of some values (including future lives) above an individual life."[2] He admonished scholars to "devot[e] themselves to the development of a workable but not too obvious control system, rather than to the spinning-out of theories of consent,"[3] because "[t]otally free consent is simply too rare an animal."[4] While I assign greater significance to consent as a mechanism of control than Guido does, I agree with him that "consent by itself is not enough."[5]

Informed consent is a hybrid concept which speaks both to physicians' disclosure obligations and patients' willingness to undergo a particular treatment. Throughout this essay I intend to give prominence to the disclosure aspect of informed consent and its implications for improving the quality of patient consent. I would go further than Guido did, when he wrote that "*some form of consent* should always be required,"[6] because I have greater faith in the crucial role that consent can play in doctor-patient decisionmaking once physicians learn to differentiate, which they have not, between acquiescence and consent. I shall have more to say about all this as I go along. In his recent, intriguing article, *Do We Own Our Bodies?*, while addressing problems of organ transplantation, Guido comes close to issues that I shall explore in this essay:

> I admit I am still an individualistic Kantian libertarian ... I find it very hard to conceive of a situation in which the state should properly say: "Guido, you must give up that magnificent hair, blood, or marrow, to someone else regardless of your will.... We owe it to ourselves ... to do more thinking about something which seems, at first glance, outlandish—like the question: Do we own our own bodies?"[7]

Guido raised his "outlandish" question with respect to state-mandated interventions. How might he answer the question, "Do we own our own bodies?" in the context of the physician-patient relationship? I shall argue that physicians take too much license with patients' bodies and that the common law doctrine of informed consent has insufficiently addressed the question of who owns our bodies. In a different vein, Guido speaks to this question in *Ideals, Beliefs, Attitudes, and the Law*:

> Have the lives we have prolonged been, in some sense, fruitful and rewarding (even if terribly handicapped)? Have we adhered to those beliefs, ideals and attitudes (including the ideal of letting people hold to their own kooky ideals) which may be dearer to us than an extra month on a life expectancy table?[8]

Physicians, as I shall argue later, have always placed greater value on longevity than on quality of life. To resolve these and other value conflicts alone requires searching conversation between physicians and patients. Without such conversation, informed consent will remain a hollow aspiration and preclude patients from exercising greater control over decisions which, in the end, only they can make.

Like Guido, though perhaps with modification, I too am "an individualistic Kantian libertarian," and thus I give greater weight to autonomy and self-determination than perhaps he does. As I observed years ago:

> Physicians have always maintained that patients are only in need of caring custody.... The idea that patients may also be entitled to liberty, to sharing the burdens of decision with the doctors, was never [at least until recently] part of the ethos of medicine. Being unaware of the idea of patient liberty, physicians did not address the possible conflict between notions of custody and liberty.[9]

In this essay I shall also argue that formidable problems exist which require study and resolution before informed consent can ever safeguard patient autonomy and self-determination. The likely outcome of such inquiries will be to return ownership of bodies to patients and to not allow caring custody to mislead physicians and patients into believing that ownership must temporarily be transferred to doctors' "discretion." Law has an important role to play here by prodding physicians to be more attentive to patients' rights regarding decisionmaking authority. Such prodding, as I have already suggested, is necessary because the idea that patients have rights to autonomy and self-determination has been an alien one throughout the history of medical practice. Ultimately, medicine and not law must formulate a doctrine of informed consent which is responsive not only to the proddings of law but also to the realities of medical practice (i.e., to the complex caretaking and being-taken-care-of interactions that are the essence of all interactions between patients and their physicians). Finally, I shall argue, as I have already noted, that greater emphasis has to be given to disclosure rather than consent and, therefore, that the inadequacies in current disclosure practices are to begin with the greater obstacle to fashioning an informed consent doctrine which is not a charade.

Guido will soon be a judge on the United States Court of Appeals for the Second Circuit. He, of course, will often return to Yale Law School and, thus, this essay is not written in the spirit of saying farewell to him but of expressing my admiration, at a decisive moment in his professional life, to a wonderful person who over the last thirty-six years has meant so much to me and to my school. I can give him no better present than my thoughts on a topic in which we share a common interest. I hope that in the informed consent cases which will surely come before him, he will address some of my concerns about the persisting inadequacies in the physician-patient decisionmaking process.

I. The Pre-History of Informed Consent in Medicine

The idea that, prior to any medical intervention, physicians must seek their patients' informed consent was introduced into American law in a brief paragraph in a 1957 state court decision,[10] and then elaborated on in a lengthier opinion in 1960.[11] The emerging legal idea that physicians were from now on obligated to share decisionmaking authority with their patients shocked the medical community, for it constituted a radical break with the silence that had been the hallmark of physician-patient interactions throughout the ages. Thirty-five years are perhaps not long enough for either law or medicine to resolve the tension between legal theory and medical practice, particularly since judges were reluctant

to face up to implications of their novel doctrine, preferring instead to remain quite deferential to the practices of the medical profession.

Viewed from the perspective of medical history, the doctrine of informed consent, if taken seriously, constitutes a revolutionary break with customary practice. Thus, I must review, albeit all too briefly, the history of doctor-patient communication. Only then can one appreciate how unprepared the medical profession was to heed these new legal commands. But there is more: Physicians could not easily reject what law had begun to impose on them, because they recognized intuitively that the radical transformation of medicine since the age of medical science made it possible, indeed imperative, for a doctrine of informed consent to emerge. Yet, bowing to the doctrine did not mean accepting it. Indeed, physicians could not accept it because, for reasons I shall soon explore, the nature of informed consent has remained in the words of Churchill, "an enigma wrapped in a mystery."

Throughout the ages physicians believed that they should make treatment decisions for their patients. This conviction inheres in the Hippocratic Oath: "I swear by Apollo and Aesculepius [that] I will follow that system of regimen which according to *my* ability and judgment *I* consider for the benefit of *my* patients...."[12] The patient is not mentioned as a person whose ability and judgment deserve consideration. Indeed, in one of the few references to disclosure in the Hippocratic Corpus, physicians are admonished "to [conceal] most things from the patient while attending to him; [to] give necessary orders with cheerfulness and serenity, ... revealing nothing of the patient's future or present condition."[13] When twenty-five centuries later, in 1847, the American Medical Association promulgated its first Code of Ethics, it equally admonished patients that their "obedience ... to the prescriptions of [their] physician should be prompt and implicit. [They] should never permit [their] own crude opinions ... to influence [their] attention to [their physicians]."[14]

The gulf separating doctors from patients seemed unbridgeable both medically and socially. Thus, whenever the Code did not refer to physicians and patients as such, the former were addressed as "gentlemen" and the latter as "fellow creatures." To be sure, caring for patients' medical needs and "abstain[ing] from whatever is deleterious and mischievous"[15] was deeply imbedded in the ethos of Hippocratic medicine. The idea that patients were also "autonomous" human beings, entitled to being partners in decisionmaking, was, until recently, rarely given recognition in the lexicon of medical ethics. The notion that human beings possess individual human rights, deserving of respect, of course, is of recent origin. Yet, it antedates the twentieth century and therefore could have had an impact on the nature and quality of the physician-patient relationship.

It did not. Instead, the conviction that physicians should decide what is best for their patients, and, therefore, that the authority and power to do so should remain vested in them, continued to have a deep hold on the practices of the medical profession. For example, in the early 1950s the influential Harvard sociologist Talcott Parsons, who echoed physicians' views, stated that the physician is a technically competent person whose competence and specific judgments and measures cannot be competently judged by the layman and that the latter must take doctors' judgments and measures on "authority."[16] The necessity for such authority was supported by three claims:

First, *physicians' esoteric knowledge, acquired in the course of arduous training and practical experience, cannot be comprehended by patients.* While it is true that this knowledge, in its totality, is difficult to learn, understand and master, it does not necessarily follow that physicians cannot translate their esoteric knowledge into language that comports with patients' experiences and life goals (i.e., into language that speaks to quality of future life, expressed in words of risks, benefits, alternatives and uncertainties). Perhaps patients can understand this, but physicians have had too little training and experience with, or even more importantly, a commitment to, communicating their "esoteric knowledge" to patients in plain language to permit a conclusive answer as to what patients may comprehend.

Second, *patients, because of their anxieties over being ill and consequent regression to childlike thinking, are incapable of making decisions on their own behalf.* We do not know whether the childlike behavior often displayed by patients is triggered by pain, fear, and illness, or by physicians' authoritarian insistence that good patients comply with doctors' orders, or by doctors' unwillingness to share information with patients. Without providing such information, patients are groping in the dark and their stumbling attempts to ask questions, if made at all, makes them appear more incapable of understanding than they truly are.

We know all too little about the relative contributions which being ill, being kept ignorant, or being considered incompetent make to these regressive manifestations. Thus, physicians' unexamined convictions easily become self-fulfilling prophesies. For example, Eric Cassell has consistently argued that illness robs patients of autonomy and that only subsequent to the act of healing is autonomy restored.[17] While there is some truth to these contentions, they overlook the extent to which doctors can restore autonomy prior to the act of healing by not treating patients as children but as adults whose capacity for remaining authors of their own fate can be sustained and nourished. Cassell's views are reminiscent of Dostoyevsky's Grand Inquisitor who proclaimed that "at the most fearful moments of life," mankind is in need of "miracle, mystery and authority."[18] While, in this modern age, a person's capacity and right to take responsibility for his or her conduct has been given greater recognition than the Grand Inquisitor was inclined to grant, it still does not extend to patients. In the context of illness, physicians are apt to join the Grand Inquisitor at least to the extent of asserting that, while patients, they can only be comforted through subjugation to miracle, mystery and authority.

Third, *physicians' commitment to altruism is a sufficient safeguard for preventing abuses of their professional authority.* While altruism, as a general professional commitment, has served patients well in their encounters with physicians, the kind of protection it does and does not provide has not been examined in any depth. I shall have more to say about this later on. For now, let me only mention one problem: Altruism can only promise that doctors will try to place their patients' medical needs over their own personal needs. Altruism cannot promise that physicians will know, without inquiry, patients' needs. Put another way, patients and doctors do not necessarily have an identity of interest about matters of health and illness. Of course, both seek restoration of health and cure, and whenever such ends are readily attainable by only one route, their interests indeed may coincide.

In many physician-patient encounters, however, cure has many faces and the means selected affect the nature of cure in decisive ways. Thus, since quality of life is shaped decisively by available treatment options (including no treatment), the objectives of health and cure can be pursued in a variety of ways. Consider, for example, differences in value preferences between doctors and patients about longevity versus quality of remaining life. Without inquiry, one cannot presume identity of interest. As the surgeon Nuland cogently observed: "A doctor's altruism notwithstanding, his agenda and value system are not the same as those of the patient. That is the fallacy in the concept of beneficence so cherished by many physicians."[19]

II. The Age of Medical Science and Informed Consent

During the millennia of medical history, and until the beginning of the twentieth century, physicians could not explain to their patients, or—from the perspective of hindsight—to themselves, which of their treatment recommendations were curative and which were not. To be sure, doctors, by careful bedside observation, tried their level best "to abstain from what is deleterious and mischievous," to help if they could, and to be available for comfort during the hours, days or months of suffering. Doing more curatively, however, only became possible with the advent of the age of medical science. The introduction of scientific reasoning into medicine, aided by the results of carefully conducted research, permitted doctors for the first time to discriminate more aptly between knowledge, ignorance and conjecture in their recommendations for or against treatment. Moreover, the spectacular technological advances in the diagnosis and treatment of disease, spawned by medical science, provided patients and doctors with ever-increasing therapeutic options, each having its own particular benefits and risks.

Thus, for the first time in medical history it is possible, even medically and morally imperative, to give patients a voice in medical decisionmaking. It is possible because knowledge and ignorance can be better specified; it is medically imperative because a variety of treatments are available, each of which can bestow great benefits or inflict grievous harm; it is morally imperative because patients, depending on the lifestyle they wish to lead during and after treatment, must be given a choice.

All this seems self-evident. Yet, the physician-patient relationship—the conversations between the two parties—was not altered with the transformation of medical practice during the twentieth century. Indeed, the silence only deepened once laboratory data were inscribed in charts and not in patients' minds, once machines allowed physicians' eyes to gaze not at patients' faces but at the numbers they displayed, once x-rays and electrocardiograms began to speak for patients' suffering rather than their suffering voices.

What captured the medical imagination and found expression in the education of future physicians, was the promise that before too long the diagnosis of patients' diseases would yield objective, scientific data to the point of becoming algorithms. *Treatment*, however, required subjective data from patients and would be influenced by doctors' subjective judgments. This fact was overlooked in the quest for objectivity. Also overlooked was the possibility that greater scientific understanding of the nature of disease and its treatment facilitated better communication with patients. In that respect contemporary Hippocratic practices remained rooted in the past.

III. *The Impact of Law*

The impetus for change in traditional patterns of communication between doctors and patients came not from medicine but from law. In a 1957 California case,[20] and a 1960 Kansas case,[21] judges were astounded and troubled by these undisputed facts: That without any disclosure of risks, new technologies had been employed which promised great benefits but also exposed patients to formidable and uncontrollable harm. In the California case, a patient suffered a permanent paralysis of his lower extremities subsequent to the injection of a dye, sodium urokan, to locate a block in the abdominal aorta. In the Kansas case, a patient suffered severe injuries from cobalt radiation, administered, instead of conventional x-ray treatment, subsequent to a mastectomy for breast cancer. In the latter case, Justice Schroeder attempted to give greater specifications to the informed consent doctrine, first promulgated in the California decision: "To disclose and explain to the patient, in language as simple as necessary, the nature of the ailment, the nature of the proposed treatment, the probability of success or of alternatives, and perhaps the risks of unfortunate results and unforeseen conditions within the body."[22]

From the perspective of improved doctor-patient communication, or better, shared decisionmaking, the fault lines inherent in this American legal doctrine are many:

One: The common law judges who promulgated the doctrine restricted their task to articulating new and more stringent standards of liability whenever physicians withheld material information that patients should know, particularly in light of the harm that the spectacular advances in medical technology could inflict. Thus, the doctrine was limited in scope, designed to specify those minimal disclosure obligations that physicians must fulfill to escape *legal* liability for alleged non-disclosures. Moreover, it was shaped and confined by legal assumptions about the objectives of the laws of evidence and negligence, and by economic philosophies as to who should assume the financial burdens for medical injuries sustained by patients.

Even though the judges based the doctrine on "Anglo-American law['s] ... premise of thorough-going self-determination,"[23] as the Kansas court put it, or on "the root premise ... fundamental in American jurisprudence that 'every human being of adult years and sound mind has a right to determine what shall be done with his own body,'"[24] as the Circuit Court for the District of Columbia put it in a subsequent opinion, the doctrine was grounded not in battery law (trespass), but in negligence law. The reasons are many. I shall only mention a compelling one: Battery law, based on unauthorized trespass, gives doctors only one defense—that they have made adequate disclosure. Negligence law, on the other hand, permits doctors to invoke many defenses, including "the therapeutic privilege" not to disclose when in their judgment, disclosure may prove harmful to patients' welfare.

Two recent opinions illustrate the problems identified here. First, in a rare opinion, the Supreme Court of Pennsylvania reconfirmed its adherence to the minority view among American jurisdictions that battery, not negligence, is the appropriate cause of action whenever lack of informed consent is alleged. The court held that whenever "the patient ... demonstrated, and the jury found, that he was not advised of ... material facts, risks, complications and alternatives to surgery which a reasonable man would have considered significant in deciding whether to have the operation ... the causation inquiry ends. The sole issue remaining [is] a determination of damages."[25] Earlier in its opinion, the court quoted, with approval, a prior Pennsylvania decision:

> [W]here a patient is mentally and physically able to consult about his condition, in the absence of an emergency, the consent of the patient is "a prerequisite to a surgical operation by his physician, and an operation without the patient's consent is a *technical assault*."[26]

Second, the Court of Appeals of California, in a ground-breaking opinion, significantly reduced the scope of the therapeutic privilege by requiring that in instances of hopeless prognosis (the most common situation in which the privilege has generally been invoked) the patient be provided with such information by asking, "If not the physician's duty to disclose a terminal illness, then whose?"[27] The duty to disclose prognosis had never before been identified specifically as one of the disclosure obligations in an informed consent opinion.

Thus, the appellate court's ruling constituted an important advance. It established that patients have a right to make decisions not only about the fate of their bodies but about the fate of their lives as well. The California Supreme Court, however, reversed. In doing so, the court made too much of an issue raised by the plaintiffs that led the appellate court to hold that doctors must disclose "statistical life expectancy information."[28] To be sure, disclosure of statistical information is a complex problem, but in focusing on that issue, the supreme court's attention was diverted from a more important new disclosure obligation promulgated by the appellate court: the duty to inform patients of their dire prognosis. The supreme court did not comment on that obligation. Indeed, it seemed to reverse the appellate court on this crucial issue by reinforcing the considerable lee-

way granted physicians to invoke the therapeutic privilege exception to full disclosure: "We decline to intrude further, either on the subtleties of the physician-patient relationship or in the resolution of claims that the physician's duty of disclosure was breached, by requiring the disclosure of information that may or may not be indicated in a given treatment context."[29]

Two: The doctrine of informed consent was not designed to serve as a *medical* blueprint for interactions between physicians and patients. The medical profession still faces the task of fashioning a "doctrine" that comports with its own vision of doctor-patient communication and that is responsive both to the realities of medical practices in an age of science and to the commands of law. As I said years ago,

> [T]ranslating the ingredients of [the informed consent] process into legal and useful medical prescriptions that respect patients' wishes to maintain and surrender autonomy, as well as physicians' unending struggles with omnipotence and impotence in the light of medical uncertainty, is a difficult task [which the medical profession] has not pursued ... in any depth.[30]

Thus, disclosure practices only changed to the extent of physicians disclosing more about the risks of a proposed intervention in order to escape legal liability.

Three: Underlying the legal doctrine there lurks a broader assumption which has neither been given full recognition by judges nor embraced by physicians. The underlying idea is this: That from now on patients and physicians must make decisions jointly, with patients ultimately deciding whether to accede to doctors' recommendations. In *The Cancer Ward*, Solzhenitsyn captured, as only a novelist can, the fears that such an idea engenders. When doctor Ludmilla Afanasyevna was challenged by her patient, Oleg Kostoglotov, about physicians' rights to make unilateral decisions on behalf of patients, Afanasyevna gave a troubled, though unequivocal, answer: "But doctors *are* entitled to the right—doctors above all. Without that right, there'd be no such thing as medicine."[31]

If Afanasyevna is correct, then patients must continue to trust doctors silently. Conversation, to comport with the idea of informed consent, ultimately requires that both parties make decisions jointly and that their views and preferences be treated with respect. Trust, based on blind faith—on passive surrender to oneself or to another—must be distinguished from trust that is earned after having first acknowledged to oneself and then shared with the other what one knows and does not know about the decision to be made. If all of that had been considered by physicians, they would have appreciated that a new model of doctor-patient communication, that takes informed consent seriously required a radical break with current medical disclosure practice.

Four: The idea of joint decisionmaking is one thing, and its application in practice another. To translate theory into practice cannot be accomplished, as the Judicial Council of the American Medical Association attempted to do in one short paragraph. The Judicial Council stated that "[t]he patient should make his own determination on treatment. Informed consent is a basic *social* policy...."[32] To translate social policy into *medical* policy is an inordinately difficult task. It requires a reassessment of the limits of medical knowledge in the light of medical uncertainty, a reassessment of professional authority to make decisions for patients in light of the consequences of such conduct for the well-being of patients, and a reassessment of the limits of patients' capacities to assume responsibility for choice in the light of their ignorance about medical matters and their anxieties when ill. Turning now to these problems, I wish to highlight that, in the absence of such reassessments, informed consent will remain a charade, and joint decisionmaking will elude us.

IV. Barriers to Joint Decisionmaking

A. Medical Uncertainty

The longer I reflect about doctor-patient decisionmaking, the more convinced I am that in this modern age of medical science, which for the first time permits sharing with patients the uncertainties of diagnosis, treatment, and prognosis, the problem of uncertainty poses the most formidable obstacle to disclosure and consent. By medical uncertainty I mean to convey what the physician Lewis Thomas observed so eloquently, albeit disturbingly:

> The only valid piece of scientific truth about which I feel totally confident is that we are profoundly ignorant about nature.... It is this sudden confrontation with the depth and scope of ignorance that represents the most significant contribution of twentieth-century science to the human intellect. *We are, at last facing up to it.* In earlier times, we either pretended to understand ... or ignored the problem, or simply made up stories to fill the gap.[33]

Alvan Feinstein put this in more concrete language: "Clinicians are still uncertain about the best means of treatment for even such routine problems as ... a fractured hip, a peptic ulcer, a stroke, a myocardial infarction.... At a time of potent drugs and formidable surgery, the exact effects of many therapeutic procedures are dubious or shrouded in dissension."[34]

Medical uncertainty constitutes a formidable obstacle to joint decisionmaking for a number of reasons: Sharing uncertainties requires physicians to be more aware of them than they commonly are. They must learn how to communicate them to patients and they must shed their embarrassment over acknowledging the true state of their own and of medicine's art and science. Thus, sharing uncertainties requires a willingness to admit ignorance about benefits and risks; to acknowledge the existence of alternatives, each with its own known and unknown consequences; to eschew one single authoritative recommendation; to consider carefully how to present uncertainty so that patients will not be overwhelmed by the information they will receive; and to explore the crucial question of how much uncertainty physicians themselves can tolerate without compromising their effectiveness as healers.

To so conduct oneself is most difficult. For, once doctors, on the basis of their clinical experience and knowledge, conclude which treatment is best, they tend to disregard, if not reject, the view of other colleagues who treat the same condition differently. Consider the current controversy over the management of localized prostate cancer: surgery, radiation or watchful waiting.[35] Some of the physicians involved in the debate are not even willing to accept that uncertainty exists, or at least they minimize its relevance to choice of treatment. Most who advocate treatment strongly prefer one type over another based on professional specialization (radiologists tend to recommend radiation; surgeons surgery).

Moreover, acknowledgment of uncertainty is undermined by the threat that it will undermine doctors' authority and sense of superiority. As Nuland put it, to feel superior to those dependent persons who are the sick, is after all a motivating factor that often influences their choice of medicine as a profession.[36] All of this suggests that implementation of the idea of informed consent is, to begin with, not a patient problem but a physician problem.

B. Patient Incompetence

Earlier, I touched on physicians' convictions that illness and medicine's esoteric knowledge rob patients of the capacity to participate in decisionmaking. Yet we do not know whether this is true. The evidence is compromised by the groping, half-hearted, and misleading attempts to inform patients about uncertainty and other matters which can make doc-

tors' communications so confusing and incomprehensible. If patients then appear stupid and ignorant this should come as no surprise; nor should patients' resigned surrender to this dilemma: "You are the doctor, you decide."

It is equally debatable, as Thomas Duffy has contended, that "[p]aternalism exists in medicine ... to fulfill a need created by illness."[37] It led him to argue, echoing Cassell, that "obviously autonomy cannot function as the cornerstone of the doctor-patient relationship [since] the impact of disease on personal integrity results in the patient's loss of autonomy.... In the doctor-patient relationship, the medical profession should always err on the side of beneficence."[38] If Duffy is correct, however, then informed consent is *ab initio* fatally compromised.

C. Patient Autonomy

Duffy's invocation of beneficence as the guiding principle is deeply rooted in the history of Hippocratic medicine. It finds expression in the ancient maxim: *primum non nocere*, above all do no harm, with "harm" remaining undefined but in practice being defined only as physical harm. Before presenting my views on the controversy over the primacy of autonomy or beneficence, let me briefly define their meaning.

In their authoritative book *Principles of Biomedical Ethics*, Thomas Beauchamp and James Childress defined these principles:

> Autonomy is a form of personal liberty of action where the individual determines his or her own course of action in accordance with a plan chosen by himself or herself. [Respect for individuals as autonomous agents entitles them] to such autonomous determinations without limitation on their liberty being imposed by others.[39]

Beneficence, on the other hand,

[r]equires not only that we treat persons autonomously and that we refrain from harming them, but also that we contribute to their welfare including their health. [Thus the principle asserts] the duty to help others further their important and legitimate interests ... to *confer* benefits and actively to prevent and remove harms ... [and] to *balance* possible goods against the possible harms of an action.[40]

Beauchamp and Childress' unequivocal and strong postulate on autonomy contrasts with the ambiguities contained in their postulate on beneficence. What do they mean by "benefits" and "harms" that allow invocation of beneficence? Do they mean only benefits and harms to patients' physical integrity, or to their dignitary integrity as choice-making individuals as well? Furthermore, what degree of discretion and license is permissible in the duty "to balance"? I have problems with balancing unless it is resorted to only as a *rare* exception to respect for autonomy. While human life is, and human interactions are, too complex to make any principle rule absolute, any exceptions must be rigorously justified.

I appreciate that mine is a radical proposal and constitutes a sharp break with Hippocratic practices. If informed consent, however, is ever to be based on the postulate of joint decisionmaking, the obligation "to respect the autonomous choices and actions of others,"[41] as Childress has put it, must be honored. Otherwise, informed consent is reduced to doctors providing more information but leaving decision-making itself to the authority of physicians.

As one physician once told me, echoing only an all too prevalent belief (and he was a physician allegedly deeply committed to informed consent), "I must first make the judgment which treatment alternative is best for patients, and only after I have exercised that professional judgment, will I discuss the risks and benefits of *the* recommended treat-

ment." This story illustrates the emphasis doctors place on risk disclosures rather than alternatives. The latter, however, is more crucial to joint decision-making than the former. Such a view, however, again encounters the issue of disclosure of medical uncertainty inherent in any forthright discussion of treatment alternatives. Physicians remain most reluctant to acknowledge uncertainty to themselves, and even more to their patients.

V. Respect for Autonomy

It should be evident by now that physicians must embark on a prolonged period of self-examination about how to interact with patients in new ways in an age of medical science and informed consent. Physicians must cease to complain about lawyers forcing them "to do silly things." Whenever doctors do so, they often observe that they can easily present their disclosures in ways that lead patients to agree with what they had thought to be the best alternative in the first place. This contention is a correct assessment of what transpires in customary practices that continue to eschew joint decisionmaking. Therefore, as I have already suggested, informed consent in today's world, is largely a charade which misleads patients into thinking that they are making decisions when indeed they are not.

Any meaningful change in Hippocratic decision-making practices first requires a new and revolutionary commitment to one principle: that physicians must respect patients as autonomous persons. The most crucial reason for my placing such high value on autonomy and self-determination is because doing so safeguards, as nothing else can, the recognition by the other that the person before him or her is as much a person as he or she is. Beneficence can readily reduce persons to non-persons by "taking care of them" in all of the many not only caring, but also, non-caring meanings of this phrase.

Before continuing, I must interject a few comments about my usage of the concept of autonomy.

The principle of autonomy has been subjected to criticism because its invocation can so readily consign human beings to abstract categories which defy reality. I wrote about this problem in my book *The Silent World of Doctor and Patient*: "Abstract principles tend to express generalizations about conduct that are ill-suited for application to actual cases in which human capacities to exercise rights must be considered."[42] Thus, I spoke instead about "psychological autonomy," to distinguish my conception of autonomy, for example, from that of Kant who restricted it to individuals' capacities to reason without any reference to their emotional life and their dependence on the external world. Instead, I wanted to convey by psychological autonomy, or better by respect for psychological autonomy, that human autonomy is fragile and that its optimal exercise requires both physicians and patients to pay caring attention to their capacities and incapacities for self-determination. In their interactions with one another, they must therefore through obligatory conversation, support and enhance their real, though precarious, endowment for reflective thought.

My views on psychological autonomy have been criticized as reintroducing paternalism into the physician-patient relationship. In particular, critics have argued that my emphasis on the *obligation* of patients to participate in such conversations constitutes an invasion of their privacy. While the criticism has merit, without such an obligation, autonomy is reduced to an abstraction that is inattentive to the psychological reality of both the strength and fragility of the human mind.

My views have also been misunderstood to require a lengthy, even "psychoanalytic," exploration of patients' minds. This was not my intention. I merely wished to suggest that it is possible to go to some length of subjecting thoughts and contemplated actions to clarification through dialogue which, in turn, may lead to a better understanding of what is at stake in the medical decisions to be made. Doing more is impossible and doing that much may

not persuade patients to choose a course of action that is "in their best interests." But, as Justice Stevens once put it, "[I]t is far better to permit some individuals to make incorrect decisions than to deny all individuals the right to make decisions that have a profound effect upon their destiny."[43]

In such conversations the principle of beneficence, often invoked as a counterpoise to autonomy, finds its rightful but delimited expression. Beneficence, in my view, requires physicians to enhance patients' capacities to arrive at the best autonomous choices they are capable of making by clearly and respectfully providing them with the information they need. The inherent tensions between the two principles, therefore, must be resolved, as I have already suggested, by giving primacy to autonomy. My reasons are twofold: (1) Autonomy assures that ultimate authority about treatment decisions resides with patients, including the decision to authorize doctors to decide for them. Since it is their bodily integrity that is at stake, no one but they can decide what should be done for them. (2) In the past, beneficence has served too unquestionably as justification for the unilateral exercise of physicians' authority to make decisions on behalf of patients. Although in rare circumstances it may trump autonomy, beneficence should only ensure that physicians will caringly assist patients to make their own choices, informed by the clarification physicians can provide about the medical consequences of the available options, particularly, of course, the consequences of patients' preferences for an option with which their doctors disagree.

Adherence to the principle of autonomy, in the ways I have defined it, demands that physicians respect patients' autonomy as choice-making individuals, and that their ultimate choices (except under the rarest and most carefully defined circumstances) be honored. It is based on the assumption that many patients are capable of comprehending what they need to know in order to decide what is best for themselves and that, therefore, they must be treated as adults possessed of the capacity for self-determination.

It is beyond the scope of this essay to explore decisionmaking between physicians and patients incompetent by virtue of severe mental illness, brain damage, or age. Throughout, I have limited my inquiry to doctors' interactions with *competent* patients often considered "*incompetent*" by doctors for reasons set forth above. To be sure, decisions by patients, like those of all human beings, are influenced by rational and irrational thoughts, rational and irrational emotions and rational and irrational judgments derived from the world of knowledge, experience and beliefs in which they have lived their lives. Respect for patient autonomy only postulates that patients, like human beings generally, have considerable capacity to listen, learn and reflect; that they can and must learn a great deal from doctors about the world of medicine as it affects their disease and dis-ease; and that they can choose and act better on their own behalf than doctors can act for them.

VI. The Current State of Physician-Patient Decisionmaking

In his recent book, entitled *How We Die*, Sherwin Nuland, a distinguished surgeon, reflects with profundity and insight on his lifelong interactions with patients. In a chapter on cancer and its treatment he speaks movingly about "death belong[ing] to the dying and to those who love them."[44] Yet, that privilege is often wrested from them when,

> [d]ecisions about continuation of treatment are influenced by the enthusiasm of the doctors who propose them. Commonly, the most accomplished of the specialists are also the most convinced and unyielding believers in biomedicine's ability to overcome the challenge presented by a pathological process.... [W]hat is offered as objective clinical reality is often the subjectivity of

a devout disciple of the philosophy that death is an implacable enemy. To such warriors, even a temporary victory justifies the laying waste of the fields in which a dying man has cultivated his life.[45]

Looking back at his work, he concludes that "more than a few of my victories have been Pyrrhic. The suffering was sometimes not worth the success.... [H]ad I been able to project myself into the place of the family and the patient, I would have been less often certain that the desperate struggle should be undertaken."[46]

In his view, a surgeon,

> [t]hough he be kind and considerate of the patient he treats ... allows himself to push his kindness aside because the seduction of The Riddle [the quest for diagnosis and cure] is so strong and the failure to solve it renders him so weak. [Thus, at times he convinces] patients to undergo diagnostic or therapeutic measures at a point in illness so far beyond reason that The Riddle might better have remained unsolved.[47]

Speaking then about the kind of doctor he will seek out when afflicted with a major illness, Nuland does not expect him to "understand my values, my expectations for myself ... my philosophy of life. *That is not what he is trained for and that is not what he will be good at.*"[48] Doctors can impart information, but "[i]t behooves every patient to study his or her own disease and learn enough about it. [Patients] should no longer expect from so many of our doctors what they cannot give."[49]

Nuland's views, supported by a great many poignant clinical vignettes, sensitively and forthrightly describe the current state of physician-patient decisionmaking, so dominated by physicians' judgments as to what is best. He presents many reasons for this state of affairs. One is based on doctors' "fear of failure":

A need to control that exceeds in magnitude what most people would find reasonable. When control is lost, he who requires it is also a bit lost and so deals badly with the consequences of his impotence. In an attempt to maintain control, a doctor, usually without being aware of it, convinces himself that he knows better than the patient what course is proper. He dispenses only as much information as he deems fit, thereby influencing a patient's decisionmaking in ways he does not recognize as self-serving.[50]

I have presented Nuland's observations at some length because they illustrate and support my contentions that joint decisionmaking between doctors and patients still eludes us. My critics had claimed earlier that my work on informed consent was dated because informed consent had become an integral aspect of the practice of medicine. In the paperback edition of *The Silent World of Doctor and Patient*, I argued that they have dismissed too lightly my central arguments:

> [T]hat meaningful collaboration between physicians and patients cannot become a reality until physicians have learned (1) how to treat their patients not as children but as the adults they are; (2) how to distinguish between their ideas of the best treatment and their patients' ideas of what is best; (3) how to acknowledge to their patients (and often to themselves as well) their ignorance and uncertainties about diagnosis, treatment, and prognosis; [and to all this, I now want to add, (4) how to explain to patients the uncertainties inherent in the state of the art and science of medicine which otherwise permits doctors on the basis of their clinical experience to leave unacknowledged that their colleagues on the basis of

their clinical experience have different beliefs as to which treatment is best].[51]

Nuland pleads for the resurrection of the family doctor[52] because he believes that the specialist is inadequate to the task of shouldering the burdens of decision with his patients. About this I differ with him. I believe that physicians (and surgeons as well) *can*, and *must*, learn to converse with patients in the spirit of joint decisionmaking. Physicians can and must learn to appreciate better than they do now that the principle of respect for person speaks to the caring commitment of physicians in old and new ways: *Old* in that it highlights the ancient and venerable medical duty not to abandon patients, and *new* by requiring doctors to communicate with them and remain at their sides, not only while their bodies are racked with pain and suffering but also while their minds are beset by fear, confusion, doubt and suffering over decisions to be made; also *new* in that implementation of the principle of psychological autonomy imposes the obligations on physicians both to invite, and respond to, questions about the decisions to be made, and to do so by respecting patients' ultimate choices, a new aspect of the duty to care.

The moral authority of physicians will not be undermined by this caring view of interacting with patients. Doctors' authority resides in the medical knowledge they possess, in their capacity to diagnose and treat, in their ability to evaluate what can be diagnosed and what cannot, what is treatable and what is not, and what treatment alternatives to recommend, each with its own risks and benefits and each with its own prognostic implications as to cure, control, morbidity, exacerbation or even death.

The moral authority of physicians resides in knowing better than others the certainties and the uncertainties that accompany diagnosis, treatment, prognosis, health and disease, as well the extent and the limits of their *scientific* knowledge and *scientific* ignorance. Physicians must learn to face up to and acknowledge the tragic limitations of their own professional knowledge, their inability to impart all their insights to all patients, and their own personal incapacities—at times more pronounced than others—to devote themselves fully to the needs of their patients. They must learn not to be unduly embarrassed by their personal and professional ignorance and to trust their patients to react appropriately to such acknowledgment. From all this it follows that ultimately the moral authority of physicians resides in their capacity to sort out *with* patients the choices to be made.

It is in this spirit that duty and caring become interwoven. Bringing these strands together imposes upon physicians the duty to respect patients as persons so that care will encompass allowing patients to live their lives in their own self-willed ways. To let patients follow their own lights is not an abandonment of them. It is a professional duty that, however painful, doctors must obey.

Without fidelity to these new professional duties, true caring will elude physicians. There is much new to be learned about caring that in decades to come will constitute the kind of caring that doctors in the past have wished for but have been unable to dispense, and that patients may have always yearned for.

I do not know whether my vision of a new physician-patient relationship defies medical reality. Thus, I may be wrong and I am willing to entertain this possibility as long as my critics are willing to admit that they too may be wrong. *As a profession we have never examined and tested in a committed manner what I have proposed.* It is this fact which, in conclusion, I want to highlight. For, I believe that in this age of medical science and informed consent the category of patient is in need of a radical reconceptualization. Throughout medical history, patients have been viewed as passive, ignorant persons whose welfare was best protected by their following doctors' orders, and physicians and patients were socialized to interact with one another on that basis. Throughout this essay, I have argued that such

a view of the physician-patient relationship was dictated by doctors' inability to explain to themselves what was therapeutic and what was not in the practice of medicine. The advent of the age of medical science has changed all that and for the first time in medical history doctors now can distinguish better between knowledge, ignorance and conjecture. In turn, this permits physicians to take patients into their confidence.

Finally, my purpose in writing this essay is twofold: (1) To argue, notwithstanding any theories of tort law and cost containment to the contrary,[53] that patients must ultimately be given the deciding vote in matters that effect their lives; and (2) to suggest that informed consent will remain a fairy tale as long as the idea of joint decisionmaking, based on a commitment to patient autonomy and self-determination, does not become an integral aspect of the ethos of medicine and the law of informed consent. Until then, physicians, patients and judges can only deceive themselves or be deceived about patients having a vital voice in the medical decisionmaking process. Of course, there are alternatives to joint decisionmaking. One that I have briefly explored elsewhere suggested that we need a number of informed (and uninformed) consent doctrines depending on the nature of the decisions to be made, with the implication that only in certain medical contexts must informed consent rise to the rigor advanced in this essay.[54] Another alternative is to fashion an informed consent doctrine for law and medicine that is *not* based on "[t]he root premise ... fundamental in American jurisprudence, that '[e]very human being of adult years and sound mind has a right to determine what shall be done with his own body.'"[55] It is not a road on which I would like to travel and thus, I leave that task to others. It is important that those who disagree with me set forth their premises about who decides what; otherwise physicians and patients are condemned to interact with one another, under the rubric of what is now called "informed consent," by deception of both self and the other.

NOTES

* Elizabeth K. Dollard Professor Emeritus of Law, Medicine and Psychiatry and Harvey L. Karp Professorial Lecturer in Law and Psychoanalysis, Yale Law School.

** This essay is a revised and extended version of an address given at the Institute de droit de la santé de l'Université de Neuchâtel and the Institute universitaire Kurt Boesch (IKB)-Sion on 6 September 1993. The address was published in the Institute's proceedings under the title *Le Consentement Eclairé Doit-Il Rester un Conte de Fées?* (1993).

I wish to thank Sherwin Nuland and my research assistants Steven D. Lavine and Katherine Weinstein for their thoughtful contributions to earlier drafts of this essay. My wife, Marilyn A. Katz, as always, has commented on the many drafts and I am grateful for her critical wisdom which is reflected throughout this essay.

1 Guido Calabresi, "Reflections on Medical Experimentation in Humans," *Daedalus* Vol. 98: 387 (1969).

2 Ibid. at 405.

3 Ibid.

4 Ibid. at 391.

5 Ibid. at 404.

6 Ibid. (emphasis added).

7 Guido Calabresi, "Do We Own Our Bodies?" *Health Matrix* Vol. 1: 17-18 (1991).

8 Guido Calabresi, *Ideals, Beliefs, Attitudes, and the Law* 10-11 (1985).

9 Jay Katz, *The Silent World of Doctor and Patient* (New York: Free Press, 1984) 2.

10 *Salgo v. Leland Stanford Jr. Univ. Bd. of Trustees*, 317 P.2d 170, 181 (Cal. Dist. Ct. App. 1957).

11 *Natanson v. Kline*, 350 P.2d 1093 (Kan. 1960).

12 Hippocrates, "Oath of Hippocrates," in Hippocrates 299-301 (W.H.S. Jones trans., 1962).

13 Hippocrates 297 (W.H.S. Jones trans., 1962).

14 "American Medical Association: Code of Ethics" (1847), reprinted in Katz, *supra* note 9, at 232.

15 Hippocrates, *supra* note 12, at 301.

16 Talcott Parsons, *The Social System* 464-65 (1951).

17 Eric Cassell, "The Function of Medicine," *Hastings Center Rep.*, Dec. 1977, at 16, 18.

18 Fyodor Dostoyevsky, *The Brothers Karamazov* 307 (A.P. MacAndrew trans., 1970).

19 Interview with Sherwin Nuland (1993).

20 *Salgo v. Leland Stanford Jr. Univ. Bd. of Trustees*, 317 P.2d 170 (Cal. Dist. Ct. App. 1957).

21 *Natanson v. Kline*, 350 P.2d 1093 (Kan. 1960).

22 Ibid. at 1106.

23 Ibid. at 1104.

24 *Canterbury v. Spence*, 464 F.2d 772, 780 (D.C. Cir. 1972).

25 *Gouse v. Cassel*, 615 A.2d 331, 335 (Pa. 1992).

26 Ibid. at 333-34 (emphasis added) (quoting *Moscicki v. Shor*, 163 A. 341, 342 [Pa. Super. Ct. 1932]).

27 *Arato v. Avedon*, 11 Cal. Rptr. 2d 169, 181 n.19 (Cal. Ct. App. 1992), *vacated*, 858 P.2d 598 (Cal. 1993).

28 *Arato*, 11 Cal. Rptr. 2d at 177.

29 *Arato*, 858 P.2d at 607.

30 Katz, *supra* note 9, at 84.

31 Alexander Solzhenitsyn, *The Cancer Ward* 77 (N. Bethell and D. Burg trans., 1969).

32 Judicial Council of the Am. Medical Ass'n, "Current Opinions of the Judicial Council of the American Medical Association," 25 (1981) (*emphasis added*).

33 Lewis Thomas, *The Medusa and the Snail* 73-74 (1979).

34 Alvan R. Feinstein, *Clinical Judgment* 23-24 (1967). Even though written 27 years ago, he has not changed his views. Interview with Alvan R. Feinstein (1994).

35 Gerald W. Chodak et al., "Results of Conservative Management of Clinically Localized Pros-

tate Cancer," *New Eng. J. Med.* Vol. 330: 242 (1994).

36 Interview with Sherwin B. Nuland (1994).

37 Thomas P. Duffy, "Agamemnon's Fate and the Medical Profession," *W. New Eng. L. Rev.* Vol. 9: 21, 27 (1987).

38 Ibid. at 30.

39 Thomas L. Beauchamp and James F. Childress, *Principles of Biomedical Ethics* 56, 58 (1st ed. 1979).

40 Ibid. 148-49 (2nd ed. 1983).

41 James F. Childress, "The Place of Autonomy in Bioethics," *Hastings Center Rep.*, Jan.-Feb. 1990, at 12, 12-13.

42 Katz, *supra* note 9, at 107.

43 *Thornburgh v. Am. College of Obstetricians & Gynecologists*, 476 U.S. 747, 781 (1986).

44 Sherwin B. Nuland, *How We Die* 265 (1994).

45 Ibid.

46 Ibid. at 266.

47 Ibid. at 249.

48 Ibid. at 266 (emphasis added).

49 Ibid. at 260.

50 Ibid. at 258.

51 Jay Katz, *The Silent World of Doctor and Patient* xi (1986).

52 Nuland, *supra* note 44, at 266.

53 See, e.g., Peter H. Schuck, "Rethinking Informed Consent," *Yale L.J.* Vol. 103: 899 (1994).

54 Jay Katz, "Physician-Patient Encounters 'On a Darkling Plain,'" *W. New Eng. L. Rev.* Vol. 9: 207, 221-22 (1987).

55 *Canterbury v. Spence*, 464 F.2d 772, 780 (D.C. Cir. 1972).

◆ ◆ ◆ ◆ ◆

ALLEN E. BUCHANAN AND
DAN W. BROCK

Standards of Competence

VII. Different Standards of Competence

A number of different standards of competence have been identified and supported in the literature, although statutory and case law provide little help in articulating precise standards.[1] It is neither feasible nor necessary to discuss here all the alternatives that have been proposed. Instead, the range of alternatives will be delineated and the difficulties of the main standards will be examined in order to clarify and defend [our decision-relative analysis]. More or less stringent standards of competence in effect strike different balances between the values of patient well-being and self-determination.

A. A Minimal Standard of Competence

An example of a minimal standard of competence is that the patient merely be able to express a preference. This standard respects every expressed choice of a patient, and so is not in fact a criterion of *competent* choice at all.[2] It entirely disregards whether defects or mistakes are present in the reasoning process leading to the choice, whether the choice is in accord with the patient's own conception of his or her good, and whether the choice would be harmful to the patient. It thus fails to provide any protection for patient well-being, and it is insensitive to the way value of self-determination itself varies both with the nature of the decision being made and with differences in people's capacities to choose in accordance with their conceptions of their own good.

B. An Outcome Standard of Competence

At the other extreme standards that look solely to the *content* or *outcome* of the decision—for example the standard that the choice be a reasonable one, or be what other reasonable or rational persons would choose. On this view, failure of the patient's choice to match some such allegedly objective outcome standard of choice entails that it is an incompetent choice. Such a standard maximally protects patient well-being—although only according to the standard's conception of well-being—It fails adequately to respect patient self-determination.

At bottom, a person's interest in self-determination is his or her interest defining, revising over time, and pursuing his or her own particular conception of the good life. [With so-called ideal or objective] theories of the good persons, there are serious practical or fallibilist risks associated with a purportedly objective standard for the correct decision—the standard may ignore the patient's own distinctive conception of the good and may constitute enforcement of unjustified ideals or unjustifiably substitute another's conception of what is best for the patient. Moreover, even such a standard's theoretical claim to protect maximally a patient's well-being is only as strong as the objective account of a person's well-being on which the standard rests. Many proponents of ideal theories only assert the ideals and fail even to recognize the need for justifying them, much less proceed to do so.

Although ascertaining the correct or best theory of individual well-being ? the good for persons is a complex and controversial task, ... any standard individual of well-being that does not ultimately rest on an individual's own underlying and enduring aims and values is both problematic in theory and subject to intolerable abuse in practice. There may be room in some broad policy decisions or overall theories of justice for more "objective" and interpersonal measures of well-being that faithfully to reflect differences ? individuals' own views of their well-being,[3] but we believe there is *much room* for such purportedly objective measures in the kind of judgments concern here—judgments about appropriate treatment for an individual patient. Thus, a standard that judges

competence by comparing the content of a patient's decision to some objective standard for the correct decision may fail even to protect appropriately a patient's well-being.

C. A Process Standard of Decision-Making Competence

An adequate standard of competence will focus primarily not on the content of the patient's decision but on the *process* of the reasoning that leads up to that decision. There are two central questions for any process standard of competence. First, process standard must set a level of reasoning required for the patient to be competent. In other words, how well must the patient understand and reason to be competent? How much can understanding be limited or reasoning defective and still be compatible with competence? The second question often passes without explicit notice by those evaluating competence. How certain must those persons evaluating competence be about how well the patient has understood and reasoned in coming to a decision? This second question is important because it is common in cases of marginal or questionable competence for there to be a significant degree of uncertainty about the patient's reasoning and decision-making process that can never be eliminated.

VIII. Relation of the Process Standard of Competence to Expected Harms and Benefits

Because the competence evaluation requires striking a balance between the two values of respecting patients' rights to decide for themselves and protecting them from the harmful consequences of their own choices, it should be clear that no single standard of competence—no single answer to the questions above can be adequate for all decisions. This is true because (1) the degree of expected harm from choices made at a given level of understanding and reasoning can vary from none to the most serious, including major disability or death, and because (2) the importance or value to the patient of self-determination can vary depending on the choice being made.

There is an important implication of this view that the standard of competence ought to vary in part with the expected harms or benefits to the patient of acting in accordance with the patient's choice—namely, that just because a patient is competent to consent to a treatment, it does *not* follow that the patient is competent to refuse it, and vice versa. For example, consent to a low-risk lifesaving procedure by an otherwise healthy individual should require only a minimal level of competence, but refusal of that same procedure by such an individual should require the highest level of competence.

Because the appropriate level of competence properly required for a particular decision must be adjusted to the consequences of acting on that decision, no single standard of decision-making competence is adequate. Instead, the level of competence appropriately required for decision making varies along a full range from low/minimal to high/maximal. Table 1 illustrates this variation, with the treatment choices listed used only as examples of any treatment choice with that relative risk/benefit assessment.

The net balance of expected benefits and risks of the patient's choice in comparison with other alternatives will usually be determined by the physician. This assessment should focus on the expected effects of a particular treatment option in forwarding the patient's underlying and enduring aims and values, to the extent that these are known. When the patient's aims and values are not known, the risk/benefit assessment will balance the expected effects of a particular treatment option in achieving the general goals of health care in prolonging life, preventing injury and disability, and relieving suffering as against its risks of harm. The table indicates that the relevant comparison is with other available alternatives, and the degree to which the net benefit/risk balance of the alternative chosen is better or worse than that for opting alternative treatment options. It should be noted that a choice might properly require only low/minimal competence, even though its expected risks exceed its expected benefits or it is more generally a high-risk treatment, because other available alternatives have substantially worse risk/benefit ratios.

Table 1 also indicates, for each level of competence, the relative importance of different *grounds* for believing that a patient's own choice best promotes his or her well-being. This brings out an important point. For *all* patient choices, other people respon-

Table 1. Decision-Making Competence and Patient Well-Being

The patient's choice	Others' risk/benefit assessment of that choice in comparison with other	Level of decision-making competence required	Grounds for believing patient's choice best promotes/protects own well-being
Patient consents to lumbar puncture for presumed meningitis	Net balance substantially better than for possible alternatives	Low/minimal	Principally the benefit/risk assessment made by others
Patient chooses lumpectomy for breast cancer	Net balance roughly comparable to that of alternatives	Moderate/median	Roughly equal from the benefit/risk assessment made by others and from the patient's decision that the chosen alternative best fits own conception of own good
Patient refuses surgery for simple appendectomy	Net balance substantially worse than for another alternative or alternatives	High/maximal	Principally from patient's decision that the chosen alternative best fits own conception of own good

sible for deciding whether these choices should be respected should have grounds for believing that the choice, if it is to be honored, is reasonably in accord with the patient's well-being (although the choice need not, of course, *maximally* promote the patient's interests). When the patient's level of decision-making competence need be only at the 10 minimal level, as in the agreement to a lumbar puncture for presumed meningitis, these grounds derive only minimally from the fact that the patient has chosen the option in question; they principally stem from others' position assessment of the choice's expected effects on the patient's well-being.

At the other extreme, when the expected effects of the patient's choice for his or her well-being appear to be substantially worse than available alternatives, as in the refusal of a simple appendectomy, the requirement of a high/maximal level of competence provides grounds for relying on the patient's decision as itself establishing that the choice best fits the patient's good (his or her own underlying and enduring aims and values). The highest level of competence should assure that no significant mistakes in the patient's reasoning and decision making are present, and is required to rebut the presumption that the choice is not in fact reasonably related to the patient's interests.

When the expected effects for the patient's well-being of his or her choice are approximately comparable to those of alternatives, as in the choice of a lumpectomy for treatment of breast cancer, a moderate/median level of competence is sufficient to provide reasonable grounds that the choice promotes the patient's good and that her well-being is adequately protected. It is also reasonable to assume that as the level of competence required increases (from minimal to maximal), the instrumental value or importance of respecting the patient's self-determination increases as well, specifically the part of the value of self-determination that rests on the assumption that persons will secure their good when they choose for themselves. As competence increases,

other things being equal, the likelihood of this happening increases.

Thus, according to the concept of competence endorsed here, a particular individual's decision-making capacity at a given time may be sufficient for making a decision to refuse a diagnostic procedure when foregoing the procedure does not carry a significant risk, although it would not necessarily be sufficient for refusing a surgical procedure that would correct a life-threatening condition. The greater the risk relative to other alternatives—where risk is a function of the severity of the expected harm and the probability of its occurrence—the greater the level of communication, understanding, and reasoning skills required for competence to make that decision. It is not always true, however, that if a person is competent to make one decision, then he or she is competent to make another decision so long as it involves equal risk. Even if the risk is the same, one decision may be more complex, and hence require a higher level of capacity for understanding options and reasoning about consequences.

In the previous section, we rejected a standard of competence that looks to the content or outcome of the decision in favor of a standard that focuses on the process of the patient's reasoning. This may appear inconsistent with our insistence here that the appropriate level of decision-making capacity required for competence should depend in significant part on the effects for the patient's well-being of accepting his or her choice, since what those effects are clearly depends on the content or outcome of the patient's choice. However, there is no inconsistency. The competence evaluation addresses the process of the patient's reasoning, whereas the degree of defectiveness and limitation of, and uncertainty about, that process that is compatible with competence depends in significant part on the likely harm to the patient's well-being of accepting his or her choice. To the extent that they are known, the effects on the patient's well-being should be evaluated in terms of his or her own underlying and enduring aims and values, or, where these are not known, in terms of the effects on life and health. Thus in our approach there is no use, an "objective" standard for the best or correct decision that is known to be in conflict with the patient's own underlying and enduring aims and value which was the objectionable feature of a content or outcome standard of competence.

The evaluation of the patient's decision making will seek to assess how well the patient has understood the nature of the proposed treatment and any significant alternatives, the expected benefits and risks and the likelihood of each, the reason for the recommendation, and then whether the patient has made a choice that reasonably conforms to his or her underlying and enduring aims and values. Two broad kinds of defect are then possible; first, "factual misunderstanding about the nature and likelihood of an outcome," for example from limitations in cognitive understanding resulting from stroke or from impairment of short-term memory resulting from dementia; second, failure of the patient's choice to be based on his or her underlying and enduring aims and values, for example because depression has temporarily distorted them so that the patient "no longer cares" about restoration of the function he or she had valued before becoming depressed.[4]

A crude but perhaps helpful way of characterizing the proper aim of the evaluator of the competence of a seemingly harmful or "bad" patient choice is to think of him or her addressing the patient in this fashion: "Help me try to understand and make sense of your choice. Help me to see whether your choice is reasonable, not in the sense that it is what I or most people would choose, but that it is reasonable for you in light of your underlying and enduring aims and values." This is the proper focus of a *process* standard of competence.

Some may object that misguided paternalists will always be ready to assess that their interference with the patient's choice is "deep down" in accord with what we have called the patient's "underlying

and enduring aims and values or at least with what these would be except for unfortunate distortions." If there is no objective way to determine a person's underlying and enduring aims and values then the worry is that our view will lead to excessive paternalism. We acknowledge that this determination will often be difficult and uncertain, for example, in cases like severe chronic depression, leading to genuine and justified uncertainty about the patient's "true" aims and values. But any claim that the aims and values actually expressed by the patient are not his underlying and enduring aims and values should be based on evidence of the distortion of the actual aims and values independent of their mere difference with some other, "better" aims and values. Just as the process standard of competence focuses on the process of the patient's reasoning, so also it requires evidence of a process of distortion of the patient's aims and values to justify evaluating choices by a standard other than the patient's actually expressed aims and values....

NOTES

1 See especially Roth, L.H., Meisel, A., and Lidz, C.W. (1977), "Tests of Competency to Consent to Treatment," *American Journal of Psychiatry* Vol. 134, 279-84; what they call "tests" are what we call "standards." An excellent discussion of competence generally, and of Roth, et al.'s tests for competence, in particular, is Freedman, B. (1981), "Competence, Marginal and Otherwise," *International Journal of Law and Psychiatry*, Vol. 4, 53-72.

2 Cf. Freedman, *op. cit.*

3 For example, John Rawls makes such claims for an objective and interpersonal account of "primary goods" to be used in evaluating persons' well-being within a theory of justice; cf. Rawls, J. (1971), *A Theory of Justice* (Cambridge, MA: Harvard University Press). Cf. also Scanlon, T. (1975), "Preference and Urgency," *Journal of Philosophy* Vol. 72, 655-69.

4 This second kind of decision-making defect illustrates the inadequacy of the tests that Roth, Meisel and Lidz call "the ability to understand" and "actual understanding" tests (cf. Roth, et al. [281-82], *op. cit.*). The clinically depressed patient may evidence no failure to understand the harmful consequences of his choice, but instead evidence indifference to those consequences as a result of his depression.

◆ ◆ ◆ ◆ ◆

DAN W. BROCK

Surrogate Decision Making for Incompetent Adults: An Ethical Framework

My role in this discussion is to add a philosophical perspective to the consideration of surrogate decision making. In the medical ethics literature, substantial, though not universal, consensus has developed that health care decision making should be shared between the physician and the competent patient. Typically, in medical practice, the physician brings his or her knowledge, training, expertise, and experience to the diagnosis of the patient's condition and provides the prognoses associated with different treatment alternatives, including the alternative of no treatment. The patient brings his or her own aims and values to the decision-making process and ideally evaluates the alternatives, with their particular mixes of benefits and risks.[1]

What values underlie a commitment to shared decision making, and what ends are we seeking to promote with it? The first, and most obvious, is the promotion and protection of the patient's well-being. Shared decision making rests in part on the presumption that competent patients who have been suitably informed by their physicians about the treatment choice they face are generally, though of course not always, the best judges of what treatment will most promote their overall well-being.[2] The other value is respecting the patient's self-determination. I mean by self-determination the interest of ordinary persons in making significant decisions about their own lives themselves and according to their own values. It is by exercising self-determination that we have significant control over our lives and take responsibility for our lives and the kind of person we become. These then are the values that guide shared decision making.

For incompetent patients we still want shared decision making, but then the patient lacks the capacity to participate and a surrogate must take the patient's place. My aim in this paper is, therefore, to sketch an ethical framework for surrogate decision making about medical treatment for incompetent adults and for thinking about the ethical issues that arise in that decision making.[3] Surrogate decision making should seek to extend the ideals of health care decision making for competent adults, with suitable changes required by and reflecting the patient's incompetence. Before considering who should be a surrogate and how the surrogate should decide, we must consider which patients should have a surrogate to decide for them.

Determining Competence

In health care, if the patient is competent, the patient is entitled to decide and to give or refuse informed consent to treatment. If the patient is incompetent, a surrogate must be selected to decide for the patient. The concept, standards, and determination of competence are complex; and there is space here to emphasize only a few important points about competence and incompetence (see especially 3, ch. 1). Adults are presumed to be competent unless and until found to be incompetent. In questionable or borderline cases, competence should be understood as decision relative, that is, a patient may be competent to make one decision but not another. First, decisions can vary in the demands they make on a patient, for example, in the complexity of the information relevant to the choice. Second, from the effects of medications, disease, and other factors, patients can change over time in the capacities they bring to the decision-making process.

Three distinct capacities are needed for competence in treatment decision making: the capacity for understanding and communication; the capacity for reasoning and deliberation; the capacity to have and apply a set of values or conception of one's good. Though people possess these capacities in different degrees, it is important to recognize that the determination of competence is not a comparative judgment. Because the competence determination in health care (and in the law) is used to sort the patient into either the class of patients who are competent to decide for themselves or into the class of patients who must have a surrogate to decide for them, it must be recognized as a threshold determination. The crucial question about competence in borderline cases then, is how defective or impaired a person's decision making must be to warrant a determination of incompetence.

Two central values are at stake when a patient is judged competent or incompetent, and so two kinds of dangers should be balanced in this determination. One value is protecting the patient from the harmful consequences of his or her choice when the patient's decision making is seriously impaired. The other value is respecting the patient's interest in deciding for him or herself. The dangers to be considered are failing adequately to protect the patient from the harmful consequences of a seriously impaired choice, which must be balanced against failing to permit the patient to decide for him or herself when sufficiently able to do so. There is no unique objectively correct balancing of these two values and dangers. Instead, the proper balancing is inherently an ethically controversial choice.

Process as the Standard

The evaluation of a patient's competence should address and evaluate the process of the patient's decision making; the standards should not be an outcome standard that simply looks to the content of the patient's choice. Given the values at stake in the competence determination it follows that the standard for competence should vary according to the consequences for the patient's well-being of accepting his or her choice. The standard should vary along a continuum from high (when the choice appears to be seriously in conflict with the patient's well-being) to moderate (when the patient's choice appears to be comparable to other alternatives in its effect on the patient's well-being) to low (when the choice will clearly best serve the patient's well-being).

One controversial consequence of this account of the competence determination is that a patient might be competent to consent to a particular treatment, but not to refuse it, and vice versa. This follows from two facts. First, the process of reasoning to be evaluated will inevitably be different if it leads to a different choice. Second, the effects on one of the values to be balanced (the patient's well-being—if the patient's choice is accepted) can be radically different depending on whether the patient has consented to or refused the recommended treatment. Treatment refusal may reasonably trigger an evaluation of the patient's competence, though it should also trigger a revaluation by the physician both of the treatment recommendation and of the communication of that recommendation to the patient; some studies have shown that the most common cause of treatment refusals is failure of communication between physician and patient, and most refusals are consequently withdrawn when the recommendation is better explained.[4]

The critical question to answer is, Does the patient's choice sufficiently accord with the patient's own underlying and enduring aims and values for it to be accepted and honored, even if others, including the physician, may think it not the best choice?

Selecting a Surrogate

Assume now that a patient has been found incompetent to make a particular treatment choice, so that a surrogate must act for the patient. Who should serve as surrogate? What standards should guide the surrogate's decision? If we are to respect the incompetent patient's wishes, then the surrogate should be the person the patient would have wanted to act as surrogate. In a number of states, by executing a Durable Power of Attorney for Health Care (DPOA), it is possible for a person, while, competent, to legally designate a surrogate who will make health care decisions in the event of later incompetence. This document also allows a person to give instructions to the surrogate about one's wishes concerning treatment. Ethically, an oral designation by a person of a surrogate should have nearly the same weight as a formal DPOA. Competent patients should be encouraged to designate who will decide for them in the case of later incompetence. In fact, physicians have a responsibility to seek this information early in treatment and while patients are still competent, especially if a period of later incompetence is likely.

Often an incompetent patient will not have explicitly designated a surrogate. It is then reasonable and common to act on a presumption that a patient's close family member is the appropriate surrogate. (In most jurisdictions, a close family member lacks explicit legal authority to act as the patient's surrogate until formally appointed by a court as the guardian. States should consider adopting legislation like the recently enacted Health Care Decisions Act in the District of Columbia which formally authorizes a family member to act as surrogate for an incompetent patient without recourse to guardianship proceedings.) Only the most important considerations that support this presumption for a family member acting as surrogate can be discussed here.

First, usually a family member will be the person the patient would have wanted to act as surrogate for him or her. Second, the family member will know the patient best and will be most concerned for the patient's welfare. It is important to underline that the claim is only that the practice of using a close family member as surrogate will result overall in better decisions for patients than any feasible alternative practice, such as appointing an attorney to act as the patient's guardian. Third, in our society the family is the central social and moral unit assigned responsibilities to care for its dependent members. Although dependent children are the most obvious example, dependent adults are another important instance of this responsibility. The family is also the main place in which most people pursue and realize the values of intimacy and privacy. Both to fulfill these responsibilities and to realize these values, the family must be accorded significant, though not unlimited, freedom from external oversight, intrusion, and control.

These grounds for presuming a close family member to be an incompetent patient's surrogate do not imply that such a surrogate must always make the optimal choice. On the other hand they also make it clear that family members' authority as surrogate decision makers is limited. When the grounds do not hold—for example, when there is no close relation between patient and family member, or when there is a clear conflict of interest between patient and family member—the presumption for family members as surrogates can be rebutted. In such cases, an incompetent patient's physician can have a positive responsibility not to allow the family member to act as surrogate.

Sometimes no family member is available to serve as surrogate. Most reasons that support a family member serving as surrogate will then also support using a close friend who is available and willing to serve. When no family member or friend is available, institutional flexibility is desirable because of the wide range of different decisions that must be made. Institutions only need a settled and public policy insuring that decision making in such cases does not become paralyzed from lack of a natural surrogate. For example, a hospital might have a policy for a specified range of decisions (such as decisions to forgo life-sustaining treatment or resuscitation) requiring that the attending physician's proposed decision be referred to the chief of service who could review the decision and take any further steps deemed appropriate (perhaps referral to an ethics committee or to the courts).

How Surrogates Should Decide

Advance Directives

What standards should a surrogate employ in deciding for an incompetent patient? Three ordered principles can guide decision making: advance directive; substituted judgment; best interest. These are ordered principles in the sense that the surrogate should employ the first if possible; if not it, then the second if possible; and if neither the first or second can be used, then the third. The advance directive principle tells the surrogate that if there is a valid advance directive from the patient, there is a strong presumption that it should be followed. Formal advance directives take two principal forms, living wills and durable powers of attorney for health care. Living wills are given legal force in approximately 40 states; DPOAs at present have legal force in far fewer jurisdictions.

Several common features limit the usefulness of living wills. I shall mention two. First, they are usually formulated in vague terms for describing both the patient conditions ("terminally ill") and the treatments ("extraordinary measures," "aggressive treatment"). Because they are executed well in advance of the decision to be made, this is to some extent inevitable and means that others must interpret how they should now apply. Second, probably in response to worries about potential abuses, enabling statutes in many states place limitations on the circumstances in which living wills can either be executed (for example, the person must already have been diagnosed terminally ill with death imminent) or applied (for example, the decision cannot cover nutrition and hydration). When persons follow these restrictions and limitations, in many circumstances their living wills will fail to apply. Since living wills are rarely brought into court for enforcement, but function primarily as a means of informing others about the patient's wishes, restrictive formulations may be inadvisable.

Except for those who have no surrogate, DPOAs are the more desirable form of advance directive for most persons. First, they allow a person to give more detailed instructions to the surrogate about wishes regarding treatment, though it is important to avoid letting greater detail narrow the application of the instructions. Second, they address the issue of later interpreting the patient's instructions by allowing the patient to designate the interpreter.

Although there is a strong presumption that a valid advance directive should be followed, there are reasons why advance directives should not have the same degree of binding force as the contemporaneous decision of a competent patient. The decision of a competent patient can be made attending to the full and detailed context, whereas advance directives must inevitably be formulated before the precise context of future decisions is known. This means that occasionally a treatment decision will arise in circumstances radically different from those imagined by the patient when executing the advance directive; in such cases, following the letter of the directive may be contrary to following its spirit. Moreover, concern over whether the patient would have changed his or her mind about treatment does not arise for a competent patient. Finally, a decision by a competent patient that appears significantly contrary to his or her interests usually will be challenged by the care givers, thereby testing understanding and resolve to an extent not possible with advance directives. Despite these limitations, there are good reasons to accord a strong presumption to any patient's advance directive.

Substituted Judgment

At present, and probably for the forseeable future, most patients do not have advance directives. Then the substituted judgment principle should be followed. This principle tells the surrogate to attempt to decide as the patient would have decided, if competent, in the circumstances that now obtain. In effect, the principle directs the surrogate to use his or her knowledge of the patient and the patient's aims and values to infer what the patient's choice would have been.

Physicians have an important responsibility in helping surrogates to understand their role in applying substituted judgment. Rather than asking, "What do you now want us to do for your mother?" the physician should say, "You, of course, knew your mother better than I did, so help us decide together what she would have wanted done for her now." Confirmation that asking the right question matters in the choices surrogates make can be found in Tomlinson.[5] This substituted judgment approach is helpful for arriving at decisions which are more in accordance with the patient's wishes. The approach also has the practical advantage of making the psychological and emotional burdens easier for surrogates to carry and facilitating their effective participation in decision making.

"Do everything" is nearly always an inadequate and unhelpful answer. Surrogates should be assured that appropriate care will always be given, including all care needed to maintain the patient's comfort and dignity. But what care is appropriate will often change with changes in the patient's condition and prognosis, and surrogates must be helped to understand that all possible care is not automatically appropriate care.

Two features of substituted-judgment decision making should be explicitly noted. First, the substituted judgment model will let surrogates take account of how the interests of others will be affected by the decision, to the extent there is evidence that the patient would have weighed those interests. Second, it will allow surrogates to assess the patient's quality of life, both at present and as it will be affected by treatment decisions, according to the patient's own values. For consideration of forgoing life-sustaining treatment only a limited judgment of quality of life is relevant: Is the best anticipated quality of life with life-sustaining treatment sufficiently poor that the patient would have judged it to be worse than no further life at all? No judgments about social worth or the social value of the patient are warranted under substituted judgment.

Best Interest

When no information is available about what this particular patient would have wanted in the situation at hand, the "best interest" principle directs the surrogate to select the alternative that furthers the patient's best interests. This, in effect, amounts to asking how most reasonable persons would decide in these circumstances, an approach which is justified by the absence of any information about how this patient differs from others. Treatment choices based on best interests can be especially difficult when reasonable: persons can and do disagree about the choice. It is, therefore, important, where possible, to avoid having to appeal to best interests by determining patients' wishes about future treatment options when patients are still competent.

Ordering These Three Principles

Strict ordering of these guidance principles would be an oversimplification. Evidence bearing on the patient's wishes concerning the decision at hand, whether from an advance directive or from the surrogate's knowledge of the patient, is not either fully determinate and decisive on the one hand, or completely absent on the other. Instead, such evidence ranges along a broad continuum in how strongly it supports a particular choice. In all cases physicians and surrogates should seek confidence that the choice made is reasonably in accord with the patient's wishes or interests. The better the evidence about what this particular patient would have wanted, the more one can rely on it. The less the information and evidence about what this patient would have wanted, the more others must reason in terms of what most persons would want.

What constitutes adequate evidence about the patient's wishes has been at issue in several recent court cases, most notably the O'Connor case in New York and the Cruzan case in Missouri, recently upheld by the US Supreme Court.[6] In the New York case the court imposed an extremely high standard of evidence for forgoing life-sustaining treatment by surrogate order, requiring clear and convincing proof that the patient had made a settled commitment while competent, to reject the particular form of treatment under circumstances such as those now obtaining. Where there is any significant doubt, the court reasoned, the decision must be on the side of preserving life. This decision set a very difficult standard in New York for patients and their surrogates to satisfy, and thereby establishes a strong presumption in favor of extending the lives of incompetent patients with life-sustaining treatment. In Cruzan, the US Supreme Court upheld the right of the State of Missouri to impose this same strong presumption, though without endorsing the wisdom of doing so.

Such a presumption undervalues patients' interest in self-determination and fails to recognize adequately the extent to which patients' well-being is determined by their own aims and values. But is it not reasonable, the Court might ask, always to err on the side of preserving life when there is any doubt about the patient's wishes? Several decades ago, when medicine only rarely had the capacity to extend life in circumstances where doing so would have been unwanted and no benefit to patients, such a policy would have been reasonable. Medicine, however, has vastly enlarged its capacities to extend life. Patients' lives can now often be extended when they would not want this done, and, as a result, New York's and Missouri's strong presumption in favor of extending life, when there is any significant doubt about the patient's wishes, can no longer be justified. Though the US Supreme Court found no constitutional bar to the clear and convincing evidence standard, good reasons remain for other states not to adopt it.

Conclusion

I want to conclude with a plea for "preventive ethics" aimed at reducing the necessity to resort to surrogate decision making. This can only be accomplished by persons, while still competent, talking with their physicians and families about their treatment wishes should they become seriously ill. Such preventive measures are especially appropriate for persons with chronic, progressive diseases in which both a possible period of incompetence and the nature of later treatment decisions likely to arise are relatively predictable. Physicians have an important role in encouraging their patients to reflect on their wishes and to make those wishes known to those who are likely to be involved in their treatment decisions. The need for surrogate decision making in health care will never be eliminated, nor can all difficult decisions be avoided. But it should be possible greatly to reduce the number of cases in which physicians and surrogates must decide about an incompetent patient's care in the absence of knowledge of the patient's wishes when that information could have been obtained earlier had it been sought.

REFERENCES

1 Some respects in which this division of labor is oversimplified are explored in Brock, D.W., "Facts and Values in the Physician/Patient Relationship," in Veatch R., Pellegrino E., eds.,

Ethics, Trust, and the Professions (Washington, DC: Georgetown University Press, 1991).

2 For a discussion of different kinds of cases in which competent patients make irrational choices, and the responsibilities of their physicians in such circumstances, see Brock, D.W., Wartman, S.A., "When Competent Patients Make Irrational Choices," *N Engl J Med* (1990) Vol. 322 (May 31): 1595-99.

3 I draw freely here on prior published work I have done on this topic, some of it collaborative work with Allen Buchanan. See especially Buchanan, A.E., Brock, D.W., *Deciding for Others: The Ethics of Surrogate Decision-Making* (Cambridge, England: Cambridge University Press, 1989).

4 Applebaum PS, Roth LS. Treatment refusal in the medical hospital. In: *President's Commission for the Study of Ethical Problems in Medicine and Biomedical Behavioral Research. Making health care decisions: the ethical and legal implications of informed consent in the patient-practitioner relationship*, vol. 2 Appendices. Washington, DC: U.S. Government Printing Office, 1982.

5 Tom Tomlinson, et al. An empirical study of proxy consent for elderly persons. *Gerontologist* 1990; 30(1): 54-60.

6 In re O'Connor, No. 312 (NY Court of Appeals, October 14, 1988); Cruzan v. Director, Missouri Department of Health, 110 Sct 2841 (1990).

CASE STUDY

THE SCHIAVO CASE AND END-OF-LIFE DECISIONS
WALLY SIEWERT

Case Description

On February 25, 1990, Florida resident Theresa (Terri) Schiavo, daughter of Robert and Mary Schindler, and wife of Michael Schiavo, suffered a cardiac arrest leading to brain damage from a lack of oxygen. During the course of the immediately following hospitalization and attempts at rehabilitation Michael Schiavo was appointed as Ms. Schiavo's guardian and the Schindlers did not object. Over the next few years Ms. Schiavo received intensive therapy at various institutions, including experimental brain and thalamic stimulator treatments. In November of 1992 Ms. Schiavo was awarded over a million dollars in two malpractice suits against doctors involved in her treatment, $300,000 of which went to Michael

Schiavo, and another $750,000 was placed in a trust fund for Ms. Schiavo's medical care.

In 1993 Ms. Schiavo's parents and Michael Schiavo had a disagreement over the course of Ms. Schiavo's therapy. As a result, on July 29th, the Schindlers petitioned the courts to have Mr. Schiavo removed as guardian for the first time. A guardian ad litem, who had no decision making power, but who was to represent Terri's best interests before the court was appointed. The guardian's report stated that Michael Schiavo had acted appropriately and attentively towards Terri and the petition to remove Michael as guardian was later dismissed.

In May of 1998 Michael Schiavo petitioned the court for the first time to authorize the removal of Terri's feeding tube (known as a PEG tube). His petition was opposed by the Schindlers, who maintain that Terri would have wanted to stay alive. A second guardian ad litem was appointed. He agreed that Ms. Schiavo was in a persistent vegetative state without possibility of improvement, but stated that Michael Schiavo's decision making may be influenced by his prospective inheritance of her estate.

On February 11, 2000, Pinellas-Pasco County Circuit Court Judge George Greer ruled that Ms. Schiavo would have chosen not to live in such a condition and ordered the PEG tube removed. On April 24, 2001, upon the denial of several appeals, the PEG tube was removed for the first time. Two days later the Schindlers filed a new civil suit against Michael Schiavo, and the tube was re-inserted.

During the ensuing court battle the Schindlers alleged that Ms. Schiavo was abused by her husband, leading to her condition, an attempt at mediation between the Schindlers and Michael Schiavo failed, and Governor Jeb Bush filed a federal court brief in support of the Schindler's efforts. On October 15, 2003 the PEG tube was removed once again on the court's orders. On October 20th and 21st respectively, the Florida House of Representatives and Senate passed "Terri's Law," allowing the governor to issue a "one time stay in certain cases." As a result, Governor Bush issued an executive order and the PEG tube was reinserted for the second time. By this time, in addition to a maze of court proceedings, the case had become a national media event. President Bush publicly praised his brother Jeb Bush's handling of the case. Pope John Paul II spoke out on "Life Sustaining Treatments and Vegetative state," defending the obligation to keep Ms. Schiavo alive. And Randall Terry, the founder of the nationally recognized pro-life group Operation Rescue, made media appearances with the Schindlers. In both the Florida and the US congresses bills were introduced which would, to varying degrees, limit the right of legal guardians in such cases to remove sustenance without the express written consent of the patient themselves.

On September 23, 2004 the Florida Supreme Court declared Terri's Law unconstitutional, and on March 18th of the following year Ms. Schiavo's PEG tube was removed for the third and final time. In the resulting scramble to have the tube re-inserted Governor Jeb Bush reported that a neurologist, Dr. William Cheshire, claimed that Ms. Schiavo was not, after all, in a persistent vegetative state. Despite this, several federal and state appeals failed and on March 31st at 9:05 a.m. Terri Schiavo died. A post-mortem revealed that she was indeed in an irreversible vegetative state.

Ethical Analysis

There are three primary areas of ethical concern involved in the Terri Schiavo case. First is the question of decision-making procedures at the end of life. The initial consideration in such cases is always the autonomous will of the patient herself. The right of Ms. Schiavo to request the removal of her PEG tube had been established by the Nancy Cruzan case. Ms. Cruzan's feeding tube was removed and she died in December 1990, after her family presented what was considered clear and convincing evidence that this would have accorded with her wishes. Since Ms. Schiavo left no written evidence of her preferences regarding continued treatment, or the abrogation thereof, the decision was left entirely up to her legal guardian. Michael Schiavo was Terri's legal guardian during the entire period from her cardiac arrest to her death. He maintained consistently that the removal of the PEG tube was what Terri herself would have wanted. The court's acceptance of his decisions regarding Ms. Schiavo's treatment was blocked, however, by the legal actions of her parents. Robert and Mary Schindler repeatedly claimed themselves as the rightful legal guardians, and the courts were obligated to hear their case before acceding to Mr. Schiavo's requests for euthanasia. The Schindlers also claimed that, contrary to Mr. Schiavo's testimony, their daughter would have preferred to stay alive.

The court's discretion in deciding whose legal guardianship is in the best interests of an incapacitated patient placed it in a very difficult position.

The second area of ethical concern involved in the Terri Schiavo case is the question of the scope of the right to privacy. The courts were petitioned by the litigants in the case, Robert and Mary Schindler and Michael Schiavo. They were therefore rightful participants in the dispute. Governor Jeb Bush, the Florida Congress, and the US Congress were not petitioned as such and had, by some accounts, no business inserting themselves into what should have been a private decision. Others claim that the removal of the PEG tube and Terri Schiavo's subsequent death was an act against moral law, and therefore the activities of said politicians, as well as other public personalities such as Pope John Paul II and Randall Terry, were justified.

Finally we must consider the status of Terri's "right to die." While precedent has established such a right under certain circumstances, its implementation is still limited to the removal or withholding of treatment. The removal of a PEG tube commences the slow and painful process of starvation. While it is unclear if Terri could do so, it is clear that some patients who ask to die in this manner can feel this pain. Terri began this process and was abruptly re-nourished twice. If what patients in these situations seek is a "good death" (the very definition of euthanasia) would a less painful and quicker injection be preferable?

Study Questions

1. Given clear testimonial evidence that the removal of the PEG tube is what the patient would have wanted, but lacking a written statement by the patient to that effect, should the courts and/or medical establishment allow the removal of PEG tubes, or euthanasia of any kind? What guidelines could you recommend to make such decisions easier in the future?

2. Regardless of the outcome, should end-of-life decisions be private? Does the fact that the decision involves the intentional, though presumably voluntary, ending of a life justify the involvement of politicians? Why or why not?

3. If you were in a persistent vegetative state, would you want to be unplugged? Would you perhaps prefer an injection? Why or why not? Since we are afforded a right to die, should this right be extended to the right to die in the most humane way possible?

Sources

Abdolmohammadi, J. Mohammad and Mark R. Nixon. "Ethics in The Public Accounting Profession." *A Companion To Business Ethics*. Edited by Robert E. Fredrick. Oxford: Blackwell Publishing, 2002. Reprinted by permission of Blackwell Publishing.

Brock, Dan W. "Surrogate Decision Making for Incompetent Adults: An Ethical Framework." *The Mount Sinai Journal of Medicine* 58.5 (October 1991): 388–92. Reprinted by permission of the Mount Sinai Hospital.

Buchanan, Allen E. and Dan W. Brock. "Standards of Competence," from *Deciding for Others: The Ethics of Surrogate Decision Making*. Cambridge: Cambridge University Press, 1989. Reprinted by permission of Cambridge University Press.

Cohen, Elliot D. "Pure Legal Advocates and Moral Agents: Two Concepts of a Lawyer in an Adversary System." *Criminal Justice Studies* 4.1 (1985): 38–59. Reprinted by permission of Taylor and Francis Ltd.

Davis, Michael. "Is There a Profession of Engineering?" *Science and Engineering Ethics* 3.4 (1997): 407–28. Reprinted by permission of Opragen Publications. "Professional Responsibility: Just Following The Rules?" *Business and Professional Ethics Journal* 18.1 (1999): 65–87. Reprinted by permission of Michael Davis.

De George, Richard T. "Ethical Responsibilities of Engineers in Large Organizations: The Pinto Case." *Business and Ethical Journal* 1.1 (September 1981): 1–14. Reprinted by permission of Richard De George.

Detmer, David. "The Ethical Responsibilities of Journalists." Copyright © David Detmer. Reprinted by permission of the author.

The Economist. "The Lessons From Enron." Originally published in *The Economist* February 7, 2002. Copyright © 2002 The Economist Newspaper Ltd. All rights reserved. Reprinted with permission. Further reproduction prohibited. <www.economist.com>.

Emmanuel, Ezekiel J. and Linda L. Emmanuel. "Four Models of the Physician-Patient Relationships." *Journal of the American Medical Association* 267.16 (April 1992): 2221–26. Reprinted by permission of the American Medical Association.

Frantz, Linda Rush. "Engineering Ethics: The Responsibility of the Manager." *Engineering Management International* 4.4 (1988): 267–72. Reprinted by permission of Elsevier Science and Technology Journals.

Freedman, Monroe H. "Professional Responsibility of the Criminal Defense Lawyer: The Three Hardest Questions." *Michigan Law Review* 64.8 (1966): 1469–84. Reprinted by permission of the Michigan Law Review.

Glasser, Theodore L. "Objectivity Precludes Responsibility." *The Quill* (February 1984): 13–16.

Gowthorpe, Catherine and Oriol Amat. "Creative Accounting: Some Ethical Issues of Macro- and Micro-Manipulation." *Journal of Business Ethics* 57.1 (2005): 55–64. Reprinted with kind permission from Spring Science and Business Media.

Greenwood, Ernest. "Attributes of a Profession." *Social Work* 2 (July 1957): 45–55. Copyright © 1957, National Association of Social Workers, Inc. Reprinted by permission of the National Association for Social Workers.

Gutmann, Amy. "Can Virtue Be Taught to Lawyers?" *Stanford Law Review* 45 (1993): 1745–71. Reprinted by permission of the *Stanford Law Review*.

Katz, Jay. "Informed Consent—Must It Remain a Fairy Tale?" *Journal of Contemporary Health Law and Policy* 10.96 (1994): 73–74. Reprinted by permission of the Catholic University of America.

Kipnis, Kenneth. "A Defense of Unqualified Medical Confidentiality," from *Economic Justice: Private Rights and Public Responsibilities.* Totowa, NJ: Rowman and Allanheld, 1985. Kenneth Kipnis and Diana T. Meyers. Copyright © 1985 Kenneth Kipnis. Reprinted by permission of Kenneth Kipnis.

Ladd, John. "Bhopal: An Essay on Moral Responsibility and Civic Virtue." *Journal of Social Philosophy* 22.1 (1991): 73–91. Reprinted by permission of Blackwell Publishing.

Landesman, Bruce M. "Confidentiality and the Lawyer-Client Relationship." Originally published in the *Utah Law Review* 4 (1980): 765–86. Reprinted by permission of the *Utah Law Review* and of Bruce Landesman.

Lichtenberg, Judith. "Truth, Neutrality, and Conflict of Interest." *Business and Professional Ethics Journal* 9.1/2 (1990): 65–78. Reprinted by permission of Judy Lichtenberg.

Lippke, Richard L. "Justice and Insider Trading." *Journal of Applied Philosophy* 10.2 (1993): 215–26. Reprinted by permission of Blackwell Publishing Ltd.

Luban, David. "The Adversary System Excuse," from *The Good Lawyer.* Totowa, NJ: Rowman and Allanheld (1983): 83–122. A revised and expanded version of this paper appears in David Luban's *Legal Ethics and Human Dignity.* Cambridge: Cambridge University Press, 2007. Reprinted by permission of the author.

Machan, Tibor R. "What is Morally Right with Insider Trading." *Public Affairs Quarterly* 10.2 (1996): 135–42. Reprinted by permission of *Public Affairs Quarterly.*

Martin, Mike W. "Whistleblowing: Professionalism, Personal Life and Shared Responsibility for Safety in Engineering." *Business and Professional Ethics Journal* 11.2 (1992): 21–40. Reprinted by permission of Mike W. Martin.

McCuen, Richard H. "Engineering Research: Potential for Fraud." *Journal of Professional Issues in Engineering* 109.3 (July 1983): 185–94. Reprinted by permission of the American Society of Civil Engineers.

Melé, Domenèc. "Ethical Education in Accounting: Integrating Rules, Values, and Virtues." *Journal of Business Ethics* 57.1 (2005): 97–109. Reprinted with kind permission from Spring Science and Business Media.

Pellegrino, Edmund D. "The Virtuous Physician and the Ethics of Medicine," from *Virtue and Medicine: Explorations in the Character of Medicine.* Edited by Earl Shelp. Dordrecht: Reidel Publishers, 1985.

Pizzimenti, Lee A. "Informing Clients About Limits to Confidentiality." *Business and Professional Ethics Journal* 9.1–2 (Spring 1990): 207. Reprinted by permission of Lee Pizzimenti.

Pritchard, Michael. "Responsible Engineering: The Importance of Character and Imagination." *Science and Engineering Ethics* 7.3 (2001): 391–402. Reprinted by permission of Michael Pritchard and of Opragen Publications.

Quinn, Aaron. "Accepting Manipulations or Manipulating What's Acceptable?" Originally published in the Australian Computer Society publication *Computers and Philosophy* 2003. CRPIT Volume 37. Reprinted by permission of Aaron Quinn and John Roddick.

Robertson, Lori. "Ethically Challenged." *American Journalism Review* 23.2 (March 2001): 20–29. Reprinted by permission of *American Journalism Review*.

Rockness, Howard and Joanne Rockness. "Legislated Ethics: From Enron to Sarbanese-Oxley, the Impact on Corporate America." *Journal of Business Ethics* 57.1 (2005): 31–54. Reprinted with kind permission from Spring Science and Business Media.

Ryan, Michael. "Journalist Ethics, Objectivity, Existential, Standpoint Epistemology, and Public Journalism." *Journal of Mass Media Ethics* 16.1 (2001): 3–22. Reprinted by permission of Lawrence Erlbaum Associates Inc.

Sanders, John T. "Honor Among Thieves: Some Reflections on Codes of Professional Ethics." *Professional Ethics* 2 (Fall/Winter 1993): 83–103. Reprinted by permission of John T. Sanders.

Siegler, Mark. "Confidentiality in Medicine—A Decrepit Concept." *New England Journal of Medicine* 307.24 (1982): 1518–21. Copyright © 1982 Massachusetts Medical Society. All rights reserved. Reprinted by permission of the Massachusetts Medical Society.

Simon, William H. "Ethical Discretion in Lawyering." *Harvard Business Review* 101 (1988): 1083–145. Copyright © 1988 Harvard Law Review Association. Reprinted by permission of Harvard Law Review Association.

Thomasma, David C. "Telling the Truth to Patients: A Clinical Ethics Exploration." *Cambridge Quarterly of Healthcare Ethics* 3 (1994): 375–82. Reprinted by permission of Cambridge University Press.

Thompson, Dennis F. "Privacy, Politics, and the Press." *The Harvard International Journal of Press/Politics* 3.4 (Fall 1998): 103–13. Reprinted by permission of Sage Publications.

Turnock, Terry L. "Public vs. Client Interests: An Ethical Dilemma for the Engineer." *Engineering Issues, Journal of Professional Activities* 101.1 (January 1975): 61–65. Reprinted by permission of the American Society of Civil Engineers.

Weil, Vivian. "Is Engineering Ethics Just Business Ethics? What Can Empirical Evidence Tell Us?" *International Journal of Applied Philosophy* 8.2 (Winter/Spring 1994): 9–15. Reprinted by permission of the Philosophy Documentation Center, Charlottesville, Virginia.

Welch, Don. "Just Another Day at the Office: The Ordinariness of Professional Ethics." *Professional Ethics* 2 (1993): 3–13. Reprinted by permission of Don Welch.

Werhane, Patricia H. "The Ethics of Insider Trading." *Journal of Business Ethics* 8.11 (1989): 841–45. Reprinted with kind permission from Spring Science and Business Media.

Wilkins, Lee. "Journalists and the Character of Public Officials/Figures." *Journal of Mass Media Ethics* 9.4 (1994): 157–68. Reprinted by permission of Lawrence Erlbaum Associates Inc.

Winch, P. Samuel. "Moral Justification for Privacy and Intimacy." *Journal of Mass Media Ethics* 11.4 (1996): 197–209. Reprinted by permission of Lawrence Erlbaum Associates Inc.

Wolfram, Charles W. "A Lawyer's Duty to Represent Clients, Repugnant and Otherwise," from *The Good Lawyer*. Totowa, NJ: Rowman and Allanheld, 1983. Pages 214–35. Reprinted by permission of David Luban.